Tunisia's Economic Development

This book identifies the differences in growth and development, and the various factors lying behind them, across both Middle East and North African (MENA) and East Asian countries over the 1960–2020 period. It considers a very wide range of factors, compares initial situations, institutions, and government policies, the dynamic responses to changing circumstances, and discusses the inability of the governments of the MENA region to achieve not only political reform, but also the kinds of economic reform that would allow their citizens to prosper in an increasingly globalized world. The book focuses on Tunisia. Since its independence in 1956 until 2010, Tunisia had considerable success relative to many other MENA countries, but was somewhat less successful relative to East Asian countries. Since 2010, however, while transitioning away from autocracy to democracy, it has been in rather serious economic decline. The book highlights how both the factors identified as enabling Tunisia's initial success and those leading to its subsequent decline can provide many useful insights for improving the management of economic development across the whole MENA region and perhaps also to developing countries throughout the world.

Mustapha K. Nabli has been Professor of Economics at the University of Tunis, Chairman of the Tunis Stock Exchange, Minister of Planning, Regional and Economic Development in the Government of Tunisia, Chief Economist and Director of the Social and Economic Development Department for the Middle East and North Africa Region at the World Bank, and Governor of the Central Bank of Tunisia.

Jeffrey B. Nugent is Professor of Economics at the University of Southern California, USA. He has worked on and in various countries of both the MENA and East Asian regions including for the United Nations, the World Bank and the International Monetary Fund. He has also served on the Board of both the Cairo-based Economic Research Forum and as President of the Middle East Economic Association.

The Routledge Political Economy of the Middle East and North Africa Series

Series editor: Hassan Hakimian

Professor of Economics and Director, Middle Eastern Studies Department, College of Humanities and Social Sciences (CHSS), Hamad Bin Khalifa University (HBKU), Qatar

10 Iran's Struggle for Economic Independence
Reform and counter-reform in the post-revolutionary era
Evaleila Pesaran

11 Economic and Trade Policies in the Arab world: Employment, Poverty Reduction and integration
Edited by Mahmoud A.T. Elkhafif, Sahar Taghdisi-Rad and Mutasim Elagraa

12 Iran and the Global Economy
Petro populism, Islam and economic sanctions
Edited by Parvin Alizadeh and Hassan Hakimian

13 State-Business Alliances and Economic Development
Turkey, Mexico and North Africa
Işık Özel

14 Social Policy in Iran: Main Components and Institutions
Edited by Pooya Alaedini

15 Tunisia's Economic Development
Why Better than Most of the Middle East but Not East Asia
Mustapha K. Nabli and Jeffrey B. Nugent

Tunisia's Economic Development

Why Better than Most of the Middle East but Not East Asia

Mustapha K. Nabli
and Jeffrey B. Nugent

Routledge
Taylor & Francis Group
LONDON AND NEW YORK

First published 2023
by Routledge
4 Park Square, Milton Park, Abingdon, Oxon OX14 4RN

and by Routledge
605 Third Avenue, New York, NY 10158

Routledge is an imprint of the Taylor & Francis Group, an informa business

British Library Cataloguing-in-Publication Data
A catalogue record for this book is available from the British Library

Library of Congress Cataloging-in-Publication Data
A catalog record has been requested for this book

ISBN: 978-1-032-31399-3 (hbk)
ISBN: 978-1-032-31400-6 (pbk)
ISBN: 978-1-003-30955-0 (ebk)

DOI: 10.4324/9781003309550

Typeset in Times New Roman
by KnowledgeWorks Global Ltd.

Contents

Tables

Figures

Acknowledgement

Earlier papers on which this book is based were presented at the conference 'Development without Developmental States: Latin America and Middle East North Africa Compared' at the University of California, San Diego, April 25–26, 2008 and The First International Development Conference of Syria 'Emerging Role of Civil Society in Development,' Damascus, Syria, Jan 23–25, 2010. This book has been extended, updated and revised considerably during the period 2019–2021.

The authors are grateful to Annie George, Jiaxuan Lu, Jamal Ibrahim Haidar, Meng Song, Hamzah Ahmed, Haoliang Chu, Daphne Nugent, and Utku Kumru for assistance in obtaining and organizing some of the data and carrying out some of the empirical analysis, to Rahel Schomaker for useful references, and to Jim Rauch and other participants at the University of California at San Diego and Syrian conferences for comments on earlier papers. The authors are especially appreciative of Hassan Hakimian, several members of his Editorial Board, and Peter Sowden for their comments on the first draft of our proposal for the inclusion of this book in the Routledge Political Economy of the Middle East and North Africa Series edited by Professor Hakimian. Finally, we express our appreciation to the Cairo-based Economic Research Forum, with which we have been involved since its beginning over 25 years ago, for allowing us to be aware of so much of the relevant literature and data sets that we have been able to draw upon in this book.

Acronyms

AA	Agadir Agreement
ADB	Asian Development Bank
AFC	Asian Financial Crisis
AfDB	African Development Bank
ALMP	Active Labor Market Programs
API	Agence de la Promotion de l'Industrie
BDET	Banque de Développement Economique de Tunisie
BNDT	Banque Nationale de Développement Touristique
BRI	Belt and Road Initiative (of China)
CBI	Central Bank Independence
CBR	Collective Bargaining Rights (An Index Based on Rigidity)
CBT	Central Bank of Tunisia
CE	Civil Engineering
CEPEX	Centre de Promotion des Exportations
CGC	Caisse Générale de Compensation
EFC	Entrepreneurial Framework Condition
ES	Enterprise Surveys of the World Bank
ESCWA	Economic and Social Commission for Western Asia
ExS	External Stability
ETAP	Entreprise Tunisienne d'Activités Pétrolières
EU	European Union
FAMEX	Fonds d'Accès aux Marchés d'Exportation
FAO	Food and Agriculture Organization
FDI	Foreign Direct Investment
FODEC	Fonds de Développement de la Compétitivité
FOPRODI	Fonds de Promotion et de Décentralisation Industrielle
FOPRODEX	Fonds de Promotion des Exportations
FTA	Free Trade Area
GAFTA	Greater Arab Free Trade Area
GCC	Gulf Cooperation Council
GDP	Gross Domestic Product
GNP	Gross National Product

GE	Gender Equality
GEM	Global Entrepreneurial Monitor
GFC	Global Financial Crisis
GFCF	Gross Fixed Capital Formation
GG	General Government
GNI	Gross National Income
GNP	Gross National Product
GVC	Global Value Chains
HC	Human Capital
ICRG	International Country Risk Guide
ICT	Information and Communications Technology
ILO	International Labor Organization
IMF	International Monetary Fund
INS	Institut National de la Statistique
INV	Investment Rate
IPRI	International Property Rights Index
IT	Inflation Targeting
ITCEQ	Institut Tunisien de la Compétitivité et des Etudes Quantitatives
KOF	Konjunkturforschungsstelle
LAMRIG	Labor Market Rigidities Index
LPI	Logistics Performance Index
MENA	Middle East and North Africa
MENA ES	MENA Enterprise Survey countries
MDG	Millennium Development Goals
MFN	Most Favored Nation
MIT	Middle Income Trap
MS	Macroeconomic Stability
NGO	Non-Governmental Organization
NIEs	New Industrializing Economies
NTBs	Non-Tariff Barriers
OECD	Organization for Economic Cooperation and Development
PI	Physical Infrastructure
PIRLS	Progress in International Reading Literacy Study
PISA	Programme for International Student Assessment
PNAFN	Programme National d'Aide aux Familles Nécessiteuses
PPI	Public Private Infrastructure
PPP	Purchasing Power Parity
PRA	Property Rights Alliance
PWT	Penn World Tables
R&D	Research and Development
REER	Reel Effective Exchange Rate
SMEs	Small and Medium Size Enterprises
SOEs	State-Owned Enterprises

SR	Structural Reform
SSA	Sub-Saharan Africa
SWF	Sovereign Wealth Fund
TIP	True Industrial Policy
TFP	Total Factor Productivity
TIMSS	Tends in International Mathematics and Science Study
TOT	Terms of Trade
UAE	United Arab Emirates
UGTT	Union Générale Tunisienne du Travail
US	United States
USD	United States Dollar
UN	United Nations
UNDP	United Nations Development Programme
UTAP	Union Tunisienne de l'Agriculture et de la Pêche
UTICA	Union Tunisienne de l'Industrie, du Commerce et de l'Artisanat
VAT	Value Added Tax
WBG	West Bank and Gaza
WDI	World Development Indicators
WID	World Inequality Database
WTO	World Trade Organization
WVS	World Value Survey
WWI	World War I
WWII	World War II

Preface

The governments of the Arab world and more broadly of the Middle East and North Africa (MENA) region have received widespread criticism for their inability to achieve, not only political reform, but also the kind of economic reforms that would allow their citizens to prosper in an increasingly globalized world. As a result, they are widely perceived as being in a crisis from which they are unlikely to emerge, and which may prevent them from being able to provide adequate employment opportunities for their rapidly growing numbers of job-seekers (both youths in general and women in particular).

This book focuses on one of the region's comparative success stories, Tunisia. It demonstrates, via a variety of development indicators and indexes, that Tunisia's economy performed better than those of most other MENA countries over the 50 years since its independence up until 2010 on many, but certainly not all, of these indicators. For comparison purposes, the book compares Tunisia and other MENA countries with a sample of six East Asian countries (China, Indonesia, Korea, Malaysia, Philippines, and Thailand). This sample is chosen because it includes both some of the 'East Asian Miracle' countries, but also some others whose growth has lagged behind. While Tunisia has done as well as some of these East Asian countries in some of these indicators over that same pre-2010 period, it has quite definitely *not* done as well as most of these East Asian countries since the Arab Uprisings of 2011. Indeed, since 2011 Tunisia has lagged substantially behind not only its earlier progress but also many of its fellow MENA countries and all the East Asian countries in the sample.

The objective of this study is to ferret out as clearly as possible the factors lying behind Tunisia's success relative to many other MENA countries but also the factors lying behind its comparative lack of success relative to East Asian countries.

For why Tunisia has done better than most other MENA countries in the pre-2010 period, two sorts of explanations are identified: (1) favorable initial conditions and (2) the relative success of the several different strategies and policies adopted by the country's policy-makers at different times since independence. While the favorable initial conditions undoubtedly played a role, the evidence suggests that, neither individually nor even collectively, could they constitute the primary explanation. The strategies adopted in different periods differed quite remarkably in some respects but also had some underlying consistencies that have proved beneficial.

But what are the deeper policy and institutional differences that have distinguished the growth experience of Tunisia from those of the East Asian countries, and how can they help to explain the divergent outcomes in terms of aggregate GDP and productivity growth, employment growth, living standards levels, technological progress, and structural transformation? Tunisia had many of the same structural features observed in the successful East Asian countries: a developmental state and strong state capacity. It followed the same broad policy directions and policies we observe in East Asia, such as a focus on human capital, pragmatism and adaptability in policy, market orientation, role of the private sector, and a strong outward orientation in its trade and investment policies. While we find insufficient divergence in any single important policy, or set of policy choices, to which one could attribute the gap in performance between Tunisia and East Asian counties, at the same time we do find very considerable divergence between them in terms of the extent of implementation of the policies and their adaptation to changing circumstances. These differences relate to the following features of Tunisia vis-à-vis the East Asian countries: its (1) limited success in achieving higher rates of savings and capital accumulation, (2) absence of land reform and wealth equalization measures, (3) limited success in stimulating technological progress, (4) skills mismatches and shortcomings in the quality and efficiency of use of human capital, (5) weak financial development, (6) weak fiscal policy, and perhaps most importantly (7) lesser exposure to competition in world markets. We argue that the deeper factors behind these weaknesses are the continued heavy hand of the state, the insufficient use of markets and enduring distortions of different types, and the limited success in making the private sector the engine for investment and productivity growth. Unlike the successful East Asian countries, Tunisia limited the scope of development of markets and of the private sector which otherwise could have allowed more efficiency, greater innovation, and stronger investment.

Political economy considerations underlie these differences, with Tunisia being unable to adapt its policies and institutions sufficiently strongly and quickly to changing circumstances. Among the major political economy failures were the excessively slow progress in allowing civil society organizations like business groups to form freely in non-rent-seeking ways through the open discussion of policy issues so as to find ways of resolving deep-seated economic inefficiencies and conflicts, and making improvements in several other institutional measures that have not kept pace with the rise in its still fragile democracy index since 2011.

Notably, despite its relative success prior to 2011, Tunisia was the first country in the MENA region to face the popular uprisings in December 2010/

January 2011. These uprisings led both to the collapse of its existing political regime, and to contagion effects to many countries throughout the region. During the almost full decade of political transition, Tunisia has indeed achieved substantial gains in terms of its democracy index (placing it above all countries in the region and among the highest in the world in this respect). Yet, the main results from this democratic gain so far have been both economic collapse and the failure of government to improve the country's institutions so as to allow the economy to grow faster and more steadily. Simply put, Tunisia has neither found a way to regain even the kind of development which it had achieved earlier, nor been able to resolve the major challenges which gave rise to the uprisings. These challenges included access to good jobs, more equitable development, a more efficient economy, and a higher standard of living. Without such access, during this most recent decade, Tunisia's institutional quality has deteriorated, trust in its institutions has declined, and the prospects for success have become much grimmer. The same political economy factors have continued to hamper change and adaptation in Tunisia, thereby explaining its economic collapse and the major reversals in relative performance experienced during this last decade.

In the search for even more fundamental, but not yet well understood, key reasons for the success of East Asia and the comparative failure of other countries like Tunisia to match the East Asian performance, we identify three major hypotheses: (i) the eventual disappearance in Tunisia of leadership capable of leading the country through changing but efficient development strategies, (ii) Political Economy Constraints which Limited Tunisia's Ability to Adapt and Adjust, Strengthened Resistance to Change and Induced a Middle-Income Trap, and (iii) The Neighborhood effect which made it impossible for Tunisia to take advantage of felicitous complementarities with its geographic neighbors. While we believe that the three different factors identified in these hypotheses have played an at least significant role in explaining these differences and in particular the more disappointing outcome in Tunisia, we admit that there remains a most serious challenge lying ahead for future research, namely, the ability to quantify their relative importance and the extent to which and how they may have changed over time.

1 Introduction

Tunisia's Economic and Social Outcomes in Comparative Perspective

Given the length of the time period under consideration, roughly 1960–2020, the inter-connectedness of modern growth theory, and the multiplicity of institutional and structural factors which have justifiably been recognized to be important in explaining long-term growth, the task of explaining the comparative successes and failures of Tunisia relative to both other Middle East and North Africa (MENA) countries and East Asian countries is understandably an extremely challenging one. The period under consideration starts in the 1960s immediately following Tunisia's independence in 1956. It covers several subperiods. The first several subperiods cover the period until 2010 during which Tunisia's development proceeded under the same quite autocratic political system. The last subperiod starts in 2011 following the popular 'Uprisings' which led to the fall of the previous regime and the beginning of a political transition toward democracy. In our analysis this last sub-period, depending on availability of data, goes up to 2019 the year preceding the COVID-19 pandemic which of course has led to new difficulties and challenges to all countries, but varying considerably from one to the other.

In this book, both the MENA and East Asian regions are defined quite broadly. MENA has been defined in the same way as by the World Bank, so as to include all the countries in both North Africa (ranging from Morocco in the West to Egypt and Djibouti in the East) and the Middle East (ranging from Lebanon and Syria in the Northwest to Iran in the Southeast). It includes both the richest country in the world (Qatar) and some of the very poorest ones (such as Yemen). Yet, our sample of MENA countries deliberately excludes Turkey and Cyprus, because they are much more integrated with Europe than with other MENA countries, and also Sudan, Comoros, and Mauritania because they are more closely associated with other East African and sub-Sahara African countries than with MENA countries. Another reason for excluding Sudan was that it was divided into two countries (Sudan and South Sudan) during the period under consideration.

Similarly, East Asia has been defined broadly enough as to include both some 'East Asian Miracle' countries, such as China and Korea, and some poorer and less successful countries, such as the Philippines and Thailand,

DOI: 10.4324/9781003309550-1

but we focus on a much smaller sample of countries, six in total, namely, Indonesia and Malaysia, in addition to the aforementioned four. As pointed out by Studwell (2013), not only are these East Asian countries from slightly different regions, Korea and China from East Asia proper, and the other four from Southeast Asia, but also they are at quite different levels of development, the former along with Japan and Taiwan being quite highly developed, but the latter four being somewhat less developed. Three of the South East Asian countries, Indonesia, Malaysia, and Thailand, started their transformation early on in the 1950s and 1960s and were much more successful than the Philippines, but were much less successful than China or Korea. Other countries of both Asian regions were omitted from the sample so as to keep them as comparable as possible to the MENA countries. For example, Vietnam was excluded because it split into North and South Vietnam, during the period, and Japan was excluded because it was already a highly developed country before the 60-year period under consideration. Since Tunisia and all the other MENA counties (with the exception of Qatar) included were of at least reasonable size and including both rural and urban areas, two other East Asian countries (Hong Kong and Singapore) were excluded because they are single island, largely urban, economies unlike the MENA countries.

One common approach to comparative development and political economy within and around the MENA region taken in the past is by way of comparative economic histories, though to do so in any depth in a single paper or volume has usually limited these comparisons to only a few countries as in Issawi (1982), Anderson (1986), Owen (1992), Owen and Pamuk (1999), Hansen (1991), and Henry (1996); though to a few more in Noland and Pack (2007), Richards and Waterbury (1990), and Henry and Springborg (2010) which are somewhat more broadly descriptive of recent periods. Somewhat related have been studies involving a larger number of countries but narrowing the focus within long-term development to a more specific topic like trade, as in Hakimian and Nugent (2004); business and political economy, as in Beblawi and Luciani (1987) and Hertog et al. (2013); the state and political economy, as in Bellin (2002), Cammett (2007), and Acemoglu and Robinson (2012); macro-economic growth, as in Nugent and Pesaran (2007); and public sector reforms, as in Beschel and Yousef (2021). Still another approach taken in a recent and very comprehensive volume is one by Hakimian (2021) with separate chapters on a wide variety of relevant topics, in most cases comparing the experiences across MENA countries.

At the other extreme are quantitative empirical studies which might include a large number of countries, although for data availability reasons, typically are limited to relatively short and recent periods, and also for hypothesis testing reasons, focused on a particular aspect of development or common policy area, such as dealing with the problems of natural resource-rich countries and hence fiscal management problems, as in Elbadawi and Selim (2016) and Mohaddes et al. (2019), or the pros and cons of various reforms as in Abdelbary (2021).

In this study, we want to keep the search for the key factors that may, potentially at least, have been contributing to either long-term growth or disruptive cycles as open and all-encompassing as possible. We describe this process as like looking for the 'needle in the haystack.' To that end, while we draw heavily on some historical analyses, as well as some econometric results in certain circumstances, so as to pay a lot of attention to finding and presenting comparable data of many kinds deemed relevant to explaining time-varying growth performance of Tunisia relative to both other MENA countries and the sample of six East Asian countries.

Because of the importance of institutions, but also the wide variety of institutions of possible relevance, much of our data gathering effort has been devoted to institutions. The fact that institutions often change only very slowly over time, but that, when they do change, many other things change as well, their determinants and effects are often difficult to sort out. While much of the data presented on the effects of institutions are at the country level, since the effects of any given set of rules can vary across different kinds of firms, individuals, or regions, we also deem it important to examine the effects of different rules or institutions at the firm, sector, or regional levels. Among the studies that have been able to analyze the determinants and effects of different institutions and policies are some which have deliberately narrowed the scope of their analyses to focus on hypothesized factors that are believed to make a difference in certain very specific types of countries or situations. Among MENA countries, this has often led to exclusive focus on those oil exporting countries with fixed exchange rates, where monetary policy is irrelevant indicating that the analysis of policy and institutional changes can be focused on fiscal policy. Alternatively, in non-resource-rich countries of the MENA or other regions, appropriate analyses might involve comparisons between countries with similar types of agricultural or manufactures specializations, or countries dominated by state-owned enterprises or alternatively private enterprises.

Given the broader scope of this study focusing on virtually all MENA countries and six representative East Asian countries, it will draw, not only on broad historical changes in aggregate growth, factors of production, and technological change, but also on economic structure, trade and investment, and, quite importantly, institutions. We will deal with both country-level and firm-level analyses, and identify the relevance of a wide variety of institutional factors and policies and interactions with other countries in the form of trade and investment.

In any case, after drawing on a wide variety of methods and data sources at both the macro- and micro-levels, our comparisons across countries and the two regions show that, up until the 2000s, the story of the MENA was straightforward. Despite the very substantial natural resource endowments possessed by some of them, the countries of the MENA region as a whole had gained a reputation for having lagged behind East Asian countries in economic and political reforms and for having achieved only rather modest average rates of economic growth, and with unusually large variability in those growth rates over time (Henry and Springborg 2010; Noland and Pack 2007). Some countries, like Oman and the United Arab Emirates (UAE) among oil exporters, and Tunisia among non-oil countries, were looked at as comparatively successful.

As an essay on the region in the *Economist* (July 25, 2009) indicated, shortly after that (by about 2010), many analysts saw the region as in crisis, and with the potential for, if not political revolution, at least a social revolution. According to this view, the citizens of the region should have been increasingly aware of what was going on in the world, both economically and politically. Yet, they were still seeing little prospect for achieving either greater freedoms or more meaningful jobs, and especially those in the private sector. The difficulty of finding jobs in the private sector by MENA citizens was particularly discouraging, given the great success in these respects of countries in East Asia and Eastern Europe, and the rapidly growing numbers of new entrants to the labor force in MENA countries resulting from their 'youth bulge.' These same sources pointed to the fact that the MENA region's shares of world manufacturing value added, manufacturing exports and foreign direct investment had generally been declining for the last several decades before 2009 or 2010.

Then came the big shock and the uprisings which started in Tunisia at the end of 2010, as its old political regime became increasingly rigid and corrupt. These uprisings soon spread throughout the region in 2011, leading to major changes in the political landscape, including major upheavals in many countries. The existing political regimes totally collapsed in 2011 in four countries (Tunisia, Egypt, Libya, and Yemen) and in two others later on (in 2019, in Algeria and Sudan). Three countries lapsed into quite devastating civil wars (Libya, Yemen, and Syria), and another (Iraq) was already in what could be regarded as a civil war after the overthrow of its government subsequent to the invasion of that country in 2003 by the US and other forces. Other countries were significantly affected, such as Bahrain with unrest in 2011, and Lebanon and Jordan due to migration flows and other spillovers from the conflicts in neighboring countries. Lebanon has continued to be riddled with political instability and ineffective government since then, as has Yemen to an even greater extent. Indeed, as a result of both conflict and disease, in recent years, Yemen has gained recognition for being the site of the greatest Humanitarian disaster in the world by the United Nations, and Lebanon for its unusually sharp decline from a rather prosperous middle-income country to one of state failure and widespread poverty.

The fact that the uprisings started in Tunisia was quite a surprise, given that Tunisia appeared to have had reasonably satisfactory economic performance over the preceding decades. Indeed, Tunisia was a country where life expectancy at birth had risen very sharply, and child mortality, poverty rates, and income inequality had all fallen more sharply than in most other countries of either MENA or East Asia. Moreover, Tunisia also turns out to be the only country where the prospects for a successful democratic transition remain distinctly alive, despite the general transition from 'Arab Spring' to 'Arab Fall' or reversion between 2010 and 2019 to strict autocracy in most of the MENA countries that had experienced the Arab Uprisings. These distinctions are only two of several which make the comparative study of Tunisia's experience interesting, relevant, and important.

As will be shown below, having achieved Gross Domestic Product (GDP) growth in real terms averaging almost 5% per annum over the period 1962–2010 and having achieved considerable growth in its share of manufacturing in GDP to well over 19% in the 1990s, Tunisia had to be regarded as a comparative success story within the MENA region. At the same time, however, Tunisia, and virtually all the other comparatively successful countries in the MENA region, even during that 1960–2010 period, had fallen far short of the growth of the successful East Asian countries.

In the many data tables and comparisons presented in this book, we distinguish not only between MENA and East Asian countries (and in a few particular circumstances to a few other countries as well), but also, within MENA, between three groups of MENA countries depending on the extent of their relative natural resource wealth. The first group includes nine countries which are not major exporters of hydrocarbons (Djibouti, Egypt, Jordan, Lebanon, Morocco, Syria, Tunisia, WBG, and Yemen). All the other countries in this group constitute close comparators to Tunisia, even though some of them are very low-income (Djibouti, Yemen[1]). The second group includes four countries (Algeria, Iran, Iraq, and Libya) which are major exporters of hydrocarbon products, but are not part of the Gulf Cooperation Council (GCC). The third group consists of the six GCC countries (Bahrain, Kuwait, Oman, Qatar, Saudi Arabia, and UAE) which have the highest oil and gas rents per capita.

To show that Tunisia's generally superior economic and social performance has not been confined narrowly to a single indicator of our choosing, we begin by presenting four tables (Tables 1.1–1.4) comparing commonly used development outcomes in Tunisia with those not only in the other MENA countries under study here but also with those six East Asian countries.

The first of these tables relates to one of the more broadly accepted perspectives on development stemming from the work of Amartya Sen (1973, 1985a, 1985b, 1988, 1999) who stressed the importance of human capabilities in any country's development. That emphasis led to the construction of an ever-improving set of human development indicators, with emphasis on the importance of public goods in their development and their importance in sustainable development as reflected in the work of the United Nations Development Program and its Human Development Index. Several of those more specific indicators will be dealt with later (e.g., in Tables 2.11–2.14 and 4.6). Yet, we begin our comparative analysis of Tunisia and other MENA and the six East Asian countries with Table 1.1. This table

Table 1.1 Human Development Indicators, 1960–2019

Country	*Life expectancy at birth (years)*				*Mortality rate under 5 (per 1000 live births)*				*Illiteracy rates/ population 15 years and over (%)*			*Average years of schooling/ population 15 years and over*		
	1960	*2010*	*Change 1960–2010*	*2019*	*1962*	*2010*	*Change 1962–2010*	*2019*	*Circa 1980*	*Circa 2010*	*Circa 2018*	*1970*	*1980*	*2010*
MENA non-major oil exporters	**47.5**	**71.2**	**23.6**	**73.2**	**224.0**	**31.6**	**−197.6**	**26.5**	**54.0**	**21.0**	**14.3**	**2.8**	**3.9**	**7.8**
Djibouti	44.0	60.1	16.0	67.1	..	76.4	..	57.5	..	..	..	..	..	..
Egypt, Arab Rep.	48.0	70.3	22.3	72.0	296.3	28.8	−267.5	20.3	61.8	28.0	28.8	1.8	3.6	8.0
Jordan	52.7	73.4	20.8	74.5	138.2	20.2	−118.0	15.6	33.2	7.4	1.8	6.0	7.0	9.9
Lebanon	63.3	78.4	15.1	78.9	71.5	10.3	−61.2	7.2		8.8	4.9	..	..	..
Morocco	48.5	74.4	25.9	76.7	228.3	31.8	−196.5	21.4	69.7	32.9	26.2	1.7	2.7	6.8
Syrian Arab Republic	52.0	72.1	20.1	72.7	154.1	19.0	−135.1	21.5	44.3	19.2		3.3	4.3	7.5
Tunisia	**42.0**	**75.0**	**33.0**	**76.7**	**269.7**	**18.4**	**−251.3**	**16.9**	**51.8**	**20.9**	**21.0**	**3.7**	**5.3**	**9.1**
West Bank and Gaza	..	71.2	..	74.1	..	23.2	..	19.4	..	5.1	2.8	..	..	..
Yemen	29.9	65.5	35.6	66.1	409.8	56.0	−353.8	58.4	62.9	45.9	..	0.3	0.7	5.5
MENA major oil exporters	**45.4**	**72.4**	**26.9**	**74.3**	**218.7**	**24.6**	**−192.5**	**18.7**	**51.2**	**20.6**	**15.8**	**3.2**	**5.4**	**9.0**
Algeria	46.1	74.9	28.8	76.9	242.0	27.4	−214.6	23.3	50.4	24.9	18.6	3.0	4.8	7.4
Iran, Islamic Rep.	44.9	73.9	29.0	76.7	..	19.7	..	13.9	63.5	16.4	14.5	3.7	6.2	10.8
Iraq	48.0	68.6	20.5	70.6	171.0	34.6	−136.4	25.9	..	27.3	14.4	3.1	4.8	8.3
Libya	42.6	72.0	29.4	72.9	243.2	16.6	−226.6	11.5	39.8	13.9	..	2.9	5.8	9.4

(Continued)

Table 1.1 Human Development Indicators, 1960–2019 *(Continued)*

Country	*Life expectancy at birth (years)*				*Mortality rate under 5 (per 1000 live births)*				*Illiteracy rates/ population 15 years and over (%)*			*Average years of schooling/ population 15 years and over*		
	1960	*2010*	*Change 1960–2010*	*2019*	*1962*	*2010*	*Change 1962–2010*	*2019*	*Circa 1980*	*Circa 2010*	*Circa 2018*	*1970*	*1980*	*2010*
MENA GCC	**52.0**	**75.9**	**23.9**	**77.3**	**202.2**	**10.0**	**−192.4**	**7.8**	**29.0**	**8.7**	**4.8**	**4.0**	**5.0**	**8.5**
Bahrain	51.9	76.1	24.2	77.3	166.0	8.5	−157.5	6.9	30.2	9.0	2.5	5.2	6.3	8.5
Kuwait	59.3	74.4	15.0	75.5	122.9	10.4	−112.5	7.9	32.5	5.5	3.9	4.2	5.2	5.7
Oman	42.7	75.7	33.0	77.9	339.5	11.7	−327.8	11.4	..	13.1	4.3	..	..	..
Qatar	61.1	79.1	18.0	80.2	..	9.1	..	6.5	24.4	8.8	4.4	5.4	5.7	9.1
Saudi Arabia	45.6	73.9	28.3	75.1	..	11.9	..	6.6	29.2	5.6	6.5	3.1	3.6	9.1
United Arab Emirates	51.5	76.3	24.8	78.0	180.3	8.5	−171.8	7.5	28.8	10.0	6.8	2.1	4.3	10.0
East Asia	**53.6**	**73.7**	**20.1**	**76.1**	**125.5**	**17.9**	**−107.2**	**13.3**	**25.3**	**5.2**	**4.1**	**5.9**	**7.2**	**10.2**
China	43.7	74.4	30.7	76.9	..	15.8	..	7.9	34.5	4.9	3.2	5.7	7.0	9.3
Indonesia	46.7	69.2	22.5	71.7	211.6	33.9	−177.7	23.9	32.7	7.2	4.3	4.2	4.8	8.2
Korea, Rep.	55.4	80.1	24.7	83.2	101.7	4.1	−97.6	3.2	..	..	..	8.4	10.3	12.5
Malaysia	60.0	74.5	14.5	76.2	80.5	8.1	−72.4	8.6	30.5	6.9	5.1	6.6	8.1	12.0
Philippines	61.1	69.8	8.7	71.2	97.4	31.7	−65.7	27.3	16.7	3.6	1.8	6.0	7.3	8.8
Thailand	54.7	74.2	19.5	77.2	136.3	13.6	−122.7	9.0	12.0	3.6	6.2	4.8	5.6	10.5

Sources: World Bank – World Development Indicators (WDI).

Notes: Average years of schooling: Barro-Lee data from WDI.

presents data on each of four different dimensions of human development, that is, life expectancy at birth, the mortality rates of those under 5, illiteracy rates of those aged 15 and over, and the average years of schooling in the population aged 15 and over.

As shown in the first set of columns in Table 1.1, over the five decades 1960–2010, Tunisia, along with Oman and Yemen, achieved the largest increases among MENA countries in the level of life expectancy at birth. Tunisia's life expectancy at birth rose between 1960 and 2010 by more than any of the East Asian countries. Although it began in 1960 with the lowest life expectancy outside of Yemen, by 2010 Tunisia's life expectancy at birth had risen to be tied with that of China, and almost as high as the average for the oil-rich GCC countries, and higher than the average for the East Asian countries.

Similarly, as shown in the second set of columns in the table, even though the data coverage on (under 5) child mortality was more limited for some countries in 1962, Tunisia started with the fourth highest such mortality rate of all the countries listed in the table, and the decline in Tunisia's rate was the fourth largest among all countries in the table, and only slightly behind those of the top three, Yemen, Oman, and Egypt. Hence, by 2010 at least, Tunisia's under five mortality rate had declined to about the average rate of the East Asian countries, and to below the averages of both the non-major oil-exporting and major oil-exporting countries.

In the third set of columns in Table 1.1, one can see that, although the illiteracy rates presented only go back to 1980, Tunisia started with the fifth highest such rate in 1980 out of all the countries in the table, but experienced the fourth largest decline in such illiteracy rates between 1980 and 2010. Tunisia's commitment to education has been clear since its beginning from a number of important actions. (1) In particular, in 1958, the Tunisian government stated that 'The State guarantees the right to free public education in public schools for all school-aged children.' (2) Because of the widespread failure of Tunisian children in rural areas of the country to attend school, in 1991 a new law made school attendance in primary education mandatory and imposed fines on families who failed to comply. (3) In its Education Act of July 23, 2002, the State committed itself to raising the quality of education which induced a greater commitment to education in the country's budget. (4) As noted in a United Nations report (United Nations 2004), Tunisia had made an impressive commitment to the Millennium Development Goals (MDGs) which included eliminating illiteracy and raising enrollment rates at various levels. Notably, however, Tunisia's reduction in its illiteracy rate was well below those of Iran, Morocco, and Egypt, and its 2017 average level of illiteracy was still more than twice those of WBG, Jordan, Lebanon, Libya, all GCC and as well as of all East Asian countries. Furthermore, between 2010 and 2018, its decline in illiteracy was among the smallest in the whole table and its level was still about three times as high as any of the East Asian countries.

Relatedly, in the third to last column of the table, one can see that in 1970, the average years of schooling in the 15 years and older population in Tunisia were below those of four other MENA countries (Bahrain, Jordan, Kuwait, and Qatar), and well below the years of schooling of all six East Asian countries. Indeed, it should be recognized that virtually all MENA country educational levels were among the lowest in the world in 1970. Not surprisingly, from the last two columns in Table 1.1, it can be seen the improvements in years of education since then (at least until 2010) for MENA countries have been quite impressive. Indeed, by 2010, Tunisia's rate had risen since 1970 by 143% compared to the rate in East Asia of only 73%. But those of Algeria, Egypt, Iran, Iraq, Libya, Morocco, Saudi Arabia, UAE, and Yemen had all grown more rapidly than that of Tunisia. As a result, even in 2010, the average years of education (of those 15 years of age and above) in Tunisia of 9.1 years was still below those of four other MENA countries and below those of four of the six East Asian countries.

Comparing the first two sets of columns reflecting health with those in the last two sets comparing education, it is fairly clear that at least by 2010, Tunisia's comparative success was much greater in heath indicators than in educational ones. Yet, even in the education indicators, it had caught up significantly, so that in average years of education, Tunisia and several other MENA countries had come to exceed not only the MENA averages but also those of at least two East Asian countries.

Recognizing that averages can hide major shortfalls in human capabilities among some disadvantaged groups, Sen also emphasized the need to be concerned with poverty and income inequality measures that compare different segments of the population. To that end, Table 1.2 presents comparable data on these indicators for our sample of MENA countries, and Table 1.3 does the same for the sample of East Asian countries. Because comparable estimates for the different countries over time are available only for slightly different poverty line measures, in both tables we present comparisons for each of five different definitions of poverty lines for as many years as possible. The alternative definitions are $1.25 per day (in 2005 PPP prices)[2] in column (1), $1.9 per day (in 2011 PPP prices) in column (2), $2 per day (in 2005 PPP prices) in column (3), $3.2 per day (in 2011 PPP prices) in column (4), and finally the national poverty rate (though the poverty line is not the same across countries) in column (5). As can be seen by comparing the two tables, the information at the individual country level is slightly less complete for columns (1), (3), and (5) for East Asian countries but nevertheless is available for the region as a whole, and they are available at the country level in columns (2) and (4). The data on these indicators over time are also in general somewhat more limited than for those in Table 1.1. Hence, fewer MENA countries are included and, as indicated above for East Asian countries, in some cases only for the regional average. Also, the time coverage differs to a greater extent across countries than in Table 1.1. Then in

Table 1.2 Poverty Rates and Inequality – MENA, 1981–2018

Country/ year	***Poverty rate (PPP $ 2005) $1.25/ day (%)***	***Poverty rate (PPP $ 2011) $1.9/day (%)***	***Poverty rate (PPP $ 2005) $ 2.0/day (%)***	***Poverty rate (PPP $ 2011) $ 3.2/day (%)***	***Poverty rate national poverty line (%)***	***Gini index of inequality***
Algeria						
1981	3.8		15.5			
1987/1988	**6.6**	6.3	**23.8**	24.9	8.0	40.2
1990	6.2		22.8			
1995/1996	**6.8**	5.6	**23.6**	23.9	14.0	35.3
1999/2000	8.2		26.4			
2005	4.2		18.1			
2011		0.4		3.9	5.5	27.6
Djibouti						
2002		20.2		47.3		40.0
2012		18.2		38		45.1
2013		22.3		44.2		
2017		17		39.8	21.1	41.6
Egypt						
1981	12.0		42.4			
1987	7.2		33.9			
1990/1991	**4.5**	8.7	**27.6**	40.5	24.2	32.0
1995/1996	**2.5**	5.6	**26.3**	41.6	19.4	30.1
1999/2000	**1.8**	2.4	**19.3**	26.7	16.7	32.8
2004/2005	**2.0**	5.2	**18.4**	35.4	19.6	31.8
2008		4.7		33.5		
2010		2.2		23.7	25.2	31.5
2012		1.5		19		
2015		1.6		18.2	27.8	31.8
2017		3.8		28.9	32.5	31.5
Iran						
1986						47.4
1990		6.2		20.1		43.6
1994		2.9		14.1		43.0
1998	**0.5**	2.6	**8.3**	14	23.3	44.1
2005	**0.5**	0.6	**8.0**	4	8.1	43.6
2009		1.1		4.5		42.1
2013		0.2		1.7		37.4
2014		0.4		3.2		
2015		0.4		3.2		
2016		0.4		3.1		40.0
2017		0.4		2.9		
2018		0.5		3.1		42.0
Iraq						
2006		1.5		15.7	22.4	28.6
2012		1.7		14.8	18.9	29.5
Jordan						
1981	0.0		2.6			32.3
1986/1987	**0.0**	0.0	**1.7**	2.6	3.0	36.1
1992/1993	**2.8**	2.7	**14.9**	16.7	15.0	43.4

(Continued)

Table 1.2 Poverty Rates and Inequality – MENA, 1981–2018 *(Continued)*

Country/ year	***Poverty rate (PPP $ 2005) $1.25/ day (%)***	***Poverty rate (PPP $ 2011) $1.9/day (%)***	***Poverty rate (PPP $ 2005) $ 2.0/day (%)***	***Poverty rate (PPP $ 2011) $ 3.2/day (%)***	***Poverty rate national poverty line (%)***		***Gini index of inequality***
1996/1997	**1.9**	1.5	**12.7**	13.4	21.3		36.4
2002	**1.1**	1	**11.0**	8.6	14.2		37.0
2005/2006	**0.4**	0.3	**3.5**	3.9			33.9
2008		0.1		2.8	13.3		32.6
2010		0.1		2	14.4		33.7
2018					15.7		
Lebanon							
2011		0.0		0.1	27.4		31.8
Morocco							
1981	10.3		32.8				
1984/1985	**8.4**	10.6	**28.7**	31.9	21.0		39.7
1987	5.9		23.3				
1990/1991	**2.5**	2.9	**15.9**	19.3	13.0		39.2
1996	4.6		19.9				
1998/1999	**6.6**	6.4	**24.4**	26.7	16.3		39.5
2000/2002	**6.2**	5.8	**24.3**	26.7	15.3		40.6
2005	3.0		16.2				
2006	**2.5**	3.0	**14.0**	16.2	8.9		40.7
2013		0.9		7.3	4.8		39.5
Qatar							
2009							41.1
2012							40.4
Syria							
1996		2.1		16.8			
2003		0.9		15.3	30.1		35.8
Tunisia					Old method	New method	
1966/67					33.0		50.3
1981	9.7		27.0		20.1		45.5
1984/1985	**8.6**	15.0	**25.1**	37.9	9.6		43.4
1987	8.1		23.8				
1990	**5.9**	10.7	**19.0**	30.5	6.7		40.2
1995/1996	**6.5**	11.8	**20.5**	31.7	8.1		41.7
2000	**2.6**	6	**12.8**	22.9	4.1	25.4	40.8
2005	1.1	3.4	7.3	15.2		23.1	37.7
2010		2.0		9.2		20.5	35.8
2015		0.2		3		15.2	32.8
West Bank and Gaza							
2004		0.8		4.8			34.0
2005		0.7		5			
2006		0.3		3.9			
2007		1.5		7.4			35.6
2009		0.3		2.6			
2010		0.2		3.2	25.7		35.3

(Continued)

Table 1.2 Poverty Rates and Inequality – MENA, 1981–2018 *(Continued)*

Country/ year	*Poverty rate (PPP $ 2005) $1.25/ day (%)*	*Poverty rate (PPP $ 2011) $1.9/day (%)*	*Poverty rate (PPP $ 2005) $ 2.0/day (%)*	*Poverty rate (PPP $ 2011) $ 3.2/day (%)*	*Poverty rate national poverty line (%)*	*Gini index of inequality*
2011		0.2		3.0	29.2	33.7
2018		0.8		4.5		
Yemen						
1981	9.1		26.1			
1987	3.8		13.4			
1992/1993	**9.1**		**26.1**		19.1	39.0
1996	4.9		34.0			
1998	**12.9**	7	**36.3**	26.9	42.0	35.0
2005	**17.5**	9.4	**46.6**	37.7	34.8	34.7
2014		18.3		51.2	48.6	36.7
MENA						
1981	7.9		26.7			
1984	6.1		23.1			
1985		8.6		31.4		
1987	5.7	8.3	22.7	31.0		
1990	4.3	6.5	19.7	27.1		
1993	4.1	6.7	19.8	29.0		
1996	4.1	6.0	20.2	28.6		
1999	4.2	3.7	19.0	21.5		
2002	3.6	3.4	17.6	20.1		
2005	3.6	3.1	16.9	18.9		
2008		2.8		16.7		
2010		2.0		13.8		
2013		2.1		12.6		
2016		5.2		16.5		
2018		7.0		19.9		

For international poverty lines:

Sources: World Development Indicators 2008 and Poverty data Supplement. Other figures are estimates from PovCalNet. For MENA and EAP: Chen and Ravallion (2008).

Notes:
Columns for $1.9/day and $3.2/day are for International 2011 PPP dollars, downloaded from World Bank July 2021.
Columns for $1.25/day and $2.0/day are for international PPP 2005 dollars.
Figures in bold indicate year of actual survey.

For national poverty lines:

Sources: From World Bank database, updated July 2021.

World Bank (1999) for Algeria, Kheir-El-Din and el-Laithy (2006) for Egypt, Lahouel (2007) for Tunisia, World Bank (1996) and World Bank (2002) for Yemen, and World Bank Poverty Database, PovCalNet, for other countries.

Data for Gini index: World Bank, downloaded July 2021.

Note: Tunisia national poverty line (using World Bank methodology): new methodology starting in 2000 uses higher poverty lines and results in higher poverty rates.

Table 1.3 Poverty Rates and Inequality – East Asia, 1981–2019

Country/ year	*Poverty rate (PPP $ 2005) $1.25/day (%)*	*Poverty rate (PPP $ 2011) $1.9/day (%)*	*Poverty rate (PPP $ 2005) $ 2/day*	*Poverty rate (PPP $ 2011) $3.2/day (%)*	*Poverty rate national poverty line (%)*	*Gini index of inequality*
China						
1990		66.2		90.0		32.3
1993		56.6		83.4		
1996		41.7		72.9		35.3
1999		40.2		68.3		38.7
2002		31.7		57.7		42.1
2005		18.5		43.2		41.0
2008		14.8		34.6		42.9
2010		11.2		28.5	17.2	43.7
2013		1.9		12.1	8.5	39.7
2015		0.7		7.0	5.7	38.6
2016				5.4	4.5	38.5
2017					3.1	
2018					1.7	
Indonesia						
1984		71.4		90.6		32.4
1987		71.4		91.6		30.6
1990		58.8		85.4		31.2
1993		58.5		84.9		32.0
1996		47.4		77.6		34.4
1998		66.7		88.8		31.1
2000		39.3		77.2	19.1	28.5
2005		21.1		57.3	16.0	33.0
2008		21.8		53.9	15.4	35.1
2010		15.7		45.0	13.3	36.4
2013		9.4		37.6	11.4	39.9
2015		7.2		30.5	11.2	39.7
2016				28.6	10.9	38.1
2017		5.7		24.6	10.6	38.1
2018				21.5	9.8	37.8
2019				19.9	9.4	38.2
Korea, Rep.						
2006		0.2		0.5		31.7
2008		0.2		0.5		32.3
2010		0.5		0.7		32.0
2012		0.5		0.5		31.6
2014				0.5		31.2
2016				0.2		31.4
Malaysia						
1984		2.9		12.9		48.6
1987		2.1		12.7		47.0
1989		1.6		11.7		46.2
1992		1.3		11.8		47.7
1995		1.8		11.5		48.5
1997		0.4		7.3		49.1
2004		0.4		2.6		46.1

(Continued)

Table 1.3 Poverty Rates and Inequality – East Asia, 1981–2019 *(Continued)*

Country/ year	*Poverty rate (PPP $ 2005) $1.25/day (%)*	*Poverty rate (PPP $ 2011) $1.9/day (%)*	*Poverty rate (PPP $ 2005) $ 2/day*	*Poverty rate (PPP $ 2011) $3.2/day (%)*	*Poverty rate national poverty line (%)*	*Gini index of inequality*
2007		0.5		3.4		46.1
2008		0.7		4.2		45.5
2011		0.1		1.2		43.9
2013		0.0		0.4		41.3
2015		0.0		0.3	7.6	41.0
2018					5.6	
Philippines						
1985		28.1				
1988		25.1				
1991		26.6				
1994		25.0				
1997		17.7				
2000		14.5		37.9		47.7
2003		13.1		36.0	24.9	46.6
2006		14.7		38.2	26.6	47.2
2009		10.7		34.0	26.3	46.3
2012		12.0		33.3	25.2	44.6
2015		7.8		25.7	23.5	42.3
2018				17.0	16.7	
Thailand						
1981		19.6		42.8		45.2
1988		14.3				43.8
1990		9.4		35.9		45.3
1992		6.6		28.8		47.9
1994		3.2		19.2		43.5
1996		2.2		15.0		42.9
1998		1.8		14.3		41.5
2000		2.5		18.3	42.3	42.8
2002		1.1		11.8	32.4	41.9
2004		0.8		8.7	26.8	42.5
2007		0.3		4.3	20.0	39.8
2010		0.1		2.4	11.4	39.4
2012		0.1		1.4	12.6	39.3
2015		0.0		0.5	7.2	36.0
2017		0.0		0.4	8.6	36.5
2018				0.5	7.9	36.4
2019				0.3	9.9	34.9
East Asia and Pacific						
1981	77.4	80.2	92.6	93.4		
1984	65.5	69.7	88.5	90.8		
1987	54.2	58.8	81.6	86.3		
1990	54.7	60.9	79.8	85		
1993	50.8	53.3	75.8	79.4		
1996	36.0	40.2	64.1	70.1		
1999	35.5	37.9	61.8	66.6		
2002	27.6	29.1	51.9	56.6		

(Continued)

Table 1.3 Poverty Rates and Inequality – East Asia, 1981–2019 *(Continued)*

Country/ year	*Poverty rate (PPP $ 2005) $1.25/day (%)*	*Poverty rate (PPP $ 2011) $1.9/day (%)*	*Poverty rate (PPP $ 2005) $ 2/day*	*Poverty rate (PPP $ 2011) $3.2/day (%)*	*Poverty rate national poverty line (%)*	*Gini index of inequality*
2005	16.8	18.4	38.7	44.6		
2008		14.8		37		
2010		10.8		30		
2013		3.3		16.9		
2016		1.7		10.3		
2019		1		6.3		

For international poverty lines:

Sources: World Development Indicators 2008 and Poverty data Supplement. Other figures are estimates from PovCalNet. For MENA and EAP: Chen and Ravallion (2008).

Notes:
Columns for $1.25/day and $2.0/day are for international PPP 2005 dollars.
Columns for $1.9/day and $3.2/day are for International 2011 PPP dollars, downloaded from World Bank July 2019.

For national poverty line:

Sources: From World Bank database, updated July 2019. Data for Gini index: World Bank, downloaded July 2021.

the last column of both tables, we present the best over time coverage of the Gini coefficient of income inequality calculated primarily on the basis of census or sample survey data on gross expenditures or incomes of households by the World Bank.

Starting with the data on the cross-country comparable poverty rates among different MENA countries in the first four columns of Table 1.2, it can be seen that by 2005 using $1.25 and $2.0 per day poverty lines, or alternatively by 2010 using $1.9 and $3.2 per day lines, poverty rates in Tunisia had fallen to levels among the lowest among MENA countries, quite similar to Iran or Jordan.[3] While, as shown in Table 1.3, the absolute reduction in those poverty rates between 1981 and either 2005 or 2015 was larger still in East Asia than in Tunisia (from Table 1.2), Tunisia's poverty rates in 2005, 2010, or 2015 were less than one-third of those for the East Asian average in all four columns. Moreover, as shown by Lowe (2006, Figure 1), Tunisia is the only MENA country to have reduced its poverty rate after 1990 by enough to suggest that it would be able to more than attain Target 1 of the Millennium Development Goals (MDG 1) of reducing the percentage of people living on less than $1 a day by 50%. Lowe (2006) also showed that, while the percentage of the population in MENA as a whole suffering from quantitative malnutrition (MDG 2) had risen from 6.8% to 8.5% between 1990 and 2001, even by that date (2001), Tunisia had already succeeded in reaching the MDG target of reducing its rate by 50% by 2015.

The last column in Table 1.2 shows that Tunisia's Gini index of income/expenditures inequality had fallen significantly from 45.5 in 1981 (or even more from 50.3 in 1966–1967) to 37.7 in 2005 and then further to 32.8 in 2015, by far the largest reduction in the Gini of any country shown in the table, though to a level that was still not below those of Algeria, Egypt, Iraq, or Lebanon. While in the 1980s, Tunisia's income inequality measure was higher than for some East Asian countries (as shown in Table 1.3) for which data are available (China, Indonesia) but similar to Malaysia, by the mid-2000s it was lower than China, Thailand, Malaysia, and the Philippines. Moreover, by 2015, Tunisia's inequality index of 32.8 had fallen below those of all East Asian countries, except possibly Korea.[4]

As the relationship between GDP growth and per capita GDP growth, on the one hand, and income inequality, on the other, has become more controversial over time (reflected, e.g., in the famous book by Piketty 2014), increasing emphasis has been given to the different ways of measuring income inequality, such as pre-tax or post-tax and on income received as opposed to income spent, and on inequality over the whole spectrum of incomes as in the Gini coefficient or alternatively over the extremes such as the ratio of the income of some of the top percentiles of income earners relative to that of the bottom percentiles of income earners.

In keeping with this important concern and to give this important relation greater attention, Table 1.4 provides additional data on income inequality for the slightly narrower time period for which the data are most complete (1980–2019) taken from the World Inequality Database (WID). In this case, the inequality calculations are based on pre-tax income and by both the ratio of the income of the top 10% to income of the bottom 50% (in the first five columns of the table) and by the Gini Coefficient in the next five columns of the table. The data are admittedly of uneven quality, the figures presented in some cases being only for a year somewhat near the year at the top of the column. Especially weak are the calculations for the GCC for which the data sources are especially limited. The data for East Asian sample countries, however, are of generally quite high quality.

Even though the measures of income inequality and the data source used in Table 1.4 are quite different than those in Table 1.3, the messages from Table 1.4 about the levels of, and changes in, inequality over time are broadly consistent with those derived from Tables 1.2 and 1.3, but with a few differences.

In particular, at the start of period (in the 1980s), by any measure of income inequality, Tunisia's level of income inequality was somewhat higher than that of most non-oil exporting countries in MENA and East Asia (some exceptions being Yemen and to a lesser extent Syria among the non-oil exporting MENA countries, and Thailand among the East Asian countries). Tunisia's measures of inequality were, however, not higher than those of most oil-exporting countries in MENA (exceptions being Algeria and Libya).

Table 1.4 Indicators of Inequality in MENA and East Asia from WID, 1980–2019

	Ratio of income of top 10% to income of bottom 50% (pre-tax national income)					***Gini coefficient (pre-tax national income, adults)***				
Country	***1980***	***1990***	***2000***	***2010***	***2019***	***1980***	***1990***	***2000***	***2010***	***2019***
MENA non-major oil exporters	**20.7**	**20.6**	**21.2**	**22.5**	**21.4**	**61.3**	**61.3**	**61.9**	**62.4**	**61.5**
Djibouti	17.8	17.8	17.8	20.8	18.9	59.0	59.0	59.0	61.7	60.0
Egypt, Arab Rep.	14.0	14.0	17.6	15.4	17.1	55.2	55.2	59.6	57.1	58.9
Jordan	17.8	21.3	17.7	20.2	17.5	59.4	62.4	59.3	62.0	59.2
Lebanon	21.5	21.5	21.5	26.7	27.1	62.4	62.4	62.4	65.6	65.9
Morocco	18.1	18.5	19.1	18.8	18.2	59.2	59.6	60.4	60.2	59.6
Syrian Arab Republic	23.8	23.7	24.7	27.0	27.0	64.4	64.4	64.9	66.0	66.0
Tunisia	**21.7**	**17.5**	**18.9**	**13.8**	**12.5**	**62.4**	**58.9**	**60.1**	**54.5**	**52.8**
West Bank and Gaza	22.1	22.1	22.8	25.9	21.4	62.9	62.9	63.2	65.0	62.1
Yemen, Rep.	29.3	29.3	30.6	33.7	32.5	67.0	67.0	67.9	69.7	69.0
MENA major oil exporters	**21.2**	**19.6**	**17.7**	**16.4**	**16.1**	**62.1**	**60.7**	**59.2**	**56.9**	**56.7**
Algeria	19.2	17.6	12.5	10.2	10.0	60.8	59.1	52.9	49.1	48.8
Iran, Islamic Rep.	26.0	21.3	22.0	20.1	20.0	66.0	62.7	63.1	61.3	61.5
Iraq	24.1	24.1	21.4	21.8	20.7	64.7	64.7	64.7	63.0	62.0
Libya	15.6	15.2	14.9	13.4	13.5	56.9	56.4	56.1	54.1	54.4
MENA GCC	**29.1**	**29.1**	**29.2**	**29.2**	**26.3**	**66.7**	**66.7**	**66.8**	**66.8**	**65.1**
Bahrain	27.1	27.1	26.6	27.4	28.9	66.2	66.2	65.8	66.2	67.3
Kuwait	25.9	25.9	25.9	24.8	23.3	65.5	65.5	65.5	65.2	64.7
Oman	32.0	32.0	32.0	32.0	32.0	67.8	67.8	67.8	67.8	67.8
Qatar	31.2	31.2	31.2	31.4	31.5	67.4	67.4	67.7	67.7	67.9
Saudi Arabia	28.1	28.1	28.0	28.1	25.2	66.4	66.4	66.4	66.5	65.0
United Arab Emirates	28.5	28.5	28.9	29.9	19.5	66.5	66.5	66.6	66.7	60.2
East Asia	**15.2**	**16.4**	**16.3**	**17.4**	**15.6**	**53.4**	**55.4**	**56.2**	**58.3**	**56.5**
China	5.6	7.2	10.3	15.5	14.5	38.2	43.2	49.7	56.6	55.5
Indonesia	13.2	16.3	11.5	14.9	19.4	54.0	57.6	51.5	56.0	60.0
Korea, Rep.	7.1	8.0	10.6	14.8	14.5	42.1	44.4	49.7	55.7	55.3
Malaysia	17.2	16.1	16.1	14.8	11.6	58.9	57.7	57.6	56.0	51.2
Philippines	19.0	20.7	22.2	20.0	16.1	60.5	61.8	63.1	61.0	57.5
Thailand	29.0	29.8	27.0	24.1	17.6	66.9	67.5	65.8	64.7	59.2

Source: World Inequality Database, World Inequality Lab.

Note: For many countries, data points are for only a few years, and the rest is extrapolated.

Over the 1980–2019 period, however, Tunisia experienced one of the largest declines in inequality compared to the same groups of countries: the only exceptions being Thailand which started from a much higher level of inequality and experienced a very large decline, and Malaysia which started from a low level and experienced a large (but smaller) decline as well

By 2010 and even more so in 2019, inequality levels were lower in Tunisia than in all non-oil exporting countries in MENA and indeed all MENA countries except Algeria. Moreover, by 2019, Tunisia's inequality measures were below those of all East Asian countries except Malaysia.

From the last two columns in the table, it can be seen that both measures of inequality were also falling between 1980 and 2019 for most oil exporting countries in MENA (especially in Algeria and the UAE), exceptions being Bahrain and Qatar where they increased slightly. On the other hand, for most East Asian countries, inequality increased over the period, most sharply in fast growing China and Korea, the exceptions in this case being slower growing Malaysia and Philippines. Lee and Shin (2021) relate some of these differences in growth and inequality patterns to different types of capitalism and changes therein. They argued that the high but slightly declining growth of Korea combined with sharp increases in income inequality reflected a major change in Korea's economic system which has become more similar to western forms of capitalism in which open finance and short-termism dominate, resulting in higher levels of inequality. They noted that Korea's inequality, as measured by the ratio of top 10% to bottom 50% which more than doubled between 1980 and 2019 (from 7.1 to 14.5) to become much closer to the high levels of income inequality in the United States and UK to which Piketty (2014) had called attention. They also related this form of capitalism to slower growth as in western countries, though the two East Asian countries with the greatest increases in income inequality, Korea and China, have quite definitely not become slow-growing countries. This phenomena of rising inequality and falling growth rates will be discussed more thoroughly in Chapters 5 and 6 where the phenomena of globalization and the Middle-Income Trap will be discussed and especially in the context of China where growth has been maintained at unusually high rates for several decades, but income inequality has also increased. Consistent with its progress in lowering income inequality, Tunisia also achieved major gains in the access of its population to basic public services which were broadly at a par with or better than other MENA and East Asian countries. By the year 2000, almost 95% of the population was connected to the electricity grid, and by 2017, almost 100%. Likewise, the share of the population with access to safe drinking water was 41% in 2000, but increased significantly to 86.3% by 2010, and even 92.7% by 2017. Similarly, based on data from the World Development Indicators (WDI), the share of the population using basic sanitation services reached 77% in 2000 and 90% in 2017. These improvements, quite naturally, are likely related to the substantial improvements in Tunisia's health measures in the first several columns of Table 1.1, which were among the best of all countries in the table.

After having investigated what is believed to be some of the most basic underlying ingredients for successful economic development in Tables 1.1–1.4, in Tables 1.5 and 1.6 we turn to the most common overall measures of macroeconomic performance for both classical and neoclassical economic growth analysis, namely, GDP per capita levels and GDP growth rates. The first three columns of Table 1.5 present comparable data on levels of GDP per capita in constant international US dollars of 2011 for three different years (1990, 2010, and 2019, respectively) and, as in the preceding tables for both MENA and the six East Asian countries. In column (4) are the ratios of 2019 levels relative to those of 1990, a crude measure of the growth of per capita GDP over the period. In columns (6), (7), and (8), we present the average rates of overall GDP growth at constant prices, of per capita GDP growth and of population growth, respectively, over the longest possible period of time as indicated in column (5). Population growth rates for the years 1970–2010 are presented in column (9), and in the last three columns of the table are absolute population sizes for the years 1990, 2010, and 2019, respectively.

Columns (6) and (7) of Table 1.5 highlight Tunisia's quite satisfactory growth rates of GDP growth at constant prices of 4.8% per annum and in per capita terms of 2.8% per annum, respectively, over the period 1966–2010. However, by comparing with other countries' GDP and GDP per capita growth, over as much as possible of the five decades (1960–2010), one can see that Tunisia was by no means the strongest performer. Over the long period, among the countries for which sufficient data were available, Oman was the star performer in MENA with an average GDP growth of 7.0% per year and a GDP per capita growth of 3.3%. Indeed, according to the Commission on Growth and Development (2008) report, Oman is one of only 13 countries in the whole world to have achieved sustained growth of at least 7% per year for at least 25 years. Oman, moreover, was followed quite closely by Egypt among MENA countries with corresponding growth rates of 5.5 and 3.2%, respectively, and until 2007 at least, by Syria in GDP growth, though not in its GDP per capita growth rate. A few major oil-exporters, namely, Qatar, Kuwait, Libya, Iraq, and Bahrain and, among non-oil exporters, also Lebanon, achieved slightly higher growth rates than Tunisia but only over much shorter periods of time. The stronger performance of Lebanon was also rather exceptional and largely attributable to the fact that this shorter period was immediately after its long civil war, during which it had lost a lot of its population and businesses, but then after which it was undergoing something of a recovery. Hence, in general Tunisia, though not exactly a star, was performing quite well in terms of growth compared to other MENA countries. However, at the same time, Tunisian GDP growth rates were well behind all the East Asian countries except the Philippines. Tunisia's comparatively better performance in per capita growth than in

Table 1.5 GDP, GDP Per Capita, and Population, 1990–2019

Country	GDP per capita (constant PPP 2017 international $) 1990	GDP per capita (constant PPP 2017 international $) 2010	GDP per capita (constant PPP 2017 international $) 2019	Ratio GDP per Capita PPP 2019/1990	GDP and population growth period	Growth rate of GDP (constant prices) (%)	Growth rate of GDP per capita (constant prices) (%)	Annual population growth rate (%)	Annual population growth 1970–2010 (%)	Population (Millions) 1990	Population (Millions) 2010	Population (Millions) 2019
Weighting of regional averages	*Weighted by population*				*Unweighted simple averages*				*Unweighted*			
MENA non-major oil exporters	**5553**	**9635**	**10648**	**1.9**		**5.0**	**2.2**	**2.8**	**2.5**	**122.278**	**187.098**	**217.403**
Djibouti	..	..	..	..	..	..	..	..	4.1	0.590	0.840	0.974
Egypt, Arab Rep.	6087	10340	11763	1.9	1961–2010	5.5	3.2	2.3	2.3	56.134	82.761	100.388
Jordan	7924	11316	10071	1.3	1977–2010	4.3	0.6	3.7	3.7	3.566	7.262	10.102
Lebanon	7553	19499	14552	1.9	1989–2010	6.1	3.1	2.9	2.0	2.803	4.953	6.856
Morocco	3817	6281	7537	2.0	1967–2010	4.4	2.6	1.9	1.8	24.807	32.343	36.472
Syria	..	..	..		1961–2007	5.4	2.2	3.2	3.1	12.446	21.363	17.070
Tunisia	**5432**	**10113**	**10756**	**2.0**	**1966–2010**	**4.8**	**2.8**	**2.0**	**2.0**	**8.243**	**10.635**	**11.695**
West Bank and Gaza	..	5411	6245		1995–2010	4.3	1.5	2.8	0.0	1.978	3.786	4.685
Yemen	..	..	..	..	1991–2010	4.7	1.4	3.3	3.7	11.710	23.155	29.162
MENA Major Oil Exporters	**8527**	**12487**	**11919**	**1.4**	..	**4.3**	**1.9**	**2.4**	**2.6**	**103.981**	**145.680**	**172.054**
Algeria	8746	10971	11511	1.3	1961–2010	3.9	1.4	2.5	2.3	25.759	35.977	43.053
Iran, Islamic Rep.	8631	13806	12389	1.4	1961–2010	2.8	0.1	2.7	2.5	56.366	73.763	82.914
Iraq	7866	8955	10815	1.4	1969–2010	5.4	2.6	2.8	2.8	17.419	29.742	39.310
Libya	..	22540	15174		2000–2010	5.2	3.7	1.5	2.7	4.437	6.198	6.777

(Continued)

Table 1.5 GDP, GDP Per Capita, and Population, 1990–2019 *(Continued)*

Country	*GDP per capita (constant PPP 2017 international $) 1990*	*GDP per capita (constant PPP 2017 international $) 2010*	*GDP per capita (constant PPP 2017 international $) 2019*	*Ratio GDP per Capita PPP 2019/1990*	*GDP and population growth period*	*Growth rate of GDP (constant prices) (%)*	*Growth rate of GDP per capita (constant prices) (%)*	*Annual population growth rate (%)*	*Annual population growth 1970–2010 (%)*	*Population (Millions) 1990*	*Population (Millions) 2010*	*Population (Millions) 2019*
Weighting of regional averages	*Weighted by population*				*Unweighted simple averages*				*Unweighted*			
MENA GCC	**46294**	**48545**	**50952**	**1.1**	..	**6.3**	**0.7**	**5.6**	**5.2**	**22.942**	**45.102**	**57.694**
Bahrain	38601	44600	45060	1.2	1981–2010	4.8	0.8	3.9	4.0	0.496	1.241	1.641
Kuwait	..	58810	49854		1991–2010	5.2	3.2	2.0	5.9	2.095	2.992	4.207
Oman	26563	33871	27299	1.0	1966–2010	7.0	3.3	3.7	3.6	1.812	3.041	4.975
Qatar	..	95908	90044		2001–2010	14.1	0.9	13.1	6.1	0.476	1.856	2.832
Saudi Arabia	41393	44037	46962	1.1	1969–2010	2.8	−1.2	4.0	3.9	16.234	27.421	34.269
United Arab Emirates	111454	54922	67119	0.6	1976–2010	4.2	−2.8	6.9	7.8	1.828	8.550	9.771
East Asia	**2561**	**9731**	**16092**	**6.3**	..	**6.6**	**4.7**	**2.0**	**1.8**	**1495.951**	**1818.463**	**1929.742**
China	1424	8885	16092	11.3	1961–2010	8.8	7.4	1.5	1.2	1135.185	1337.705	1397.715
Indonesia	4533	8287	11812	2.6	1961–2010	5.5	3.5	2.1	1.9	181.413	241.834	270.626
Korea, Rep.	12656	34394	42719	3.4	1961–2010	8.6	7.3	1.3	1.1	42.869	49.554	51.709
Malaysia	10306	20536	28364	2.8	1961–2010	6.7	4.2	2.5	2.5	18.030	28.208	31.950
Philippines	4232	5918	8915	2.1	1961–2010	3.6	1.0	2.6	2.5	61.895	93.967	108.117
Thailand	7101	14397	18451	2.6	1961–2010	6.6	4.8	1.8	1.5	56.558	67.195	69.626

Source: Authors' calculations based on data from World Bank WDI.

Notes:
Total GDP growth rate: calculated using a linear regression on the logarithmic transformation of GDP in constant local currency.
Total population growth rate: calculated using a linear regression on the logarithmic transformation.
GDP per capita is the difference of the total GDP growth rate and population growth rate, slightly different from figures in Table 1.6.
Average GDP per capita for groups of countries is weighted by population.
Average growth rates are simple averages population.

aggregate GDP growth is attributable to its somewhat slower rate of population growth shown in columns (8) and (9) of the table. Tunisia's relatively low population growth can largely be attributed to the relatively early rise in its female labor force participation rate and greater gender equity (to be documented in Tables 2.11 and 2.12).[5]

Table 1.6 presents for each of the same countries, wherever possible, the average growth rates of GDP per capita by decade, beginning with 1961–1970 in column (1) to 2011–2019 in column (6). For comparison purposes, it also presents in column (7) the growth rates for the longest period possible before 2011. Careful inspection of the per capita GDP growth rate data for individual countries over as many decades as the data in the different columns permit helps to detect an important contributor to the comparatively greater success in per capita GDP growth of Oman, Egypt, Tunisia, and most East Asian countries over the 1960–2010 period. This is their considerably lower volatility in growth rates over time. In particular, notice that, of the countries with growth rates available for at least four different decades, the only countries without negative average growth rates for at least one decade were the overall strong growth performing countries, Egypt, Morocco, Oman, and Tunisia among MENA countries and all except Philippines among East Asian countries. Note also that even Tunisia's volatility in growth rates was considerably greater than that in five of the six East Asian countries. That negative effect on growth for MENA countries is formalized in Nugent (2021) which reports a significantly negative effect of growth volatility on long-term growth of GDP per capita in a virtually complete sample of MENA countries.

The six tables already presented (i.e., Tables 1.1–1.6) and this very brief introductory chapter call attention to the main differences in growth performance over the last 60 years in MENA and East Asian countries, which are the comparatively successful growth performance of Tunisia and a couple of other MENA countries like Oman and Egypt relative to most of the other MENA countries, but at the same time that the growth rates of these relatively successful countries have fallen well short of that of almost all of the East Asian countries in the sample.

We conclude this introductory chapter with a brief sketch of what lies ahead. In particular, going beyond the broad developmental outcome indicators discussed in this chapter, we draw in Chapter 2 upon additional statistical data to go into greater depth to compare the economic performance of Tunisia, with its fellow MENA countries and with our sample of six East Asian countries. As we shall show, there are many dimensions or indicators on which Tunisia seems to have performed relatively well, that is, better than most, but perhaps not all other, countries of the MENA region. That conclusion is reached on the basis of both a relatively large set of development outcomes as well the major features of development dynamics.

Then, in Chapter 3 we provide a review of the factors which have been at play to explain Tunisia's performance. We start by identifying some

Table 1.6 Real GDP Per Capita Growth (%), 1961–2019

Country	*Average growth rates of real GDP per capita by decade (%)*						*Average growth rate of GDP per capita for available years period (%)*	*Actual period*
	1961–1970	*1971–1980*	*1981–1990*	*1991–2000*	*2001–2010*	*2011–2019*	*1961–2010*	
MENA non-major oil exporters (weighted average)	**3.1**	**4.5**	**2.3**	**2.2**	**2.9**	**−0.3**	**2.6**	..
MENA non-major oil exporters (simple average)	**2.9**	**5.8**	**0.5**	**2.4**	**2.9**	**−0.4**	**2.1**	..
Djibouti	..	..	..	..	..	4.94	..	..
Egypt, Arab Rep.	2.36	4.51	3.36	2.54	3.16	1.43	3.12	1961–2010
Jordan		10.47	−2.56	0.95	3.14	−1.31	0.59	1976–2010
Lebanon				5.05	3.08	−2.88	3.04	1989–2010
Morocco	5.74	3.26	3.00	1.41	3.69	1.97	2.50	1967–2010
Syrian Arab Republic	0.99	6.22	−1.82	2.19	2.23		2.12	1961–2007
Tunisia	**2.41**	**4.45**	**0.70**	**2.96**	**3.55**	**0.91**	**2.72**	**1966–2010**
West Bank and Gaza					3.39	1.47	1.49	1995–2010
Yemen				1.45	1.16	−9.57	1.39	1991–2010
MENA major oil exporters (weighted average)	**6.8**	**1.5**	**−1.8**	**1.9**	**2.6**	**0.5**	**1.0**	..
MENA major oil exporters (simple average)	**5.7**	**3.4**	**−1.1**	**2.9**	**2.5**	**0.2**	**1.9**	..
Algeria	2.28	4.02	−0.30	0.05	2.43	0.70	1.33	1961–2010
Iran, Islamic Rep.	9.04	−2.24	−3.00	0.85	3.42	−0.17	0.08	1961–2010
Iraq	..	8.31	−0.11	7.75	0.20	1.95	2.52	1969–2010
Libya	..	..	..	..	3.94	−1.61	3.65	2000–2010

(*Continued*)

Table 1.6 Real GDP Per Capita Growth (%), 1961–2019 *(Continued)*

Country	*Average growth rates of real GDP per capita by decade (%)*						*Average growth rate of GDP per capita for available years period (%)*	*Actual period*
	1961–1970	*1971–1980*	*1981–1990*	*1991–2000*	*2001–2010*	*2011–2019*	*1961–2010*	
MENA GCC (weighted average)	17.9	3.5	−5.6	−0.5	0.1	0.3	−0.8	
MENA GCC (simple average)	**31.5**	**2.8**	**−2.8**	**0.0**	**−0.4**	**−0.3**	**0.2**	
Bahrain			−1.03	2.07	−0.82	0.46	0.81	1981–2010
Kuwait				−2.91	2.20	−2.40		1966–2010
Oman	31.49	1.68	4.03	2.31	0.16	−2.24	3.17	1966–2010
Qatar					0.83	−0.85	0.83	2001–2010
Saudi Arabia		4.27	−7.44	−0.69	1.07	0.40	−1.18	1969–2010
United Arab Emirates		2.33	−6.73	−0.64	−6.02	2.57	−2.58	1976–2010
East Asia (weighted average)	**3.3**	**4.2**	**7.5**	**7.8**	**8.6**	**5.9**	**6.4**	
East Asia (simple average)	**3.6**	**5.0**	**4.6**	**4.3**	**4.7**	**4.1**	**4.6**	
China	3.47	3.99	8.71	9.46	10.27	6.74	7.26	1961–2010
Indonesia	0.61	4.61	3.05	2.36	3.95	3.93	3.39	1961–2010
Korea, Rep.	6.92	8.31	9.11	5.80	4.07	2.47	7.19	1961–2010
Malaysia	3.53	5.39	2.54	4.35	2.93	3.71	4.07	1961–2010
Philippines	1.74	3.11	−1.69	0.89	3.05	4.84	0.99	1961–2010
Thailand	5.08	4.57	5.65	2.99	3.96	2.85	4.72	1961–2010

Source: Authors' calculations based on data from World Bank WDI.

Notes:
GDP per capita, constant prices, local currency.
GDP growth rates: calculated from regression of logarithm of GDP per capita when number of observations is 7 or more and linear exponential growth for shorter periods.
Weighted averages are by population.

favorable initial conditions which may have contributed to Tunisia's comparative success. But, initial conditions are not enough. Tunisia has had to face major economic challenges in the 50–60 years following independence and hence a major part of Tunisia's success must also be attributed to the policies adopted in facing these challenges. To that end, the rest of the chapter is devoted to identifying the economic strategies and policies that Tunisia has chosen to deal with these challenges. Notably, these have evolved over time and hence this chapter distinguishes between several different stages and time periods in Tunisia's experience. While in some ways, these strategies and policies can be traced back to the early Bourguiba days and the other favorable initial conditions, in other ways these policies have shown Tunisia to be a relatively early mover in adjusting its policies to changing circumstances and, unlike many of its neighbors in the MENA region, in encouraging both exports and industrial growth.

The next three chapters look into the factors explaining the relative success of Tunisia compared to other MENA countries, and its relative failure compared to the most successful East Asian countries. Chapter 4 identifies factors which explain the relative success of Tunisia compared to other MENA countries. These factors, however, generally do not differentiate Tunisia's development path from that of the East Asian countries. That chapter is followed by two key Chapters (Chapters 5 and 6) which explore and pull together the deeper policy and institutional contributors to Tunisia's relative failure compared to East Asia.

Chapter 5 identifies a set of seven economic features, as well as policy and institutional factors which we believe are the major proximate determinants of Tunisia's much weaker performance compared to the more successful East Asian countries. In Chapter 6, we delve deeper into the root causes of these relative weaknesses in Tunisia. As such, the focus is on what might lie at the core of the differences in policies and institutional features, namely, in how the state and markets have been used to allocate resources and improve efficiency, how countries have dealt with both market and government imperfections, and in the roles that the private and public sectors have played in the development process.

Since Tunisia was the first country to go through the phenomena which have come to be known as the 'Arab Spring,' but more appropriately called the 'Arab Uprisings,' and the country which has gone through it more completely than other MENA countries, Chapter 7 is devoted more exclusively to this experience. It focuses first on identifying and explaining the factors lying behind the 2010/2011 uprisings in Tunisia, which led to a major change in the political regime. It then goes on to review Tunisia's economic performance during the transition period toward its higher, though still fragile, democracy, but at the same time its multidimensional economic decline. Once again, considerable emphasis is given to comparisons with both other MENA countries and the East Asian sample countries.

Finally, Chapter 8 draws lessons and conclusions, regarding what we learned about past experiences and understanding what happened. It also suggests some forward-looking lessons and their implications for the future, as the country continues to face its long-standing challenges, goes through a muddled democratic transition, but also faces new challenges as the global environment evolves, driven by digitalization and technological change, a changing context for globalization and climate change.

Notes

1 It should be noted, moreover, that even poverty-stricken Yemen did discover oil in 1984 and developed as a supplier of oil to the world so that by 2016 it was producing about 22 thousand barrels a day, justifying it to be ranked 79th in the world and had proven reserves of about 4 million barrels. Indeed, its oil exports have been accounting for large shares of its total exports but these are not expected to last very far into the future, and the civil war, through which the country has been going for much of the last decade, has meant that it has not been able to take advantage of its not insignificant amounts of oil.

2 PPP: Purchasing Power Parity prices.

3 That rate for Jordan, moreover, had started at a rate below its 2005 level, but was subsequently pushed up by the severe debt problems it got into as a result of its support for Iraq prior to and during the Gulf War and hence Iraq's failure to pay off its large debts to Jordan.

4 Notably, Salehi-Isfahani (2016, 44–45) related Tunisia's lower level of income inequality to lower inequality in access to education, and to the lowest inequality in educational quality among all MENA countries, based on test scores for eighth-grade boys on the internationally standardized educational quality scores (TIMSS).

5 When fertility rates fall, this results in slower growth in population, other things being equal. While there can be various factors contributing to declining fertility such as the greater availability of contraceptive devices, increases in the benefits of working while young for women can be one such cause. Even if not the cause, rising labor force participation rates of females are likely to correspond to falling fertility and population growth rates.

2 Structural Transformation and Long-Term Growth in Tunisia and Across Sample Countries

While not contradicting the earlier approaches of Amartya K. Sen and others discussed in Chapter 1, many of the more recent and 'modern' approaches to understanding long-term economic growth, especially in developing countries, stress the importance of more structural and dynamic aspects of growth and development. Indeed, in this Chapter, we find it necessary to paint a somewhat more mixed picture of Tunisia's performance when we explore five major features of its structural and developmental dynamics. The examination of these underlying economic features helps to identify some of the most important similarities and differences among the countries in our sample. Despite its several aforementioned areas of considerable strength and success in development, we show that Tunisian development exhibited only very limited structural transformation, quite low overall productivity growth and slow technological progress, weak labor market dynamics, and only slight improvements in the gender equity in its labor markets.

A. Limited Structural Transformation in General and Industrialization in Particular

The aforementioned essay in the Economist (July 25, 2009) in Chapter 1 indicated that, even at that pre-Arab Uprisings date, perhaps the most notable area in which MENA countries lagged behind, not only behind East Asia but really behind most of the world, was in manufacturing, which is deemed very important for developing countries in generating the employment opportunities for their rapidly growing labor forces and in reducing poverty. Indeed, many different theoretical and empirical perspectives have pointed to the critical role of manufacturing and industrialization in overcoming the problems of underdevelopment.

Historical studies of developed countries have called attention to the rise of manufacturing in raising GDP per capita in England, Netherlands, elsewhere in Western Europe and subsequently in the United States. But also in the developing country context, beginning in the 1960s much of the credit for their 'East Asian Growth Miracle' was attributed to their unusually rapid

DOI: 10.4324/9781003309550-2

industrial growth in these East Asian countries. Among the mechanisms cited as lying behind these cases of rapid industrial growth have been those of economies of scale in many manufacturing activities, and the increasing division of labor which would lead to specialization and technological change from classical growth theories of Adam Smith. Another mechanism identified in the post-war period of the 1950s and 1960s was the ability to take advantage of the 'surplus labor' that was deemed to be so prevalent in low-income countries according to W. Arthur Lewis (Lewis 1954). Subsequent to Lewis, various other scholars in the field of Development Economics developed strategies for how to achieve this objective. One of these was the 'Big Push' of Nurkse (1953) and another took the form of the backward and forward linkages of Hirschman (1958).[1] It is clear, therefore that there are numerous reasons to believe that, if it could be accomplished, manufacturing growth could be an important means of achieving long-term economic development.

In order to examine the comparative success of Tunisia, other MENA countries and the East Asian countries in this respect, Table 2.1 presents comparative data on both agriculture and manufacturing value added as percentages of GDP from 1965 to 2019. In so far as the data are available, it is clear from this table that the shares of manufacturing in GDP have varied quite considerably both across countries and over time from 1965. Consistent with the early analysis of the 'East Asian miracle,' the evidence suggests that all East Asian countries (except perhaps Philippines which was generally regarded as untouched by the East Asian miracle) had shares of manufacturing which grew quite rapidly from 1965 until at least 2005, before declining somewhat after that (Asian Development Bank 2020; World Bank 1993). Consistent with the aforementioned 'surplus labor' theory, the rapid increase in manufacturing in these countries was achieved largely at the expense of agriculture, the shares of which in GDP had started to fall in all these countries from shares which were over 30%, but by 2005 were down to less than 14%. Since agriculture almost everywhere is a relatively low-income sector, the rise of manufacturing and decline in agriculture in East Asia was associated with rapidly increasing GDP per capita. After 2005, however, by which time agriculture's share in GDP had been substantially reduced in East Asia, further growth in its GDP began to be associated with an increase in the share of services (much of which was technology oriented) and in several of these East Asian countries also with a modest decline in the manufacturing share of GDP.

Notably, the shares of Agriculture and Manufacturing in GDP within the MENA region, and the changes therein over time were very different from those of East Asia, with a few notable exceptions. With the single exception of Oman, there was no MENA country with an agriculture share in GDP as high as 30% in 1965, or indeed in any year. The closest other MENA country to that 30% threshold was Syria in 1995 which had done very well in spreading irrigation, accounting for the impressively high growth rates

Table 2.1 Structure of Production, 1965–2019

Country	*Agriculture value added as % of GDP*							*Manufacturing value added as % of GDP*						
	1965	*1975*	*1985*	*1995*	*2005*	*2010*	*2019*	*1965*	*1975*	*1985*	*1995*	*2005*	*2010*	*2019*
MENA non-major oil exporters	**21.0**	**17.7**	**14.4**	**14.0**	**10.2**	**8.3**	**7.1**	**11.6**	**12.7**	**14.7**	**15.4**	**13.0**	**13.6**	**11.9**
Djibouti	..	..	..	..	..	..	1.3	..	..	..	..	..	..	2.8
Egypt, Arab Rep.	25.7	27.7	17.1	15.7	14.0	13.3	11.0	..	16.7	14.1	16.3	16.7	16.1	15.9
Jordan	14.1	6.9	4.9	3.7	2.8	3.6	4.9	10.9	7.8	9.6	12.9	16.0	18.9	17.7
Lebanon	..	..	..	6.8	3.6	3.9	3.1	..	..	..	12.5	7.5	7.7	5.6
Morocco	23.4	17.9	13.3	13.5	11.8	12.9	12.2	15.7	17.1	20.1	18.9	16.8	15.6	14.9
Syrian Arab Republic	..	..	20.8	28.2	20.7	..	..	..	..	..	13.8	..	..	..
Tunisia	**20.8**	**18.5**	**15.8**	**11.4**	**9.2**	**7.5**	**10.3**	**8.1**	**9.1**	**15.1**	**19.0**	**15.7**	**16.5**	**14.8**
West Bank and Gaza	..	..	..	11.8	9.0	9.0	7.1	..	..	..	17.5	11.3	12.4	11.2
Yemen, Rep.	..	..	..	20.5	10.6	8.2	..	..	..	..	12.3	7.1	8.0	..
MENA major oil exporters	**18.6**	**7.3**	**13.6**	**16.6**	**5.9**	**6.7**	**9.3**	**10.8**	**8.0**	**9.4**	**8.4**	**17.6**	**18.0**	**13.5**
Algeria	..	..	..	..	7.7	8.5	12.4	..	..	..	..	49.0	39.0	23.8
Iran, Islamic Rep.	18.6	6.7	12.8	12.6	6.5	6.5	12.2	10.8	9.1	8.9	15.3	15.0	12.8	14.8
Iraq	..	7.8	14.4	20.6	6.9	5.2	3.3	..	6.8	9.9	1.4	1.3	2.3	2.0
Libya	..	..	..	..	2.5	..	..	..	..	..	..	5.1	..	..
MENA GCC	**60.6**	**1.4**	**2.1**	**2.3**	**1.4**	**0.9**	**1.0**		**3.0**	**9.0**	**11.6**	**11.2**	**10.4**	**10.7**
Bahrain	..	..	1.2	0.9	..	0.3	0.3	..	..	10.1	19.1	..	14.5	17.7
Kuwait	..	..	..	0.4	0.3	0.5	0.4	..	..	..	11.0	7.3	6.0	7.2
Oman	60.6	2.8	2.8	2.8	1.6	1.4	2.4	0.4	..	..	..	8.6	10.7	10.5
Qatar	..	..	..	..	0.1	0.1	0.2	..	..	..	..	19.8	12.5	7.8
Saudi Arabia	..	0.9	3.7	5.9	3.3	2.6	2.2	..	5.0	8.0	9.6	9.5	11.0	12.5
United Arab Emirates	..	0.5	0.9	1.8	1.4	0.8	0.7	..	0.9	8.9	6.8	10.6	7.9	8.7
East Asia	**33.0**	**28.9**	**20.7**	**14.3**	**9.7**	**10.0**	**7.6**	**16.3**	**20.8**	**21.5**	**25.1**	**27.8**	**26.2**	**22.9**
China	37.5	32.0	27.9	19.6	11.6	9.3	7.1	..	..	..	..	32.1	31.6	26.8
Indonesia	..	..	23.8	17.1	13.1	13.9	12.7	..	..	16.4	24.1	27.4	22.0	19.7
Korea, Rep.	37.5	24.5	11.8	5.3	2.6	2.1	1.6	17.1	20.1	24.4	25.8	25.7	27.4	25.3
Malaysia	31.0	30.7	20.3	12.9	8.3	10.1	7.3	10.2	18.7	19.7	26.4	27.5	23.4	21.4
Philippines	27.2	30.3	24.6	21.6	13.5	13.7	8.8	23.6	25.7	25.2	23.0	24.3	21.9	18.5
Thailand	31.9	26.9	15.8	9.1	9.2	10.5	8.1	14.2	18.7	21.9	26.2	29.6	30.9	25.6

Source: Data from database: World Bank, World Development Indicators.

in its agricultural value added in the 1980s and early 1990s. Even though China's agricultural share of GDP was not especially high in 1960 (the start of the period under study) as a result of its collectivization to avoid famine just before this (Lin 1990), beginning in the late 1970s, an impressive reform in rural property rights was undertaken which allowed the share of agriculture in China to remain relatively high at 19.6% until the mid-1990s (Lin 1988) despite extremely rapid urbanization. Within the next two decades came the spread of private property rights in China to private sector manufacturing and China's membership in the World Trade Organization, allowing the country to take advantage of manufactures exports in increasing its industrial share very significantly, further decreasing the share of agriculture in GDP.

Among MENA countries, the subsequent declines in agriculture were more modest than in East Asia except in some of the non-GCC major oil exporting countries of the region (such as Algeria, Iran, Iraq, and Libya) where currency appreciation took place as a result of the so-called 'Dutch disease' analyzed by Corden (1984). The GCC countries were largely on fixed exchange rates pegged to the United States (US) dollar and hence were not as adversely affected and their oil revenues allowed these countries to import foreign workers from low-income countries to work in agriculture and other sectors. These issues will be discussed further in Chapter 4.

With respect to the shares of Manufacturing in GDP, there were a few MENA countries, namely, Algeria, Bahrain, Iran, Iraq, Kuwait, Syria, and West Bank and Gaza, which relatively early on had shares of manufacturing in GDP that were at least somewhat comparable to those in East Asia. In several of these cases, this was partly the result of the heavy influence of the public sector, but quite definitely not reflecting competitive private manufacturing sectors in these countries. While virtually all MENA countries had prioritized manufacturing growth over the period shown in the table, the average of manufacturing shares in GDP in MENA non-major oil exporting countries rose by only 3.8 percentage points between 1965 and 1995, whereas the corresponding average manufacturing share of East Asia had increased by 8.8 percentage points, that is, by over two times as much. While among MENA countries, Iran, Jordan, Morocco, Saudi Arabia, UAE, and perhaps even Bahrain and Syria, may also have increased their shares of manufacturing in GDP between 1965 and 1995, the star performer in this respect was Tunisia which increased its manufacturing share by over 10 points from 8.1% in 1965 to 19% in 1995.

Later on, however, during the most recent two decades, that is, between 1995 and 2019, the regional averages of those manufacturing shares in GDP declined by 3.5 percentage points in the MENA countries outside the major oil exporting countries whereas the East Asian countries as a whole maintained an average manufacturing share of about 25%. The only countries to experience increasing shares of manufacturing in GDP during these last two decades among MENA countries were

Jordan (from 12.9% to 17.7%) and Saudi Arabia (from 9.6% to 12.5%). Two East Asian countries, namely, Korea and Thailand, saw their manufacturing shares increase until 2010, but decline again to reach around 25%. For the East Asian countries as a whole, the average share of manufacturing has been declining since 2005 (while it was moving in the direction of rising shares of services).

What about Tunisia? Tunisia's manufacturing share fell after 1995 by a full 4.2 points to 14.8% by 2019, but keeping it still well above the average for its MENA sub-group and a full 8 points below the East Asian average. The rise and subsequent fall in Tunisia's manufacturing share is especially meaningful, given the fact that industrial development has been such a basic objective of Tunisian policy-makers ever since the country's independence as will be documented below. One interesting feature to notice is that, while Tunisia's share of value-added in manufacturing in GDP has been declining in recent years, its share of manufacturing exports in GDP was increasing as will be discussed below (Table 4.8). More importantly, significant diversification was taking place within the manufacturing exports sector, as the share of medium-technology exports in total manufacturing exports increased from 10.3% in 1995 to 30.2% in 2010, while that of high-technology exports increased from 3% to 15.2% (Ghali and Nabli 2020). The share of low-technology exports, mainly clothing and apparel, however, collapsed from 87.8% to 54.5%. The fact that the ability to export manufactures seems to be so important to even the maintenance of Tunisia's still fairly impressive share of manufacturing in GDP makes raising that share further especially challenging.

That sharp decline in the manufacturing share of Tunisia between 1995 and 2019 is also representative of the much greater volatility in these shares across time among MENA countries than among East Asian countries, and also the rather considerable variation from one country to another within the MENA region in contrast to the rather amazing consistency in the industrial shares among East Asian countries in virtually every given year. It should also be noted that the two MENA countries, Algeria and Oman (which are of course major oil exporters) with unusually large shares of manufacturing, for example, in 1995 and 2010, are statistical artifacts resulting from the fact their oil companies which also run refineries and other derivatives from oil have their value added classified as manufacturing value added. Hence, if the oil and derivatives from it were excluded from the manufacturing sector in these countries, the gap between the averages for MENA sub-groups and average East Asian manufacturing shares would have been even greater.

The fact that manufacturing shares in GDP had come to fall since 1995 in a majority of MENA countries including Tunisia, and had leveled off in East Asian countries has led to considerable recent empirical analysis as to whether or not it might now be possible to bypass industrialization as a means of achieving long run growth in GDP per capita, jumping to the services sector whose share in GDP seems to be rising everywhere. This has been suggested by Dasgupta and Singh (2005) based on the Indian experience and by Rodrik (2008, 2009) and Timmer and de Vries (2009) based on that of other regions. Jorgenson et al. (2005) have also questioned whether it is aggregate manufacturing (as a whole) or only some more specific high-tech components within manufacturing that are very important for long-term growth.

In an impressively comprehensive test of such ideas vis-à-vis the traditional view that a large manufacturing sector share in GDP is needed for success in long-term economic growth, Szirmai and Verspagen (2015) undertook a study of 88 countries over the period 1950–2005, separating also by decade and taking into consideration the initial levels of both GDP per capita relative to that of the U.S. and of education in terms of the average years of schooling in the population over the age of 15. Their results provided no support for the importance of the Service Sector in long-term growth, but showed that the manufacturing share was a highly significant contributor to long-term growth primarily only during the 1970–1990 period. Notably, however, The Economist (2020) has pointed to some promising indications that Sub-Saharan Africa may finally be making some progress in industrialization and with it increasing per capita income.[2]

The aforementioned study of Szirmai and Verspagen (2015) also showed that the effect of the share of manufacturing on long-term growth was stronger when interacted with the measure of years of education of population over 15 but weaker when interacted with the country's initial level of GDP per capita relative to that of the US. Since MENA countries including Tunisia are considerably lower than East Asian countries in that educational measure but higher than East Asian countries in terms of GDP per capita, this would seem to suggest that raising the share of manufacturing relative to GDP may have been somewhat less beneficial for long-term growth in MENA countries than in the East Asian countries. For the specific case of Tunisia, however, it would point to its failure to put as much emphasis on raising the quantity and quality of education as it did on health and life expectancy which as shown in the previous Chapter was well above that of many other MENA and East Asian countries. If it had done so, these results suggest that Tunisia would have been able to derive more of the long-term benefits of industrialization on the level of economic development.

In any case, the growth of manufacturing in developed countries historically is widely known to have come at the expense of declining shares of agriculture. By comparing the trends in agriculture shares and manufacturing shares, the same can be seen in Table 2.1 among most countries. Among MENA countries, the largest declines in the shares of value added in agriculture between 1975 and 2010 were by 14 percentage points in Egypt, and by 11 percentage points in Tunisia. Yet, even these declines were quite small compared to those in all six of the East Asian countries, and especially China, Korea, and Malaysia, where these declines exceeded 20 percentage points.

While the unusually large (and perhaps mistakenly large) share of agriculture in Oman accounts for why the decline of agriculture's share in GDP in the GCC was as large as indicated in Table 2.1, the decline in the average agriculture share in GDP for both non-GCC sub-groups of MENA countries was much smaller than that in East Asia between 1965 and 2010. Similarly, the increases in the share of manufacturing in GDP in both MENA's non-major oil exporters (including Tunisia) and in the GCC were considerably smaller than those in East Asian countries.[3]

Another comparative perspective on agricultural transformation can be seen from Table 2.2 which shows the changes over time for this sector in: (a) its share in employment (available only since 1991), (b) its labor productivity, and (c) the growth of its value-added. Even by 1991, the share of employment in agriculture was still quite high in many East Asian countries, such as China (59.7%), Indonesia (54%), the Philippines (44%), and Thailand (60.3%). It was much higher in these East Asian countries than in Tunisia (22.1%)[4] and in all MENA countries, except Morocco and Yemen. But the decline in this share has been dramatic in East Asian countries, reaching 25.3% in China in 2019 and 31.4% in Thailand, reflecting much greater declines there than what was taking place in MENA. Labor was moving out of agriculture much more rapidly in East Asian countries than in MENA, including Tunisia. The Asian Development Bank (2020) report provides data on employment shares for a longer period. Indeed, according to the data from that source, the shares of employment in agriculture declined from 76.4% in the 1970s to 25.6% in 2018 in China and from 61.1% to 32.1% in Southeast Asia.[5]

The implication is that, despite a rate of growth of value-added in agriculture which was typically lower in East Asia, than in MENA countries, productivity growth was much higher there than in MENA during the period since 1991. Growth of labor productivity in agriculture in MENA countries was similar to that of Malaysia, Philippines or Thailand, but much lower than that in the other East Asian countries. Labor productivity increased by almost 200% from 1991 to 2010 in China and by 140% in Korea, but by only 20% in Tunisia and 50% in Egypt. This higher productivity growth was driven by the gains achieved through the green revolution (i.e., new crop varieties and techniques), greater diversification, expanded irrigation, use of fertilizers, and the development of food value chains. For instance, yields in rice production increased from around 2 tons per hectare in the early 1960s to 7 tons per hectare by the mid-2010s in East Asia and to 4 tons per hectare in Southeast Asia. For wheat, the increase during the same period was from 1 ton per hectare to 5 tons in East Asia and to 3 tons per hectare in Southeast Asia.[6] This gain in yields was much greater than in Tunisia where the production of wheat per hectare increased only from 0.5 ton in the early 1960s to 1.6 in 2017. Clearly, climate change combined with already much more arid climatic conditions point to increasing challenges to MENA countries in trying to increase

Table 2.2 Agricultural Transformation, 1961–2019

	Share of agriculture in total employment (%)				***Ratio of labor productivity in agriculture***		***Average Annual Growth Rate of Agriculture value added (%)***					
Country	***1991***	***2000***	***2010***	***2019***	***2010/1991***	***2019/1991***	***1961–1970***	***1971–1980***	***1981–1990***	***1991–2000***	***2001–2010***	***2011–2019***
MENA non-major oil exporters	**30.4**	**27.4**	**20.9**	**16.6**	**1.4**	**1.5**	**3.5**	**4.4**	**4.8**	**3.7**	**5.5**	**2.5**
Djibouti	41.2	40.1	32.8	24.5								7.7
Egypt, Arab Rep.	39.0	29.6	28.3	20.6	1.5	2.5	2.1	2.3	2.9	3.1	3.4	3.1
Jordan	4.8	4.2	3.4	2.5	1.0	1.2		6.8	5.9	−1.5	9.3	2.0
Lebanon	21.0	18.8	14.4	11.3	1.3	1.6				6.8	0.8	3.6
Morocco	46.9	45.4	40.6	33.3	1.1	1.5	7.3	2.0	6.6	5.1	8.2	2.7
Syrian Arab Republic	28.2	32.9	14.5	10.1					3.1	6.7	9.1	
Tunisia	**22.1**	**20.3**	**18.0**	**13.8**	**1.2**	**2.0**	**1.2**	**6.5**	**5.3**	**3.9**	**1.9**	**3.9**
West Bank and Gaza	15.5	14.1	11.8	6.1						0.4	8.9	1.4
Yemen, Rep.	54.8	40.8	24.1	27.5	2.5	0.0				4.8	2.7	−4.5
MENA major oil exporters	**27.7**	**25.5**	**18.7**	**15.4**	**1.3**	**1.5**	**4.1**	**4.0**	**5.1**	**0.8**	**4.0**	**4.2**
Algeria	24.9	22.3	11.9	9.6						−4.6	7.2	4.9
Iran, Islamic Rep.	25.0	24.4	19.2	17.4	1.4	1.8	3.6	5.6	5.1	3.4	3.2	4.3
Iraq	31.5	28.7	23.1	18.3	1.2	1.2	4.6	2.5	5.1	3.6	1.8	3.3
Libya	29.2	26.5	20.6	16.4								

(Continued)

Table 2.2 Agricultural Transformation, 1961–2019 *(Continued)*

	Share of agriculture in total employment (%)				***Ratio of labor productivity in agriculture***		***Average Annual Growth Rate of Agriculture value added (%)***					
Country	***1991***	***2000***	***2010***	***2019***	***2010/1991***	***2019/1991***	***1961–1970***	***1971–1980***	***1981–1990***	***1991–2000***	***2001–2010***	***2011–2019***
MENA GCC	**5.9**	**4.5**	**2.9**	**1.9**	**1.4**	**2.0**	**2.7**	**7.8**	**11.0**	**3.1**	**1.6**	**5.1**
Bahrain	2.4	1.6	1.1	0.9							0.3	2.5
Kuwait	2.3	2.4	2.4	1.8								1.8
Oman	9.9	6.4	5.2	4.0						4.1	2.6	10.9
Qatar	4.4	2.6	1.5	1.2							7.1	10.8
Saudi Arabia	7.9	6.1	4.2	2.4	1.4	2.0	2.7	7.8	11.0	2.1	2.3	1.8
United Arab Emirates	8.5	7.9	3.4	1.4							–4.3	2.7
East Asia	**42.9**	**35.0**	**27.8**	**20.6**	**1.8**	**2.8**	**4.6**	**3.4**	**3.7**	**1.8**	**3.0**	**2.3**
China	59.7	50.0	36.7	25.3	2.9	5.9	5.6	1.6	6.3	3.8	4.1	3.8
Indonesia	55.5	45.3	39.1	28.5	1.7	2.7	2.7	3.5	3.5	2.1	3.5	3.9
Korea, Rep.	14.6	10.6	6.6	5.1	2.4	2.8	4.8	2.4	4.1	2.1	1.4	0.7
Malaysia	22.5	18.4	13.3	10.3	1.4	1.7		4.8	3.2	0.9	3.1	2.0
Philippines	44.9	37.1	32.9	22.9	1.4	2.0	4.3	4.1	1.2	2.1	3.5	2.0
Thailand	60.3	48.8	38.3	31.4	1.2	1.6	5.6	4.0	3.9	–0.4	2.2	1.3

Source: Data from database: World Bank, World Development Indicators.

their agricultural productivity. Even serious attempts to increase the efficiency of water use by metering in Tunisia and neighboring countries have been problematic, making it difficult to achieve higher levels of efficiency in water use.[7]

With wage and profit rates known to being higher in manufacturing than in agriculture, there can be little doubt that the sharp declines in agriculture shares of GDP and rising manufacturing shares in Egypt and Tunisia contributed to the findings concerning falling rates of poverty in these countries (Table 1.2) and perhaps even to their relatively large increases in educational achievement and declining mortality rates shown in Table 1.1.

Agriculture and manufacturing are not the only sectors with interesting implications for comparative performance and relevance to long-term growth. Another interesting sector for countries of the MENA region, including oil countries and their diversification from oil, is the tourism sector. There are several other reasons besides diversification why this sector can be important. First, even in countries in which the public sector is generally important as it has generally been in manufacturing and banking, usually tourism is run largely by the private sector. Second, since tourism in these countries is largely international, tourism revenues can contribute very positively to a country's balance of payments. Third, many MENA countries (but also East Asian countries) may be deemed to have some comparative advantage in this sector based on (1) their warmer climates relative to those in countries like Europe and North America from which tourists come), (2) their lovely sandy beaches, and (3) their many important historical sites based on early civilizations. Table 2.3 presents data, for the period since the 1990s, for the same set of comparator countries for foreign exchange receipts from tourism as a % share of GDP. Not surprisingly, these tourism shares tend to be higher in small countries than in larger ones like China or Indonesia in East Asia. For some MENA countries, including Bahrain, Egypt, Lebanon, Jordan, Morocco, and Tunisia, tourism became a significant contributor to the balance of payments, similar to some Asian countries such as Thailand, Indonesia, and Malaysia. Notably, even though still rather modest in size, the tourism sectors of both UAE and Qatar have increased with the attempts of these countries to develop museums and host important sporting events and conferences.

With data for a longer time period (dating from the 1960s), Table 2.4 reveals Tunisia's significant diversification into the tourism sector in greater detail. In terms of growth over time Tunisia started with a tiny share of tourism in GDP in the 1960s (less the 1%) but grew that share to reach almost 6% by the end of the 1990s. Indeed, its share in current balance of payments receipts reached almost 20% in the mid-1970s but declined somewhat after that as manufacturing exports started growing as well. Although both these shares had fallen sharply by 2010, even then tourism revenues accounted for 10% of total revenues in the balance of payments and 5% of GDP. Yet, both of these

Table 2.3 International Tourism, 1996–2019

	International tourism receipts (% of GDP)				
Country	*1996–2000*	*2001–2005*	*2006–2010*	*2011–2015*	*2016–2019*
MENA non-major oil exporters	**6.49**	**8.32**	**9.35**	**6.70**	**6.95**
Djibouti	1.30	0.70	0.50	0.48	0.71
Egypt, Arab Rep.	4.68	6.21	7.07	2.98	3.61
Jordan	13.34	12.71	15.63	14.74	13.93
Lebanon	5.42	23.58	22.18	15.42	15.55
Morocco	4.85	7.72	9.51	8.24	8.09
Syrian Arab Republic		6.45			
Tunisia	**9.23**	**8.13**	**8.42**	**5.79**	**5.31**
West Bank and Gaza	6.59	1.05	2.16	3.68	1.48
Yemen, Rep.				2.28	
MENA major oil exporters	**0.24**	**0.77**	**0.46**	**0.63**	**0.86**
Algeria			0.26	0.16	0.11
Iran, Islamic Rep.	0.40	0.82	0.53	0.75	0.99
Iraq			0.82	0.97	1.49
Libya	0.09	0.72	0.23		
MENA GCC	**4.13**	**3.74**	**3.01**	**3.16**	**5.52**
Bahrain	10.03	10.50	8.45	6.48	11.26
Kuwait	1.30	0.70	0.50	0.48	0.71
Oman		2.48	2.05	2.52	3.85
Qatar				4.68	8.82
Saudi Arabia			1.49	1.31	2.23
United Arab Emirates	1.06	1.28	2.54	3.49	6.28
East Asia	**3.51**	**3.63**	**4.08**	**4.20**	**4.76**
China	1.35	1.36			
Indonesia		2.17	1.28	1.17	1.54
Korea, Rep.	1.49	1.12	1.11	1.41	1.35
Malaysia	5.38	7.40	8.21	6.98	6.26
Philippines	2.54	2.44	2.37	1.94	2.59
Thailand	6.80	7.27	7.41	9.52	12.07

Source: Data from database: World Bank, World Development Indicators.

tourism shares have fallen sharply since 2010, showing that from 1990 and even more since 2010, the pattern in tourism revenue shares constitutes another example of the extremely large stall in its structural transformation since the 1990s as well as in its ability to accumulate foreign exchange earnings. Between 1990 and 2015, the absolute numbers of both hotels and beds stagnated, and both occupancy rates and average duration of stay fell sharply (by over 50%) although recovering somewhat between 2015 and 2019, the average duration of stay recovered from 4.7 days to 5.4 days and the average occupancy rate from 26.1% to 44.6%.

Table 2.4 Tunisian Tourism, 1965–2019

	1965	*1970*	*1975*	*1985*	*1995*	*2000*	*2005*	*2010*	*2015*	*2019*
Number of hotels	85		273	420	612	736	816	856	862	876
Number of hotel beds (thousands)	8.7		62.4	93.3	161.5	197.5	229.8	241.5	241.4	236.0
Non-resident entries (thousands)	166	411	1014	2003	4120	5057	6378	6903	4201	7984
Receipts per night (TND deflated by CPI base 2010), average last 3 years		69.7	96.1	116.2	91.7	86.5	95.0	109.7	133.5	135.8
Receipts per night (US dollars deflated by CPI base 2010), average last 3 years		87.7	140.0	98.5	79.5	64.4	68.4	79.6	84.3	65.8
Occupancy rate (%)	47		51	46	50	55	49	51	26.1	44.6
Average duration of stay (days)	8.0		8.6	7.2	5.7	6.6	5.3	4.7	2.7	5.4
Receipts as % of balance of payments current revenue		16.5	19.1	16.6	15.8	16.0	11.9	10.0	6.2	8.83
Value added as % of GDP market prices, current prices	0.9	3.2	3.9	3.2	5.8	5.9	5.4	5.0	3.9	4.8

Source: Various national sources.

B. Rapid Urbanization

Urbanization is another aspect of structural transformation, as people tend to be increasingly attracted to living in urban centers where job opportunities, living conditions, access to education, health care, electricity, and other public services are better and their quality also tends to be higher. It represents one of the aspects of the economic structural transformation associated with the growing role of industry and services and the relative decline of lower productivity agriculture.

As shown in Table 2.5, by 1960 Tunisia had already reached a level of urbanization (37.5%) which was much higher than all East Asian countries in our sample. It was also higher than in most MENA countries except for small city states or highly urbanized ones such as Jordan, Lebanon, or Iraq. Over the following decades, the process of urbanization continued at a rapid pace in Tunisia as well as in all the comparator MENA countries. But urbanization was much faster still in East Asia. Indeed, the rate of urbanization of Tunisia was exceeded by that of Korea by 1980, and by that of Malaysia by 2010. The rate of urbanization almost tripled on average in East Asia between 1960 and 2019, while it increased only by 85% in Tunisia. While the rate of growth of the urban population in Tunisia was similar to that of East Asia, the lower overall population growth implied a relatively faster rate of urbanization in East Asia. Despite its relatively early start in urbanization compared to East Asia, by the end of the period, Tunisia's urbanization rate was not much higher than the average of this region. Indeed, since 2000 its annual growth in urbanization has been only about half that of East Asian countries, again contributing to why industrialization was slower in Tunisia and contributing less to growth in per capita GDP than in East Asia.

C. Low Overall Productivity Growth

Much of the literature on long-term development, stemming from the contributions of Solow (1956, 1957), has emphasized that total factor productivity (TFP) growth is perhaps *the* most important factor to be considered in explaining long-term growth differences across countries. It is deemed to be especially important in that it is generally believed to be the source of growth that comes at the lowest social cost, reflecting to a large extent technological progress. TFP differences are also believed to reflect differences in policy or institutional quality and/or changes therein over time, and the associated structural transformation. The computation of TFP and TFP growth, however, is by no means yet entirely standardized and requires much more detailed data on capital stocks and other factors like factor shares and elasticities of substitution among the different factors of production in the aggregate production function of countries across time than are currently available in many cases. As a result, estimates of TFP growth over substantial periods of time are by no means universally available.

Table 2.5 Urbanization, 1960–2019

	Percentage of population in urban areas (%)							*Average annual growth rate of urban population (%)*					
Country	*1960*	*1970*	*1980*	*1990*	*2000*	*2010*	*2019*	*1961–1970*	*1971–1980*	*1981–1990*	*1991–2000*	*2001–2010*	*2011–2019*
MENA non-major oil exporters	**37.6**	**45.3**	**51.9**	**57.8**	**61.2**	**64.4**	**66.8**	**5.3**	**4.5**	**4.2**	**3.4**	**2.8**	**2.2**
Djibouti	50.3	61.8	72.1	76.0	76.5	77.0	77.9	8.5	9.7	5.5	2.0	1.6	1.8
Egypt, Arab Rep.	37.9	41.5	43.9	43.5	42.8	43.0	42.7	3.5	2.8	2.5	1.9	1.9	2.1
Jordan	50.9	56.0	60.0	73.3	78.3	86.1	91.2	7.1	3.9	6.1	4.3	4.4	4.3
Lebanon	42.3	59.5	73.7	83.1	86.0	87.3	88.8	5.8	3.3	2.0	3.5	2.7	3.8
Morocco	29.4	34.5	41.2	48.4	53.3	58.0	63.0	4.2	4.0	3.8	2.5	2.0	2.2
Syrian Arab Republic	36.8	43.3	46.7	48.9	51.9	55.6	54.8	4.9	4.2	3.8	3.4	3.3	–2.7
Tunisia	**37.5**	**43.5**	**50.6**	**57.9**	**63.4**	**66.7**	**69.3**	**3.4**	**3.8**	**3.9**	**2.5**	**1.4**	**1.5**
West Bank and Gaza	44.0	54.3	62.4	67.7	72.0	74.1	76.4				4.5	2.9	2.7
Yemen, Rep.	9.1	13.3	16.5	20.9	26.3	31.8	37.3	5.3	4.7	6.2	6.2	4.8	4.3
MENA major oil exporters	**33.6**	**46.6**	**57.2**	**63.5**	**67.2**	**71.3**	**74.9**	**6.4**	**5.3**	**4.2**	**2.7**	**2.2**	**2.4**
Algeria	30.5	39.5	43.5	52.1	59.9	67.5	73.2	5.3	3.8	4.7	3.3	2.7	2.9
Iran, Islamic Rep.	33.7	41.2	49.7	56.3	64.0	70.6	75.4	4.6	4.9	5.0	2.8	2.1	2.0
Iraq	42.9	56.2	65.5	69.7	68.5	69.1	70.7	5.8	4.7	3.1	2.8	2.4	3.3
Libya	27.3	49.7	70.1	75.7	76.4	78.1	80.4	9.8	7.6	4.0	2.0	1.7	1.3
MENA GCC	**51.6**	**62.7**	**73.5**	**80.7**	**83.1**	**85.3**	**88.3**	**8.3**	**8.7**	**6.0**	**3.4**	**6.5**	**3.9**
Bahrain	82.3	83.8	86.1	88.1	88.4	88.6	89.4	2.9	5.5	3.4	3.0	6.3	3.2
Kuwait	74.9	85.7	94.8	98.0	99.0	100.0	100.0	11.5	7.1	4.6	3.7	3.9	3.8
Oman	16.4	29.7	47.6	66.1	71.6	75.2	85.4	8.6	9.4	7.8	3.0	3.4	6.9
Qatar	31.3	48.7	65.9	76.6	79.8	82.1	84.1	8.7	7.3	7.9	2.6	11.6	4.8
Saudi Arabia	31.3	48.7	65.9	76.6	79.8	82.1	84.1	8.0	8.1	6.7	2.8	3.1	2.7
United Arab Emirates	73.5	79.8	80.7	79.1	80.2	84.1	86.8	10.1	14.8	5.6	5.5	10.5	1.8
East Asia	**22.5**	**27.1**	**34.1**	**42.8**	**49.5**	**56.9**	**62.0**	**4.3**	**4.5**	**4.3**	**3.2**	**2.8**	**2.0**
China	16.2	17.4	19.4	26.4	35.9	49.2	60.3	2.8	2.9	4.6	4.1	3.7	2.7
Indonesia	14.6	17.1	22.1	30.6	42.0	49.9	56.0	4.3	5.1	5.3	4.7	3.1	2.5
Korea, Rep.	27.7	40.7	56.7	73.8	79.6	81.9	81.4	6.4	5.0	3.8	1.7	0.8	0.4
Malaysia	26.6	33.5	42.0	49.8	62.0	70.9	76.6	5.1	4.7	4.4	4.7	3.3	2.2
Philippines	30.3	33.0	37.5	47.0	46.1	45.3	47.1	3.9	4.1	4.9	2.1	1.7	2.0
Thailand	19.7	20.9	26.8	29.4	31.4	43.9	50.7	3.6	5.0	2.7	1.7	4.0	2.0

Source: Data from database: World Bank, World Development Indicators.

In Tables 2.6a and 2.6b, however, we present alternative estimates of TFP growth by decade for Tunisia as well as for several other MENA countries and for each of the same six East Asian countries. These start with the decade 1961–1970 and end with 2011–2019. The TFP growth rates by country and decade presented in this table have been constructed in the standard growth accounting way, that is, as a residual. This method requires construction of a time series on capital stock and its growth based on investment flows data, assuming a reasonable depreciation rate for capital and the use of the perpetual inventory method for constructing capital stocks, as well as the time series data on growth of both the labor force and GDP in real terms. In Table 2.6a, data on GDP growth and employment are taken from the World Bank, while capital stock and labor shares are taken from the Penn World Tables (PWT). In Table 2.6b, we present the TFP calculations using fully the data and methodology of the PWT, but which is unfortunately available only for a smaller number of countries.[8]

As can be seen in the row for Tunisia in Table 2.6a, the estimated rates of TFP growth for Tunisia at the aggregate level, although never very high (and well below those of China and Korea) have always been positive, averaging about 1.67% a year over the period 1961–2010. During the 1980s when its balance of payments and economic conditions reached crisis levels and the distortions and inefficiencies of its import substitution regime (to be discussed in detail in Chapters 4 and 5) became more apparent, its average TFP growth (to be described below) was at its lowest despite some reforms that were instituted late in that decade. With increasing liberalization and the resumption of growth since then, TFP growth had gradually recovered but remained weak. Indeed, especially with the rising importance of the higher technology of its auto parts industry and record FDI inflows during the 2001–2010 decade, Tunisia's TFP growth rate for this period reached 1.8% per annum, that is, close to that reached in the 1960s.[9] While Tunisia's TFP growth was by no means stellar, as can be seen from the other rows of the top section of the table, it has been steadier and higher on average over the whole period 1961–2010 than that of all other MENA countries with the minor exception of Syria. Although its TFP growth was marginally lower on average than that of Syria, Tunisia's TFP growth rates were much less volatile than those of Syria, whose TFP growth rate had collapsed to −1.8% per annum during the 1980s, while in Tunisia TFP growth during that decade fell only to a positive 0.122. Almost all MENA countries (except Morocco and Oman) experienced sharp falls in TFP growth during the 1980s and which continued for many countries through the 1990s. On the other hand, among the comparator East Asian countries, China and Korea maintained since the 1980s relatively steady rates of TFP growth and ones that were higher than those of Tunisia and Morocco. While TFP growth was weaker and more variable for the other East Asian countries, in none of them was the overall average rate over the period negative while it was negative for no less than nine countries in the MENA region. The Philippines

Table 2.6a Total Factor Productivity – World Bank Growth Data, 1961–2019.

Country	*Total factor productivity growth (TFP) in percent*						*Average for available years period 1961–2010*
	1961–1970	*1971–1980*	*1981–1990*	*1991–2000*	*2001–2010*	*2011–2019*	
MENA non-major oil exporters	**2.202**	**2.132**	**−3.740**	**0.974**	**1.338**	−1.327	**0.275**
Djibouti						1.853	
Egypt, Arab Rep.	1.182	−0.466	−0.864	−1.098	−0.321	0.773	−0.313
Jordan		5.075	−4.015	−0.377	1.650	−1.862	0.583
Lebanon			−17.022	6.086	2.513	−3.314	−2.808
Morocco	3.752	−0.689	1.127	−0.035	1.837	1.008	1.198
Syrian Arab Republic	2.113	3.926	−1.786	2.104	2.143		1.700
Tunisia	**1.759**	**2.813**	**0.122**	**1.906**	**1.768**	**0.601**	**1.674**
West Bank and Gaza				−1.377	1.433	−0.752	0.028
Yemen, Rep.				0.586	−0.316	−8.921	0.135
MENA major oil exporters	**3.146**	**−2.018**	**−0.849**	**2.067**	**−0.441**	**−1.100**	**0.244**
Algeria	2.348	0.167	−1.389	−0.147	0.473	−0.738	0.290
Iran, Islamic Rep.	3.945	−8.081	−0.413	0.430	0.897	−1.702	−0.645
Iraq		1.860	−0.743	5.920	−2.694	−0.856	1.086
Libya							
MENA GCC		**−0.360**	**−3.068**	**1.012**	**−2.399**	**−2.652**	**−1.661**
Bahrain			−3.350	2.007	−1.548	−1.246	−0.964
Kuwait					−2.177	−3.776	−2.177
Oman		−2.299	1.627	1.125	−3.352	−4.130	−0.725
Qatar					−2.890	−5.486	−2.890
Saudi Arabia		−0.908	−6.033	0.269	−2.230	−2.226	−2.225
United Arab Emirates		2.125	−4.515	0.646	−2.195	0.950	−0.984
East Asia	**2.460**	**1.446**	**1.193**	**1.270**	**2.405**	**1.727**	**1.755**
China	1.104	1.105	3.970	5.312	4.964	2.691	3.291
Indonesia	2.964	2.382	−1.125	−1.148	1.727	0.997	0.960
Korea, Rep.	5.287	2.925	3.745	1.946	1.684	0.692	3.117
Malaysia	1.932	−0.145	−0.342	0.289	1.518	1.112	0.651
Philippines	0.496	0.452	−1.959	−0.304	1.793	2.207	0.096
Thailand	2.979	1.956	2.868	1.523	2.746	2.662	2.414

Source: Authors calculations using standard Cobb-Douglas production function and data from World Bank – World Development Indicators on GDP and employment, and Penn World Tables data on capital stock and labor shares. When data on labor shares not available, those of a similar country used.

Table 2.6b Total Factor Productivity – Penn World Tables Data, 1961–2019

Country	*Total factor productivity growth (TFP) in percent*						*Average for available years period 1961–2010*
	1961–1970	*1971–1980*	*1981–1990*	*1991–2000*	*2001–2010*	*2011–2019*	
MENA non-major oil exporters	**2.354**	**−0.367**	**−1.865**	**−0.973**	**0.558**	**−0.220**	**−0.059**
Djibouti							
Egypt, Arab Rep.	1.970	−1.285	−0.890	−1.371	−0.932	0.207	−0.501
Jordan	−2.102	−0.721	−5.210	−1.750	1.083	−1.731	−1.740
Lebanon							
Morocco	4.993	−1.269	−0.309	−1.580	1.272	1.148	0.621
Syrian Arab Republic							
Tunisia	**4.555**	**1.808**	**−1.053**	**0.807**	**0.810**	**−0.504**	**1.386**
West Bank and Gaza							
Yemen, Rep.							
MENA major oil exporters	**−3.719**	**−3.835**	**−3.087**	**2.320**	**−1.725**	**−1.466**	**−1.730**
Algeria							
Iran, Islamic Rep.	−3.719	−7.585	−0.627	−0.242	−0.513	−1.958	−2.537
Iraq		−0.085	−5.546	4.880	−2.938	−0.974	−0.922
Libya							
MENA GCC		**−9.426**	**−6.038**	**1.643**	**−2.920**	**−3.588**	**−4.185**
Bahrain		−3.901	−5.650	0.852	−1.636	−1.277	−2.584
Kuwait		−17.875	−8.657	4.164	−2.603	−4.608	−6.243
Oman							
Qatar		−5.346	−3.155	1.506	−4.184	−5.705	−2.795
Saudi Arabia		−10.581	−6.689	0.051	−3.254	−2.764	−5.118
United Arab Emirates							
East Asia	**1.486**	**0.445**	**−0.392**	**−0.095**	**1.538**	**0.796**	**0.617**
China	0.958	−0.993	−0.144	0.580	2.972	−0.604	0.674
Indonesia	1.145	1.926	−1.372	−1.464	1.298	1.277	0.307
Korea, Rep.	1.810	1.308	2.541	1.059	1.084	0.046	1.560
Malaysia	1.183	−0.127	−1.826	−0.685	0.963	0.831	−0.098
Philippines	−0.230	−0.326	−2.398	−0.822	1.512	1.609	−0.453
Thailand	4.651	0.883	0.849	0.764	1.400	1.615	1.709

Sources: Authors calculations using standard Cobb-Douglas production function, using Penn World Tables data, with adjustments for human capital and capital services.

Penn World Table: Feenstra et al. (2015).

was the worst performer in East Asia with almost no TFP growth during the 1960–2010 period.

While the TFP results are sensitive to the data and methodology used, and in many cases differ considerably between Tables 2.6a and 2.6b, from the latter table where the PWT method for calculating TFP growth has been used consistently across the countries included, the overall message is consistent. Notably, the TFP calculations in Table 2.6b quite appropriately adjust employment for human capital and use a measure of capital services, rather than capital stock, implying lower rates of growth of TFP over the long run, even though they tend to be higher during the 1960s when the most rapid structural transformation was taking place. Indeed, in this table, Tunisia's TFP growth rates during the period 1961–2010 are shown to have been much higher than those of Morocco and of any other MENA country and similar to those of Korea and Thailand. But, overall, TFP growth performance was much weaker among MENA countries than among East Asian countries. Indeed, the overall growth rates of TFP were positive among all but two of the East Asian countries (Malaysia and the Philippines), whereas the corresponding average was negative for eight of the ten MENA countries with such data.

The TFP growth rates of most MENA countries including Tunisia dropped substantially after 2010, the average growth rates becoming negative in all three MENA subregions in Tables 2.6a and 2.6b, but remaining positive for the East Asian region. While in Table 2.6b, the differences in TFP growth rates between MENA and East Asia became a little less extreme in that last 2011–2019 period in general, in this period Tunisia's TFP growth rate became negative and the worst it had since the 1980s.

While the data in Table 2.6b do not fully conform to the Asian Development Bank (2020) hypothesis of increasing contribution of TFP growth over time, the table does show that TFP growth has been much larger in East Asian countries since the 2000s, except for Korea. On the other hand, the trend in Tunisia was the reverse, having been highest in the 1960s but becoming significantly negative after 2010. Clearly, except for the 1960s, the country has not been successful in harnessing technological progress and structural transformation to achieve higher economic growth.

The ingredients of the success of East Asia have been the subject of much debate, especially as to whether it was more attributable to capital and employment growth or to growth in TFP. Some authors have argued that the rapid pace of East Asian growth was mostly due to the accumulation of factors of production, which may not be sustainable.[10] Notably, the Asian Development Bank (2020) report argues that the contribution of TFP and technological progress to total GDP growth changed over time. For between 21 and 25 of all Asian countries, while TFP growth was negligible or even negative during the 1970–1985 period, it constituted 21.9% of GDP growth during 1995–2005 and 40.8% of such growth during 2010–2017. Interestingly, this report argues, based on a larger set of global experiences, that this contribution of TFP growth was 10% for economies which remained middle-income, but reached 28.3% for countries which moved from middle-income to high-income status.

The same story can be gleaned from comparative data on labor productivity growth, which are available for the period since 1991, and shown in Table 2.7. Over a 28-year period (1991 to 2019) Tunisia's labor productivity

Table 2.7 Labor Productivity, 1991–2019

	GDP per person employed (Constant PPP 2017 US Dollars)			***Labor productivity growth (annual %)***		
Country	***1991***	***2019***	***Ratio 2019/1991***	***1991–2000***	***2001–2010***	***2011–2019***
MENA non-major oil exporters	**28910**	**37654**	**1.5**	**1.1**	**2.1**	**0.5**
Djibouti						
Egypt, Arab Rep.	23976	43930	1.8	2.2	1.6	2.8
Jordan	41845	46175	1.1	−0.5	2.2	−0.8
Lebanon	42095	43807	1.0	1.7	2.0	−3.6
Morocco	15445	25402	1.6	−0.1	2.5	2.8
Syrian Arab Republic						
Tunisia	**21191**	**36017**	**1.7**	**2.3**	**2.2**	**1.1**
West Bank and Gaza		30593				
Yemen, Rep.						
MENA major oil exporters	**32534**	**45993**	**1.8**	**3.7**	**0.8**	**−1.0**
Algeria	41683	44185	1.1	0.4	−0.9	1.2
Iran, Islamic Rep.	42572	40975	1.0	−1.0	2.3	−2.0
Iraq	13347	46829	3.5	11.7	0.5	1.6
Libya		51984			1.4	−4.9
MENA GCC	**139375**	**92351**	**0.6**	**0.0**	**−3.0**	**−1.0**
Bahrain	96677	76445	0.8	1.3	−3.3	−0.3
Kuwait		88493			−0.2	−2.7
Oman	87107	51626	0.6	1.7	−2.8	−4.3
Qatar		120185			−1.8	−0.6
Saudi Arabia	161584	119170	0.7	−1.4	−1.0	−0.9
United Arab Emirates	212131	98188	0.5	−1.4	−8.8	2.7
East Asia	**16847**	**41654**	**3.6**	**3.6**	**4.0**	**3.6**
China	2784	30074	10.8	8.8	9.6	7.0
Indonesia	11643	24426	2.1	1.2	3.5	3.2
Korea, Rep.	31385	80707	2.6	5.1	3.5	1.5
Malaysia	28955	59390	2.1	3.6	2.0	2.2
Philippines	11497	21832	1.9	0.5	2.2	4.2
Thailand	14817	33495	2.3	2.2	3.2	3.2

Source: World Development Indicators, World Bank.

increased by 70%, the highest rate (along with Egypt) of any MENA country, not taking into consideration Iraq which started from a war year in 1991. The annual growth rate was a healthy 2.2% per year during the 1990s and 2000s. It was higher than in all oil-exporting countries where productivity growth was mostly negative (an exception is Iraq during reconstruction periods), and higher than in non-oil exporting countries, (with the exception of Morocco during the 2000s). But the 28-year increase in labor productivity in Tunisia was lower than in all East Asian countries, where the increase was 90% or more, reaching almost a 1000% in China. The annual growth rate was typically higher than 3% per year in East Asian countries. Note once again that Labor Productivity growth slowed down considerably since 2011 in Tunisia following the political upheavals, becoming only a small fraction of those of most East Asian countries, although still higher than those of nine other MENA countries. It is worth noting that even by 2019, from column (2) of the table, the level of labor productivity was still higher in Tunisia than in all East Asian countries except Korea and Malaysia.

D. Strong Population Pressures and Weak Labor Market Dynamics

As many analysts have pointed out, and as a result of their early declines to relatively low levels of infant mortality (shown in Table 1.1) and a little later some quite sharp declines in fertility rates from their unusually high levels in the 1960s, by the 1980s Tunisia and many other MENA countries began to have the advantage of relatively high 'youth bulges' (relative to those in East Asian countries). The 'youth bulge' was thought to serve as a considerable advantage since countries with larger percentages of youths would indicate that these countries would then (or soon thereafter) be experiencing larger year-to-year increases in their labor forces than other countries. Especially with education also rising, this would imply more rapid growth in both the quantity and quality of labor.

Table 2.8 presents comparable data on the individual countries of the MENA and East Asian regions on this potentially important demographic indicator, namely, the percentage share of youths (15–24) in the total population. This indicator has been believed by many economists (e.g., Beck and Dyer 2016; Sayre and Yousef 2016; Yousef 2004) to be a very important contributor to economic growth. Since youths aged 15–24 in any particular year can be expected to be entering the labor force over either the present or subsequent decade, when this share is high, and especially when youths are healthy and better educated as is usually the case and already shown to have been true especially for MENA countries, it can constitute an important source of growth. Many analysts have referred to this as the youth bulge and noted that over the 1980–2000 period it became especially high in MENA.

Table 2.8 Share of Youths in Total Population, 1950–2020

Country	Share of youths of both genders aged 15–24 in total population (%)									Change	Average
	1950	1960	1970	1980	1990	2000	2010	2015	2020	1960–1980	1980–2000
MENA non-major oil exporters	**19.0**	**17.8**	**18.2**	**19.9**	**20.1**	**20.4**	**20.3**	**19.1**	**17.7**	**0.9**	**20.1**
Djibouti	19.3	20.3	18.8	20.4	19.7	20.5	20.8	19.4	18.3	0.1	20.2
Egypt, Arab Rep.	19.3	15.7	18.8	19	18.2	20.3	20	18	16.7	3.3	19.2
Jordan	17.5	20	18	19.6	21.6	21.2	19.4	19.3	19.4	–0.4	20.8
Lebanon	19.1	15.4	18.4	20.5	21.3	18.8	19.5	18.4	17.1	5.1	20.2
Morocco	22.1	16.9	16.7	21.8	20.6	20.9	19.1	17.4	15.8	4.9	21.1
Syrian Arab Republic	20	16.2	18.8	19.8	20.5	22.3	20.6	19.6	18.2	3.6	20.9
Tunisia	**17.7**	**16.6**	**17.6**	**20.9**	**19.7**	**20.3**	**18.7**	**15.5**	**13.6**	**4.3**	**20.3**
West Bank and Gaza	17.6	19.7	18.5	19.2	20.1	19.5	21.6	21.8	19.9	–0.5	16.5
Yemen	18.5	19.3	18.6	18.2	19	19.7	22.9	22.1	20.5	–1.1	19.0
MENA major oil exporters	**18.7**	**17.2**	**17.9**	**18.9**	**20.5**	**22.6**	**20.5**	**17.5**	**15.7**	**0.3**	**20.7**
Algeria	19.4	17.9	18.5	20.2	20.6	22.7	20.8	16.7	13.5	2.3	21.2
Iran, Islamic Rep.	19.4	15.9	18.4	19.9	18.7	24.3	21.5	15.9	13.2	4	21.0
Iraq	17.4	17.2	18	18	21.2	20.9	19.9	20.2	19.8	0.8	20.0
Libya	18.4	17.9	16.6	17.5	21.4	22.6	19.9	17.2	16.1	–0.4	20.5
MENA GCC	**19.2**	**18.7**	**19.0**	**18.9**	**16.3**	**17.0**	**16.3**	**13.2**	**11.3**	**–0.3**	**17.4**
Bahrain	19.1	17.6	17.9	22.1	16.4	16.6	15	13.2	10.6	4.5	18.4
Kuwait	21.8	19.5	18.2	17.9	17.8	16.2	15.2	11.2	10.1	–1.6	17.3
Oman	18.9	19.4	18.6	17.6	15.9	21.4	21.1	14.7	10.6	–1.8	18.3
Qatar	18.5	19.4	20.8	20.1	13.8	13.8	14.4	14.1	11.9	0.7	15.9
Saudi Arabia	18.4	18.3	18.4	17.9	18.4	18.2	18.5	15.2	13.1	–0.4	18.2
United Arab Emirates	18.5	17.9	20.3	17.7	15.7	16	13.5	10.7	11.2	–0.2	19.6
East Asia	**18.5**	**17.8**	**18.8**	**20.9**	**20.6**	**18.0**	**16.9**	**16.0**	**14.8**	**2.4**	**19.8**
China	17.8	16.1	19.3	19.6	21.7	15.6	16.7	13.2	11.8	3.5	19.0
Indonesia	20	19	17.1	20.2	20.9	20.4	17.3	17	16.8	1.2	20.5
Korea, Rep.	17.1	18	18.6	22.4	20.6	16.5	13.2	13.2	11.1	4.4	19.8
Malaysia	17.9	17.3	19.7	21.3	19.2	18.7	20.2	18.8	17.1	4	19.7
Philippines	17.9	17.9	19.9	21	20.1	19.8	19.5	19.5	18.8	3.1	20.3
Thailand	20.1	18.7	18.2	20.9	21.2	17.1	14.3	14	13.2	2.2	19.7

Source: United Nations, World Population https://population.un.org/wpp/DataQuery/.

The oil exporting countries of the Gulf had the advantage that, since their huge oil revenues allowed them to become heavy importers of labor, their labor forces could grow much faster than their fertility rates would suggest. What is interesting, however, is that neither the non-major oil exporters among MENA countries nor the GCC countries, which were as a result able to import foreign labor, seemed to have noticeably larger youth bulges than most East Asian countries. Between 1960 and 1980, the youth bulge increased more rapidly in Lebanon, Morocco, and Bahrain than in the top East Asian country (Republic of Korea) where it grew by 4.4 percentage points. Note that Tunisia's increase of the share of youth by 4.3 percentage points during this period was fourth highest in the MENA region and was well above the average youth share increases in both East Asia and each of the sub-groups of MENA countries. But several MENA countries did not have increases in these youth shares between 1960 and 1980, and as a result the average shares of youths in MENA sub-groups were virtually the same as that for East Asia. Yet, it was not until the 1980–2000 period that the youth shares in MENA and East Asia really jumped. Tunisia's share jumped to 20.3% although, even then, it was still below those of Algeria, Morocco, Iran, and Jordan, and only slightly above the East Asian average of 19.8%.

But, how did these youth bulges convert into growth rates of the working age population? Table 2.9 provides comparable data on the growth rates of working age populations in both the MENA and East Asian countries by decade from the 1960s to 2011–2019 period. These figures show considerable variation by country and decade. In East Asia the growth rate of working age population peaked in the 1980s and declined to well below 3% per year in all countries except Malaysia which lagged behind, through the 2000–2010 decade and to 1% per annum in the 2011–2019 period. Because of rising oil prices between 2000 and 2010 and their ability to import foreign labor, the growth rates of working age population in GCC countries were much higher, rising by 4% per annum in 1990–2000 and by 8.4% per annum in 2000–2010, before falling to a still very impressive 3.7% per annum during 2011–2019. Among the other two groups of MENA countries, the rates of growth of their working age populations averaged about 3.5%, 3.0%, and 2.1% for the non-oil exporters, respectively, during these three different decades and 3.4%, 2.4%, and 1.8% for the non-GCC major oil-exporters, respectively, during these same decades. Tunisia's per annum growth rates in working age population were a little below these, closer to those of East Asia.

As Yousef (2004) and Beck and Dyer (2016) had pointed out, these high and growing youth bulges since 1960 subsequently did lead to extremely rapid growth rates of the labor force in MENA countries since 1980. Indeed, coupled with the rapidly increasing health and educational characteristics of their youths, since 1990 these growth rates of effective labor force in MENA were considerably higher (though somewhat less so in Tunisia) than those in East Asia, Latin America, or anywhere else, potentially contributing substantially to higher economic growth rates. Yet, as shall be

Table 2.9 Growth Rates of Working Age Population, 1961–2019

	Average annual growth rates of working age population (%)					
Country	***1961–1970***	***1971–1980***	***1981–1990***	***1991–2000***	***2001–2010***	***2011–2019***
MENA non-major oil exporters	**3.2**	**3.3**	**3.4**	**3.5**	**3.0**	**2.1**
Djibouti	6.3	8.6	5.5	2.6	2.9	2.1
Egypt, Arab Rep.	2.7	2.4	2.6	2.7	2.6	1.8
Jordan	6.2	2.5	4.8	4.9	3.8	4.5
Lebanon	2.5	1.6	0.9	4.1	3.2	3.7
Morocco	1.9	3.2	2.7	2.3	1.8	1.4
Syrian Arab Republic	3.2	3.3	3.8	4.0	3.3	–1.9
Tunisia	**1.5**	**2.9**	**3.3**	**2.6**	**1.8**	**0.7**
West Bank and Gaza				4.2	3.6	3.0
Yemen	1.1	1.6	3.6	4.6	4.2	3.2
MENA major oil exporters	**2.6**	**3.2**	**3.6**	**3.4**	**2.4**	**1.8**
Algeria	2.2	3.0	3.6	3.3	2.4	1.3
Iran, Islamic Rep.	2.5	3.2	3.4	3.5	2.6	1.0
Iraq	2.3	2.8	2.7	3.7	2.5	4.0
Libya	3.2	3.9	4.5	3.2	2.2	1.0
MENA GCC	**6.4**	**8.4**	**5.6**	**4.0**	**8.4**	**3.7**
Bahrain	2.1	7.7	3.4	3.3	8.3	3.2
Kuwait	9.1	7.0	5.8	5.6	4.5	4.0
Oman	2.2	5.2	4.6	3.7	4.8	6.3
Qatar	10.0	7.6	8.8	2.3	15.3	4.4
Saudi Arabia	3.4	5.4	5.7	3.1	4.3	3.2
United Arab Emirates	11.5	17.2	5.4	6.3	13.3	0.9
East Asia	**2.7**	**3.1**	**2.9**	**2.1**	**1.6**	**1.0**
China	2.1	2.4	2.5	1.5	1.3	0.1
Indonesia	2.1	2.9	2.9	2.3	1.6	1.5
Korea, Rep.	2.8	3.0	2.3	1.3	0.6	0.3
Malaysia	3.2	3.3	3.1	3.1	2.7	1.8
Philippines	3.4	3.3	3.1	2.8	2.5	2.0
Thailand	2.7	3.4	3.3	1.7	1.0	0.2

Source: Data from database: World Bank, World Development Indicators.

shown later on, because of increasing unemployment, this meant that the potential growth arising from these youth bulge increases has become vastly underutilized. The reason for this is that the potential benefits of the youth bulging and growing working age population can be realized only if their employment levels are increased sufficiently to take advantage of this labor supply growth.

Indeed, as shown in Table 2.10, even in the 1990s and beyond (by which time the youth bulge advantages would have kicked in), average employment rates in non-GCC countries including Tunisia, remained stagnant and quite low, typically around 40%, rates which are much lower than those in East Asian countries, where they have been consistently high (in the 60 to 80% range).

Even more telling perhaps are the high average rates of unemployment beginning in the 1980s shown in the same table. Indeed, the simple averages of unemployment in non-major oil exporting and major oil exporting MENA countries were 12.1% and 18.3%, respectively, during the 1990s, with Tunisia averaging about 15.4% in considerable contrast to the average unemployment rate of the East Asian countries which rarely ever exceeded 5%.

Hence, it is quite clear that the youth bulge has in fact not benefitted MENA countries. The exception is the GCC countries, where a very peculiar dual pattern in the labor market developed since the 1970s. This is one in which nationals are mostly employed in the public sector and non-national 'guest' workers are employed primarily in the private sector. As a result, their employment rates have been increasing and, by the 2000s decade, their levels typically exceeded the average employment rates of East Asia, and their unemployment rates were also very low.

Next in Table 2.11, we turn to overall labor force participation rates, shown in the first six columns of the table, and female labor force participation rates in the last six columns. Consistent with the cross-country differences in average employment rates in Table 2.10, Table 2.11 shows that the overall labor force participation rates are low in non-GCC countries of the MENA region, and much higher in all the East Asian countries and in recent years higher still in the GCC countries with the highest shares of non-nationals in the labor force like, Bahrain, Kuwait, Qatar, and the UAE. It is the data on the female labor force participation rates in the last six columns of Table 2.11 that explain virtually all the aforementioned patterns. Notably, by the 1980s those female labor force participation rates had come to average over 50% in East Asia, reaching 72% in China, but were below 30% in all other MENA countries, except for tiny Djibouti in the 1990s[11] and for a few GCC countries with imported female labor (Kuwait, Qatar, UAE). In some GCC countries (Oman, Saudi Arabia), and despite the importance of female imported labor in their labor forces, participation of their national women in the labor force remained low. Among non-GCC MENA countries, Tunisia, with a female labor force participation rate of slightly over 25% had one of the highest such rates, but clearly only about

Table 2.10 Employment and Unemployment, 1970–2019

Country	*Average employment rate (%)*					*Average rate of unemployment (%)*					
	1970s	*1980s*	*1990s*	*2000s*	*2010s*	*1960s*	*1970s*	*1980s*	*1990s*	*2000s*	*2010s*
MENA non-major oil exporters	**43.2**	**40.5**	**40.9**	**38.0**	**36.1**	**3.9**	**4.0**	**10.8**	**11.7**	**12.8**	**15.6**
Djibouti					23.9						26.1
Egypt, Arab Rep.	40.5	38.1	40.7	38.8	41.0	2.4	2.9	6.3	9.4	9.7	11.7
Jordan			34.5	33.4	32.8			11.6	15.4	13.8	14.6
Lebanon			42.9	40.0	43.3				8.6	7.7	11.4
Morocco		42.9	43.5	43.4	43.5			15.2	16.9	10.5	9.3
Syrian Arab Republic	46.0		50.2	42.3		5.4	5.1	4.9	7.3	9.7	
Tunisia		**40.3**	**39.3**	**40.2**	**39.5**			**16.1**	**15.4**	**13.4**	**16.1**
West Bank and Gaza			36.0	30.2	33.3				10.6	21.7	22.4
Yemen			40.6	35.5	31.4				9.9	15.8	13.5
MENA major oil exporters	**21.2**	**32.7**	**37.0**	**36.3**	**37.7**			**16.8**	**18.3**	**12.3**	**13.0**
Algeria	21.2	31.9		31.7	36.8			19.5	26.6	16.7	10.8
Iran, Islamic Rep.		33.5	37.0	39.2	37.6			14.2	10.1	11.6	11.7
Iraq				38.1	37.8					8.7	10.6
Libya					38.7						19.0
MENA GCC	**54.5**	**48.2**	**54.6**	**65.2**	**71.7**		**2.0**	**1.9**	**2.7**	**3.1**	**2.6**
Bahrain	35.8	39.4	43.5	61.6	70.5			3.1		3.6	2.6
Kuwait		57.0	61.3	71.8	73.7			1.5	0.7	1.5	2.4
Oman			27.8	55.8	67.5					4.1	2.5
Qatar			73.1	83.6	88.3					0.7	0.2
Saudi Arabia			47.9	46.9	51.5				5.4	5.5	5.7
United Arab Emirates	73.2		73.8	71.4	78.8		2.0	1.2	2.0	3.1	2.1
East Asia	**56.9**	**64.7**	**65.2**	**64.1**	**64.3**	**5.7**	**3.2**	**4.1**	**4.2**	**3.8**	**3.1**
China			75.3	72.6	68.2		5.2	2.4	2.8	4.1	4.2
Indonesia	68.0	66.0	63.5	61.3	64.1		1.8	2.6	4.4	6.9	4.3
Korea, Rep.	40.9	56.0	59.2	60.1	60.7	4.7	4.1	3.5	3.4	3.3	3.3
Malaysia		62.3	63.3	61.4	64.9			5.9	3.2	3.5	3.2
Philippines	42.4	59.8	58.3	59.1	59.1	6.7	4.4	6.9	9.7	3.7	3.0
Thailand	76.5	79.5	71.3	70.3	69.1		0.6	3.1	1.9	1.5	0.6

Source: Data from database: World Bank, World Development Indicators.

Table 2.11 Labor Force Participation, 1961–2019

	Average labor force participation rate, total (%)						*Average female labor force participation rate (%)*					
Country	***1960s***	***1970s***	***1980s***	***1990s***	***2000s***	***2010s***	***1960s***	***1970s***	***1980s***	***1990s***	***2000s***	***2010s***
MENA non-major oil exporters	**43.4**	**42.7**	**45.0**	**45.4**	**43.4**	**42.6**	**6.1**	**12.0**	**17.0**	**22.4**	**17.9**	**19.0**
Djibouti						32.3				48.7		18.2
Egypt, Arab Rep.	43.0	41.9	42.3	45.4	43.7	46.5	5.8	6.6	16.2	19.9	20.1	21.4
Jordan	40.6	42.2		39.4	38.8	38.4	4.4	8.5		12.3	13.0	14.2
Lebanon		44.6		46.8	44.5	48.8		15.4			21.3	29.3
Morocco		45.6	48.4	51.4	48.4	47.6		12.6	21.0	26.3	25.3	24.8
Syrian Arab Republic	44.8	48.3	39.9	45.9	46.8	43.4	8.6		9.8	16.9	16.7	14.8
Tunisia	**44.9**	**50.4**	**49.4**	**48.5**	**44.3**	**47.3**	**5.5**	**19.5**	**21.1**	**23.3**	**23.5**	**25.9**
West Bank and Gaza				40.3	38.6	42.9				12.3	12.8	16.7
Yemen		25.8		45.8	42.1	36.3		9.4		19.3	10.2	6.0
MENA major oil exporters	**45.0**	**43.4**	**41.1**	**40.0**	**41.2**	**43.2**	**6.4**	**9.1**	**8.5**	**9.2**	**14.3**	**19.4**
Algeria	40.7	32.6	33.7	33.2	38.2	41.0	2.9	3.5	6.2	8.6	14.1	15.8
Iran, Islamic Rep.	50.4	46.8	45.8	44.6	43.6	41.8	12.2	10.6	9.0	10.3	16.5	15.4
Iraq		48.6	43.9	42.3	41.7	42.2		15.8	10.5	8.8	12.2	12.8
Libya	44.0	45.7				47.8	4.1	6.5				33.8
MENA GCC	**44.7**	**58.3**	**63.0**	**59.9**	**67.1**	**72.0**	**6.0**	**12.6**	**25.9**	**26.9**	**36.7**	**42.4**
Bahrain	29.2	43.4	54.3	65.7	64.1	71.3	2.4	7.4	20.3	32.1	36.5	43.0
Kuwait	60.2	57.2	59.4	59.2	73.4	75.6	9.5	17.5	29.8	36.4	53.4	53.4
Oman				36.0	57.2	62.8				12.7	24.7	28.6
Qatar			75.5	72.9	84.1	87.6			27.5	33.4	47.8	55.6
Saudi Arabia				50.6	49.6	54.4				15.7	17.2	20.8
United Arab Emirates		74.3		75.2	74.1	80.2		13.0		31.3	40.6	52.7
East Asia	**56.2**	**57.8**	**69.6**	**68.0**	**66.7**	**66.3**	**33.3**	**42.7**	**56.3**	**54.7**	**53.7**	**53.5**
China			79.0	76.8	73.9	70.7			71.8	70.6	63.7	
Indonesia	59.2	65.0	67.6	66.6	65.8	67.0	31.2	44.0	51.0	50.6	48.6	51.6
Korea, Rep.	54.0	46.5	58.1	61.3	62.1	62.8	34.9	34.8	43.8	48.0	50.4	52.1
Malaysia		60.4	65.9	64.2	63.6	67.0		40.1	46.4	44.7	46.9	54.6
Philippines	55.4	41.6	64.7	65.2	61.9	60.9	34.0	27.8	48.2	48.5	47.8	47.5
Thailand		75.4	82.2	73.7	72.9	69.6		66.9	76.7	65.7	64.9	61.6

Source: Data from database: World Bank, World Development Indicators.

Note: Data are averages of available observations available for each decade, based on national sources.

half that of the East Asian countries, even though they, too, have been experiencing at least slightly declining rates since the 1980s or 1990s.

Even more importantly, Table 2.12 provides comparable data on the percentages of population over 15 years of age with completed secondary education and tertiary education by country and year from 1950 to 2010 at 10-year intervals. Note that among MENA countries, Tunisia was a strong performer, the share of those over 15 with secondary education increasing from 1.4% in 1950 to 16.4% in 2010 and that of those with tertiary education increasing from 0.3% in 1950 to 8.4% in 2010. The only MENA countries which did even better than this were perhaps Iran and Libya outside of the GCC and Qatar and UAE among GCC countries in which much of the labor force was foreign-born. Yet, for East Asia as a whole these shares started higher at 2.6% and 0.6%, respectively, in 1950 but grew to considerably higher percentages, that is, 27.2% and 10.9%, respectively, in 2010.

The largest source of shortfall in in effective labor supply of Tunisia and other MENA countries relative to the sample of East Asian countries is that revealed in Table 2.13 showing the percentages of male workers with completed secondary and higher education by country and period who were unemployed. Note, for example, that for the non-oil exporting countries as a whole the male unemployment rates among those over 15 years of age with completed tertiary education increased from 7.1% in 1996–2000 to 14.4% in 2011–2015. The corresponding rates for Tunisia started at 7.3% in 1995–2000 but rose to well above that average to 18.2% in 2011–2015. On the other hand, the average unemployment rates for males aged 15 and over with tertiary education in East Asia actually fell from 5.6% to 4.7%, even though they had increased somewhat just before and during the world financial crisis. These data pertain only to males but since males outnumber females in the labor markets of pretty much all countries, these are quite representative of the labor forces across countries in general. Hence, the data show that the high unemployment rates in MENA countries including Tunisia for educated workers means that the firms employing workers in MENA countries actually employ considerably smaller percentages of the potentially employable highly educated workers than would be the case on the basis of demographics and education by themselves.

E. Lagging Gender Equity in Labor Markets

Another specific feature of labor markets dynamics relates to the role of women and gender equity. While Table 2.11 showed the very low rates of female labor force participation in Tunisia and all non-GCC MENA countries, Tables 2.12 and 2.13 illustrate another source of underutilization of human capital in MENA countries. While there has been rising percentage of populations with higher educational levels, unemployment rates are higher among males with advanced education since 2005 in Tunisia, unlike in East Asian countries. Table 2.14 provides a few more indicators on

Table 2.12 Educational Achievement, 1950–2010

	Percentage of population age 15+ with completed secondary schooling							*Percentage of population age 25+ with completed tertiary schooling*						
Country	*1950*	*1960*	*1970*	*1980*	*1990*	*2000*	*2010*	*1950*	*1960*	*1970*	*1980*	*1990*	*2000*	*2010*
MENA non-major oil exporters	**1.0**	**1.9**	**3.2**	**5.0**	**10.2**	**14.2**	**18.5**	**0.3**	**0.4**	**0.8**	**1.5**	**3.0**	**3.7**	**5.5**
Djibouti														
Egypt, Arab Rep.	0.7	1	1.8	6.2	14.5	20.4	26.4	0.6	1.0	1.8	2.2	3.1	3.1	6.8
Jordan	2.9	6.3	8.4	8.9	22.0	32.0	27.1	0.4	0.7	1.6	4.1	6.1	5.4	5.6
Lebanon														
Morocco	0.7	1.3	2.4	3.8	5.9	8.5	12.1	0.0	0.0	0.1	0.4	3.0	5.1	6.3
Syrian Arab Republic	0.3	0.8	2.4	3.8	5.1	4.1	18.1	0.2	0.2	0.8	1.4	3.2	3.5	4.1
Tunisia	**1.4**	**2**	**4.2**	**7.3**	**10.6**	**14.0**	**16.4**	**0.3**	**0.3**	**0.6**	**1.1**	**2.5**	**4.0**	**8.4**
West Bank and Gaza														
Yemen, Rep.	0.0	0.0	0.0	0.2	2.9	6.0	10.7	0.0	0.0	0.0	0.0	0.3	0.9	1.7
MENA major oil exporters	**0.5**	**1.1**	**3.4**	**8.5**	**15.4**	**18.7**	**20.3**	**0.2**	**0.3**	**0.6**	**1.5**	**3.0**	**5.6**	**10.8**
Algeria	0.5	1.1	3.3	7.6	14.4	15.4	17.1	0.2	0.2	0.2	0.6	2.1	4.0	6.8
Iran, Islamic Rep.	1.0	2.0	6.4	14.0	21.2	27.6	30.5	0.2	0.4	0.9	2.1	3.9	9.3	15.8
Iraq	0.5	1.0	2.6	6.1	10.8	14.2	17.4	0.3	0.5	1.0	2.2	4.2	6.1	9.5
Libya	0.1	0.4	1.2	6.3	15.4	17.8	16.0	0.1	0.1	0.3	1.1	1.9	3.0	11.3
MENA GCC	**2.8**	**4.7**	**9.0**	**14.1**	**19.8**	**23.9**	**27.8**	**1.5**	**2.2**	**3.8**	**5.4**	**8.6**	**10.3**	**9.4**
Bahrain	2.2	3.1	11.2	17.5	25.5	32.5	32.1	1.5	1.5	2.7	4.1	11.4	12.7	9.1
Kuwait	2.6	5.6	9.9	16.4	21.9	20.1	18.7	1.3	2.0	2.9	6.3	8.4	6.9	5.5
Oman														
Qatar	4.5	6.0	8.9	12.0	15.4	18.6	23.6	1.8	3.4	6.6	7.9	8.8	11.0	12.6
Saudi Arabia	2.9	4.1	5.5	8.6	12.8	18.1	29.1	1.8	2.3	3.7	4.9	7.4	9.1	9.2
United Arab Emirates	1.8	4.5	9.3	16.1	23.5	30.0	35.7	1.0	1.8	3.0	3.9	7.2	11.8	10.7
East Asia	**2.6**	**4.3**	**6.6**	**12.2**	**18.2**	**23.5**	**27.2**	**0.6**	**1.2**	**2.3**	**3.5**	**5.0**	**6.8**	**10.9**
China	1.8	2.9	5.1	9.4	19.9	27.5	22.9	0.2	0.4	0.7	0.6	1.3	2.9	2.4
Indonesia	0.5	0.9	2.1	5.2	10.9	9.7	22.1			0.3	0.4	1.5	1.8	5.0
Korea, Rep.	4.3	8.7	13.4	26.1	39.0	39.6	35.5	0.7	1.4	4.3	6.6	11.5	20.8	34.8
Malaysia	2.0	3.2	7.2	15.4	17.1	35.0	39.8	0.4	0.5	0.7	0.6	2.8	3.1	5.9
Philippines	5.6	7.9	9.8	13.1	16.6	17.9	23.8	1.5	3.4	7.0	9.8	8.7	8.0	7.2
Thailand	1.5	1.9	2.0	4.2	6.0	11.5	19.0	0.3	0.3	0.9	2.9	4.4	4.4	10.0

Sources: World Bank, World Development Indicators and Barro and Lee (2013).

Table 2.13 Unemployment by Educational Level, 1991–2019

	Unemployment with intermediate education, male (% of male labor force with intermediate education)						***Unemployment with advanced education, male (% of male labor force with advanced education)***					
Country	*1991–1995*	*1996–2000*	*2001–2005*	*2006–2010*	*2011–2015*	*2016–2019*	*1991–1995*	*1996–2000*	*2001–2005*	*2006–2010*	*2011–2015*	*2016–2019*
MENA non-major oil exporters		**8.6**	**17.8**	**12.7**	**15.0**	**15.2**	**12.6**	**7.1**	**15.1**	**11.2**	**14.4**	**15.8**
Djibouti						26.1						14.1
Egypt, Arab Rep.				7.6	11.3	9.6				11.6	14.6	14.9
Jordan						8.9						18.3
Lebanon				9.8		10.3				10.8		12.8
Morocco			20.8		14.6		22.0		22.8			
Syrian Arab Republic												
Tunisia			**12.2**	**12.8**	**17.4**	**15.7**	**3.3**	**7.3**	**9.9**	**13.9**	**18.2**	**18.2**
West Bank and Gaza		8.6	20.4	17.7	16.5	20.6		6.9	12.7	12.9	13.0	16.5
Yemen, Rep.				15.4	15.2					7.0	12.0	
MENA major oil exporters			**21.1**	**7.4**	**5.1**	**11.6**			**16.5**	**7.2**	**5.1**	**13.5**
Algeria			21.1						16.5			
Iran, Islamic Rep.						11.6						13.5
Iraq				7.4	5.1					7.2	5.1	
Libya												

(Continued)

Table 2.13 Unemployment by Educational Level, 1991–2019 *(Continued)*

	Unemployment with intermediate education, male (% of male labor force with intermediate education)						***Unemployment with advanced education, male (% of male labor force with advanced education)***					
Country	*1991–1995*	*1996–2000*	*2001–2005*	*2006–2010*	*2011–2015*	*2016–2019*	*1991–1995*	*1996–2000*	*2001–2005*	*2006–2010*	*2011–2015*	*2016–2019*
MENA GCC	**2.3**	**10.5**	**2.8**	**6.1**	**2.5**	**2.5**	**1.8**	**1.8**	**2.3**	**3.4**	**1.3**	**1.9**
Bahrain												
Kuwait												
Oman		10.5						1.8				
Qatar					0.1						0.1	
Saudi Arabia				6.1	4.8					3.4	2.5	
United Arab Emirates	2.3		2.8			2.5	1.8		2.3			1.9
East Asia	**6.3**	**9.2**	**12.5**	**6.5**	**5.3**	**5.1**	**5.0**	**5.6**	**13.1**	**6.2**	**4.7**	**4.4**
China												
Indonesia	9.4	11.7	12.0	11.8	7.6	6.9	6.9	8.4	10.2	8.5	5.1	4.3
Korea, Rep.	3.3	6.7			3.4	3.7	3.0	2.8			3.8	4.0
Malaysia				4.2	3.5	3.9				3.2	3.1	3.6
Philippines			12.9	9.0	11.1	9.8			16.0	11.5	10.4	8.5
Thailand				0.9	0.8	1.0				1.6	1.2	1.5

Source: Data from database: World Bank, World Development Indicators.

Table 2.14 Gender Equity, 1991–2019

Country	*Ratio of female to male unemployment rates*							*Female percent of employment outside of agriculture*							*Gender inequality index (GII)*					
	1991	*1995*	*2000*	*2005*	*2010*	*2015*	*2019*	*1991*	*1995*	*2000*	*2005*	*2010*	*2015*	*2019*	*1995*	*2000*	*2005*	*2010*	*2015*	*2019*
MENA non-major oil exporters	**1.51**	**1.52**	**1.64**	**1.75**	**2.09**	**1.99**	**2.03**	**17.0**	**17.4**	**18.7**	**18.9**	**19.4**	**19.2**	**19.5**	**0.615**	**0.611**	**0.550**	**0.507**	**0.498**	**0.477**
Djibouti	0.96	0.95	0.97	0.99	1.00	1.04	1.02	34.4	35.6	37.2	39.2	39.7	40.5	41.0						
Egypt, Arab Rep.	3.67	3.24	4.49	3.42	4.64	2.64	3.06	15.1	17.0	15.8	14.2	15.6	16.3	17.4	0.668	0.637	0.579			0.449
Jordan	1.66	2.47	1.71	2.02	2.09	2.06	1.82	10.8	11.2	13.3	12.8	16.3	16.0	16.6	0.667	0.627	0.560	0.487	0.481	0.450
Lebanon	1.37	1.27	1.26	1.24	2.06	2.05	1.96	21.6	22.7	22.9	21.0	22.5	22.8	23.3				0.424	0.448	0.411
Morocco	0.96	0.91	0.95	1.07	1.06	1.14	1.22	17.8	18.4	19.3	18.8	17.1	16.7	16.8	0.722	0.700	0.564	0.533	0.471	0.454
Syrian Arab Republic	2.73	2.58	2.80	3.80	3.53	3.47	3.52	13.4	11.4	10.0	11.8	12.9	14.2	14.6	0.503	0.481	0.490	0.513	0.494	0.482
Tunisia	**1.11**	**1.10**	**1.11**	**1.26**	**1.74**	**1.78**	**1.75**	**22.1**	**22.6**	**23.7**	**24.7**	**24.1**	**25.5**	**25.0**	**0.515**	**0.412**	**0.312**	**0.286**	**0.275**	**0.296**
West Bank and Gaza	0.72	0.74	0.72	0.81	1.01	1.70	1.82	10.6	10.9	11.8	13.3	15.3	16.2	15.9						
Yemen, Rep.	0.40	0.46	0.72	1.12	1.64	2.05	2.09	6.9	6.5	14.1	14.5	11.1	5.0	5.0		0.807	0.796	0.799	0.819	0.795
MENA major oil exporters	**1.44**	**1.25**	**1.30**	**1.34**	**1.75**	**2.00**	**2.18**	**14.3**	**15.4**	**16.8**	**18.7**	**18.7**	**19.3**	**18.8**	**0.682**	**0.627**	**0.467**	**0.472**	**0.439**	**0.429**
Algeria	0.78	0.94	1.00	1.22	2.35	1.67	2.17	15.5	15.1	15.1	16.2	16.6	18.4	16.9	0.682	0.624	0.552	0.507	0.427	0.429
Iran, Islamic Rep.	2.57	1.71	1.84	1.73	1.73	2.10	1.93	9.8	12.0	14.2	16.5	14.9	14.7	17.3	0.657	0.593	0.511	0.519	0.507	0.459
Iraq	0.82	0.83	0.83	0.82	1.31	2.60	3.02	10.3	10.6	11.7	14.0	14.1	14.0	10.8	0.707	0.664		0.575	0.566	0.577
Libya	1.58	1.50	1.53	1.58	1.59	1.63	1.59	21.7	23.8	26.2	27.9	29.2	30.0	30.3			0.339	0.287	0.256	0.252

(Continued)

Table 2.14 Gender Equity, 1991–2019 *(Continued)*

	Ratio of female to male unemployment rates							***Female percent of employment outside of agriculture***							***Gender inequality index (GII)***					
Country	***1991***	***1995***	***2000***	***2005***	***2010***	***2015***	***2019***	***1991***	***1995***	***2000***	***2005***	***2010***	***2015***	***2019***	***1995***	***2000***	***2005***	***2010***	***2015***	***2019***
MENA GCC	**3.94**	**3.00**	**3.46**	**4.69**	**6.69**	**7.56**	**9.53**	**16.1**	**16.3**	**17.7**	**17.6**	**16.7**	**17.5**	**16.8**	**0.612**	**0.598**	**0.472**	**0.373**	**0.311**	**0.213**
Bahrain	8.63	6.05	6.90	11.93	8.36	9.23	19.75	17.5	18.9	20.9	20.8	20.7	21.4	19.8			0.321	0.247	0.236	0.212
Kuwait	7.43	5.06	4.66	3.17	1.99	3.67	5.19	24.6	24.0	25.2	24.1	27.3	27.0	24.7	0.588	0.586	0.381	0.228	0.328	0.242
Oman	2.13	1.85	1.90	1.98	2.71	6.09	9.00	14.7	12.7	16.9	18.5	15.7	12.5	12.0			0.387	0.328	0.325	0.306
Qatar	3.14	2.61	3.56	5.20	19.24	14.21	11.68	16.1	16.7	16.3	16.1	11.6	13.6	13.8				0.557	0.524	0.185
Saudi Arabia	0.68	1.03	2.47	3.06	5.04	8.76	7.67	11.9	12.8	13.8	13.8	13.4	14.3	13.4			0.679	0.646	0.277	0.252
United Arab Emirates	1.65	1.37	1.24	2.82	2.80	3.42	3.88	11.9	12.6	13.0	12.2	11.4	15.9	17.2	0.635	0.609	0.592	0.233	0.175	0.079
East Asia	**1.15**	**1.15**	**0.97**	**1.03**	**1.01**	**1.00**	**1.01**	**42.2**	**42.2**	**42.8**	**42.2**	**42.7**	**43.1**	**43.3**	**0.430**	**0.376**	**0.338**	**0.316**	**0.312**	**0.292**
China	0.78	0.78	0.78	0.78	0.78	0.78	0.78	50.5	49.9	49.2	47.9	46.6	46.2	45.6		0.269	0.224	0.194	0.172	0.168
Indonesia	1.25	1.36	1.18	1.48	1.25	0.97	0.94	35.7	37.4	36.9	34.7	38.3	38.3	40.5	0.574	0.563	0.550	0.508	0.494	0.480
Korea, Rep.	0.74	0.73	0.72	0.85	0.82	0.97	0.90	38.4	38.7	40.0	40.6	41.0	41.6	42.3	0.280	0.194	0.100	0.098	0.076	0.064
Malaysia	1.29	1.34	1.03	1.08	1.09	1.16	1.22	36.6	36.9	37.5	36.9	37.0	39.9	39.9	0.357	0.304	0.285	0.273	0.270	0.253
Philippines	1.12	1.19	1.16	1.19	1.09	1.08	1.24	48.2	46.5	46.1	45.6	45.5	45.4	43.6	0.503	0.493	0.481	0.457	0.436	0.430
Thailand	1.74	1.49	0.96	0.82	1.00	1.03	0.97	44.0	43.6	47.0	47.3	47.5	47.3	47.6	0.434	0.435	0.386	0.364	0.424	0.359

Source: United Nations Human Development Report Database.

gender equity: namely, (a) the ratio of female to male unemployment rates, (b) female percent of employment outside agriculture, and (c) a gender equity index. The various indicators show that, while Tunisia performs relatively well among MENA countries in most aspects of gender equity, it lags considerably behind the East Asian countries. Not only were the male Unemployment rates shown in Table 2.13 so much higher than those in East Asian countries, but from the data in Table 2.14, especially since the 2000s in Tunisia, it can be seen that the unemployment rates for females have generally been much higher than those for males, whereas for East Asian countries the ratios of the male and female rates were almost identical. The ratio of female to male unemployment shown in the table has also been increasing in almost all MENA countries until 2010. In the following period, it continued to increase in the GCC countries but has stabilized in most other MENA countries.

The second set of columns show what has happened to the percentages of females working outside of agriculture over time. The share of women employed outside agriculture has risen modestly in many MENA countries, but it has stagnated or even declined recently in several other MENA countries (Morocco, Oman, Qatar and Yemen). The notable exception is tiny Djibouti where that share in 2019 of 41% was even close to the shares of 43% for East Asian countries. Tunisia's share of 25% in 2019 was second highest in non-oil MENA countries (after Djibouti)

The last set of columns in the table show the changes over time in the Gender Inequality Index of the United Nations Development Program constructed as part of their Human Development Reports. As such, it includes measures of both reproductive health (i.e., maternal mortality and adolescent birth rates) and empowerment (in the form of seats in parliaments, and labor force participation). The higher the index, the greater is the disparity between males and females in terms of these aspects of human development. As can be seen, these indexes have declined over time in virtually all countries, indicating increasing gender equity. Exceptions are Syria and Yemen among MENA countries and to a very limited extent the Philippines among East Asian countries. Korea is again the star performer, having reduced its Gender Inequality Index from 0.28 in 1995 to 0.06 in 2019. Next most impressive was China. Among MENA countries, the GCC countries (especially the UAE and Kuwait), have achieved the largest reductions in their Gender Inequality Indexes. Among the non-GCC, Tunisia has also reduced its Gender Inequality Index quite substantially over this period as have Algeria, Egypt, Jordan, Morocco, and Iran. In the case of Tunisia, the reduction was much more substantial between 1995 and 2005 than after that.

Overall, despite the great progress in some aspects of gender equity in Tunisia relative to many other MENA countries and even relative to some East Asian countries, its achievements in the labor markets remain very weak and constitute a major drag on the economic performance of the country, with much of the blame on relatively low female labor force participation rates, high male unemployment rates, and low employment rates among the more educated (both males and females).

Notes

1 The former strategy stressed that, because any industrial firm, especially at the beginning stages of industrialization, would be very specialized, individual firms could only receive sufficient demand for their products to be viable if there was balanced growth, i.e., simultaneous development of firms in virtually all sectors of the economy. See Murphy et al. (1989) for an articulation of various ways in which this might be accomplished and Magruder (2013) for an example of success in this respect in one of the East Asian countries (Indonesia). The Hirschman strategy had the same objective but, because it identified decision making capability to be the main constraint on industrial and overall development, stressed the value of the linkages in triggering dynamic sequences of decisions to develop industries in quite unbalanced growth paths. Yotopoulos and Nugent (1973) carried out a test of this across countries and over time. Holz (2011) has more recently tested the role of China's State-owned Enterprises (SOEs) in achieving growth by way of unbalanced growth in China across provinces and over time.
2 This was based on at least anecdotal evidence of some local African conglomerates succeeding in attracting foreign electric bicycle producers and foreign car assembly plants to locate in various African countries. Yet, no solid evidence of increasing technical efficiency in Africa's manufacturing industry was cited.
3 The volatility during the 1980s and 1990s in the figures of the shares of manufacturing for Iran and Iraq is much related to the war between the two countries.
4 The share of agriculture in employment was already a low 37.5% of total employment in 1975 in Tunisia.
5 Asian Development Bank (2020, Table 3.1b).
6 From Asian Development Bank (2020, Chapter 4, page 125).
7 See, for example, Matoussi and Seabright (2014), Devlin (2016, Chapter 4), United Nations (2002). It is especially challenging in Tunisia which, unlike quite a few MENA and East Asian countries, has no major river.
8 Data for GDP growth may differ considerably, between the World Development Indicators database (World Bank) and the Penn World Tables, especially for the earlier years in the 1960s and 1970s. For details on the Penn World Tables and their measures, see Feenstra et al. (2015).
9 The appropriateness of attributing some of the inter-temporal variation in TFP growth to variations in the strength of economic reform is supported by comparisons of TFP growth across sectors according to their exposure to international competition. Indeed, some World Bank calculations show that TFP growth has been higher in sectors that were more open to international competition than in ones that remained more protected (World Bank 2008b).
10 See, for example, Krugman (1994) and Young (1995).
11 The figure for Djibouti during the 1990s may be a statistical artifact, as the rate of female labor force participation in the 2010s is much lower, similar to that of other MENA countries.

3 A Historical Perspective on Tunisia's Development

Initial Conditions, Strategies, and Policies

In this chapter, we review what we believe to be the most important explanations for not only the long-term developmental outcomes of Tunisia but also those outcomes by each of several subperiods which have been identified in the two preceding chapters. We find it convenient to group the various explanations into two main groups. The first of these grouped explanations for Tunisia's success can be identified as favorable initial conditions at independence. These conditions are historical, geographical, and structural in nature. The second type are the quite different strategies, policies, and institutions which have been selected and implemented in Tunisia at different points of time since independence, and each one of which has exerted relatively strong influences during the various stages of experience over the approximately 60 years under study (1960–2019).

A. Favorable Initial Conditions for Tunisia's Success

Among the possible explanations for Tunisia's comparative success are several that would have to be considered as extremely favorable initial conditions. These include: (1) the country's favorable historical heritage in terms of state capacity, itself a multidimensional characteristic, (2) the homogeneity of its population and relatively low inequality[1], (3) its favorable geographic location and characteristics, and (4) the fortuitous emergence of a strong and relatively progressive leader in Habib Bourguiba, the country's first president after independence in 1956. The purpose of this section is to identify and briefly explain each of these.

1. The Favorable Heritage in Terms of State Capacity

One early and important component of Tunisia's favorable heritage is that it was the locus of the long reign of the Hafside dynasty which lasted for three and a half centuries (1228–1574) (See M'Rabet 2008). The basics of a functioning and autonomous state were laid down during that period. One member of an aristocratic family that played an important role in that Hafside dynasty and which had settled in Tunisia was Ibn Khaldun, an administrator-scholar

DOI: 10.4324/9781003309550-3

who had come to appreciate the role of the city-state in attracting entrepreneurs and artisans in such a way as to increase the size of the market and generate socio-political stability and economic growth. After having been born in Tunis in 1332 and educated there, he then spent time in other locations within the North Africa region as an administrator and political leader (although sometimes landing in jail for going against the interest of a particular political leader). He returned to Tunis, however, in 1378 to teach law and utilize an excellent library there to write a History of the world, the first part of which was his famous book, *The Muqaddimah.*[2]

As nicely articulated by Boulakia (1971), in *The Muqaddimah* Ibn Khaldun drew on historical events, including many he had himself seen in the region, to identify policy mistakes that had been made, but in the process constituting a coherent theory of economic growth that incorporated all of the following: 'a theory of production, a theory of value, a theory of distribution and a theory of cycles' (Boulakia 1971, 1106). This growth model consisted of three key contributing groups or sectors: (1) production as orchestrated by the artisans and entrepreneurs, (2) exchange carried out by money changers and intermediaries, and (3) public services (provided by the state). From Boulakia's exposition of Ibn Khaldun's theory, it was remarkably like that of Adam Smith's *Wealth of Nations* although written some four hundred years before Smith's book. The crux of it was to show that, in order to maintain growth in any such society over time, a careful balance (or equilibrium) among product prices, wage rates, profit rates, and taxes would have to be maintained. While we know of no particular testimony by Bourguiba or any other Tunisian leader linking Tunisian policy-making to Ibn Khaldun's theory and practice of successful development, the fact that Ibn Khaldun's residence and his writings are known to virtually any of the elites raised in Tunisia or elsewhere in the region makes it hard to deny that the remarkable success of the Hafsides and/or the logic and earlier applicability of Ibn Khaldun's economic theory and historical applications must have played an important (even if rather hidden) role in Tunisian policy-making since its independence.[3]

Many scholars (e.g., Besley and Persson 2009; Bockstette et al. 2002; Englehart 2009; Tilly 1990) have argued that state capacity is an important ingredient of a country's ability to withstand and/or adjust to the various challenges, such as was proposed in Ibn Khaldun's theory. Such ideas would suggest the desirability of constructing a measure of state capacity. Admittedly state capacity is difficult to measure. Yet, since this capacity is central to our explanation of why Tunisia has done better than many of its neighbors in the MENA region, in the following paragraphs, we shall pay attention to several such measures and the way in which they are alleged to foster growth and development.

One way of measuring it, as suggested by Bockstette et al. (2002), is by the number of years in which a state has existed in the current borders of the country. They show that this measure is positively correlated with various performance indicators such as the level of income per capita and even growth rates. Alternatively, Englehart (2009), O'Brien (2005), and Besley and Persson (2009) measure state capacity in terms of the ability to collect taxes, and some of these authors also bring in the ability to control corruption and to provide law and order since these, too, would be closely related to, if not absolute preconditions for, the ability to raise revenues. Tilly (1990) and O'Brien (2005) have made use of historical studies of Europe to demonstrate the relevance of wars and conflicts, arguing that it is wars and conflicts that stimulate the need for states to find new ways of raising revenues, and then again that success in war may enhance the power of the state and its ability to raise revenues. Englehart (2009) uses panel data for a large number of countries to show that, although each of three different measures of state capacity (tax revenue as a percentage of GDP, Freedom from Corruption, and Law and Order) could in principle be used to limit or suppress human rights, in practice each such measure has a positive effect on various indicators of human rights. Indeed, this may be due to the fact that the state will be able to raise more revenues if individuals are allowed (or even encouraged) to invest, and if the government itself invests so as to raise the tax base. For the same reason, the state may want to foster property rights (Epstein 2000) so that greater state capacity may be associated with more developed and stronger property rights (once again not so different from the model of Ibn Khaldun).

Besley and Persson (2009) have built on this literature by developing a rich theoretical model demonstrating how both wars on the one hand, and accumulated wealth on the other can be linked to superior performance in development by way of enhanced state capacity and its links to both private and public investment. In their case, state capacity is measured in terms of two broad components: (1) fiscal capacity and (2) legal capacity. These two components are believed to be complementary to one another. The latter is deemed relevant because of the complementary relation between legal capacity and the strength of property rights which affect the ability to collect taxes, settle disputes and induce investments, and thereby to provide a route to higher income per capita. In their empirical analysis, they measure Legal Capacity in terms of credit to the private sector, contract enforcement and the rule of law, and examine both the determinants and effects of state capacity. In the latter respect, they show that state capacity raises both the level of financial development and the quality of institutions, and thereby economic growth as well. While our comparative examination of rule of law and other institutional indexes will be postponed until our presentation of Tables 4.11 and 4.12 in the next chapter, we hasten to point out also that our Table 5.3 in Chapter 5 shows that, although Tunisia started from low levels of financial indicators, it made considerable progress in raising its financial development indicators in the way suggested by Besley and Persson (2009). This is, therefore, a finding consonant with the notion that state capacity causes development in the way espoused by the aforementioned economic historians, as well as by Besley and Persson (2009).

On the basis of this literature, we now turn to the specific case of Tunisia prior to its independence. As will be shown, we find several reasons to believe that the last hundred years or so prior to independence may have provided a background conducive to its subsequent political stability and economic development by way of increasing state capacity. Masri (2017) has argued that Tunisia was an 'anomaly' in the Arab region, with its unique features in terms of a history of early reforms of its institutions, its cultural norms, and its openness.

The first such reason, and one that is especially consistent with the aforementioned measure of state capacity advocated by Bockstette et al. (2002), is that Tunisia had several quite long stretches of history in which it was a more or less independent state. Among these were the periods of Carthaginian prominence (814BC–146BC), the aforementioned Hafside dynasty that lasted more than three and a half centuries (1228–1574), and the Husseinite dynasty that lasted for two and a half centuries (1705–1957), (see Guellouz 2010 and Smida 2010).[4] Even during the period when it was part of the Ottoman Empire, Tunisia's distance from Istanbul meant that it was largely left on its own, though benefiting from the relatively free trade regime of the empire. The Husseinite Dynasty was particularly important and favorable in this respect in that this was a period characterized by the consolidation of an independent and structured state. During this period, it operated as a virtual nation state with considerable stability under a succession of beys for several centuries, and the ability of the state to collect revenues and mobilize defense forces. Even more impressive and more reflective of the state's ability to provide a stable government was the promulgation of a constitution in 1861 (Anderson 1986, 80–95). During the latter part of this dynasty, under the reforming Prime Minister Kheireddine (1873–1877), Sadiki College, the country's first modern secular educational institution, was founded. The elites of this dynasty believed that the increasing influence of Europeans and European society could only be curbed by the selective adoption and adaptation of the concepts and technology from which the West had derived its strength (Perkins 1997, 8).

Second, while the colonial experience (1881–1956) had its costs in terms of political and economic discrimination, expropriation, and repression; it also brought progress in a number of areas (Boularès 2011, 561–562). When Tunisia became a Protectorate of France, the Tunisian Bey was reduced to being a figurehead and the French came to dominate the key posts in the administration, but nevertheless quite a few Tunisians were involved in government, especially in the latter years of the Protectorate. European settlers grew in numbers and importance after World War I (WWI) to constitute 10%or more of the population. They were important and privileged, but not to the same extent that French settlers were in Algeria where, according to Young (1994), they played a role in the French parliament adopting policies to assist them, too often at the expense of regular Algerians.

A major contribution of the French in the case of Tunisia was the extent to which the administration of the country was centralized and made more efficient relative to the way it had been under the beys. Indeed, Cammett (2007) argues that this contributed in an important way to the relative strength of the state in post-Independence Tunisia.[5] The French put considerable emphasis on private sector development based on private property rights, but experimented with a variety of mechanisms, including various colonization schemes with important infrastructure investments designed to attract French private capital. Major investments were placed in the railways in 1878, and in the ports of Tunis, Bizerte, Sousse, and Sfax between 1865 and 1913 (Issawi 1982). This demonstrated the important potential complementarities between private and public investment that could be realized by an effective state and served as a demonstration case for the subsequent need for state-provided social overhead capital investments in the form of highways, port facilities, and utilities in order to encourage private investment activities (Young 1994).

Since any such investments as well as important government services, such as those provided by an effective bureaucracy and judicial system, have to be financed, one of the key requisites for state capacity and success in private sector activities and in the accumulation of capital – both private and public – is the ability to collect taxes. The importance of this was probably never more important and challenging than in the post-WWI period and especially during the great depression when the French colonial authorities in Tunisia were forced to strictly prioritize their investments according to their anticipated economic payoff and the need for local financing of their expenditures.[6]

Third, the Protectorate also served to stimulate human capital investments and institutions that could facilitate such investments. Prudential associations were formed for risk pooling and to form the basis of a primitive credit system. Even though these schemes did not work very well, since Tunisians were excluded from most of them due to their lack of education, this motivated a social and political movement to increase educational access for Tunisians. Sadiki College grew so as to become an incubator for the modern, university-educated elite whose outlook came to dominate Tunisia after independence (Moore 1965, 23). In the early 1900s, the first Tunisian political movement, the Young Tunisians, emerged, pushing *against* both the confiscation of land in favor of the colonials and the lack of representation of the locals in government but *for* more schools for the local population (Boularès 2011). As a result of this pressure from the Young Tunisians, in 1907, the protectorate's 'Conférence Consultative'[7] admitted Tunisians for the first time. When subsequently Protectorate policy was temporarily reversed and the party's youthful elites were bypassed, this sparked a strong anti-French opposition. It was this opposition which led eventually to independence and, in the meantime, to push for modern, secular education for which Tunisia has become well known (Moore 1965, 23). Even in the presence of French intervention, Tunisian elites came to become quite national in scope. As Anderson (1986, 231–269) points out, these Tunisian elites came to be established as a recognized, national-in-scope social structure that contrasted quite sharply with the situation of the local population in neighboring Libya, which in no way became a national society, only a tribal and very regionally divided one. Notably, Anderson went on to explain how that fundamental difference eventually resulted in a state in the case of Tunisia under Bourguiba, but absolutely no state, only tribes, in the case of Libya. None of those aforementioned state-like innovations that had been instituted in Tunisia in the 19th Century, such as its capitation tax, conscription laws, and constitution, had been undertaken in Libya.

Fourth, as time went on, grievances against the French regime in Tunisia increased.[8] By the 1920s local agitation was pressuring the government to distribute domain land to Tunisians. The first real political party, the 'Destour,' was created in 1920.[9] By the 1930s workers had expressed their collective grievances against their French, Italian, and other employers. Habib Bourguiba, the son of a minor government official in Monastir (in the coastal agricultural Sahel region of the country), took advantage of his Sahelian connections and these grievances of workers to broaden the existing Destour Party (that had been based rather exclusively on a narrowly defined urban elite). By integrating workers, small merchants, professionals, and medium-sized farmers into it, in 1934 Bourguiba transformed the party into the Néo-Destour Party. Many members of the latter groups came from the Sahel where local landowners had resisted incursions of the French and invested in the education of their children, often in France, just as had been done with Bourguiba himself. In addition, Bourguiba defended some indigenous business groups from the French authorities and as a result obtained their support that allowed him to subdue the old Destour party (Belev 2001). All through this transformation of the old party into the new one, education continued to be a major objective of the party (Powell 1970; United Nations, Food and Agricultural Organization (FAO) 1994).

At least one well-known political scientist, Samuel Huntington, claims that Bourguiba's skillful integration of medium-sized commercial farmers into the party was in itself a crucial contribution to Tunisia's subsequent success. In particular, Huntington (1991) argues that rural-based coalitions provide considerably greater stability than urban ones and indeed cites Tunisia as evidence in support of his argument. Given the strength of its rural base, in 1949 the party assisted in the creation of a farmers' organization, the Union Générale des Agriculteurs Tunisiens, which subsequently provided the core of Tunisia's 'liberation army' in Tunisia's fight for independence (King 1998).

Despite the growing list of grievances against the French administration, the Protectorate provided Tunisia with relative stability and some major institutional changes. It permitted the development of political roots, social codes (including civil/religious rights, and a constitution), and systems of trade and communication, each of which was superior to those of Tunisia's neighbors (Perkins 1997, 8). For his part, Bourguiba was also careful to defend those aspects of the French influence that he saw as modern and developmental, such as education, law, centralized administration, and infrastructural development. Notably, during World War II (WWII), despite some opposition from other elements of the local population, Bourguiba took a strong stance in support of the Allies side in the war (which of course included France).

Fifth, under Bourguiba's leadership, the main objectives of the party, both before and after independence, were modernization and development. These were consistently given priority over democratic, civil and political liberties. This was an objective that most Tunisians, and especially the new middle class, could espouse. In his speeches Bourguiba repeatedly stressed that the most urgent battle was against underdevelopment (economic and social objectives), not against foreigners or for political liberties (political objectives). Hence, this too could explain why no democratic 'revolution' has yet fully come into power in Tunisia (Brown 1964; Moore 1965; Anderson 1986; Cammett 2007).[10]

Hence, in all these ways, and its having experienced long periods of relatively independent self-rule prior to independence, including the development of a centralized administration capable of making major infrastructural and human capital investments, and providing law and order, Tunisia's early experience demonstrated both (a) the usefulness of combining and coordinating public and private investment, and (b) the need to finance its brief war of independence and the purchase of French-owned capital. A major benefit was having obtained the fortuitous leadership of Habib Bourguiba. As a result, therefore, even at independence Tunisia was relatively well endowed with the various ingredients of each of the different definitions of state capacity identified above. In addition, all these factors can be seen as providing strong support for the 'state capacity causes development thesis' articulated by Besley and Persson (2009).

2. *Homogeneity of Population*

Relative to many of its neighbors in Africa and Western Asia, Tunisia enjoyed much greater homogeneity in its populace. Being small, and without high mountains of the type that would limit mobility, even its citizens living in the country's more distant regions have never been very distinct. They all spoke the same language (a dialect of Arabic) and, except for a small Jewish minority, many of whom left Tunisia after independence, they share the Islamic religion, and indeed the Malikite Sunni school of Islam

(Murphy 1999). This is very different from the countries of sub-Saharan Africa which are inhabited by many tribes, each with a different culture and language, and whose institutions were destroyed by the slave trade (Nunn 2005). This is also at least fairly different from its neighbors in North Africa which also have sharper tribal, ethnic and in some cases religious differences. Many of the other MENA countries such as Algeria, Iran, Oman, and Yemen, moreover, have high, mobility-reducing mountains that lead to distinct regional differences in their populations (Lacouture 1970, 136, 157). The widespread popularity of its liberation movement also provided Tunisians with a common bond, giving the Néo-Destour party (which as pointed out above was founded by Bourguiba), and the Tunisian people in general greater uniformity and homogeneity than they would have had without going through the drive for independence.

3. A Favorable Geographic Location

Tunisia's location close to the heart of Western Europe was certainly another major advantage. The country is in especially close proximity to France and Italy, whose businessmen and professionals had played an important role in the pre-independence economic life of the Protectorate. Access to the prosperous European market was facilitated further by the fact that, as a former protectorate of France, Tunisia received privileged access to the market of the European Community for a time without duties and quotas on most of its products in the immediate post-independence period. This allowed both policy-makers and entrepreneurs in Tunisia to see the opportunities for them and their products in Europe. Yet, since Morocco, and especially Libya and Algeria, benefited to a similar extent from this favorable location but did not manage to take advantage of it to the extent that Tunisia did, it is clear that the policy approaches taken by Tunisia's policy-makers deserve a good bit of the credit.[11]

4. The Fortuitous Emergence of Habib Bourguiba as Its First President

The early independence period saw extreme political tensions with the struggle over political leadership between Habib Bourguiba and Salah Ben Yousef, who was another leader of the Néo-Destour party. The two leaders had different political visions and competing ambitions, and this created deep divisions within the party and the population. But the conflict was quickly resolved, Bourguiba prevailed and became the dominant political leader in the country. Despite this conflict, due to his role in the independence movement and having been in jail under the French, at independence, Bourguiba, his government, and the Tunisian state were all viewed as very legitimate. This was in great contrast to many of the leaders in other parts of the MENA region and especially those in Tunisia's neighborhood who inherited thrones or took power by military coup.[12]

Many political economy researchers have called attention to the importance of what happens during the so-called 'honeymoon period' immediately after a new popular leader takes over a government. They emphasize that the honeymoon period is likely to be potentially more important and significant when the new leader comes to power as the result of an election or a mass movement as Bourguiba did. As indicated above, at independence, Bourguiba was in an especially good position to act without much interference. And act he did! He undertook strong social reforms, such as strengthening women's legal rights, and encouraging women to be educated and to participate actively in the economic and political life of the country. He weakened the religious establishment by abolishing the religious educational institutions, and launching an alternative secular educational system (Bechri and Naccache 2007; Bsaies 1989). These were reforms that were way ahead of other MENA countries, and undoubtedly controversial at that time in Tunisia. But, because of Bourguiba's popularity and that these were undertaken immediately during the honeymoon period; these reforms proved to be difficult to block or subsequently to be reversed. Some regard these reforms as some of the most fundamental to Tunisia's subsequent development. Notably, Tunisia became one of the first countries in the MENA region to achieve gender equity in education and to reduce its fertility rate, and quite likely also its infant mortality rate. Clearly, Bourguiba's social reforms contributed substantially to these developments. Bourguiba's agenda was that of 'modernity' with the coexistence of, and a fine balance between, religiosity and secularism (Masri 2017).

In office, Bourguiba quickly showed himself to be adept at putting down opposition with both carrot and stick policies, sticks to impose stiff penalties on those who opposed him, and carrots to reward those who were loyal to him.[13] His willingness to use strong-arm tactics to preserve his position in power was not unlike some of the equally strong-armed leaders in East Asia, such as Korea's President Park, China's Zhou Enlai and Deng Xiaoping, Singapore's Lee Kuan Yew, Malaysia's Mahathir bin Mohamed or Thailand's Thanom Kittkachorn, who also led their countries to economic success. In the Asian case, where growth in GDP per capita over the period 1965–1990 was double that of any other region of the world and was accomplished along with declining inequality and poverty rates, this became known as the Asian Miracle. Notably, in their well-known assessment of the Asian Miracle, Campos and Root (2001) pointed to the fact that much of their success should be attributed to their success in making the policies they chose credible to both their business communities and their citizenry, not simply to their military or politically powerful. In the Tunisian case, moreover, the need for the strong-armed tactics was probably reduced by the fact that few if any could question Bourguiba's deep and enduring commitment to the goal of modernization and development of his country (Lacouture 1970, 146–155).[14]

Some would also attribute Tunisia's subsequent political and social stability to the breadth of the dominant Néo-Destour political party that Habib Bourguiba had created well before independence. At independence, party functionaries took over the positions in government previously held by the French. By the mid-1960s, the Néo-Destour became the single party which controlled the state, with the president of Tunisia also being the president of the party (Cammett 2007, 59). After a successful and peaceful coup in 1987 against the then aging and ailing Bourguiba, Zine-el-Abidine Ben Ali, Tunisia's second president, changed the name of the party from Néo-Destour to Rassemblement Constitutionnel Democratique. But little changed either structurally or ideologically. Because of (1) the party's breadth (with substantial rural elements in it), (2) its strong grassroots organization, and (3) its leaders being largely recruited from the middle class but generally also with considerable support from labor unions, the party managed to remain accepted by the population, even if not exactly popular following the change in leadership.

Some of these considerations, especially its relatively long experience as a relatively autonomous state even under the Ottoman Empire, its relatively benign colonial experience, its relatively inexpensive war of independence, and the fortuitous emergence of Bourguiba as the leader of its independence, made the management of Tunisia's economic and political life after independence much smoother than it otherwise would have been, and thus much smoother than in many other developing countries after their independence. Yet, in other aspects, such as its climate and proximity to Europe, it was not appreciably better off than some of its North African neighbors. For this reason, and because major problems remained after independence and numerous new challenges were lying ahead, in our view, Tunisia could not have been successful over the 60 plus years since independence without having been able to (1) adopt strategies capable of meeting these new challenges and changing circumstances, and especially (2) take advantage of the opportunities to which these changing circumstances gave rise.

B. Strategies and Policies Followed Since Independence and Their Effects on the Country's Economic Performance

Despite its favorable historical heritage and other circumstances identified in the previous section, Tunisia was not without problems and would not be without problems throughout much of the over 60 years following independence. At independence, the new country faced extremely high land inequality, with more than half of the large properties owned by the French. Its agricultural productivity, especially that on Tunisian owned or controlled lands, was extremely low; literacy and educational attainment levels were low (though on their way up); fertility was very high (the total fertility rate being well over 7 children per woman) and the country was heavily dependent on foreign professionals and foreign enterprise. It had few entrepreneurs with any experience in industry. Aside from services and agriculture, the only non-agricultural activities of any importance were phosphate mining in the Southwest of the country and olive oil in the East and North.

1. The Early Years of Independence (1956–1961): Private Sector Encouragement

At Tunisia's independence in 1956, most newly independent developing countries were already well along in their import-substituting industrialization modes. Following such a strategy seemed natural, and Tunisia proved no exception. Given the dearth of entrepreneurial and worker experience in virtually any industry in the country, Bourguiba could well have led the country immediately toward state ownership as was common in Egypt and many other countries of the region. To a certain extent, he did so. Over the first several years of independence, the Tunisian state bought out the French investments in mining and fertilizers, utilities, and transportation. Because these were very capital intensive, private entrepreneurs were in no position to buy or even manage these enterprises. Hence, these became state enterprises. But, beyond that, his emphasis was on encouraging private enterprise. In part, this may have been due to the foreseen importance of taking advantage of foreign aid from France and the US to develop the country's infrastructure while recognizing that such aid might be jeopardized if state enterprise was emphasized. One group, namely, the old wealthy merchants who had collaborated with the French, were not among the private entrepreneurs encouraged. To the independence movement and the Néo-Destour Party at least, these merchants were seen as traitors. Indeed, by instigating in 1957 two important laws, the Law of Ill-Gotten Gains and the Law of National Indignity, the government gained the power to confiscate the property of, and to impose harsh sentences on, those accused of collaborating with the French (Bellin 2002). But others, merchants and non-merchants alike, were encouraged to undertake new industrial ventures, however small. The confiscation of private property, moreover, was limited to this small contingent of traitors. Among non-traitors, private property was very much respected and, in the case of industry and many services, it was much encouraged

While the industrialization strategy adopted by Bourguiba and his new government was not based on what might be called free market policies, it represented a continuation of pre-existing policies under the Protectorate, such as guaranteed loans and favorable tax treatment for those investing in industry along with generally heavy regulation.

Yet, despite this rather aggressive means of encouraging private sector investment in industry, investment, industrial output and GDP per capita all stagnated during the first five years of independence. By 1961, capital flight became a serious problem and GDP per capita began to decline. Few of the small enterprises during these years proved viable. Foreign investment largely avoided Tunisia because of uncertainty about future relations with

France and economic policy. While the state also encouraged the transfer of public and foreign-owned agricultural land to Tunisian farmers, this, too, gave very disappointing results.

2. State-Led Development and Planning 1961–1969

Recognizing the limited success of the aforementioned efforts at private sector development, and without wanting to give up on the goal of industrial development, by appointing former labor union leader Ahmed Ben Salah as Minister of Planning in 1961 and later as Minister of Finance as well, Bourguiba made a rather radical about-face. The state adopted state planning and state enterprise. Bechri and Naccache (2007) argue that Bourguiba's choice of Ben Salah as the main Minister in charge of economic and social development during this period was motivated by the desire to co-opt and neutralize the main labor organization, l'Union Générale Tunisienne du Travail (UGTT). Cooperatives became an important form of organization (essentially under government and ruling party control) and were used as a means of generating forced saving and investment, although not necessarily in the same line of activity (Grissa 1973). Since the major organization of entrepreneurs, l'Union Tunisienne de l'Industrie, du Commerce et de l'Artisanat (UTICA), was also largely under government control, this meant that the potentially important non-government interest groups were inactive, thereby giving the government the ability to act and coordinate without obstruction or delay by organized interest groups.

Much of agriculture was nationalized during this period (including foreign owned land in 1964) and placed in the hands of cooperatives. Cooperative agriculture, however, turned out to be even more of a disaster than it had been in the preceding years, alienating the peasants and farmers who had been such an important component of the Néo-Destour Party. The peasants found themselves working in the cooperatives with little say in the use of cooperative funds and little incentive to work. As a result, the cooperatives became very unproductive. The landowners and shopkeepers were even more resentful because of the alienation of their lands and commercial property which too were placed at the disposal of the cooperatives.

Meanwhile, an active import-substitution industrialization strategy was pursued, with the state playing a leading role. Trade protection was used extensively as an instrument for promoting import-substitution, and most of foreign trade was put in the hands of state monopolies. Some of these developments were not unlike some of those in neighboring Algeria. Moreover, following upon discovery and rapid development of oil in Algeria, the Tunisian state declared ownership of natural resources like oil but also contracted with foreign companies with licenses to explore for oil in Tunisia. Oil was discovered in 1964 and production began in 1965 with estimated reserves of 0.5 billion barrels. A large oil refinery (Societe Tunisienne des Industries de Raffinage) was built and some of its production was exported.

Thanks in part to the oil sector whose exports grew rapidly from the late 1960s and through the 1970s with rising oil prices, both long- and short-term financings of the new enterprises were made possible by new financial institutions. Enormous investments were made through state banks into rather capital-intensive public enterprises, often with little relation to the country's comparative advantage. By 1969 more than 80 state enterprises had been set up in the industrial sector, and the public sector accounted for almost 85% of total investment in industry between 1961 and 1969 (Bellin 2002, 22). Investors in new activities were also to be given licenses and protection in the form of both tariffs and quotas (or even prohibitions of imports in certain sectors) (Bellin 2002). In textiles, a sector in which private sector activities had managed to grow more than in other sectors, a coordinating institution was created, namely, the 'Office National des Textiles.' Its purpose was to coordinate development of the textile sector. Given the lack of experience of Tunisians in industry, the government sent students to France to study subjects like textile engineering (Cammett 2007, 69).

Oil production grew from something like 20,000 barrels per day (bbd) in the late 1960s to a peak of 120,000 bbd in the late 1970s. The oil part of the oil and gas industry came to be managed by the Ministry of Energy and Mines. Exploration licenses were issued for both on-shore and off-shore exploration throughout much of the country, the largest pools being found in El Borma in the South near the Algerian border, in the Center at Sidi-el-Kilani and the offshore field of Ashtart in the Gulf of Gabès. Likewise, production licenses were issued to foreign firms in collaboration with the Tunisian National Oil Company (Entreprise Tunisienne d'Activités Pétrolières). Gas production was located primarily in El Borma and offshore in Miskar and was sold to the national company in charge of production of electricity (Société Tunisienne d'Electricité et de Gaz).

In contrast to many developing countries, the Tunisian state dealt with the private sector it was trying to encourage in a relatively transparent bureaucratic way, not in a cozy, patron-client way in which only some insiders would be encouraged (Cammett 2007). The new banks and other financial institutions created during those early years are, for the most part, still operative and important in the finance of Tunisian enterprises.

Much of the state's revenues came from (a) the newly acquired public enterprises in phosphate mining, (b) its modest at first but fast-growing oil and gas sector, (c) the forced savings of cooperatives, and (d) some of its new industrial public enterprises. Indeed, according to data on Fuel Exports as a percent of Total Merchandise Exports (obtained from the World Bank and as computed from the UN ComTrade database), this percent rose from nil in 1965 to over 25% in 1970 and, thanks to the quadrupling of oil prices in the 1970s and early 1980s, to 54% by 1982 before falling to 6% in 1992 with subsequent oil price declines and diversification from oil after that.

For several years in the 1960s, very sizable investments were made in public sector industrial activities. But generally, these were not very profitable.

Since French aid and access to French markets had been cut off as a result of the nationalization of French land and other assets, despite the fuel revenues and considerable growth in the industrial sector, by 1969 the state was no longer able to keep financing its investments at such high rates. This was especially true because of the very limited quantity of Tunisia's oil and gas reserves, very different from the GCC and other countries of the region including Algeria.

As documented by Esfahani and Squire (2007), throughout the 1970s and 1980s, to encourage industrial development, Tunisia maintained both high effective tariff rates and substantial non-tariff barriers, very different from the major oil exporting countries of the MENA region, and even higher ones than in most of the non-oil MENA countries. Naturally, a consequence of these protective measures imposed by Tunisia and other countries outside the large oil exporters was a reduction in the overall openness of their economies. Esfahani and Squire undertook a comparison for all MENA countries (and for a number of other developing countries) between each country's *actual* Openness to Trade score and that which would be *predicted* on the basis of its country size, population size, geographic proximity to trading partners, access to the sea, and notably also the percentage of fuel in total exports. In part because of Tunisia's relatively large share of fuel exports for the period up to 1985, they found that its actual openness to trade lagged well behind its predicted extent of Openness to Trade, and to a greater extent than for any of the other MENA countries in our analysis until 1975 and, indeed except for Syria, even beyond that until 1985. This finding was also consistent with their finding of higher tariffs and non-tariff barriers in Tunisia and most other MENA countries outside the GCC than in the other developing countries.

As a result, not surprisingly, some of the industries that Tunisia tried to protect were inefficient, non-competitive internationally, and still heavily dependent on imports. Eventually, the non-sustainability of state-led import-substituting industrialization became evident.

Despite the general inefficiency of the state-led industrial development, and the 'collectivization' of agriculture, as a result of the high levels of investment the economy had grown considerably, and the state sector, including the bureaucracy, had demonstrated that it could coordinate the many things that had to be done in proper sequence. As shown in Table 1.6, despite these inefficiencies, Tunisia's growth rates of per capita GDP were quite high during the decade of the 1960s, as they were in many of the MENA countries during this period. Besides this, the state seemed to have provided all the inducements necessary to encourage the rapid growth of tourism, to provide engineering and on-the-job training in industry, and to allow public enterprise managers and civil servants to become capable of functioning properly. Notably, with the ability to collect the taxes and other revenues to finance infrastructural and other investments, design, and implement incentives to the private sector, to coordinate both private and public sector activities, as well as to provide training for managers and engineers of state enterprises, the young Tunisian state was already well along in the development of state capacity.[15]

However, with the expansive fiscal policies of the early 1960s, including increased expenditures on infrastructure and on wages, as early as 1964 the country came to face its first macroeconomic crisis which led to a major devaluation. While the economy recovered quickly, by the end of the 1960s Tunisia ran into another major macroeconomic crisis, as the trade deficit increased sharply over the decade and became clearly unsustainable. There was also strong and active opposition to the policy of 'collectivization' of not only agriculture but also of many trade and service activities. This led to a political crisis as well and the firing of Ben Salah and the repudiation of the 'socialist' development strategy that he had promoted.

3. Strong Social Policies and Inclusion

As part of the 'socialist' development agenda of the 1960s, Tunisian government pursued very active policies for poverty reduction, improved standards of living and social protection. These policies, which were continued and even expanded over the decades, contributed to a large extent to the strong performance in terms of poverty reduction and lower inequality observed in Tunisia, especially prior to 1990 as shown in Table 1.2. A variety of policy instruments were used to achieve better inclusion: investment in education, health and housing, consumer price subsidies, incomes policies, and social protection schemes (Economic and Social Commission for West Asia 2016; World Bank 2015).

First, since the early independence years, there was an emphasis on access to education, health, and housing. As will be discussed further in Chapter 4, the government allocated the major share of its expenditures to education and health, achieving major gains in terms of enrollment in education and improved health indicators. Investment in social housing, with subsidies and long-term credit, was also expanded to allow access to home ownership for the largest segments of the population.

Second, in order to protect the poor from the volatility of commodity prices, a system of subsidies of basic food products was introduced in response to the surge in food commodity prices during the early 1970s. A budgetary fund called the Caisse Générale de Compensation (CGC) was created to finance subsidies of prices for basic food commodities, and smooth out their variations for the consumer. Initially it included mainly bread, other cereals products, and vegetable oil prices. This system, which was expected to be temporary, has remained in place until now, and its scope has varied over time, with some products, such as energy products sometimes added and others sometimes withdrawn.

Third, an active income protection policy was pursued since the 1960s. A minimum wage was introduced for agricultural and non-agricultural workers, and regularly adjusted. A workfare program has been implemented, and used until the present, to fund public works for poor unemployed people, for a limited number of days per year. Since 1986, a program of cash transfers to the neediest families has been in place. This Programme National d'Aide aux Familles Nécessiteuses (PNAFN) has expanded steadily over the decades to become a significant part of the poverty reduction agenda (Ben Cheikh and Bibi 2017).

Fourth, an extensive social protection system was developed for old-age and health insurance. A publicly managed 'pay-as-you go' system of retirement benefits both public sector and private sector employees. Many schemes for health insurance have been introduced for various groups, including for the most vulnerable, who have free access to the public health system. The coverage for social protection has expanded steadily to cover a large part of society, but it remains incomplete and not universal.

4. Macroeconomic Institutions, Policies, and Reforms

There is a broad consensus in the development literature that the macroeconomic framework plays a critical role in the success of countries in achieving strong and steady economic growth and the transformation of economies. A stable and predictable environment with low and stable inflation, predictable and reasonable taxation, and absence of financial crises depend on sound policies and institutions. Tunisia has been, at least until 2010, generally successful in developing and implementing adequate fiscal and monetary institutions and policies.

Fiscal Policies and Institutions

From early in the 1960s, Tunisia has anchored its fiscal policies within a planning medium-term framework. This approach has remained to a large extent in place until now. While the multi-year plan framework was initially for 3 or 4 years, since the 1980s it has been for 5-year periods. Each such plan was prepared and adopted according to schedule, providing both the general policy framework and the government's (including state enterprises) investment plan. The annual budgets are prepared within this framework, but also with a lot of flexibility.

Until the 1990s, the government plans were implemented under the overall supervision of the Ministry of Planning, which vets investment projects and follows up the actual funding and implementation with the relevant agencies. The Ministry of Finance is in charge of resources and the current expenditures budget. This set-up has changed since the end of the 1990s when all budget operations were merged within the Ministry of Finance.

Tunisia has succeeded in increasing tax revenue significantly reaching more than 20% of GDP since the 1970s (See Chapter 4). The tax system has been continuously improved with a major reform of both personal and corporate income taxes in the early 1990s and the introduction of a Value-Added Tax (VAT) system. The share of direct taxes in total taxes has increased steadily from around 20% in the 1980s to almost 45% recently. However, the tax system still suffers from many weaknesses including its complexity, uneven coverage, the multiplicity of its tax regimes and tax exemptions, and lack of transparency.

The institutional set-up and the effective mobilization of tax revenue have allowed the country to pursue prudent fiscal policies, which were development-driven but generally cautious on deficits and financing. Of course, political conditions led sometimes to major excesses, such as in the early 1980s, or during the recent post-uprisings period, in which large budget deficits and excessive borrowing have occurred.

Central Bank Independence and Inflation

The Central Bank of Tunisia (CBT) was created in 1958 following a decision to exit from the colonial monetary arrangement within the French Franc area. A new currency, the 'Dinar' was launched, and an autonomous monetary policy conducted by the new monetary authority, with a relatively flexible exchange rate arrangement. From the beginning the CBT was relatively autonomous, if not fully independent in the modern sense, from the fiscal authorities. This relative independence was maintained throughout the decades despite attempts from time to time at making the CBT submissive to the authority of the Ministry of Finance. This has contributed to the mostly conservative monetary policy of CBT and the relatively moderate inflation rates for Tunisia over the long run, as can be seen from Table 3.1.

The Tunisian monetary policy arrangement has moved slowly towards a formal Central Bank Independence (CBI) arrangement for monetary policy, as has become a favored in macroeconomic circles since the 1980s. The argument is that, only if it establishes complete independence from government pressures to pursue other objectives of the government through its actions, can the Central Bank focus on achieving the most basic objective of monetary policy, namely, to create price stability and limit growth-inhibiting volatility in income over time. For elaboration of the theory and evidence concerning the effects of CBI, see Berger et al. (2008).

The empirical findings concerning the impact of CBI on monetary stability, however, have sometimes proved controversial, in part because of different ideas about the most appropriate way to measure it, how to mitigate selection and endogeneity biases, how to test for the direction of causality, to allow for possible interactions with other institutional characteristics such as the extent of democracy, and different choices of the most appropriate outcome variables (such as inflation, volatility, and growth). Chief among the choice of measures are several of the *de jure* type, based largely on the laws and regulations of each country's central bank, and several of the

Table 3.1 Inflation, 1961–2019

	Inflation, consumer prices (average annual change %)						
Country	*1961–1970*	*1971–1980*	*1981–1990*	*1991–2000*	*2001–2010*	*1961–2010*	*2011–2019*
MENA non-major oil exporters	**2.69**	**9.23**	**11.21**	**8.28**	**5.31**	**7.85**	**6.77**
Djibouti			4.35		3.66	4.39	2.08
Egypt, Arab Rep.	3.22	9.49	16.96	9.08	8.40	9.43	12.66
Jordan		11.34	7.53	3.52	4.12	6.61	2.59
Lebanon							3.01
Morocco	2.30	8.60	7.32	3.95	1.81	4.80	1.17
Syrian Arab Republic	1.73	10.71	22.62	5.83	5.73	9.33	20.73
Tunisia	**3.50**	**6.01**	**8.49**	**4.52**	**3.33**	**5.24**	**5.27**
West Bank and Gaza				5.25	4.05	4.40	1.32
Yemen, Rep.				25.78	11.36	18.57	12.13
MENA major oil exporters	**3.34**	**8.80**	**12.00**	**45.41**	**9.61**	**18.01**	**9.05**
Algeria		8.52	9.74	16.93	3.58	9.62	4.73
Iran, Islamic Rep.	1.74	12.89	18.52	24.39	14.67	14.44	21.38
Iraq	2.32	7.19		134.73	19.88	42.81	2.03
Libya	5.97	6.60	7.74	5.57	0.30	5.17	8.06
MENA GCC	**1.97**	**11.34**	**2.28**	**1.67**	**3.58**	**4.00**	**1.85**
Bahrain	2.22	12.79	1.96	0.63	1.84	4.07	1.94
Kuwait		8.43	3.88	2.33	3.68	4.38	2.66
Oman					3.01	3.01	1.43
Qatar			3.43	2.74	5.29	3.92	1.61
Saudi Arabia	1.73	12.80	−0.13	0.97	2.74	3.74	1.92
United Arab Emirates					4.90	4.90	1.53
East Asia	**46.64**	**12.97**	**8.26**	**7.20**	**3.90**	**14.10**	**2.71**
China			11.84	7.48	2.16	5.99	2.52
Indonesia	210.57	17.47	8.61	14.14	8.59	51.88	4.71
Korea, Rep.	13.98	16.49	6.39	5.10	3.18	9.03	1.59
Malaysia	0.93	5.98	3.25	3.55	2.20	3.18	2.19
Philippines	5.41	14.93	15.03	8.41	4.64	9.68	2.93
Thailand	2.30	9.98	4.43	4.53	2.62	4.77	1.40

Source: Data from database: World Bank, World Development Indicators.

Note: Tunisia data, completed and corrected from domestic sources.

de facto type, most commonly the frequency of changes in the Governors of the central bank or in the selection of board members.

While much of the early literature focused on relations between inflation and CBI in developed countries, where the rules were clearly identified, over time increasing attention has been devoted to the measurement and analysis of CBI in developing countries. Examples of such studies in all regions include de Haan and Kooi (2000) and most recently Garriga and

Rodriguez (2020), in transition countries those of Lougani and Sheets (1997) and Lybek (1999), in Latin American countries by Gutierrez (2003), and in MENA countries by Gisolo (2008), Economic and Social Commission for West Asia (2011) and Selim (2019) (although in the latter case only for the oil exporting countries of the MENA region).

The most up-to-date and comprehensive study of CBI and its effects on inflation rates in developing countries we have found is the aforementioned study of Garriga and Rodriguez (2020) which makes use of time series data on *de jure* measures of CBI and on several of its different components as well as on inflation rates over the period 1980–2013 for 118 developing countries, including not only 18 different MENA countries but also many Asian countries and all six of our comparator East Asian countries. Table 3.2 shows

Table 3.2 Central Bank Independence Indicators, 1970–2012

	Garriga indexes of CBI						*Cukierman*
	1970	*1980*	*1990*	*2000*	*2006*	*2012*	*2012*
MENA non-major oil exporters	**0.345**	**0.335**	**0.372**	**0.410**	**0.513**	**0.513**	**0.527**
Djibouti				0.454	0.575	0.575	
Egypt, Arab Rep.	0.491	0.441	0.410	0.441	0.516	0.516	0.380
Jordan	0.514	0.514	0.514	0.514	0.514	0.514	0.458
Lebanon	0.365	0.365	0.365	0.365	0.365	0.365	0.708
Morocco	0.119	0.119	0.119	0.119	0.622	0.622	0.708
Syrian Arab Republic				0.400	0.400	0.400	0.417
Tunisia	**0.237**	**0.237**	**0.450**	**0.450**	**0.575**	**0.575**	**0.438**
West Bank and Gaza							
Yemen, Rep.				0.540	0.540	0.540	0.582
MENA major oil exporters			**0.426**	**0.376**	**0.463**	**0.501**	**0.703**
Algeria					0.338	0.488	0.750
Iran, Islamic Rep.	0.021	0.507	0.507	0.507	0.507	0.507	0.583
Iraq					0.702	0.702	0.708
Libya			0.344	0.244	0.306	0.306	0.770
MENA GCC		**0.424**	**0.424**	**0.430**	**0.478**	**0.478**	**0.510**
Bahrain					0.504	0.504	0.770
Kuwait		0.400	0.400	0.400	0.400	0.400	0.520
Oman		0.497	0.497	0.497	0.497	0.497	0.375
Qatar		0.263	0.263	0.293	0.507	0.507	0.645
Saudi Arabia	0.421	0.421	0.421	0.421	0.421	0.421	0.167
United Arab Emirates		0.538	0.538	0.538	0.538	0.538	0.582
East Asia	**0.293**	**0.310**	**0.31**	**0.519**	**0.495**	**0.586**	**0.532**
China	0.269	0.269	0.269	0.603	0.497	0.497	0.220
Indonesia	0.294	0.294	0.294	0.864	0.826	0.826	0.645
Korea, Rep.	0.330	0.366	0.366	0.444	0.444	0.444	0.582
Malaysia	0.363	0.363	0.363	0.441	0.441	0.559	0.582
Philippines	0.425	0.492	0.492	0.685	0.685	0.685	0.645
Thailand	0.077	0.077	0.077	0.077	0.077	0.505	0.520

Source: Ana Carolina Garriga website, Cukierman et al. (1992).

the available CBI data for selected years between 1970 and 2012 for all the comparator countries in MENA and East Asia. The CBI de jure measures in that table are based on a modified version of the commonly used index (originally developed by Cukierman et al. (1992) but labeled Garriga Indexes in the table). For comparison purposes, in the last column of the table are the corresponding scores for 2012 using the original Cukierman et al. coding. Note that in general from the last two columns in the table, it can be seen that the two different coding systems do yield quite different scores, though neither one is always larger than the other. Comparing the Garriga indexes over time, one can see that for almost half the countries in the table there were no changes over time but that of the others, except Libya, the trend was upward. Notably, Tunisia was one of the MENA countries with a substantial upward trend, the underlying sources indicating that the reforms took place in 1988, 2000, 2001, and 2006 (specifically, Loi 1988–119 of November 1988, Loi 2000–37 of April 2000, Loi 2001–65 of July 10, 2001, and Loi 2006–26 of May 15, 2006). While this upward trend in CBI for Tunisia through 2006 was not as sharp as that for Algeria, it was certainly well above average for MENA countries.[16] Note, however, that every one of the East Asian countries also registered upward changes in their CBI measures over the period, with exceptionally sharp rises in Indonesia and Thailand. The East Asian average scores, however, showed that they were rather similar to those of Tunisia in almost all years, again confirming the stylized pattern observed throughout this study, in that Tunisia has scored better on most relevant performance indicators than most other MENA countries but not better than East Asian countries, although in this case also *not worse* than the East Asian countries.

More recently, Tunisia adopted a full CBI framework with the new Central banking Law of 2016 although the Garriga CBI scores in Table 3.2 do not go beyond 2012.

Among studies distinguishing Tunisia from other countries, Gisolo (2008) classified Tunisia as among the two or three MENA countries with the highest both *de jure* and *de facto* CBI measures. Yet, on Accountability, measured by timely publication of statements about Central Bank activities and objectives, Tunisia's Central Bank was ranked lowest in the region, and on Policy Formulation (in turn based on four sub-indicators Monetary Policy, Foreign Exchange Policy, Coordination, and Resolution) it was ranked second lowest in the region (higher only than Morocco). Consistent with the importance of CBI for reducing inflation, Tunisia's relatively high CBI index over the 1996–2005 was found to result in an inflation rate about 1% below the average for the region. In view of the rather sizable differences between countries on the related sub-indicators and without total consensus on how they should be weighted, the author chose not to go further in his overall assessment of the importance of CBI, especially for developing countries and especially going to outcomes beyond inflation. This study did not focus on changes over time and indeed for Tunisia used only the

1959 law establishing the Central Bank as the basis for coding its CBI and comparing it with that of other countries. Notably, in their study of CBI in Algeria, Zouache and Ilmane (2008) called attention to significant changes over time indicating an important trend toward greater CBI in that country.

Not surprisingly, given the very different contexts of the different countries and regions studied, the empirical results from other studies have sometimes differed quite substantially. For example, Selim (2019) found that none of the Central banks of MENA oil exporting countries were at all independent, but also that for the GCC exporters this would not matter because they all had exchange rates pegged to the US dollar. However, in the absence of fixed exchange rate regimes but also with weak institutions in general, Selim argued that non-GCC oil exporters would have benefitted from CBI. In their study of MENA countries using both the aforementioned *de jure* and *de facto* measures of CBI, Economic and Social Commission for West Asia (2011) found the results to differ, not only between oil exporters and non-oil exporting countries but also between the *de-jure* and *de facto* measures. Legal or *de jure* CBI significantly reduced inflation in non-oil exporting countries but not in oil exporting countries, but *de facto* CBI reduced inflation in all MENA countries in their sample, (a sample which did not include Tunisia). They also went on to examine both the effects of these different CBI measures on the volatility of inflation rates (often thought to be a contributor to slower economic growth). The determinants of inflation rate variability were shown to be similar to those obtained for inflation rates themselves. The study also sought to identify the most important rules or characteristics within the *de-jure* measure of CBI. In the latter respect, they found that clarifying and prioritizing price stability as the objective of the Central Banks was the most important such characteristic.

Some important contributions of Garriga and Rodriguez (2020), aside from its much greater time and country coverage, are the following:

1 It did rather strongly confirm the finding that higher CBI scores tend to lower inflation rates across countries and over time.
2 It showed that this relation is stronger in democratic countries than non-democratic ones but still significant in relatively non-democratic ones.
3 It showed that these findings were robust to different model specifications, methodologies[17], measures of CBI (applying almost identically to the *de facto* measure of CBI as to the *de jure* measure), inflation rates and other possible control variables, the introduction of various lags, and to the use of different samples (across regions and over time)[18];
4 After including CBI, democracy, and their interactions, it showed that other control variables having significant effects on current inflation rates were capital account openness, pegged exchange rates, world inflation rates, all with negative effects, and lagged inflation and political instability, both with positive effects; and

5 Perhaps most importantly, it showed that the effects of different components of the CBI measures were quite different, those of personnel independence and Central Bank objectives being much more important than Financial Independence and especially policy independence.

Inflation Targeting

One of the operational implications of CBI is the focus by Central Banks on price stability through Inflation Targeting (IT). Under IT, the target would be only to keep inflation rates within a certain band for a specified period of time, while allowing short-term deviations within that band so as to pay at least partial attention to other important economic contingencies and objectives.

Ayres et al. (2014) track the timing of acceptance of IT across a relatively large sample of developing countries in different regions of the world and examine the impacts thereof on both inflation rates and economic growth rates in the two quarters following the transition to IT. That switch was estimated to have occurred in only 17 countries in their sample, but four of them being East Asian countries (Korea beginning in 1998, Thailand in 2000, Philippines in 2002, and Indonesia in 2005) and two of them being Middle Eastern countries, namely, Israel beginning in 1992 and Turkey beginning in 2002, neither of which is included in our MENA sample. Most of the other countries they identified as having adopted IT were in Eastern and Southern Europe and in Latin America. Their primary finding was that the impacts of the adoption of IT on economic growth differed quite substantially across regions. In general, the effects were negative on growth in the first quarter subsequent to completing the transition to IT, but were then offset by a positive effect in the subsequent quarter. The respective magnitudes were found to be considerably greater in Israel and Turkey than in any of the other regions, possible indicating their greater vulnerability to growth volatility.

Tunisia has never formally adopted IT as its monetary policy operational objective. However, while it has sometimes targeted the real exchange rate, or a mix of objectives the CBT has always considered price stability as its main objective. Even since the adoption of CBI in 2016, the CBT has not formally moved to IT, and Boughrara (2007) and Boughrara et al. (2008) have expressed doubts that they ever would be able to.

Chockri and Frihka (2011) investigate the transmission channels through which the IT strategy would normally operate and conclude that, if Tunisia were to be completely successful in IT, its Central Bank would have to have greater CBI, its exchange rate should be more flexible, and its fiscal policy would have to be improved. This would seem to suggest that the policy changes needed to overcome Tunisia's shortcomings in the growth benefits that could be derived from the adoption of IT should include CBI but should not be limited to it. Kadria and Ben Aissa (2014) focus on the relationships over time among inflation, money supply, exchange rate, and interest rate in Tunisia and show that these relations have been very unstable and the relationships among them not statistically significant in the short run. Despite some slight improvement over time in the stability and predictability in these relationships over time, especially given the rise in inflation in Tunisia in recent years shown in Table 3.1, the authors argue that further improvements in the *transparency* of Central Bank operations and objectives would require strengthening of the overall economic structure of its financial system, increased flexibility of its exchange rate, and the role of interest rates in Central Bank operations as well as in the overall economy to be clarified. That same study also stressed that, as a result of the regime overthrow in 2011 and the increasing fiscal and balance of payments deficits that have taken place after that, substantial efforts should also be made to reduce these deficits through improved fiscal policy.

In any case, despite all the discussion of the potential of IT in Tunisia, Boughzala and Moussa (2011) predicted that Tunisia would be unlikely to even stick to IT, and furthermore argued that it would not be desirable to do so anyway.[19]

5. Back to the Private Sector but with Special Incentives for Exports 1970–1986

To its credit, the Bourguiba administration was still sufficiently pragmatic to see the failure of many of its policies of the 1960s and the need for a change of course. Moreover, despite the failed policies, Bourguiba was also still sufficiently powerful politically so that he could accomplish this quickly by changing prime ministers.[20] The new one, Hedi Nouira, was from Bourguiba's hometown and a long-time ally. He brought to the job the perspective of an economist since he had been serving Bourguiba, first as Minister of Finance, and later as head of the Central Bank. It was Nouira who led the country away from the public sector-led strategy and back toward strong encouragement of the private sector. While from the experience of the oil and gas industry, the state was already able to deal with private foreign oil companies by issuing the exploration and production licenses, this time, the emphasis was on assisting the domestic private sector, especially in manufacturing, in the ability to penetrate international markets.

While it was at first very small, the domestic private sector received very substantial support from the government. One way in which this was done, and common to many other developing countries at the time, was by raising tariffs on imported goods that made local production of industrial goods more profitable (Bellin 1994, 429). Another and more unique way used by the Tunisian government was to provide an opportunity for civil servants or public enterprise employees to get a 'leave of absence'[21] for up to two years which would allow them to undertake a new private business venture (Bellin 1994). This arrangement provided significant security for these 'new entrepreneurs' as they are able to go back to their previous job in case their project should fail. Many of today's owners of major private sector business groups have benefited from this mechanism and built their businesses partly on the basis of their intimate knowledge of government rules, regulations, and networks. These 'new entrepreneurs,' as well as others, also came to benefit from another specially designed financing vehicle for small and medium-sized enterprises (SMEs), namely, a popular lending program called 'Fonds de Promotion et de Décentralisation Industrielle' (FOPRODI), discussed further below.

While much of the emphasis in the new strategy was again on industrial development, agriculture was by no means ignored. Irrigation was supported with credit and infrastructural projects that contributed to raising agricultural productivity and the subsequent reduction in income gaps between rural and urban areas (Lahouel 2007). Agriculture and domestic commerce were put back in the hands of the private sector, a reform that proved very popular, thus serving to solidify the country's orientation toward the strengthening of private property rights. With the return to private ownership and to normalcy in French-Tunisian relations, the European Community contributed to the encouragement of Tunisian agriculture, its private sector, and its pro-Western orientation by way of an accord it signed in 1976 with Tunisia (and Morocco as well) to allow these countries, in addition to privileged access of manufacturing exports, rather sizable quotas free of tariffs for their olive oil and other agricultural exports (White 2001).

As time went on, however, the European Community and subsequently the European Union's (EU) agriculture policy became increasingly protectionist, accentuating the importance of reforms conducive to the development of industrial exports. Among the further incentives that Tunisia took in support of private industrial activities were credit, training, and still greater protection from imports. Thanks to new licensing requirements for domestic investment and production, industrial producers could even be protected from other domestic producers. New investment codes were introduced to encourage industrial exports and foreign direct investment into industrial production. New institutions were created to help the private sector, in particular, the industrial promotion agency (Agence pour la Promotion de l'Industrie or API) to identify profitable investment opportunities, evaluate investment proposals and provide credit guarantees to all approved proposals. Once they had the appropriate approvals from API, industrial investors could also benefit from complementary infrastructure such as roads and access to utilities. While most of these fiscal and other incentives were for domestic and foreign-owned firms investing in manufacturing, in 1981, a law was adopted which granted incentives even to multinational firms which were investing in certain needed services, such as warehousing and distribution (Bellin 2002).

Another new element was the creation of a second tier in the banking system. Foreign banks and development banks were allowed to enter as 'off-shore' banks, thereby free of the rather stringent regulations of the Central Bank, but at the same time unable to accept deposits from residents in Tunisia. Several of these banks were funded by the Gulf States which, because of the oil price boom, found themselves with huge fiscal surpluses and the need to find earnings opportunities abroad.

While protection to all industrial activities in Tunisia increased, the new emphasis on export industries signified a variant on the 'two track' system that had been used for some time very successfully in Korea and subsequently China (Lin 2009). In this system, the normal protective regime applied to industries aimed at the domestic market but new special incentives for exports were applied to those industries aimed at foreign markets. The incentives of the new second track included tariff rebates and exemptions on imported inputs intended for export activities, and complete tax holidays on the incomes generated from the profits of such investments. These benefits were designed to offset the disadvantages of maintaining an overvalued exchange rate.

Despite its intended benefits, any two-track system like the one adopted in Tunisia inevitably introduced its own distortions. For example, the structure of protection tended to be highly inequitable. Indeed, the highest rates of effective protection were applied to industries producing finished goods for the smallest domestic markets, and the lowest ones (often negative) applied to industries producing intermediate goods. This can lead to enormous inefficiencies in resource allocation. It also led to the separation of the economy into two quite different segments, that is, those producing finished goods and those producing intermediate goods, but with no links between them, even when both segments are engaged in similar and potentially related forms of manufacturing.

Yet, the two-track system also had several distinct advantages relative to a more free market approach that would have involved dismantling protection and instituting a more realistic uniform exchange rate. First, the two-track reform did not necessarily lead to the sudden bankruptcy of the large portion of industrial activities that sold primarily to the domestic market, but which are small in scale and not very efficient. This is because these activities remained highly protected and hence able to sell to the domestic market at prices high enough to cover costs. As a result, this approach can avoid the risk of large-scale unemployment that would have arisen from the sudden shut down of much industrial activity in a liberalized single-track system. Second, because the export-oriented activities must be competitive in international markets, in relatively capital-scarce Tunisia, they became typically much more labor-intensive than those aimed at domestic markets, thereby reflecting to a much greater degree the comparative advantage of a developing country like Tunisia than would otherwise have been the case.

In political economy terms, therefore, such reforms were more likely to be feasible and, once implemented, also sustainable. Given the many reasons why opening up reforms may not be undertaken, for example, due to uncertainty about which firms will succeed and which ones fail (Fernandez and Rodrik 1991), this two-track approach could be advantageous. On the other hand, however, there may be little incentive to move beyond the two-track system into a more complete market-oriented reform. And, the lack of linkage between the firms producing for those two different market segments (i.e., domestic and foreign markets) implies that some viable industrial production opportunities would go untapped and the import bill could become greater than necessary. This is because wholly exporting firms may have little incentive to use domestically produced inputs and thus remain rather isolated, thereby failing to generate positive demand externalities for the rest of the economy.

In any case, this new system which Tunisia has adopted since the early 1970s proved much more successful than either the earlier single-track system of support to private sector industrial activities or the 'socialist' planning period of the 1960s. Instead of having its investment, output, and employment in the private industrial sector all stagnate as in the 1956–1961 period, the number of industrial firms grew rapidly over the 1970s and early 1980s. Indeed, the number of private manufacturing enterprises increased from 865 in 1970 to 2866 by 1983, in both the 'off-shore' and 'on-shore' segments. The rapid growth in numbers of firms was visible not only in a single sector but in quite a few different sectors, including food, construction materials, chemicals, textiles and clothing, leather, and 'other' sectors. While the vast majority of these firms were small, by 1983 there were 334 firms with over 100 employees, two-thirds of which were in textiles and clothing. The relative importance of the private sector in industrial activities increased sharply, the share of the private sector in manufacturing value added coming to exceed 80% in both 'textiles and leather,' and 'other' industries by 1983. Their contribution to exports also grew significantly but starting from what in 1970 was a very low level. The traditional sectors, petroleum and petroleum products, phosphates and minerals and olive oil accounted for the bulk of exports through the mid-1970s. By 1980, however, the relative importance of both phosphates and olive oil in exports had declined sharply while that of textiles and chemicals had grown so as to more than take their place. With the decline in the prices of petroleum and petroleum products after 1982, the contribution of that sector declined so that, by 1986, textiles had become the leading export sector, accounting for 28% of the total (Bellin 2002, 33). Indeed, in the mid-1980s, it was estimated that 87% of the employment growth and 54% of the investment growth that followed from the key fiscal incentives law of 1972 were realized in the textiles, clothing, and leather industries (Cammett 2007, 74–75).

The textile sector is of course a broad one, comprised of spinning (thread manufacture), weaving (cloth making), and finished clothing. The relatively capital-intensive weaving sector was geared mainly towards the domestic market. However, it was the finished clothing sector (within textiles) that developed most rapidly after the new laws of the early 1970s were introduced. This sector, by contrast, was labor-intensive, largely foreign owned, and operated on the basis of subcontracting arrangements with European clothing producers such as Levi's and Coopers. These operations depended heavily on imported inputs and sold their production almost exclusively abroad. Much of this activity took place outside of large towns and made almost exclusive use of female labor. This allowed wage rates to be lower than they would have been had the activities been located in Tunis, and this system was facilitated by the fact that administratively the free zone rules on imported inputs were not restricted to a very specific area. Even without this restriction, because they were located on the site of these enterprises, customs officials could prevent the duty-free imports of inputs from spilling over into the domestic market.

There were other notable institutional developments that took place during this second phase of encouragement of the private sector. Some of these were especially useful to the SMEs that made up the bulk of the clothing, food, and leather industries (Bechri 1989). One of these was the requirement issued by the Central Bank that commercial banks should make at least minimal credit allocations to SMEs and agriculture throughout much of the period. Another was the aforementioned very special program of small loans known as FOPRODI specifically designed for SMEs. The latter was a very popular program designed to facilitate provision of relatively long-term loans without requiring collateral, an opportunity which Tunisia's new entrants into SMEs had not previously enjoyed. As with some of the other incentives, API approvals and related credit guarantees played an important role in the allocation of FOPRODI funds.[22] Given these guarantees, the banks became willing to make these loans. A stated purpose of FOPRODI was also to decentralize economic activity away from the major cities, and in fact some 80% of the applications were from firms located outside of the major cities. Naturally, this raised the transaction costs to the banks and to API of investigating the projects and subsequently monitoring firm compliance with the stated purposes of their loans. But, it also contributed substantially to the relatively equitable development of Tunisian manufacturing compared to manufacturing in many other developing countries where manufacturing has become highly concentrated in a few large firms or groups with holdings across sectors in only a few large cities (Cammett 2007, 76–77). The degree of concentration in Tunisian manufacturing may also have been limited by the fact that family business groups have tended to diversify horizontally, leading to less concentration at the product or sectoral level. As a result, the various groups have tended to compete with each other for the same business opportunities than would otherwise have been the case.

Even well into this second period of private sector support, the public sector continued to grow and remained dominant in chemicals, construction materials, mining, utilities, and the more capital- and technology-intensive segments of even those sectors in which the private sector was dominant.

Hence, public enterprise still constituted over 50% of manufacturing value added and 25% of GDP. This continued growth of the public sector was attributable to the country's more than ten-fold increase in oil and phosphates revenues in the 1970s and early 1980s. Growth of the public sector contributed to regime stability by lowering unemployment, the rate of rural-urban migration, and regional imbalances.

But all those benefits arising from high oil and phosphate prices disappeared with the decline in both these prices after 1983. Tunisia's current account balances and economic growth were also severely damaged by the fall in remittances from Tunisian workers in Europe that had been induced by the recession in Europe which in turn has been induced by the higher prices for energy and tight monetary policies aimed at controlling inflation. There was also a falloff in tourism revenues following the US bombing of Libya and, during the mid- to late-1980s, the same deleterious terms of trade decline as in many other MENA countries. All these factors combined to cause a sharp deterioration in Tunisia's current account balances and economic growth.

Its continued reliance on import substitution in the 'first track' was leading to negative productivity growth, a collapse of investment and low employment growth (Nabli 1981). When, on top of all these negative developments, Tunisian agriculture suffered from a severe drought in 1986, Tunisia found itself in both a severe balance of payments crisis and an economic crisis (marked by a substantial decline in real GDP).

In view of the 'hard state' character of Tunisia's leadership until then, one might wonder how the government had allowed the crisis to get so bad. Part of the explanation at least for this was that in 1981 Prime Minister Nouira had to be replaced for health reasons. Bourguiba replaced him with Mohamed Mzali, a close confidant but a man with no political strength of his own and no experience with economic issues. To try to overcome his political weakness, Mzali lightened the suppression of the labor and Islamic movements and even allowed major wage increases which had a strong inflationary impact. However, after the 1984 riots that emanated from reactions of the local populace to a reduction in price subsidies for bread, the government became sharply divided on the choice of what action to take. Two new prime ministers were appointed in short order, constituting a sharp, though temporary, departure from its long-standing 'hard state' commitment to development and stability. This outcome was also related to Bourguiba's aging, weakening hold on power, and eventually to the struggle over his succession.

6. The Structural Adjustment Reforms of 1986–1995

With few alternatives available and mounting foreign debt, the Tunisian government chose to sign structural adjustment programs with the International Monetary Fund (IMF) and World Bank. These programs called for a number of reforms aimed at strengthening the competitiveness of the private sector and privatizing some public enterprises. The Tunisian government, which by 1987 was led by the new President Ben Ali, implemented many components of the structural adjustment program. It deregulated product prices (that had been very rigidly regulated throughout the post-independence period), largely eliminated quantitative restrictions on imports, replacing them in some cases with tariffs, and terminated industrial licensing and approvals by API, except in cases where financial incentives were involved. It implemented financial sector reforms including deregulation of interest rates and devaluation of the Tunisian dinar which, together with deregulation of imports, made the dinar almost fully convertible as far as current account transactions were concerned. From then on, the Tunisian dinar was allowed to float in a way that both avoided the kind of real currency appreciation which has served to lower the competitiveness of manufacturing in many other developing countries, and at the same time encouraged remittances that have averaged over 4% of GDP ever since (Lahouel 2007). As demonstrated by Adams and Page (2003), these remittances have played a substantial role in reducing poverty and income inequality in Tunisia and several of the other non-oil MENA countries. Interestingly, and again encouraged by the IMF, Algeria had also initiated a structural adjustment program at the same time as that of Tunisia, but Algeria's program wound up as a complete disaster. Dillman (1998) attributed much of Tunisia's relative success in this to (1) the fact that the size of Tunisia's public sector was considerably smaller than that of Algeria, (2) its political leadership was much more united and able to exercise coordination, and (3) that Tunisia already had in place a number of mechanisms in place for facilitating the creation of private firms.

These accomplishments earned Tunisia high praise from the IMF. Notably, key economic ministers during this reform period were technocrats with considerable training in economics and experience in international institutions, a characteristic that Nugent (1997) has shown to be conducive to reforms based on reform episodes from around the world. In order to attain the targets of its structural reform program (with substantial support from the IMF and World Bank), as in most countries, government expenditures had to be cut substantially. Significantly, however, given the need for legitimacy on the part of Ben Ali (who had obtained his position in a manner which could certainly be seen as less legitimate than that of his predecessor), Tunisia was the only MENA country whose state did not retreat under such pressure from international agencies from programs such as food subsidies and health programs supplying basic needs of the population during the economic crisis and its aftermath (El Said 2008). Much to its credit, the cost to the country's fiscal balances of its food subsidies, through the CGC, was kept much lower than in many other countries, thanks to its better targeting of those subsidies to those in the greatest need (Lahouel 2007).

Two other areas where Tunisia did drag its feet on reforms were in the reduction in tariffs on imported manufactures and in privatization. In both cases, this was done in fear of the possible adverse consequences thereof on its already high unemployment rate. It may also have been the case that Tunisia's leadership may have felt that, to be regarded as legitimate, the regime had to rededicate itself to the goals of industrial development and social equity. While both maximum tariff rates and the dispersion in tariff rates were reduced, average tariff rates remained well over 20%. Without complete liberalization, therefore, even with the structural adjustment reforms, Tunisia's economic system retained its two-track character.

Hence, because of these important limitations, collectively the reforms of this period still did not allow market forces to play a much more important role in economic performance and resource allocation than in the past (more on this in Chapter 6). In fact, between 1987 and 1994, on average, the Ministry of Social Affairs registered 117 enterprises per year as being 'in difficulty,' but not altogether bankrupt (Bellin 2002, 39). Notably, the government intervened to save many of these firms from bankruptcy. Indeed, laws were passed and regulations implemented to help prevent such firms from going bankrupt. For example, the new Central Bank regulations in 1988 entitled 'Measures to Help Enterprises and Sectors in Difficulty' and some new financial funds, such as the Fonds de Développement de la Compétitivité (FODEC), helped financially troubled firms to consolidate their debts with low interest rate loans and by reducing their social security taxes. Further, a new program was created to help firms in potentially threatened industries improve their productivity so as to become more competitive internationally.

Nevertheless, the reforms did, at least to some extent, increase the role of market forces. With such financial help to both new and existing firms, the private sector continued to grow. Indeed, the overall number of private enterprises more than tripled between 1986 and 1995 to well over 10 thousand. Manufacturing employment growth accelerated from 12,000 added jobs in 1986 to an estimated 17,000 new jobs in 1995. Indeed, by 1995 the private sector's share in investment in manufacturing in Tunisia rose to a then all-time record of 78%. Also, by 1995 the almost entirely private textile, clothing and leather sectors continued to increase their share of exports to about 50%. As was shown in Table 2.1, the share of manufacturing in GDP, which had been a mere 8.1% in 1965 and 9.1% in 1975, reached 15.1% in 1985, and 18.9% in 1995, putting Tunisia on a par with most European countries in this respect, and highest in the MENA region. Notably, however, as pointed out above and in that table, the share of manufacturing in GDP has declined quite significantly since 1995.

7. Further Integration into the World Market Since the Mid-1990s

By the mid-1990s, however, Tunisian exports to Europe began to face increasing competition from China and other transition and developing countries. The Civil War in Algeria, the rising perception of a threat from

Islamists in the region as a whole, and the Gulf War and its aftermath also contributed to the decline in FDI in Tunisia and elsewhere in the region, with adverse consequences for the Tunisian economy (White 2001). The decline in FDI was also the result of both a recession in much of Western Europe and Europe's growing interest in those Eastern European countries which became candidates for joining the EU.

To make matters still worse for Tunisian exports and growth, in 1995 an agreement by the World Trade Organization (WTO) members was reached to gradually phase-out by 2005 the quotas on large Asian exporters of clothing under the Multi Fiber Agreement. This led to the loss of much of Tunisia's privileged access to the European market in the textiles and clothing sector that had become so important to Tunisia (and Morocco).

But once again, Tunisian policy-makers responded vigorously. These pressures induced them to attract the type of FDI that could help diversify its exports away from textiles and clothing. To that end, in preparing for full membership in the WTO, in 1990 Tunisia adopted an entirely new trade and tariff classification system which had the effect of somewhat lowering its previously extremely high rates of effective tariff rates. To encourage industrial exports from the 'off-shore' processing zones that had been established since 1972, in 1992 it loosened somewhat the labor regulations on activities within these areas. Then, in 1993 it adopted a new and much more comprehensive investment code which streamlined the complex system of incentives, eliminating them for some sectors such as tourism, and reducing them for others. The investment code emphasized incentives which targeted 'horizontal objectives' such as exports, food security, regional development, technological development, or environmental protection. Generous incentives for exports were continued and stronger incentives were given for investments into lagging and poorer regions. That new Investment Code reduced restrictions on foreign direct investment, especially for services. For the latter activities, according to the new code, only those foreign investments where the foreign share in the firm's total capital exceeded 50% still required prior approval by the National Investment Commission.[23]

Then in 1995 and 1996, as part of the Barcelona Process and EU concerns about excessive in-migration of workers from North Africa and other parts of Africa, the EU offered an opportunity for Southern and Eastern Mediterranean countries to sign Association Agreements with the EU. Tunisia was the first country to sign such an agreement, a process facilitated by a concession by the EU to allow Tunisia's duty-free quota of olive oil imports to remain at 46,000 tons per year, a somewhat more favorable arrangement than obtained by other MENA region countries (White 2001). Certain reforms on the part of Tunisia were suggested as a pre-condition for the agreement, but were not strictly enforced in most cases. One such reform that Tunisia did undertake in this context was a legal reform, namely, one substantially simplifying its dispute resolution procedures

(Duc and Lavallée 2006). In return for the EU's agreement to waive tariffs and quotas on most exports from Tunisia, Tunisia also had to commit to the same for those imports from the EU in certain 'sensitive' sectors, but was given a relatively lengthy adjustment period to accomplish this. In some of these highly protected sectors like textiles, the tariff reduction required was very large indeed (from about 100% in 1996 to 4% in 2006). It was Tunisia's hope that, by freeing its trade with Europe, Tunisian enterprises and skilled professionals would become more deeply embedded in Europe's industrial complexes (World Bank 2008b). Tunisia also had to commit to some broader reforms such as increasing the extent of privatization that was allowed both within those firms which retained majority ownership by the state, and within sectors where full privatization was allowed, as in the case with cement after 2000. As Ben Jelili (2005) has also shown, foreign investment, increased firm size, and technical training (some financed by the EU) all contributed to improving TFP at the firm level. Finally, Lahouel and Maskus (2000) assert that Tunisia also committed itself to removing the rather high 20% margin in favor of domestic firms in public procurement, a move they believed would both stimulate competition and TFP growth on the part of Tunisian firms, and encourage FDI.

Tunisia also signed rules of origin agreements with other individual countries and groups of countries and signed onto various agreements aimed at liberalizing trade among MENA countries. One such agreement was the Agadir Agreement on free trade with Jordan, Egypt, and Morocco. To better prepare Tunisian firms for competition with European and other firms in the absence of protection, and to face the gradual loss of its favored position in the textiles and clothing markets of Europe due to the phasing out of quotas on Asian producers by 2005, in 1996 Tunisia instituted (with EU funds) an upgrading program that covered technology, marketing, organizational, and financial restructuring.

Another facet of Tunisia's trade promotion effort was an interesting system introduced since the 1990s, which created incentives for European automobile companies to subcontract production of auto-components in the country. At that time, the different European automakers were lobbying the Tunisian authorities for increases in their company-specific import quotas. According to World Bank (2008b, 15), the Tunisian government decided to make this possible by halting the domestic assembly of private cars but at the same time negotiating with European automakers 'local content rules' for the import of European cars. As a result, starting in 1998, foreign automakers were authorized to export larger numbers of their vehicles to Tunisia but only in exchange for the commitment by those foreign automakers to purchase motor vehicle components manufactured by Tunisian firms up to an agreed-upon portion of the value of the imported automobiles. This resulted in substantial investments by French, Italian, and German carmakers in partnership with Tunisian firms in the mechanical and auto components sector. The program turned out to be so successful that Tunisian firms soon became able to export more than the amounts agreed upon. This represents another example of a rather unorthodox trade policy of the two-track type that Tunisia has taken advantage of to the benefit (as will be demonstrated below) of industrial development and exports.

Indeed, an important development along these lines has been a shift toward trade-facilitation, and in particular the creation of trade-facilitating institutions. Several programs now aim at helping exporters overcome information and other market failures inherent in penetrating new markets, and in obtaining insurance and finance for exports. The Export Promotion Fund (Fonds de Promotion des Exportations (FOPRODEX), set up in 1985, grants loans and transport subsidies to exporters, carries out international marketing surveys, assists enterprises with canvassing and advertising, and helps them strengthen their internal structure. The Centre de Promotion des Exportation (CEPEX) was established to provide a one-stop shop for exporters, to implement the export promotion strategy developed by the Ministry of Trade, to manage the computerized trade database Trade Net, and to organize training missions, in-country trade fairs, and exhibitions. An Export Market Access Fund (Fonds d'Accès aux Marchés d'Exportation or FAMEX) was created under a World Bank loan that provided 50% non-reimbursable co-financing to help individual firms implement investments in market research and export promotion (such as establishing export service offices abroad, searching for partnerships, export planning and training, and modifying product designs). FAMEX also provides 70% co-financing to professional associations, such as export associations, chambers of commerce, and professional consulting organizations, to support groups of Tunisian firms working under a specific common export plan. Another trade-facilitating program is the Pre-shipment Export Finance Guarantees program which seeks to encourage financial institutions to provide pre-shipment working capital to emerging exporters with viable export contracts (World Bank 2008b, 14).

In the wake of these further steps in introducing market forces but still with very considerable pro-active government intervention, further changes in performance of the private sector have been visible. The various efforts to increase FDI became successful. While FDI fluctuates from year to year and FDI stocks have fallen somewhat from earlier years, inflows of FDI came up to an average of more than 3% of GDP during the 1992–2010 period, demonstrating the importance of the legal changes in 1992 and 1993 designed to encourage FDI in off-shore export activities. In 2008, FDI hit an all-time high of over 5.8% of GDP and, as shown in Table 4.9, reached a decade length average high of 3.72% over the entire 2001–2010 period. In addition to the 30% of FDI inflows that have been directed to manufacturing, in recent years FDI has also entered into those subsectors of services undergoing privatization. The special pact with the European carmakers seems to have had considerable effect inasmuch as while the share of manufacturing FDI in textiles and clothing, which had been 43.3% in 1990–2000, fell to only 21.3% in 2001–2013, to at least partially compensate for this loss the share in mechanical and electrical industries and engineering jumped from 16.1% to 32.1%[24]. As a result, the share of mechanical and electrical products in Tunisia's exports rose from 13.7% in 1995 to 41.8% in 2015, while that of textiles and clothing declined from 50% to 21.7%.[25] As we will discuss further in Chapter 6, however, these accomplishments in terms of increased competitiveness of private sector activities in manufacturing and services and in exports have fallen well short of what would have been necessary for Tunisia to live up to the amazing success of several of the East Asian Miracle countries.

Notes

1 Numerous scholars, for example, Easterly and Levine (1997), have provided empirical evidence (though not without some shortcomings) suggesting that ethnic, linguistic, religious, and income differences within countries have contributed substantially to the demise of growth in sub-Sahara Africa.
2 See its translation, Ibn Khaldun (1967).
3 Indeed, it is no accident that one of the leading associations of economists specializing in the Economic Development of MENA countries, namely, the Middle East Economic Association, has been offering for each of the last twenty years the Ibn Khaldun prize to a young member judged to have presented the best paper at one of the conferences it has organized in any country during that year.
4 Moalla (1992) presents a detailed history of state building.
5 Kohli (2004) argues that South Korea also gained much in terms of its state capacity from its colonial experience under Japan.
6 Once again, note the similarity of this approach involving state capacity to the coordination and balancing one (already discussed above) provided some 600 years earlier by Ibn Khaldun.
7 This council, created in 1891, included initially only representatives of the 'colonials.' The council played an advisory role to the Résident Général, a French national designated by the French government, to serve effectively as the highest government authority in Tunisia.
8 Many revolts took place during this period: in Kasserine-Thala in 1906, in Tunis (events of the Djellaz Cemetery in 2011, and Tramway in 1912), and in the South of the country (which was under military rule in 1915–1917) (Boularès 2011).
9 Le Parti Liberal Constitutionnel Tunisien.
10 Indeed, Anderson (1986, 229) drew on this historical experience in which the basic ingredients of a modern, functioning state had been created to come to the following conclusion. 'For Tunisia, the incorporation of the hinterland population into the purview of a continuous state administration had been accomplished by the time the country became independent. The rise to power and capture of the state by the provincial elite represented by the leaders of the Neo-Destour were facilitated by their control and extension of the networks of clientele that had developed around state administration and the commercial economy. The Protectorate period had fostered the development of broad-based interest groups, however, whose interest was obscured by the refusal

of the French to permit genuine participation by the common interest of all Tunisians in independence. The story of independent Tunisia would demonstrate the importance of the identity of those who controlled the state and who would make state policy structuring political organization'.

11 White (2001) suggests that Tunisia's smaller size may have contributed to its greater and certainly earlier inclination to open up to Europe and world trade and investment than these other and generally larger countries of the region.

12 Gamal Abdel Nasser in Egypt was one of the more popular leaders in the region, but, as Lacouture (1970, 137) notes, he lacked the broad-based, flexible, organized support that Bourguiba enjoyed. Moreover, Nasser attained power by conspiracy, and hence was not seen as fully legitimate by some.

13 An interesting example of giving carrots to those loyal to him is the monopolistic power that the government under Bourguiba conferred on the union of porters in the wholesale market of Tunis for their role in the independence movement (Azabou et al. 1989). As these authors point out, this was done at considerable cost in terms of the economic efficiency of the market. For various examples of his stick policies to would-be opponents, see Lacouture (1970, 162), and Moore (1965).

14 Interestingly enough, the 'sacrifice' that Bourguiba exemplified for all to see was being put in jail under the Protectorate as a result of his demonstrations against the French before independence. His success also resulted from his willingness and ability to explain his policies and maintain their consistency with the goals proclaimed for the country at independence. This combination seems to fit remarkably well with the model of Hermalin (1998) for explaining how leaders can get followers to follow even without having to resort to strong-armed tactics.

15 See Ayubi (1997), Richards and Waterbury (1990), Waterbury (1989) and Cammett (2007), among others, for documentation of the rather substantial mobilization of resources and the commitments of state resources to industrialization, management of the economy and human capital in Tunisia during these relatively early years post-independence. All of this is evidence of strong state capacity.

16 While there is no data on the CBI index of Garriga before 2006, the papers by Gisolo (2008) and Zouache and Ilmane (2008) indicated that, prior to that date, there may have been a decline in CBI for Algeria or alternatively an especially weak link between its CBI and its ability to reduce inflation.

17 These different methodologies included the use of Generalized Method of Moments estimators designed to mitigate endogeneity concerns.

18 In particular, they found the effects of CBI on inflation to be very similar between MENA and Asia, although in both cases somewhat weaker than in Eastern Europe but stronger than in South America and in very low-income countries. They also found the impacts of CBI on inflation to be somewhat higher during the period 1980–2006 during which the debate on CBI was so great.

19 Schnabl and Schobert (2009) point to another factor contributing to Tunisia's overall monetary stability, namely, the tendency of Tunisia's Central Bank to hold most of its assets in the form of foreign assets (indeed as much as to exceed total money in circulation) and until 2004 at least refraining from large liabilities (though those to banks denominated in foreign currencies had increased sharply since 2004). While desirable for financial stability, these authors argued that this has also led to somewhat less of an increase in liquidity and credit creation than otherwise might have been the case. Indeed, on page 78 the authors point to how the expansionary effect of the government's

sale of its shares in the national Telecom company (Tunisie Telecom) was offset by a corresponding increase in the Central Bank liability to the government in the form of government deposits at the bank.

20 The position of Prime Minister exists under the Constitution of 1959, but it was not actually filled until 1970. Prior to that there was only a 'coordinator' position of government.

21 This mechanism is called 'Mise En Disponibilité' and allows public sector employees to go on leave for an extended period for personal of professional reasons.

22 In practice, however, once banks complained about not getting repaid sufficiently promptly by the guarantee fund on defaulted loans, the banks started to require collateral anyway. Default rates were generally sufficiently high so that, despite the popularity of the program with entrepreneurs, the program collapsed in 1997. For more details on the problems of FOPRODI and how it worked, see Bechri et al. (2001).

23 See Lahouel (1998) for details on these important reforms.

24 This data is from Dhaoui and Samoud (2016).

25 These figures come from the Institut National de la Statistique database.

4 Why Has Tunisia Been More Successful in Growth and Development than Other MENA Countries?

As suggested in Chapter 3, some of the credit for the relative success of Tunisia should be attributed to favorable initial conditions. Yet, to fully take economic advantage of these initial conditions, Tunisian policy-makers had to undertake certain specific actions. More broadly, the discussion in Chapter 3 has suggested that Tunisia's development strategy has shared a number of the ingredients which had been found to be common to the highly successful growth experiences around the world identified by the Commission on Growth and Development (2008). Out of this, in the present chapter we proceed to identify seven different broadly defined factors which seem to have contributed to Tunisia's comparative success through 2010. Each of these factors will be explained and briefly substantiated in separate sections (Sections A–G), while Section H summarizes our results. We believe that these seven factors go a long way toward explaining Tunisia's relative success among MENA countries both (1) in reducing its poverty rates (Table 1.2), and (2) in achieving relatively high real per capita GDP growth rates (Tunisia's growth rates having been the second highest among MENA countries between 1990 and 2010 and the third highest over the full period 1965–2010, as shown from Table 1.5). Recall also that the one MENA country which grew faster than Tunisia during both these periods was Oman. Oman, however, had started in the 1960s from an extremely low level of development, having been an extremely closed society in many ways, and of course benefitted from its sizeable oil and gas resources.[1]

As will be discussed below, for each of these factors there were no significant differences between the experience of the most successful East Asian countries and Tunisia. As a result, while these factors explain Tunisia's comparative success until the 2000s relative to other MENA countries, they do not explain why Tunisia's overall development performance has not matched that of most East Asian countries. That task will be left to Chapters 5 and 6, and the identification of the factors that help explain the failure of Tunisia to achieve as successful performance in development as in East Asia.

Before going into these seven factors in detail, we deem it relevant to present the results of a quantitative analysis, making use of a formal neoclassical growth model developed by Nabli and Véganzonès-Varoudakis (2007) to

DOI: 10.4324/9781003309550-4

explain long-term growth in GDP per capita over both the 1980s and the 1990s. What makes this study and its results especially useful in this context is that, in its quantitative analysis, it included not only lags (to get closer to true causal relationships) and different kinds of physical capital (measured by investment (INV), and physical infrastructure (PI)) and human capital growth (HC), but also indicators representing more institutional characteristics, like macroeconomic stability (MS), external stability (ExS), and structural reform (SR). The study also allowed for interactions among those latter more institutional measures in order to detect the extent of substitutability, or alternatively complementarity, between them. Its estimates were based on pooled time series and cross-section data for a substantial number of countries (from both MENA and non-MENA regions) over the 1980s and 1990s. For five of these six measures, specifically, MS, ExS, SR, PI, and HC, moreover, each such measure is an aggregate of more than one indicator.

Table 4.1 presents the results broken down into these six separate sources of long-term growth for Tunisia, and the other countries of the MENA and Asia[2] regions, and separately for each of the two decades. Of the standard factors of production, shown in the first three rows of the table, both HC and PI turned out to have the largest positive effects on growth in Tunisia, and both the MENA and Asia regions for both decades, while notably the investment rate (INV) did not. The weaker impact of investment is due to both lower average percentage changes in the ratio of investment to GDP (which was declining in most MENA countries during the 1980s), and the lower elasticity of GDP per capita growth with respect to the investment

Table 4.1 Contributions of Various Factors to Economic Growth, 1980–2019 (percentage points)

	Tunisia		*MENA*		*Asia*	
Factor	***1980–1989***	***1990–1999***	***1980–1989***	***1990–1999***	***1980–1989***	***1990–1999***
Human Capital (HC)	1.2	0.9	1.1	0.9	0.7	0.7
Physical Infrastructure (PI)	1.3	1	1.4	1	1.5	1.1
Investment (INV)	0.1	–0.1	–0.3	–0.1	0.2	0.2
Macroeconomic Stability (MS)	0.2	0.4	–1.3	0.4	0.1	0.5
External Stability (ExS)	0.1	0.3	–1	1	0.2	0.5
Structural Reform (SR)	0.6	0.7	0.2	0.2	0.9	0.6
Total Contribution to growth	3.5	3.2	0.1	3.4	3.6	3.6
Growth Rate of GDP per Capita	1.6	3.2	0	1.7	3.4	3.9

Source: Nabli and Véganzonès-Varoudakis (2007, Tables 2.3, 2.4, 2.5, 2.6, 2.7, 2.8, A12-6).

Note: The impact of MS includes a direct effect and an indirect effect conditional on Structural Reforms. The impact of SR is conditional on MS. See details in paper.

ratio.[3] In all three cases also, the contributions were larger for the 1980s than for the 1990s. These variables are of course measures of productive factors that were accumulating over time and contributing directly to growth. Hence, neither of these would correspond exactly to the estimates of TFP growth shown in Table 2.6a.

Instead, it would be the measures of the institutional factors, MS, ExS, and SR in the next three rows of Table 4.1 that are presumably more closely related to TFP growth. These macroeconomic indicators were also shown to matter for the complementarity or substitutability between them. In particular, SR was shown to have been complementary to MS and ExS (based on their positive interaction terms). Because of changes in the various indicators of the explanatory variables over time, the estimated contributions of these factors were also shown to have varied across countries, regions, and time periods. The results shown in the table are based on an aggregation of the influences of the individual indicators into the aforementioned MS, ExS, and SR categories of reforms.

From the fourth and fifth rows of the table it can be seen that, during the 1980s, MENA countries tended to suffer from instability in both their macroeconomic and external stability indicators, This was reflected in the fact that the contributions of both MS and ExS to per capita growth were negative for that period, but became positive for the 1990s. Indeed, the MS result for MENA for the 1980s indicates that MS lowered the growth rate of GDP per capita in the MENA region as a whole by 1.3% per annum. The experience of Tunisia was similar to that of Asian countries, with MS having a positive contribution, even though it was in the 1980s only half that in the 1990s. The same was true for ExS, except that in the 1990s, the contribution of ExS to growth was smaller for Tunisia and Asia than for MENA as a whole, reflecting the fact that not much progress was made in reducing Tunisia's debt to GDP ratio during this period, which also coincided with the Asian financial crisis. But, taken together, these two influences had very different impacts on per capita GDP growth in Tunisia and Asia than in other MENA countries during the 1980s.

The final factor of note in Table 4.1 is SR. In both periods, the contributions of SR to per capita growth were considerably larger for Tunisia and Asia (for Tunisia 0.6% and 0.7% per annum, and for Asia 0.9% and 0.6% per annum in the 1980s and 1990s, respectively) than for MENA as a whole (0.2% per annum). In general, however, as weak as the growth performance was in Tunisia during the 1980s, it is quite plausible that the various reforms adopted by Tunisia during the latter part of this decade identified in Section B of Chapter 3, and which were much more substantial than those undertaken in most other MENA countries, contributed to Tunisia's better performance in TFP growth over the 1980s and its comparatively better growth performance over all.

While this quantitative study neither went back to the 1960s and 1970s nor did it go forward to the most recent years, from what has been discussed above, the contributions of both PI and HC would most certainly have been even greater at least during earlier decades than during the 1980s and 1990s. But, on the other hand, the contributions of MS, ExS, and especially SR would have been weaker for Tunisia and probably most of the other MENA countries for the earlier periods. SR, however, would have been more positive in the 1970s for Tunisia. From all this, it would seem clear that, for earlier decades, it would have been the major investments in HC and PI that best explained the quite satisfactory growth of Tunisia and other MENA countries in the years prior to the 1980s. Yet, according to the results in Table 4.1, during the more recent decades Tunisia's advantage over the other MENA countries would seem more attributable to its larger values of MS, ExS, and SR which should also reflect a greater role of TFP growth in the overall growth of GDP per capita.

After examining this quantitative background, we now turn to expositions of each of the seven factors which we feel have been most important in explaining Tunisia's relative success in long-term growth.

A. Leadership, with a Consistent and Broadly Shared Vision, a Committed and Capable Government, and Ever-Strengthening State Capacity

First, one strength of Tunisian experience is that its development policies have remained remarkably and consistently fixed on the goals of social progress, modernization, and industrialization. With political stability maintained throughout more than five decades (up until 2010), Tunisia's leadership succeeded in focusing on these widely shared goals. The common acceptance of this vision has been re-enforced by the government's strong and rather consistent focus on poverty reduction and social progress.

The government's ability to consistently pursue this vision and implement the developmental policy priorities deemed conducive to the attainment of these goals has been made possible by Tunisia's **strong state capacity.** This finding is consistent with that of Kohli (2004) based on the country case studies he examined (South Korea, Brazil, India, and Nigeria). Specifically, he concluded '...the creation of effective states in the developing world has generally preceded the emergence of industrializing economies. This is because state intervention in support of investor profits has proved to be a precondition for industry to emerge and flourish in late-developers.' As demonstrated in the previous Chapter, in the Tunisian case that capacity has been reflected in its generally strong bureaucracy and its ability to (1) ensure domestic peace, stability, and security of property, (2) successfully coordinate the various components of economic policy design and implementation, (3) raise the taxes and other revenues needed to invest in human development, build infrastructure, and provide the incentives for both private sector development and entry into international markets, (4) recognize the need for policy changes in the face of the new problems faced and changing circumstances, and then (5) design and implement appropriate policy changes (including the need for diversification to reduce risk). Just as Kohli showed it to be in his case studies, Tunisia's state capacity was built on progress made during the colonial period and further emphasized by its leaders at, and since, independence. Notably, the relatively few and rather short periods in which state capacity and political leadership had been quite weak (e.g., 1982–1987), were precisely the periods when state agents were unable to take decisive action, and hence existing problems were allowed to develop into full-fledged crises and, moreover, some backsliding on reforms occurred.[4]

Lying behind strong state capacity is the ability to tax and mobilize resources for development (see below). Tunisia's capacity to mobilize both tax and non-tax revenue allowed it to deliver public goods for development, as illustrated by the large share of expenditures and health and education shown in Table 4.5.

One interesting example of Tunisia's promotion and use of strong state capacity to achieve both desirable productivity enhancement and industrial diversification, on the one hand, and political solidarity, on the other hand, is its Industrial Upgrading Program. We will discuss this program and its effectiveness further in Chapter 5, but it is an example of the capacity of government to undertake complex tasks and pursue them over long periods of time.

Section G provides a more detailed discussion of various indicators of state capacity such as property rights, various other institutional features and scores related to doing business.

B. Stable and Limited Distortions in Macroeconomic Environment

Second, Tunisia benefitted at independence from a number of favorable historical factors including a relatively strong state capacity, strong leadership, and over time the country's abilities to generate tax and other revenues grew further so as to finance needed infrastructure, to provide incentives for the private sector, and to make investments in public enterprises. While data are not shown here, Tunisia's tax and government revenue to GDP ratios were higher than for most comparator East Asian countries, as well as for all non-major oil exporting MENA countries. By the 1970s, some 40% of gross national expenditures originated in the public sector. Since the 1980s, Tunisia's tax revenues averaged more than 20% of GDP as shown in Table 4.2. The share in GDP of total government revenue, reached 33% during the early 1980s, reflecting the large revenues from phosphates and oil since the early 1970s. With expenditures increasing at a faster rate, the larger gap between revenues and expenditures eventually led to the macroeconomic crisis of the mid-1980s and the adoption of its structural adjustment program, which supported a quick return to stability.

Table 4.2 Budget Revenues and Expenditures in Tunisia, 1981–2019 (% of GDP)

	1981–1985	*1986–1990*	*1991–1995*	*1996–2000*	*2001–2005*	*2006–2010*	*2011–2015*	*2016–2019*
Tax revenue	23.5	20.4	20.6	20.6	19.1	19.6	21.8	22.8
Total revenue	32.7	29.4	26.8	25.0	22.3	23.4	25.1	25.6
Total expenditures	40.5	33.1	30.9	28.5	25.0	25.0	29.3	30.5
Budget deficit	−7.8	−3.8	−4.1	−3.6	−2.7	−1.6	−4.2	−4.9

Sources: 1986–2019: Ministère des Finances, Tunisia; 1981–1985: VIIè Plan de Développement Economique et Social 1987–1991, Ministère du Plan et du Développement Economique.

As in East Asia, the overall experience of Tunisia is characterized by the relatively steady growth in real GDP per capita, which was shown in Table 1.6, and, as will be shown in what follows, in terms of low inflation, low internal and external deficits and sustainable debt. The incidence of fiscal, banking or currency crises was limited, both in Tunisia and East Asia. Tunisia, however, was by no means totally immune to macroeconomic crises. The first ones occurred in the 1960s (1964 and 1969), but again during the mid-1980s, not unlike many East Asian countries which experienced macroeconomic crises, including the major 1997–1998 financial crisis. Tunisia even avoided some of the mistakes made by East Asian countries such as the premature liberalization of their capital accounts.

Like most MENA and East Asian countries, Tunisia followed sound monetary management, with a progressive shift from more direct credit management tools to more market-oriented mechanisms for monetary policy. Table 3.1 presents estimates of the average rate of inflation in Tunisia by decade, along with those of the other comparator countries from MENA and East Asia. Overall, by avoiding having even any individual years with extremely high inflation rates, it would appear that Tunisia's monetary policy was contributing to macroeconomic stability. Note that from the next to last column, with the overall average rates of inflation 1961–2010, that Tunisia's average rate of inflation of 5.24% was below that of most MENA countries and below those of each of the East Asian countries except Malaysia and Thailand. The table shows that those MENA countries with pegged exchange rates, especially those from the GCC and a few other countries (Djibouti, Jordan, Lebanon, Libya, or Morocco), generally had inflation rates that were lower than Tunisia's. Yet, compared to other MENA countries, which experienced considerable currency depreciation over the period, such as Algeria, Egypt, Iraq, Iran, Syria, and Yemen, Tunisia's inflation rates were lower and less volatile during this period.

With the exception of its inflation spike in the middle of the 1980s, which was simultaneous with the major macroeconomic crisis described in the previous Chapter, in no period did its decade average inflation rate get much above 6 % per annum, and for every decade since the 1970s, Tunisia's average inflation rate was below the averages of both the major and non-major oil exporting MENA countries and even below that of East Asia except in the 1980s and after 2011, the latter being a period which, as will be shown below, was far from politically stable. While in all regions and especially East Asia, the inflation rates fell quite substantially during the 2011 to 2019 period (the East Asian average of 14.1% in 1961–2010 driven by the Indonesia high inflation during the 1960s, fell to 2.71% in 2011–2019), there was a slight increase for Tunisia from 5.24% to 5.27%.

As discussed in Chapter 3, the relative autonomy, if not full independence in the modern sense, of the Central Bank of Tunisia may have contributed to greater monetary stability and hence the lower inflation rates for Tunisia shown in Table 3.1. But, of course Central Bank Independence is of much less relevance to the operation of fiscal policy which comes more under the Ministry of Finance, where discipline seems to have been much weaker; contributing to Tunisia's considerably weaker performance on External Debt and Debt Service Payments.

For purposes of comparing Tunisia with the other countries with respect to external debt, Tables 4.3 and 4.4 present comparable estimates of external debt as a percentage of Gross National Income (GNI), and service on external debt as a percentage of exports of goods and services by decade, respectively. On both of these indicators, Tunisia's figures look much *less* impressive relative to other MENA countries and East Asian countries than in the case of inflation. Although sometimes reaching high levels, Tunisia's debt and debt service relative to exports were mostly in the middle of the range for non-major oil exporting countries in MENA.[5] One favorable characteristic is that, compared to these other MENA countries, these debt ratios have been less volatile over time. Yet, they were also in most years quite a bit higher than the corresponding averages for East Asia. Not surprisingly, Tunisia's debt and debt service shares compared most unfavorably in 2019, well into its period of overall political instability. To its credit, Tunisia had reduced its debt and debt service ratios from their highs in the 1980s through to 2010, but then after 2010 it allowed both of these ratios to jump up to alarmingly high ones in 2019.

From the first set of columns in Table 4.4, it can be seen that Tunisia compared favorably to the non-major oil exporting countries of MENA on its overall external balance as a share of GDP throughout the periods. But the Tunisia-East Asia average comparisons were unfavorable to Tunisia in all years, the East Asian countries often enjoying significant trade surpluses.

These results in terms of macroeconomic stability reflect to a large extent the policies which determined macro-level prices such as average real wages, real interest rates, and real exchange rates. While comparative data on such prices are not available, Tunisia did not allow any major distortions to develop and/or to persist. One major exception was the macroeconomic crisis of the mid-1980s when major distortions prevailed at the same time.

During the second half of the 1970s and first half of the 1980s, however, the available data show that real wages increased by an average of 5% per year, which was a much higher rate than the growth of labor productivity

Table 4.3 External Debt Stock, 1970–2019

	Stock of external debt (% of GNI)							
Country	***1970***	***1980***	***Highest in 1980s***	***1990***	***Highest in 1990s***	***2000***	***2010***	***2019***
MENA non-major oil exporters	**27.3**	**57.4**	**106.1**	**100.8**	**113.2**	**62.3**	**54.2**	**74.0**
Djibouti	..	..		..		52.5	67.0	79.0
Egypt, Arab Rep,	22.6	94.7	132.7	78.8	86.6	29.1	17.1	39.4
Jordan	18.1	47.3	181.7	211.2	243.6	129.2	63.5	75.7
Lebanon	..	..	30.3	51.6	57.3	57.3	126.1	144.9
Morocco	25.0	45.7	111.9	85.4	72.2	54.6	29.7	46.8
Syrian Arab Republic	..	..		..		..	..	..
Tunisia	**43.7**	**41.8**	**74.0**	**64.7**	**65.9**	**55.3**	**53.8**	**100.8**
West Bank and Gaza	..	..		..		..	..	..
Yemen, Rep,	..	..		113.2	153.4	58.0	22.4	31.3
MENA major oil exporters	**19.8**	**26.3**	**28.6**	**27.2**	**60.0**	**28.5**	**4.3**	**3.3**
Algeria	19.8	47.8	50.9	47.1	83.5	48.9	4.5	3.3
Iran, Islamic Rep,	..	4.7	6.3	7.2	36.5	8.0	4.1	..
Iraq	..	..		..		..	..	..
Libya	..	..		..		..	..	..
MENA GCC								
Bahrain	..	..		..		..	..	..
Kuwait	..	..		..		..	..	..
Oman	..	..		..		..	..	..
Qatar	..	..		..		..	..	..
Saudi Arabia	..	..		..		..	..	..
United Arab Emirates	..	..		..		..	..	..
East Asia	**28.6**	**36.8**	**57.7**	**47.0**	**88.9**	**58.5**	**25.0**	**26.6**
China	..	..	13.6	15.3	19.4	12.2	12.3	14.8
Indonesia	38.1	30.2	72.7	69.2	168.2	93.5	27.0	37.0
Korea, Rep,	..	..		..		..	..	..
Malaysia	..	..		..		..	..	..
Philippines	33.5	54.4	98.8	70.2	71.9	63.8	28.2	20.2
Thailand	14.1	25.9	45.9	33.4	96.0	64.4	32.5	34.4

Source: Data from database: World Bank, World Development Indicators.

(less than 2% per year as shown in Figure 4.1) This was one of the main factors contributing to the major macroeconomic crisis of the mid-1980s. Over the long run, for the period 1983–2010 both variables moved very much in parallel: the average real wage increased by 48% while total labor productivity increased by 57%. But, as also shown in Figure 4.1, there were also periods when wages moved much faster than productivity. While the adjustment program after 1986 led to stagnation of real wages for almost a decade, a major discrepancy characterized the 2000s when real wages were

Table 4.4 External Balance and External Debt Service, 1980–2019

	External balance on goods and services (% of GDP)					Total debt service (% of exports of goods, services and primary income)						
Country	*1980s (average)*	*1990s (average)*	*2000s (average)*	*2010*	*2019*	*1980*	*Highest in 1980s*	*1990*	*Highest in 1990s*	*2000*	*2010*	*2019*
MENA non-major oil exporters	**–24.7**	**–20.5**	**–16.1**	**–17.8**	**–13.6**	**22.9**		**23.9**		**15.7**	**12.3**	**25.0**
Djibouti				..	8.99	..		..	5.4	6.9	7.9	1.5
Egypt, Arab Rep.	–11.95	–6.12	–3.91	–5.24	–8.24	19.0	42.3	28.6	22.1	9.8	6.2	16.1
Jordan	–35.04	–23.87	–27.95	–20.23	–13.02	12.3	41.6	24.4	28.8	20.1	5.9	19.2
Lebanon	–77.57	–43.97	–22.64	–25.05	–25.32	..		..		..	50.5	88.2
Morocco	–7.08	–4.84	–7.27	–10.78	–8.92	44.2	58.4	28.4	52.5	29.7	11.8	9.2
Syrian Arab Republic	–10.56	–5.22	2.74	..	..	..		..		..	3.1	..
Tunisia	–6.29	–3.81	–2.89	–5.15	–10.67	16.3	32.9	27.0	26.5	22.1	10.5	15.7
West Bank and Gaza		–55.46	–50.80	–40.25	–37.95	..		..		..	..	..
Yemen, Rep.				..	..	..		11.1	14.9	5.9	2.8	..
MENA major oil exporters	**–6.9**	**4.4**	**13.3**	**10.2**	**1.7**	**17.5**		**34.2**		**9.9**	**1.4**	**0.5**
Algeria	–3.01	4.14	15.13	7.02	–6.44	28.2	80.3	65.1	0.0	..	1.0	0.5
Iran, Islamic Rep.	–7.19	0.59	2.88	5.03	–5.64	6.9	7.1	3.2	31.2	9.9	1.8	0.5
Iraq	–10.43	8.57	6.61	5.34	7.47	..		..		..	..	..
Libya		4.42	28.44	23.51	11.27	..		..		..	..	..

(Continued)

Table 4.4 External Balance and External Debt Service, 1980–2019 *(Continued)*

	External balance on goods and services (% of GDP)					Total debt service (% of exports of goods, services and primary income)						
Country	*1980s (average)*	*1990s (average)*	*2000s (average)*	*2010*	*2019*	*1980*	*Highest in 1980s*	*1990*	*Highest in 1990s*	*2000*	*2010*	*2019*
MENA GCC	**8.8**	**7.2**	**22.2**	**25.9**	**13.5**							
Bahrain	12.03	5.93	18.67	18.60	11.32	..		..		..	..	..
Kuwait	8.55	–4.82	28.53	36.32	8.40	..		..		..	..	..
Oman	14.37	9.51	20.34	24.90	14.59	..		..		..	..	..
Qatar		16.94	32.11	38.57	14.37	..		..		..	..	..
Saudi Arabia	0.33	8.33	22.27	16.59	8.44	..		..		..	..	..
United Arab Emirates			11.15	20.61	23.98	..		..		..	..	..
East Asia	**–0.1**	**1.2**	**5.8**	**4.9**	**1.4**	**23.1**		**22.4**		**18.8**	**11.3**	**16.7**
China	–0.27	2.04	4.67	3.65	1.16	..	11.7	11.7	16.8	13.1	3.0	9.6
Indonesia	1.43	3.53	4.59	1.90	–0.56	..	40.4	33.5	37.1	22.8	18.7	39.4
Korea, Rep.	0.44	0.99	1.82	2.81	2.90	..		..		..	..	..
Malaysia	2.55	6.06	19.69	15.92	7.44	..		..		..	..	..
Philippines	–1.69	–6.11	–1.20	–0.35	–12.08	27.3	43.9	27.6	26.1	22.9	18.7	9.7
Thailand	–3.10	0.53	5.13	5.72	9.34	18.9	31.9	16.9	21.8	16.3	4.7	8.0

Source: Data from database: World Development Indicators.

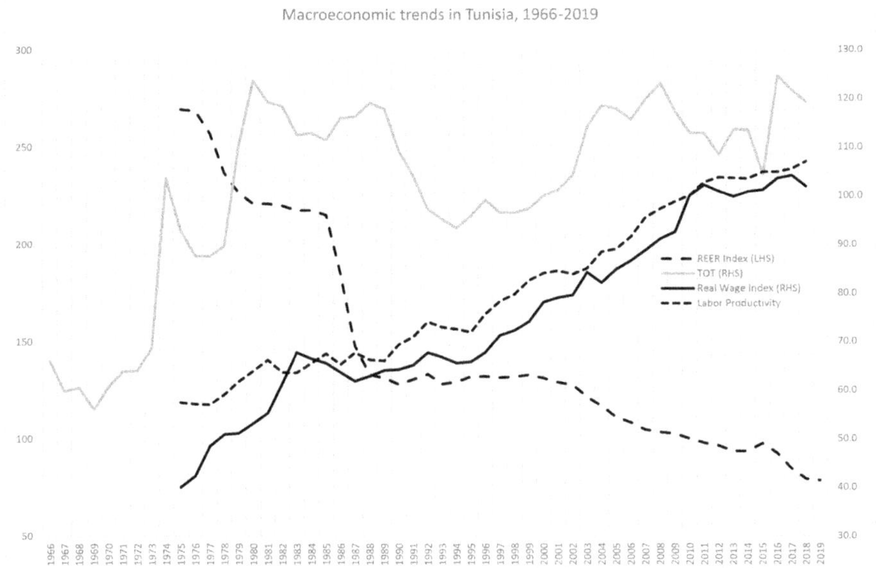

Figure 4.1 Macroeconomic Trends in Tunisia, 1966–2019

Sources:	REER (base year 2010=100)	IMF International Financial Statistics
	TOT (terms of trade base year 2000=100)	UNCTAD and INS data
	Real Wages (base year 2010=100)	Tunisian data based on National Accounts
	Labor Productivity (base year 2010=100)	Tunisia data from various sources

moving faster and slightly more than productivity. As a result, the share of labor income in total income moved up accordingly, increasing by almost 15 points from 1975 to 1983 (from 40% to 55%)[6], but then declining to 52% by 1997, and fluctuating in the range of 52%–56% since then.

Like most MENA as well as East Asian countries, Tunisia pursued a policy of financial repression during the 1960s, keeping real interest rates low and strongly directing the allocation of credit through government intervention. To illustrate, Figure 4.2 shows the benchmark money market interest rate, adjusted for inflation, since 1964. The real interest rate was negative for three years out of six for which data are available during the 1960s. These policies were reversed during the 1970s, and real interest rates became positive, except in 1975 when there was an exceptional spike in inflation. The first half of the 1980s saw a return to the negative real interest rates situation which persisted until the crisis. This resulted from the persistently high rates of inflation during the early 1980s shown in Figure 4.2. Eventually during the mid-1980s, with the structural adjustment program in effect, and financial liberalization, distortions were reduced or eliminated and real interest rates became much more market-determined. Overall, however, the reforms and changes in Tunisia lagged behind the reforms in East Asian countries, but compared favorably to most other MENA countries.

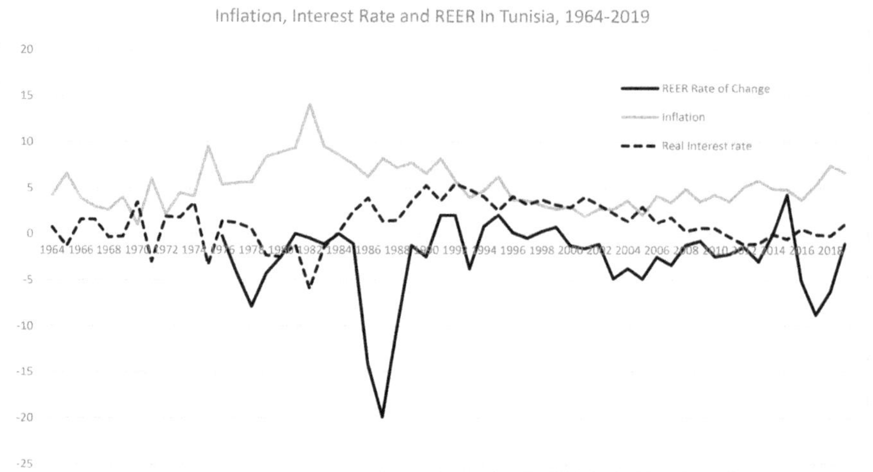

Figure 4.2 Inflation, Real Interest Rate, and Real Exchange Rate in Tunisia, 1964–2019

Sources: REER (%) IMF International Financial Statistics
Inflation (%) Institut National de la Statistique, Tunisia
Real interest rate (%) Central Bank of Tunisia, various sources

While real exchange rate distortions were of little importance to the ability of MENA's oil countries to export their oil and other natural resources, they can be quite important to countries like Tunisia once the importance of such oil exports had become increasingly less important and labor-intensive exports had become more important as they have since the 1980s. When real exchange rates are overvalued or excessively volatile, as demonstrated by Edwards (1988), Cottani et al. (1990) and Ghura and Grennes (1993), they can interfere with a country's ability to export manufactures, especially in developing countries. Nabli and Véganzonès-Varoudakis (2004) used a sample of 53 developing countries from all regions, including both Asia and some ten countries from MENA, to estimate the effect of both real exchange rate volatility and misalignment on manufactures growth 1970–1999. While the negative effects of exchange rate volatility on manufactures exports were not statistically significant, those of real exchange rate misalignment were in general highly significant, and for Tunisia had become highly costly by the 1990–1999 period due to Tunisia's unusually large share of manufactures exports in total exports at that time.

Tunisia's exchange rate management was able to avoid persistent real exchange rate appreciations,[7] even though it had led to at least short periods of substantial misalignments. As shown in Figure 4.1, the real effective exchange rate (REER) has been continuously declining over the period 1975–2018 for which data are available.[8] There was no significant episode or period of appreciation of the REER, but many episodes of major depreciations in that rate. Although not shown in Figure 4.1, there had been a major devaluation in 1964. But as shown in Figure 4.1, there were at least four other major episodes of real effective exchange depreciation since then. The first was during the period 1977–1979 (when the REER declined by 15.6%); the second deprecation was in the context of a major macro adjustment program during the years 1986–1988 (when it declined by 38%); the third one was a slow process of depreciation during the period 2003–2007 (when it declined 18%); and the last one occurred during 2016–2018 (when the REER declined by18.8%). [9] It should be pointed out that the data show that a major misalignment of the real exchange rate had been allowed to persist during the first half of the 1980s. While in the presence of major macroeconomic distortions, and expanding deficits, the REER was allowed to remain stable until 1985, a major adjustment had to be made in 1986–1987. It is noteworthy that in Tunisia, the episodes of major positive terms of trade shocks, such those during 1973–1974 and 1979–1980, were not followed by any appreciation of the real exchange rate. On the other hand, as shown in Figure 4.1, most real depreciations were not closely associated with negative terms of trade shocks.

However, we should note that many of these REER misalignments were *within* sectors (such as very different tariff rates and very specific actions taken to save those particular firms in a particular sector which were in financial trouble from having to lower their employment), rather than between sectors. This suggests that demonstrations of only limited exchange rate misalignments affecting manufacturing as a whole were overlooking a large portion of the inefficiencies, which were really among firms within particular sectors.

Overall, while large REER distortions were avoided, in Tunisia, the temporary misalignments in real exchange rates between, as well as within, sectors have certainly played a role affecting exports and overall growth over time.

C. High Levels of Investments in Human Capital, Equity, and Equality of Opportunity

Third, the development strategy followed to achieve the aforementioned and consistently held goals was buttressed by having put priority on human capital formation based on both the rapid expansion of secular public education, public health and other services, and the liberation of women. This was an important part of equalizing access to public services for, and opening up economic opportunities to, all segments of society. As discussed in Chapter 3, a very active social policy helped achieve broad-based access to education, health services, clean water, electricity, housing ownership, and other services. It included other programs, such as social protection, in-kind subsidies for basic commodities, and income support. This led to the excellent progress in terms of poverty reduction, and the health and educational improvement components of the Millennium Development Goals (MDGs) that were noted in Chapter 1.

The importance of human capital in growth and development is of course well-known from both macroeconomic studies (e.g., Mankiw et al. 1992) and microeconomic studies (e.g., Strauss and Thomas 1995). While prior to 1995 much of the literature emphasized education, soon after that it began to stress health and the complementarity between education and health in their effects on each other and on growth (Thomas and Strauss 1997).

Note from Table 1.1 (Chapter 1) that Tunisia did at least as well as the most successful MENA and Asian countries in increasing both types of human capital measures between 1960 and 2010. These indicators, however, were focused on the basics, literacy, the average number of years of education, and infant mortality. While in those tables, Tunisia's accumulation of human capital was not clearly superior to the stronger comparators both in MENA and East Asia, in the case of higher education, Tunisia's performance stands out more sharply, both in the quantity of that education and in terms of quality. This is what emerged from a more detailed recent analysis of Tunisia's higher education system by Abdessalem (2011) and from a comparison with other MENA countries by El-Araby (2011). Not only did Tunisia compare favorably in university attendance and the growth thereof, but it also compared favorably in the percent of students enrolled in sciences and engineering. It is such education which may be most relevant to explaining such important pathways to Tunisia's success as the ability of its textile industries to adopt the technology that would allow it to be competitive in Europe once restrictions on imports from low wage Asian countries had been removed and to develop entirely new higher tech industries, such as auto parts manufacturing and Information and Communications Technology (ICT) adoption. Also, the role of higher education should not be neglected in the ability of its government officials to perform the important coordinating, policy-making and implementation functions identified above.

How did Tunisia accomplish this? What the World Bank (2008a), El-Araby (2011), and Abdessalem (2011) make clear is that Tunisia did it primarily by consistently investing more than all other MENA countries in education, at first at lower levels of education, but in recent decades in higher education. Tunisia has also been among the leaders in introducing incentives in the financing of higher education and health.

As shown in Table 4.5, Tunisia's public expenditures on education rose from 5.14 to 6.6% of GDP between 1978/1982 and 2015/2019, and in every period since the 1980s its expenditures on education as a share of GDP exceeded the averages of these educational expenditure shares of all MENA sub-groups and East Asia. The same table shows that Tunisia's public expenditures on health, although available only for the period since 2000, were also quite high, at 5–7% of GDP. Although these rates were only comparable to or even sometimes lower than the levels achieved by Iran, Jordan, Lebanon, and more recently Korea, they were higher than those in all other countries in the table.

Table 4.5 Public Expenditures on Health and Education, 1971–2019

	Health expenditures (% GDP)			*Education expenditures (% GDP)*					
Country	***2000***	***2010***	***2018***	***1971/1972***	***1978/1982***	***1988/1992***	***1998/2002***	***2008/2012***	***2015/2019***
MENA Non-Major Oil Exporters	**5.8**	**5.4**	**6.0**	**3.7**	**5.2**	**4.7**	**5.9**	**4.7**	**4.7**
Djibouti	2.94	3.06	2.32				8.39	4.49	3.72
Egypt, Arab Rep.	4.92	4.15	4.95	4.53	4.94	4.39		3.76	
Jordan	9.63	8.39	7.79	2.84	4.75	4.85	4.88		3.23
Lebanon	10.84	7.44	8.35				2.70	1.84	
Morocco	3.98	5.86	5.31		5.89	4.54	5.13	5.30	
Syrian Arab Republic	4.35	3.28	..	3.58	5.27	3.83	4.70	4.86	
Tunisia	**5.05**	**5.88**	**7.29**		**5.14**	**5.86**	**6.12**	**6.33**	**6.60**
West Bank and Gaza	..	..	..					5.85	5.37
Yemen, Rep.	4.67	5.16	..				9.44	5.15	
MENA Major Oil Exporters	**3.9**	**4.7**	**6.3**	**2.8**	**5.3**	**3.7**	**3.2**	**4.0**	**3.5**
Algeria	3.49	5.12	6.22		6.89			4.34	
Iran, Islamic Rep.	4.74	6.75	8.66	2.77	6.47	3.77	4.20	3.62	3.48
Iraq	..	3.23	4.11		2.42	3.55			
Libya	3.43	3.59	..				2.26		
MENA GCC	**3.0**	**3.1**	**4.4**	**2.9**	**3.3**	**4.3**	**5.4**	**4.0**	**2.6**
Bahrain	3.56	3.84	4.13					2.57	2.50
Kuwait	2.51	2.76	5.00	3.05	3.21		6.57		
Oman	3.06	2.82	4.13			3.06	3.93	4.19	
Qatar	2.01	1.79	2.49	2.85	2.78		3.74	3.94	2.78
Saudi Arabia	4.21	3.65	6.36		4.02	5.46	7.32	5.14	
United Arab Emirates	2.37	3.88	4.23						
East Asia	**3.2**	**4.0**	**4.6**	**3.1**	**3.4**	**2.7**	**3.7**	**3.8**	**4.1**
China	4.47	4.21	5.35	1.50	2.00	1.71	1.87		3.51
Indonesia	1.91	2.96	2.87	2.79		0.87	2.55	3.17	3.58
Korea, Rep.	3.90	5.92	7.56	3.48	3.93	3.18	3.37		4.33
Malaysia	2.53	3.18	3.76	4.55	6.14	5.11	6.70	5.28	4.59
Philippines	3.15	4.31	4.40		1.90		3.20	2.56	
Thailand	3.10	3.39	3.79	3.05	2.89	2.85	4.68	4.04	

Source: Data from database: World Development Indicators.

Additional support for (a) Tunisia's commitment to equitable human capital development as being of critical importance in explaining its comparative success over the entire period from independence until the mid-2000s, (b) its unusual leadership and coordination capabilities as identified in Section A, and (c) its ability to maintain macroeconomic stability stressed in Section B, can be seen in the following beautifully written assessment by the World Bank and the Islamic Development Bank of Tunisia's accomplishments as a result of programs that these two international banks had helped fund:

> The main party responsible for the significant socioeconomic achievements of Tunisia is the country itself.... Perhaps three main attributes of Tunisia's efforts were crucial for this overall success: (i) program ownership and the explicit policy of the government to move ahead with difficult policies and reforms only after a broad consensus with labor unions, the business community and the political structure had been achieved, albeit within a regime that is governed by a strong central authority. Although this meant that the pace of reform had to be cautious and deliberate, it also meant that there have been no policy reversals and that economic agents could count on a basically predictable policy environment; (ii) the maintenance of high investment levels in human resources, which has led to a well-educated population and a well-trained and qualified labor force; and (iii) the achievement of macroeconomic stability through a combination of sound fiscal monetary and foreign exchange policies.
>
> *(World Bank and Islamic Development Bank 2005, 31)*

The increasing percentages of young people with more years of education and the expenditures on education by Tunisia and other MENA countries have been impressive as we have shown above. One important concern, however, that has been raised about education in MENA countries is its quality. One measure that has been used for quality in recent years has been scores on internally standardized tests, such as those for Math, Science, and Reading ability as shown in Table 4.6. Unfortunately, no such scores exist for Tunisia on the more widely cited TIMSS (Trends in International Mathematics and Science Study) test for Math and Science in 2015 and 2019, and the PIRLS (Progress in International Reading Literacy Study) test in 2016 for Reading ability presented in the first three sets of columns in the table. Yet, in the sixth set of columns, there are comparable test scores for Tunisia (and for as many as possible of the same sets of MENA and East Asian countries) on the 2015 PISA (Program for International Student Assessment) test. Notice that, despite the generally high shares of public expenditures on education for MENA countries in general, and Tunisia in particular, the test scores for MENA countries and even Tunisia are all low relative to the East Asian countries. Not a single MENA country in the table

Table 4.6 Educational Test Scores, 2015–2019

Country	*TIMSS 2015 Math*		*TIMSS 2015 Science*		*TIMSS 2019 Math*		*TIMSS 2019 Science*		*PIRLS 2016 Reading*	*PISA 2015*			*PISA 2018*		
	4th Grade	*8th Grade*	*4th Grade*	*8th Grade*	*4th Grade*	*8th Grade*	*4th Grade*	*8th Grade*	*4th Grade*	*Math*	*Science*	*Reading*	*Math*	*Science*	*Reading*
MENA non-major oil exporters	**383**	**404**	**352**	**397**	**383**	**413**	**374**	**408**	**344**	**381**	**394**	**372**	**387**	**397**	**377**
Djibouti															
Egypt, Arab Rep.		392		371		413			330						
Jordan	388	386		426		420		452		380	409	408	400	429	418
Lebanon		452		398		429		377		396	386	347	393	384	353
Morocco	377	384	352	393	383	388	374	394	358				368	377	359
Syria															
Tunisia										**367**	**386**	**361**			
West Bank and Gaza															
Yemen, Rep.															
MENA major oil exporters															
Algeria										360	376	350			
Iran, Islamic Rep.	431	436	426	456	443	446	441	449	428						
Iraq															
Libya															

(*Continued*)

Table 4.6 Educational Test Scores, 2015–2019 *(Continued)*

	TIMSS 2015 Math		***TIMSS 2015 Science***		***TIMSS 2019 Math***		***TIMSS 2019 Science***		***PIRLS 2016 Reading***	***PISA 2015***			***PISA 2018***		
Country	***4th Grade***	***8th Grade***	***4th Grade***	***8th Grade***	***4th Grade***	***8th Grade***	***4th Grade***	***8th Grade***	***4th Grade***	***Math***	***Science***	***Reading***	***Math***	***Science***	***Reading***
MENA GCC	**417**	**420**	**418**	**444**	**437**	**434**	**441**	**461**	**432**	**415**	**428**	**418**	**407**	**413**	**413**
Bahrain	451	454	459	466	480	481	493	486	446						
Kuwait	353	392	337	411	383	403	392	444	393						
Oman	425	403	431	455	431	411	435	457	428						
Qatar	439	437	436	457	449	443	449	475	442	402	418	402	414	419	407
Saudi Arabia	383	368	390	396	398	394	402	431	430				373	386	399
UAE	452	465	457	477	481	473	473	473	450	427	437	434	435	434	432
East Asia	**503**	**500**	**493**	**486**	**428**	**531**	**429**	**524**	**583**	**461**	**467**	**452**	**451**	**454**	**431**
China	597*	589*	555*	569*					559*	518	528	484	591	590	555
Indonesia	397		397							386	403	397	379	396	371
Korea, Rep.	608	604	589	556	607	600	561	588	606	524	516	517	526	519	514
Malaysia		465		471		461		460					440	438	415
Philippines					249		297						353	357	340
Thailand		431		431						415	421	409	419	426	393

Sources: International Education Association TIMSS and PIRLS Boston College, Pisa: www. Pisa-worldwide-ranking-average-scores-of-math-science-reading.

Note: The scores presented for China with * in this table are actually for Chinese Taipei. Those without * are for China.

has a score on any of the tests that is even close to the East Asian average score, with the exception of the UAE for Reading in 2018.[10]

Gender and population policies were a notable aspect of Tunisia's emphasis on human capital. Again, as noted in Chapter 3, even at the outset of independence, Bourguiba pursued a very active policy of gender equality which has never been reversed or even weakened. Providing equal access to both education and health services was a priority objective among social policies of the state. As noted above, these policies contributed a great deal toward reducing Tunisia's fertility rates and raising its female labor force participation rates, both factors contributing to Tunisia's relative success in economic development. The gender inequality index presented in Table 2.14 was based on a very wide range of gender differences in life, ranging from access to education and health care to property rights, legal protection, and political participation. That table showed that by 1995 with a score of 0.515 Tunisia's Gender Inequality Index score was the lowest among all MENA countries for which it was possible to construct this index at the time. Yet, at that time it was still quite far above the East Asian average score of 0.430. By 2005 and 2010, however, Tunisia had reduced its Gender Inequality Index score to be on a par with the East Asian average.

As pointed out in Chapter 1, Tunisia's achievements in poverty reduction were as impressive as those achieved in the more successful East Asian countries. Tunisia's poverty rates and income inequality measures were among the highest early on until about 1980. However, both declined steadily and quite sharply after that, so that by 2015 Tunisia's rates were among the lowest in the region and lower than those in East Asia. Even at its highest, inequality in Tunisia had never reached the high levels that it had reached in many other developing countries after independence (World Bank 1995).

East Asian countries experienced two major waves of poverty reduction (Asian Development Bank 2020, Chapter 11). The first wave was between the 1960s and the 1980s, resulting in their being identified as the 'New Industrializing Economies' (NIEs) for having achieved very high GDP per capita growth. As shown in Table 1.3, the absolute poverty rate in Korea declined from 60 to 70% in the mid-1960s to 3.4% by the mid-1980s. By the end of the 1980s, the absolute poverty rate had also declined to less than 2% in Malaysia, to 9.4% in Thailand, 26.6% in the Philippines, and 58.8% in Indonesia (Table 1.3). Based on the data in Table 1.2, at 10.6% in 1990, the absolute poverty rate in Tunisia compared very favorably even to some of these East Asian success stories. Despite a significant drop from 88.1% to 66.2% between 1981 and 1990, China's poverty rate remained very high. Yet, the second wave of poverty reduction, which took place beginning in the 1990s, was driven largely by China, which saw a dramatic decline in its absolute poverty rate from 66.2% in 1990 to 0.7% in 2015. Absolute poverty rates also continued to decline in other East Asian countries between 1990 and 2015, for example, from 58.8% to 7.2% in Indonesia, from 26.6% to 7.8% in the Philippines, and from 9.4% to 0% in Thailand (Table 1.3).[11]

The decline in poverty rates prior to 1990 in East Asia can be explained by its very high GDP per capita growth and the stable levels of inequality. Some countries in East Asia (Korea, Taiwan, China, Indonesia) started during the 1960s with especially low levels of inequality, compared to the less successful ones with considerably higher levels of inequality. But in all cases inequality remained stable during this period. Beginning in the 1990s, however, the East Asian countries started to change substantially in this respect. Those which started with low levels saw an increase in inequality such as China and Indonesia. Those which started with high levels saw a decline in inequality (Malaysia, Philippines, Thailand). The major exception was Korea where inequality remained stable. One very important policy contributing to low-income inequality early on in the period under study was land reform. Notably, Studwell (2013) pointed to the important role of land reforms in distinguishing the East Asian countries with low inequality and greater reductions in poverty from those less successful in these respects which did not undertake such land reforms, such as Malaysia and the Philippines.

For Tunisia, however, its impressive reduction in inequality over several decades was much more related to its broad, inclusionary social policy and investments in public health and education (as discussed in Chapter 3). But fiscal policy also played a role. For example, for the year 2010 the Gini coefficient was reduced by 5 points from 44 for market income to 39 for disposable income after taxes and transfers (Jouini et al. 2018). These relatively precise numbers by Jouini et al. (2018) show a greater redistributive effort in Tunisia, than in the comparable figures for other countries using the recent version of the Standardized World Inequality Database (see Solt 2020). Indeed, according to that data, the average difference in the level of the Gini Index for market income and the Gini Index for disposable income (i.e., before and after taxation and redistribution) for the years 1975–1990 was around 2.9 points for Tunisia and 1.9 points for the six East Asian countries. As a result, according to Jouini et al. (2018), thanks to its emphasis on access to education and health, as well as other active social policies which included large subsidies to commodities catering to basic needs, and the political strategy followed by Bourguiba, Tunisia's poverty rates and income inequality measures were even lower than those of most East Asian countries, and even more so if, as pointed out above, the inequality measures were based on disposable income.

One outcome of these developments has been the growth of the middle class, an outstanding feature of the Tunisian as well the East Asian experience. Economic and Social Commission for West Asia (2014) found the middle class to be 57.5% of the population in 2010 in Tunisia, the second highest among the Arab countries considered. While using a different definition of the Middle Class, African Development Bank (2011) estimated the Middle Class in Tunisia to be 89.5% of the population, the highest in Africa.[12] East Asian countries saw also a dramatic rise in their middle class. Using a definition of the middle class based on expenditures per capita ranging from $2–20 at 2005 PPP prices, the Asian Development Bank found that by the middle of the 2000s, Malaysia had the largest middle class (89.3% of the total population) followed by Thailand (with 85.8%). China experienced the largest increase in its middle class between 1990 and 2008 to reach 62.7% in 2008, and Indonesia experienced the second largest to reach 46.6% in 2008 (Asian Development Bank 2010).

D. High Levels of Investments in Infrastructure

Fourth, although there are unfortunately little reliable data on aggregate investments in infrastructure that is comparable across countries, the limited data available show that MENA countries have invested heavily in infrastructure, on about the same scale as East Asia. Based on some estimates by Fay et al. (2019), investments in infrastructure in 2011 reached between 5.4% and 8.23% of GDP in MENA, depending on the measure used.[13] Not surprisingly, the largest infrastructural investment shares among MENA countries were in some of the GCC countries, like Qatar and the UAE, contributing substantially to boosting the average of these shares in MENA as a whole. However, even Tunisia was shown to have invested heavily on infrastructure in 2011 somewhere between 4.64% and 7.2% of GDP. The comparable figures for East Asia were between 5.1% and 9.2% of GDP, excluding China, which has been an outstanding outlier, with investment in infrastructure estimated at about 16% of GDP. These numbers are consistent with more precise data from Tunisia's national accounts which show that investment in infrastructure was around 3.5–4.5% of GDP per year during the period 1997–2010.[14] This ratio for Tunisia, however, had been much higher earlier (after independence during the 1960s and 1970s), when a major drive to build up infrastructure had been implemented.[15]

The scope and extent of investment in infrastructure can also be assessed using data on physical achievements in some sectors. Table 4.7 shows energy use per capita, fixed telephone lines per 100 population and the share of the population using safely managed sanitation services. Progress on these indicators in Tunisia did not match achievements by the most successful East Asian countries, such as China, Korea, and Malaysia, or most of the major oil-exporting countries in MENA. However, it was a front runner in these respects compared to non-oil exporting MENA countries. Between 1971 and 2010 energy use per capita increased three-fold, and the percentage of the population using safe sanitation services reached 70% in 2010. The number of telephone lines per 100 population reached 12% in 2010, higher than in all non-major oil-exporting MENA countries, except Lebanon, and higher than both Thailand and the Philippines among East Asian countries.

Overall infrastructure, therefore, was a favorable factor for economic growth and improved living conditions in Tunisia, compared to other non-oil producing MENA countries. Hence, as in East Asia, insufficient

Table 4.7 Infrastructure, 1971–2019

	Energy use (kg of oil equivalent per capita)						*Fixed telephone subscriptions (per 100 people)*						*People using safely managed sanitation services (% of population)*		
Country	*1971*	*1980*	*1990*	*2000*	*2010*	*2014*	*1971*	*1980*	*1990*	*2000*	*2010*	*2019*	*2000*	*2010*	*2017*
MENA non-major oil exporters	**322.5**	**483.9**	**546.6**	**737.9**	**855.7**	**837.4**	**0.9**	**1.5**	**4.4**	**8.0**	**10.4**	**9.1**	**45.3**	**50.1**	**53.9**
Djibouti	..	..	220.3	..	..	..	0.7	0.7	1.0	1.4	2.2	3.8	25.9	30.8	36.4
Egypt, Arab Rep.	220.9	348.5	574.5	589.7	876.5	827.5	0.8	..	2.9	8.0	11.6	8.7	54.3	57.1	60.7
Jordan	272.1	640.2	918.1	949.9	978.2	917.1	1.0	2.5	6.9	12.1	6.7	3.5	75.9	79.0	80.6
Lebanon	785.2	955.4	697.1	1277.0	1287.8	1196.9	..	..	14.1	15.0	16.9	12.9	17.1	19.6	21.8
Morocco	180.7	270.5	307.1	382.7	528.1	555.1	0.6	0.8	1.6	4.9	11.6	5.6	32.2	36.9	38.8
Syrian Arab Republic	361.9	500.0	840.8	940.9	1013.9	577.3	1.3	2.7	4.0	10.2	19.0	16.7	..	..	..
Tunisia	**319.9**	**512.7**	**600.2**	**752.5**	**966.8**	**950.5**	**0.9**	**1.8**	**3.7**	**9.8**	**12.1**	**12.4**	**58.7**	**70.2**	**78.1**
West Bank and Gaza	..	..	..	..	..	..	..	..	..	8.4	8.9	9.4	53.1	57.4	61.2
Yemen, Rep.	116.9	160.1	214.6	272.7	338.3	..	..	0.2	1.1	2.0	4.5	..	..	..	..
MENA major oil exporters	**474.0**	**1117.3**	**1439.7**	**1700.8**	**2124.6**	**2158.6**	**0.8**	**1.9**	**4.0**	**8.6**	**17.2**	**17.7**	**26.5**	**27.2**	**28.3**
Algeria	232.9	583.0	861.3	869.6	1114.2	1327.5	0.7	1.6	3.2	5.7	8.1	10.8	18.5	18.1	17.7
Iran, Islamic Rep.	566.9	984.7	1230.0	1874.7	2769.5	3060.4	1.0	2.4	3.9	14.5	35.0	34.9	..	..	..
Iraq	391.5	712.1	1150.7	1104.9	1261.2	1437.9	0.9	1.8	4.1	2.9	5.8	7.3	31.7	36.3	41.1
Libya	704.7	2189.5	2517.1	2954.1	3353.5	2808.6	0.6	..	5.0	11.3	19.8	..	29.3	27.3	26.1

(*Continued*)

Table 4.7 Infrastructure, 1971–2019 *(Continued)*

Country	Energy use (kg of oil equivalent per capita)						Fixed telephone subscriptions (per 100 people)						People using safely managed sanitation services (% of population)		
	1971	*1980*	*1990*	*2000*	*2010*	*2014*	*1971*	*1980*	*1990*	*2000*	*2010*	*2019*	*2000*	*2010*	*2017*
MENA GCC	**4463.6**	**6923.6**	**7612.9**	**9617.3**	**9325.6**	**9715.5**	**3.4**	**8.9**	**14.9**	**22.0**	**15.4**	**16.6**	**87.9**	**90.2**	**93.2**
Bahrain	6394.8	7794.6	10555.4	11988.8	10207.8	10596.6	3.0	11.5	19.0	25.7	18.4	16.6	95.9	96.0	96.0
Kuwait	7665.8	7637.8	4347.3	9152.0	10721.5	9178.9	5.1	11.5	15.8	22.8	17.4	13.9	100.0	100.0	100.0
Oman	113.4	997.0	2328.3	3337.3	6154.5	6040.6	0.1	1.5	5.8	9.8	9.3	12.8	..	..	..
Qatar	7754.0	14809.7	13703.2	18431.9	14890.4	17922.7	7.4	13.7	19.3	27.0	14.5	16.3	86.3	88.5	96.0
Saudi Arabia	1206.1	3209.1	3573.1	4735.7	6764.4	6905.8	1.6	3.3	7.6	14.3	15.2	15.7	67.9	73.1	77.8
United Arab Emirates	3647.2	7093.7	11170.2	10057.9	7215.2	7648.4	..	11.8	21.7	32.5	17.3	24.2	89.6	93.4	96.3
East Asia	**433.7**	**644.9**	**982.4**	**1567.7**	**2110.4**	**2309.4**	**0.7**	**2.0**	**7.4**	**17.0**	**21.0**	**16.7**	**57.9**	**67.8**	**78.1**
China	464.9	609.5	767.0	899.0	1954.7	2236.7	..	0.2	0.6	11.2	21.5	13.3	26.6	47.6	72.1
Indonesia	297.3	377.8	543.8	735.9	877.1	883.9	0.1	0.3	0.6	3.1	16.9	3.6	..	..	..
Korea, Rep.	516.1	1082.2	2167.3	4002.7	5045.5	5289.3	1.5	7.1	30.9	54.6	57.6	48.3	85.9	95.7	99.9
Malaysia	547.2	862.0	1211.0	2107.8	2601.5	3003.5	1.0	2.9	8.8	20.0	16.3	23.3	77.8	81.5	88.6
Philippines	415.9	473.3	463.8	512.7	429.9	474.3	0.5	0.9	1.0	3.9	3.5	3.9	41.5	46.4	51.6
Thailand	360.6	464.4	741.6	1148.2	1753.7	1969.0	0.3	0.8	2.3	8.9	10.2	7.8	..	..	..

Source: Data from database: World Bank, World Development Indicators.

infrastructure did not constitute a constraining factor. As we noted in Chapter 1, access to electricity and safe drinking water was high and helped lead to much improved living conditions for Tunisia's population.

E. Leveraging Global Markets

Fifth, Tunisia has continuously relied at least moderately on leveraging global markets, particularly European ones, in order to benefit from access to ideas, technology, and potential economies of scale. Even during the state-led import substitution period of the 1960s, the encouragement of tourism meant continued openness. This leveraging of global markets was progressively strengthened during the subsequent decades. The Dinar Convertibility Act of 1993 provided free repatriation of profits and proceeds from the sale of equity capital. The Investment Incentives Law of December 1993 (a) provided tax relief for those profits which were reinvested, (b) limited the VAT tax rates to 10% on imported capital goods, and (c) provided exemptions from taxes on profits for firms whose exports constituted 80% of their total sales. Even more importantly, the Barcelona Agreement of 1995 committed Tunisia (and other MENA countries joining the Trade Agreement with the EU) to continue to reduce both formal and informal barriers to free movement of goods and services between the country and EU members, and to encourage FDI. Although with admittedly quite incomplete data, Testas (2000) found that by 1998 FDI into Tunisia (from almost 2000 foreign firms) constituted about 25% of total private investment. His empirical model, moreover, showed that EU investments had raised Tunisia's total fixed capital formation over the period 1987–1994 by 22% and, after the further liberalizations of the next several years, by 34% during the 1995–1997 period. Testas (2000) also showed that these investments had raised Tunisia's level of GDP during that short period by 6.6%.[16]

Table 4.8 presents comparative data on two different indicators of international trade over several decades beginning in the 1960s, trade openness and non-oil merchandise exports. While Bahrain, Jordan, and United Arab Emirates all had somewhat higher measures of trade openness and some of the other oil exporters had very high measures in years of relatively high oil prices, Tunisia has sustained the steadiest increase in openness among MENA countries since the 1970s. Its greater success is even more evident in the case of non-oil exports as a percent of GDP. As Table 4.8 shows, Tunisia's increasing degree of openness and its non-oil export growth rates have matched those of the more successful East Asian countries, such as China, Korea and Indonesia. The reader should also refer back to Table 2.4 which, in characterizing changes in productive structure, had shown Tunisia's tourism receipts and tourism's share in GDP to have grown impressively and to have sustained until 2010, as shown in Table 2.3, the highest shares of international tourism in GDP of any MENA country except Bahrain,

Table 4.8 Foreign Trade, 1961–2019

Country	*Trade openness (exports plus imports as a % of GDP)*						*Non-oil merchandise exports (% GDP)*					
	1961–1970	***1971–1980***	***1981–1990***	***1991–2000***	***2001–2010***	***2011–2019***	***1961–1970***	***1971–1980***	***1981–1990***	***1991–2000***	***2001–2010***	***2011–2019***
MENA non-major oil exporters	**37.3**	**66.4**	**77.3**	**75.9**	**83.0**	**108.9**	**10.2**	**11.2**	**11.0**	**12.6**	**17.0**	**18.5**
Djibouti						287.2			6.2	4.3	6.9	
Egypt, Arab Rep.	35.7	49.3	52.1	48.9	55.1	40.6	10.4	9.0	4.3	3.0	6.7	7.4
Jordan		117.7	118.9	121.8	127.6	100.7	5.4	10.5	16.9	23.7	30.6	21.2
Lebanon			113.9	68.1	82.6	80.9				4.0	11.0	9.5
Morocco	38.9	47.9	54.0	51.1	68.7	83.1	14.1	13.6	12.6	16.3	17.5	21.6
Syrian Arab Republic	38.5	52.1	43.9	66.2	73.1							
Tunisia	36.2	65.0	80.8	85.3	94.4	101.7	10.9	11.5	14.8	24.6	29.5	32.6
West Bank and Gaza				90.1	79.8	68.1						
Yemen, Rep.												
MENA major oil exporters	**49.3**	**67.8**	**50.7**	**47.8**	**77.8**	**71.1**	**4.0**	**1.4**	**0.7**	**1.4**	**2.0**	**2.8**
Algeria	56.5	63.7	48.5	51.5	67.9	60.0	7.0	2.0	0.5	0.9	0.8	0.7
Iran, Islamic Rep.	33.9	54.7	28.7	38.1	48.4	48.6	2.5	1.0		2.5	4.8	7.1
Iraq	57.5	85.1	54.9	50.8	103.4	67.6	2.4			1.3	0.9	0.1
Libya			70.8	50.7	91.5	108.1		1.0	1.0	1.0	1.7	3.3
MENA GCC	**84.5**	**134.9**	**115.1**	**96.6**	**105.0**	**115.0**	**1.8**	**2.7**	**15.1**	**13.0**	**11.0**	**16.9**
Bahrain		239.3	199.1	155.3	134.5	162.1			24.9	28.6	16.0	22.8
Kuwait	88.8	102.9	99.6	96.8	89.6	99.1	3.5	6.3	23.0	2.6	2.8	3.4
Oman	80.2	108.4	86.2	79.7	87.8	93.3		1.6	4.1	9.5	9.4	12.5
Qatar				85.8	90.9	95.9		2.7	6.6	7.4	6.3	6.5
Saudi Arabia		88.8	75.6	65.7		73.3	0.1	0.4	0.7	3.4	4.9	13.5
United Arab Emirates					122.4	166.4		2.7	31.1	26.7	26.7	42.8
East Asia	**35.3**	**47.5**	**59.0**	**84.7**	**96.5**	**83.1**	**15.2**	**20.1**	**20.5**	**34.3**	**41.0**	**32.6**
China	6.4	8.9	21.6	33.6	53.5	42.0			9.0	18.7	27.6	20.5
Indonesia	22.9	43.7	49.0	60.7	56.8	44.0	6.8	8.1	8.7	22.0	20.3	13.4
Korea, Rep.	24.9	51.7	58.1	55.1	73.8	87.3	5.6	21.8	28.0	23.8	30.6	34.6
Malaysia	85.5	91.1	116.5	185.5	190.3	136.5	38.9	38.4	40.9	76.6	79.7	56.8
Philippines	36.4	46.1	51.8	82.8	77.6	62.4	12.3	16.1	15.4	28.4	34.1	19.4
Thailand	35.4	43.6	56.8	90.7	126.8	126.4	12.5	16.3	21.0	36.2	53.7	50.9

Source: Data from database World Bank, World Development Indicators.

Jordan, Lebanon, and Morocco, and a share similar to those of Malaysia and Thailand among East Asian countries.

Since FDI is often regarded as a means of accessing foreign technology and technology transfer, Table 4.9 provides averages of net inflows of FDI as percentages of GDP by decade from the 1970s to the present decade for Tunisia and its comparators. Tunisia has been successful in attracting FDI net inflows which are steady and relatively higher than most countries in MENA and East Asia throughout the decades. They averaged 2.3% of GDP during 1971–2010. For individual decades, only a few MENA countries had net inflows of FDI as a percentage of GDP that were higher than those of Tunisia (e.g., Egypt during the 1980s, and 2000s, Bahrain in the 1990s and 2000s, and Lebanon, Jordan, and Djibouti during 2001–2010). Moreover,

Table 4.9 Foreign Direct Investment, 1971–2019

	Foreign direct investment, net inflows (% of GDP)					
Country	***1971–1980***	***1981–1990***	***1991–2000***	***2001–2010***	***1971–2010***	***2011–2019***
MENA non-major oil exporters	**0.94**	**0.42**	**1.94**	**5.01**	**2.64**	**3.01**
Djibouti		0.06	0.53	8.48	3.61	7.15
Egypt, Arab Rep.	1.27	2.48	1.20	3.97	2.23	1.96
Jordan	0.74	0.94	2.20	10.23	3.60	4.28
Lebanon		0.09	3.03	11.60	6.37	5.53
Morocco	0.17	0.33	1.36	3.02	1.22	2.66
Syrian Arab Republic		0.13	0.98	1.38	0.77	
Tunisia	**1.59**	**1.62**	**2.34**	**3.72**	**2.32**	**2.13**
West Bank and Gaza			4.05	0.92	2.09	1.22
Yemen, Rep.		–2.32	1.75	1.81	1.59	–0.82
MENA major oil exporters	**0.46**	**0.12**	**0.14**	**1.55**	**0.65**	**–0.03**
Algeria	0.80	0.00	0.36	1.48	0.66	0.73
Iran, Islamic Rep.	0.64	–0.07	0.06	1.12	0.46	0.72
Iraq	–0.05	0.00	0.25	1.19	0.35	–1.93
Libya		0.55	–0.09	2.41	1.13	0.35
MENA GCC	**0.36**	**0.90**	**2.11**	**3.29**	**1.87**	**1.71**
Bahrain		1.97	9.00	5.35	5.44	3.21
Kuwait		0.00	0.81	0.23	0.26	0.65
Oman	1.49	1.45	0.63	2.84	1.60	2.69
Qatar	0.86	–0.04	1.82	4.39	1.76	–0.02
Saudi Arabia	–1.16	1.94	0.26	3.53	1.14	1.12
United Arab Emirates	0.24	0.10	0.11	3.38	1.04	2.59
East Asia	**1.13**	**1.13**	**2.65**	**2.25**	**1.88**	**2.06**
China	0.01	0.61	4.18	3.79	2.68	2.25
Indonesia	1.80	0.47	0.78	0.93	1.00	2.09
Korea, Rep.	0.61	0.39	0.84	1.07	0.73	0.73
Malaysia	3.28	3.37	5.70	2.99	3.84	3.34
Philippines	0.48	0.72	1.88	1.22	1.08	2.01
Thailand	0.61	1.20	2.53	3.47	1.95	1.92

Source: Data from database: World Bank, World Development Indicators.

among East Asian countries, only China and Malaysia managed to attract higher averages of net FDI inflow percentages of GDP than Tunisia over the entire 1971–2010 period. Tunisia's success in increasing its FDI inflows can be attributed at least in part to Tunisia's rapid diversification of manufacturing exports toward higher technology products since the 1990s (as mentioned earlier, and shown in detail in Ghali and Nabli 2020).

The indicators for international trade and FDI discussed above are partial ones and do not provide a satisfactory overall measure of the extent of integration of a country in the global economy. The KOF research Institute[17] in Switzerland has developed a set of broad indicators of globalization, with comparable data across all the countries in our MENA and East Asia samples.[18] Table 4.10 presents these data for the two most important component indexes of Globalization: the Trade Globalization Index and the Financial Globalization Index.[19] For each of these indexes the KOF constructs one index in '*de facto*' terms designed to be most closely related to Globalization *outcomes* and another in '*de jure*' terms designed to be most related to the *policy and institutional features giving rise to those outcomes.* In many cases the two indices are relatively similar and hence we present primarily only those in *de facto* terms. Indeed, all except those in the last column of the table are the '*de facto*' indicators. Yet, since, especially for the Financial Globalization Index, there are a few sizeable differences between the '*de facto*' and '*de jure*' indexes, for comparison purposes in the last column of the table we also the corresponding '*de jure*' index for 2018.

Potrafke (2015) provides a comprehensive review of the KOF indexes and their applications in the literature, most of which has been directed to explaining the relation between globalization indexes and economic growth, although in some cases looking at the relation between globalization and inequality as in Dreher and Gaston (2008). Potrafke's (2015) review shows that most studies have shown significant positive relations between rising globalization and economic growth, though since the direction of the relation could also go from economic growth to globalization, causality in this relation has seldom been demonstrated clearly. While the earlier literature provided robust support for the strength of the relationship between globalization and economic growth, even before the global financial (GFC) crisis of 2008–2009, concerns started to be raised by Stiglitz (2002) and others that perhaps globalization had gone too far, inducing policy makers in different countries to become a little more protective rather than open to globalization.

From the Trade Globalization Indexes on the left side of Table 4.10, one can see considerable diversity in the patterns over time. Notably, the indexes for each of the East Asian countries rose substantially over time, at least doubling between 1970 and 2018 in each of the countries except Malaysia which started with one of the highest indexes of all the countries in 1970. Even for these East Asian countries, however, with the exception of Thailand, the indexes peaked sometime before 2018, most frequently in 2000, that is, before the Global Financial Crisis. For MENA countries the

Table 4.10 Globalization Indexes, 1970–2018

	Trade globalization index (de facto)						***Financial globalization index (de facto)***						***Financial globalization index (de jure)***
Country	***1970***	***1980***	***1990***	***2000***	***2010***	***2018***	***1970***	***1980***	***1990***	***2000***	***2010***	***2018***	***2018***
MENA non-major oil exporters	**44.4**	**52.3**	**57.2**	**54.4**	**62.4**	**59.8**	**36.8**	**47.5**	**55.2**	**56.8**	**58.0**	**57.0**	**52.5**
Djibouti		69.0	66.0	53.8	58.4	87.8		51.6	53.1	46.3	50.0	58.0	66.2
Egypt, Arab Rep.	49.3	50.8	49.8	43.0	52.8	53.7	14.5	43.1	52.7	41.1	47.2	53.1	50.8
Jordan	43.9	79.2	87.5	80.2	80.9	73.7	26.5	46.7	63.2	81.4	75.2	70.1	68.4
Lebanon	81.0	77.7	85.9	63.8	82.5	70.5	65.3	64.8	62.5	70.0	82.1	85.2	57.6
Morocco	29.2	28.7	33.1	47.1	64.3	67.4	19.4	28.8	42.8	45.1	51.3	51.1	49.2
Syrian Arab Republic	33.2	28.0	50.8	50.9	64.6	59.2	11.5	29.6	49.1	51.9	41.4	39.8	30.0
Tunisia	**38.7**	**57.7**	**61.8**	**56.1**	**66.9**	**66.3**	**36.8**	**43.0**	**55.4**	**57.9**	**64.2**	**62.2**	40.6
West Bank and Gaza	43.9	44.0	44.6	42.9	39.8	40.5	62.4	62.4	64.4	66.3	63.3	62.9	n.a.
Yemen, Rep.	35.7	35.6	35.3	51.8	51.6	18.7	57.8	57.4	53.6	51.3	47.0	30.3	56.8
MENA major oil exporters	**36.2**	**38.0**	**26.6**	**36.5**	**43.0**	**43.6**	**44.8**	**40.1**	**34.4**	**39.5**	**40.6**	**42.2**	**32.7**
Algeria	26.8	34.6	17.3	34.6	46.0	42.1	33.9	40.8	25.7	47.6	39.8	34.2	31.7
Iran, Islamic Rep.		24.5	22.7	31.2	25.9	25.9		15.9	8.4	15.8	19.8	20.7	29.6
Iraq	46.5	59.1	33.4	61.5	51.0	53.0	61.0	64.6	61.7	53.8	32.7	35.6	33.5
Libya	35.2	34.0	32.8	18.5	49.3	53.5	39.4	39.0	41.6	40.8	69.9	78.3	36.0

(Continued)

Table 4.10 Globalization Indexes, 1970–2018 *(Continued)*

	Trade globalization index (de facto)						Financial globalization index (de facto)						Financial globalization index (de jure)
Country	***1970***	***1980***	***1990***	***2000***	***2010***	***2018***	***1970***	***1980***	***1990***	***2000***	***2010***	***2018***	***2018***
MENA GCC	**48.6**	**68.7**	**63.5**	**68.0**	**75.1**	**76.2**	**57.9**	**59.1**	**66.5**	**65.5**	**78.4**	**80.9**	**67.4**
Bahrain	74.5	74.5	72.1	80.2	79.6	84.6	86.8	86.5	90.8	93.7	91.8	90.6	79.2
Kuwait	60.1	70.8	71.4	66.5	72.9	78.5	34.9	66.4	73.3	73.2	82.5	91.0	56.0
Oman	44.3	49.8	41.7	57.9	67.6	65.0	66.4	39.9	52.1	50.8	66.4	67.4	65.1
Qatar	67.7	67.1	52.9	59.7	66.2	73.7	74.2	69.1	71.4	74.4	85.7	85.2	68.4
Saudi Arabia	45.2	75.4	69.0	62.9	67.8	57.5	64.3	54.3	66.7	47.1	63.9	67.1	55.4
United Arab Emirates	73.3	74.5	73.7	81.0	96.3	98.0	21.3	38.6	44.9	53.8	80.0	84.1	82.5
East Asia	**27.6**	**43.2**	**46.6**	**65.7**	**61.8**	**60.5**	**26.6**	**36.1**	**43.6**	**56.1**	**57.8**	**58.6**	**57.2**
China	16.1	18.9	18.4	39.9	38.5	31.2	8.3	8.3	22.4	39.0	51.1	46.3	46.1
Indonesia	17.2	26.6	35.4	61.2	33.8	33.7	32.0	37.4	47.2	61.1	44.5	51.6	55.7
Korea, Rep.	20.5	56.9	37.4	54.9	69.4	62.4	18.5	37.3	22.6	38.2	52.0	55.7	69.9
Malaysia	61.4	72.5	80.8	89.4	87.4	85.3	45.6	57.4	69.2	74.3	78.5	76.4	64.6
Philippines	21.5	37.8	44.4	66.4	58.3	65.6	29.6	44.6	52.9	60.6	56.6	54.8	59.5
Thailand	28.7	46.9	63.2	82.5	83.3	85.0	25.8	31.3	47.3	63.6	64.1	66.5	47.7

Sources: KOF Swiss Economic Institute website. Gygli et al. (2019).

Note: The figures under 1970 for Bahrain, Qatar, and UAE are for the year 1971.

pattern over time has been much more diverse, falling since 1980 in Saudi Arabia and since 1990 in Lebanon and West Bank and Gaza, but peaking in 2018 in most of the other countries led by the UAE followed by Djibouti. Tunisia's Trade Globalization Index rose impressively from 38.7 in 1970 to 66.9 in 2010, ranked then as third highest among all MENA countries outside the GCC. Notice that these (de facto) indexes tended to be lower for some of the larger countries in each region such as Egypt, Algeria, and especially China, than in the smaller countries where trade is almost always much more important.[20]

From the Financial Globalization Indexes on the right-hand side of Table 4.10, one can see that their growth has tended to be even greater over time than for Trade Globalization. For each of the East Asian countries, this index grew by about 30 points between 1970 and its peak year. This growth was even more impressive in most of the MENA countries outside of both the GCC, Lebanon and West Bank and Gaza where international banking was already well developed by 1970 or at least by 1980. While in quite a few of both East Asian and MENA countries these indexes continued to grow all the way up to 2018, in Tunisia and especially in Jordan, Morocco, Algeria, Iraq, Yemen, and among East Asian countries Indonesia and the Philippines, they have declined in recent years.

Comparing the last two columns in the table with each other, that is, the '*de facto*' and the '*de jure*' indexes, one can see some interesting discrepancies. While in a majority of East Asian countries the '*de jure*' or more policy and institution-based indexes were higher than the more outcome-related *de facto* indexes[21] (Thailand and Korea being exceptions), notice that Tunisia along with Lebanon, Libya, and all GCC countries except the UAE, are countries where their policies and institutions are not deemed as conducive to Financial Globalization as their actual outcomes. Since in practice the '*de jure*' indexes often have the effect of inducing changes in subsequent *de facto* indexes, in the case of Tunisia, its comparatively low 'de-jure' index score in 2018 could be a predictor of a lower *de facto* score when new scores become available. The bottom line of these comparisons for Tunisia is that its progress on Globalization has been much less impressive in the case of Financial Globalization than in that of Trade Globalization and that especially in Financial Globalization from the policy and institutional '*de jure*' perspective it is has done even less well, in considerable contrast to most East Asian and GCC countries.

F. Adaptive but Broadly Predictable Policies and the Use of Both Market and Non-Market Mechanisms to Allocate Resources

Sixth, within its overall strategic developmental vision, Tunisia has consistently made use of some rather pragmatic and heterodox policies to help achieve its industrialization and economic diversification goals. There were two major reversals in policy: first, during the early 1960s when Tunisia moved toward a more socialist approach and, second, in the late 1960s when it reversed itself from that course. After that, however, the thrust of policies up to 2010 had been consistent and without major disruptions and reversals.

After its initial period of rather indiscriminate practice of import substitution, the Tunisian state has quite consistently leveraged global markets by making use of various elements of the more heterodox so-called two-track strategies that had been used in East Asia from the 1970s. Specifically, during both the second and third of the different periods identified in Chapter 3, mechanisms to encourage off-shore production and export of clothing and other manufactures via both domestic and foreign owned firms were developed. The key to their success was allowing duty-free imports of inputs, irrespective of the location of the activities, something that in many countries has proved to be administratively difficult to accomplish. As a result, elsewhere in the world most such schemes are confined to very specific geographic areas, typically in a special zone of a port city. By making it possible to exercise off-shore types of setups in more rural and interior areas where wage rates were lower, the Tunisian approach had the effect of lowering labor costs and reducing rural-urban migration. The pro-poor result of the program was further strengthened by the fact that the vast majority of its workers in this industry were women. If the government had opted for complete liberalization at that point, much of the industrial growth that had been obtained prior to this might well have gone bankrupt, and if so, the industrialization drive would have been hard to restart. Since this was, however, only one of the two tracks, it has contributed to the stability of the policy regime and made policy pronouncements more credible than they otherwise might have been.

In the period since 1990, Tunisia has made even greater use of some other policies which might be regarded as heterodox policies. First, the country signed a number of very distinctive preferential trade agreements, the most important one of which was its Association Agreement with the European Union, mutually freeing trade with European countries but continuing to apply high 'Most Favored Nation (MFN) tariffs' to the rest of the world. Second, it has made good use of a special deal with European automakers that allows duty free imports of cars into Tunisia on the condition that parts and components of an agreed-upon value would be purchased from producers in Tunisia. In the latter case, Tunisian authorities have provided the kind of incentives that helped make these new industries in Tunisia competitive.

Other examples of the heterodox two-track approach cited above are the use of special financial facilities to support SMEs, technological upgrading, debt consolidation, and trade facilitation activities. The same can be said about the unusually generous system of providing long-term finance for hotels with credit guarantees which allowed international tourism to spread rapidly throughout the country, and to provide a major source of export revenues.

G. Factors Common to All the Periods: Property Rights, Gender Equity, and Governance

Seventh and last among the factors contributing to Tunisia's long-term success in economic development are several other institutional characteristics, all related to state capacity and governance, that have stood out as having rather important effects over much of the more than sixty years since Tunisia's independence. Among these have been its rather continuous support to private entrepreneurs and private property rights, to a better business environment and to gender equity. Tables 4.11 and 4.12 provide comparable measures of relevance to these and other institutional characteristics for roughly the same set of countries as in the performance indicators of the previous tables.

The measures in Table 4.11 attempt to capture the strength of property rights, and closely related institutional characteristics, such as law and order (sometimes considered an indicator of strength of property rights enforcement, but sometimes also as a measure of state capacity). In the first four columns of the table are values of the Index of Property Rights provided by the well-known Index of Economic Freedom. As shown, Tunisia has had a score of 50 on this index since at least 1995, which put it above the MENA averages (at least of those outside the GCC) but below those of the East Asian average which in any case have been extremely volatile over the 1995–2021 period shown. The fact that Tunisia's scores on this same Index of Economic Freedom Property Rights Index have generally been much more stable over time than for any other country in the table is a sign of considerably greater consistency and credibility in such policy over time, presumably contributing more positively to confidence in property investments over time. In terms of the trends in this index over time, however, China, Malaysia and even Egypt, Jordan, Iran, Bahrain, and Qatar showed the largest improvements over time.

In the next six columns of the table, we present data taken from an agency more specialized in property rights, the Property Rights Alliance (PRA). The PRA has constructed its own International Property Rights Index (IPRI) from a number of different components, such as the Legal Aspects and the Judicial System, Protection of Physical Property (including land and other registries, and access to land) and Intellectual Property Rights (including patent protection, trademark and copyrights protection). Each component of the index is scored on a 0–10 scale. As such, the IFPRI is believed to be the most comprehensive index of property rights yet developed, even though its country coverage is as yet less comprehensive than the Index of Economic Freedom. In the first three of these six columns we present the IPRI Indexes for 2008, 2018, and 2021 (the latter only recently released). The data for year 2008 show rather clearly, that at least until the ousting of its long-standing political regime in 2011, Tunisia's IPRI of 6.7 was remarkably high, higher than that of any other MENA country except for the UAE (with a score of 6.9) and Korea (with a score of 6.8). That score was much above the average score of all regions including East Asia. However, according to the IPRI Tunisia, scores did fall somewhat after 2011 to a still very respectable 5.1 in 2021. From the changes since 2008 for the other countries, however, it can be seen that many of them raised their property rights index scores. This was especially the case for China and Indonesia among East Asian countries and for Bahrain, Egypt, Morocco, and even Algeria among MENA countries.

Given the quite different components that were integrated into the overall IPRI scores, to provide more insights into the strong and weak points in the next three columns of Table 4.11 we present the scores of each country on each of the three main components, that is, Legal and Judicial, Physical Property and Intellectual Property, for the most recent year 2021. The general pattern in the table is for the countries to receive higher score on the more traditional Physical Property Rights component than on either the Legal-Judicial or Intellectual Property Rights components. Tunisia is no exception in this respect. Notably, by 2021, Tunisia has fallen behind all six of the GCC countries on each of these components and behind all six of the East Asian countries on at least two of these component indexes. In view of the importance of Intellectual Property Rights for high tech industry and innovation, it may be somewhat alarming that China, Indonesia, Korea and Malaysia have all managed to achieve scores on the Intellectual Property Rights Index that are more than 1.5 points higher than that of Tunisia.

Finally, in the last column of the table is another somewhat related index generated by the PRA for Gender Equity in Property Rights. This index compares males and females in their access to land, to other property and to credit. This index also makes use of inheritance practices and social rights. Note that, at least in 2008, Tunisia's score was higher by far than any other MENA country and above the average for the six East Asian countries, again confirming Tunisia's long-standing commitment to gender equity.

While none of these property rights measures goes back to the 1950s or 1960s, on the basis of both the favorable initial conditions identified in Chapter 3 and the subsequent actions to protect such rights (not without some temporary reversals as in the 1960s), one can reasonably assume that these measures for the years 1995–2010 are representative of the property rights situation of Tunisia over the last 4–5 decades, prior to its possible deterioration in the last decade.

Table 4.12 presents the corresponding scores on several other well-known institutional indices from the International Country Risk Guide (ICRG) for selected years between 1994 and 2015, beginning with Government Stability and Socioeconomic Conditions in the first two sets of columns, followed by those for Military in Politics, Religious Tolerance, Ethnic Tensions,

Table 4.11 Property Rights Related Indices, 1995–2021

	IEF property rights (0–100)				***IPRI property rights index (0–10)***			***Components of IPRI property rights index (0–10)***			***PRA gender equality index (0–10)***
								Legal	***Physical Property***	***Intellectual Property***	
Country	***1995***	***2010***	***2017***	***2021***	***2008***	***2018***	***2021***	***2021***	***2021***	***2021***	***2008***
MENA Non-Major Oil Exporters	**40.0**	**38.6**	**45.5**	**47.9**	**6.7**	**4.9**	**5.0**	**3.9**	**6.5**	**4.5**	**7.3**
Djibouti				42.8							
Egypt, Arab Rep.	30.0	40.0	35.4	51.2	4.8	5.1	5.4	4.4	6.6	5.1	7.8
Jordan	40.0	55.0	60.1	66.2	5.8	6.2	6.2	5.5	7.4	5.6	5.6
Lebanon	30.0	30.0	43.8	42.3		4.3	4.2	2.9	6.2	3.6	
Morocco	70.0	40.0	55.0	67.5	5.1	5.6	5.8	4.7	7.2	5.6	6
Syrian Arab Republic	30.0	25.0	37.3	42.5							
Tunisia	**50.0**	**50.0**	**49.6**	**53.9**	**6.7**	**5.1**	**5.1**	**4.5**	**6.2**	**4.6**	**9.6**
West Bank and Gaza											
Yemen	30.0	30.0	37.3	16.5		2.8	3	1.4	5.4	2.6	
MENA Major Oil Exporters	**20.0**	**16.7**	**28.7**	**32.2**	**4.0**	**4.4**	**4.4**	**3.2**	**5.7**	**4.1**	**6.1**
Algeria	50.0	30.0	38.2	34.0	4	4.1	4.6	3.3	6	4.2	6.1
Iran, Islamic Rep.	10.0	10.0	32.4	33.5		4.7	4.1	3	5.4	4	
Iraq	10.0		37.3	44.8							
Libya	10.0	10.0	6.8	16.5							
MENA GCC	**75.0**	**52.5**	**65.7**	**69.2**	**5.8**	**6.5**	**6.5**	**5.9**	**7.7**	**5.7**	**5.7**
Bahrain	60.0	60.0	64.2	71.5	5.2	6.2	6.3	5.4	7.9	6.7	4.8
Kuwait	90.0	50.0	55.5	57.4	5.6	5.5	5.8	5.4	6.7	5.1	8.7
Oman	70.0	50.0	60.8	68.7		6.3	6.6	6.5	7.7	5.5	
Qatar	50.0	65.0	74.8	68.3	6.5	7.2	6.8	6.5	8.1	5.5	
Saudi Arabia	90.0	40.0	62.0	68.7		6.2	6.4	5.8	8	5.5	
United Arab Emirates	90.0	50.0	76.7	80.8	6.9	7.6	7.1				3.6

(Continued)

Table 4.11 Property Rights Related Indices, 1995–2021 *(Continued)*

	IEF property rights (0–100)				*IPRI property rights index (0–10)*			*Components of IPRI property rights index (0–10)*			*PRA gender equality index (0–10)*
								Legal	*Physical Property*	*Intellectual Property*	
Country	***1995***	***2010***	***2017***	***2021***	***2008***	***2018***	***2021***	***2021***	***2021***	***2021***	***2008***
East Asia	**63.3**	**41.7**	**60.0**	**67.4**	**5.3**	**5.9**	**5.9**	**5.1**	**6.7**	**5.9**	**9.2**
China	30.0	20.0	48.3	62.2	4.7	5.9	6.1	4.7	7.1	6.3	9.9
Indonesia	50.0	30.0	48.3	59.4	4.1	5.3	5.3	5.3	4.5	7	8.8
Korea, Rep.	90.0	70.0	77.8	80.7	6.8	6.4	6.7	6.2	7.3	6.5	8
Malaysia	70.0	55.0	85.3	85.1	6.2	6.5	6.7	6	7.9	6.2	8.5
Philippines	50.0	30.0	49.2	57.0	4.5	5.2	5	3.7	6.5	4.9	10
Thailand	90.0	45.0	51.3	60.0	5.4	5.9	5.4	4.6	7	4.6	9.9

Sources and Notes:

The Heritage Foundation: Index of Economic Freedom (IEF) Reports

Index of Economic Freedom (IEF) Property Rights Index with values ranging from 0 to 100.

Property Rights Alliance (PRA) International Property Rights Index (IPRI) Reports.

IPRI represents a 0–10 index based on 0–1 scores on ten different sub-indicators covering the Legal and Political Environment, Physical Property Rights and Intellectual Property Rights.

Gender equality (GE) in property rights Index based on three subcomponents covering (1) women's access to land, other property and credit, (2) inheritance practices, and (3) women's social rights. It ranges from 0 to 10.

Table 4.12 Political Risk Institutional Indexes from the International Country Risk Guide, 1984–2015

	Government stability (0–12)					*Socioeconomic conditions (0–12)*				
Country	*1984*	*1990*	*2000*	*2010*	*2015*	*1984*	*1990*	*2000*	*2010*	*2015*
MENA Non-major oil exporters	**5.6**	**6.6**	**9.6**	**9.1**	**6.7**	**5.8**	**3.9**	**5.6**	**5.2**	**4.5**
Djibouti										
Egypt, Arab Rep.	7.8	8.4	4	8.3	8.1	6	4.5	6	5	4.8
Jordan	7.1	5.9	10.5	9.1	8	9.8	3	5	4.2	4
Lebanon	2.5	2.5	10.2	8.1	6.7	3.8	1	5	5.5	5
Morocco	6.3	8	10	8.5	7.1	5	6.7	4	6.5	5.5
Syrian Arab Republic	5.7	7.3	10.5	10	6	5	4	6	5	3.5
Tunisia	**4.2**	**7.3**	**11**	**10.9**	**6.5**	**5**	**4**	**6**	**6**	**5**
WBG										
Yemen		3,8	11	9	4.6		3.8	7.3	4.5	3.8
MENA major oil exporters	**5.3**	**6.1**	**9.8**	**7.5**	**6.8**	**5.4**	**4.8**	**3.3**	**4.0**	**4.1**
Algeria	7.4	8	9.8	7.3	7.3	7.3	5.4	3	5	5.5
Iran, Islamic Rep.	5.3	6.8	9.2	5.3	7.2	4.7	4.9	5	5.5	6.2
Iraq	3.5	3.2	10.1	7.1	7	4	3	1	0.5	0.5
Libya	4.8	6.2	10	10.4	5.6	5.6	5.8	4	5	4
MENA GCC	**6.1**	**5.5**	**10.5**	**9.8**	**8.8**	**6.8**	**6.4**	**7.2**	**8.0**	**7.6**
Bahrain	5	6	11	8	7.8	6	3.7	6	7	6.5
Kuwait	6	4.3	10	7	6.6	7	5.8	8	9	8.9
Oman	6	6.3	11	11	9.5	6	6.3	9	7	6
Qatar	5	5	11	11.5	10.5	7.6	7.8	6	8	8
Saudi Arabia	7.3	6.2	9.8	10	8.4	8.6	8	6	7.5	6.8
UAE	7	5.3	10	11	10	5.7	6.8	8	9.5	9.5
East Asia	**6.9**	**5.3**	**10.0**	**7.8**	**7.2**	**7.3**	**7.1**	**4.7**	**7.5**	**7.3**
China	9	4	12	10.2	8.9	9	4.6	4	8	7
Indonesia	7	5.8	8.6	8	6.5	4.5	8.6	2.2	6.3	5.9
Korea, Rep. of	7	8.7	9.3	8.5	6.2	10	7.5	6	8.8	9.7
Malaysia	7.5	6.2	11	6.9	7.5	8.7	9.2	5.9	10	9.8
Philippines	3.3	1	8.9	6.5	6.8	4.7	3.8	5	5	4.5
Thailand	7.8	5.8	10	6.4	7.4	7	9	5	7	7

Source: ICRG International Country Risk Guide.

Note: Scales for each variable are indicated in parentheses next to each heading.

Internal Conflict, Democratic Accountability, Investment Profile, Law and Order, Bureaucratic Quality, and Freedom from Corruption. These cover a wide variety of governance characteristics, many of which relate to 'State Capacity.' As can easily be seen, there were considerable changes over time in Tunisia's scores on most of these indicators, as well as some very distinctive differences between them and also in the comparisons between

Military in politics (0–6)					*Religious tensions (0–6)*				
1984	*1990*	*2000*	*2010*	*2015*	*1984*	*1990*	*2000*	*2010*	*2015*
2.4	**2.4**	**3.6**	**3.1**	**2.7**	**1.7**	**2.7**	**3.7**	**4.1**	**3.5**
2	3	3	0.9	0	2	3	2	3	2.5
2.8	3	5	5	4.5	2	2.4	3	4	4
2	0.5	3	2	2	1	1	3	2.5	2.5
2.6	3	4	4	4	2	2	4	5	5
1	2	2	2	2	1	3	5	5	3.5
3.9	**3**	**4**	**4**	**4**	**2**	**4**	**5**	**5**	**4**
	2	4	4	2.7		3.5	4	4	2.8
1.9	**2.3**	**2.0**	**2.8**	**2.5**	**2.1**	**2.5**	**2.8**	**2.6**	**2.5**
2.4	3	0	3	2.5	5	3.6	0	2.5	2.5
3.2	4	5	5	4.5	0	1.2	2	2	2
1	1	0	0	0	2.2	3	5	1	1
1	1	3	3	3	1.3	2	4	5	4.5
3.8	**3.7**	**4.5**	**4.3**	**4.5**	**2.4**	**2.7**	**3.3**	**3.8**	**3.7**
5	5	3	3	3	3	3	3	3.5	3
4	3	5	4	5	2	3	2	4	3.8
2.8	2	5	5	5	4	4	4	4	4
4	4	4	4	4	3	3	4	4	4
3.4	4	5	5	5	1	1	3	3.5	3.5
3.8	4	5	5	5	1.3	2	4	4	4
2.6	**2.4**	**3.6**	**3.5**	**3.4**	**3.8**	**3.8**	**3.8**	**3.5**	**3.3**
3	2	2	3	3	5	6	3.2	5	4
1	0.3	1.8	2.6	2.5	2	2	1.5	1	1
2	4.9	5	4	4	5	5	6	6	6
5.7	5	5	5	5	3.3	2	4	4	4
2	1	4	3	3	2.7	3	3	3	3
1.8	1	4	3.5	3	5	5	5	2	2

(Continued)

Tunisia's scores and those of other MENA countries and the same six East Asian countries.

A rather distinctive pattern for Tunisia in general was for its governance scores to improve from 1984 to 2000 but then in most cases to decline after 2000, and especially after the Arab Uprisings events of 2011. A notable exception, of course, was Democratic Accountability. In any case, between 1984 and 2000 Tunisia' scores improved for Government Stability,

Table 4.12 Political Risk Institutional Indexes from the International Country Risk Guide, 1984–2015 *(Continued)*

	Ethnic tensions (0–6)					*Internal conflict (0–12)*				
Country	*1984*	*1990*	*2000*	*2010*	*2015*	*1984*	*1990*	*2000*	*2010*	*2015*
MENA Non-major oil exporters	**3.2**	**3.5**	**5.3**	**4.4**	**4.1**	**4.6**	**6.1**	**9.1**	**8.2**	**6.0**
Djibouti										
Egypt, Arab Rep.	4	3	6	5	5	7	5.8	8	7.9	5.6
Jordan	3	3	5	4.4	3.5	6.1	4.6	7.8	9.5	6.5
Lebanon	0	0.2	5	5	5	0.2	1.5	9	7.1	5.5
Morocco	3	4	5	4.5	4.5	4.7	6	9.3	7.5	7.2
Syrian Arab Republic	3.9	4	6	3	2.5	3.9	7	11.9	10	5
Tunisia	**5**	**6**	**5**	**5**	**5**	**5.4**	**9**	**11**	**10.2**	**7.9**
WBG										
Yemen		4	5	4	3.2		9	7	5.5	4.6
MENA major oil exporters	**2.5**	**3.0**	**3.2**	**3.6**	**3.6**	**4.8**	**5.8**	**4.0**	**8.6**	**7.0**
Algeria	3.9	4	2	3.5	3.5	9.4	9.1	4.9	8.5	7.8
Iran, Islamic Rep.	1	3	5	3.5	3.5	2	5	7.2	8.1	8.8
Iraq	1.1	1	2	2.5	2.5	3	3	3.2	6.2	5.2
Libya	4	4	3.7	5	5	4.7	6	0.8	11.5	6
MENA GCC	**2.7**	**3.0**	**4.8**	**5.1**	**5.0**	**5.7**	**6.2**	**10.8**	**9.3**	**8.6**
Bahrain	2	2	4	4.5	4	5	5	8	9.8	7
Kuwait	2.3	1.7	5	5	4.8	5.6	5	11	8.5	8.3
Oman	4	4	5	5	5	8	8	12	10	9.5
Qatar	4	4	6	6	6	7	7	12	8.5	9.5
Saudi Arabia	2	4	5	5	5	4.7	7.3	9.9	8.8	8
UAE	1.8	2	4	5	5	4.1	5	12	10	9
East Asia	**3.5**	**2.7**	**4.3**	**3.6**	**3.9**	**8.0**	**7.7**	**8.2**	**8.7**	**8.3**
China	4	3	4	3.5	3.5	10.1	10	10	9.2	7
Indonesia	2.8	2	2	2	2	8	6	4.1	8.4	8.5
Korea, Rep. of	6	4	6	6	6	9.4	8	9.6	9.7	10
Malaysia	2	1	4	4	4	10	10	9	9.7	9.5
Philippines	2	2	5	4	4	2.6	4	6.5	7.5	7.8
Thailand	4	4	5	2	4	7.8	8	10	7.8	6.7

Socioeconomic Conditions, Military in Politics, Religious Tensions, Internal Conflict, Investment Profile and Law and Order. In some of these cases, the improvements were large, the scores approximately or more than doubling as in Government Stability, Religious Tensions, Internal Conflict, Investment Profile, and Law and Order. The exceptions were a slight decline between 1984 and 2000 in Democratic Accountability and no change in Bureaucratic Quality and Freedom from Corruption. With

Democratic Accountability (0–6)					*Investment Profile (0–12)*				
1984	*1990*	*2000*	*2010*	*2015*	*1984*	*1990*	*2000*	*2010*	*2015*
2.1	**3.0**	**3.0**	**3.0**	**3.3**	**5.6**	**3.8**	**8.0**	**8.0**	**6.9**
3.3	4.7	2	2	2	6.2	2.4	10	6.5	6.9
1.8	3.6	4	3	3	8	2	10	10	9
2	1	5	5	5	3.8	3.1	4	8.5	7.9
2	2	3	4.5	4.5	6	7	9	9.2	8
1.2	2	1	1	1	4.4	3.1	5	5.5	4
2.5	**4**	**2**	**2**	**4.5**	**5.3**	**5.2**	**10**	**8.5**	**7.9**
	3.5	4	3.5	2.8		4	8	8	4.8
1.8	**2.8**	**1.7**	**3.1**	**3.1**	**5.1**	**3.9**	**6.2**	**7.4**	**6.9**
2	4.6	2.6	3.5	3.5	7.4	3.9	6.9	7.8	8.5
1.6	2	3.3	4	3	5	4.2	5	4.9	6.2
1.9	2.5	0	4	4	3.4	3.3	4	7.7	6.5
1.7	2	1	1	2	4.7	4.3	8.8	9	6.5
2.1	**2.0**	**1.3**	**2.3**	**2.4**	**7.6**	**6.0**	**8.0**	**10.9**	**9.4**
2	2	0	4.5	3.5	6.8	4.9	9	11.5	4.5
2	1.2	3	3	3	8	6.2	5	10.5	9
3	3	1	1	2	8.4	6.5	8	11.5	11
2	2	2	2	2	6	6	10	10	10
1.8	2	0	1	1.1	8.7	5.9	8.7	11	10.3
1.6	2	2	2.5	2.5	7.7	6.7	7	11	11.5
3.3	**3.4**	**3.7**	**4.4**	**4.2**	**7.4**	**6.5**	**7.5**	**8.5**	**7.9**
4	3.3	1	1.5	1.5	8.6	5	8.4	6.5	6
3	3	4	5	4	6.5	8.3	5	8.9	7.4
2	2	6	6	5.5	8.8	7.4	7.6	10	10
5	5	2.1	4.5	4	7.5	7.3	7.2	9.3	8.2
2.8	3.8	5	5	5	5.1	3.2	8	9	8.2
3	3	4	4.5	5	8	7.6	8.7	7.5	7.5

(Continued)

the notable exception of Democratic Accountability, by 2000, Tunisia scores on these indexes had exceeded the average scores of non-GCC MENA and East Asian countries and had become among the very highest scores among MENA countries. Yet, after 2000 and especially after 2010, there were declines in most of these indexes, especially sharp ones in the case of Government Stability, Internal Conflict, Investment Profile and Freedom from Corruption. The very notable exception was in Democratic

Table 4.12 Political Risk Institutional Indexes from the International Country Risk Guide, 1984–2015 *(Continued)*

	Law and Order (0–6)				
Country	***1984***	***1990***	***2000***	***2010***	***2015***
MENA Non-major oil exporters	**1.6**	**2.0**	**4.3**	**4.1**	**3.9**
Djibouti					
Egypt, Arab Rep.	2.7	2	4	3.5	3
Jordan	2	2	4	4	4
Lebanon	1	1	4	4	4
Morocco	2	2	6	5	4.5
Syrian Arab Republic	1.6	2	5	5	4.5
Tunisia	**2**	**2**	**5**	**5**	**5**
WBG					
Yemen	0	3	2	2	2
MENA major oil exporters	**1.4**	**1.8**	**3.3**	**3.1**	**3.1**
Algeria	2	2.2	2	3	3
Iran, Islamic Rep.	1.7	1	5	4	4
Iraq	1	2	2	1.5	1.5
Libya	1	2	4	4	4
MENA GCC	**3.3**	**3.2**	**5.0**	**4.8**	**4.6**
Bahrain	4	4	5	5	4.5
Kuwait	2.7	1.8	5	5	4
Oman		4	5	5	5
Qatar		3	6	5	5
Saudi Arabia	3.7	3.6	5	5	5
UAE	2.7	3	4	4	4
East Asia	**2.7**	**2.6**	**3.8**	**3.5**	**3.3**
China	2.9	3	4.8	4.1	3.5
Indonesia	1.5	2.6	2	3	2.5
Korea, Rep. of	3	2	4	5	5
Malaysia	4.7	3	3	4	4
Philippines	1	1	4	2.5	2.5
Thailand	3	4	5	2.5	2.5

Accountability, in which by 2015 Tunisia had become tied for the highest (with Morocco) among MENA countries and well above the average of the East Asian countries.

Tables 4.13a and 4.13b present comparable scores on nine different Doing Business Indicators, namely Starting a Business, Getting Electricity, Dealing

Bureaucratic Quality (0–4)					*Freedom from Corruption (0–6)*				
1984	*1990*	*2000*	*2010*	*2015*	*1984*	*1990*	*2000*	*2010*	*2015*
1.6	**1.6**	**1.7**	**1.8**	**1.8**	**2.6**	**2.3**	**2.5**	**2.4**	**2.0**
2	2	2	2	2	2	2	2	2	2
2	2	2	2	2	3	3	3	3	3
1	0	2	2	2	3	1	1	1.8	2
3	2	2	2	2	2	2	3	3	2.5
1	1	1	1.5	1.5	2	2	2.8	2	1
2	**2**	**2**	**2**	**2**	**3**	**3**	**3**	**2.8**	**2.5**
0	2	1	1	1	3	3	3	2	1
1.0	**1.5**	**1.3**	**1.6**	**1.5**	**3.0**	**3.0**	**2.8**	**1.6**	**1.4**
1	3	2	2	2	3	3.9	2	1.9	2
1	1	2	2	2	3	3	4	1.6	1.5
1	1	0	1.5	1.5	3	2	1	1.5	1
1	1	1	1	0.5	3	3	4	1.5	1
2.2	**2.2**	**2.2**	**2.2**	**2.2**	**2.8**	**2.7**	**2.3**	**2.7**	**3.3**
3	3	2	2	2	3	3	3	2.4	2.6
2	2	2	2	2	3	3	2	3	3
2	2	2	2	2	3	3	3	2.5	3
1	1	2	2	2	2	2	2	2.5	4
3	3	2	2	2	3	2	2	2.4	3
2	2	3	3	3	3	3	2	3.3	4
2.0	**1.8**	**2.7**	**2.5**	**2.5**	**2.5**	**2.6**	**2.4**	**2.4**	**2.4**
2	2	2	2	2	4	4	1.1	2	2
0	0	3	2	2	1	0.3	1.9	3	3
3	3	3	3	3	2	2	3	3	2.5
3	2	3	3	3	5	4	3	2.5	2.5
1	0	3	3	3	0	2	2.4	2	2.5
3	3.5	2	2	2	3	3	2.8	2	2

with Construction Permits, Getting Credit, Registering Private Property, Paying Taxes, Protecting Minority Investors, Trading Across Borders, and Resolving Insolvencies. Table 4.13a provides the scores for the earlier period 2004–2015, for which the indicators are comparable over time since the same methodology was used. These indicators, unfortunately, do not go

Table 4.13a Doing Business Scores, 2004–2015

Country	*Starting a business*		*Getting electricity*		*Dealing with construction Permits*		*Getting credit*		*Registering property*		*Protecting minority investors rights*		*Paying taxes*		*Trading across borders*		*Resolving insolvency*		*Overall ease of doing business*	
	2004–2008	*2015*	*2010*	*2015*	*2004–2008*	*2015*	*2004–2008*	*2014*	*2004–2008*	*2015*	*2006*	*2014*	*2006–2008*	*2016*	*2006–2008*	*2015*	*2004–2008*	*2015*	*2010*	*2014*
MENA non-major oil exporters	**38.5**	**76.2**	**74.5**	**75.9**	**51.3**	**61.3**	**16.4**	**39.1**	**58.2**	**63.6**	**37**	**43**	**65.1**	**74.1**	**60.1**	**72.5**	**35.4**	**36.4**	**56.0**	**57.5**
Djibouti	24.4	62.8	38.8	51.6	63.4	60.7	6.3	12.5	47.9	50.7	23.3	23.3	82.5	75.4	50.8	78.6	42.1	48	45.7	50.5
Egypt, Arab Rep.	33	81.2	81.4	82.6	25	63	18.8	56.3	31.7	64.3	33.3	36.7	41.1	58.9	48.3	71.6	33.6	39.3	57.2	59.9
Jordan	23.8	85	82.2	82.6	36	61.7	12.5	12.5	57.9	63.5	30	30	89.4	81.3	60	78.9	30	30.2	56.3	57.6
Lebanon	53.7	79.8	86.5	86.8	41.5	42.4	18.8	50	63	63.2	50	50	79.4	81.7	63.3	72	26.5	29.9	60.2	61.1
Morocco	46.8	88.7	75	74.4	70	81.3	18.8	50	57.1	58.3	26.7	46.7	57.8	78.9	70.5	84.6	37.3	33.8	60.4	64.8
Syrian Arab Republic	43	68.4	77.1	77.9	44.4	58.1	6.3	25	54.2	55.5	43.3	46.7	67.5	67.9	55.4	58.6	31	27.6	50.4	46.8
Tunisia	**59.2**	**81.6**	**82.7**	**84.6**	**63.8**	**71.5**	**25**	**50**	**67.6**	**69.1**	**33.3**	**56.7**	**60.4**	**75.4**	**77.2**	**80.4**	**54**	**54.7**	**66.5**	**68.4**
West Bank and Gaza	47.9	64.3	75.5	75.9	37.4	37.4	25	56.3	70	68.5	53.3	53.3	73.8	80.3	64.8	64.4			50.1	52.3
Yemen	15	73.6	71.3	66.7	80.1	75.4			74.6	79.2	40	40	33.6	66.7	50.3	63.5	28.7	27.5	57	56.4
MENA major oil exporters	**67.6**	**72.6**	**66.3**	**69.7**	**40.9**	**61.2**	**25.0**	**31.3**	**56.0**	**59.7**	**29**	**34**	**59.2**	**61.2**	**32.1**	**50.8**	**42.5**	**43.2**	**50.7**	**47.7**
Algeria	68.1	74.6	62	60	35.2	50.5	18.8	18.8	38.3	50.7	30	30	32.2	44.7	49.6	64.2	49.2	49.2	48.8	48.7
Iran, Islamic Rep.	63.4	67.5	60.8	67	17.3	62.4	43.8	62.5	65.8	65.9	30	36.7	65.6	67.8	38.3	56.8	35.7	37.2	55.9	57.9
Iraq	71.3	74	76	72.7	70.3	70.8	12.5	12.5	63.9	62.6	43.3	43.3	79.8	77.3	8.3	20.5			47.3	48.6
Libya		74.3		79.1							13.3	26.7		54.8		61.7				35.4

(Continued)

Table 4.13a Doing Business Scores, 2004–2015 *(Continued)*

Country	*Starting a business*		*Getting electricity*		*Dealing with construction Permits*		*Getting credit*		*Registering property*		*Protecting minority investors rights*		*Paying taxes*		*Trading across borders*		*Resolving insolvency*		*Overall ease of doing business*	
	2004–2008	*2015*	*2010*	*2015*	*2004–2008*	*2015*	*2004–2008*	*2014*	*2004–2008*	*2015*	*2006*	*2014*	*2006–2008*	*2016*	*2006–2008*	*2015*	*2004–2008*	*2015*	*2010*	*2014*
MENA GCC	**58.3**	**77.4**	**81.1**	**82.5**	**68.4**	**74.2**	**27.1**	**51.1**	**82.6**	**84.1**	**48**	**53**	**93.4**	**96.3**	**72.6**	**77.6**	**39.9**	**41.1**	**66.1**	**68.3**
Bahrain	72.1	76.1	79	79	71.9	72.7	37.5	43.8	90.4	88.7	50	50	87.8	94.4	74.6	77.3	42.8	44.2	66.3	67.3
Kuwait	63.3	70.4	70.7	70.8	43.2	52.8	37.5	43.8	64.3	65.6	50	53.3	92.5	92.5	60.7	68	38.4	39.1	60.3	61.2
Oman	48.4	75	82.3	82.4	73.2	76.3	25	56.3	78.7	81.8	50	50	93.2	92.4	72.9	78	41.8	43.9	65.6	68.6
Qatar	81.2	80.6	84	84	80.5	80.5	18.8	43.8	83.8	83.8	43.3	43.3	100	99.4	73	77.8	37	37.9	66.2	68.7
Saudi Arabia	20.8	74	81.6	81.5	67.6	76.4	18.8	62.5	87.8	87.8	56.7	66.7	92.9	99.6	70.3	73			66.1	67.6
United Arab Emirates	63.9	88.5	89	97.4	73.7	86.4	25	56.3	90.7	96.7	40	53.3	93.9	99.4	84	91.5	39.4	40.4	71.8	76.1
East Asia	**67.3**	**79.4**	**90.9**	**85.6**	**64.7**	**64.3**	**59.4**	**71.9**	**63.9**	**68.5**	**59**	**65**	**67.7**	**74.3**	**74.3**	**82.2**	**53.7**	**65.9**	**71.1**	**70.7**
China		80.9		66.4		30.7				74.4	43.3	50		64.4		71.7		55.3		61
Indonesia		64.1		78.2		56.8				60.7	56.7	60		67.1		77.5		67.7		62
Korea, Rep.	58.6	91.9	99.8	99.8	85.6	86	68.8	75	68.3	71	60	66.7	75.9	84.5	78.6	93.5	81.1	82.2	80.9	83
Malaysia	72.6	89.3	90.4	92.5	53.4	80.7	87.5	100	50.8	71.2	86.7	90	70.3	84.3	88.6	89.9	39.4	62.5	74.6	80.9
Philippines	62.3	67.2	87.6	90.8	54.7	61.6	25	50	62.9	62.8	43.3	43.3	57.3	66.9	72.6	77.2	35.1	55.2	55.2	62.2
Thailand	75.7	82.7	85.8	85.9	65.2	69.8	56.3	62.5	73.6	70.9	63.3	80	67.4	78.6	57.4	83.6	59	72.2	73.8	75.3

Source: World Bank, Doing Business Database.

Notes: Scores are calculated in such a way as to range from 0 to 100 from the worst to best performer on any indicator. Methodology used for various indicators in Doing Business Reports 2004 to 2014.

back to earlier decades so as to be comparable over time to the many other indicators presented in preceding tables. Nevertheless, since development of the private sector is the area in which many analysts[22] have said that MENA countries are the weakest, even if available only since 2004,[23] the comparisons between Tunisia and both other MENA countries and East Asian countries over this period is of considerable relevance to our overall comparisons of Tunisia with the same sets of MENA and East Asian countries.

Similar to the familiar pattern of the earlier tables, Tunisia ranks among the top MENA countries, and at least not too far from the East Asian country average, on most of these indicators. For 2004 or the earliest available year after that, Tunisia received scores that were below the average of those of the East Asian and GCC countries for most indicators but were above those of other MENA countries and at least one of the East Asian countries. But for almost all indicators, Tunisia made considerable improvements so that by about 2015 Tunisia's scores on these indicators were better than almost all non-GCC MENA countries. Three notable exceptions were Tunisia's relatively very low scores for Protecting Minority Shareholders Rights, Getting Credit and Resolving Insolvency. The latter two are undoubtedly interrelated, since if insolvency of a firm cannot be easily resolved, it suggests that banks may be more reluctant to provide credit to firms. Note also that Resolving Insolvency was the one such indicator for which Tunisia made no significant improvement between 2004–2008 and 2015, leaving it in 2015 behind all six of the East Asian countries, although above all other MENA countries. As indicated in the last column of Table 4.13a, by 2014 Tunisia's overall score on the Ease of Doing Business indicator was sufficiently high to exceed those of all other countries except Oman, Qatar and the UAE among MENA countries and Korea, Malaysia, and Thailand among East Asian countries.

Table 4.13b provides the same indicators but for the most recent period 2015–2019 in which a revised methodology was used in constructing them but which are again comparable among each other over time. Between 2015 and 2019, Tunisia seems to have continued to make some progress in terms of reforming its institutions relevant to firms and business, but its progress has become slower than for most comparator countries. Indeed, on the overall Ease of Doing Business indicator Tunisia's score fell to below Morocco, Bahrain, Oman, and the UAE among MENA countries and below all except Philippines among East Asian countries. It failed to make any progress on either Resolving Insolvency or Paying Taxes and as a result found itself behind Djibouti and all East Asian countries on Resolving Insolvency, and behind Djibouti, Jordan, Lebanon, Morocco Syria, West Bank, and Gaza and all GCC countries among MENA countries and all East Asian countries on Paying Taxes. Table 4.13c provides further data on institutional characteristics

Table 4.13b Doing Business Scores, 2014–2019

Country	***Starting a business***		***getting electricity***		***Dealing with Construction permits***		***Getting credit***		***Registering property***		***Protecting minority investors rights***		***Paying taxes***		***Trading across borders***		***Resolving insolvency***		***Overall ease of doing business***	
	2015	***2019***	***2015***	***2019***	***2015***	***2019***	***2014***	***2019***	***2016***	***2019***	***2014***	***2019***	***2016***	***2019***	***2015***	***2019***	***2015***	***2019***	***2016***	***2019***
MENA non-major oil exporters	**76.2**	**81.1**	**64.9**	**71.1**	**66.0**	**67.1**	**33.8**	**46.3**	**57.9**	**59.6**	**41**	**50**	**68.3**	**68.9**	**64.7**	**64.3**	**36.4**	**39.6**	**53.1**	**55.9**
Djibouti	62.8	84.0	38.7	64.2	63.9	69	5	25	40.5	58.2	14	52	62.8	62.7	59.4	59.4	48	60.9	44.3	58.4
Egypt, Arab Rep.	81.2	83.8	61.9	71.4	70.6	70.8	50	65	54.2	55	40	62	50.8	52.6	51	42.2	39.3	42.3	54.7	58.5
Jordan	85	84.4	77.6	80.5	64.6	59.9	45	50	66.4	66.4	42	50	69.9	71.7	78.9	79	30.2	30.3	56.7	61.3
Lebanon	79.8	78.6	65.1	62.7	55.2	54.2	40	40	60	59.4	40	40	68.1	67.9	57.9	57.9	29.9	29.5	54.7	54.4
Morocco	88.7	93	80.8	81.3	82.6	82.5	40	45	59.7	59.4	54	64	83.8	85.7	81	84.8	33.8	52.8	67.4	71.7
Syrian Arab Republic	68.4	81	58.4	52.1			15	15	50.3	45.2	54	54	74	74	29.9	29.8	27.6	21.1	43	41.5
Tunisia	**81.6**	**88.5**	**82.2**	**82.4**	**73.7**	**77.1**	**40**	**50**	**61.9**	**62.7**	**56**	**62**	**62.2**	**62.2**	**72.5**	**74.6**	**54.7**	**54.2**	**64.6**	**67.2**
West Bank and Gaza	64.3	69.4	69.4	74.2	48	56	35	80	62.7	65	44	44	69.2	68.9	86.7	86.7			54.2	59.7
Yemen	73.6	67	50.1		69				65.2	65.2	26	26	74.1	74.1			27.5	25.9	38.4	30.7
MENA major oil exporters	**72.6**	**74.0**	**59.3**	**65.5**	**63.2**	**67.7**	**27.5**	**30.0**	**54.8**	**57.0**	**31**	**31**	**56.7**	**60.1**	**39.2**	**47.0**	**43.2**	**42.4**	**43.8**	**46.1**
Algeria	74.6	77.9	57.5	71.9	57.9	64.6	10	10	43.8	44.3	20	20	46	53.9	27.7	38.4	49.2	49.2	44.2	48.5
Iran, Islamic Rep.	67.5	67.8	65.9	69.3	69.3	70.8	45	50	64.9	69	40	40	53.8	59.5	45.9	66.2	37.2	35.6	55.4	58.6
Iraq	74	76.5	54.5	61.7	62.3	67.6			55.8	57.7	46	46	63.3	63.5	25.3	25.3			42.9	44.7
Libya	74.3	73.6	59.3	59.1							18	18	63.6	63.6	57.9	57.9			32.6	32.7

(Continued)

Table 4.13b Doing Business Scores, 2014–2019 *(Continued)*

Country	*Starting a business*		*getting electricity*		*Dealing with Construction permits*		*Getting credit*		*Registering property*		*Protecting minority investors rights*		*Paying taxes*		*Trading across borders*		*Resolving insolvency*		*Overall ease of doing business*	
	2015	*2019*	*2015*	*2019*	*2015*	*2019*	*2014*	*2019*	*2016*	*2019*	*2014*	*2019*	*2016*	*2019*	*2015*	*2019*	*2015*	*2019*	*2016*	*2019*
MENA GCC	**77.4**	**87.4**	**76.0**	**82.3**	**75.9**	**76.2**	**36.7**	**50.0**	**78.0**	**80.6**	**54**	**61**	**91.8**	**91.7**	**64.8**	**67.7**	**41.1**	**43.2**	**65.9**	**68.9**
Bahrain	76.1	89.6	74.9	74.8	74.5	73.4	35	45	81.1	86.2	52	64	94.4	93.9	75.3	77.8	44.2	44.6	66.6	70.1
Kuwait	70.4	81.4	68.7	71.8	62.9	61.4	35	45	63	68.4	60	64	92.5	92.5	48.8	50.5	39.1	39.3	60.7	62.6
Oman	75	93.4	61.8	86.5	75.6	75.1	35	35	74.7	71.1	52	52	90.6	90.2	74.3	79.2	43.9	44.1	66.3	68.8
Qatar	80.6	86	78.6	81.1	80.3	84.2	30	45	82.4	84.1	44	28	99.4	99.4	69.2	71.5	37.9	38.1	66.5	66.7
Saudi Arabia	74	80.1	76.8	79.9	77.3	76.7	45	60	78.2	84.1	60	80	74.7	75	48.5	54.3			59.2	63.8
United Arab Emirates	88.5	94.1	95	99.9	84.8	86.5	40	70	88.8	89.6	54	78	99.4	99.4	72.7	72.7	40.4	49.7	76.3	81.6
East Asia	**79.4**	**85.1**	**83.6**	**94.0**	**66.2**	**74.1**	**52.5**	**63.3**	**67.4**	**70.6**	**64**	**71**	**70.1**	**74.9**	**77.4**	**80.7**	**65.9**	**67.6**	**69.5**	**74.7**
China	80.9	93.4	65.4	92	38	65.2	50	60	74.5	80.8	52	62	60.5	67.9	70.7	83.4	55.3	55.8	63.1	74
Indonesia	64.1	79.4	75	86.4	64.3	65.9	50	70	53.2	60	60	70	67.5	68.4	62.8	66.5	67.7	67.9	62.1	68.2
Korea, Rep.	91.9	93.4	99.9	99.9	77.8	84.4	65	65	76.2	76.3	70	74	86.9	86.9	92.5	92.5	82.2	83	83.1	84
Malaysia	89.3	82.8	94.3	99.3	82.2	88.8	70	75	76.3	79.5	86	88	73.5	76.1	83.7	88.5	62.5	67.2	78.6	81.3
Philippines	67.2	69.3	83.8	87.5	64.5	68.6	35	40	56.7	57.6	40	44	62.7	72.2	70.6	68.4	55.2	55.2	58.2	60.9
Thailand	82.7	92.3	83.2	98.6	70.5	71.9	45	70	67.4	69.5	78	86	69.6	77.7	84.1	84.6	72.2	76.6	71.9	79.5

Source: World Bank, Doing Business Database.

Notes: Scores are calculated in such a way as to range from 0 to 100 from the worst to best performer on any indicator. Methodology used for various indicators in Doing Business Reports 2015 to 2019.

Table 4.13c Conditions Constraining Credit to the Private Sector and Especially SMEs, 2009–2020

Country	*Getting credit* (1)		*Strength of legal rights* (2)		*Depth of credit* (3)		*Credit registry coverage (% of adults)* (4)		*Credit bureau coverage (% of adults)* (5)		*Outstanding guarantees in 2009 as % of GDP* (6)	*Average value of guarantees issued in 2009 scaled by GDPPC* (7)	*Standardized fee per annum on loan guarantees* (8)	*Time to complete insolvency* (9)	*Recovery rate (in %)* (10)
	2014	*2020*	*2014*	*2020*	*2014*	*2020*	*2014*	*2020*	*2014*	*2020*	*2009*	*2009*	*2009*	*2020*	*2020*
MENA non-major oil exporters	**30**	**46.7**	**1.2**	**4.4**	**3.8**	**5.1**	**8**	**12.2**	**4.4**	**9.5**	**0.36**	**25.25**	**1.84**	**2.74**	**30.9**
Djibouti	5	40	1	8	0	0	0.3	0.4	0	0				1.5	44
Egypt, Arab Rep.	50	65	2	5	8	8	5.3	9.5	19.6	31.3	0.07	22	2	2.5	23.3
Jordan	45	50	0	11	0	8	2	5	0	22.9	0.07	10		3	27.3
Lebanon	40	40	2	2	6	6	19.2	21.3	0	0	0.9	14.6	2.5	3	30.8
Morocco	40	45	2	2	6	7	0	0	19.6	31.6	0.4	60	2	3.5	28.7
Syrian Arab Republic	15	15	1	1	2	2	7	7.8	0	0				4.1	21.1
Tunisia	**40**	**50**	**3**	**3**	**5**	**7**	**28.8**	**36.4**	**0**	**0**	0.5	33.5	0.6	1.3	51.3
West Bank and Gaza	35	80	0	8	7	8	8.8	22.9	0	0	0.3	11.4	2.1	No practice	No practice
Yemen	0	35	0	0	0	0	1	1.3	0	0				3	21
MENA major oil exporters	**13.75**	**15**	**1.0**	**1.0**	**1.75**	**2**	**22.2**	**17.5**	**8.32**	**15.1**	**0.01**	**5.0**		**1.4**	**43.5**
Algeria	10	10	2	2	0	0	2.4	3.6	0	0				1.3	50.8
Iran, Islamic Rep.	45	50	2	2	7	8	41.6	60.3	33.3	60.7				1.5	36.1
Iraq	0	0	0	0	0	0	0	1.3	0	0	0.01	5		No practice	No practice
Libya	0	0	0	0	0	0	0.5	0.6	0	0				No practice	No practice

(Continued)

Table 4.13c Conditions Constraining Credit to the Private Sector and Especially SMEs, 2009–2020 *(Continued)*

	Getting credit		*Strength of legal rights*		*Depth of credit*		*Credit registry coverage (% of adults)*		*Credit bureau coverage (% of adults)*		*Outstanding guarantees in 2009 as % of GDP*	*Average value of guarantees issued in 2009 scaled by GDPPC*	*Standardized fee per annum on loan guarantees*	*Time to complete insolvency*	*Recovery rate (in %)*
	(1)		*(2)*		*(3)*		*(4)*		*(5)*		*(6)*	*(7)*	*(8)*	*(9)*	*(10)*
Country	*2014*	*2020*	*2014*	*2020*	*2014*	*2020*	*2014*	*2020*	*2014*	*2020*	*2009*	*2009*	*2009*	*2020*	*2020*
MENA GCC	**36.7**	**51.7**	**1.2**	**2.7**	**6.2**	**7.7**	**10.1**	**15.1**	**21**	**30.1**	**0.03**	**13.00**		**3.14**	**34.4**
Bahrain	35	55	1	3	6	8	0	0	26	40.9				2.5	41.3
Kuwait	35	45	1	1	6	8	10.9	16.8	29	31.6				4.2	32.2
Oman	35	35	1	1	6	6	21	27.1	0	0				3	41.1
Qatar	30	45	1	1	5	8	22.7	34.7	0	0				2.8	30
Saudi Arabia	45	60	1	4	8	8	0	0	44.3	56.7	0.03	13		No practice	No practice
United Arab Emirates	40	70	2	6	6	8	5.8	12	27	51.3				3.2	27.7
East Asia	**52.5**	**63.3**	**4**	**5**	**6.5**	**7.7**	**20.7**	**44**	**38.9**	**49.9**	**3.2**	**6.4**	**1**	**1.63**	**51.28**
China	50	60	4	4	6	8	30.2	100	0	0				1.7	36.9
Indonesia	50	70	4	6	6	8	41.2	30.9	0	40.4				1.1	65.5
Korea, Rep.	65	65	5	5	8	8	0	68.2	100	100	5	7	1.2	1.5	84.3
Malaysia	70	75	7	7	7	8	52.9	64.9	77.2	89.1	1	9.4		1	81
Philippines	35	40	1	1	6	7	0	0	6.9	13.5				2.7	21.1
Thailand	45	70	3	7	6	7	0	0	49.2	56.5				1.5	70.1
Taiwan											3.5	3	0.8	1.9	82.3

Sources: Columns (1–5, 9–10) from World Bank Doing Business Database, Columns (6–8) from Saadani et al. (2011).

of special relevance to the provision of credit to private sector SMEs for selected years between 2009 and 2020. The discussion of this table, however, will be postponed to the next chapter (Chapter 5) which is more focused on such matters.

H. Some Recapitulation and the Relation to Growth

Nevertheless, from all the materials that have been shown and discussed in this chapter, it is clear that in the case of numerous measures of institutional strength, such as the strength of property rights, the strength of the judicial system and especially gender equality, and other measures of state capacity, Tunisia has been ranked comparatively well, not only now, but over much of the last 50–60 years. Since, as pointed out above, all three of these institutional characteristics have been related to higher levels of development, higher growth rates or both in the literature, we deem it appropriate to argue that these factors could well have contributed to Tunisia's relative success in development in terms of the various dimensions identified in Tables 1.1–1.6, at least up to the year 2010. Since then, however, its institutional improvements have been more limited in general and have even reversed in some important respects.

While, as indicated above, some credit for the relative strength of Tunisia in each of the more positive areas should be given to favorable initial conditions and the fortuitous early leadership provided by the leader of its drive for independence Habib Bourguiba, these early advantages have been effectively built upon and subsequently strengthened by reinvesting in them, in some cases rather continuously, but in others at least, at certain strategic points in its history since independence.

Gender equity and women's rights provide a good example. The country's constitution and Code of Personal Status of 1956 granted women the right to vote, to stand for public office, to deny consent to their own marriage, and for widowed women the right of custody to their minor children. It also allowed for judicial divorce and abolished both polygamy and marriage before the age of 17. Various laws and amendments in the 1990s further strengthened these women's rights and gender equity.[24] Thanks to the clothing and other labor-intensive segments of export industries, female labor force participation increased rapidly, and because of the fact that female wages are lower than male wages, this contributed to the ability of Tunisian exports to compete in European markets with other producers from all over the world (Baud et al. 1977; Joekes 1982; Ross 2008).[25]

Both human capital investments among females and of their participation in professional life has been encouraged by the Tunisian leadership rather consistently since independence. Subsequently, the employment primarily of women in the crucially important clothing sector, gave rise to the growing participation of Tunisian women in economic life and government

(Charrad 2001; Ross 2008).[26] Not surprisingly, the gender gaps in education have virtually disappeared, and as a result women's participation in government, politics, business, and professional life has increased sharply. Perhaps the most important effect of the consistent advocacy of gender equity has been that on fertility rates, those in Tunisia having fallen earlier and more sharply than in other MENA countries, so as to now be at, or below, replacement rates.

Similarly, as noted above and as reflected in the indicators of Tables 4.11–4.12, there have been numerous instances in which property rights, state capacity, and other important institutional indices have been strengthened over time. Indeed, each has complemented and provided feedbacks to the other. For example, strengthening the legal system has allowed property rights to be strengthened and sharpened, and stronger property rights, in turn, have strengthened investment, incomes, and the ability of the state to accumulate resources to finance both infrastructure and the provision of government services including health, education, the judiciary, and legal services. While the dynamics of these processes over time are extremely complex in practice, one cannot help but notice how closely the Tunisian experience over time fits with the rather simple model and related empirical evidence on the roles of state capacity and property rights and changes therein over time in financial development and overall economic growth provided by Besley and Persson (2009).

The presence of these seven ingredients identified above explains why Tunisia's development performance has been superior to that of most other MENA countries over the first 50 plus years since independence, although somewhat less so in the most recent 2011–2019 period. While a few of these ingredients may have been present in some other MENA countries, with the exception of Oman (which had over time transformed from an extremely closed economy and being pre-occupied by major conflicts, into an emerging oil exporting country), in none of the others were they present to the same extent. Every one of the MENA countries which achieved relative success in growth and development until the last decade, such as Jordan, Egypt, Syria, or Morocco, had one or more of these ingredients missing or present only in a weak way. Jordan, has perhaps come closest to Tunisia is terms of the presence of most of these ingredients, but had more serious macroeconomic crises which led to its more complete collapse of growth in the 1980s and 1990s; and until quite recently had not used global markets as a leverage for growth as much as Tunisia. Egypt also failed to use global markets as the main driver for growth, continuing for too long with inward orientated policies and being slower in adopting more market-friendly policies. Egypt has also been hurt by its inability to link its capital-intensive and protected textiles sector with its export-oriented, labor-intensive garments industry, in large part because the former (textiles) remains in the hands of state enterprise (Nugent and Abdel Latif 2009). In contrast to Tunisia, Morocco has not invested as heavily in human capital or as consistently adopted the kinds of social policies that would reduce poverty.

It is, however, probably the first ingredient, that of its leadership and commitment to a broadly shared vision of development and capable government, which most clearly distinguishes Tunisia from all other countries in MENA, with the exception of Oman which has indeed shared this dimension. Even for Oman, its high average rate of growth over the long period would not have been as high as Tunisia, had it not been for its oil boom which generated its double-digit growth rates in the 1960s. Panagariya (2008), in his wide-ranging review of India's development experience over 50 years, notes four common features which explain why that country's economic growth never collapsed like that of many other developing countries. These features are macroeconomic stability, gradual, and predictable change in policies with no major unpredictable shifts, political stability, and the capacity to implement whatever policies the government should adopt. It is striking that these same four features were present throughout the first 50 years of Tunisia's experience since independence, even though Tunisia has never had the democratic institutions that India has had. Not only did Tunisia, like India, avoid the major collapses in growth that occurred from time to time in many other MENA countries, but it was more successful than India, at least until the 1990s. This was because it adapted and reformed more readily than India and followed more market-friendly and open policies. Despite this relative success, however, Tunisia failed to achieve the success of many East Asian countries or even that of India since the 1990s, and it seems to have slipped somewhat further after 2011, issues to be dealt with in the following two chapters.

Notes

1 One ingredient which was found by the Commission on Growth and Development (2008) to be important for growth in countries around the world was high levels of investment in infrastructure, and the role played by governments in ensuring that this takes place. More data and analysis would be needed to determine the extent to which this dimension played a distinguishing role in determining the growth outcomes in Tunisia. However, from casual observation at least, and the information presented in the previous Chapter, it would appear as if the government of Tunisia did play an active role in ensuring that adequate and timely infrastructure investments for development were undertaken in both urban and rural areas.

2 The sample of MENA countries used in these growth regressions consisted of Algeria, Egypt, Iran, Jordan, Morocco, Syria, and Tunisia. The sample countries for Asia included the following five from our sample of East Asian Countries (Indonesia, Korea, Malaysia, Philippines, and Thailand), and four South Asian countries (Bangladesh, India, Sri Lanka, and Pakistan). It did not include China.

3 The estimate of this is only 0.065.

4 Interestingly enough our claim that strong state capacity was an important contributor to Tunisia's relative long-term success contrasts sharply with the otherwise very well informed views of White (2001) who described the Tunisian state as being 'precarious' or fragile because it was caught in a squeeze between the competitive pressures of the international economy favoring low wages, informality and open doors and the 'state in society' view in which the state should respond primarily to the needs of its own citizens.
5 Indeed, note that the debt to GDP ratios of several MENA countries (Egypt, Jordan, Morocco, Syria, and Yemen) had been allowed to reach crisis levels of well over 100%, and in some of these countries on several different occasions. This has also happened in Djibouti more recently.
6 The labor share of GDP is calculated using GDP at market prices and adjusting the wage bill by the ratio of total employment to the number of salaried workers. This method assumes that the imputed average wage of non-salaried workers is equal to the average for those salaried. The ILO has recently started producing estimates of labor income shares which take into consideration self-employed workers, using micro-data on their characteristics and wages, and show a share in the 44–46% range over the period 2005–2019.
7 Indeed, it is because Tunisia's real exchange rate misalignment has seldom been large that we have not included a table for real exchange rates among our tables.
8 Real Effective Exchange Rates are from the IMF and are defined so that an increase means appreciation and a decline represents depreciation.
9 While it has become standard to find that currency depreciation should help improve the current account balance and currency appreciation should do the opposite, very recently Bahmani-Oskooee et al (2019) used time series data on exchange rates and sectoral trade balances for Tunisia over the 1980–2016 period to question this finding. Their paper made use of quite sophisticated time series analysis (Auto Regressive Distributed Lag model) but allowing also for non-linearities in the relationships to be estimated. While the overall positive influence of exchange rate depreciation on the trade balance in the medium and long run was retained, their results revealed some asymmetries in the sectoral trade balances, the balances in some sectors improving, but in others getting worse. This showed that the currency depreciation phases may well have had very different effects on firms, even of the same type (e.g., exporters), but in different sectors and especially in the short to medium term. This illustrates the fact that, even a well-intended or even necessary policy reform, could have very different effects on different private firms of the same general type.
10 Note once again, that Korea is clearly the star performer among East Asian countries on this index. It should also be noted that the relatively low scores for Tunisia on the 2015 PISA test, were from the recent 2011–2019 decade, during which as will be explained further below Tunisia's performance in many respects was falling significantly.
11 Although not in our East Asian sample, it is also interesting to note that Vietnam's absolute poverty also declined extremely sharply, indeed, from 76.3% in 1981 to 2.4% in 2015.
12 The African Development Bank study uses the $2–20 2005 PPP prices definition of the middle class, while Economic and Social Commission for West Asia uses its own relative income definition.
13 Both of these measures are based on national accounts data: one on gross fixed capital formation (GFCF) by general government (GG) adjusted to account for Public Private Infrastructure (PPI) (GFCF/GG+PPI) and the other gross

fixed capital formation expenditures on civil engineering (CE) works (GFCF/CE). See Fay et al. (2019, Table 7).

14 This measure includes investments in energy, water, telecommunications and general government investment in transportation, sanitation and urban infrastructure.

15 Based on a slightly different measure, which includes energy, water, telecommunications and transportation (by general government and enterprises), the rate of investment was 6% of GDP in 1975 and 8% in 1980.

16 Yet, as will be pointed out in Chapter 5, its achievements in this respect were rather pale and shallow relative to those of most East Asian countries, especially the small and medium-sized ones like Malaysia, Singapore, and Thailand.

17 KOF refers to the name of Institute Konjunkturforschungsstelle.

18 See Dreher (2006), Gygli et al. (2019), and the KOF Swiss Economic Institute website.

19 Other globalization indexes developed by the KOF are those for Social Globalization (including personal contact, information flows, and cultural proximity) and Political Globalization (involving the number of embassies in other countries, international treaties, memberships in international organizations).

20 The indexes are adjusted to take into consideration country size.

21 Among MENA countries, this was also true for Yemen and Iran.

22 See, especially the collaborative volume between the European Bank for Reconstruction and Development, the European Investment Bank and the World Bank (2016), which will be discussed in greater detail in Chapter 6.

23 While the earliest year for each given indicator that is available for most countries is given in the column heading for the early entry, even in these cases, although the Tunisian entries do match that date, not all other countries have entries going back that far.

24 Among the amendments made in the 1990s were (1) The Code of Personal Status, replacing an earlier clause stating that 'a woman must obey her husband and respect his prerogatives' with one stating that both spouses should 'treat each other with mutual respect and assist each other in managing the household and the children's affairs,' (2) the creation of a fund for alimony and child support for women who are divorced and gain custody of the children, (3) a provision allowing both spouses to apply for loans for purchasing a residence, (4) another extending the rights of women to run for parliament, and finally (5) one strengthening women's rights with respect to community property. Several official organizations including the Ministry of Women and the Family have also been set up to monitor implementation of these laws and to advise the government on the need for further legislative or administrative action.

25 This is a pattern that has also been observed in other countries that have developed in large part through clothing and textile exports, such as in Turkey (Baslevent and Onaran 2004; Ozler 2000), Korea (Ross 2008) and Morocco (Joekes 1982). Ross (2001) attributed the coincidence of female employment growth and political and legal strength, on the one hand, and textile exports, on the other hand, to the virtual absence of natural resources or emigrant remittances in these three countries compared to the oil-rich countries of the world. This was the result of an empirical demonstration by Ross showing that female labor force participation is discouraged in oil-rich countries because oil exports have the effect of raising the reservation wage for women to work and making it unnecessary for governments to adopt measures to promote manufactures exports. We hasten to point out, however, that in the early period when Tunisia was just getting started in manufacturing, Tunisia's

oil sector was by no means negligible and more recently emigrant remittances have been quite important. As a result, both these cases have operated against textile exports and female labor force participation.

26 Even between the mid-1990s and 2003, Ross (2008) cites World Bank statistics showing that the number of women running for local office tripled and the fraction of parliamentary seats held by women increased in Tunisia from 0.6% to 23%. This was a level more than double the percent of any other country in the MENA region.

5 Why Has Tunisia Not Done as Well in Economic Growth and Economic Development as the Most Successful East Asian Countries?

In the previous chapter, we focused on evidence, and then explanations, for Tunisia's overall comparative success in development performance relative to most other MENA countries. In the tables presented and in some parts of the text, it has also been noted that in many respects it did not perform as well or grow as fast as several East Asian countries. Tunisia's long run real GDP growth rate in per capita terms of about 2.7 per cent per annum (from Table 1.6) was consistently above that of most MENA countries except Oman, but was significantly lower than both the unweighted average of East Asian countries (4.6% per annum) and their weighted average growth rate of 6.4% per annum, and even further behind those of the two faster growing countries of the East Asian sample, China and Korea, over the same five decades. Tunisia has also been shown to have lagged behind East Asia in terms of structural transformation (including manufacturing), diversification of its economy, technological upgrading, and overall employment growth, and at least more recently in property rights.

One could argue that Tunisia's economic performance was in fact weaker than what one would have expected it to be, given the advantages it had over other MENA and perhaps even some Asian countries in terms of initial conditions, homogeneity, and social stability, as explained in Chapter 2. This is especially so because in quite a few respects Tunisia has shared with East Asian countries several aspects of their development experience. Indeed, both Tunisia and several East Asian countries had experienced relatively stable macroeconomic environments, reasonably strong state capacities, large investments in both human capital and infrastructure, adaptable and flexible policy agendas, and early adoption of outward oriented policies.

In a sense, therefore, the Tunisian paradox is not why it has been successful compared to other MENA countries, but why it has failed to achieve the same success as that of many East Asian countries despite having, seemingly at least, followed a very similar path and model of development.

Some have attributed the limited success of Tunisia and other MENA countries compared to East Asia to prevailing cultural values which are not supportive of growth and development. Diwan et al. (2018) have discussed some of these but also shown such explanations to be mostly unfounded.

DOI: 10.4324/9781003309550-5

For example, based on World Values Survey data, Arab citizens are found to hold similar values to the citizens of other regions about embracing market economies and competition, individual desires for a good life, strength of work ethics, preferences for work in the private sector, and support for income redistribution. The authors did find, however, that Arab citizens, in Tunisia specifically, have much weaker views compared to people in other countries about preferences for thrift, acceptance of female work outside of household, and levels of trust in national institutions. These latter factors may well have contributed to Tunisia's weaker performance compared to the successful East Asian countries, but the differences were relatively small and unlikely to explain all of that gap.

In this chapter, we seek to identify the major differences in policies and other features between Tunisia and East Asian countries which may help to explain the divergent outcomes in terms of aggregate GDP and productivity growth, employment growth, living standards levels, technological progress, and structural transformation. One striking observation from these comparisons is the strong similarity in the broad directions of policies pursued by both Tunisia and the successful East Asian countries. As we observed above, Tunisia followed the same type of policies with the priority given to human capital, especially education, the attention given to technological progress, the role given to markets and the private sector, the active role of the state, and an outward orientation. We find no divergence in any major single policy, or set of policy choices, to which one could attribute the gap in performance between Tunisia and East Asian counties. On the other hand, we do find lots of divergence in terms of the extent of implementation of the policies and their adaptation to changing circumstances. For this reason, we also wish to identify the most important explanations for these differences in the extent of implementing these policies and adapting them to Tunisia's circumstances. While there is considerable overlap and interdependencies among the various factors, as in the previous chapter, we find that they can be broadly divided into a number of different categories, once again seven.

The seven categories of shortcomings for Tunisia relative to East Asia are: (1) its lower rates of saving and capital accumulation, (2) its failed land reform, (3) its limited success in stimulating technological progress and transfer, (4) its miss-matching of skills and the inefficient allocation of human capital, (5) its mixed success in financial development, (6) its weak fiscal policies, and (7) its insufficient use of global markets. Some of these factors were identified by the influential Commission on Growth and Development (2008) when it compared growth across countries more generally. In any case, we feel that these factors can be expanded on and developed more thoroughly. In doing so, we feel that, collectively at least, these factors can explain why East Asian countries could achieve and sustain GDP growth rates of as much as 7 per cent per annum or higher for some time whereas at best Tunisia could do so for at most 5% per annum and to do so only for shorter periods. In each of these categories, we identify some ingredients for the success of the rapidly growing East Asian countries which were found to be either entirely missing or only slightly apparent in Tunisia.

Each of these categories of shortcomings will be taken up in each of the following seven sections (A–G). Once again, wherever possible we try to take advantage of relevant data, either presented in tabular form for suitable measures, or in terms of relevant findings from other related studies.

A. Tunisia's Limited Success in Achieving High Rates of Savings and Physical Capital Accumulation

Table 5.1 provides data on three macroeconomic indicators over the decades since the 1960s or 1970s. The first two sets of columns show the average rates of gross national savings and gross domestic capital formation as percentages of GDP, and the last set of columns shows the average Current Account Balances (again a measure of national saving with respect to the rest of the world) by decade.

During the 1960s, as shown in Table 5.1, Tunisia's rate of Gross Fixed Capital Formation (GFCF) was very respectable, indeed averaging 23% of GDP, and during the 1970s, Tunisia raised that rate to about 25% to be only slightly below those of the East Asian countries and above those of at least a few MENA countries. Similarly, its gross savings rate was also about 25% and roughly on a par with East Asian countries. This was aided by the facts that during this period, Tunisia had become an at least somewhat important oil exporter and oil prices tripled over the course of the decade. Even in the 1980s, when oil was no longer so important, Tunisia's GFCF as a share of GDP rose further to 27%, almost keeping up with East Asia's rise to an average of 27.8%. Yet over the next couple of decades, as oil exports became much less important and oil prices less favorable, Tunisia's gross savings rates plummeted to 22.7% in the 1990s and 21.8% during the 2000s, and then collapsed after the change in political regime to 11.8% in 2011–2019. Its GFCF rates started to lag well behind those of most MENA countries and far behind those of all East Asian countries. In particular, while East Asia's average GFCF rate rose to about 30% in the 1990s, Tunisia's rate fell to 25.1% in the 1990s and 23.5% in 2001–2010.

Lying behind these rising gross savings rates in East Asia were its rising household and corporate savings rates as shown by the Asian Development Bank (2020). Indeed, for most East Asian countries, corporate savings were the main driver. In China and Thailand, corporate savings reached 20% or more of GDP, while in Tunisia they remained in the order of 9–10% during the 1990s and 2000s. Various factors have been mentioned explaining the high rates of corporate savings in East Asian countries, such as the high profitability of their firms, their especially large production platforms, their containment of wages due to the limited activities of labor unions, low interest rates, and low dividend payments (Asian Development Bank 2020).

Table 5.1 Savings, Investment and Current Account Balance, 1961–2019

Country	*Gross savings (% GNI)*					*Gross fixed capital formation (% of GDP)*						*Current account balance (% of GDP)*				
	1971–1980	*1981–1990*	*1991–2000*	*2001–2010*	*2011–2019*	*1961–1970*	*1971–1980*	*1981–1990*	*1991–2000*	*2001–2010*	*2011–2019*	*1976–1980*	*1981–1990*	*1991–2000*	*2001–2010*	*2011–2019*
MENA non-major oil exporters	**25.3**	**23.9**	**20.6**	**19.1**	**14.7**	**15.7**	**25.5**	**27.2**	**26.7**	**23.5**	**22.7**	**–4.4**	**–3.1**	**–3.4**	**–4.7**	**–8.9**
Djibouti					27.04						28.18			14.45	–0.74	–1.15
Egypt, Arab Rep.	23.46	26.71	23.87	20.33	12.99	14.36	19.65	30.00	22.77	18.79	14.89	–5.57	–3.19	1.49	1.02	–3.24
Jordan	31.28	23.57	24.39	23.11	15.15		34.55	26.67	26.80	25.55	19.43	–0.08	–3.33	–4.31	–5.02	–10.22
Lebanon				3.91	–1.07			31.31	29.93	23.11	22.83				–16.36	–21.34
Morocco	18.15	26.47	25.74	32.44	28.17	12.12	21.72	26.12	24.49	29.20	29.76	–11.32	–4.09	–1.14	0.14	–5.79
Syrian Arab Republic	27.87	18.25	19.33	24.76		13.19	25.99	21.87	22.74	21.54		2.02	0.02	0.94	3.31	
Tunisia	**25.89**	**24.46**	**22.70**	**21.83**	**11.76**	**23.17**	**25.63**	**27.12**	**25.10**	**23.47**	**20.17**	**–7.16**	**–4.76**	**–4.16**	**–2.76**	**–8.74**
West Bank and Gaza			7.33	7.03	9.15				34.91	22.63	23.35			–31.03	–18.37	–16.21
Yemen, Rep.															–3.38	–4.43
MENA major oil exporters	**33.9**	**22.8**	**35.0**	**49.4**	**39.0**	**31.2**	**33.7**	**26.9**	**17.9**	**21.4**	**25.4**	**–1.1**	**2.2**	**4.0**	**15.3**	**–1.6**
Algeria	37.23	28.06	34.16	54.09	42.61	31.82	37.98	31.21	25.61	27.11	37.60	–7.21	–0.49	5.18	15.91	–5.00
Iran, Islamic Rep.	30.55	17.46	35.91			30.49	38.98	30.85	30.61	30.72	23.59	5.11	–0.46	3.16		
Iraq				40.19	35.37		24.14	31.63	3.18	10.71	14.99				6.69	6.93
Libya				54.00				13.87	12.33	17.22			7.61	3.675	23.25	–6.82

(Continued)

Table 5.1 Savings, Investment and Current Account Balance, 1961–2019 *(Continued)*

	Gross savings (% GNI)					*Gross fixed capital formation (% of GDP)*						*Current account balance (% of GDP)*				
Country	***1971–1980***	***1981–1990***	***1991–2000***	***2001–2010***	***2011–2019***	***1961–1970***	***1971–1980***	***1981–1990***	***1991–2000***	***2001–2010***	***2011–2019***	***1976–1980***	***1981–1990***	***1991–2000***	***2001–2010***	***2011–2019***
MENA GCC	**50.8**	**31.6**	**15.2**	**38.5**	**36.7**	**15.4**	**22.8**	**22.7**	**19.0**	**23.3**	**24.0**	**18.8**	**7.3**	**–5.5**	**15.1**	**10.5**
Bahrain	54.79	38.60	15.44	33.44	31.06		30.82	29.38	17.03	26.07	26.13	6.00	2.71	–3.77	5.60	2.87
Kuwait	57.73	38.31	10.69	44.39	39.16	15.53	12.22	18.56	21.90			46.94	28.78	–8.81	29.90	25.14
Oman	40.18	29.26	15.55	35.23	23.13	16.71	29.67	20.75	17.98	24.52	25.42	8.03	3.79	–3.74	8.37	–2.25
Qatar					53.73											17.93
Saudi Arabia	50.45	20.21	19.19	40.86	36.39	14.05	18.59	22.18	19.23	21.01	24.14	14.04	–6.12	–5.87	16.35	9.01
United Arab Emirates										21.71	20.20					
East Asia	**26.6**	**28.4**	**32.7**	**34.6**	**34.4**	**16.9**	**24.3**	**27.8**	**30.9**	**26.6**	**29.6**	**–2.9**	**–2.4**	**–0.5**	**4.4**	**2.6**
China		35.52	39.45	46.38	46.41	19.56	27.28	28.56	32.06	38.91	43.07		0.04	1.52	5.18	2.04
Indonesia		23.37	26.22	26.72	32.15	8.94	19.28	25.26	26.33	24.36	32.30		–3.21	–0.43	2.05	–2.03
Korea, Rep.	28.37	34.27	37.16	33.45	35.35	18.69	28.01	30.85	35.16	30.66	29.82	–3.95	–0.85	0.50	1.49	4.96
Malaysia	28.26	29.59	37.35	37.01	29.71	16.73	24.39	30.51	35.53	22.36	24.85	2.57	–2.98	–0.46	12.73	4.59
Philippines	27.68	21.19	21.50	33.44	31.76	19.01	22.67	21.89	22.20	18.77	23.09	–4.99	–3.57	–3.10	2.03	2.00
Thailand	21.91	26.52	34.37	30.42	31.26	18.68	24.21	29.83	34.17	24.59	24.39	–5.40	–4.11	–1.21	2.69	4.16

Source: Data from database: World Bank, World Development Indicators.

In Tunisia households' savings remained in the order of 8–9% of GDP during the 1990s and 2000s, but they reached 20% or more in China. Some of the main explanatory factors for increasing households' savings rates in East Asia have been their declining dependency rates, the limited nature of their official social insurance schemes, and their limited access to financial institutions (Asian Development Bank 2020). We would also like to add their more rapid urbanization and thus their greater need to save to finance urban housing for newly married and recently migrated households.

One result of these lower gross savings and capital formation rates in Tunisia than in East Asia, especially after 1990 was that Tunisia's capital stock was estimated to have grown by only about 3–4% per annum since 1990 compared to 8–12% per annum in East Asia during the 1990s and 5–13% per annum since then.[1]

From the last set of five columns in Table 5.1, it can be seen that Tunisia has been the only country, except for Jordan, in either region to have incurred negative average Current Account Balances over all five decades, whereas at least by the last two decades five East Asian countries were averaging surpluses over these decades. One positive characteristic for Tunisia in all three sets of columns is that its rates were less volatile than those of many of the other countries, greater volatility having been known to impede growth as pointed out in Chapters 1 and 2.

But what could be the cause of Tunisia's low savings and investment rates? Although a difficult thesis to prove, Diwan et al. (2018) argued that a weaker preference for thrift by Tunisians may have played a role. The earlier demographic transition, the decline in the dependency ratios, and the weaker social safety nets may have favored East Asian countries in terms of savings. One factor that we deem more important is the strikingly weak role of the private sector in the case of Tunisia. In East Asia, and other countries experiencing high growth episodes, such as India since the 1990s, the main driver for the increase in savings and investment was the private sector. The dynamism of the private sector and the high productivity growth rates have not surprisingly induced higher rates of savings and investment by private agents in East Asia.

But, why did the private sector in Tunisia not reveal the dynamism and growth that the East Asian countries experienced, especially considering the several very positive ingredients that were operating in Tunisia identified in Chapters 3 and 4? While each of the following sections in this chapter will contribute to the explanation for this, we will also take up this issue more fully in Chapter 6, where it is of most critical importance.

B. Land Reform: A Missing Ingredient?

Land reform has been the subject of much debate and study, and the experience with it has varied considerably across the globe in the extent of land reforms, and their impact on economic growth and poverty reduction

(Deininger 2003). Studwell (2013) argues that land reform was the most critical policy shaping the extent of success of the development experience in East Asia, and distinguishing between two groups of countries within that broad region. The first of these two groups were the Northeast Asian countries which undertook extensive, deep, and effective land reforms. This started in Japan under the Meiji restoration, but it became most important and effective since the late 1940s and early 1950s as a new wave of land reforms occurred in Japan, (South) Korea, Taiwan, and China.

In South Korea, as described by Shin (1976), the need for land reform had been made very clear prior to and through WWII because the bulk of agricultural land had come to be expropriated from Korean farmers and given to the businesses and government of Japan (its colonial power) from whom the Korean workers had to rent small parcels at exploitative rents. Under Japanese occupation, most of the land was held by large landlords (many non-resident) who rented their land out to landless rural workers at high and exploitative rents in a way that provided no incentive for upgrading productivity, efficiency, or collaboration. Even though achieving land reform was a top priority after World War II when Korea was liberated from Japanese rule, for quite a few years neither the US nor Korean governments were able to implement a new well-designed land reform. Only in 1950, and even if a far-from-optimal one, land reform was initiated there that made it possible for well over a million small farmers to receive the land confiscated from the Japanese and other large exploitative landlords. Even after a few years under that system, only a modest share of the farm households which received the small parcels of land were able to pay back the government for the land they were given, and few of these small farmers were able to learn how to improve their farming methods. The Korean War which followed (1950–1953) made matters even worse. Nevertheless, not very long after this, Korean agriculture became successful in entering some export markets and providing some critical raw materials for its rapidly growing manufacturing industry, and leading Shin (1976, 12) to conclude as follows: 'The land reform improved the prospects for raising production and productivity since new incentives for increased work and investment were created as a result of abolishing tenancy and accomplishing more equitable redistribution of lands.' It may be safe to say that the land reform of 1950 provided a turning point for the modernization of agriculture and of rural communities in Korea.

Although land reforms were also initiated, sustained, and expanded in Japan and Taiwan, in China the early post-WWII reforms were reversed in the mid-1950s and replaced with collectivization which acted as a severe drag on China's development. In 1978, however, a new reform took Chinese agriculture out of collectivism and into private farming. This reform is known as the Household Responsibility System. It was first initiated in one province in China. But, with its success there, the reform spread rapidly throughout the country. In this new system, the farmer needs only to pay the government a fixed quota from his (her) output, thereby greatly increasing the incentive for both greater effort on the part of the farmers and increasing productivity. This important land reform in the late 1970s is generally credited with the launching of China's rather amazing resurgence (Lin 1988), re-launching its household farming and constituting an important factor lying behind the doubling of its real GDP growth rates beginning in the 1980s (as shown in Table 1.6). It could also have been an important contributor to the sharp rise in China's TFP growth (from Table 2.6a)[2], and also to, not only the unusually large share of agriculture in total employment in 1991, but also the sharp decline in that share after that (as shown in Table 2.2) and the sharp rise in urbanization after 1980 on Table 2.5. All these developments, traceable in part at least to China's land reform of the late 1970s, could be said to be consistent with the ingredient to successful development, allowing the '*surplus labor*' of developing countries to be put to use (an objective to which the famous development economist Arthur Lewis (1954) had called the world's attention).[3]

On the other hand, in the second group of Asian countries discussed by Studwell (2013), the mainly Southeast Asian countries, Indonesia, Malaysia, the Philippines, and Thailand, land reforms were either extremely limited or even reversed.

Earlier analysis by other well-known development economists had already called attention to the role of land reforms in expanding the number of small household farmers who work on their own land and contribute strongly to triggering a virtuous circle for development. The importance of this had been indicated by the findings of Deininger and Squire (1998) showing that inequality in land tended to have a more negative effect on growth than inequality in income. In some of the countries where land reforms were undertaken, they were shown to have involved 30–40% of total cultivated land, such as in Japan, Korea, and Taiwan, affecting two-thirds of rural households (Deininger et al. 2007). In many Latin American countries, such as Bolivia, Nicaragua, Peru, and Mexico, land reforms affected sizeable portions of their arable land and benefited up to one-third of the rural population. These reforms were not always successful, as in most cases in Latin America, Africa, or South Asia. But when they did succeed as in Japan, Korea, Taiwan, and later on in China, they were shown to have reduced inequality and social tensions, increased labor use in agriculture, and smoothed the rural-urban migration process. They also led to increased yields in agricultural production and rural incomes, reductions in poverty, increased human capital accumulation, improved nutrition, and increased demand for manufacturing production. The greater agricultural surpluses also led to higher savings, greater capital accumulation, and improved trade balances, thereby also reducing the pressure on the balance of payments and relaxing the foreign exchange constraint.

Tunisia, however, did not undertake any real land reform. There was an attempt at collectivization during the 1960s, similar with what had been implemented in China in the mid-1950s. The objective was to create larger land properties in order to exploit economies of scale and increase productivity and efficiency. The large land properties expropriated in 1964 from the foreign 'colons' were included in the process of land consolidation. But this attempt in Tunisia, like in other countries, failed and agricultural production fell sharply. There was not much of an increase in the use of farm labor and opposition to this policy became very strong so that by the end of the 1960s this program was abandoned, and land was returned to its owners, but without any change in the structure of land holdings. The large properties, which had been nationalized from 'colons' in the 1960s became state property and were managed directly by the government. Since the 1990s, some of this land has been (long-term) leased to private 'agricultural enterprises' mostly large businesses but without yielding any noticeable benefits in terms of productivity. As a result, Tunisia's experience with land reform was similar to that of the less successful South East Asian countries, but clearly very inferior to the experience of the North East Asian countries (like Korea and China) which did undertake serious land reforms. As a result, Tunisia did not achieve either the rapid productivity gains in agriculture or the surge in rural incomes and reduction in rural poverty that those North Asian countries did.

In his explanation of the success of the Northeast Asian countries, Studwell (2013) argues that effective and large-scale land reform is just the first and most basic ingredient for increasing productivity in agriculture, raising incomes and releasing surplus labor and that it should be complemented with two other ingredients for success. One of these is the expansion of manufacturing to supply the low-skill intensity products demanded by the rural population and for use in exports. This development absorbs the available supply of labor, gives rise to surplus income that can be invested in manufacturing, and can lead to additional foreign exchange receipts. The final ingredient is a set of financial institutions which are geared toward the financing of agriculture and the emerging manufacturing sector (which will be discussed further in Sections E and G).

One of the main benefits of land reform, of course, is to lower income inequality and thereby to lower poverty rates. Unfortunately, as pointed out by Bauluz et al. (2020) in their recent survey of data for the World Inequality Database, land censuses in the MENA region have been almost as scarce as industrial and other censuses and even the agricultural surveys and censuses, which do exist across the world and over time often suffer from a number of idiosyncrasies undermining their comparability. For example, many of them lack data on land values, the presence of landless persons, and ownership. While the Food and Agriculture Organization (FAO) has been trying to orchestrate consistency in land censuses across countries and over time, and in their Food and Agricultural Organization (2021) volume they do have at least basic data on the number and average size of landholdings for quite a few MENA as well as Asian countries, generally these do not contain information on ownership. That volume shows that the size distributions of agricultural land parcels varied significantly across countries. Over time, however, the average size of farms had fallen between the time of the earliest (in 1930) FAO-led censuses (International Institute of Agriculture 1939) through the year 2000 but have risen slightly since then. Since inequality in ownership is more relevant than inequality in land per se (because smaller farms are often of higher quality land than large ones), Bauluz et al. (2020) combined the census data with household surveys to measure inequality in ownership. They were able to do this only for 13 countries, none in MENA, but China was one of them (the rest being mainly from South Asia, Sub-Sahara Africa, and Latin America). Interestingly, thanks to its impressive land reform in such an enormous country, China turned out to have the second lowest inequality in land ownership in terms of both land area and land value out of their sample of 13 countries.

An especially relevant study on wealth inequality is that of Hlasny and AlAzzawi (2018) comparing Tunisia with Jordan and Egypt and also Egypt over time. This study is based on the information on incomes earned and assets owned by different households obtained from the household and labor market surveys in these countries. Perhaps reflecting the absence of a major land reform, asset inequality in 2014 was found to be slightly higher in Tunisia than in either Jordan or Egypt although the top 1% of households owned much larger percentages of the wealth in Jordan than in either Egypt or Tunisia. These authors also traced the observed wealth gaps back to certain demographic differences. Especially among those in the higher wealth deciles, the two most important sources of wealth gaps were urban-rural differences and educational differences. In both these categories, these differences contributed more to the wealth gaps among the relatively wealthy in Tunisia than in either of the other countries. This is also consistent with the consistent efforts over the years by the Tunisian government to encourage education and urbanization. Since the Tunisian survey used in that study was slightly more recent (2014) and hence could have been affected by its abandonment of some of the inequality-reducing and efficiency-promoting institutions and policies, suggesting that wealth inequality in Tunisia in 2014 could have been higher than it had been earlier, in contrast to Egypt where the surveys showed quite clearly that wealth inequality had been declining. Even so, however, the fact that income inequality at that time was lower than asset inequality in Tunisia would seem to reflect the continued influence of some of the other inequality reducing forces identified above over much of Tunisia's post-independence period.

C. Limited Success in Stimulating Strong Technological Progress and Technology Transfer

A notable feature of East Asian development has been the rapid pace of its technological progress which constituted a major ingredient of its rather remarkable structural transformation and high total factor productivity growth. It translated into continuous technology upgrading, diversification, and complexification of production and exports, the deepening of the process of innovation and the accumulation of patents. At least during the first few decades of development since the 1960s, this produced the so-called 'flying geese' pattern of industrialization in the region, with technological upgrading and diffusion of production across countries according to their comparative advantage and the evolution of their technological capabilities.

Various methods and mechanisms have been used in these East Asian countries to stimulate technological progress including exchange of experts, contracting foreign licenses, reverse engineering, import of machinery and equipment, trade and FDI, and research and development.[4] The relative importance of these different methods varied across countries and over time, depending on the stage of technological development reached by each country.

For example, among the government policies critical to this success in East Asia have been a variety of instruments and incentives justified by the 'public goods' nature of these activities, and the presence of major externalities. In particular, national innovation systems were put in place, including universities, research institutions, national laboratories, and science parks. Legal and institutional arrangements were also put in place, including intellectual property rights regimes. Incentives, subsidies, and credit were deployed by governments to support private research and development.

Notably, Tunisia has given much attention to technology and introduced policies and measures quite similar to those in East Asia. For instance, the level of expenditures on research and development hovered around 0.7% of GDP on average, which as shown in Table 5.2 was comparable to or higher than in other East Asian countries and higher than in all MENA countries. Yet, it did not reach the exceptionally high levels of Korea or China. Ghali (2018) describes the very diversified and rich institutional system used in Tunisia to support research and innovation, including universities, research centers, and technical centers, led by various public institutions, agencies, and funding mechanisms. These supported research and innovation by providing technical assistance, subsidies, and incentives. Research and development expenditures were further boosted significantly after 1996 from 0.28% of GDP in 1996 to reach a high of 0.73% in 2004.

However, the contribution of the business sector itself in that process remained quite small, not exceeding 30%. Since the 2000s, a new mechanism was introduced in the form of technology parks, indeed no less than ten of them between 2001 and 2010, some sectoral in nature but others even multisectoral, but all of them fully driven by government initiatives.

The overall assessment of the Tunisian experience of these technology parks and innovation systems by Ghali (2018) concludes that, despite some successes, the results and performance of the innovation system as a whole were weak, and well below the achievements of East Asia. For instance, the number of patents registered in Tunisia by Tunisian residents remained

Table 5.2 Research and Development, 1996–2018

	Research and development expenditure (% of GDP)				
Country	***1996–2000***	***2001–05***	***2006–10***	***2011–15***	***2016–18***
MENA non-major oil exporters					
Djibouti					
Egypt, Arab Rep.	0.20	0.26	0.33	0.61	0.70
Jordan		0.34	0.43		0.71
Lebanon					
Morocco	0.27	0.59	0.66		
Syrian Arab Republic				0.02	
Tunisia	0.38	0.62	0.68	0.67	0.60
West Bank and Gaza			0.29	0.49	
Yemen, Rep.					
MENA Major Oil Exporters					
Algeria		0.20			0.54
Iran, Islamic Rep.		0.54	0.44	0.33	0.83
Iraq			0.04	0.04	0.04
Libya					
MENA GCC					
Bahrain					
Kuwait	0.20	0.15	0.09	0.20	0.07
Oman				0.20	0.24
Qatar				0.50	0.51
Saudi Arabia		0.05	0.22	0.86	
United Arab Emirates				0.69	1.13
East Asia					
China	0.70	1.13	1.51	1.96	2.15
Indonesia	0.07	0.05	0.08	0.08	0.24
Korea, Rep.	2.19	2.43	3.14	4.08	4.53
Malaysia	0.36	0.63	0.86	1.17	1.44
Philippines		0.13	0.11	0.14	
Thailand	0.18	0.24	0.22	0.47	0.89

Source: Data from database: World Bank, World Development Indicators.

very low, compared to other countries. The number patents registered in the United States, Europe, or other developed countries remained even smaller, and their rate of acceptance in those countries low. During the 1977–2015 period, the US Patent Office accepted 43 patents from Tunisia, while the comparable numbers of accepted patents were 2690 from Malaysia, 1043 from Korea, and 333 from Indonesia. These results were due to the lack of coordination between institutions, weak governance, and the failure to build strong connections between the public institutions in charge of innovation, on the one hand, and academic research institutions and especially the world of private business, on the other.

One major program of this sort in Tunisia, as mentioned earlier, was the Industrial Upgrading Program, initiated in the 1990s, motivated by the country's Free Trade Agreement (FTA) with the European Union. It aimed to achieve productivity upgrading and industrial diversification through technology transfer. Such an objective was needed to offset the loss of labor-intensive industries that resulted from the phasing out of the import quotas on textiles from China in Europe and North America but it had the effect of giving Tunisia's government more control of its private sector and market activities. Specifically, the Tunisian government called for grant applications for such upgrading from the private sector and from both large and small enterprises under Tunisia's Industrial Upgrading and Modernization Program.

Between 1996 and 2010, almost 3500 applications were approved to receive help from this program, resulting in investment plans averaging 6.1% of manufacturing value-added per year, and a subsidy rate of 13.7% on these investments (Ghali and Nabli 2020). For the period 2011–2019 an additional 2714 applications were approved, with investments worth 4.8% of value-added and a subsidy rate of 12.7%. The program included incentives for both 'material' and 'immaterial' investments to 'upgrade' industrial firms.

There is, however, only limited evidence on the effectiveness of this program. Some studies mention some cases in which positive results were reported (World Bank 2008b, 16). Yet, an evaluation by Institut Tunisien de la Compétitivité et des Etudes Quantitatives (2010) did not find any conclusive evidence on the program's effectiveness. In the case of textiles and clothing, the technical assistance and credit for upgrading technology and product quality was meant to help firms face much of the increased competition from low-wage Asian countries by moving somewhat higher up in the quality and price spectrum of such products. This may have happened in a few cases, but the rapid decline of exports of clothing and apparel since the great recession is hardly a positive indicator of success.

Interestingly, Marouani and Marshalian (2019) made use of a data set from tax authorities and created a 'treated group' of firms which, based on their characteristics, were considered beneficiaries of such assistance, and a control group of firms which were not beneficiaries. Their results showed that most of the benefits of loans to large firms had the effect of benefitting the owners of those firms, whereas those to small firms had the effect of benefitting the workers (by raising wage rates, employment, and net job creation), in each case serving to benefit a quite different group but not the citizenry as a whole.

Among the objectives of the Industrial Upgrading Program was one to support investments in Information and Communications Technology (ICT). Applications for three different types of ICT were called for: Software, Hardware, and Network Communications. The government then evaluated these applications, not only on efficiency grounds, but also based on location and other characteristics. Not surprisingly, some studies, for example, by Murphy (2006) and especially Ben Khalifa (2018), have indicated that geographic factors and personal characteristics apparently played a role in their selection. The latter study made use of an important Industrial Upgrading Survey carried out in 2016 by Tunisia's Ministry of Industry and Trade to evaluate the effectiveness of subsidies to firms over the 2004–2014 period in stimulating individual firm's 'technical upgrading of each of those three types, Software, Hardware and Network Communications. The firms in the sample included 140 which had received the subsidies they had applied for and another 98 which had not received any subsidies. The Ben Khalifa analysis first used a wide variety of background characteristics on firms and their location within Tunisia to come up with matched likelihoods across firms in the total sample to undertake technological upgrading of each of these three types. Based on the matched samples, their estimates of Average Treatment Effects on the treated indicated that the subsidies did in fact significantly increase technological upgrading of each type, indeed by 1.1 adoptions for Software, 0.4 adoptions for Hardware, and 0.48 for Network communications. This is indeed seemingly rather impressive evidence of the extent to which Tunisia's government could use incentives in the form of subsidies to stimulate technological upgrading by individual firms.

While the study had shown that the subsidies offered by the government to applications of individual firms to increase the adoption of Software, Hardware, and Network Communication technologies had succeeded in increasing the number of these adoptions significantly, this did not necessarily reflect causality. In his subsequent analysis, Ben Khalifa (2018) showed that, when investigating the geographic pattern of these technological up-gradings, most of the upgrading had occurred primarily in the already technologically developed regions, like Tunis (the capitol region) and Center-East where the increases may have occurred more as a result of prior acceptance of such innovations among neighboring firms than on the basis of the programmed subsidies to the firms which had applied for the subsidies. This interpretation was supported by the fact that the strong differences between the regions as to which of the three types of technological adoption was most important remained very much the way they were before the program. Ben Khalifa's policy conclusion was that for the Tunisian government to be truly more successful in inducing technological upgrading, it would have to do more to reduce the degree of 'digital divide' between regions and to involve local and regional governments to coordinate in encouraging firms to engage with each other through partnerships among firms, business associations, and civil society and the broadening of existing technological networks.

As a result, despite using the same modalities and instruments to support innovation and technological development, it is not at all clear that Tunisia succeeded in achieving the degree of technological upgrading that East Asian countries had. As shown in Chapter 2, it seems that the process of structural transformation remained limited, the process of increasing the complexity of production and exports remained slow, and the productivity gains quite low. East Asia's policies to stimulate technological progress were more strongly supported by higher trade intensity, larger FDI inflows and especially more dynamic competitive markets in which the private sector played a much larger role.

D. Skills Mismatches and Shortcomings in the Quality and Efficient Utilization of Human Capital in the Form of Education over Time

As noted in Chapters 1, 2, and 4, since independence, the Tunisian leadership has put an unusually large emphasis on the promotion of education and gender equity, accounting for why Tunisia has consistently rated fairly well in many of the human capital indicators in Tables 1.1 and 1.2.

Tunisia's emphasis on human capital was similar to that observed in East Asian countries. It has given top priority to education and has even invested more heavily than East Asia. Public spending on education has been consistently much higher: for instance in 2008/2012 Tunisia allocated 6.3% of GDP to education while this ratio was only on average about 3.8% of GDP in the East Asian countries (Table 4.5).

But there were major differences in policy. As in East Asian countries, Tunisia introduced compulsory education, but unlike them, it failed to achieve broader access through various mechanisms of enforcement or educational assistance to households. And most importantly, East Asian countries have strived continuously to align education development with the changing needs of the economy. They have given significant attention to technical and vocational education which is connected to the market and the development strategies (Asian Development Bank 2020). On the other hand, Tunisia has done little in this respect. As noted below, this resulted in many differences in outcomes and in efficiency.

First, Tunisia's achievements remained well below those of most East Asian countries. By 2010 illiteracy rates remained much higher in Tunisia than in East Asian countries and the average number of years of schooling of 9.1 in Tunisia remained much lower than in Korea, Malaysia, or Thailand which reached 10.5–12.5 years (Table 1.1).

Second, a striking feature of labor market dynamics which differentiates Tunisia (as well as other MENA countries) from East Asian countries is the way educational achievements of the population match demand. For Tunisia, the mismatches between education and needs of the market have led to high unemployment rates for the tertiary education graduates. At the same time, the social and cultural norms on the role of women in society (Diwan et al. 2018) have resulted in low levels of participation of women in the labor force and high unemployment rates. As a result, a major potential source of employment and productivity growth in Tunisia has to a large extent been wasted.

Table 2.12 shows the ratio of the population with completed intermediate and higher education at ten-year intervals since 1970. While each country in both the MENA and East Asia regions made great progress in raising the percentages of its population with completed secondary and completed tertiary schooling levels, Korea was clearly the star performer, raising its percentages of population with secondary and tertiary education to 35.5% and 34.8%, respectively, by 2010. The only MENA countries raising their percentages of population over 25 years of age with tertiary education to more than 10.7% (still only 30% as high as Korea's) were Iran, Qatar, Libya, and UAE, all important oil exporting countries with substantial and increasing portions of their populations which were foreign-born. Of the non-oil countries, Tunisia with 8.4% did the best among the non-major MENA oil exporting countries and wound up slightly ahead of all the other East Asian countries except Thailand (10%). In the case of the shares of over 15 population with completed secondary education in 2010, among non-GCC countries, only Iran, Jordan, and Egypt with 30.5%, 27.1%, and 26.4%, respectively, came close to the average for East Asian countries (of 27.2).

But, have these increased numbers of highly educated people been put to good use everywhere? Table 2.13 provides data over time on unemployment rates among *male* members of the labor force for both those with secondary and higher education, respectively. Although the data in this table are much less complete, especially over time, based on the estimates for the most recent periods (2011–2015 and 2016–2019) in the last columns of the two parts of the table, it can be seen that, while unemployment rates for both educational levels are quite low (lower than 5%) for all East Asian countries except for the Philippines, and also for most of the oil exporting countries of MENA, for non-major oil exporters of MENA (as well as for Algeria), the unemployment rates for tertiary education graduates are high, indeed over 14% in Egypt, Tunisia, and West Bank and Gaza (WBG). While this demonstration of the much more serious underutilization of the increasingly educated work force throughout MENA, but especially among non-major oil exporting countries including Tunisia, applies only to male workers, Table 2.11 showed that in MENA countries as a whole the female labor force participation averaged only 18% for these countries in the 2000s compared to an average in the East Asian countries of 54%. While Tunisia's female labor force participation rate was higher than those of most MENA countries, at 23.5% during that same decade, it was still less than half the average for East Asian countries.

The data from Tables 2.11–2.13 do indeed illustrate the exceptional case of South Korea with spectacular progress in both secondary and tertiary education, low unemployment rates for all groups of the population, and relatively high rates of female labor force participation. Among MENA countries, most GCC countries, as well as Iran, have achieved great progress in the percentages of population with completed secondary education similar to what was achieved by Korea or Malaysia, but even for them, their female labor force participation rates have been lower and their male unemployment rates higher, even in recent years, than those of all East Asian counties, and especially than Malaysia and Korea.

Progress on secondary educational achievement in other MENA countries has been similar to that achieved by the East Asian countries other than Korea and Malaysia. Yet, their outcomes in terms of unemployment rates are strikingly different: high rates in MENA countries, and low ones in Asian ones. The large numbers of secondary education graduates find adequate jobs in economies undergoing deep structural transformation. Yet, in MENA countries many graduates do not find jobs and hence their unemployment rates have been increasing.

The data for tertiary education are even more striking. With the exception of South Korea, Asian countries did not invest too heavily in higher education, and hence their percentages of population with tertiary degrees remained moderate, ranging from 2.4% to 10% in 2010 (Table 2.12). By contrast, non-GCC countries in MENA achieved great progress with rates similar to, or even exceeding those of, East Asian countries in 2010. But, with much more limited economic structural transformation, the demand for those skills has remained weak. The result has been the skyrocketing rates of unemployment of male tertiary education graduates in many MENA countries, reaching 22.8% in Morocco and 16.5% in Algeria in 2001–2005, 18.2% in Tunisia in 2011–2015, 15% in Egypt during 2011–2019, and 16.5% in WBG in 2016–2019 shown in Table 2.13. In contrast, they remain lower than 10% in East Asian countries, and even much lower in Korea, Malaysia and Thailand. While not shown in that table, the situation is much worse for female unemployment of tertiary education graduates.

Naturally, governments and their policies and job placement efforts can potentially at least be used to fix these mismatches and Tunisia has been active in this respect. Indeed. Youth employment was seen for a long time as a key priority in its successive Development Plans and resulted in the adoption of many Active Labor Market policies, which included subsidies to support the insertion of tertiary education graduates, training programs, and job matchings. Zrelli Ben Hamida et al. (2017) made use of data in 2010 on each of over 100,000 graduates on whether or not each had been engaged in a form of Active Labor Market Program (ALMP) and then information about their employment status in 2013 by job type. The results did show that 60% of the graduates had become involved in an ALMP program, but that less than 20% had been employed at any point over those subsequent three years (a period in which economic conditions declined sharply). The results also showed that graduates in specialties in short supply pharmacists, engineers, and architects had the best prospects for ALMP participation and for being employed at the end of the three years. But, female graduates and somewhat older graduates had significantly lower prospects in both respects. But most discouragingly, only those from the more developed East where the economic activities were much more developed including Tunis, benefitted from an ALMP and subsequent employment. The region in which the

ALMP offices were located had no significant effects, implying the effects of ALMP participation depend almost entirely on one's skills and training, and not on the government activities, leaving job prospects very poor for all those without the training in the few specialties in the shortest supply.

Third, another (though somewhat related) dimension of the inefficiency in the education sector, is the quality of education. Among all 15-year-old (8th grade) students taking the internationally comparable tests for Math, Science Literacy, and Reading in the Programme for International Student Assessment (PISA) in 2015, as shown in the column labeled PISA 2015 in Table 4.6, the scores of Tunisian students on these three tests of 367, 386, and 361, respectively, were ranked only 65th out of 69 countries, slightly ahead of Algeria but behind Jordan and well behind all the East Asian countries covered.[5] According to the White Book of Tunisia's Ministry of Education (2016), teacher absenteeism has been high (especially in recent years) and credentials have deteriorated over time, inducing parents to hire private tutors. These tutors, moreover, are often the teachers themselves and are suspected of rewarding the students of the wealthier parents who can afford to pay for that tutoring. These findings induced Limam and Ben Hafaiedh (2017, 5) to conclude that 'learning is sacrificed for grades, and the whole education system becomes more focused on passing exams than on learning experience' and of little relation to the needs of firms. They also (on p. 6) point to Tunisia's extremely inefficient allocation of resources within higher education and its overly selective and rigid tracking system as factors related to this unfortunate outcome.

Fourth, the skill mismatches and the low quality of education have resulted in low returns to education in Tunisia (as in many other Arab countries) in comparison with other countries, even though as expected they do vary by location and level of education. Notably, Zouari-Bouatour (1998) showed that in the mid-1990s these rates in Tunisia were very low (5.6%) for primary education, but were 19.2% for secondary education and 24.6% for higher education. The overall rate of return to education at that time in the mid-1990s was estimated to be 9.5%. Quite alarmingly, using similar methods and data, Zouari-Bouatour et al. (2014) estimated that the overall rate of return to education had fallen to 5.9% in 2009. While Limam and Ben Hafaiedh (2017) found the rate to have risen moderately to 7.3% by 2014, they demonstrated that the rate of return to education in Tunisia was at least then remaining remarkably low relative to other countries (the world average being 10% according to Montenegro and Patrinos (2014)).

Fifth, another dimension of the inefficiency in allocation of resources within the educational system, is the unusually large discrepancies in the level of education, the wage rates, unemployment rates, and the returns to education across levels, regions, rural-urban (within regions), and genders.

The rates of return to education in Tunisia are considerably higher in urban areas than in rural areas and for females than for males. In contrast to comparable studies for other countries where the rate of return quite naturally declines with the number of years of education, the fact that in Tunisia it is several times higher at the tertiary level than at the elementary level is rather unique. As suggested by Limam and Ben Hafaiedh (2017), this may be attributable to the signals sent by the public sector which offers some of the most preferred jobs, but largely because of their more favorable fringe benefits, working hours etc. and wage rates that rise sharply with years of education, rather than reflecting higher productivity. Other indicators of the inefficiencies in the allocation of education and labor across sectors that these authors report are (1) that those individuals with 17 years of schooling working in the public sector earn on an hourly basis a wage rate that is 37% higher than those in the private sector and (2) that those in the formal private sector earn wages that are 59% higher than those in the informal sector. These results point to the exaggerated influence of segmentation in the labor markets. A substantial drawback of living in a rural area or in an underdeveloped region derives from the lack of employment opportunities in these preferred segments of the labor market.

E. Tunisia's Mixed Success in Financial Development

As indicated above financial development may be another area in which Tunisia may be lagging behind in terms of long-term economic growth and development. Yet, the importance of this weakness may depend on the direction of causality between these two variables. As a result, various studies have tested for this. A study by Ghali (1999) demonstrated that Granger causality does go from financial development to economic growth in Tunisia. The study by Ghali was based on annual time series data for a relatively long time period (1963–1993) on broad money stock, both GDP and GNP and two alternative measures of financial development, namely, bank deposits as a share of nominal GDP and the ratio of bank claims on the private sector to nominal GDP. It showed that long run causality was definitely in the direction going from financial development to growth (rather than the other way around), leading to the conclusion that at least to that date 'There is a high degree of confidence that development of the financial sector is an effective policy towards promoting Tunisia's economic growth' but at the same time suggesting that much more could and should be done in enhancing financial deepening.

The basic underlying framework for financial development in Tunisia was similar to that used by East Asian countries. At least until the financial crisis of 1997–1998, in East Asian countries bank-finance was the dominant source of finance, and governments intervened extensively through public development banks and directed credit, just as they did in Tunisia. Also, and until the 1980s, moderate interest rate repression was prevalent in East Asia (Asian Development Bank 2020). Especially impressive has been the success of East Asian countries in getting their SMEs appropriate access to finance, even though the specific mechanisms for accomplishing this have varied from country to country and even across sectors (Levy et al. 1999, especially Ch. 6).

As compared to East Asia, however, the development of an efficient financial system in Tunisia has posed four main challenges in the way they relate to the growth of the private sector and of markets: (i) access to bank credit of any type by the private sector and especially by SMEs, (ii) dominance of state banks in the credit market, (iii) availability of the harder to obtain long-term credit, and (iv) the development of stock markets. Tunisia has made significant progress on all four fronts, but in each case its success has remained mixed and insufficient.

1. Access of the Private Sector to Bank Credit

As in East Asia, the banking system has been the main mechanism for financing the economy in Tunisia over the whole period. Even during the period of financial repression from the 1960s to the mid-1980s, there was significant financial deepening. Banks were highly regulated and interest rates were kept low, indeed negative in real terms.

With the Structural Adjustment Program of the mid-1980s, Tunisia undertook a strong program of reforms of the financial sector, with regulations on the administrative allocation of credit lifted and interest rates liberalized. Bank loan rates in real terms became positive by 1985, and time deposit rates in real terms became positive after 1987–1988, indicating progress toward greater equilibrium in bank finance and credit markets. However, the money market rate remained highly controlled by the Central Bank, and interest margins were liberalized only in 1994. At the same time, entry (domestic and foreign) remained very restricted and competition in the credit market was also weak (Nabli et al. 2002).

Table 5.3 presents comparable indicators of banking finance development for different MENA and East Asian countries for three different indicators of banking finance development, namely, those for bank deposits, domestic bank credit to the private sector as a share of GDP and the bank credit to deposits ratio for each of six different decades beginning in the 1960s. With respect to the ratio of Bank deposits to GDP Tunisia showed fairly impressive gains more than doubling between the 1960s to the 2000s, but, even so, its growth in this ratio was lower than that of many other MENA countries and very far behind the average of East Asian countries which started below that of Tunisia but wound up in the most recent decade some 45% higher than that of Tunisia.

However, the more relevant measures of financial development, and especially with respect to the role of the private sector, are the figures on bank credit to the private sector as a share of GDP in the second set of columns in Table 5.3. As can easily be seen for most countries, these shares vary considerably from one country to another but have also tended to rise over time. Note that in the 1960s, Tunisia's bank credit to the private sector as a

Table 5.3 Banking Finance Indicators, 1961–2019

	Bank deposits						***Domestic bank credit to private sector***						***Bank credit to deposits ratio (%)***					
	(% of GDP)						*(% of GDP)*											
Country	***1961–1970***	***1971–1980***	***1981–1990***	***1991–2000***	***2001–2010***	***2011–2017***	***1961–1970***	***1971–1980***	***1981–1990***	***1991–2000***	***2001–2010***	***2011–2019***	***1961–1970***	***1971–1980***	***1981–1990***	***1991–2000***	***2001–2010***	***2011–2017***
MENA	**24.5**	**39.6**	**56.8**	**54.0**	**76.9**	**86.1**	**18.6**	**20.1**	**35.0**	**37.1**	**42.9**	**48.0**	**119.6**	**76.1**	**65.2**	**60.9**	**56.4**	**59.2**
Non-Major Oil Exporters																		
Djibouti			51.9	50.7	62.1	75.0			51.5	39.7	24.4	23.9			83.7	77.4	39.4	38.6
Egypt, Arab Rep.	17.7	21.6	56.1	61.7	70.0	62.2	14.8	15.1	26.8	35.5	47.5	28.5	83.5	62.9	44.4	51.1	62.6	43.4
Jordan	21.6	38.3	63.5	79.4	97.3	95.3	17.1	29.3	58.0	66.3	78.7	70.3	89.4	80.8	86.5	79.7	77.2	74.1
Lebanon	66.0	124.6	185.9	123.6	208.8	230.9			66.0	59.8	74.2	93.2	82.4	71.4	49.3	44.8	35.1	38.5
Morocco	15.5	17.1	24.1	40.9	68.3	86.7	12.0	14.3	15.1	30.4	50.1	66.0	81.5	68.2	61.3	66.8	79.5	76.0
Syrian Arab Republic	6.8	13.1	24.3	26.9	44.6		15.7	5.5	7.3	9.7	11.7		241.0	42.4	28.0	33.7	27.8	
Tunisia	**19.7**	**22.9**	**32.5**	**34.1**	**43.6**	**54.6**	**33.2**	**36.4**	**50.0**	**51.1**	**49.9**	**63.9**	**140.1**	**131.1**	**138.1**	**135.8**	**124.2**	**131.5**
West Bank and Gaza				55.0	78.2	63.1						**33.2**				29.5	29.7	47.5
Yemen, Rep.			16.2	14.1	19.3	20.7			**5.2**	**4.6**	**6.9**	**5.1**			30.4	29.1	32.5	24.3
MENA Major Oil Exporters	**12.4**	**18.4**	**42.6**	**31.0**	**29.6**	**64.6**	**15.0**	**26.3**	**42.7**	**18.7**	**16.5**	**26.5**	**90.5**	**103.3**	**88.5**	**53.8**	**46.3**	**46.9**
Algeria	17.0	29.2	45.5	25.9	40.4	44.8	17.2	47.5	63.9	9.7	12.3	18.8	76.0	146.4	134.6	38.1	27.6	39.3
Iran, Islamic Rep.	16.2	23.9	39.8	30.1	37.6	58.2	16.9	21.6	21.6	19.7	40.3	55.4	101.0	84.6	52.2	56.8	95.6	91.3
Iraq	9.1	8.9			12.6	21.1	11.0	9.6			2.8	7.7	118.5	95.3			21.0	33.4
Libya	7.1	11.6		36.9	27.9	134.1				26.8	10.7	24.2	66.5	87.0	78.8	66.5	41.1	23.5

(Continued)

Table 5.3 Banking Finance Indicators, 1961–2019 *(Continued)*

	Bank deposits						***Domestic bank credit to private sector***						***Bank credit to deposits ratio (%)***					
	(% of GDP)						*(% of GDP)*											
Country	***1961–1970***	***1971–1980***	***1981–1990***	***1991–2000***	***2001–2010***	***2011–2017***	***1961–1970***	***1971–1980***	***1981–1990***	***1991–2000***	***2001–2010***	***2011–2019***	***1961–1970***	***1971–1980***	***1981–1990***	***1991–2000***	***2001–2010***	***2011–2017***
MENA GCC	**17.3**	**18.5**	**37.1**	**43.2**	**44.3**	**60.7**	**11.5**	**17.9**	**35.2**	**32.5**	**45.4**	**64.7**	**83.0**	**88.1**	**91.7**	**88.2**	**104.8**	**104.3**
Bahrain		35.7	48.5	53.4	59.9	71.6		37.6	39.4	43.1	51.7	69.2	62.0	92.6	74.0	68.1	80.4	94.5
Kuwait	26.6	27.0	73.6	90.5	62.6	76.6	12.0	21.7	75.9	35.6	60.2	78.0	34.1	68.9	100.0	39.7	91.8	98.4
Oman		11.6	19.2	25.6	29.4	41.7		13.6	19.7	31.0	37.2	59.7		94.0	93.3	112.3	118.8	125.8
Qatar	23.3	17.9			47.1	68.6	14.9	14.0			37.1	63.8	55.5	74.5	73.4	74.8	70.6	76.1
Saudi Arabia	2.2	4.9	12.5	15.4	19.3	32.8	7.5	4.9	16.0	22.1	34.5	46.1	180.5	105.8	122.1	137.6	167.9	135.9
United Arab Emirates		14.0	31.9	31.1	47.8	72.7		15.7	24.6	30.5	51.8	71.0		92.6	87.0	96.7	99.2	94.8
East Asia	**16.3**	**23.6**	**36.6**	**50.4**	**63.5**	**79.2**	**16.2**	**26.9**	**50.6**	**79.8**	**81.9**	**97.1**	**95.7**	**101.0**	**151.9**	**156.7**	**117.4**	**123.7**
China			18.5	25.7	41.9	47.5			74.6	94.5	115.1	145.9			371.3	339.3	254.0	280.9
Indonesia		8.2	15.0	34.8	33.7	32.9		9.5	23.9	46.5	23.4	31.8		78.9	104.2	107.6	60.3	89.5
Korea, Rep.	11.5	24.2	27.7	36.0	57.9	100.9	17.0	33.8	43.5	52.9	120.5	135.5	127.6	125.1	147.3	141.9	140.3	116.2
Malaysia	19.3	42.7	89.9	87.5	107.5	121.0	14.1	33.8	79.6	123.5	110.5	118.4	66.0	62.6	78.8	122.2	95.3	94.1
Philippines	15.5	14.3	19.7	37.6	47.1	58.5	19.4	25.9	23.1	35.4	30.0	39.8	108.1	140.8	102.7	80.2	58.0	62.3
Thailand	18.8	28.5	48.9	81.1	92.8	114.3	14.2	31.4	59.0	125.9	91.7	110.9	80.9	97.7	107.4	148.7	96.9	99.4

Sources: Domestic bank credit to the private sector, World Bank, World Development Indicators. Bank deposits, from Financial Structure Database (World Bank 2019 version). Bank credit to deposits ratio from Financial Structure database (World Bank 2019 version).

share of GDP of 33.2% was the largest of any country in the table with the information available. Even in the 1970s by which time this information became available for other countries, it was only slightly behind two oil exporting countries of the MENA region, namely, Algeria and Bahrain[6] and still above these rates of all East Asian countries with the available data. While Tunisia's bank credit to the private sector as a percent of GDP rose to 51.1% by the 1990s, by then it was already behind those of Jordan and Lebanon among non-oil exporters in MENA where these shares of GDP were about 60% or more, and especially far behind that of the East Asian average which was about 80% of GDP. After a slight decline in the 2001–2010 decade, Tunisia's bank credit to the private sector as share of GDP rose to 63.9% during the 2011–2019 period. However, by then that share of GDP was below those of, not only Jordan, Lebanon, and Bahrain, but also those of Morocco, Kuwait, and the United Arab Emirates among MENA countries and well behind the East Asia average of 97.1%, and less than half of those of all East Asian countries except Indonesia and Philippines. Clearly, therefore, despite a very positive start in the 1960s of getting credit to the private sector, doing better than most other MENA countries and also East Asian ones, in recent years Tunisia has fallen significantly behind the others in this relevant measure of financial development.

From the last set of columns in Table 5.3, namely, those for the Bank Credit to Deposit Ratios, it can be seen that some of the blame for Tunisia's quite disappointing ability to increase more significantly bank credit to the private sector could be directed to its failure to increase its bank credit to deposit ratios. But this was in large part because Tunisia started in the 1960s with one of the highest such ratios (140%), one which could not be maintained and indeed actually fell after that. That initially high bank credit to deposits ratio was partly attributable to the fact that the Tunisian banks were often intermediating, not only from regular deposits but also very significantly from government and external sources. This ratio was higher in Tunisia than in most MENA countries, except in some major oil exporting countries (Algeria in the 1970s and Saudi Arabia during most of the periods and) especially during the years following surges in their oil revenues, when presumably government revenue was being recycled to the private sector through banks.[7] Some of the East Asian countries, especially China and Korea, also had high credit to deposits ratios as bank credit was being used with state involvement as a major tool for financing industrial development. One should not forget, however, that countries can get into trouble when the bank credit to deposits ratios get too high. It was such excessive bank lending which contributed substantially to the East Asian financial crisis towards the end of the 1990s, as can be seen from the high ratios for China, Thailand, Korea, and Malaysia in that period. Note that each of the six East Asian countries managed to reduce its credit to deposits ratio substantially after that.

While several other MENA countries also started with high Bank Credit to Deposit Ratios which then fell over time, within the non-oil exporting

MENA countries a notable exception was the WBG which started with a lower ratio in the 1990s and 2000s of 29.5%, but then experienced a sharp increase in that ratio to 47.5% in the most recent period. The WBG example may offer some clue into what Tunisia or other countries in MENA might do to increase their Bank Credit to Deposits ratio as a means of getting more credit to their firms and especially their SMEs. In particular, the World Bank's Doing Business Reports called attention to an important collateral reform that was introduced in the WBG in 2016, and Hrenko and Nugent (2021) go on to apply a synthetic controlled experiment (along the lines of Abadie et al. 2015) on a panel of countries similar to the WBG but without this reform to show causal effects of the reform on credit and then conduct a detailed analysis of a panel of WBG firms before and after the reform to show positive effects of the reform on the supply of credit to firms, and its effects on investment and employment in WBG firms, especially among SMEs. This reform was one which allowed not just land and buildings (assets seldom owned by SMEs) but also moveable equipment (more frequently possessed by SMEs) to be used as collateral in obtaining loans. If managed properly, this kind of a reform can well be a useful means of increasing financial credit to SMEs whose investments may contribute to increasing employment and/or technological improvement.

In the case of the East Asian Miracle countries, various analysts (Page 1994; World Bank 1993, and especially Cherif and Hasanov 2019) have also made much of the link in these countries between finance and investment, on the one hand, and the ability of their firms to upgrade technology and boost TFP growth, on the other. Yet for Tunisia, Nabli et al. (2002) argued that the link between bank financing and growth and competitiveness in these respects was at best only rather mixed. On the one hand, they said that Tunisia's initially high level of financial intermediation and subsequent financial deepening may have contributed to TFP growth over the long run. In particular, they pointed out that Tunisia succeeded in achieving high ratios of medium to long-term loans as a share of total loans, increasing them from 30% in the 1970s to more than 40% in the early 1980s (see more on this below). In addition, they found evidence of 'success' of the banking system in allocating credit to successful manufacturing activities and tourism, and in supporting export growth and economic diversification. Yet, Nabli et al. (2002) also provided evidence of wide-ranging distortions which increased economic inefficiency and lowered economic growth in Tunisia. In particular, they found that limited protection of creditor rights, weak accounting standards, and contract enforcements, together with wide-ranging policy distortions, combined to induce a misallocation of resources toward low-performing public enterprises, some SMEs and excessive investment in some sectors such as tourism, thereby limiting the efficiency and performance of the credit allocation mechanism. They also found no correlation between changes in TFP growth over the decades and changes in the level of financial intermediation.

For Tunisia and most other MENA countries, Gazdar and Cherif (2015) have also shown that their financial development indicators were insufficient for triggering significant positive effects on growth. They used a series of financial development indicators from both the banking and the stock market sources of finance, and combined these with various governance indexes, such as those presented in Table 4.12, to show that the MENA financial development indicators would be insufficient for stimulating satisfactory economic growth rates unless the relevant and highly complementary governance indicators, like Investment Profile, and Law and Order, could be raised above certain thresholds, which was definitely not the case.

Also, using time series data from 1990 to 2008, Rachdi and Mensi (2013) showed that, among all MENA countries, trade as a share of GDP was an even more important contributor to growth than any measure of financial development. Yet, when interacted with one or another of the World Bank's governance indicators, especially Investment Profile, External Conflicts, and Socioeconomic Conditions, only one such measure, namely, Central Bank Assets, was found to raise the rate of economic growth.

Moore (1991) traced the gradual improvements in the functioning of Tunisia's banking system from its infancy in the Bourguiba days when there were close ties between the top leaders and the few most important banks which were mostly public sector banks until the late 1980s. Yet, he pointed out that, even as late as 1985, all Tunisian banks were under the strict supervision of Tunisia's Central Bank so that, even the private banks acted like 'virtual state agencies,' (p. 65) and were not very competitive. While these state regulations, especially the rules of Tunisia's Central Bank, on banks were loosened quite significantly in the late 1980s, resulting in greater competition among banks in trying to attract deposits, the public sector banks remained the largest ones, and as a result competition in the credit market remained weak.

Henry (1996), moreover, pointed out that even as late as 1989, Tunisia's largest banks were state-owned or foreign-owned and that all but one of the public sector owned banks had more than 20% of its outstanding loans classified as 'problem' loans and with very substantial capital shortfalls. These shortfalls seriously constrained the desire of the government to liberalize and grow the economy by reducing interest rates on loans to the private sector. Notably, at the same time, these banks, through their own close-knit business association, resisted new entries so as to make it easier for them to hold onto their depositors without having to raise interest rates on bank deposits any further than they already were. The Tunisian government also objected, until recently, to the entry of Islamic banks. The problems of the public sector banks were in large part attributable to the requirement that they offer loans to debt-ridden public sector companies.

Hence, with the exception of the bank credit to deposits ratio, where Tunisia may have maintained it at too high a level and allocated that credit to inefficient and problematic firms, Tunisia's progress in financial development, as exemplified by the measures in Table 5.3, has been quite modest. With respect to the measures we deem most relevant, namely, the share of bank credit to the private sector in GDP (from the middle columns of Table 5.3), it can be seen that Tunisia less than doubled that share over the sixty-year period between the 1960s to the 2010s while both the GCC countries and the six East Asian countries as a whole increased these shares at least six-fold.

Another source of credit to the private sector in some, especially low income, countries is Micro Credit of the type pioneered by the Grameen Bank in Bangladesh. Microfinance has been helpful in providing credit to the very smallest of firms, typically single person firms and firms unable to access credit from banks. While consistent data sources comparing the magnitude of Micro Credit across countries are lacking, those available surveys, such as that by Symbiotics (2017), have shown the MENA region to be the region with the smallest incidence of Micro Credit. Its presence seems to have been limited to only seven MENA countries with a total of no more than 400,000 clients. While there is one such Micro Credit institution in Tunisia (Enda Inter Arabe) founded in 1987, it has never been among the largest in MENA, and ranks well behind those in Egypt and Morocco. Turkey is host to the largest microfinance in the broader region but, even if Turkey were included in MENA, the region would rank well behind East Asia and South Asia and probably also Sub-Sahara Africa, in the importance of credit from microfinance institutions.

2. *Dominance of State Banks in the Credit Market*

To move down from the macro-level to the level of individual banks in Tunisia and throughout the MENA region, we take advantage of an interesting study based on a panel of individual banks over the period 2001–2008 by Farazi et al. (2011). Their survey showed that in 1970 state banks in the MENA region accounted for a little over half the assets of all banks and that this was not very different from the shares of state banks in other regions like Sub-Sahara Africa, Latin America, and East Asia and was somewhat below those in Eastern Europe, Central Asia, and South Asia. Tunisia's shares of assets in state banks relative to assets in all banks were near the overall average across countries and regions and were far below those of Libya, Algeria, Syria, and even Egypt. Yet, whereas the shares of state banks in other regions of the world and even Syria and Egypt within MENA had fallen substantially by 2008, the share of state banks in total bank assets in Tunisia remained well above 40% and well above the state bank shares in East Asia, and within MENA in Saudi Arabia, Bahrain, Kuwait, Jordan, Lebanon, and Oman where these shares were 0% for the last four countries. In situations where credit markets and banking are very underdeveloped, state banks can be very useful in getting credit to firms including private firms, but in general as banks and credit markets have expanded over time, this benefit of state banks has been deemed, both in this and many other studies, to be less important.

Moreover, Farazi et al. (2011) rather clearly identified several quite specific shortcomings of dependence on state banks. These were that the presence of state banks tended (1) to lower the willingness of foreign banks to enter the country, thereby constraining the ability to lure foreign finance, (2) to lower the emphasis on incentives given to individuals to make deposits in local banks, (3) to raise the ratio of costs of personnel expenses (wages, salaries, pension costs, etc.) a potentially important source of inefficiency, (4) to earn significantly lower rates of return to both assets and equity, and (5) to have larger shares of non-performing loans (which in turn raise the costs of credit to the borrowers by having to include compensation for such losses in current loan rates).

Using a somewhat similar panel of individual banks over an overlapping period, Kobeissi and Sun (2010) pointed to the many advantages of foreign ownership in banks, not only in attracting foreign capital and overall efficiency but also in bringing in technical improvements that could be adopted by domestic banks. They also showed that Tunisia had the second lowest percentage of foreign banks in the total number of banks among all countries in the region (second only to Syria which had none). Tunisian banks also had the lowest return on assets, the lowest deposits to assets ratios, and second highest loans to assets ratios, and the second lowest average of total assets, the latter two indicators signaling greater vulnerability to risk.

Motivated by those findings and to get down closer to the microlevel and who gets the credit from banks, in a related study making use of the responses of firm managers to questions addressed to them in surveys, such as in the aforementioned Doing Business Surveys and Enterprise Surveys, Rocha et al. (2011) and Saadani et al. (2011) made use of the detailed Enterprise Surveys conducted in MENA countries and elsewhere between 2006 and 2009 to show that the percentages of private small and medium-sized enterprises (SMEs) with loans or other lines of credit from banks was exactly 20% (on a par with those in Sub-Sahara Africa), but well below the averages of about 40% in the East Asia and Pacific, and even Eastern Europe and Central Asia, and Latin America and the Caribbean regions (Rocha et al. 2011, Figure 1b). Similarly, the percentage of SMEs with Investment Finance in MENA countries was only about 10% compared to an average of about 20% in the latter three regions (Rocha et al. 2011, Figure 1c). With respect to the share of loans to SMEs in total bank loans, they found this share to be only 7.59% in MENA countries but 16.2% in a larger sample of banks in 38 developing countries and to averages well over 25% in Organization for Economic Cooperation and Development (OECD) countries (Rocha et al. 2011, Table 1.4). While the percentages in all regions were somewhat higher among large enterprises, the financing of SMEs is very important since they are generally the newer enterprises, with potential to grow and to innovate.[8] This percentage was a little higher in Tunisia (15%) than for the non-GCC average of 13%, but Tunisia's shares of SMEs with loans were considerably lower than those in Lebanon, Yemen, and Morocco (Rocha et al. 2011, Figure 3a).

These two studies went on from there to conduct detailed surveys of individual banks in 16 MENA countries to try to identify factors lying behind the disappointingly low shares of lending to private SMEs by banks. One thing that they did find was that private banks were less likely to provide such loans to SMEs than state banks. Compared to the answers received to similar bank surveys in other regions, they found that the banks in MENA countries pointed much more uniformly to the greater importance of weaker financial infrastructure including the legal and contractual environment than did those in other countries. Among private banks, in MENA countries virtually all the banks identified 'SME Transparency' as an important obstacle to the provision of lending to SMEs, and well over 60% of them pointed to Lack of Reliable Collateral, Credit Information Systems and Weak Creditor Rights as important obstacles to such lending. Lying behind the collateral problems is that fixed collateral is often not likely to be available for SMEs to take to banks, but only moveable collateral, such as specific machinery, and that for such moveable assets, some 70% of the banks said that they faced significant problems in trying to sell such assets, implying that they would also be very reluctant to accept any such assets as collateral. In their Tables 8.1 and 8.3, Rocha et al. (2011) ran multiple regressions to compare the relative strength of these various factors in affecting the shares of lending to SMEs in total loans. The results showed that the weakness of legal rights (captured by the entries in column pair (2) in Table 4.13c) was among the most important factors, and one in which (as shown in that table) Tunisia was especially weak, even in 2020.

Following up on the discussion of Table 4.13b in Chapter 4 concerning the ability of individual firms to get access to various services including credit, in the first pair of columns in Table 4.13c, we further update the comparative data on Getting Credit to 2014 and 2020, showing Tunisia to have been as usual slightly above the MENA average but well below the East Asian average. Then in the subsequent column pairs (2)–(5), we present the corresponding scores assigned by individual firms in the same list of countries to each of the four more specific factors that the bank surveys pointed out to be the key ones contributing to getting more loans from banks to private SMEs. These are all scores computed on the basis of averages among all the responses of individual firms in the specific country and year from the World Bank's Doing Business Database. Note that by 2020, while Tunisia remained well above the averages of most MENA sub-regions on Strength of Legal Rights, Depth of Credit, and Credit Registry Coverage, it remained far below the East Asian averages and not even close to any of these regions with respect to Credit Bureau Coverage. Although not up to date, in columns 6–8 of Table 4.13c, we place the scores that Saadani et al. (2011) had obtained in 2009 from their queries to banks about Loan Guarantees as a device to raise the willingness of banks to lend to private SMEs. In all these respects but no more recently than 2009, it can be seen that Tunisia was doing as well as the East Asian average in terms of the use of loan guarantees. Yet, in all the other respects captured by the other entries in Table 4.13c (including columns (9) and (10) which pertain to 2020), like many other MENA countries, Tunisia is shown to have more recently been lagging considerably behind East Asia in the various other factors identified by Rocha et al. (2011) as encouraging bank lending to SMEs.[9]

3. Long-term Credit and Development

For many years, access to long-term finance has been recognized as a major constraint to jump-starting development in any particular sector in developing and middle-income countries. The development of long-term finance allows firms to match the maturity of their assets and debts, contributing to increased efficiency and improved performance. The initial solution used by the Tunisian government during the 1990s was the direct involvement of the State in mobilizing, mostly through foreign bilateral and multilateral channels, long-term finance to fund not only infrastructure but also capital-intensive commercial projects. However, this was achieved primarily through the creation of SOEs, not through the private sector where innovation and technological change might have been expected to be more telling.

According to Nabli et al. (2002), the government used many instruments to enhance long-term finance in Tunisia to both the public and private sectors. A first instrument was the requirement of commercial banks to allocate a minimum of 10% of deposits to medium and long-term credit for priority activities. A second instrument was the direct government direction of credit through state-owned banks or through Central Bank approval procedures to preferred sectors and/or firms. The third instrument was through provision of subsidized credit through lower interest rates and direct subsidies to some activities which have assets with long-term maturity such as tourism and agriculture. The fourth instrument was the use of external lines of credit from bilateral and multilateral sources to channel such credit to the private sector in the form of long-term maturities.

But it was quickly recognized that each of these instruments (and especially the last one) was insufficient and there was a need to channel long-term credit to the private sector through development banks specialized in long-term finance. Indeed, each of the aforementioned instruments was found to be extensively used in Tunisia through *development banks* to supply long-term credit and direct resources to preferred sectors and activities.

The first one, 'La Banque de Développement Economique de Tunisie' (BDET), was created in 1959. Afterwards, three sectoral institutions specialized in long-term credit were launched: one created in 1969 was to focus on tourism ('La Banque Nationale de Développement Touristique' (BNDT)[10]), one for agriculture (Banque Nationale de Développement Agricole was created even earlier (in 1959) but was enlarged and merged with another development bank in 1969 and one for housing ('Caisse Nationale d'Epargne Logement,' which was created in 1974, but then became the 'Banque de l'Habitat' in 1989). Further expansion of this mechanism took place during the early 1980s with the creation of many joint-development banks between Tunisia and individual GCC countries, which helped channel oil-revenue resources from these countries to Tunisia. Four different development banks were created with GCC countries (one each with Saudi Arabia, the UAE, Kuwait, and Qatar), and two others were created with Algeria and Libya. As a result, by the 1990s, there were a total of eight development banks operating in Tunisia.

Indeed, the relative importance of long-term lending to the private sector has been noted to have become a rather distinctive characteristic of Tunisia's financial development by Nabli et al. (2002). This allowed the share of long-term debt in total capital to become unusually high and especially so in the most rapidly growing industrial firms. By 1985 development banks accounted for 22% of total credit of the overall banking system (including development banks). The share of medium-term and long-term credit in total credit of the whole banking system (including development banks) increased from 27% in 1970 to reach 43% in 1985.[11]

Based on a sample of 163 manufacturing firms over the period 1984–1994, the ratio of long-term debt to assets was found to be in the upper range of what is observed in developing countries as a whole, even though it was in the lower range of that in advanced economies (Nabli et al. 2002, Table 8.11). The ratio of long-term debt to assets averaged 19% during 1984–1986, but has trended downwards in the subsequent periods. But, notably, the success in terms of increased availability of long-term finance, driven by such heavy government intervention *was not focused on the private sector* and therefore may not have increased its efficiency. Indeed, relatively more of the credit from development banks was channeled toward public enterprises, which were in many cases less efficient. The ratio of long-term debt to assets was twice as high for SOEs as for private firms (27% compared to 14%). Also following the credit liberalization that has been occurring in Tunisia since the mid-1980s, the overall ratio of long-term debt to assets has declined, especially in low-growth firms.

This lack of efficiency in the development of long-term credit in Tunisia, all done under the heavy hand of the state, translated into very low profitability rates and the accumulation of a large portfolio of non-performing loans by the development banks, most of which became insolvent by the end of the 1990s. Some of these were integrated with commercial banks to form so-called 'universal banks,'[12] while others were left as they were, but privatized. This led to a sharp decline of the share of medium and long-term credit in total credit from its high of 40–45% in 1980–1990 to 33% in 2005. Hence, the declining availability of long-term credit during the last three decades has no doubt contributed to the slower progress in the development of private enterprise. Needless to say, even less of this otherwise quite impressive growth of long-term credit reached Tunisia's private sector SMEs.

4. Direct Finance and Stock Markets

In East Asia, the role of capital markets remained very small until the 1997–1998 financial crisis. Active policies, however, were pursued soon after that to expand and encourage direct finance through capital markets (mainly stock markets). In Tunisia, however, as with its banking system, the contribution of the stock market to the financing of the business sector remained marginal. The Tunisian stock market was created in 1969 (towards the end of the socialist experiment and at the beginning of the opening up of the economy), but it remained almost completely inactive throughout the first two decades of its existence. Major reforms were undertaken in 1989–1990 with a full overhaul of the rules and regulations on the conditions for the listing of public companies, on transparency and financial disclosure rules, and the operation of market transactions. Following these reforms, the stock market capitalization to GDP ratio increased sharply from 4% in 1990 to 23% in 1995. During the 1993–1995 period, as a nascent stock market, the Tunis Exchange experienced a major price bubble. Indeed, the price index increased threefold between the end of 1992 and the end of 1995, and by more than 100% during 1994 alone.[13] While some of that bubble was the result of improving economic conditions, quite a bit of it was attributable to false expectations and greed in the context of a market beset with lack of transparency, weak information and actors still learning how a stock market works. While not focused on any specific sector of economic activity, the stock market price bubble quickly burst and prices declined by 10% in 1996 and by 20% in 1997. This led to further reforms, some beginning as early as 1994, with the creation of a separate regulatory capital markets authority and the strengthening of rules and regulations. Additional reforms and incentives were introduced in the 2000s to encourage the development of the capital market. By the late 2000s, the market had regained its dynamism such that Tunisia's stock market capitalization to GDP ratio had come once again to exceed 20%.

Table 5.4 provides a comparison of various indicators of stock market development across countries and over time. These include the number of listed companies and stock market capitalization (as % of GDP) in the first two sets of columns of the table, and then value of the stocks traded (as % of GDP), stock turnover ratios (as % of market capitalization), and market capitalization in value terms, in the remaining columns of the table. The indicators for Tunisia remained very weak compared to similar MENA countries (Egypt, Jordan, Morocco, Lebanon, and even the WBG) and even farther behind all six GCC countries, and extremely low compared to the East Asian countries. Indeed, despite the aforementioned reforms in the 1990s, Tunisia has clearly failed to use stock markets as a

Table 5.4 Finance through Stock Markets, 1995–2019

Country	*Stock exchanges*	*Year of establishment*
MENA Non-Major Oil Exporters		
Djibouti		
Egypt, Arab Rep.	Egyptian Exchange (formerly Cairo and Alexandria Exchanges)	1883
Jordan	Amman Stock Exchange	1999
Lebanon	Beirut Stock Exchange	1920
Morocco	Bourse de Casablanca	1929
Syrian Arab Republic	Damascus Stock Exchange	2009
Tunisia	Bourse de Tunis	1969
West Bank and Gaza	Palestine Exchange	1995
Yemen		
MENA Major Oil Exporters		
Algeria	Bourse d'Alger	1993
Iran, Islamic Rep.	Stock Exchange of Teheran	1967
Iraq	Iraq Stock Exchange	2004
Libya	Libyan Stock Exchange	2007
MENA GCC		
Bahrain	Bahrain Stock Exchange	1987
Kuwait	Kuwait Stock Exchange	1984
Oman	Muscat Securities Market	1988
Qatar	Qatar Exchange	1997
Saudi Arabia	Tadawul	1984
United Arab Emirates	Abu Dhabi Securities Exchange, Nasdaq Dubai	2000
East Asia		
China	Shanghai Stock Exchange, Shenzhen Stock exchange	Shanghai: 1990 but earlier dated back to 1860s; Shenzhen: 1990
Indonesia	Indonesian Stock Market	1912
Korea, Rep.	Korean Exchange	
Malaysia	Bursa Malaysia	1964
Philippines	Philippine Stock Exchange	1927
Thailand	Stock Exchange of Thailand	1962

Source: World Bank Data, from World Federation of Exchanges database.

Note: figures in italics and underlined are for nearest year to that indicated in column heading.

significant mechanism for financing development, especially in marked contrast to what has happened in the GCC and East Asia. Even well after the aforementioned reforms, by 2010 Tunisia's capital market capitalization did not exceed 25% of GDP compared to 48% or more in East Asia as a whole, and reaching 160% in the case of Malaysia. Moreover, in contrast to many

	Listed domestic companies (Number, end of year)					
Ownership Structure	***1995/1996***	***2000***	***2005***	***2010***	***2015***	***2019***
	171	**229**	**181**	**114**	**115**	**92**
Public	654	1075	744	227	250	246
Public	126	163	201	277	228	
Public	6	12	11	10	10	10
Mutualized	44	53	54	73	74	74
Public						
Mutualized	**24**	**44**	**45**	**56**	**78**	**81**
Private		25	28	39	49	48
	142	**285**	**408**	**369**	**318**	**331**
State Owned						
	142	285	408	369	318	331
Mutualized						
State Owned						
	65	**107**	**125**	**90**	**100**	**107**
State-Owned	35	36	40	44	44	43
Public	45	77	147			
State-Owned	114	208	235	114	116	111
State-Owned				43	43	47
State-Owned			77	146	171	204
State-Owned				104	125	130
	404	**668**	**847**	**1001**	**1182**	**1436**
State-Owned	323	1086	1377	2063	2827	3777
	237	286	336	420	521	668
	721	1242	1616	1781	1948	2262
	523	787	1015	948	892	919
	205	228	235	251	262	265
	416	381	504	541	639	725

(Continued)

of the other countries, Tunisia's use of the stock market (via all four measures in Table 5.4) after 2010 actually declined.

Among the factors lying behind the small size of stock market finance in Tunisia and most other MENA countries has been (a) the dearth of investments by insurance companies, pensions, mutual funds, and other

Table 5.4 Finance through Stock Markets, 1995–2019 *(Continued)*

	Market capitalization of listed domestic companies (% GDP)					
Country	***1995/1996***	***2000***	***2005/2007***	***2008/2010***	***2015***	***2017/2019***
MENA Non-Major Oil Exporters	**19.92**	**10.87**	**45.88**	**52.09**	**33.08**	**29.96**
Djibouti						
Egypt, Arab Rep.			*86.99*	38.50	16.59	14.58
Jordan				115.18	66.90	48.09
Lebanon	*17.50*	9.00	22.37	33.03	22.79	14.50
Morocco				74.18	45.39	55.10
Syrian Arab Republic						
Tunisia	**22.34**	**13.11**	**8.73**	**24.18**	**20.43**	**21.92**
West Bank and Gaza		10.50	65.43	27.49	26.35	*25.55*
Yemen						
MENA Major Oil Exporters	**9.50**	**12.44**	**8.11**	**8.93**	**11.66**	**12.30**
Algeria		0.52	0.14	0.07	0.09	*0.21*
Iran, Islamic Rep.	9.50	24.35	16.09	17.80	23.23	*24.39*
Iraq						
Libya						
MENA GCC	**47.38**	**48.70**	**101.51**	**61.26**	**65.77**	**108.28**
Bahrain	*77.21*	73.09	108.74	78.01	61.85	69.69
Kuwait	47.70	51.60	128.37			
Oman	17.23	21.41	49.12	49.64	60.12	22.24
Qatar			*119.81*	*66.39*	88.14	87.24
Saudi Arabia				66.91	64.36	303.52
United Arab Emirates				45.37	54.41	58.70
East Asia	**97.25**	**44.16**	**58.52**	**87.75**	**81.83**	**78.93**
China			17.58	66.17	74.02	59.37
Indonesia	32.94	16.25	28.48	47.73	41.04	46.76
Korea, Rep.	32.11	29.72	76.80	95.44	84.00	
Malaysia	240.97	120.65	125.77	160.26	127.08	110.76
Philippines	*97.35*	31.05	37.05	75.50	77.93	73.06
Thailand	82.87	23.12	65.44	81.42	86.92	104.70

institutional investors and even more so (b) by the dearth of investments by international investors. According to the OECD (2012) report, this has made share prices in these exchanges more volatile than they would otherwise have been, and especially when political uncertainty tended to arise with the Arab Uprisings in 2011 in Egypt, Syria, and Tunisia. Without a sovereign wealth fund (SWF) or even a large pension fund, the Tunisian exchange has been without some of the share price stabilization benefits that SWFs have provided to stock listings in the stock exchanges of GCC countries.

In a sense, the pattern of changes in the different stock exchange indicators for Tunisia presents something of a puzzle. Although the figures have

Stocks traded (% GDP)					
1995/1996	*2000*	*2005/2006*	*2010*	*2013/2015*	*2017/2019*
4.78	**4.35**	**53.59**	**11.48**	**3.68**	**2.96**
		45.00	17.00	4.44	3.68
8.66	5.49	186.57	32.08	9.34	*5.60*
0.49	0.67	4.20	4.88	1.01	0.37
6.27	8.12	12.66	6.54	2.88	2.75
3.71			**4.17**	*1.86*	
	3.11	19.51	4.20	2.53	*2.42*
0.58	**4.07**	**3.18**	**3.49**	**2.19**	**2.64**
0.58	4.07	3.18	3.49	2.19	*2.64*
8.82	**2.95**	**100.11**	**13.86**	**21.09**	**9.10**
1.81	2.71	4.40	1.12	0.94	1.97
22.70	*3.34*	114.32		*23.16*	
1.95	2.81	11.76	5.80	5.20	2.23
		34.09	14.71	14.93	7.27
		335.97	38.09	66.78	27.84
			9.56	15.55	6.17
28.76	**39.34**	**39.79**	**68.81**	**101.19**	**60.99**
10.55	62.13	17.16	135.66	355.52	132.79
7.11	7.82	9.75	13.83	8.72	10.53
32.52	85.97	128.33	142.45	125.79	117.38
67.79	55.99	31.10	45.01	36.99	29.78
19.79	8.81	4.98	10.68	12.54	7.96
34.80	15.29	47.44	65.21	67.61	67.53

(Continued)

shown a gradual increase in the number of listed companies over time, those numbers are still not large, even compared only to other MENA exchanges. More importantly, that growth in number of listed firms has not yielded a corresponding increase in the magnitude of finance through its stock exchange that one might have expected. The OECD (2012) Report on MENA stock exchanges attributed this to the fact that Tunisia's exchange, like many others in the region, was unable to assure investors that activity in the exchange would be subject to high standards of governance. That study pointed out that, unlike some of the exchanges in the GCC, the Tunisian exchange does not have a specific corporate governance program. While

Table 5.4 Finance through Stock Markets, 1995–2019 *(Continued)*

	Turnover ratio (% of capitalization, yearly)					
Country	***1995/1996***	***2000***	***2005/2006***	***2010***	***2013/2015***	***2017/2019***
MENA Non-Major Oil Exporters	**9.71**	**14.85**	**33.43**	**21.35**	**11.33**	**8.91**
Djibouti						
Egypt, Arab Rep.			51.73	44.16	26.74	25.26
Jordan				27.86	13.97	8.01
Lebanon	2.80	7.49	18.76	14.78	0.00	2.53
Morocco				8.82	6.36	4.98
Syrian Arab Republic						
Tunisia	**16.62**	7.45		**17.23**		**5.38**
West Bank and Gaza		29.60	29.82	15.26	9.59	7.29
Yemen						
MENA Major Oil Exporters	**6.05**	**16.72**	**19.75**	**19.61**	**9.44**	**25.28**
Algeria						
Iran, Islamic Rep.	6.05	16.72	19.75	19.61	9.44	25.28
Iraq						
Libya						
MENA GCC	**20.90**	**7.33**	**39.01**	**22.78**	**31.89**	**7.33**
Bahrain	3.75	3.71	4.04	1.43	1.53	2.83
Kuwait	47.60	5.15	89.06			3.13
Oman	11.34	13.13	23.93	11.69	8.66	10.04
Qatar					16.94	8.34
Saudi Arabia				56.93	103.77	9.17
United Arab Emirates				21.08	28.57	10.51
East Asia	**44.92**	**95.66**	**68.27**	**84.26**	**129.04**	**79.72**
China			97.64	205.02	480.29	223.66
Indonesia	21.59	48.12	34.21	28.98	21.24	22.53
Korea, Rep.	101.25	289.24	167.09	149.26	149.75	129.83
Malaysia	28.13	46.41	24.73	28.09	29.11	26.89
Philippines	31.63	28.38	13.45	14.14	16.09	10.90
Thailand	42.00	66.16	72.50	80.09	77.79	64.49

the exchange does post a 'Code of Best Practice of Corporate Governance' for a firm to be listed on the exchange, compliance with that Code of Best Practice is strictly voluntary. One of the aforementioned reforms which it has made was to allow for different listing tiers (just as the exchanges of Egypt, Jordan, Algeria, Iraq, WBG, and even Syria have done) but there are no governance requirements for any of these tiers, again making adherence of firms of any type to any code strictly voluntary. So, too the Tunisian exchange was found not to have any 'Self-Regulatory Organization,' indeed making Tunisia's exchange one of the few exchanges in MENA not to have one. While the Tunis Exchange does have certain disclosure requirements

Market capitalization (billions current USD, end of year)					
1995/1996	*2000*	*2005/2006*	*2010*	*2013/2015*	*2017/2019*
3.21	**1.61**	**26.07**	**35.02**	**25.02**	**25.11**
		93.50	84.28	55.19	44.20
			30.86	25.45	21.04
2.40	1.55	4.81	12.70	11.38	7.74
			69.15	45.93	65.42
4.03	**2.82**	**2.82**	**10.65**	**8.82**	**8.50**
	0.45	3.16	2.45	3.34	3.76
9.16	**13.49**	**18.29**	**43.37**	**44.79**	**160.52**
	0.29	0.14	0.11	0.14	*0.37*
9.16	26.69	36.44	86.64	89.43	320.67
6.69	**10.09**	**45.45**	**133.32**	**163.77**	**571.62**
4.71	6.62	17.36	20.06	19.25	26.88
12.97	19.46	103.72			
2.38	4.18	15.27	28.32	41.12	17.12
				142.56	160.05
			353.41	421.06	2406.82
			131.49	194.84	247.21
151.22	**178.75**	**326.30**	**1096.05**	**1848.10**	**2066.20**
		401.85	4027.84	8188.02	8515.50
66.58	26.81	81.43	360.39	353.27	523.32
181.95	171.26	718.01	1091.91	1231.20	*1413.72*
286.65	640.46	592.84	661.10	728.49	1100.11
80.65	25.98	39.80	157.32	238.82	*275.30*
140.28	29.22	123.88	277.73	348.80	569.23

for listing, from the questionnaires circulated as part of the OECD (2012) study, not a single case was identified in which the Tunisian exchange de-listed any company for violating these requirements. Not surprisingly, not a single one of the 25 largest listed companies in the MENA region was listed on the Tunisian exchange.

Some exchanges in Asia and in developed countries have encouraged greater transparency on the part of firms by also opening up trading for corporate debt. This was because, quite naturally, buyers of a firm's assets or debts would want to have greater access to information about the firm's accounts. Since some of the same companies would be listed in both asset and debt markets, this would improve informational access to potential buyers of stock shares for those firms. Yet, this has not yet happened in the Tunisian exchange or indeed in most other exchanges in the MENA region.

Attempts to develop the bond market in Tunisia and many other MENA countries have failed, not only for bond issues of the private sector, but even for government bonds. While there has been some development in the primary market, especially for government bonds, the secondary market has remained embryonic. The development of the bond market has been undermined in part because of the capture of this market by the banks, themselves. The banks have become the main brokers in government securities and continued to dominate that market by having given priority to increasing the share of government bonds in their own portfolios. As a result, the secondary market for government bonds has remained almost non-existent, and direct acquisition by individuals and businesses of government bonds has remained small.

On the positive side, Amico (2014) did credit the securities regulator of the Tunisian exchange for intervening to freeze shareholdings of the companies and other property owned by the Ben Ali family and their corrupt collaborators, paving the way for the eventual confiscation of these assets.

In any case, however, Tunisian firms have continued to depend mainly on the credit market to finance their development. The volume of initial equity public offerings and bond issues by business firms was a comparatively very low 3% of total private investment as recently as 1990. While it did increase to 10% in 1995, it then fell sharply to 4% in 2000,[14] before recovering partially to averages of 7.1% during the 2000s and 8.6% during the 2010s.[15]

Another harmful implication of Tunisia's comparative shortcomings in the development of its stock market is that underdevelopment of the stock market can also lower the efficiency and raise operating costs of banks and thereby make bank credit less available and more costly to private firms. In particular, Ben Naceur and Omran (2011) used data from 10 different MENA countries including Tunisia over the period 1989–2005 and showed[16] that banks have lower operating costs and can lower borrowing costs for firms when local stock markets are more developed and when bank ownership is less concentrated. Both of those conditions have been shown to contribute to why private firms in Tunisia have not had better access to finance than firms in other MENA and especially East Asian countries.

F. Tunisia's Weak Fiscal Policy

While the only very modest rise in the share of bank credit to the private sector in GDP, and the very limited role of the stock markets in financing business, were certainly important contributors to Tunisia's relative weakness in both generating savings, investment, and financial development, they were not the only contributors. Indeed, fiscal policy and the budgetary system would seem to be another important contributor. Boughzala (2001) provided an account of the strengths and weaknesses of Tunisia's budgetary and fiscal systems prior to 2000. The first law enacted by the Tunisian government in 1960 was the Budget Law, which remained in force, but with amendments in crisis times in 1967 and 1996, respectively. Boughzala's account of the budgetary system pointed to several somewhat perennial problems in it, but with rises as well as declines in their severity over time. Among these were (1) the relative importance of off-budget items which would not go through the normal disclosure procedures, (2) the fact that during some periods (e.g., in the 1970s) the individual ministries had considerable bargaining power in getting their desired expenditures approved at the expense of the otherwise dominant position of the Finance Minister and the President, (3) variations in the comprehensiveness of coverage of expenditures treated as investment (as opposed to current consumption) expenditures which were programmed in multi-year plans (which made it difficult to achieve overall control of the total budget), (4) lack of coordination between those in the Ministry of Finance responsible for authorizing and allocating budgetary funds and those agencies following up on the authorized expenditures, and perhaps most importantly (5) the absence of program evaluation or any other means for evaluating the efficiency and effectiveness of expenditures, except in the case of special funds provided through foreign aid. As a result of these shortcomings, Tunisia's fiscal deficits have become endemic, and in some years quite large. For example, these fiscal deficits exceeded 5% of GDP in 1978, 1983, 1984–1987, and 1991–1992, the deficits always adding to the country's foreign debt. When these debts grew to crisis proportions as in the mid-1980s, it led to intervention by the IMF which brought in reforms leading to greater inclusiveness of the budget, stricter rules such as that, when the deficits were severe (perhaps because of revenue shortfalls), the Minister of Finance could cut items that had previously been approved. As shown in Table 4.3, the large size of Tunisia's external debt in the mid-1980s also gave rise to its peak share of Total External Debt Service in Total Exports. Note, however, that Tunisia was by no means the only country to run such high deficits, debt and debt service, especially in the period before 1990. But, over the whole period, Tunisia's share of Foreign Debt to GDP doubled while those same shares in both GCC countries and East Asian countries as a whole fell.

While such sizable fiscal deficits and great volatility in fiscal policy over time posed real challenges, there are clearly numerous shortcomings in Tunisia's fiscal policy that one could point to. Notably, Chebbi (2019) calls attention to one relatively simple change which, if carried out, might well reduce both the volatility and the size of fiscal deficits and also increase overall economic efficiency. This has to do with fuel taxes/subsidies and how these change as the world oil price changes over time. The context is seen as one where the retail price of each type of fuel paid by the consumer might well differ from the concessionary price that the distributor of fuels (a public enterprise) would receive. Chebbi diagnosed the severity of the problem that was occurring was due the traditional tendency of relatively autocratic governments to keep fuel users happy by keeping the prices to consumers low while allowing public enterprise inefficiencies to grow, contributing to fiscal deficits. Given that the rich consume much more fuel than the poor, this makes for an extremely inequitable subsidy and a far from optimal fuel pricing system. Chebbi proposed the adoption of a gradual price and subsidy adjustment program which would improve consumer surplus while at the same time lowering instability of fiscal policy and vulnerability to oil price shocks. Since the determinants of demand for each fuel type would be different, Chebbi recommended that different adjustment rules should be designed for each fuel type. Even if it were applied to gasoline alone, the study showed that it could reduce the overall fiscal deficit by 10%.

G. Tunisia's Insufficient Use of Global Markets and Limited Diversification

We observed in Chapter 4 that Tunisia was relatively more successful than other MENA countries in leveraging global markets, increasing its exports and attracting FDI. As shown in Tables 4.8 and 4.9, its performance in terms of non-oil exports and FDI even matched those of some of the most successful East Asian countries. But Tunisia has failed to reap the level of benefits achieved by these East Asian countries in terms of diversification and sophistication of production and exports, and the ensuing employment and productivity growth stemming from that. In that respect, we have pointed out above Tunisia's inability to make use of exports as a means of providing the markets needed to generate sufficient demand for its increasing numbers of more highly educated workers and to finance higher levels of saving and investment. Moreover, we are by no means the first to suggest that insufficient use of global markets has been one of the main shortcomings of Tunisia. Indeed, several important volumes focusing on the MENA region have pointed this out, not only about Tunisia, but also about many other countries in the region. See, for example, Henry and Springborg (2010, Chapters 1, 2, 5, and 8) and Devlin (2010, Chapters 3, 7–9).

While those studies were rather general and not especially quantitative, other more quantitative analyses have also identified the shortcomings of MENA countries in general, and Tunisia in particular, in taking advantage of global markets. Miniesy et al. (2004) and Nugent and Yousef (2005) both made use of panel data on bilateral trade flows among a large sample of countries over time showing that Tunisia and virtually all MENA countries were engaged in significantly less trade, especially with other neighboring and MENA trade partners, than would have been predicted on the basis of standard Gravity Models trade determinants, such as GDP and geographic size, distance between countries, contiguity, commonalities in terms of language and legal systems and the existence of trade or currency unions.

In the light of these findings, these studies pointed to the potential usefulness of developing more special trade agreements among MENA countries for generating more trade and for diversifying their economic structures. This appeal was very much in line with trying to realize the benefits that East Asian countries had taken advantage of and that East Asian scholars had credited as playing a substantial part of their success. For example, as Justin Yifu Lin of Peking University in China and a former Chief Economist at the World Bank put it, 'If the government pays a facilitating role, enabling firms to *exploit the economy's comparative advantages*, its economy will develop successfully' (Lin 2009, 93). Lin (2009, 2012a, 2012b, 2012c) saw this as being quite different than what governments in many developing countries tend to do, which is to promote favored industries but which go against their true comparative advantages.

The sad story is that the only important trade arrangements that Tunisia and its neighboring MENA countries have engaged in until 2007 were with the EU, commencing in the 1960s, deepening in the 1970s and even more in the late 1990s. While as noted above, Tunisia was quite successful in deriving some benefits from this agreement for the development of both olive oil exports and automobile parts manufacturing, these agreements were in fact fairly restrictive as far as these countries' comparative advantages in agriculture were concerned. Tunisia's attempt to engage in trade agreements with neighboring MENA countries, moreover, has been even less successful.

The primary such agreement of special relevance to Tunisia was the Agadir Agreement (AA) which came into force only in 2007 between Tunisia, Egypt, Jordan, and Morocco (but without Algeria as had been attempted). There seems to be agreement among the various evaluators of this scheme (Freund and Portugal-Perez 2012; Khodeir 2017; World Trade Organization 2018; Kourtelis 2021) that this scheme has not been successful, though with some disagreements as to why. While it did reduce tariffs between countries, it seems to have allowed other taxes to be increased and failed to reach any satisfactory system of settling disputes. The most recent of these evaluations, that is, Kourtelis (2021), makes the case that one of the shortcomings of the agreement was excessive reliance on the framework of the EU in its agreements with Mediterranean countries and giving these far less qualified country level partners the same kinds of power that more experienced and less political EU partners would have. This was said to allow the individual countries to push their own favorites but thereby undermining the potential for effective integration along the lines of comparative advantage. It also argues that the concern of each country for collecting revenues from tariffs as in the case of trade with the EU undermined their interest in tariff-free trade under the AA and has prevented the AA from allowing its members to trade among each other somewhat higher value products than those it exports to the EU.

There is also an even grander trade agreement among Tunisia and a larger number of MENA countries known as the Greater Arab Free Trade

Area (GAFTA) which was cultivated by the Arab League. Fourteen Arab countries concluded an agreement to join GAFTA as early as 1997, but some others including some of the larger ones like Algeria only signed onto it as recently as 2009. It was designed to come into effect by the beginning of 2007. While tariff barriers among those countries which had signed onto GAFTA had been removed by 2005, the elimination of the more complicated and divisive non-tariff barriers (NTBs) has been very sporadic. As evaluated in its early stages by Abedini and Peridy (2008), using a standard gravity model to estimate trade between all pairs of member countries, they did find that intra-regional trade among the 17 GAFTA members had been increased by 16–24% between 1997 and 2005. This was at least fairly impressive. Yet, the bulk of that intra GAFTA trade (indeed 70% of it) was confined to the GCC countries which also had their own and much simpler FTA, and almost half of all the intra-GAFTA trade was in the form of primary products mostly agriculture and fuels, thereby representing very little in the way of diversification of economic activity. Tunisia was found to be one of the few countries outside the GCC which was generating at least a small surplus in that trade. But, as with all the Maghreb countries, the growth in its trade with the EU was considerably greater than that from GAFTA. In recent years, however, there has been increasing concern for shortcomings in both the design and implementation of GAFTA.

According to the useful and more recent review of GAFTA in 2017 by Malkawi (2017), some serious problems remain, preventing its full implementation. Most important among these is the Rules of Origin which is of considerable importance since free trade among members is only supposed to be granted to products which are produced entirely within GAFTA. Yet, the rules that were developed for this purpose occupied 13 pages of text and a number of alternative methods proposed but none agreed to by all. For this reason, even in 2019, newspaper articles appeared concerning a new attempt by the GAFTA to construct a simpler set of rules, but apparently these have still not been finalized. Especially as a result of the difficulties with the Rules of Origin, many disputes have arisen but Dispute Settlement within GAFTA has also been found wanting. The promise of GAFTA has been found to be especially disappointing for relatively small exporting and importing firms which have found the administrative costs and time delays to obtain the necessary approvals to be so great as to not justify the attempts to obtain them.

Prior to the AA and GAFTA and early in the experience with the agreements with the EU, but of special importance to manufactures, Meon and Sekkat (2004) used panel data on a large number of countries over the 1990s to show very specifically that all MENA countries exported less manufactured goods and attracted less FDI than they should have because of their especially weak political risk and governance institutions. Since Tunisia was considered better off in quite a few other respects (especially along the lines we have identified in Chapter 4), their estimates suggested that the exports and FDI of Tunisia (and to a lesser extent also of Egypt) could have been boosted more by improvements in their political risk and governance institutions than those in any of the other MENA countries.

Yet, given Tunisia's relatively small size, we feel it necessary to focus more specifically on this problem in Tunisia, especially since it is one of the smaller countries in the MENA region. We observed in Chapter 3 that in the 1960s Tunisia had followed an inward-oriented development strategy with very high protection of domestic activities, import-substitution, and little use of global markets. Beginning in the early 1970s, however, it changed course and pursued a more export-oriented strategy, and one promoting foreign direct investment and integration into the global economy. Indeed, this process was similar with what happened in East Asia. With large variations in the timing, speed, and substance of their liberalization and integration into the global economy, the different East Asian countries have varied more in these respects from one country to another than have the MENA countries. They moved through these three stages quite smoothly even though the movement and timing from one stage to the next varied from country to country and was often cautious and pragmatic. Sometimes it involved the coexistence of the previous system of protection with the more liberalized new system, such as through special economic zones. During the first stage, that of import-substitution and self-reliance, starting in the 1950s and 1960s, this involved high tariffs and quantitative restrictions on imports, overvalued exchange rates, and extensive government intervention in trade and production. The second stage started with the newly industrializing economies (NIEs) in the late 1960s as they moved toward more outward-oriented and export promotion strategies. Relevant policies of the East Asian countries during this period included subsidies, favorable allocations of foreign exchange, preferential allocation of credit, tax incentives, and even under-valued exchange rates. The third and last stage came in the 2000s and was characterized by a movement from inter-industry to intra-industry trade and the dominance of Global Value Chains (GVCs), and from inter-regional to intra-regional trade and direct investment. It was driven by increased liberalization of trade, lower cross-border transportation and communications costs, and regional trade agreements (Asian Development Bank 2020).

Most MENA countries, however, began to liberalize only in the late 1980s or 1990s, whereas some Asian countries (like Korea and Taiwan) started in the 1950s but others like China and Malaysia in the 1980s and Indonesia, Vietnam and the Philippines only more recently. This has meant that within the Asian region, there have been greater differences in factor endowments, stages of development and hence greater opportunities for developing intra-industry trade and trading networks than within MENA or even between Tunisia and other MENA countries with their neighbors in Europe. As a result, neighborhood effects for Tunisia in MENA and the

Mediterranean have been much less favorable than those enjoyed by many countries from the more dynamic East Asia region.

Without having had to face the competition of world markets to the extent that would have been expected were it not for Tunisia's continued adherence to its protected trade regime, Tunisia has generally been unable to take full advantage of the available global markets and integrate into the world economy to the extent that Asian countries have. In Japan, Korea, Taiwan, Singapore, and Hong Kong, subsequently China, and more recently Vietnam and the Philippines, this has resulted in a continuous upward movement in the technological and organizational sophistication of industry, allowing these economies to take advantage of their increasing human capital stocks and to remain competitive internationally despite rising wage rates. While Tunisia has been able to achieve significant diversification of its manufacturing exports since the 1990s toward higher technology products, its traditional low-technology products, which developed nicely in the 1970s and 1980s, slowed significantly during the 1990s and almost totally stalled with the great recession of 2008–2009. While its medium and high technology exports expanded rapidly, driven to a large extent by FDI, this process remained much weaker in Tunisia than what was observed in East Asia.

As a result, despite the potential suitability of special subsectors of manufacturing for Tunisian conditions, the share of manufacturing in total employment fell from 20% in 1990 to 19% in 2016 (Boughzala 2018). One factor deterring Tunisian firms from being able to increase manufacturing production and other exports has been the weak technical abilities of Tunisian firms. Numerous analysts, including both Bustos and Yildirim (2017) and Samoud and Dhaoui (2019), have pointed to the need for Tunisian firms to increase their own technical abilities in a low-cost manner or at least to make it easier to work with foreign firms in GVCs. Bustos and Yildirim made use of an Economic Complexity index which showed that, despite Tunisia's rise in both per capita income and exports per capita over the period 1995–2010, its Economic Complexity Index only stagnated, suggesting that this failure should be overcome by picking sectors, technologies and particular foreign markets in which Tunisian firms would be able to make this transition into complexity at low cost. Samoud and Dhaoui, on the other hand, using a longer time horizon on Economic Complexity showed that its Economic Complexity Index has in fact increased, although, especially since 1995, by considerably less than any of its three MENA neighbors, Egypt, Algeria, and especially Morocco.[17]

To do better in raising its Economic Complexity Index, Samoud and Dhaoui (2019) suggested using an alternative strategy, namely, to take greater advantage of GVCs, as a lower cost and more appropriate means of achieving the same objective. The advantage of the GVC strategy is that the individual country (like Tunisia) would not need to attract all the complementary industries for it to be successful in a highly desirable sector like Computers, Electronic, and Electrical Equipment Manufacturing which many analysts have identified as an ideal one for Tunisia to take advantage of, given its excess supply of well-educated youths. Instead of trying to attract such a large complex of firms in different industries to the country, it would only need to take advantage of trading opportunities to and from foreign firms already deeply involved in GVCs. A country with heavy emphasis on GVCs would be expected to have relatively large percentages of intermediate goods rather than final ones in both its imports and exports. Yet, Samoud and Dhaoui (2019) showed (p. 5–6) that in both cases Tunisia's shares of intermediate goods were considerably lower than those of its neighbor Morocco. They did identify Textiles, Chemicals, and especially the Computers, Electronic, and Electrical Equipment sector, as sectors in which Tunisia scored well on the GVC Participation Index and accounting for why Tunisia scored above most of its MENA neighbors and at least above Indonesia (among the East Asian countries). Indeed, its high GVC score in Computers, Electronic, and Electrical Equipment was most impressive, showing the country's integration into three different important GVCs, namely, Aeronautics, Aircraft Maintenance and especially Automotive (in which no less than 230 companies were engaged).

Given the importance of intermediate goods imports in those sectors with relatively high GVCs, it is relatively easy to attribute Tunisia's success in this respect to its use of the offshore regime which, as mentioned above, exempted such firms from having to pay import duties on goods that will be incorporated into exports, and to its trade integration with the European Union in 1995 which has exempted their imports of manufactures from Tunisia from customs duties. Yet, this GVC Participation Index, by focusing on the early phase of GVCs, does not account for the intermediate goods supplied by a country that appear in the exports of other countries and the use by the country itself of imported intermediate goods from other countries in its own productive inputs. Samoud and Dhaoui (2019) go on to make use of a GVC Position Index (developed by Koopman et al. 2010). This measure is the ratio of the use of intermediate goods supplied by a country in the exports of all other countries to the use by the country of its intermediate imports in its own production. Not surprisingly, since Tunisia's strength was in the share of intermediate imports in its offshore production process, Samoud and Dhaoui (2019, 12) show that Tunisia ranks quite low on the GVC Position Index as of 2015, indicating that the country has a long way to go to make an enlarged and higher tech manufacturing sector viable.[18]

This is illustrated by recent developments showing that Tunisia has lost ground even to other MENA countries. In particular, its neighbor Morocco has since about 2014 managed to take great advantage of GVCs, with imported inputs constituting over 50% of the gross value added of its exports of motor vehicles, machinery, and coke and petroleum products (OECD 2018). Also since 2013, it has been taking advantage of a strategic partnership with a new foreign investor to the region, China. Under that country's huge Belt and Road Initiative (BRI), free trade zones, and other special programs with huge amounts of FDI have been established in Morocco, such as the Atlantic Free Trade Zone in Kenitra, the Mohammed VI Tangier Mediterranean Port Complex (within which there is a growing logistics complex), and the Casablanca Finance City (Ghafar and Jacobs 2019). As a result, by 2014–2015 the World Economic Forum (2014) identified Morocco as the most competitive economy in North Africa.

One determinant of the relative success of countries in engaging in exports, technological upgrading through R&D expenditures and participating in GVCs with backward and forward linkages is the strength of their logistics. High quality logistics is often seen as an important vehicle for private firms to access modern technology and to link in to GVCs. One measure of this factor is the Logistics Performance Index (LPI). Unfortunately, this LPI index does not contain any entries before 2007 and its country coverage even since then is a bit incomplete (with no coverage at all of the WBG). In any case, Table 5.5 presents the corresponding LPI scores for selected years between 2007 and 2018 for each of our MENA and East Asian sample countries. The LPI is scored on a 0–5 basis.

With its score of 2.76 in 2007 Tunisia was the top scoring country among the non-oil MENA countries although considerably below each of the GCC countries, and also below all except the Philippines among the East Asian countries. While Tunisia's score rose fairly sharply to 3.17 in 2012 just after the uprisings which was accompanied by an explosion of use of electronics, by 2018 its LPI score had fallen quite sharply to 2.57 which was only in the middle of the pack of non-oil MENA countries and well below the LPI scores of all GCC and East Asian countries. It is notable that Morocco's score caught up with and even surpassed that of Tunisia. From information on the components of the LPI from World Bank (2018) which included its applicability to trade (Customs, Infrastructure, International Shipments Logistics Quality and Competence, Tracking and Timeliness) Tunisia's scores in 2018 were especially low for the most basic components (Infrastructure and Logistics Quality). That same report of the World Bank (2018, Chapter 2) called attention to the role of Logistics Performance in giving rise to 'Technology Rising Star Products' and to participation in high value GVCs and also suggested that raising their LPI score would be a very useful means of increasing both their intra-MENA and extra-MENA trade.[19]

The value of GVCs in reducing poverty in a broad range of developing countries (Ferreira et al. 2010), in promoting gender equity (Rocha and Winkler 2019), and more broadly in promoting trade and growth through a number of mechanisms, including technological change and attracting FDI, has been further articulated by the World Bank (2020) in its comprehensive analysis of GVCs as a vehicle for trade, growth, and equity, in developing countries. Based on detailed sectoral productivity and value-added growth data for 40 countries (both developed and developing but not including Tunisia or any other MENA countries), Yanikkaya et al. (2020) showed

Table 5.5 Logistics Performance Index, 2007–2018 (score 0-5)

Country	*2007*	*2010*	*2012*	*2014*	*2016*	*2018*
MENA non-major oil exporters	**2.35**	**2.74**	**2.70**	**2.58**	**2.56**	**2.57**
Djibouti	1.94	2.39	1.80	2.15	2.32	2.63
Egypt	2.37	2.61	2.98	2.97	3.18	2.82
Jordan	2.59	2.74	2.56	2.87	2.96	2.69
Lebanon	2.37	3.31	2.58	2.73	2.72	2.72
Morocco	2.38		3.03		2.67	2.54
Syrian Arab Republic	2.09	2.74	2.60		1.60	2.30
Tunisia	**2.76**	**2.84**	**3.17**	**2.55**	**2.50**	**2.57**
West Bank and Gaza						
Yemen	2.29	2.58	2.89	2.18		2.27
MENA Major Oil Exporters	**2.29**	**2.34**	**2.34**	**2.48**	**2.45**	**2.32**
Algeria	2.06	2.36	2.41	2.65	2.77	2.45
Iran, Islamic Rep.	2.51	2.57	2.49		2.60	2.55
Iraq		2.11	2.16	2.30	2.15	2.18
Libya		2.33	2.28	2.50	2.26	2.11
MENA GCC	**3.13**	**3.22**	**3.18**	**3.22**	**3.40**	**3.24**
Bahrain	3.15	3.37	3.05	3.08	3.31	2.93
Kuwait	2.99	3.28	2.83	3.01	3.15	2.86
Oman	2.92	2.84	2.89	3.00	3.23	3.20
Qatar	2.98	2.95	3.32	3.52	3.60	3.47
Saudi Arabia	3.02	3.22	3.18	3.15	3.16	3.01
United Arab Emirates	3.73	3.63	3.78	3.54	3.94	3.96
East Asia	**3.22**	**3.29**	**3.31**	**3.38**	**3.34**	**3.32**
China	3.32	3.49	3.52	3.53	3.66	3.61
Indonesia	3.01	2.76	2.94	3.08	2.98	3.15
Korea, Rep.	3.52	3.64	3.70	3.67	3.72	3.61
Malaysia	3.48	3.44	3.49	3.59	3.43	3.22
Philippines	2.69	3.14	3.02	3.00	2.96	2.90
Thailand	3.31	3.29	3.18	3.43	3.26	3.41

Source: World Bank (2018) and lpi.worldbank.org.

Note: Country-years with missing data are left blank.

quite clearly, and with results that were robust to different measures of the relevant variables, that forward GVC participation significantly raised TFP growth of manufacturing as a whole over the period studied (1996–2009). Yet, at the same time, the World Bank (2020) report has pointed out that joining GVCs, need not be easy and that the growth of GVCs declined sharply with the Global Financial Crisis of 2008–2009, and then again more recently with destabilizing protective actions by large trading countries like the U.S. and China. The usefulness of GVCs is also being undermined by increased policy uncertainty throughout much of the world.

Even without GVCs, however, participation in global markets can pay off via spillovers in economic growth across countries. Just as in the case of how the widely applied gravity model of trade between countries leads one to think that trade between countries can be strengthened by geographic proximity, common language and judicial systems, one would think that geographic proximity, common language and legal systems and other cultural similarities would make it likely that the growth rates of Tunisia and other MENA countries would be positively related and could provide positive spillovers to each other and to related third countries. The investigation of such hypotheses has led to the use of spatial econometric models, as in Bivand and Brundstad (2006), Fingleton and López-Bazo (2006), and Blonigen et al. (2007) in which the growth rate of an individual country would be allowed to be affected by lagged growth rates of other countries of varying distance from that country.

Although perhaps not yet finalized, a recent paper on the role of spatial clustering on trade and growth by Alaya (2020) has made use of growth rate data on 73 countries over the period 1996–2014, including 17 MENA countries, 33 European countries, and 23 Asian countries. The results show that most European countries and most Asian ones were highly clustered (i.e., with growth rates among nearby countries that were more highly correlated among each other), whereas in the case of MENA countries clustering was statistically insignificant in all countries, with the minor exception of Kuwait where there was at least marginally significant clustering. The paper then went on to check the degree of autocorrelation in this respect among neighboring countries, finding this to be characteristic of 13 of the 16 Asian countries but for none of the MENA countries. Tunisia and Lebanon were identified as among the countries where their clustering pattern differed most substantially from those of their neighbors. From there, the paper went on to run spatial regression models for growth which included as explanatory variables, the various within-country factors lying behind growth, such as the initial level of GDP per capita, physical capital, human capital, labor, technology, capital depreciation rates, exports, and both an average of five governance indexes, and the lagged growth rates of other countries, weighted by their distance from that country. Given that the impact of the latter externalities impacts could be modeled in different ways, three different models were employed to detect the robustness of the results to different modeling assumptions.

When this was done for the full sample, the results revealed highly significant externalities in all models, the results in one such model even identifying certain specific mechanisms (especially FDI) wherein these externalities are realized. When separate samples were utilized for Europe and also Asia, in each case similar results were found for two of the three models. Yet, when the same models were run only on the MENA sample, the results revealed positive and significant externalities in only one of the models (and even in this case the externalities are only fairly marginally significant). From this result, Alaya drew the conclusion that MENA countries seem to be disconnected (i.e., outside the clustering process either within the MENA region or with either Asia or Europe). As a result, neither geographic proximity nor economic and political proximity seems to be preventing Tunisia and other MENA countries from falling behind in capturing the benefits of growth externalities.

Given that services account for some 60% of Tunisia's GDP and that various services are especially important in GVC participation, another priority area for improvement in Tunisia is trade reforms in services industries. Dee and Diop (2010), moreover, have argued that trade reforms in services would be less likely than other trade reforms to lead to difficulties for some Tunisian firms. Based on a detailed study by the OECD in 2005 of regulatory conditions outside of manufacturing (i.e., OECD 2005a, 2005b and 2005c) comparing Tunisia with China, Korea, Malaysia, Vietnam, Turkey, Morocco, Australia, New Zealand, Mexico, Canada, Japan, the U.S., and at least 12 different European countries, Dee, and Diop found Tunisia's regulations to be among the two most restrictive among all countries surveyed in Postal Services, Passenger Transport, Accounting and Legal Services, and the fifth most restrictive for banking services. These authors also showed that, as a result of Tunisia's unusually tight regulations on services, the prices of all these services except for telecommunications ranged from 5% to 20% higher than they otherwise would need to be for both foreign and domestic providers.

Notes

1 Data from the Conference Board Total Economy Database, downloaded April 2019.
2 Not also that Korea's earlier start in land reform could well have contributed to its extremely high TFP growth rates in years prior to this.
3 While China had lost two decades of progress between the collectivization of agriculture in 1956 until the Household Responsibility System in the late 1970s, it rapidly made up for this after 1978.
4 Chapter 5 of Asian Development Bank (2020) provides an up-to-date detailed description of these modalities. See Levy, Berry and Nugent (1999) for earlier evaluations of Japan, Korea and Indonesia.
5 The country coverage of PISA tests and other similar ones like the TIMSS and PIRLS tests in this same Table 4.6 are quite limited. Both Tunisia and most of the rest of the MENA countries for which such test scores are available have scores that are well below the average scores for the East Asian countries and especially China and Korea. The 2015 scores for Tunisia were by no means an aberration as the available PISA scores for 2003 and 2012 were very similar.
6 The figures for Algeria should be treated with caution, given (1) the nature of the economic system of this country during this period, where the role of the private sector was very limited, and (2) the numbers for the private sector are likely to include some at least partially state-owned enterprises.
7 And oddly Syria during the 1960s.
8 See, especially Ayyagari et al. (2011).
9 Note once again from the entries for Getting Credit and the Strength of Legal Rights how much greater improvement the West Bank and Gaza made between 2014 and 2020, reflecting the impressive collateral reform that the West Bank and Gaza carried out in 2016 referred to in Section E-1. Indeed, in

2014, the score of the West Bank and Gaza on Strength of Legal Rights had been 0.0 but in 2020 it was up to 8, i.e., one of the highest of all the countries and its score on Getting Credit jumped from 35 to 80 (higher than that of any other country in the table).

10 It was initially created as the 'Compagnie Financière et Touristique'.

11 Based on data from various issues of the Bulletin de Statistiques Financières, Banque Centrale de Tunisie.

12 In 1989 the 'Banque Nationale de Développement Agricole' merged with the Banque Nationale de Tunisie (to become the current 'Banque Nationale Agricole'). In 1999 the two main development banks (BDET and BNDT) were absorbed by the main state-owned bank, the 'Société Tunisienne de Banque'.

13 These figures refer to the price index of the Bourse des Valeurs Mobilières de Tunis and are taken from the Banque Centrale de Tunisie, Bulletin de Statistiques Financières, various issues.

14 Conseil du Marché Financier (2002, 22).

15 Conseil du Marché Financier (2003 to 2019).

16 Using Generalized Method of Moments estimation procedures.

17 For an in-depth discussion of the importance of complexity and its measurement, see Hausmann et al. (2014).

18 Given the broad range of factors identified above (from high wage rates, and labor regulations of various sorts to offshoring and GVCs), note should be made of the attempt by Ben Salha (2013a, b, c) to use time series data on aggregate and sectoral real wage rates, and sectoral labor demand to identify the relative importance of the different factors in the Tunisian environment that were changing over the period 1983-2009 and which may have been contributing to these industrial development outcomes. Among the changing factors were an index of globalization (reflecting the influence of international trade), and three sets of labor market policies: the minimum wage rate, active labor market policies (policies designed to encourage employment by subsidies to start-up self-employment), and changes in labor regulations (such as the introduction of short-term contracts, and the loosening of conditions on firing workers). The results showed that globalization boosted aggregate labor demand, but at least during that period primarily only in the low wage agricultural sector, where it also had the effect of raising the real wage rates. He also showed that the active labor market policies and partial de-regulation of the labor market both had the effect of slightly reducing real wage rates in both the manufacturing and service sectors, but the minimum wage rate increases over time had the opposite effect in all three sectors.

19 Unless Tunisia can succeed in dramatically increasing its participation in GVCs via technological upgrading and logistics performance, more traditional means of increasing exports, such as further liberalization of both tariffs and non-tariff barriers via a new more Deep and Comprehensive Euro-Med Agreement, will likely be necessary, Gasiorek and Mouley (2018) have estimated that the two sectors which would benefit the most from this would be Agriculture and Food Products Manufacturing.

6 A Political Economy Analysis of the Balance over Time between the Roles of the State and Markets and the Private Sector

We have shown in Chapter 2 that Tunisia has achieved only limited structural transformation, had weak labor market dynamics and its TFP growth has remained relatively low at 1–1.2% per annum since the 1990s, especially after having recovered from the negative growth of the late 1980s. Chapter 2 also showed that Tunisia continued to have lower levels of *efficiency* than the successful East Asian countries. In Chapter 5, we identified seven major differences in policies and other proximate determinants of performance between Tunisia and the most successful East Asian countries, namely, Tunisia's: (i) lower levels of savings and capital accumulation, (ii) the absence of a progressive land reform, (iii) limited success in stimulating strong technological progress and technology transfer, (iv) skills mismatches and shortcomings in the quality and efficient utilization of human capital in the form of education over time, (v) mixed success in financial development, (vi) weak fiscal policy, and (vii) insufficient use of global markets with which to diversify its economy and stimulate the ever-increasing competition experienced in East Asia.

In this Chapter, we attempt to identify the root causes of these relative weaknesses in Tunisia. The discussion in Chapter 5 suggested at different points that what might lie at the core of such differences are policies and institutional features with regard to how the state, on the one hand, and markets, on the other hand, have been used to allocate resources and improve efficiency, and further examined the role that the private sector played in the development process.

As shown in the preceding chapters, Tunisia and each of the East Asian countries have witnessed the exercise of a strong role for the state in their development process. Indeed, in Sections C and D of Chapter 4, it was shown that in Tunisia the State has played the dominant role in undertaking heavy investments in both human capital and physical infrastructure (as it had in the East Asian countries as demonstrated in the World Bank 1993). In both Tunisia and most of the East Asian countries, the state has also played a large role in development planning. Yet, in those areas where one might like to have seen the private sector play a more important role in that process, such as it did in product market development and globalization in East

DOI: 10.4324/9781003309550-6

Asia, in Tunisia the relative importance of the private sector and markets in that process has been relatively slight, and from our perspective distinctly suboptimal, though varying considerably across sectors and over time.

Moreover, compared to East Asia, the balance in Tunisia has remained tilted toward heavier government interventions, and with insufficient emphasis on market development and innovation. In our view, the result for Tunisia has been the persistence of inefficiencies and comparative underdevelopment and the lack of competitiveness of its private sector, in contrast to most of the East Asian countries where private sector firms have in several cases become world leaders.

In Tunisia, despite the many policy changes and reforms taken by the Tunisian government over time, in general the state has continued throughout the decades to intervene heavily in markets and the allocation of resources. Seemingly, as a result, Tunisia has come to experience more and longer persisting distortions and suffer from the costs thereof in terms of greater economic inefficiency and slower and more volatile growth than most of the East Asian countries in our sample. As a result, we find that Tunisia lacked the enduring success of the private sector, which has occurred in the East Asian Miracle countries through a process of continuous competition and globalization, resulting in continuous technological upgrading.

In this chapter, we pay attention to the roles of failures of both the private sector and the state at different points along the way and also attempt to identify the reasons lying behind why Tunisia has chosen somewhat different ways to respond to crises, and to confront common impediments such as the MIT, with different policies and strategies than those used by the East Asian countries. This chapter articulates the roles of both the state and the private sector in each of the main channels for affecting economic growth lying beyond that of human capital formation. Although the East Asian countries have varied in the extent of importance of the private sector and institutional policies relative to it and over time, we identify numerous ways in which Tunisia has fallen way short of the more successful East Asian countries in encouraging private sector development, stimulating innovation, R&D expenditures, and continuous technological upgrading by taking advantage of dynamic comparative advantage.

While we find many parallels in the comparisons between Tunisia and East Asia at various points in time and even within some of these different channels, over time we find a quite distinctive difference in trends. In East Asia, we see a steady but clear upward trend in the roles of markets and private sector agents in most of these various different areas, whereas in the case of Tunisia we find much less of a distinct upward trend in the roles of markets and the private sector (and instead growing cyclicality and even some decline). As a result, we confirm the explanation of Cherif and Hasanov (2019) for the rather miraculous growth of some of the East Asian countries and identify rather specific ways in which Tunisia (and most other MENA countries) have fallen far short of the most successful East Asian countries in globalization, innovation and R&D investments, that otherwise might have allowed Tunisia to compete with the East Asian countries in these respects.

While political economy perspectives are involved in all the other chapters, we believe that they are most central to this chapter and hence will be emphasized in the different sections of the chapter.

Since we feel that the difference between the way East Asia and Tunisia have been trying to find a balance between state and markets may be central to the overall difference in economic development performance over the last 60 years, we start in Section A by reviewing briefly the state of knowledge about how the most successful East Asia countries succeeded in breaking through the MIT and sustaining economic growth. Key political economy lessons of this experience are the ability to maintain close dialogue between the state and the private sector and the need to adjust the relevant rules and policies of the public sector in such a way as to overcome any problematic outcomes that arise over time and push the private sector to continuously upgrade its technology and eventually to maintain international competitiveness of its much higher tech firms through participation in GVCs. This provides a benchmark from which to assess the Tunisian experience.

Then in Section B, we review Tunisia's experience during the 30-year period following independence. This includes a discussion of how the Tunisian state has responded to the pervasiveness of market failures in the 1950s and 1960s, by relying on the development of an expansive state-owned enterprise (SOE) system complemented by a few major policies targeted at specific sectors. This strong and heavy intervention of the state continued until the mid-1980s when there was an important change in the direction of policy toward a more open-orientation and greater encouragement of the private sector.

In Section C, we discuss how the new more open and liberal policy orientation, which had been evolving in Tunisia since the mid-1980s, in which there was greater preference for 'horizontal' industrial policies, has still failed to lead the country to be one in which the role of markets and the private sector would be much greater, instead leaving the heavy hand of the state in the economy very clearly in place.

Section D shows that in contrast to the East Asian countries Tunisia had a much more limited success in making the private sector as a main engine for investment and productivity growth. Using an extensive set of data and analyses it reviews the main constraints and obstacles to the emergence and growth of dynamic private firms. It shows that much of the competition of Tunisian firms is that between formal firms and the many informal firms which arise in response to non-optimal and costly regulations that have arisen in recent years, and made even worse by the increasing political instability. Then, in the final Section E, we bring all these considerations together in deriving their implications for the development outcomes in Tunisia, with an emphasis on the largest shortcomings relative to most East Asian countries, in terms of low savings and investment, low productivity growth, limited structural transformation, weak technological change and innovation, weak financial sector, and insufficient use of global markets.

A. Breaking through the Middle-Income Trap and Sustaining Growth in East Asia

The successful path that East Asia has taken to prosperity has been the subject of extensive analysis and debates and there have been strong disagreements as to what has made for its success. For example, while Balassa (1988) viewed the East Asian experience as the outcome of a standard neoclassical model in which the relative prices and the private sector played an important role in constraining efficiency-reducing interventions by the state, the Asian countries making use of their relatively low-cost labor to achieve breakthroughs in labor-intensive manufacturing while at the same time maintaining low income inequality. Yet, Amsden (1992) taking advantage of the Korean experience and Wade (1990) more of other cases, put forward a developmental state explanation in which it is the state which rises to constrain the otherwise distortionary influences of domestic and international markets by providing finance and appropriate incentives for the appropriate activities. Considerable attention was also devoted to some significant patterns of such changes over time, thereby distinguishing between the early industrialization experiences of Korea, Taiwan, and Singapore with later ones in Malaysia, Thailand, and China.[1] Some of the processes cited by the alternative theories were simply occurring at different points in time in different countries.

More recent and encompassing analyses have led to a broader consensus that its success was built on an elaborate mixture of reliance, not only on state intervention and institutions, but also on markets and private sector growth (Asian Development Bank 2020; World Bank 1993). The relative roles of the state versus markets have never been uniform or static in East Asia. Indeed, they have varied considerably across countries and over time. But, after World War II, Japan and the four newly industrializing countries (NIEs), namely, Hong Kong, Korea, Taiwan, and Singapore, and more recently China and to some extent even Malaysia and Thailand, have tended to call upon markets, prices and competition to play the dominant role in allocating resources and driving economic growth. Indeed, liberalizing markets and promoting external trade became major features of the East Asian experience, but to a large extent accomplished with the help of the state.

At first, in all East Asian countries the state was called on to play a major role in providing public goods and complementary factors of production, such as infrastructure and education, just as it has been shown above to have done also in MENA (see, for example, Birdsall and Sabot 1993). Yet, as stressed by Acemoglu et al. (2006) and Cherif and Hasanov (2019), instead of lingering in the middle-income category and eventually falling into 'the middle-income trap' as many other developing and middle income countries did, the 'miracle growth' East Asian countries also used the state to develop and undertake more 'active' industrial policies designed to guide and facilitate innovation, structural transformation, and globalization. Notably, these developments included an ambitious innovation-based strategy and the maintenance of vigorous competition, thereby encouraging both managers and workers to continuously learn and upgrade and to prevent insider firms from constraining that competition. As argued forcefully by Lin (2012a), a major feature of the East Asian countries, especially in Korea and China, has been a gradual, pragmatic, and evolving reform agenda which combines market and state intervention in such a way as to adhere to and take advantage of their ever-evolving, *dynamic comparative advantages*. Such a process of structural transformation can be efficient and successful, however, primarily only when it is continuously adapting to changing relative factor endowments and trading opportunities. From that perspective, a country's industrial policies and industrial upgrading should not be going 'against' its comparative advantage (as e.g., in traditional import substituting industrialization). Rather, it should be responding to changes in the economy's endowments in terms of basic labor, human capital, and 'tangible' infrastructure, by taking advantage of technological changes and international market opportunities so as to be able to produce increasingly sophisticated products. In their quite recent analysis of the East Asian Miracle and related empirical analysis, Cherif and Hasanov (2019) called this process the adoption of 'True Industrial Policy' (TIP).

Indeed, these authors cited the speeches of Korean President Park Chung Hee in 1964 and other Asian leaders as examples of government leaders announcing ambitious state-led programs of long-term development to be sustained over time in such a way that all these elements of innovation and increasing export sophistication would be incorporated. This would be achieved by linking the state and its industrial policies to long-term development by way of their private firms operating in a continuously competitive environment. They contrasted this ambitious, more dynamic, and long-sustained approach (which they called 'high geared TIP') with other more gradual or shorter term approaches (which they called lower geared versions of TIP) and argued that high-geared TIP would require much more comprehensive coordination so as to internalize the benefits of the strategy which would otherwise leak out to others in the form of externalities. While Cherif and Hasanov (2019) remained focused primarily on the miracle growth countries of East Asia, they showed that in their attempts to upgrade technology through diversification away from oil, some GCC countries within the MENA region (on p. 28 of their study) have also managed to improve technology in non-tradeable goods sectors outside of oil, like construction and services. However, even these GCC successes have not managed to do so in internationally competitive sectors, as Japan, Korea, and Taiwan have done, and as China has been doing more recently. They acknowledged that the state had to intervene heavily to get such processes started and overcome early market failures. Notably, the entries into up-grading in East Asian countries have not been confined to agriculture and labor-intensive manufacturing but have come to include automobile manufacturing, ship-building and electronic equipment. To be sustainable, however, these interventions have had to be efficient and market-promoting and have had to remain competitive as they up-graded and competed with higher income countries.

In their empirical analysis, Cherif and Hasanov (2019) also built on Rodrik (2016) in showing that the rising share of output and employment in manufacturing was not short-lived in these Miracle East Asian countries, as it was in so many other developing and middle-income countries that went through lower-geared TIP. Moreover, not only did the output and employment shares of manufacturing continue to grow, but so too did manufacturing TFP, especially in the Republic of Korea. They also cited Singapore as an East Asian success story in which much of this technological upgrading has been in tradeable services, such as transportation (including air transport), business services and finance, instead of non-tradeable services, like retail and storage as in some of the GCC countries. Notably, they also cited empirical studies of the International Monetary Fund (2018) showing evidence that service inputs have been growing in importance in manufacturing in recent years and also that the share of R&D expenditures in such services have been rising over timc. Thcy also pointed out that much of the explanation for why Malaysia's otherwise quite impressive industrial growth did not live up to the phenomenal growth of Korea, Singapore, and Taiwan was due to its much lower degree of technology creation (as measured by its smaller numbers of patents, shares of the chip manufacturing industries, R&D spending and shares of university graduates in engineering, manufacturing, and construction).

Given the predominance of SMEs in the total number of firms, employment growth, and their rising importance in technological upgrading especially in East Asian countries, the rise of SMEs in both manufacturing production and exports has been seen as a central part of the success in East Asian countries. In their volume aimed at showcasing relatively successful country experiences of SMEs, especially in export activities, Levy et al. (1999) chose four countries, three of which were from East and South East Asia: Japan, Korea, and Indonesia. In each case, they traced their success back to three important forms of support, namely, support in finance, technology and marketing. In each case, they distinguished between such support coming from the public sector, from industry associations and NGOs and other firms or groups thereof. Yet, even from the latter sources, public policy tended to play an important role. While in Indonesia that success was limited primarily to only one of the three industries studied, namely, furniture, much of which was due to taking advantage of the Chinese ethnicity of many of its firm leaders and their links to other Chinese in countries around the world but especially in the East Asian region, a common mechanism across countries was the launching of trade fairs. This competitive networking was much broader and deeper in Japan where subcontracting relationships linked SMEs to the already experienced and technically sophisticated large enterprises. Korea was perhaps an even more spectacular example, where through both domestic subcontracting and international exporting the share of SMEs in exports more than doubled from 20% in 1983 to over 42% by 1994 (Kim and Nugent 1999). Across the East Asian countries in the sample, in general, when well-staffed and motivated, public agencies, such as the special SME Finance organizations and credit guarantee systems, and Export Promotion Agencies, were available to them, both industry associations and subcontracting relationships were also reported to be very useful by the SMEs surveyed (Levy et al. 1999, especially Chapters 1, 6, and 7).

Onis (1991) builds upon the specialized studies on East Asian countries to point to additional contributors to success. Given that help for industry from the state for firms to become internationally competitive is required for this strategy to be successful, this would be excessively costly and give rise to fiscal and current account deficits if to do so required very large agencies. Expansion of the numbers of well-paid bureaucrats has thus been a source of budgetary crises in many developing and middle-income countries. Instead, most East Asian countries have managed to supply the high-quality services needed by firms, even while keeping these agencies small. By keeping them small also, more highly qualified workers would have greater incentive to seek employment in the private sector, thus providing a nice link to the labor market as well. At the same time, Onis (1991, 114) argued that: 'Rigorous standards of entry not only ensured a high degree of bureaucratic capability, but also generated a sense of unity and common identity on the part of the bureaucratic elite. Hence the bureaucrats were imbued with a sense of mission and identified themselves with national goals which derived from a position of leadership in society. The common educational backgrounds plus the high degree of intra-elite circulation were instrumental in generating an unusual degree of cooperation among the bureaucrats, the executive and the entrepreneurial elites'.

In successive waves, East Asian countries moved from what, at first, were extensive import substitution and state interventions to more outward and market-oriented policies. This pattern was initiated by Japan soon after World War II, but then followed by the NIEs of Hong Kong, Korea, Taiwan, and Singapore beginning in the 1960s. Other Southeast Asian countries, in particular, Indonesia, Malaysia, and Thailand, have followed this pattern beginning in the early1970s, and mainland China has done so since 1978. Finally, another wave started beginning in the mid-1980s with Vietnam, Cambodia, and Laos, and more recently Myanmar.

In their economic and social transformation, East Asian countries faced the same political economy constraints to reform as have other developing countries. Prominent among these obstacles to reform were typically: (i) overcoming ideological baggage, (ii) the weight of patronage, (iii) rent-seeking and vested interests, (iv) bureaucratic inertia, (v) economic pain resulting from reform and popular resistance, and (vi) disconnect between short termism of the political actors and the longer-term perspectives of technocrats (Arroyo 2008; Hill 2013). The relative importance of these different constraints quite naturally has varied depending on the time and the country.

Those East Asian countries which were successful showed an ability to deal with these challenges and to undertake timely and effective reforms. Their strategies varied considerably and depended largely on domestic considerations, with history, and geopolitics playing the central role. Specific stratagems were used in different countries to deal with each of these constraints and there has been no single political economy strategy underpinning all the successful experiences in East Asia. The extent of success in their reforms has also varied, explaining their different levels of success in outcomes. However, three features seem to have been identified in the more successful political economy performances, allowing them to adopt and subsequently implement suitable reforms in a timely way.

First, the successful political economy strategies were not static. They evolved over time, adapting to new circumstances and conditions, such as whether the political system was democratic or autocratic, or the relative strength of the major players, such as large private sector actors, or the relative importance of its industrial development.

Second, the institutional set-up around the concept of 'embedded autonomy' seems to have been one of the most important characteristics in the successful strategies (Evans 1995). This concept implies that the efficacy of the developmental state depends on combining 'corporate coherence' and 'connectedness'. Corporate coherence requires a meritocratic bureaucracy, with a strong sense of corporate identity. Connectedness requires a dense set of institutionalized links to industrial capital and labor and more generally to private elites. As Evans (1995, 12) has stated, such a set-up provides 'institutional channels to the continuous negotiation and renegotiation of goals and policies.'

Third, as stressed by Lin (2009, especially in Chapter 9 where he focuses on the different East Asian countries), the countries were generally able to succeed by taking advantage of changing comparative advantage. For example, the earliest successes in Korea and Taiwan involved timely but rather clear structural shifts going from heavy reliance on competitive comparative advantage in the primary sector to that in labor intensive manufacturing, and especially in Korea's case again to more capital-intensive and high-tech manufacturing somewhat later on. Even the communist party-led and planned economy countries, like China and Vietnam, were able to become more efficient and internationally competitive in industry by allowing their state enterprises to sell any of their outputs above the levels identified in their plans for delivery to the state in competitive international markets, and at the same time, allowing firms to pay wage rates above previously set rates so as to induce workers to help make this happen. Lin interpreted this experience of successful East Asian countries to following a principle of dynamic comparative advantage from firms competing with and learning from their experience in international markets.

In the following paragraphs, we draw on both some attempts by other specialists on the region to come up with general patterns and their explanations, as well as of explanations of certain differences across countries and over time. These involve identifying the specific constraints that arose in these countries and the political economy of what they did and how to relax or get around these constraints and thereby help accomplish their rather amazing success in achieving ever-increasing levels of technology and international competitiveness. Moreover, these findings were remarkably consistent with the aforementioned assessments that their success was achieved while taking advantage of their dynamic comparative advantages in ways in which their private sectors came to play very important roles.

Walter and Zhang (2012) have provided a general framework for how capitalist development and institutional regimes have evolved, and in many cases also about how these have been changed over time. Specifically, their analysis suggests that East Asian states have been more actively involved in guiding economic outcomes than most of their counterparts in other regions, but also that the extent of state intervention in East Asia has declined somewhat over time, although with some increases again recently but of a somewhat different kind. The ways in which the state and capitalist groups interact has tended to vary (1) by the relative extent of state organization of the economy, on the one hand, and on the other (2) by the way business systems are organized (such as the concentration of ownership, and relationships among owners, managers and workers), their financial sources (such as the relative roles of the state, banks, or stakeholders), and also (3) by the way welfare is provided to individuals.

We start with some analyses of Korea which is generally regarded as the most impressive among the East Asian Miracle countries, focusing on changing conditions over time and the reforms which seemed to help. Joong-Woong (1988) pointed to the growing crises that were hitting Korea in the late 1970s and were reflected in high and accelerating inflation rates, government budget deficits, current account deficits, money supply growth, and what he regarded as increasing fragmentation and rigidity of the country's financial and other markets. Most of these problems were attributed to the continuing heavy hand of the state, its growing inability to raise more revenues for the government and to attract financing for domestic economic activity from outside the government. Until that time, while the economy was still rather simple and not very diversified, the state had been able to mobilize investment that powered growth. But once the economy became more diversified, efficiency in the allocation of resources across sectors and factors of production and their coordination became more important, calling attention to the benefits of a well-functioning flexible relative price mechanism. The aforementioned problems in Korea in the late 1970s were said to have resulted in three important shortcomings of the financial system: (1) because of the hyperinflation caused by excessive monetary growth and dominant influence of the state, the price mechanism had been rendered incapable of allocating financial resources efficiently, (2) the total lack of innovation in the financial sector because of its virtually total ownership and control by the government, and (3) the fact that so many of the government's chosen investments were inefficient, leaving the entities making those investments unable to pay off their loans to the banks.

In particular, Joong-Woong (1988) pointed to several key reforms beginning in 1980 to relax and get around the growing constraints arising from these shortcomings. One such reform was the Anti-Monopoly and Fair Trade Act of 1981 and the liberalization of external transactions. This had the effect of increasing the interest of foreign banks and other financial institutions in investing and doing business in Korea. A second was the revision of the General Banking Act in 1982 to denationalize the four large commercial banks and free the banks from domination by large shareholders and the government so that they could be run on profit-maximization lines rather than merely to carry out government priorities. Among the mechanisms was one which allowed (1) the interest rates charged to vary with the demonstrated credit-worthiness of the borrowers, (2) all banks and financial institutions to compete with each other, and (3) both government and corporate bonds to be sold within a more universal banking system in which commercial banks were encouraged to try to attract deposits from individuals, businesses, and foreign firms and individuals and to encourage foreign firms to be listed in Korea's equity market. All these actions greatly mitigated the three shortcomings of the financial system identified above. They made the whole financial system more competitive, increased the supply of financial funds from other sources, and stimulated continuing technical innovations in the financial sector.

Reforms in the financial markets and other institutions have also been given considerable credit by Sheng (1988) for why Malaysia's financial system had become rather well developed by the mid-1980s. Key reforms in Malaysia were the abolition of central administration of interest rates of commercial banks in 1978, allowing banks to determine freely their interest rates on both deposits and loans, giving rise to new financial instruments in the form of bankers' acceptances and negotiable certificates of deposits. Malaysia also created a large stock exchange (the Kuala Lumpur Stock Exchange) which benefitted considerably by linking it to its neighbor's large Singapore Stock Exchange, thereby taking advantage of an important regional linkage. To meet the needs of its Muslim population in 1983, an Islamic Bank was also introduced in Malaysia, once again diversifying the kinds of financial institutions and financial resources available.

On the other hand, Malaysia's financial development was not directly boosted by private sector and market-oriented institutional development. As pointed out by Gomez and Jomo (1997), the pressures for further strengthening the state and public sector in Malaysia exploded in the aftermath of the bloody race riots that broke out between the more well-off and business-oriented Chinese and the Malay majority in 1969. This resulted in the formation and long-lasting leadership of a gigantic political party consisting primarily of Malay nationals to accomplish inequality-reducing and growth promoting policies and institutions. Then, the Asian financial crisis of the late 1990s induced the Malaysian governmental coalition to turn more strongly in a different direction, namely, encouraging foreign investment and opening up the economy as detailed in Zhang and Whitley (2013). Private business grew rapidly but without huge businesses or business associations having to play much of a role.

Even if not one of the East Asian Miracle countries, Thailand's experience represents still another quite different way in which, over the same period of time, the country opened up to the world economy and became quite successful in technological change and development. In this case, as shown by Zhang and Whitley (2013) and Jomo et al. (1997), it did so largely through the private sector. Indeed, over much of the period, SOEs and government investment represented the smallest share in total investment of any of the East Asian economies. While early on, the Thai state was said to be ruled by a rather arrow coalition of the military with the civilian bureaucracy, in which powerful individuals of virtually any background were able to exert significant influence on the economy, over time the trend was toward the disintegration of networked based coalitions in favor of neo-liberal market reforms that encouraged arms-length transactions.

While many of the differences between East Asian and MENA and other countries occurred between 1960 and the Global Financial Crisis of 2008–2009, Kalinowski (2015) called attention to some of the differences triggered by that serious financial crisis and the increasing competition through GVCs and ongoing technological change in the world economy since then. Focusing on Korea and China among countries in our East Asian sample but also including Japan, this author pointed out the rather striking fact that East Asian countries spent much more in the way of fiscal stimulus to pull their economies out of that Global Financial Crisis than did Western countries which were most directly impacted by that crisis. Indeed, in the case of China, its fiscal stimulus spending during 2008–2010 was more than double that in the US (of slightly more than 5% of GDP) which was perhaps the highest among western countries. Moreover, there was an even more important difference in the type of stimulus offered, in the west largely demand-oriented and directed to public consumption and health and education, whereas in the East Asian countries it was supply-oriented, providing increased lending for investment by various sectors and public infrastructure for technology upgrading (much in the form of more green technology) and designated in some cases to some large enterprises but primarily to SMEs which provide more jobs. Because of the high level of interdependence between trade and investment in East Asia, the exceptionally large fiscal stimulus exerted by China significantly increased the stock markets in Japan, Korea, and other East Asian countries. Also, China's extremely ambitious BRI initiative initiated in 2016 to bring so many countries, not only of East Asia but also of South Asia, Africa, and Eastern Europe, into a huge infrastructure, trade, and investment network, has contributed even further to this initiative. Moreover, according to Lu and Nugent (2021), the BRI may well have been motivated in part by wanting to lower pollution and other problems in China about which its citizens were increasingly complaining. Nevertheless, the conclusion of Kalinowski (2015) about this more recent move on the part of Korea, Japan, and China is not a return to the old 'developmental state' which characterized their earlier political economy orientation but rather was a move toward a more 'neo-developmental state' in which the objective is much more micro than macro-level-oriented and a process characterized by allowing winners to emerge with less direct intervention from the government.

In the following section, this wide variety of positive, dynamic, and adaptive processes used in East Asia is to be contrasted with the more hesitant and weak process of change in Tunisia.

B. Market Failures and the Central Role of the State as Major Driver in Structural Transformation and Diversification in Tunisia

From the early years of its independence, Tunisia's newly installed government authorities realized the existence of many impediments to development and to the emergence of a modern more productive economy. The need to overcome market failures was a predominant concern among Tunisian policy-makers and was interpreted to imply the need for the state to play a heavy hand in this process. It was recognized that the private sector and markets suffered from many failures which impeded their role in achieving growth and structural transformation. These included limited entrepreneurship, the lack of large and long-term sources of capital, and the low quality of human skills. Due to the pervasiveness of market failures, markets were recognized to be insufficient and unable to generate sufficiently rapid structural transformation and diversification of the economy.

This led to the use of development planning as a tool to manage its development programs. Since the early 1960s multi-year plans were prepared and adopted through an extensive process of analysis, evaluation, consultation, and consensus building. While the earlier versions tended to be more directive and constraining, planning later became somewhat more flexible and indicative in nature. As shown by Nabli (1997) and Malinvaud and Nabli (1997), in the Tunisian context planning came to be used as a mechanism to deal with market and private sector failures, on the one hand, and government failures, on the other hand. Government interventions were used to mitigate and overcome market failures, sometimes through subsequent guidance and the coordination of expectations. Yet, these government interventions have often had their own failures, although in some cases these have been mitigated through coordination, target setting, and recurrent evaluation. As such, the planning mechanisms have been used so as to ensure better public sector choices over time and better implementation of both policies and projects. As a result, these policy planning mechanisms have been lying at the heart of trying to find an appropriate balance between the state and markets.

Within this general view, however, and over the course of the three decades following independence, two quite different transitions in policy orientation in the country were experienced. First, after the apparent failure of its initial liberal approach to development (discussed in Section B-1 of Chapter 3) during the second half of the 1950s, the country embarked during the 1960s on a socialist experiment (Section B-2 of Chapter 3), in which the state became the central player, not only in the development of human capital and infrastructure, but indeed in the entire economy. But then in the early 1970s, government policy moved back in the direction of greater openness and private sector involvement, as discussed in Section B-5 of Chapter 3. However, throughout both these periods and until the mid-1980s, the role of the state continued to be pervasive. From a political economy perspective, therefore, this entire period to the mid-1980s could be characterized by two major features: first, the emergence of a strong SOE sector, and then later the emergence of a private sector, but one closely linked to the state.

1. The Emergence of a Strong and Broad-Based SOE Sector

During the period of the 1960s and the 'socialist experiment', overcoming market failures in Tunisia was achieved through a combination of: (i) direct intervention through SOEs and (ii) sectoral policies combining SOEs with the private sector by providing incentives to the private sector through a broad array of specific support mechanisms, and incentive schemes designed to provide trade protection, restrictions on entry by others, funding for investment, and subsidies for production. These policies continued in place, at least to a large extent, after the aforementioned change in policy track during the 1970s. The development of its SOEs would have major political economy implications for policies and the relative roles of the state, on the one hand, and markets on the other hand.

In the early 1960s, the obvious solution for the pervasiveness of market and private sector failures was considered to be for the state to take on the role of entrepreneur and develop new sectors and activities through SOEs. The state was to develop projects, mobilize the financing, organize and fund the training of personnel, and provide for their proper management.

In addition to the relatively long existing, mostly nationalized activities of network services (electricity and gas, water, telephone and telegraph, and railways), from the 1960s onwards, SOEs were extensively used to develop new activities. Indeed, during the 1970s, Tunisia continued the strong development of the SOE sector, fueled by the accumulation of large export revenues from natural resources, primarily phosphates and oil products.

Table 6.1 provides data for our set of comparator countries on the shares of the private sector in GDP and in total GFCF, while Table 6.2 shows, for Tunisia only, the evolution of the shares of investment by public enterprises in GDP and in business investment. By the 1960s, the share of investment in GDP by the private sector had already reached 17–20% of GDP in Korea

Table 6.1 Private Sector Gross Fixed Capital Formation, 1961–2019

Country	*Gross fixed capital formation, private sector (% of GDP)*						*Private sector share in total gross fixed capital formation (%)*					
	1961–1970	*1971–1980*	*1981–1990*	*1991–2000*	*2001–2010*	*2011–2019*	*1961–1970*	*1971–1980*	*1981–1990*	*1991–2000*	*2001–2010*	*2011–2019*
MENA non-major oil exporters	**8.5**	**13.0**	**16.3**	**15.5**	**14.9**	**15.5**	**36.9**	**45.0**	**58.2**	**59.5**	**65.4**	**72.2**
Djibouti						19.38						68.78
Egypt, Arab Rep.			11.87	8.46	10.14	7.79			39.58	37.15	53.93	52.32
Jordan		17.08	15.55	18.64	19.94	16.19		49.43	58.31	69.55	78.05	83.33
Lebanon			30.65	24.71	20.57	21.36			97.90	82.55	89.01	93.57
Morocco												
Syrian Arab Republic		11.11	9.76	12.01	10.05			42.74	44.65	52.80	46.66	
Tunisia	**8.55**	**10.96**	**13.69**	**13.89**	**13.95**	**12.69**	**36.89**	**42.75**	**50.49**	**55.32**	**59.43**	**62.93**
West Bank and Gaza												
Yemen, Rep.												
MENA major oil exporters	**23.2**	**25.2**	**19.3**	**20.1**	**12.6**	**19.6**	**74.2**	**65.6**	**62.2**	**71.6**	**45.3**	**83.1**
Algeria	25.82	27.77	17.69	19.04			81.14	73.12	56.67	74.33		
Iran, Islamic Rep.	20.52	22.63	20.91	21.06	22.06	19.61	67.31	58.05	67.79	68.82	71.79	83.12
Iraq												
Libya					3.22						18.723	
MENA GCC		**7.7**	**5.9**	**9.1**	**16.4**	**16.4**		**25.9**	**28.5**	**52.7**	**68.0**	**68.9**
Bahrain				12.59	19.91	21.65				73.92	76.36	82.83
Kuwait												
Oman		7.67	5.92	5.66				25.85	28.53	31.51		
Qatar												
Saudi Arabia												
United Arab Emirates					12.96	11.09					59.68	54.88

(Continued)

Table 6.1 Private Sector Gross Fixed Capital Formation, 1961–2019 *(Continued)*

	Gross fixed capital formation, private sector (% of GDP)						***Private sector share in total gross fixed capital formation (%)***					
Country	***1961–1970***	***1971–1980***	***1981–1990***	***1991–2000***	***2001–2010***	***2011–2019***	***1961–1970***	***1971–1980***	***1981–1990***	***1991–2000***	***2001–2010***	***2011–2019***
East Asia	**18.2**	**19.3**	**21.7**	**25.3**	**22.1**	**24.3**	**73.3**	**77.3**	**76.7**	**80.0**	**73.2**	**78.0**
China				30.05	34.45	37.47				93.73	88.53	87.00
Indonesia												
Korea, Rep.	19.72	22.60	25.35	29.48	25.26	25.18	76.30	80.69	82.16	83.86	82.39	84.47
Malaysia			21.89	23.26	10.98	16.04			71.75	65.45	49.09	64.57
Philippines		17.76	16.83	18.50				78.35	76.85	83.36		
Thailand	16.69	17.64	22.69	25.16	17.89	18.53	70.30	72.86	76.06	73.65	72.78	75.98

Source: Data from database: World Bank, World Development Indicators.

Note: Tunisia: for private GFCF the figures from WDI for the period 1997–2010 seem to be inaccurate. We use figures for 2001–2017 obtained from the National Accounts.

Table 6.2 Tunisia: Gross Fixed Capital Formation by Public Enterprises (%), 1961–2017

Period	***1961–1963***	***1964–1966***	***1967–1970***	***1971–1973***	***1974–1976***	***1977–1980***	***1981–1983***	***1984–1986***	***1987–1990***
Share of public enterprises in business investment (%)	53.20	66.29	54.90	51.00	54.63	63.08	54.71	51.44	44.90
Investment by public enterprises as share of GDP (%)	4.63	8.54	5.73	6.15	8.67	11.32	10.37	8.14	6.05
	1991–1993	***1994–1996***	***1997–2000***	***2001–2003***	***2004–2006***	***2007–2010***	***2011–2013***	***2014–2017***	
Share of public enterprises in business investment (%)	44.38	n.a.	n.a.	31.12	28.84	25.67	24.89	26.53	
Investment by public enterprises as share of GDP (%)	6.49	n.a.	n.a.	4.26	3.90	3.96	3.26	2.76	

Source: Tunisia National Accounts, various documents.

and Thailand, but remained quite low (at less than 9%) in Tunisia. On the other hand, the share of public enterprises in business investment in Tunisia surged to reach more than 66% during 1964–1966 (Table 6.1).

Early in this evolution, SOEs were deeply involved in the extraction and transformation of Tunisia's natural resources, including: (i) Chemicals based on phosphates (Compagnie des Phosphates de Gafsa, and Groupe Chimique), (ii) Oil exploration and extraction (Entreprise Tunisienne d'Activités Pétrolières in 1972), refining and distribution (Société Tunisienne des Industries du Raffinage since 1960), (iii) Paper pulp based on alfalfa, and (iv) Cement and concrete products from sand and gravel. The second category of SOEs, consisting of those involved in new activities and not based on available natural resources, was in general developed opportunistically. They constituted a large array of enterprises starting with heavy industries, such as iron and steel (the firm El-Fouledh created in 1962 and a steel mill started in 1965). Another domain was that of transportation activities: air transport (Tunis Air), sea transport (Compagnie Tunisienne de Navigation), and a large number of public companies for land transportation (at the city, regional and inter-regional levels). Other activities in which SOEs were established were those in light manufacturing, such as textiles and clothing (Société Générale des Industries Textiles), and in ceramics, as well as electrical and mechanical industries.

While SOEs were used to develop a large range of activities, many of them were part of more sector-oriented development policies. Three such sectors were specifically targeted. The first sector was that of the phosphates-based chemicals industry. In this case, the policy was pursued exclusively through the public sector and SOEs. It involved the downstream transformation of phosphates into chemical products, mostly fertilizers. This activity was mainly export-oriented and had to meet the market test of competitiveness. It became a major part of Tunisian exports.

The second sector targeted early on for development was tourism. As indicated in Section A of Chapter 2, tourism was greatly favored by Tunisia's natural endowment in terms of climate and sunny weather, sandy beaches and historical sites, and location in close proximity to the much cooler countries of Europe. In this case, however, while strongly encouraged by the state, management of the tourism sector was left largely to the private sector. This was both because it was thought to be a sector in which private management would be suitable and because, being dependent on foreigners to visit the country, it was thought to be risky and well beyond the control of government. But, for tourism to succeed, hotels and perhaps other infrastructure would require substantial amounts of financing as well as both promotion abroad and well-qualified management. Moreover, all this had to be coordinated so as to be in the right sequence. Fortunately, as noted above, the Tunisian state was already reasonably capable of serving this coordination function. To help serve the needed coordinating function, new specialized institutions were established. Among these were the

'Office National du Tourisme et du Thermalisme de Tunisie'[2], the public sector 'Société Hotelière et Touristique de Tunisie' created in 1959, and in the 1970s several other institutions. In particular, the Société Hotelière et Touristique de Tunisie promoted and created its own hotel units, which were fully publicly owned. The government also provided tax incentives to privately owned hotels and other tourism-related businesses that were equally generous as those in industry, and also made large amounts of long-term credit (with credit guarantees) available from the development and other banks to finance this rather capital-intensive industry. The procedures for starting hotel projects were also much simpler than those in industry. As shown in Section E-3 of Chapter 5, a specialized development bank was created to provide long-term finance for tourism development.

The favorable financial incentives and credit facilities for the sector continued until the 1990s. It is interesting to note that the hotel owners group became an important business group in the country and obtained far more cheap credit and fiscal incentives than their contribution to GDP would seem to justify as suggested by Nugent (1989). Because of the extremely generous amounts of long-term credit made available for tourism projects, hotel owners (both foreign and domestic) could build their hotels without having to have much capital of their own. Such financing, moreover, was highly subsidized. Hotel tourism was, therefore, a very popular outlet for private entrepreneurial activity. The government appropriately realized that earning a reputation for quality in tourism was important for long-term success. To help achieve a reputation for quality, the government also set up training institutes for both employees and managers, and helped to provide international marketing and ancillary infrastructure, such as roads, buses, and taxis. As a result, international tourism soon became a major earner of foreign exchange for the country.

As was shown in Table 2.4, in the years between 1965 and 2000 the growth of the tourism sector in Tunisia was high, raising the share of value added in this sector by more than six-fold to almost 6% of GDP in 2000, making it a very significant activity.

The third sector identified for development and to benefit substantially from the systematic support and direct action by the state was agriculture. Support for agriculture took various forms to encourage agricultural production, support modernization, and diversification (African Development Bank 2012; Boughanmi 1995). One such form consisted of the heavy investments by the government in infrastructure, especially for water mobilization and distribution (dams, deep wells, water transportation, and irrigation zones). Other interventions included tariffs, and various price and non-price incentives. For instance, SOEs were tasked to buy and market agricultural products at pre-announced support prices, such as cereals or olive oil, and to supply inputs to the farmers at subsidized prices (water, fertilizers). Other incentives included subsidized credit, direct subsidies, and the provision of infrastructure. In particular, a specialized institution was created to provide long-term finance for agriculture, namely, the Banque Nationale de Développement Agricole, and one commercial bank was created to focus on agriculture (the Banque Nationale de Tunisie).[3] In addition to the encouragement of traditional Tunisian crops, such as olives, cereals, and dates, other activities which were promoted included cattle raising, milk production, cultivation of fruits, and fishing in the deep waters. While some of these activities, such as sugar beets, were utter failures, others endured, but often remained dependent on subsidies.

2. *The Emergence of a Private Sector Closely Linked to the State*

As indicated above, one major reorientation in Tunisian policy took place beginning in the early 1970s, when greater emphasis was placed on the private sector and the existing socialist policies were abandoned. In fact, this was when a two-track strategy was pursued in Tunisia aimed at protecting the large import-substituting SOE sector, but at the same time allowing for the emergence of a new and dynamic private sector mainly in the export-oriented manufacturing sector. As a result, the private sector expanded rapidly, especially in export-oriented sectors, such as clothing and tourism, and import-competing sectors like construction, agriculture, and other manufacturing.

As a result, as shown in Table 6.2, the share of public enterprises in business investment moderated to 51% in the early 1970s and the share of the private sector increased significantly. But, as shown in Table 6.1, the share of private investment in GDP remained stubbornly low in Tunisia at 11–13%, compared to the higher rates achieved in East Asia at an average of 19%.

Through this two-track strategy, Tunisia's private sector became closely linked to the state through many channels. One such channel was through its continued dependence on finance from commercial banks as well as development banks, which were mainly state-owned. A second channel was through access to land, whereby industry, tourism or agriculture continued to depend on public sector supply of that land, and the approval of such access to land for these specific purposes by political authorities. A third channel, primarily for import-competing activities, was for the state to continue to tailor protection and benefits to the requirements of business firms. An especially unique and innovative channel was to convert former 'bureaucrats' into businessmen with continuing close links to the state apparatus. In order to succeed via this channel, individual entrepreneurs had to build and entertain close links with state institutions and the political system, something that made the bureaucrats rather happy.

3. *Political Economy and Its Role*

Bechri and Naccache (2007) argue that the adoption of 'collectivism' and socialist-oriented policies during the 1960s, which was assisted with heavy government intervention, was mainly driven by the political strategy followed by Habib Bourguiba, Tunisia's leader from its independence into the 1980s. This strategy of Bouguiba was to 'coopt' Ahmed Ben Salah, the leader of the major labor union (UGTT) and thereby to weaken the threat of rivalry from Ben Salah's former organization. Bouguiba co-opted Ben Salah by having the government itself adopt the program and the views of development which had previously been followed and elaborated on by the UGTT. This both neutralized the further pressures for change by the labor union and thereby strengthened Bourguiba's hold on power. The other large organizations of political relevance, such as those of businesses and farmers, were weak and could not oppose these policy choices of the state even if they wanted to.

It should be noted that the increasingly heavy role of the state provided President Bourguiba with additional political benefits. The more pervasive role of the state opened opportunities to Bourguiba to distribute rents to supporters of the regime, either in the form of jobs in leading government and SOE positions, and/or in the form of economic rents from the many extensive controls and regulations. As a result, the existing political regime, which faced a major test in the early 1960s of a plot against it, was able to strengthen its grip on power. Indeed, with the mounting economic difficulties and an increasingly vocal opposition, the 'socialist/collectivist' experiment was abandoned in 1969. Even the core support for the regime within the ruling party became openly opposed to that socialist orientation and a new policy approach was adopted, under the leadership of Bourguiba's new Prime Minister, Hedi Nouira.

All in all, over the period from the early 1960s to the mid-1980s, Tunisia developed one of the most extensive SOE sectors in the world, both in terms of number of firms and shares of SOE employment or production. According to Bechri and Naccache (2007), the number of SOEs increased from 25 in 1960 to 185 in 1970, and reached 285 in 1984. Yet, this count seems to be based on a restrictive definition, including only firms where the state has a dominant position (presumably controlling 34% or more of the firm's capital). Alternatively, according to Durupty (1986), using an alternative criterion for what would count as public enterprise, the total number of public enterprises in 1985 was considerably larger, indeed 550. While only about 165 of them were said to be owned fully and directly by the state, the vast majority of them were indirectly owned subsidiaries, with at least 10% of public ownership. In addition to the main public services, such as electricity and water, telephone, transportation, mining of phosphates and oil, SOEs were developed in almost all sectors of activity, including banking and insurance, construction materials, mechanical and electrical activities, tourism, textiles and clothing, construction and housing, and trade services. It was estimated that the public enterprise system contributed 25% of Tunisia's GDP, one-third of its capital formation, and employed 10% of its labor force.

Notably, even the new and more liberal policies pursued in Tunisia since 1970 did not lead to a major change with respect to the continued strong role of the state. The views developed during the 1960s continued to dominate with respect to the need for a major role of the state, have tended to continue guiding Tunisian policies through all the subsequent decades until the present, although not without some important adjustments and changes over time. Indeed, throughout this early period, that is, after the collapse of the 'socialist' experiment and the full eviction of the radical Ahmed Ben Salah from power, until the mid-1980s, the SOE sector itself was a major player in the political economy of reform and adaptation in Tunisia. By the early 1970s, the SOE sector had become entrenched, and formed the bedrock of the labor union movement. Constituting a strong base, the labor union movement became also the major pressure group defending existing public enterprises and pushing up against contestability and liberalization of markets. Constituting the main reservoir of membership for the UGTT labor union, the SOE sector became a major proponent of continuing the central role of the state. Even when policies were changed to emphasize more openness and markets, the earlier 'skepticism' with respect to importance of markets continued to be pervasive. At the same time, the private sector remained weak and heavily dependent on the state. The balance of power remained in favor of the heavy hand of the state, despite the openly expressed liberal choices of Tunisia's leaders.

The critical role of the main labor union in shaping the policy directions and the actual policies implemented can be clearly seen through the union's involvement in the major street riots of 1978 and 1984. Since the mid-1970s, there was continuous tension between the labor union and the government on almost all economic and social issues, involving not only wages but also many other policies like prices, employment, and labor regulations. Two important political crises emerged from this tension, the first crisis occurring in January 1978 when the government's attempted repression of the labor union resulted in 'blood on the streets'. The second such crisis occurred in 1984 following the large increases of prices of foodstuffs, mainly bread, which once again led to riots and repression.

In addition to the critical role of the labor unions in constraining policy reforms, we should also acknowledge the role of the newly emerging political threat in the form of the Islamists. They became increasingly active beginning in the early 1980s and were posing real threats to the political regime, which became increasingly reluctant to undertake policy actions which would create political opportunities for Islamists to exploit. This threat was greatest during the mid-1980s, when Islamists undertook various violent actions against the state, including terrorist attacks on hotels and citizens. This happened exactly when the economic situation was worsening, and reforms were most urgently needed. As a consequence, the implementation of the IMF supported adjustment program coincided with the strong repression by the state of Islamists during 1986–1987.

C. Horizontal Industrial Policies and the Continued Heavy Hand of the State, and Tunisia's Insufficient Use of Competition and Markets for Allocating Resources and Reducing Its Many Inefficiencies

Like the East Asian countries, Tunisia began the 1970s characterized by heavy state intervention, thanks to the extensive controls of markets and import-substitution that had been introduced in the 1960s, but from there embarked on a certain degree of market liberalization and the adoption of export-oriented policies. As mentioned in the previous section, the targeting on certain sectoral and other specific activities continued after Tunisia's change in the direction of policy in the 1970s. This was achieved, not only through its SOEs, but also through setting up innovation and technical support centers, and industrial upgrading programs.

The legacy of the central role of the state in driving structural transformation throughout the period from the 1950s until the mid-1980s, left Tunisia with the challenge of trying to find a better way to balance the respective roles of the state and markets. Yet, in fact, the tradition of state intervention continued even after the implementation of the Structural Adjustment Program of the mid-1980s, as was discussed in Section B-6 of Chapter 3.

1. The Two-Track System and the Shift toward Horizontal Industrial Policies

Since its rather radical transformation from liberal to socialist and back to neo-liberal policies in the 1960s and 1970s, Tunisia has approached policy changes only quite slowly and often has tried to get around problems by creating new mechanisms, such as the dual-track trade policy regimes. Even with the implementation of the Structural Adjustment Program in the mid-1980s, the two-track system continued to be in place, despite repeated attempts to discard it in favor of a more uniformly open regime.

In an effort to increase the role of the private sector and to offer more market-compatible incentives, in the 1970s the country started to move toward more 'horizontal' industrial policies, in which export promotion was the main objective, and away from sector-specific targeting as discussed in Section B-5 of Chapter 3. This involved a set of reforms designed to create a more level playing field for the private sector and to provide a greater role for markets. The objective of export promotion and diversification of the economy was pursued through an elaborate incentive system which gave significant benefits to exporters through processing zones and extremely generous tax-incentives. This led to a surge in exports of low-skilled manufacturing products, especially clothing and garments as has been pointed out in Section B-5 of Chapter 3.

Tunisia's elaboration of its Investment Code of 1993 provided an opportunity to go further in the adoption of horizontal industrial policies. The main economic objectives of this code were: (i) export promotion, (ii) regional development, (iii) technological progress and research and development, and (iv) the promotion of young entrepreneurs and SMEs. While specific sectoral incentives were eliminated for tourism, they were maintained for agriculture and were extended further into new activities related to the reduction of pollution and environmental protection.

Subsequently, by taking advantage of the free-trade area agreement offered by the European Union to Tunisia and other MENA countries in 1996 (Tunisia being the first to enter into such an agreement), Tunisia was able to better implement its more horizontal policy, through the industrial upgrading program discussed in Chapter 5. More recently, a new framework for investment was developed and put into practice during 2016/2017 (Loi 2016–71 du 30 September 2016, the Law on Investment and Law 2017–8 of February 14 2017) via reform of fiscal benefits. The main objectives for the granting of financial and other incentives were 'horizontal', that is, making them widely applicable and including: (i) the enhancement of productivity and competitiveness, (ii) regional development, (iii) sustainable development, (iv) the promotion of both exports and innovation, and (v) encouragement of projects of national interest and larger size (measured in terms of investment and employment). However, in addition to agriculture which has always remained a sectoral priority as a result of its having been ruled out from the EU- Southern Mediterranean FTAs, the new system introduced a new broad array of 18 specific sectoral priorities in industry and services.

Ghali and Nabli (2020) undertook a thorough assessment of the effectiveness of such policies and found that there would have been limited, or even no, success in diversification of exports without either horizontal or vertical policies (or especially with both types of policies together). In other words, no significant diversification took place without the presence of explicit and well-designed export diversification policies, and almost all cases of successful diversification were in fact supported by some kind of industrial policies.

They also found that the greatest successes with industrial policy were almost never based on attempts at picking winners. Rather the successes tended to occur by building on emerging dynamism in some export activities and trying to support their expansion, in a way which was consistent with comparative advantage. Only in such circumstances did such interventions have clear potential for success. These interventions tried to deal with the 'market' failures which were hindering the diversification process. This highlights the significance of existing market failures and the usefulness of policies to mitigate these failures and thereby to support exports.

In Tunisia there have been quite a few cases in which only 'horizontal' policies or only 'vertical' policies were successful. Yet, more targeted policies, such as those supporting the diversification of olive oil exports into higher value-added packaging or in furthering higher quality dates have also been successful when they have built upon natural comparative advantage.

The 'off-shore' system of incentives used to support manufacturing beginning in the early 1970s was broad-based and did not focus on any specific activity. It was successful in launching the process of diversification into low-technology exports. But it did so only for two decades, and especially only while the quota sanctions on East Asian exports were in place and hence Tunisian products could be competitive.

Yet, in the case of the 'horizontal' industrial policies introduced in the 1990s, it has been more difficult to determine clearly whether or not they succeeded in promoting diversification and increased sophistication of exports in Tunisia. Indeed, there are no empirical studies showing convincingly such an impact. The empirical evidence that does exist seems to show that diversification was concentrated in only a few activities, products, and sectors, although not entirely precluding the possibility that 'horizontal policies' may have contributed to some of these successes through natural comparative advantage, market dynamics and private entrepreneurship.

More importantly, however, Ghali and Nabli (2020) conclude that the Tunisian experience suggests that the choice in industrial policy should not be seen as one between 'horizontal' and 'vertical' policies. In fact, the most successful cases in diversification and upgrading were found to be supported by an appropriate combination of both types of policies. While 'horizontal' policies create the appropriate environment and overall set of incentives, targeted sectoral policies support the growth and expansion of specific products and industries. This was the case for the mechanical, electric, and electronics sector with its auto-components as well as non-auto components activities developed from opportunities made possible by Tunisia's Trade Agreement with the EU.

2. *The Increased Difficulties with the Two-Track System*

While as indicated above, the two-track system has had some important benefits, over the longer run, it has also tended to let inefficient situations persist, leading to deteriorating conditions in industrial development, in the financial system and in other respects. As a result, Tunisian growth has displayed much more of a 'stop and go' character than has been the case in the countries of East Asia, although perhaps a little less 'stop and go' than in most other MENA countries. Surges in growth have been interrupted by crises during the 1960s, mid-1980s, and especially after 2010. As a result, Tunisia has not yet been able to sustain economic growth rates of more than 5% per year over a period as long as a decade. East Asian countries have also been deliberate in their policy changes but have rather consistently displayed an ability to commit to timetables for gradual liberalization. South Korean policy-makers offered protection to infant industry producers just as Tunisia's have, but they limited that protection to explicit, and generally rather short, periods of time, and often conditional on demonstrations of success in exporting. In contrast to the Korean and other East Asian experience, in many cases Tunisia's protection to infant or other industry has not diminished at all over several decades.

Given the fact that Tunisia's tariff reductions have been primarily limited to those with the EU, there has existed since 2007 a huge discrepancy between the average tariff rate applying to goods from the EU of 4% and the average MFN rate of 24.7% applied to other countries. The MFN tariff rates also vary sharply from one sector to another. For example, in agriculture they range between 50 and 75%, whereas in manufactures they are generally within the 20–30% range, and worst of all, they vary substantially within these broad classes of goods, a characteristic which can lead to corruption in the form of bribes to customs officers who may be able to use his (her) discretion as to the specific category so as to reduce the effective tariff that the importer has to pay in return for a 'gift' or bribe. The several preferential trade regimes that Tunisia has signed with other countries, especially other Arab countries, are largely non-operative because of quantitative restrictions that have been imposed to prevent large-scale fraud (to which they would otherwise be vulnerable because of conflicting rules of origin and difficulties in monitoring them among MENA countries).[4]

Much of Tunisia's rise in manufactures exports was due to the aforementioned growth of its textiles and clothing industry in the 1970s and 1980s. But, Tunisia's loss in competitiveness to East Asian and other countries in this industry, as suggested by Cammett (2007), may have been due to the greater ability of such countries to take advantage of current trends in the industry (such as those in the direction of higher quality products)[5], through more full integration with floor-ready merchandise fostered by their gradual movement toward more complete liberalization. This trend is motivated by the perceived need to reduce the effects of the substantial distortions that had arisen from the two-track system as well as from other policies undertaken to achieve the country's industrialization goal. These difficulties must have been exacerbated by the temporary misalignments in the real exchange rate, discussed in Chapter 4, and have certainly played a role in negatively affecting exports and overall growth.

Another example of the difficulties arising from Tunisia's use of a two-track system, and sectoral targeting (and one very specific to Tunisia) is its continued use of a highly subsidized hotel financing scheme, which, at least until the mid-1990s imposed large costs on the relevant parties. Table 2.4 in Chapter 2 presented some data showing the evolution of some of these benefits and costs over the period 1965–2019. On the benefits side, that table showed the explosive growth in the numbers of hotels, beds, non-resident entries (tourists) and foreign exchange receipts until the early 2000s. However, note should also be taken of some other, rather tell-tale, signs of inefficiencies. For one, the occupancy rate rarely exceeded 50%, which is low by international standards. For another, despite the ever-increasing investment in hotels, the average duration of stay has been declining. More importantly, receipts per night, once adjusted for inflation and exchange rate changes, have been declining in real terms since the 1980s.[6] With both receipts per night and duration of stay declining, it is clear that Tunisia has been facing rapidly diminishing returns to these investments and indeed many hotels have fallen into bankruptcy. Abdallah and Adair (2007) show that the rate of return to such investments is low and considerably lower than in Morocco where greater corresponding effort has gone into working with travel agents abroad so as to raise the occupancy rate, construct travel packages of high quality and avoid overinvestment.

Similarly, many of the two-track elements evident in Tunisia's financial markets and institutions have also given rise to large scale inefficiencies and in some cases market failures. For example, schemes like the aforementioned FOPRODI, and central bank regulations mandating at least minimal credit allocations to designated sectors, such as agriculture, SMEs and hotels, along with credit guarantees and preferential interest rates, have given rise to extremely large interest rate differentials across different borrowers, as well as to large numbers of non-performing loans. In some cases, as a result of both adverse selection and moral hazard incentives, these have resulted in market failures in that the banks have refused to lend, even with so-called credit guarantees.

One implication has been the rising costs of these distortions in terms of rising percentages of non-performing loans in the banking system, the relatively high debt to GDP ratios, and the country's rather extreme reliance on European markets for exports and FDI despite the partial diversion of EU interest in the direction of Eastern Europe and Tunisia's failure to take advantage of its proximity to several Sub-Sahara African countries where trade has started to grow. That extreme reliance on the EU is also the result of the institutional shortcomings in the FTAs with Arab countries which have impeded the implementation of these agreements and contributed to the failure to liberalize MFN tariffs, quotas, and eliminate the monopolistic trading boards in specific commodities. Other problems lie in the facts that privatization remains quite partial and that services are still neither deregulated nor open to international competition despite the fact that, world-wide, trade in services is growing much faster than merchandise trade. Note that other countries have gone well ahead of Tunisia in liberalizing services trade. As a result, Tunisia's international trade in services is severely restricted by existing regulations and the absence of mechanisms undertaken jointly with other countries to liberalize them.

The cost of the aforementioned inefficiencies in Tunisia is most dramatically reflected in the labor markets in the form of persistently high unemployment rates, particularly among young people and women. As was shown in Table 2.10, Tunisia's overall unemployment rate remained stubbornly high (around 15–16%) over the 1980s and 1990s and has risen to still higher levels in recent years. Even worse, is that it has been highest (and rising most rapidly) among youths and those with relatively high levels of education (Abdessalem 2011). The latter finding is especially disturbing given the relatively high quality of Tunisia's higher education and the heavy investment that has been made in such education by the Tunisian government.[7] That inefficiency has had the effect of lowering the rates of return to schooling in Tunisia for both males and females. Indeed, they ranged from 2.7% to 5.5% in 2001 for primary and secondary education, which is well below such rates for many MENA countries and far below those of the more successful developing countries (like most of the East Asian countries) as shown by Tzannatos et al. (2016) where these rates are in the range of 8–10% (World Bank 2008a, 216–217).

An especially revealing study, pointing to the sizeable allocative inefficiencies in the Tunisian economy over the period between 1983 and 1996, is that of Ghali and Mohnen (2004). In line with the fact that over this period, resource allocation in Tunisia was, at least partially, affected by the series of five-year development plans that the country adopted over this period, these authors constructed a linear programming model consisting of some 15 different productive sectors, and six factors of production (capital and five different categories of labor of specified levels of availability by skill and educational level) designed to maximize the level of final demand in each year subject to the technology reflected in annual input output tables. Their findings demonstrate the importance of numerous bottlenecks and sources of inefficiency. In particular, if resource allocation had been optimal, the levels of final demand that could have been satisfied would have been 15–20% higher than they actually were in each year. Certain sectors, like food processing, construction materials, electrical and mechanical goods, were producing far below the levels that would have been optimal if resources had been more mobile, while other sectors like textiles and other manufacturing were producing far above their optimal levels. Under the optimal allocation, the shadow wage rates of labor skill level 2 (machine operators) would have been raised significantly while those of highly skilled labor would have been lowered, consistent with the aforementioned fact that unemployment rates have remained so high throughout the entire post-1980 period for this type of labor. The authors did detect some improvement over time since 1986 which was when the aforementioned Structural Adjustment Program was introduced. Yet, even so, this study highlights the many distortions in the allocation of Tunisia's labor and capital resources across sectors and also in international trade.

3. *The Political Economy of Liberalization Reforms*

Why did the structural adjustment program and the reforms undertaken by Tunisia between the mid-1980s and 2010 not lead to greater dependence on markets, to smaller and fewer inefficiencies, and to a greater role for the private sector?

The major macroeconomic crisis of the mid-1980s resulted from the conjunction of three factors: (i) an expansive fiscal policy facilitating increased wages and public expenditures aimed at meeting social demands,

(ii) deteriorating terms of trade (resulting from a major drop in major commodity export prices, including oil, and resulting in lower government revenues), and (iii) increased inefficiencies in the economy reflected in significant productivity declines. The political sclerosis and infighting within the power structure made things worse as no decisions and actions could be undertaken, and, when they were undertaken as in the case of the sharp bread price increases in 1984, this led to riots and a political crisis.

That crisis, and the macroeconomic adjustment program with the IMF that resulted from it, provided an opportunity for a shift toward more market-oriented reforms driven by the private sector and with less direct control by the state. The change in political regime in 1987 which removed Bourguiba from power and introduced more coherence to government could and should have supported such a process.

There were also many other factors favorable to the deepening and strengthening of reforms. First, the political momentum and the success of the Structural Adjustment Program in restoring macroeconomic stability and economic growth should have favored the continuation, broadening, and deepening of reforms. Second, the political regime did succeed in taming the potentially distortionary power of the three major interest groups: the labor union (UGTT), the business organization (UTICA), and the agricultural organization (Union Tunisienne de l'Agriculture et de la Pêche, UTAP). Third, the global environment in which the engine of globalization was roaring was supportive of further reforms and Tunisia's integration into the global economy. Fourth, the free-trade agreement with the European Union was a major trigger of supportive action and the EU had hoped that the agreement would lead to further trade agreements among MENA countries.

While it is true that reforms were undertaken to liberalize prices and markets, reduce trade protection, liberalize the financial market, and even to privatize public enterprises, the process eventually stalled. Indeed, the heavy hand of the state was maintained and some reforms were even reversed. The aforementioned factors were not sufficient and, for a number of different reasons, the movement toward a greater role for markets and the private sector did not proceed.

First, there was the incentive within the political system to maintain the rents made possible through a strong interventionist state so that they could continue to be available for redistributing them to supporters and to penalize opponents (Acemoglu and Robinson 2012). As the political regime became entrenched and felt the need to strengthen its grip on power, the attractiveness of adopting a more open economic system became even weaker, contributing strongly to the stall of reforms. Second, and in the same vein, the political regime became increasingly aware that a stronger private sector may well contain the kinds of leaders who could constitute a political threat to the existing regime. Third, as in the 1980s, the continued existence of the Islamist political threat, despite its repression, made the state reluctant to undertake any reforms which could provide opportunities to foment dissent and riots and, as a result, opportunities for the Islamists to seriously intervene.

While the lack of reforms during the 1980s was accompanied by more political openings toward Islamists, the situation changed completely beginning in the early 1990s. With increased activism and threats from Islamists, the solution, as in many other MENA countries, called for more repression of political opponents. As a result, the political regimes in MENA and especially Tunisia became more autocratic. The emphasis on security and political stability required slowing down and even reversing economic reforms. When such reforms were undertaken, they were imposed by decree and required no more adhesion by main stakeholders.[8]

Adding these considerations to the continued threat of opposition by the labor union, even though it was now weaker and more accommodative, meant that momentum for reform and further opening of the economy were lost. Above all, in the reversal of reforms was the predatory behavior of the political leadership, and of the Ben Ali family in particular, which hardened the various regulations and restrictions on competitive markets (especially those on foreign investment and tariffs), in order to allow Ben Ali family members to take advantage of them, but thereby further weakening the private sector as a whole and its competitiveness and discouraging entrepreneurship.

While all this allowed the Ben Ali family to show off at least some success stories in the economy, it was soon seen to be an extreme form of corruption and of further distortions between and within sectors. In any case, the state continued to intervene heavily in the economy, including playing an active role in promoting diversification during the 2000s and 2010s. For instance, the state was the main promoter of technology parks which oversaw the development of ICT-enabled activities. It introduced, as recently as 2018, the Start-up Act Law which provides a specific set of incentives addressed to the digital economy. Yet, in the following subsections, we present three important examples illustrating the difficulties faced by further liberalization reforms in Tunisia: namely, the stalled privatization program, the difficulties of the repeated attempts at dismantling the two-track system, and the forever-postponed reform of the price subsidy scheme.

4. A First Example: the Stalled Privatization Program

The privatization program is a telling example of the dynamics of reform. A major component of the Structural Adjustment Program was the privatization of SOEs. Many different objectives were pursued as part of this program, including increasing the efficiency of many low-performing SOEs, opening sectors, and activities to the private sector for increased efficiency, reducing the cost of loss-making SOEs to the budget, and reducing the burden of those non-performing loans to the banking system that were attributable to SOEs. The chosen approach was to start with the SOEs which operate in competitive sectors and to proceed with either their liquidation or privatization. This approach was indeed pursued in a few different sectors, such as tourism, textiles, and construction materials. As a result, many SOEs were either dismantled or forced to sell off many of their assets, while others were privatized with or without financial restructuring.

Indeed, according to Bechri and Naccache (2007), the number of SOEs (presumably using the same definition referred to above) declined by about 100 units over 20 years, falling from 285 in 1984 to 187 in 2004. Yet, the core system of SOEs remained in place, going well beyond the 'strategic' SOEs, operating in non-competitive sectors and mainly providing public services such as in transport and communications. The sell-off of SOEs did not go very far and came to an almost complete halt by the early 2000s.

The labor union's influence in this process was crucial. After the uprisings, during the 2010s, by which time the UGTT had once again become stronger, more vocal and freer from government containment, the UGTT repeatedly expressed the view that the privatization of SOEs is a 'red line that cannot be crossed'. Indeed, its opposition to SOE privatization became complete and strong and, as a result, the process has been almost completely stopped.

The bottom line on the failure to go further in privatizing SOE and undertaking policy reform over all the last 25 years in Tunisia is very similar to that expressed by Piro (1998) for Jordan, namely, that political economy considerations greatly impede the ability of the public sector to reform in the direction of the divestiture of state enterprises.

5. *A Second Example: the Difficulties of Dismantling the Two-Track System*

The difficulties caused by the two-track system, in which there was one set of incentives for export-oriented enterprises and another one for import-competing firms, became increasingly evident to policymakers. In addition to the fiscal cost of the incentive system, which continued to increase with the expansion of exports (derived from their exemption from taxes), the efficiency costs were increasingly evident, especially due to the disconnect and lack of integration between the two types of activities.

The reforms required to rectify this dichotomy and major source of inefficiency were straightforward. In particular, it required measures to subject revenue from exporting activities to the same tax system as that for the rest of the economy. Not surprisingly, international organizations such as the IMF and the World Bank were pushing for such reforms, and pressures were also coming from foreign (European) governments, which saw the tax incentive system in Tunisia as unfair competition, requesting that the system be dismantled. The implementation of such reforms would require an at least gradual but progressive process of increased taxation of export revenues until such tax rates were fully aligned into a uniform system for the entire country.

The first attempt at this occurred in 2006 with the adoption of Organic Law 2006–80 (18 December 2006) which introduced a corporate tax of 10%

on income from export activities, to be implemented starting in 2008. But one year later, the implementation of this decision was postponed to 2012 (Law 2007–70, 27 December 2007), and subsequently further delays were introduced from year to year.

The tax incentives for the two-track system were finally abandoned by Law 2018–56 (27 December 2018), based on a decision to apply a common tax rate of 13.5% to income from both exports and domestic sales, to be implemented starting in 2021. After 16 years, the distortionary tax incentives are still in place, and it remains to be seen whether the new system will actually be implemented in 2022.

6. *A Third Example: the Forever-Postponed Reform of the Price Subsidy Scheme*

An extensive subsidy scheme was introduced in the 1970s to smooth variations in basic consumption commodities, funded through the CGC (see Chapter 3). Of course, the volumes of the subsidies, and their shares of GDP, have varied over time depending on changes in commodity prices, and adjustments in the rates of subsidy. The system was expected to be temporary but has remained in place almost unchanged over the last 5 decades, despite various attempts to reform it beginning in the early 1980s. One attempt to adjust the subsidies at the end of 1983 resulted in the doubling of the prices of bread and cereals which triggered major riots and forced the government to cancel the price increases in January 1984. A more gradual process of price adjustments was followed since the macroeconomic adjustment program of the mid-1980s, which helped reduce the budgetary burden of the subsidies.

The effectiveness, equity, and quality of targeting of the subsidy scheme have all been seriously questioned, and as a result, there have been attempts to reform it (World Bank 2015). Cash transfer programs have been considered, and such a program was actually introduced in 1986 as an initial step towards reform. Yet, after almost 40 years, the subsidy scheme remains fully in place and recently reached unprecedented levels. The ratio of consumption price subsidies to GDP, which was only 2.3% of GDP in 2010, increased to 7.3% in 2013, although declining to 4.6% in 2018 (Nabli 2019, 70). At the same time, the cash transfer program of the PNAFN has expanded from reaching 73 thousand families in 1986 to 285 thousand in 2018, at a budgetary cost of 0.6% of GDP. The reform of the price subsidy scheme has stalled, and resistance to it has prevailed.

D. Tunisia's Limited Success in Making the Private Sector the Engine for Investment and Productivity Growth

Despite the relative success of its industrial restructuring program initiated in the 1980s, even by 2000 Tunisia's progress in this respect fell quite far short of East Asian countries. Why could Tunisian businessmen not go as far as those in East Asia? One interesting analysis of precisely this question was one by an outside specialist (Erdle 2011) in a report funded and distributed by a German Development Research Institute. As part of his conclusion (46) he said: 'As noted before, the majority of Tunisian businessmen (and the same observation also applies *grosso modo* to the majority of foreign investors active on Tunisian soil) are only prepared to invest in relatively simple and low-risk activities which promise quick and secure profits or, to put it differently, they are not ready to invest their personal fortune into economic products which take a long time (and substantial funding) to develop, require complex organizations and external investment, and/or involve extensive technological know-how and industrial research. This is also one of the reasons why neither Tunisian entrepreneurs nor their foreign counterparts have so far managed (or bothered) to produce sophisticated technological products and/or high-end consumer goods.'

Erdle (2011) attributed part of this failure to the government for at the same time it was maintaining existing public sector jobs in fear of the political implications of rising unemployment, it was also offering to private businessmen the opportunity to take advantage of easy and low-risk opportunities offered them through close connections to existing autocrats and their families. This was instead of inducing them to accept somewhat lower returns in the short run while seeking higher future returns based on more dynamic and competitive higher technology activities. In view of the heavy hand of the Tunisian state and its extensive distortions in its financial, labor, and product markets, Tunisia's success in entrepreneurship continued to depend on the entrepreneur's proximity to the political regime and to government. The state continued to have available to it a wide range of instruments, and enough discretion in the design and implementation of laws and regulations, to be able to affect the economic fate, either positively or negatively, of any private entrepreneur in any activity. Whether it was through business regulations, access to the financial markets, international trade rules and regulations, labor markets or the judiciary, the state continued to retain the ability to selectively and preferentially affect the performance of private businesses.

By contrast, the Asian countries have experienced gradual trends toward freer labor markets and toward business organizations that serve both as useful intermediaries between government and individual workers, on the one hand, and individual firms on the other, and in providing firms with information, dispute resolution, and other services. In East Asia, and especially in Korea and later on in China, as a result of freer markets, linkages developed between the large firms with the high technology and SMEs employing more labor-intensive methods. This occurred by allowing for vertical integration and lowering the transaction costs between the different types of firms in input supplying and demanding industries.

When technologies and contracting were simple and changing only slowly, international competitiveness might have been served by co-opting or suppressing unions and business associations so as to limit their rent-seeking abilities as Tunisia has done. Yet, as time went on, with globalization proceeding rapidly, and contracting and technology becoming increasingly complex, information and coordination problems have become increasingly important. The competitive private firms of East Asia became increasingly able to learn from firms in their more advanced export markets and thereby to move up the technological ladder. Early on in this process, Page (1994), in contrast to some other explanations of the East Asian Miracle, showed that the big difference between manufacturing firms in East Asia and those in other developing countries, including MENA, Latin America, and the Caribbean and South Asia, was that they were private and much more seriously engaged in exporting. He argued quite convincingly that it was the push into exporting that gave such manufacturing firms in East Asian countries greater access to best practice technology in conditions is which markets for technological information were very incomplete that made the difference, rather than sector-specific initiatives. He showed that the East Asian manufactures exporters took advantage of information-related technologies in their export destinations to increase their own TFP. Notably, he also showed that TFP growth in the whole economy, as well as in the manufacturing sector itself, of the Asian Miracle countries between 1960 and 1989 was positively related to two quite different measures of their outward or export orientation. Moreover, he also showed the positive impact of the educational quality of their labor force, thereby confirming the relevance of the educational quality to learning and TFP growth. While unfortunately, he did not have access to any data on the comparative role of business associations or interfirm connections, from what we stated above concerning the relative importance of inter-firm linkages between East Asian countries, we suspect that business linkages should also be given credit for the success of East Asian Miracle countries in TFP growth.

It is in this context of business associations that Bellin (2002, 2004) and Cammett (2007) argue that Tunisia has been missing an opportunity to have free and independent business associations that could discuss the problems of their industries openly among each other and with government so as to overcome their information problems and bring about additional policy reforms when and where needed. They argue that given their dependence on government for protection in their specific product lines and access to credit and other inputs on favorable terms, Tunisian businessmen became too timid to do this. Hence, without more open discussion of governance issues, Tunisia's political and administrative system has found it increasingly difficult to resolve deep-seated economic inefficiencies and conflicts, especially those within the manufacturing sector.[9] Indeed, it should be stressed that Tunisia's large business association UTICA was a very top-down organization which existed primarily as a means of communicating to business firms government policies but with virtually no bottom-up influence whereby business firms and especially private ones could influence government policy as described in Nugent (1989).

These pervasive interventions also have undermined the credibility of the reforms aimed at improving the business environment and encouraging the private sector to take the lead in wealth creation. Without such credibility, the persistence of pervasive selective and preferential treatment has had the effect of increasing risks to private entrepreneurs, thereby discouraging investment. Nabli et al. (2008) argue that the lack of credibility in the commitment of government to reforms and markets may be due to the unwillingness of the incumbent authoritarian rulers to commit to a broad-based and strong private sector, because such a sector, if it were to become sufficiently strong, could constitute a threat to the regime itself. While similar authoritarian regimes, including in East Asia, have found alternative commitment mechanisms to provide credibility, this has not been the case in Tunisia. (Gehlbach and Keefer 2007).

Tunisia (like most of its MENA neighbors) has lagged well-behind East Asian countries in the formation of business groups and other means of accomplishing vertical integration to facilitate both greater linkages between upstream and downstream firms in broad industry groupings, and thereby to achieve greater efficiency. Even though Tunisia and other MENA countries have firms in both textiles and clothing or in both auto parts and automobile manufacturing sectors in which vertical integration can be useful for increasing efficiency and exports, the comprehensive survey of business groups and their usefulness by Khanna and Yafeh (2007) identified no such business groups of importance in Tunisia or any other MENA country but identified such groups in each of the six East Asian countries in our tables. Indeed, in several of the East Asian cases, their business groups were identified as being among the most diversified in the world (Khanna and Yafeh 2007, 334). El-Haddad (2008, 2010, 2013) have all drawn on Williamson's (1979) classic analysis of transaction cost economics to show the relevance of vertical integration as a means of avoiding the high transactions costs arising from huge asymmetries of information between textile firms sending fabric to firms in the clothing industry. Such transaction costs are especially high in countries with institutional shortcomings like Egypt, Tunisia, and other MENA countries where the means of achieving vertical integration are likely to be costly and difficult to achieve. Their situation and experience contrasts sharply with those of South Korea.

The limited success of MENA countries in general, and Tunisia more specifically, in making the private sector an engine of growth, even after the reforms of the 1980s, can be seen from the comparative data on the rate of Private Sector Gross Fixed Capital Formation as percent of GDP shown in Table 6.1. While this table appears to identify two MENA countries, namely, Algeria and Iran, as having unusually high rates of private investment as a percent of total Investment, we believe this information to be of suspect quality. The two countries are major oil-exporting countries where the state is dominant in the economy, and the high numbers almost certainly reflect a misclassification of investments by SOEs or similar institutions (such as the

Bonyads in Iran) as part of the private sector. The high rates of private sector investment for Bahrain, Lebanon and Jordan reflect the historically weaker roles of the state in these countries. For all other MENA countries, including Tunisia, the share of private sector investment in total investment was typically not much higher than 50–52%. Only two such countries showed a positive trend prior to the 2000s for this ratio: Egypt and Tunisia. [10] Yet, even for these countries, the shares of private investment in total investment have been typically far below those for East Asian countries where they have been in the 70–80% range.[11] Given the low shares of private investment and the low total rates of investment in MENA countries, the rate of private investment to GDP remained very low, typically lower than 20%, and for many countries, including Tunisia, lower than 15%. As shown in Table 6.2, until the early 1990s the share of public enterprises in business investment in Tunisia was still at 44%, though it declined somewhat in the 2000s. This is to be contrasted with East Asian countries where during the 1990s the rate of private investment reached 30% of GDP in Korea and 25% in Thailand. Indeed, Page (1994, esp., 244–246) has given considerable credit to this in his explanation for the East Asian Miracle by pointing to the much larger shares of private investment than public investment in GDP in East Asia compared to countries in other regions.

Business associations, of course, can only become relevant for any business after that business has been created. Even more fundamental in growth of the private sector is entrepreneurship. Ismail et al. (2018) have produced a very useful and quite up-to-date survey on conditions concerning entrepreneurship and new firm creation and growth in the MENA region. This survey is related to the Global Entrepreneurship Monitor (GEM) which has been collecting information on entrepreneurship in a growing number of countries over the years. Table 6.3 shows data provided by Ismail et al. (2018, Table 6.2) on average scores collected from a sizeable number of experts for 9 different MENA countries as well as comparable averages for the MENA region as a whole and also all countries covered by GEM. Each of the columns in the table from (1) to (9) shows a measure of the extent to which that particular type of service (Entrepreneurship Framework Condition (EFC)) is deemed to be helping new firms to be created, based on a scale of 1–9. Note that on EFCs 1 (Entrepreneurial Finance), 2a (Government Policy Support and Relevance, 6 (Commercial and Legal Infrastructure), 7a (Internal Market Dynamics), and 8 (Physical Infrastructures), Tunisia scores were very close to or even slightly higher than the MENA and GEM averages. Note, however, that for EFCs 2b (Government Taxes and Bureaucracy), 4a (Entrepreneurial Education at School Stage), 4b (Entrepreneurial Education at Post-school Stage), 5 (R&D Transfer), 7b (Internal Market Burdens and Entry Regulations), and 9 (Cultural and Social Norms) Tunisia's scores are well below both the MENA and GEM averages, and even below those of MENA non-major oil-exporting countries. These categories in which Tunisia's score are well below the other averages are especially telling since they

Table 6.3 Quality Scores on Entrepreneurial Conditions in MENA, 2016–2017

		Government policies			*Entrepreneurial education*				*Internal market*			
	Entrepreneurial finance	***Support and relevance***	***Taxes and bureaucracy***	***Government entrepreneurship programs***	***At school age***	***At postschool age***	***R&D transfer***	***Commercial and legal infrastructure***	***Dynamics***	***Entry regulation***	***Physical infrastructure***	***Cultural and social norms***
Country	*(1)*	*(2a)*	*(2b)*	*(3)*	*(4a)*	*(4b)*	*(5)*	*(6)*	*(7a)*	*(7b)*	*(8)*	*(9)*
MENA	**4.2**	**3.8**	**3.4**	**3.6**	**2.4**	**3.7**	**3.2**	**4.9**	**5.2**	**3.6**	**4.8**	**4.5**
Non-major oil exporters												
Djibouti												
Egypt, Arab Rep.	3.9	3.6	3.1	3.3	1.7	3.1	2.8	3.9	5.1	4.0	0.5	4.1
Jordan	4.1	3.6	3.4	3.7	2.2	3.0	3.8	4.8	5.3	3.8	6.3	4.2
Lebanon	5.0	3.6	3.8	3.9	4.3	5.1	3.9	5.4	4.4	3.8	3.7	6.2
Morocco	3.6	4.2	4.1	3.7	1.9	4.0	2.8	4.7	4.5	3.4	6.6	4.1
Syrian Arab Republic												
Tunisia (2015)	**4.2**	**4.1**	**2.7**	**3.6**	**1.7**	**3.4**	2.8	5.8	6.9	2.9	6.7	4.1
West Bank and Gaza												
Yemen, Rep.												
MENA major oil exporters												
Algeria												
Iran, Islamic Rep.	2.9	3.4	2.6	2.2	2.5	3.2	3.1	3.2	5.0	2.8	6.3	3.6
Iraq												
Libya												

(Continued)

Table 6.3 Quality Scores on Entrepreneurial Conditions in MENA, 2016–2017 *(Continued)*

		Government policies			*Entrepreneurial education*				*Internal market*			
	Entrepreneurial finance	*Support and relevance*	*Taxes and bureaucracy*	*Government entrepreneurship programs*	*At school age*	*At postschool age*	*R&D transfer*	*Commercial and legal infrastructure*	*Dynamics*	*Entry regulation*	*Physical infrastructure*	*Cultural and social norms*
Country	*(1)*	*(2a)*	*(2b)*	*(3)*	*(4a)*	*(4b)*	*(5)*	*(6)*	*(7a)*	*(7b)*	*(8)*	*(9)*
MENA GCC	**4.3**	**5.1**	**4.7**	**4.8**	3.7	**4.7**	**3.8**	**4.9**	**5.0**	**4.3**	**6.9**	**5.4**
Bahrain												
Kuwait												
Oman												
Qatar	4.5	5.5	4.7	5.4	4.6	5.8	4.3	5.2	4.5	4.0	6.6	5.4
Saudi Arabia	3.9	3.9	4.0	3.4	2.1	3.7	3.0	3.9	4.8	4.0	6.8	4.6
United Arab Emirates	4.4	5.8	5.5	5.6	4.5	4.7	4.2	5.6	5.6	5.0	7.3	6.2
MENA Average	4.0	4.2	3.8	3.9	2.8	4.0	3.4	4.7	5.1	3.7	6.3	4.7
Global Average	4.2	4.2	4.0	4.3	3.1	4.6	3.8	4.9	5.0	4.3	6.5	4.8

Source: Ismail et al. (2018, Table 6.2).

Note: Scores are weighted averages: ranging from 1 as highly insufficient to 9 as highly sufficient.

would seem to be especially relevant for young, educated potential start-up entrepreneurs. While some of these like Government Startup Programs and Entrepreneurial Education may be rectifiable by starting up new programs, some of the others like Government Policies, Taxes and Bureaucracy, and Cultural and Social Norms while also very important to accomplish will undoubtedly take considerable time and effort to accomplish. Aside from the scores, the narrative in Ismail et al. (2018) said that virtually all the entrepreneurship services were especially lacking for those in the startup stage, and especially for those in the western and southern areas of Tunisia where access to banks is also difficult and costly. It was also stated that coops and agricultural groups have virtually no access to funding of any sort from banks or other organizations. The figures in this table also clearly identify that Tunisia has been ranking especially far below GCC countries like Qatar and UAE. Notably, Alphin and Lavine (2016) have attributed much of the success of GCC countries in entrepreneurship and innovation to their ability to encourage foreign universities and think tanks to locate branches in these countries.

While most of the evidence and assessment concerning problems and accomplishments of the private sector, including entrepreneurship, presented above has been at the country level, it is useful to look at information coming from individual and mostly private firms. A suitable source of such information is the Enterprise Surveys (ES) conducted on randomly selected private firms for a few countries and years. Unfortunately, the World Bank had been allowed to conduct only a few such surveys in MENA region countries including Tunisia before 2013 and even to this day has rarely ever been allowed to do so in a GCC country.

It was only in the context of a major large study, conducted jointly by the European Bank for Reconstruction and Development, the European Investment Bank and the World Bank during 2013 and 2014, that ESs were undertaken so that such information became available at the firm level for Tunisia and several other MENA countries and in most cases for the year 2013 alone.[12] For this reason, so as to focus on the responses of the managers of formal private firms and to draw upon differences across countries, we concentrate on these ESs in eight MENA countries and a comparison with an aggregate for other countries (mostly low and middle income countries) taken from the same Surveys. As shown in Part A of Table 6.4, the eight MENA ES countries with such data at this time are Djibouti, Egypt, Jordan, Lebanon, Morocco, Tunisia, West Bank and Gaza, and Yemen. To be included in the sample, the firms had to have at least five workers, to operate in in either the manufacturing or services sectors, and to be relatively formal in that they had to be identified from registration.

Each firm manager in these ESs was asked to identify the obstacle that he (she) deemed to be the most serious one out of a whole list of such obstacles. The entries in each of the first five columns of Part A of Table 6.4 show the relative seriousness of these obstacles to their business as perceived by the firm

Table 6.4 Concerns Expressed by the Managers of Private Firms in MENA Countries, 2012–2014

A. Percentages of firms identifying most serious obstacle to their firm's business

Country	***Political instability***	***Informality***	***Inadequately educated workforce***	***Access to finance***	***Corruption***	***Informal sector as % of GDP* (2015)***	***Electricity outage***
Djibouti		4		2	13	n.a	55
Egypt	49	3		9	6	33.9	6
Jordan	11	2		30	5	15.2	
Lebanon	56	1		5	8	29.2	10
Morocco	8	14		11	22	27.1	
Tunisia	50	14	10	8	3	30.9	
West Bank and Gaza	31	10		8	3	n.a.	13
Yemen	48	1		4	7	28.8	22
MENA ES						27.5	
All Economies						27.8	

B. Time required for firms to deal with certain issues

Country	***% of senior management time spent on government regulations***	***Days to obtain import license***	***Days to obtain operating license***	***Days to clear exports through customs***	***Days to obtain electricity connection***	***Days to obtain water connection***
Djibouti	5.3	7.7	8.8	10.4	34.1	16.1
Egypt	3.1	19.8	138.9	7.4	75.7	20.5
Jordan	5.3	2.1	1.4	4.6	13.1	21
Lebanon	4.1	28	50	4.9	56	40.2
Morocco	4.6	30.6	24.1	3.5	13.8	49.8
Tunisia	6.5	12.9	39.2	3	89.3	17.2
West Bank and Gaza	4.4	35.4	11.5	2.5	42.5	13.4
Yemen	1.9	11.6	7	11.2	25.6	35.9
MENA ES	9.4	18.5	35.1	5.9	43.8	26.8
All ES Economies	9.8	18.4	30.1	7.9	30	27.7

(Continued)

Table 6.4 Concerns Expressed by the Managers of Private Firms in MENA Countries, 2012–2014 *(Continued)*

C. Importance of females in various types of firms, sectors, and positions

Country	***Total labor force***	***Formal private sector***	***Labor-intensive manufacturing***	***Other manufacturing***	***Services***	***Top management of the firm***	***Female share in employment of firms managed by a female***
Djibouti	30	22	3	13	32	13	37
Egypt	23	12	16	8	15	7	25
Jordan	22	14	15	7	3.5	2.5	52
Lebanon	25	22	23	16	25	4	44
Morocco	26	26	53	22	28	4	46
Tunisia	27.5	33	54	21	30	7.5	48
West Bank and Gaza	20	5.5	4	5	5.5	1.5	5
Yemen	24	7	1	3	2	2.5	12
MENA ES	24	19.5	20	15	18	5.5	
All ES Economies						18	49

Source: European Bank for Reconstruction and Development, European Investment Bank and World Bank (2016).

Notes:

* Indicates that source of these data is Medina and Schneider (2018) and is an estimate for the whole economy in 2015.

ES: Enterprise Survey; MENA ES: counties in MENA for which enterprise surveys available for 2012–2014 (Djibouti, Egypt, Jordan, Lebanon, Morocco, Tunisia, West Bank and Gaza, and Yemen).

All ES economies: all countries of the world for which ESs were available for this time period.

managers. As can easily be seen from this Table, by 2013 political instability was ranked by firm managers as the most serious obstacle to their business in Tunisia. From column (2) of this part of the table we see that informality (reflecting competition from the informal sector) was identified by the second largest percentage of firms in Tunisia as the most serious obstacle to business. Note that this is consistent with the fact shown in column (6) that the share of the informal sector in GDP in 2015 was estimated to be second highest among all the countries shown. Note also that another commonly cited obstacle to business of private firms around the world, Access to Finance identified in the fourth column, was less frequently pointed to as the most important obstacle to business in Tunisia than elsewhere, even though this obstacle has quite clearly gotten much more serious in Tunisia since 2013. Note also that the responses of firm managers indicated that Corruption and Government Regulations were identified as major obstacles by significant percentages of private firms in Tunisia.

Part B of Table 6.4 shows something else can be learned from the various responses to questions posed to firm managers in the ESs, such as the time of senior management spent on government regulations and the time needed to get various important connections. Note that access to electricity connections seems to require considerably more time in Tunisia than in most other countries. On the other hand, time for exports to clear customs and to obtain water connections are relatively modest in the case of Tunisia according to the responses of firm managers in these ES surveys.

For Tunisia in particular, more details about the obstacles faced by its firms are shown in Table 6.5a, with information about the fuller list of 15 such obstacles. The first column of the table identifies the absolute number of Tunisian firms in the 2013 ES sample which identified each of these obstacles as the most severe one. Note that every one of the obstacles is identified by at least one firm as the most serious obstacle for that particular firm, pointing to the widely varying circumstances serving as obstacles to their business among firms of all different size, age, industry, and location characteristics. What the remaining columns of the table indicate is the extent to which these responses vary by industry or sector. The entries in the subsequent columns of each row in the table represent the percentages of the firms in the first column for that row which identify that obstacle as the most serious one.

Since the ESs for other countries all over the world started in 2002, we complement the assessment based on the 2013–2014 surveys for Tunisia with findings from other studies using the larger sample of ESs undertaken before 2013, which did include a limited sample of MENA countries (Algeria, Egypt, Iraq, Lebanon, Morocco, Oman, Syria, and Yemen) and which have been analyzed by Liaqat and Nugent (2015, 2016) among others. Of these two papers, the first concentrated on the MENA region as a whole and comparisons between MENA and non-MENA countries, while the second dealt with the full sample of ESs but concentrated on the effects of *labor*

Table 6.5a Tunisia Enterprise Surveys: Distribution of Each of the Most Serious Obstacles to Business Across Firms in Different Industries in 2013 (%)

			Manufacturing			
Biggest obstacle affecting the operation of this establishment	***Number of firms***	***Percentage of firms by obstacle***	***Food***	***Tobacco***	***Textiles***	***Garments***
Access to finance	51	9.0	5.88	0	0	15.69
Access to land	1	0.2	0	0	0	100
Business licensing and permits	3	0.5	33.33	0	0	0
Corruption	19	3.3	5.26	0	0	0
Courts	2	0.4	0	0	0	0
Crime, theft and disorder	5	0.9	20	0	0	0
Customs and trade regulations	21	3.7	4.76	0	0	14.29
Electricity	5	0.9	0	0	0	20
Inadequately educated workforce	59	10.4	22.03	0	0	20.34
Labor regulations	9	1.6	33.33	0	0	22.22
Political instability	286	50.3	12.24	0	2.1	16.43
Practices of competitors in the informal sector	71	12.5	12.68	0	0	19.72
Tax administration	14	2.5	14.29	0	0	14.29
Tax rates	18	3.2	11.11	0	0	16.67
Transport	5	0.9	0	0	0	0
Total	569	100.0				

Sources: European Bank for Reconstruction and Development, European Investment Bank and World Bank (2016). https://www.enterprisesurveys.org.

regulations and their enforcement. Both studies make heavy use of factors which private firm managers said constituted obstacles to their business. Two of these specifically highlighted for the MENA region are (1) the lack of relevant skills among their workers, and (2) labor regulations and their enforcement. The findings of both studies for MENA are broadly quite relevant to Tunisia even if no such study was undertaken in Tunisia itself, and even though the specifics may be different.

Based on these findings, in the remainder of this section we review each of the five factors which were found to be the most serious obstacles to private business in Tunisia: political instability, competition from the informal sector, corruption and government regulations, lack of skills and inadequate education of workforce, and labor regulations. This section is completed with some remarks about the gender dimension of the growth of the private sector and a presentation of some tentative econometric results on the impact of firm characteristics on the severity of obstacles to growth of private sector firms.

Manufacturing							
Leather	*Wood*	*Paper*	*Publishing*	*Petroleum refining*	*Chemicals*	*Plastics, rubber*	*Non-metallic Min.*
0	0	0	1.96	0	1.96	0	0
0	0	0	0	0	0	0	0
0	0	0	0	0	0	0	0
0	0	0	0	0	0	0	0
0	0	0	0	0	0	0	0
0	0	0	0	0	0	0	0
0	0	0	9.52	0	0	0	0
0	0	0	0	0	0	0	20
0	1.69	1.69	0	0	0	0	0
0	0	0	0	0	0	0	0
0.35	0	0.7	1.05	0	1.05	0.7	0.35
1.41	0	0	0	0	1.41	0	0
0	0	0	0	0	0	0	0
0	0	0	0	0	0	0	0
0	0	0	0	0	0	0	0

(Continued)

1. Political Instability

From Part A of Table 6.4, it can be seen that in 2013 firm managers viewed political instability (representing primarily policy uncertainty) as the most serious obstacle to private business in each of the countries in the MENA ES sample, except for three. These exceptions were Djibouti where electricity outage was deemed to be the most serious obstacle by over half of the firm managers, Morocco where the highest percentage of firms identified corruption as the most important obstacle, and Jordan where both Access to Finance and Competition from the Informal Sector were at least slightly more important.

Political instability is of course by no means unique to Tunisia and other MENA countries and indeed it has been noted as a potential threat from time to time in countries all over the world. Its most important link to the health of the private sector comes through its effect on policy uncertainties. There are indeed a myriad of different kinds of policy uncertainties that can worry private firms, potentially limit their investments and lead to volatility

Table 6.5a Tunisia Enterprise Surveys: Distribution of Each of the Most Serious Obstacles to Business Across Firms in Different Industries in 2013 (%) *(Continued)*

	Manufacturing				
Biggest obstacle affecting the operation of this establishment	***Basic metals***	***Fab. metal prod.***	***Machinery equipment***	***Electronics***	***Precision Instruments***
Access to finance	0	5.88	0	3.92	0
Access to land	0	0	0	0	0
Business licensing and permits	0	0	0	0	0
Corruption	5.26	0	0	0	0
Courts	0	0	0	0	0
Crime, theft and disorder	0	0	0	0	0
Customs and trade regulations	0	0	0	4.76	0
Electricity	20	0	0	0	0
Inadequately educated workforce	0	1.69	0	0	0
Labor regulations	0	0	0	0	0
Political instability	0.7	1.75	1.05	0.35	0.35
Practices of competitors in the informal sector	0	0	0	1.41	0
Tax administration	0	0	0	0	0
Tax rates	0	0	0	0	0
Transport	0	0	0	0	0
Total					

in production, employment, and especially trade. Even in developed countries, these uncertainties are often believed to induce firms to 'wait and see' what policies will eventually emerge, in the meantime discouraging investment, market development, R&D expenditures, and production and employment decisions (Bernanke 1983; Dixit and Pindyck 1994). Among the various uncertainties might be those about interest rates, credit regulations, labor and product regulations, tax rates and costs of electricity, and other vital inputs. Both Carruth et al. (2000) and Bloom (2014) have explored both theoretically and empirically the relationships between policy uncertainties and the investment and other activities of individual firms in a variety of settings.

Rarely, however, have detailed studies of this type been done on individual firms. One such study is that of Morikawa (2016) done on large samples of both manufacturing and non-manufacturing firms in Japan during a period of political transition which attempted to identify the specific policy and other uncertainties that most strongly affected the investment and other decisions of these Japanese firms over the following few years. Very detailed

Manufacturing					*Services*		
Motor vehicles	*Other transport equipment*	*Furniture*	*Re-cycling*	*Other manufacturing*	*Retail*	*Whole-sale*	*Information Technology*
0	1.96	0	0	25.49	3.92	11.76	0
0	0	0	0	0	0	0	0
0	33.33	0	0	0	0	0	0
5.26	0	0	5.26	21.05	5.26	21.05	5.26
0	0	0	0	0	50	0	0
0	0	0	0	60	0	0	0
0	0	0	0	33.33	4.76	19.05	0
0	0	0	0	20	0	20	0
0	1.69	0	0	18.64	13.56	5.08	3.39
0	0	0	0	22.22	0	0	11.11
0	0	0.7	0	14.69	7.69	11.89	2.45
0	1.41	0	0	23.94	12.68	15.49	2.82
0	0	0	0	21.43	0	28.57	0
0	0	0	5.56	22.22	22.22	5.56	0
0	0	0	0	20	20	20	0

(Continued)

measures were obtained of both the degree of policy uncertainty over a list of leading concerns to the firms (including tax policy, business licensing, labor regulations, product regulations, and social security regulations) and the extent that these uncertainties affected firm behavior in the form of investment, R&D, entry into export markets, and employment. Among the key findings of the study were (1) the relatively high degree of policy uncertainty within firms even in a developed East Asian country like Japan, (2) the strength of many of the effects of these uncertainties on the various different types of firm behavior, and (3) the substantial variations in the magnitudes of these effects between different types of firms (manufacturing and non-manufacturing) and different kinds of firm outcomes (investment, R&D, entry into export markets, and employment).

Needless to say, because of the continuing heavy hand of the state, the experience of various market failures and failed policies and the need to great uncertainties about the future direction of many types of regulations and circumstances in Tunisia, one can easily suppose (1) that those policy

Table 6.5a Tunisia Enterprise Surveys: Distribution of Each of the Most Serious Obstacles to Business Across Firms in Different Industries in 2013 (%) *(Continued)*

Biggest obstacle affecting the operation of this establishment	***Services***				
	Hotels, restaurants	***Vehicle service***	***Construction***	***Transport***	***Travel***
Access to finance	11.76	1.96	5.88	1.96	0
Access to land	0	0	0	0	0
Business licensing and permits	0	0	0	33.33	0
Corruption	5.26	0	10.53	5.26	5.26
Courts	0	0	50	0	0
Crime, theft and disorder	0	0	0	20	0
Customs and trade regulations	0	4.76	0	4.76	0
Electricity	0	0	0	0	0
Inadequately educated workforce	3.39	1.69	3.39	1.69	0
Labor regulations	0	0	11.11	0	0
Political instability	5.59	3.15	3.5	4.2	6.99
Practices of competitors in the informal sector	0	2.82	0	2.82	1.41
Tax administration	7.14	0	0	7.14	7.14
Tax rates	11.11	0	0	5.56	0
Transport	0	0	0	40	0
Total					

uncertainties would be greater in Tunisia than in Japan, (2) that they could therefore have even more serious effects on firm outcomes, and (3) that these effects could also differ greatly across different kinds of firms and different locations within Tunisia. While unable to undertake such a large-scale survey of individual firms in Tunisia as Morikawa did in Japan, in what follows we do attempt to take advantage of what firm managers say in Tunisia, other MENA countries and even other countries in which the World Bank's ESs have been undertaken.

While the finding about the serious impact of political instability in Tunisia was in 2013, during the period of transition to democracy which started in 2011, when political instability may have become stronger, it had already been known to be an important factor even before that. Political instability and uncertainty about the policies to be chosen by its government have increased compared to previous periods, and clearly this is precisely the type of obstacle which leaves private firms with high investment risk. It leaves such firms in Tunisia and other MENA countries unable to know what policies will be adopted over the near future, and of course also especially over the more distant future. Therefore, they were unable to assess whether a certain type of investment is likely to fit with the polices likely to be in effect a few years ahead, thereby greatly discouraging such investments by private firms.

Table 6.5a also shows how these responses concerning the most serious obstacle to the firm's business vary by sector, both within manufacturing and within services (the latter in the last eight columns of the table). This choice of political instability as the most important obstacle to business was shared quite widely across sectors, with at least one firm in every service sector and all but six of the 22 manufacturing sectors identifying it as the most serious obstacle. This explains why political instability has had such an important debilitating effect in the whole period since 2011 when this problem has become increasingly important. Almost every sector is adversely affected by it. Even though from the firm manager responses to the 2020 ES shown in Table 6.5b, political instability was no longer ranked as the most serious obstacle to business by many firms, the average severity assigned to it remained at almost the same level it was in 2013. Hence, it is clear that political instability has not diminished in severity as an obstacle to business on the part of Tunisian firms. Rather, what has changed between these two periods is that so many other obstacles have become more severe. Note that the percentages of firms identifying Customs and Trade as the most serious obstacle to business rose from 3.7% in 2013 to 39.4% in 2020, those identifying Courts as the most serious obstacle to business rose from 0.4% to 11.5%, Business Licenses from 0.5% to 5.4% and Labor Regulations from 1.6% to 15% during the same 2013–2020 period.

2. *Competition from the Informal Sector*

Various firm surveys in Tunisia report that large percentages of firms in some sectors cite various sources of unfair competition, such as counterfeit or illegal products, the evasion of taxes and social security contributions, and especially excessive regulations. It is, therefore, hardly surprising that in 2013 Informality was ranked as the second most serious constraint to firms with 12.5% of all the firms surveyed identifying competition from the Informal Sector as the most serious obstacle to business. This is also consistent with the relatively high share of the informal sector in GDP shown in the last column of Part A of Table 6.4.

MENA countries have generally been characterized as having fairly large informal sectors, but which vary considerably from one country to another. The relative sizes of the informal sector can be important to formal private firms since they constitute an important source of competition for such firms, as their rationale for remaining informal is to avoid the different costs that firms have to pay to comply with the different regulations (paying taxes, abiding by labor, and product market regulations, etc.). Measuring

Table 6.5b Percentages of Firms Identifying Most Serious Obstacle to Their Firm's Business in the Most Recent Year Available

Country	*Access to finance*	*Business licensing and permits*	*Corruption*	*Courts*	*Crime, theft and disorder*	*Customs and trade*	*Electricity*
MENA	**11.4**	**3.7**	**9**	**0.9**	**1.6**	**3.5**	**11.7**
Djibouti (2013)	3.8	6.6	1.7	1	4	1.9	0.8
Egypt (2020)	4.7	2.2	2.1	17.4	8.7	8.4	0.2
Iraq (2011)	4.3	7	5	15.1	16.7	4.7	10.5
Jordan (2019)	6.2	0.2	6.2	14.3	3.6	2.2	1.5
Lebanon (2019)	2.1	0.5	0.2	36.9	6.5	28.7	0.3
Morocco (2019)	0.3	3.5	3	1.9	9.1	4.3	6.7
Tunisia (2020)	5.4	5.4	3.1	11.5	8.3	39.4	0.5
West Bank and Gaza (2019)	6.1	0.3	1.2	47.4	11.7	17.7	0.4
Yemen (2013)	0.7	0.8	1.3	49	1.1	4.8	1.5
East Asian Sample							
China	1.8	13	1.9	0.8	19.6	22.4	5.6
Indonesia (2015)	6.2	1.7	1	12.8	36.7	6.3	1.2
Malaysia (2015)	4.9	0.2	7.4	8.4	29.9	0.9	6.1
Philippines (2015)	5	2.4	6.4	3.4	20	10.4	6
Thailand (2016)	0.5	2.6	8.8	20.3	5	4.6	0.9
East Asia & Pacific	**13**	**3.7**	**8.6**	**1.1**	**2.7**	**3.2**	**5.6**
Latin America	**9**	**4.4**	**9.7**	**1**	**6.7**	**4.2**	**5.4**
South Asia	**12.4**	**1.8**	**9.3**	**0.4**	**2.6**	**1.9**	**20.3**
Sub-Sahara Africa	**23.7**	**1.3**	**7.3**	**0.6**	**3.3**	**4.6**	**14.7**
All Countries	**14.4**	**2.6**	**7**	**0.9**	**2.9**	**3.5**	**9**

Sources: World Bank Enterprise Surveys. https://www.enterprisesurveys.org.

Note:

The average reported for MENA in this table by the Enterprise Survey web page uses a different definition of MENA countries than the one used in this book.

the relative importance of the informal sector, however, is never straight-forward since rarely can statistical agencies collect reliable information on them. Notably, however, those figures in Part A of Table 6.4 come from one of the most respected specialists in measuring the importance of the informal sector across countries for the period under study here, namely, Friedrich Schneider.[13] The estimates of Schneider and his co-authors shown in this table are the shares of the informal sector in GDP for each of the different MENA countries for which that information is available, as well as for the average of the 162 countries for which Medina and Schneider (2018) have been able to calculate these shares. These estimates were for the year 2015 alone, although in some cases, Schneider and his co-authors

Inadequately educated workforce	*Labor regulations*	*Political instability*	*Informality*	*Tax Administration*	*Tax Rates*	*Transportation*
8.7	**2.7**	**19.1**	**7.7**	**2.6**	**11**	**4**
1.8	12.6	0.7	0	1.3	12.4	2.6
5.8	14.6	0.2	0.5	6.3	24.4	1.5
6.4	2.9	0	1.4	1.3	4.6	0.5
1.9	15.7	1.6	0.9	2.1	28	2.9
0.6	12.1	0.1	0.2	0	6.6	0.4
4.1	15.5	3.1	3.9	14.2	15.2	8.7
4.9	15	0.5	0.4	1	3.2	0.8
2.6	1	2.1	1.2	0.2	1.1	1.7
0	7.9	0.8	7.8	0.3	0.2	0.2
0.2	1.2	2	0.3	4.2	15.1	7.2
6.8	2.5	1.3	4.3	1.2	14.3	2.9
11.1	8.2	0.4	0.3	9	9.5	1.6
4.5	11.5	0.6	3.5	4.3	9	5.2
1.5	2.3	0	1	1.7	15	16.1
6.9	2.8	12.8	15.3	3	1.6	4.8
7.8	4.5	11.1	17.4	4.4	10.9	2.2
3.4	5.1	17.9	6.2	2.7	6.9	3.6
1.7	1	10.6	10.5	4.2	9.5	2.6
8.7	3.2	11.8	11.9	4	13	3.7

have estimated these same shares of the informal sector in GDP going back to 1991. In most countries, and for each region of the world, their estimates have shown these shares of informality to have been declining slightly over time as more firms choose to take advantage of some of the benefits of formality in terms of access to credit, dispute settlement and other mechanisms. In their full sample of countries and over time these authors have shown the shares of informality to be higher in countries with lower GDP per capita, where firms may be less able to pay for the costs of registration and where firms tend to be smaller. As shown in this last column of Part A of Table 6.4, the share of the informal sector in GDP in 2015 was estimated to be slightly higher in Tunisia (30.9%) than the averages of both the MENA

ES countries (for which ESs are available) and the world of about 27%. It was also higher than that of every other individual MENA country except that of lower-income Egypt. Although GCC countries were not included in this table (because in none of them was an ES conducted in 2013), the 2015 shares of the informal sector in GDP in GCC countries were considerably lower than those of Tunisia. In particular, the 2015 estimates from Medina and Schneider (2018) showed the corresponding shares of the informal sector for GCC countries to be: for Bahrain 16.63%, Kuwait 21.72%, Oman 23.91%, Qatar 13.08%, Saudi Arabia 14.7%, and UAE 24.26%. This suggests that by 2013 the average formal private firm in Tunisia was facing above-average competition from firms in the informal sector which may be able to offer their products at a lower price because they have avoided having to abide by the various regulations that apply to formal firms. Hence, this is indeed one relevant measure of the difficulties of formal private firms in Tunisia and other countries with large shares of the informal sector in GDP.

From Table 6.5a, it can be seen that this second most commonly identified obstacle as the most serious one, Competition from and Practices of the Informal Sector, is more concentrated among firms in other manufacturing, garments, wholesale, retail, food, all relatively labor-intensive industries in which the labor cost savings of the informal sector are especially advantageous. Despite the fact that the share of firms in the informal sector has been declining over time especially in the middle and high income countries, given the considerable depression that has characterized the Tunisian economy since 2010, it would seem quite possible that in their fight for survival and avoidance of bankruptcy, the firms comprising the sample of Tunisian firms in the 2020 ES sample may have become more informal, abiding by fewer regulations of formal firms than they did earlier. This may explain why, in the 2020 ES, as shown in Table 6.5b, the percentage of firms identifying Competition from the Informal Sector to be the most important obstacle to their business declined to less than 1% whereas it had been 12.5% in 2013.

Notably, in his rather comprehensive analysis of the labor market in Tunisia, Boughzala (2018) identified the divergence in real wage rates between the formal and informal sectors, which in turn depended on both government policy, including labor regulations, and their enforcement, to be a major source of Tunisia's labor market problems. As Boughzala (2018) quite appropriately described it, the long-in-place tripartite agreement between labor unions, private sector and government, had tried to harmonize labor regulations in such a way as to preserve social peace. But, over time there were increasing differences in pressures across regions and sectors, such that increasingly the labor regulations were less well enforced, leading to increasingly divergent conditions across sectors. It was primarily only in the government and the public sector where the labor regulations (minimum wage rates or labor bargained wage rates and working conditions) were more fully satisfied. Large private companies with over 100 workers and exporters also tended to abide with the labor and other regulations including social security since in their case violations could easily be observed and they depended on many public services for finance, protection of property rights, protection against theft and customs and formal infrastructure. Yet, there were very few of these large private firms, the vast majority of firms having less than 20 workers. As a result, less than 4% of employees in the private sector were unionized and the vast majority of private firms were 'informal' in the sense that they were not officially registered and not obligated to meet the minimum wage and social security regulations. One minor exception was the relatively small group of single-person private firms which were established by the aforementioned program of subsidizing public sector employees to start up by taking advantage of special training and information programs.[14] As Boughzala depicted it, with such poor enforcement of the labor regulations which tended to support higher wage rates and better working conditions, the choice of whether to be 'formal' (and thereby abide with the regulations) or 'informal' (and thereby avoid the costs of these regulations) was entirely up to the private firm manager, the vast majority of whom chose informality, explaining the unusually small size of the formal private sector and the unusually large share of firms and workers in the informal sector, but thereby without access to credit and improved technology needed to make for international competitiveness and productivity growth.

3. Corruption and Government Regulations

Corruption and government regulations do not appear among the top five obstacles to private business in Table 6.5a, and the percentages of firms identifying corruption as the most serious obstacle declined slightly from 3.3% in 2013 to 3.1% in 2020 as shown in Table 6.5b. Nevertheless, the fuller responses of both these tables show that many firms cite tax administration, customs and trade regulations, courts and crime as major obstacles. Note, by comparing these items in the same two tables, it can be seen that the percentages of firms citing Courts, Customs and Trade, Business Licenses and Labor Regulations as the most severe obstacle to their business all increased significantly between 2013 and 2020. These are all areas of public service where corruption might play an important role in obtaining such services at lower cost or more promptly.

Most alarmingly, from the first column of Part B of Table 6.4, we notice that the senior managers of Tunisian private firms said that a whopping 46.5% of their time was spent on dealing with government regulations. This was ten times as high as in most other MENA countries and five times as high as the overall average of all countries with ESs. While it might have been especially high at that time because of a totally new government, it is outrageously high. Had it been lower, or at least like the overall average of other countries, this would presumably have allowed these managers to spend at least somewhat more of their precious time improving firm efficiency, identifying new markets and taking advantage perhaps of economies of scale. By contrast, from the comparisons across countries in the second and fourth columns, it can be seen that factors related to imports (days to obtain an Import License) and to exports (Days to Clear Exports through Customs) do not seem to be as problematic for private firms in Tunisia as for those in either other MENA or non-MENA countries. The same is true for the Number of Days to Obtain Water Connections in the last column of Part B of the table, showing that the time required for this in Tunisia is well below the averages in MENA ES countries and All ES countries. Yet, even though Tunisia was not a country where many managers identified Electricity Outage as a serious problem, from the sixth column of this part of the table, getting access to electricity (Obtaining an Electricity Connection) in Tunisia in 2013 was said to take a much longer time than in any of the other MENA ES countries and almost three times as long as the average across all ES Economies. Similarly, as shown in the third column of this portion of the table, something even more basic, Days to Obtain an Operating License also was said to require considerably more time in Tunisia than in any of the other MENA countries except Egypt and well above the world average.[15]

4. *Skills and Inadequately Educated Workforce*

Although in the interest of space and to focus on the changes in the response of managers in Tunisia over time, the data presented in Table 6.5a are limited to Tunisia, the responses by managers (1) showed 'inadequately educated workforce' to be identified as the third most serious obstacle to business. This finding is consistent with the comparisons between the MENA and non-MENA regions, by Liaqat and Nugent (2015) who identified quite sharp differences between these two groups of countries in terms of both the percentages of firms saying that the Education and Skills of their Workers was a Serious Obstacle to Their Business and the Percentages of Firms Offering Training to their Workers. Notably, while 36.4% of the managers of private MENA firms said that the lack of skills was a serious obstacle to their businesses, only 21.9% of those from non-MENA countries said so. Although ES data for Tunisia were not included in the sample used by Liaqat and Nugent (2015), and while the terminology of the questions and responses changed slightly, as shown in Table 6.5a, data from the 2013 ES for Tunisia show that over 10% of the top managers of private firms in all sectors of Tunisia's economy said that lack of adequately trained labor force was the most serious obstacle to their business. The percentages of firm managers saying this, moreover, were somewhat higher in several sectors within manufacturing. Although not shown in the table, in the survey itself over 30% of the managers said that the lack of an adequately trained labor force was at least a moderate obstacle to their business. Hence, as in so many other respects, Tunisian private firms seemed to be slightly better off than private firms in most other MENA countries in terms of skills of their workers but far worse off than those in East Asian and other non-MENA countries.

Considering the rise in the unemployment between 2013 and 2020, it is not surprising to see that, as shown in Table 6.5b, the percentage of firm managers saying that an inadequately skilled labor force was the most serious obstacle to their business had fallen from 10.4% in 2013 to 4.9% in 2020.

In another study, Muller and Nordman (2011) used two separate worker and firm surveys in Tunisia to identify firms which were offering training to their workers. This was a circumstance wherein the firm paid low wages to workers without and during training but much higher wages to workers once they had successfully completed their training.[16] In their econometric analysis, Liaqat and Nugent (2015) went on to produce a large number of regressions identifying important interactions among some of these different firm and country characteristics, helping to explain the lesser training by MENA firms to workers across countries, sectors, and firm types than in non-MENA countries.

While one might think that this difference would have prompted MENA firms to offer more training to their workers than non-MENA firms, the calculations of Liaqat and Nugent (2015) based on the managers responses showed that only 17% of the MENA firms said that they had offered such training, while in non-MENA countries 39.3% of the firm managers said that they were offering such training. Indeed 45.1% of those in East Asia and the Pacific said they were doing so, as did 39.3% in Eastern Europe and Central Asia, 43.7% in Latin America and the Caribbean, 26% in South Asia, and 31.9% of those in Sub-Sahara Africa.[17]

Liaqat and Nugent (2016) also identified the lack of skills and limited training as a major constraint on growth of private firms and went on to identify a number of possible policy reforms designed to encourage private MENA firms to undertake more training. These included (1) to somewhat lighten the labor regulations on labor, especially those on firing workers, but at the same time to increase their enforcement in ways not likely to stimulate corruption payments by firms to government agents while trying to escape enforcement of these regulations by the governments, (2) to encourage financial development in ways that could allow private firms to have access to more stable sources of finance, such as that through stock markets, large banks, and foreign finance so as to become larger, hire more experienced managers (given that corporate owners and larger firms are more likely to engage in training of their workers than non-corporate managers and those of smaller firms), and (3) to promote gender equity in firm management since female owners and/or managers seemed more likely to engage in training than males.

Each of these policies may be likely to generate some additional indirect benefits. For example, Policy (1) would have the further advantage of lowering the seriousness of competition from the informal sector as an obstacle to business. Policy (2) could make it more likely that firms could succeed in entering export markets, and engaging in innovations to further enhance their competitiveness, both contributing indirectly to long-term economic growth. At the same time, the authors caution that 'one size does not fit all' with respect to such policies, so the optimal policies should be tailored specifically to the particular circumstances of the individual country.

The significance of the lack of skills as an obstacle to the growth of the private sector found in the Liaqat and Nugent (2016) study is to be contrasted with the finding by Boughzala (2018) and others, that due to the very limited employment opportunities in the formal private sector, the vast majority of better educated youth came to prefer to find jobs in the government and public sectors. Yet, especially as public sector budgets became increasingly hard to balance, such jobs remained limited, leaving the only practical choice for such citizens to be between working in the informal sector and either unemployment or to drop out of the labor force entirely. In general, working in the informal sector became increasingly unattractive to females, explaining why unemployment rates and withdrawal from the labor force rose over time much more sharply for females than for males. Indeed, he showed that between 2006 and 2011, the unemployment rate among youths aged 15–24 increased from 15.1% to 28.2% for females, but only from 11.5% to 15.4% for males. Among youths with university level educations, by 2011 the gender gap in unemployment rates was even greater, 22.6% for males but 44.2% for females. As a result, there appears to be a sizable mismatch in Tunisia between the levels of education and aspirations of youth and the skills required by the private sector.

Another relevant study is that of Ghali and Zitouna (2018). While it focused more on the demand side of the labor market, it did so in a way that is complementary to the supply side and regulation effects discussed above. In particular, they pointed to the increasing difficulty of private firms, such as those created in 2000, to sustain their existence over time. Even among those firms which did survive until 2013, many of them were not producing as much as they had been in 2000. The only two sectors of the economy outside of the public sector that were hiring significant numbers of the increasing percentages of more highly educated workers were manufacturing and market services. Yet, these sectors were very much constrained on the demand side by insufficient markets for their products and on the supply side by inadequate skills needed to justify their employment (despite their higher years of education). Indeed, firms in these sectors said that, despite their education, 60% of their job applicants did not meet even the minimal skill requirements of these firms. The consequence was that 26% of these firms were increasingly unable to meet their sales targets and delivery deadlines, and 27% of them indicated that they were still announcing their vacancies.

5. *Labor Regulations*

From responses of managers in the 2013, ES labor regulations did not appear as a major obstacle to business in Tunisia. Indeed, as shown in Table 6.5a only 1.6% of Tunisian firms identified labor regulations as the single most severe obstacle to their business in 2013. As shown in Table 6.5b, however, based on the latest waves of the ESs (2020 in the case of Tunisia), that percent has risen quite sharply to 15%. Even before this new finding, it has often been argued that labor regulations have been a major obstacle to business in Tunisia.

While not all firms hire their workers through the formal labor market, in Tunisia and around the region, firms, especially those in competitive industries and activities, such as those engaged in exports and import-competing activities, do so and often complain about what they might see as excessively tight regulations on hiring and firing workers. Indeed, although focused more on Morocco than on Tunisia, Agénor and Al-Aynaoui (2003) used ESs data to argue that labor regulations were especially rigid and harmful to employment and exports in the MENA region.

As shown in the time series data on the many different types of regulations of formal labor markets across the countries of the world over time put together by Adams et al. (2016), Tunisia's labor regulations have never been especially rigid compared to other countries. Nugent (2016) has drawn on firm responses to the ESs in countries in various regions of the world to a special question about what the effect on their employment would be if, hypothetically, all such regulations were eliminated. He found that they would usually respond by saying they would want to both hire more workers and fire workers, but with the numbers to be hired substantially outnumbering those to be fired. This study also showed both (1) that the percentages of hiring would be considerably larger in countries where the labor regulations had been evaluated as being more rigid and restrictive and (2) that firms rate the labor regulations to be more serious obstacles to their business in those countries where, and time periods when, the labor regulations had been rated to be more rigid.[18]

Liaqat and Nugent (2015), identified such regulations as a major differentiating factor between MENA and non-MENA firms. Lying behind the greater concern of MENA managers for labor regulations as a somewhat more serious obstacle to their businesses than in non-MENA countries was evidence from comparative indexes of the rigidity of different kinds of labor regulations across countries showing that the restrictions on hiring, firing, and working hours of workers in MENA countries were typically somewhat tighter and more restrictive than in non-MENA developing and middle income countries. But, at the same time, it was found that these labor regulations seemed to be less well enforced in MENA countries than in non-MENA countries. That combination of strict labor regulations but weak enforcement of course may well have contributed to why, as mentioned above, competition from the informal sector should have been seen as recently as 2013 as a more serious obstacle in MENA countries than elsewhere.[19]

It should be pointed out, however, that labor regulations are very multifaceted and seldom quantitative in nature and can be viewed quite differently from different perspectives. The labor regulations used in the Liaqat and Nugent studies came from attempts by the assistants of the authors to construct separate indexes of the rigidity of regulations on hiring, working hours, and firing based on access to the labor laws themselves. These indexes were subsequently extended to a compendium put together into a dataset called Labor Market Rigidities Index (LAMRIG) by Campos and Nugent (2018). Country-and time period-specific scores based on LAMRIG for the MENA and six East Asian countries are presented in column group (1) in Table 6.6 for four different periods, 1970–1974, 1980–1984, 1990–1994, and 2000–2004. Higher scores represent greater rigidity based on an aggregation of the underlying scores for rigidity in hiring, working hours and firing, in turn based on large numbers of quite different regulations. These scores suggest that Tunisia managed to reduce the rigidity of its labor regulations quite significantly, especially between 1990–1994 and 2000–2004. As recently as 1990–1994, however, the rigidity of Tunisia's labor regulations was rated as considerably tighter than those of both the vast majority of both other MENA countries and East Asian countries.

Given the subjectivity of the different measures that have been used in measuring the rigidity of labor regulations, for comparison purposes in the next three groups of columns (labeled 2, 3, and 4) we present the corresponding scores for the same set of countries constructed at three different points of time (1980, 2000, and 2013) but in this case, based on a smaller number of different regulations and aggregated into three separate Collective Bargaining Rights (CBR) sub-indexes. These are for hiring and short-term contracts (CBR1), working hours (CBR2), and dismissal of workers (CBR3), respectively. Note that there are many differences between the CBR and LAMRIG indexes, both in the trends over time and in the country rankings. Yet, one thing that is quite clear from the CBR columns is that the regulations on firing (CBR3) are much more rigid than those on hiring and working hours, and especially for MENA countries.[20] Note also that in contrast to regulations on Hiring workers (CBR1) where Tunisia had loosened its regulations between 1980 and 2000 quite significantly, in the case of regulations on Firing workers (CBR3), Tunisia tightened these regulations very significantly between these dates.

One could certainly imagine that the effects of this greater rigidity in firing workers in Tunisia could have been especially difficult for firms in relatively old, labor-intensive industries like clothing, leather, and textiles which had been encouraged by the stiff quotas that developed countries, including Europe and America, had imposed on imports from China and other Asian countries, after these quotas were removed in the mid-1990s making it increasingly difficult for Tunisian firms to retain their competitiveness in exports and thereby employ these workers. Although Tunisia was never a high wage country, Bellin (2002, 287–188) presents a rather detailed table comparing average wage costs (inclusive of fringe benefits) across countries in 1990, showing that, while Tunisia's average wage rate was only 10–20%

Table 6.6 Measures of Tightness or Flexibility of Labor Regulation, 1970–2019

Country	***Overall index of labor market rigidity LAMRIG***				***Rigidity in hiring (CBR 1)***			***Rigidity in working hours (CBR 2)***			***Rigidity in dismissal of workers (CBR3)***			***Doing business ease of hiring***	***Doing business flexibility of hours***	***Doing business ease of firing***	***Doing business overall***	
	(1)				*(2)*			*(3)*			*(4)*			*(5)*	*(6)*	*(7)*	*(8)*	
	1970–1974	*1980–1984*	*1990–1994*	*2000–2004*	*1980*	*2000*	*2013*	*1980*	*2000*	*2013*	*1980*	*2000*	*2013*	*2004*	*2004*	*2004*	*2004*	*2019*
MENA	**1.51**	**1.52**	**1.45**	**1.44**	**2.95**	**2.35**	**2.98**	**3.97**	**4.13**	**4.50**	**4.39**	**4.74**	**5.27**	**44.90**	**68.00**	**41.00**	**51.60**	**56.20**
Non-major oil exporters																		
Djibouti	1.70	1.70	1.70	1.70	n.a.	n.a.	n.a.	n.a.	n.a.	n.a.	n.a.	n.a.	n.a.	n.a.	n.a.	n.a.	n.a.	58.40
Egypt, Arab Rep.	1.70	1.75	1.75	1.59	1.75	1.75	1.75	3.94	4.50	3.70	3.83	4.57	6.40	33	83	61	59	58.50
Jordan	1.70	1.70	1.70	1.46	1.75	1.75	1.75	3.72	4.48	4.37	3.16	4.50	4.50	33	82	64	60	61.30
Lebanon	1.07	1.15	1.15	1.25	n.a.	n.a.	n.a.	n.a.	n.a.	n.a.	n.a.	n.a.	n.a.	53	50	35	46	54.40
Morocco	1.32	1.39	1.39	1.62	3.67	3.67	5.47	4.27	4.55	4.67	4.34	4.34	6.70	56	63	33	51	71.70
Syrian Arab Republic	1.35	1.34	1.34	1.31	1.75	1.75	n.a.	2.94	2.94	5.24	4.42	4.42	4.75	33	79	22	45	43.50
Tunisia	**1.72**	**1.72**	**1.61**	**1.48**	**6.00**	**4.60**	**4.60**	**4.17**	**4.17**	**4.27**	**5.41**	**7.39**	**7.33**	**73.0**	**53.0**	**44.0**	**57.0**	**67.20**
West Bank and Gaza					n.a.	n.a.	n.a.	n.a.	n.a.	n.a.	n.a.	n.a.	n.a.	n.a.	n.a.	n.a.	n.a.	59.70
Yemen			0.95	1.08	2.58	1.58	1.58	4.79	4.79	4.79	5.19	5.19	5.19	33	66	28	43	30.70
MENA major oil exporters	**0.82**	**0.97**	**1.12**	**1.15**	**4.38**	**4.50**	**4.85**	**3.60**	**4.18**	**4.18**	**4.84**	**5.88**	**6.22**	**45.5**	**68.5**	**33.0**	**49.0**	**46.40**
Algeria	1.18	1.63	1.33	43.30	5.75	6.25	6.95	3.94	4.88	4.88	7.50	6.00	5.66	58	60	19	46	48.50
Iran, Islamic Rep.	1.20	1.20	1.83	1.83	3.80	2.75	2.75	3.29	3.48	3.48	2.17	5.77	6.77	33	77	47	52	59.60
Iraq	n.a.	1.22	1.25	1.30	n.a.	n.a.	n.a.	n.a.	n.a.	n.a.	n.a.	n.a.	n.a.	n.a.	n.a.	n.a.	n.a.	44.70
Libya	0.08	0.08	0.08	0.09	n.a.	n.a.	n.a.	n.a.	n.a.	n.a.	n.a.	n.a.	n.a.	n.a.	n.a.	n.a.	n.a.	32.70

(Continued)

Table 6.6 Measures of Tightness or Flexibility of Labor Regulation, 1970–2019 *(Continued)*

Country	*Overall index of labor market rigidity LAMRIG*				*Rigidity in hiring (CBR 1)*			*Rigidity in working hours (CBR 2)*			*Rigidity in dismissal of workers (CBR3)*			*Doing business ease of hiring*	*Doing business flexibility of hours*	*Doing business ease of firing*	*Doing business overall*	
	(1)				*(2)*			*(3)*			*(4)*			*(5)*	*(6)*	*(7)*	*(8)*	
	1970–1974	*1980–1984*	*1990–1994*	*2000–2004*	*1980*	*2000*	*2013*	*1980*	*2000*	*2013*	*1980*	*2000*	*2013*	*2004*	*2004*	*2004*	*2004*	*2019*
MENA GCC	**0.39**	**0.39**	**0.43**	**0.47**	**3.09**	**3.09**	**3.97**	**3.86**	**3.86**	**4.02**	**3.26**	**3.23**	**4.08**	**39.2**	**60.5**	**32.0**	**40.8**	**70.30**
Bahrain	0.17	0.17	0.20	0.25	n.a.	n.a.	n.a.	n.a.	n.a.	n.a.	n.a.	n.a.	n.a.	n.a.	n.a.	n.a.	n.a.	70.50
Kuwait	0.17	0.17	0.17	0.28	n.a.	n.a.	n.a.	n.a.	n.a.	n.a.	n.a.	n.a.	n.a.	33	40	50	41	62.60
Oman	0.17	0.17	0.17	0.02	n.a.	n.a.	n.a.	n.a.	n.a.	n.a.	n.a.	n.a.	n.a.	58	78	25	41	68.80
Qatar	0.05	0.05	0.05	0.15	2.67	2.67	2.67	3.57	3.57	3.79	3.42	3.42	4.42	n.a.	n.a.	n.a.	n.a.	74.50
Saudi Arabia	0.86	0.86	0.86	0.86	3.67	3.67	3.37	3.87	3.87	4.13	2.58	2.58	3.78	33	58	16	36	63.80
United Arab Emirates	0.90	1.10	1.10	1.19	2.92	2.92	5.88	4.14	4.14	4.14	3.79	3.70	4.04	33	66	37	45	81.60
East Asia	**1.57**	**1.56**	**1.54**	**1.41**	**2.09**	**2.98**	**4.02**	**2.41**	**3.42**	**3.55**	**4.37**	**4.68**	**5.31**	**49.2**	**63.3**	**37.8**	**50.2**	**74.70**
China	2.50	2.30	1.90	1.42	1.00	1.00	2.70	0.83	4.56	5.07	3.66	3.65	7.33	17	67	57	47	74.00
Indonesia	1.50	1.50	1.50	1.58	3.00	4.70	6.20	5.63	5.53	5.33	5.67	5.67	5.67	76	53	43	57	68.20
Korea, Rep.	1.44	1.44	1.60	1.19	2.84	4.01	6.06	1.96	2.36	2.76	5.84	5.28	5.68	33	88	32	51	84.00
Malaysia	0.80	0.80	0.80	0.87	1.50	1.50	0.50	0.88	3.15	3.23	4.37	4.87	4.87	33	26	15	25	81.30
Philippines	1.60	1.60	1.69	1.61	1.50	2.67	4.00	1.37	1.37	1.37	4.00	5.34	4.68	58	73	50	60	60.90
Thailand	1.60	1.74	1.74	1.78	2.25	4.05	4.05	3.80	3.55	3.55	2.16	3.33	3.66	78	73	30	61	79.50

Sources: That data of Column (1) from Campos and Nugent (2018) and that in column (5) are averages computed for as many years as are available during 2003–2010 from the individual years taken from the World Bank Doing Business Database The data in Columns (2–4) are taken from Adams et al. (2016), 'CBR Labour Regulation Index: Dataset of 117 Countries,' Cambridge University: Centre for Business Research (columns labeled 2, 3 and 4).

as high as those in Europe and America, it was well above those in almost all Latin American countries and several times as high as those at that time in Egypt, and Asian countries like China, Indonesia, India, Pakistan, Sri Lanka, Thailand, and the Philippines. Given the large numbers of Tunisian firms that had been established quite successfully earlier in these industries, one can easily understand why the rigidity in firing such workers could by the mid-1990s come to impede the competitiveness of such relatively old firms in competitive, labor-intensive industries such as these.

In the last five columns of Table 6.6 are inverse measures of rigidity, namely, the Ease of Hiring, Flexibility of Hours, Ease of Firing, and Overall Flexibility coming from still another source, the World Bank's Doing Business Indicators. The entries in the first four of these columns are from the 2004 Doing Business Report. The year 2004 was the first one for which Doing Business Indicators were measured. Those in the last column are the corresponding Overall Flexibility in Employing Workers from the Doing Business Database for the year 2019. Note that in the first of these Doing Business columns for 2004, the one index in which Tunisia stands out very well is in Ease of Hiring where its score is 73. That score was by far the highest among all MENA countries and roughly on a par with Indonesia and Thailand, the East Asian countries with the highest Ease of Hiring scores in 2004. Note, however, in the next two columns (Flexibility in Hours and Ease of Firing) that Tunisia's regulations of these types were deemed to be much less flexible, explaining why its overall score for Flexibility in Employing Workers in 2004 in the next-to-last column of the table was only somewhere in the middle of the pack among both MENA and East Asian countries. Clearly it is in flexibility of Hours and to a lesser extent the firing workers where Tunisia ranks much further behind, as such regulations may serve as obstacles to some private firms. Comparing the entries for Overall Ease of Employing Workers Regulations in the last two columns of the table, it can be seen that Tunisia increased its score between 2004 and 2019, indeed by more than any other MENA countries except Morocco, and the GCC countries. Note, however, that the extent to which the overall flexibility of its labor regulations increased was much below all East Asian countries except the Philippines. Although the detailed components of this overall index are not shown in the table, even in 2019 the most rigid aspects of Tunisia's labor regulations lie in rigidity of hours and rigidity in firing workers.

The greatest success enjoyed by Tunisia in this table was its reform in Hiring that occurred prior to 2004, making for that extremely high Ease of Hiring score in 2004. Indeed, when the World Bank's first Doing Business Report came out in 2004, it pointed to the Hiring and Firing of Workers as one of the most important obstacles to business and pointed to the success of Tunisia (among others). As the World Bank (2004b, 29–39) stated in documenting its own evaluation of constraints on firms arising from regulations in the Doing Business Surveys, the cause of the decline in this constraint on business of private firms was an important reform in 1996 in which it introduced fixed term contracts. These contracts made it easier to hire workers than under regular contracts (so-called permanent or long-term contracts). Such contracts are widely credited around the world as a means of helping new entrants, especially females and students, to enter the labor force and to get jobs, including part-time ones (World Bank 2004b, 29–39). The special relevance of such a reform was identified by Rama (1998) who pointed out that, just before the effect of the reform had kicked in, Tunisia's unemployment rate of 15.4 (Table 2.10) (and one of the highest in the world), would have been much more moderate had it not been for the large number of unemployed first-time job seekers (Rama 1998, 67). Rama went on to show that the matching of job opportunities with job seekers worked well for skilled and experienced workers but most definitely not for new entrants.

Since the labor market reforms of 1996, businesses in the country made use of these new more flexible labor contracts. The results of this reform are clearly observable in the relevant tables of the present study. For example, note that by the year 2000, the overall unemployment rate had fallen by a full 2% to 13.4% even though the overall rate of economic growth per capita over the decade of the 1990s was less than 3% per annum (Table 1.6). Even more notably, from column (3) of Table 1.2, it can be seen that Tunisia's Poverty rate fell from 20.5% in 1995–1996 to 12.8% in 2000 and further to 7.79% in 2005. While we certainly do not wish to attribute all of these reductions in unemployment and poverty to the loosening of regulatory constraints on short-term labor contracts, it would seem likely that the reform helped a great deal in these respects. More importantly, however, from the present section it should be clear that in terms of both flexibility of hours and Ease of Firing, there is considerable room for improvement in labor regulations which could contribute to the overall economic efficiency, and competitiveness of Tunisia's private sector with firms from East Asian and other countries. Also, of increasing concern, is the increasingly poor enforcement of labor regulations, accounting for why the vast majority of private sector firms seem to be remaining informal.

Although not included in Table 6.6 or in any of the other tables in this study, another indicator of labor market problems is the number of strikes and especially those not considered to be legal. Bellin (2002, 189–190) showed a time series of the number of strikes by year from 1970 to 1994 which can be updated by similar data from the International Labor Organization through 2007. This series showed a relatively sharp increase in the annual number of strikes in Tunisia beginning in 1981 which, since that time until 2005 at least, remained at about 500 per year. Notably, the vast majority of these strikes were illegal. Bellin argued (especially, 137–157) that this pressure of strikes by workers helped sustain the government's unwillingness to go along with the advice of the World Bank to liberalize the labor regulations, especially those on firing in the late 1990s.

The pension system in Tunisia' and how it differs between the private and public sectors would also seem to contribute to the underdevelopment of a competitive and efficient private sector. The private sector is subject to much greater uncertainties and risks than the public sector or the government itself. For this reason, even when incentives were offered to entrepreneurs to set up private firms, entering the private sector has remained riskier not only because of the aforementioned policy uncertainty, but also because of Tunisia's pension system. Ben Braham and Marouani (2016) provided a very useful description of Tunisia's 'pay as you go' pension systems, showing that they differ significantly between the public and private sectors. From this information provided in that study, one can certainly understand why any self-employed individual or employee would prefer to be in the public sector instead of the private sector since in the public sector every individual is mandated to qualify for both health and pension benefits and to be enrolled in both systems automatically but in the private sector this is by no means assured and the benefits vary across different types of workers. For this reason, too, with 100% compliance the public sector pension system (Caisse Nationale de Retraite et de Prévoyance Sociale) is bound to be sustainable, whereas, with generally far lower regular compliance in the private sector pension system (Caisse Nationale de Sécurité Sociable), it is essentially non-sustainable.

Ben Braham and Marouani (2016) calculated (among other things) the pension level that would be received at the end of a standard working career. For the self-employed, 80% of retirees would receive a pension payment that was below the minimum wage. Even for a wage worker, 60% of the retirees would receive a pension below the minimum wage and well below what could be obtained in the public sector. Moreover, unlike the public sector, the pension would not be automatically linked to the health insurance benefits. Both the benefits and sustainability of the system for private sector workers and self-employed are undermined by low 'contribution density' attributable to the relatively high frequency of periods (quarters of a year) during a career in which the private sector worker would not be likely to be registered. The authors attributed this partly to low wages and the reluctance of workers to agree to pay into their pension account in difficult periods but also due to insufficient information provided to the workers and weak enforcement. One should also bear in mind that increasing percentages of Tunisian private sector workers are being employed in the informal sector where the worker has access to neither health nor pension benefits.

6. A Gender Perspective on the Obstacles to Growth of Firms

Part C of Table 6.4 is devoted to the perspective of private firm managers on one of the long-time comparative advantages of Tunisia relative to other MENA firms noted in preceding chapters of this study, namely, its relatively high gender equality in the form of labor force participation and education. From column (1) we see (from country-level data, i.e., not from data based on the ESs) that the overall female labor force participation rate in Tunisia was second highest among the MENA countries listed in this part of the table in this respect (with only Djibouti above it). Yet, although not shown in the table, this was below most of the East Asian countries (as was shown in Table 2.11). From the second column in Part C of the table, and the ES respondents themselves, it can be seen that Tunisia's advantage over other countries is considerably greater as far as female participation in the formal private sector is concerned. While in most cases, females would most likely want to be employed in the public sector where worker protection, wage rates and working conditions are most favorable, since these jobs became limited, employment opportunities became only possible in the private sector, either formal or informal. This explains why the percentage of females in the formal private sector was as large as it is indicated to be in this table.

Similarly, in the third and fourth columns of the table, it can be seen that female labor force participation rates for Tunisia are also relatively high in both the Labor Intensive Manufacturing and Other Manufacturing Sectors, both of which are dominated by formal firms. The sixth column in Part C of the table shows that, although certainly not high in absolute terms, Tunisia is also well above the average of MENA ES sample countries in the percentage of females serving as the top manager. Indeed, as in the first column, Tunisia is second highest in this respect only to tiny Djibouti. Note, however, possibly reflecting fairness or lack of gender discrimination on the part of female managers, that Tunisia is not above average in terms of the share of employment by females within firms managed by females.

7. Firm Characteristics and Obstacles to Business

To further trace the seriousness of the most important obstacles to business back to underlying firm characteristics, Table 6.7 shows the results of some simple regressions for each of four of the most commonly cited obstacles to business discussed above, namely, (1) political instability, (2) competition from the informal sector, (3) inadequate skills and education of the work force, (4) corruption, as well as in (5) the lack of access to finance. The explanatory variables of interest are listed in the first column of the table. Then, in the remaining columns of the table are the parameter estimates obtained from estimating an ordered logit equation.[21]

In the following paragraphs, we direct the reader's attention to the firm and other characteristics that seem to be significantly related to each obstacle in the Tunisian context based on the empirical results in Table 6.7. First, with respect to firm age and its square, after controlling for all the other factors included in the table, these seem to be significantly related only to Competition from the Informal Sector, indicating that it is middle aged firms which are most adversely affected by this obstacle.

Second, with respect to the sector of the firm, firms in food, garments, and other manufacturing sectors are less severely affected by the Corruption and Political Instability obstacles. Although firms in construction are less

Table 6.7 Tunisia: Ordered Probit Estimates of Determinants of the Degree of Severity of Key Obstacles to Business

Firm characteristic	*Access to finance* (1)	*Corruption* (2)	*Inadequately educated workforce* (3)	*Political instability* (4)	*Competition from informal sector* (5)
Firm Age	–0.011	0.012	–0.009	0.026	**0.052****
	(0.021)	(0.016)	(0.019)	(0.019)	(0.024)
Age²	0.000	0.000	0.000	0.000	**–0.001***
	(0.000)	(0.000)	(0.000)	(0.000)	(0.000)
Sectors					
Food	**–0.910****	**–0.840****	–0.312	**–0.941****	–0.024
	(0.450)	(0.408)	(0.473)	(0.414)	(0.521)
Garments	0.162	**–1.079*****	–0.531	**–0.724***	0.223
	(0.411)	(0.383)	(0.420)	(0.398)	(0.467)
Fab. Metal Products	–0.115	–0.101	–0.087	–0.903	–0.153
	(1.019)	(0.478)	(0.530)	(0.668)	(0.969)
Other Manufacturing	0.320	**–0.950****	–0.566	**–0.669***	0.388
	(0.401)	(0.372)	(0.408)	(0.367)	(0.456)
Construction	**24.863*****	–0.743	**–1.244****	**13.057*****	0.000
	(1.195)	(0.611)	(0.587)	(1.220)	(.)
Hotels and Restaurants	**–9.804*****	–0.569	0.6	–1.097	**–12.512*****
	(1.504)	(0.810)	(0.835)	(0.835)	(1.594)
Transport	**–12.671*****	0.673	–0.643	0.305	**–12.224*****
	(1.125)	(0.417)	(0.443)	(0.407)	(1.148)
Regions					
Tunis	–0.123	**–0.760***	0.073	–0.219	–0.823
	(0.398)	(0.394)	(0.424)	(0.332)	(0.517)
Sfax	–0.065	–0.358	**–0.768****	–0.326	0.309
	(0.369)	(0.321)	(0.334)	(0.335)	(0.340)
Northeast	**0.745****	–0.243	–0.103	0.261	–0.091
	(0.318)	(0.297)	(0.351)	(0.321)	(0.349)
Interior	**1.288***	0.825	0.806	0.867	–0.222
	(0.715)	(0.534)	(0.496)	(0.561)	(0.619)
Legal Status					
Shareholding Co. with non-traded shares	**2.427****	0.34	–0.067	0.24	0.127
	(0.952)	(0.509)	(0.678)	(0.615)	(0.851)
Sole Proprietor	**3.744*****	0.69	0.002	0.884	1.428
	(1.044)	(0.692)	(0.847)	(0.788)	(0.979)
Partnership	**3.050*****	0.869	–0.216	0.553	1.297
	(0.976)	(0.585)	(0.715)	(0.697)	(0.860)
Limited partnership	2.420	0.573	–0.300	–0.488	**20.587*****
	(1.493)	(0.609)	(0.775)	(0.726)	(1.170)

(Continued)

Table 6.7 Tunisia: Ordered Probit Estimates of Determinants of the Degree of Severity of Key Obstacles to Business *(Continued)*

Firm characteristic	*Access to finance* (1)	*Corruption* (2)	*Inadequately educated workforce* (3)	*Political instability* (4)	*Competition from informal sector* (5)
Manager Experience (years)					
1–9 Years	0.000	0.000	0.000	0.000	0.000
	(.)	(.)	(.)	(.)	(.)
10–19	−0.768	−0.485	−0.673	−0.101	−0.285
	(0.492)	(0.478)	(0.497)	(0.512)	(0.714)
20–25	**−1.116****	**−1.104****	−0.368	−0.312	−1.109
	(0.454)	(0.481)	(0.519)	(0.484)	(0.704)
26–39	−0.753	−0.581	−0.28	−0.135	−0.199
	(0.495)	(0.482)	(0.533)	(0.472)	(0.710)
40+	−0.449	**−1.269****	−0.665	−0.557	−0.353
	(0.553)	(0.581)	(0.562)	(0.549)	(0.750)
Other					
% large owner	−0.009	−0.005	**−0.011***	**−0.009***	**−0.011****
	(0.006)	(0.005)	(0.006)	(0.005)	(0.005)
% foreign owned	−0.007	0.000	0.007	−0.003	**−0.022*****
	(0.005)	(0.005)	(0.004)	(0.005)	(0.007)
% Imported Materials	−0.006*	0.003	0.004	0.001	−0.001
	(0.003)	(0.004)	(0.003)	(0.003)	(0.003)
Export	0.090	0.380	−0.007	0.447	0.005
	(0.289)	(0.285)	(0.305)	(0.293)	(0.299)
Innovation	−0.030	**−0.748*****	−0.459	−0.271	0.196
	(0.277)	(0.262)	(0.281)	(0.246)	(0.273)
Quality certificate	−0.275	**−0.552***	−0.197	**−0.537****	−0.392
	(0.310)	(0.282)	(0.298)	(0.263)	(0.308)
Subsidy program	0.363	−0.417	**−0.933*****	0.145	−0.125
	(0.319)	(0.328)	(0.328)	(0.310)	(0.370)
N	292	292	286	291	280
pseudo *R*2	0.083	0.061	0.063	0.033	0.12

Notes:

Standard errors in parentheses. Based on the Sample of Tunisian Firms in the 2013 Enterprise Survey. The dependent variable in each column of the table is the severity of the obstacle to business identified in the column heading (each measured on a 1-5 scale).

* $p < 0.1$, ** $p < 0.05$, *** $p < 0.01$.

likely to be adversely affected by Inadequately Educated Workforces, they are much more likely to face greater obstacles in Access to Finance and Political Instability. Firms in the hotels and restaurant and transport sectors are also less likely than firms in other sectors to be adversely affected by Access to Finance and Competition from the Informal Sector.

Third, the firm's location also seems to be significantly related to the severity of some of these alternative obstacles. In particular, firms located in either the Northeast or Interior seem to rate Access to Finance as a more severe obstacle than do those in other regions. Also, those located in the Interior seem to rate the Inadequately Educated Workforce obstacle as more severe (although in this case that difference is not quite statistically significant). On the other hand, location in Tunis or Sfax seems to have the effect of lowering the severity of some of these obstacles.

Fourth and not surprisingly, compared to the excluded firm ownership type (a shareholding company with shares that are traded in the stock exchange), all four of the other ownership forms (ranging down to sole proprietorships and partnerships) are considerably more likely to experience more severe Access to Finance problems. It is limited partnership firms that are more likely to face greater severity of Competition from the Informal Sector. Note that firms whose managers have had 20–25 years of experience are much likely to face less severe obstacles in either Access to Finance or Corruption. In the latter case, the severity of this obstacle is even less severe for firms with managers with even more experience (40+ years).

Fifth, moving still further down Table 6.7, one can see that firms with larger percentages owned by large or foreign owners report facing less severe obstacles in the form of Inadequately Educated Labor Forces, Competition from the Informal Sector and Political Instability. Finally, there seem to be a number of respects in which firms which have managed to make significant improvements, such as in having undertaken innovations in the last three years, having received a quality certificate or having participated in a specific subsidy program (mostly through the aforementioned programs to improve technology), have been rewarded with less severe obstacles in the forms of Corruption and Inadequately Educated or Trained Workforces, and in one case also in Political Instability.

Sixth, and among the most notable empirical results, are those about the impact of experience, showing that the Corruption and Lack of Access to Finance obstacles seem to be less of a problem to managers with two specific years of experience levels, 20–25 and 40+.

Overall, the results in Table 6.7 add considerable value by showing the advantages of (1) location in either Tunis or Sfax, or the breadth of ownership in reducing the severity of the Access to Finance obstacle, (2) having large percentages of the firm's assets owned by large or foreign owners in reducing the severity of the Competition from the Informal Sector obstacle, and especially (3) having made technical innovations, or obtained a quality certificate or participated in a special subsidy program in reducing the severity of the Corruption, Inadequately Educated Workforce and Political Instability obstacles.

Some bottom lines coming out of this analysis from the ES for Tunisia are (1) the widespread importance of the informal sector, and hence the relatively high commonality of concerns about Competition from the Informal Sector by formal sector private firms, (2) the large percentage of sample firms (50%), which identify Political Instability as the most important obstacle to their business, and (3) that even firms with very experienced managers are likely to be seriously affected by several important obstacles.

E. How the Heavy Hand of the State and a Weak Private Sector Hindered Tunisia's Development?

In the introduction to this chapter, it was suggested that the *fundamental weaknesses* in the Tunisian development experience compared to the most successful East Asian countries were the persistently strong heavy hand of the state and the weak development of the private sector. In this section, we complete the argument and show how these fundamental weaknesses have hindered the development process in the country, and engendered the major differences in policies and performance discussed in Chapter 5.

First, one major reason for the ***low aggregate rates of savings and investment*** in Tunisia compared to East Asia, as suggested in Chapter 5, was the low corporate rate of savings and the low rate of private investment. This is obviously a direct outcome of the weak private sector and the continued excessive predominance of SMEs, which are unable to generate large savings. As noted in the previous section, political uncertainty, which in turn makes for uncertain future government policies has no doubt added greatly to the explanation for low investment rates among private firms especially after 2010.

In addition to the various constraints discussed above, there would appear to be several other contributors to Tunisia's relative failure to develop the private sector in a such a way as to increase efficiency and competitiveness. Although among the successful East Asian countries were some rather authoritarian ones, one possible contributor to that failure could be Tunisia's authoritarian character. Based on experience from around the world, Acemoglu and Robinson (2012) showed that authoritarian regimes often feel the need for relatively closed economic systems with large public sectors for generating the rents and resources required for sustaining their elites and their clients. This requires continuation of a heavy hand of the state and interventions to generate rents. The pervasive cronyism that characterized Tunisia during the last decade before the 2010/2011 uprisings is a virtually perfect example of this. It resulted in the rather complete lack of credibility for an open economy in which the private sector could play an important role. As a result, policies capable of stimulating not only private sector development, but also higher savings and investment rates were sorely lacking. In fact, as reflected in their high rates of informality, private sector firms in Tunisia have tended to avoid growth, and visibility so as not to become targets of predation.

The widespread corruption during the 2000s alienated much of the government's sources of support. leading to government overthrow and the subsequent political instability. That political instability has of course also further enhanced uncertainty about the policies to be adopted in the near future which has further discouraged investment and growth by firms in almost all sectors, but especially in those more sophisticated manufacturing sectors in which entry into global markets would seem most essential. As a result, savings and investment declined post 2000, and in the case of savings have even declined further since 2011 with the increased political uncertainty, and social turmoil and sharp decline in economic growth.

A second channel is through Tunisia's ***low productivity growth*** as the continued heavy hand of the state has contributed to the weakness and informality of the private sector which in turn led to the country's limited structural transformation and innovation, its continued importance of less efficient SOEs, and the continued pervasiveness of distortions in the economy. All these factors implied low TFP growth for Tunisia which was clearly demonstrated in Tables 2.6a and 2.6b.

Third, the ***limited structural transformation and weak innovation*** could be related to the nature of the industrial policies pursued and also the lack of support for Entrepreneurship in Tunisia as compared to East Asia. There is clear evidence that industrial policies in Tunisia failed to match the success those of East Asia. For example, Table 2.1 has shown that, while the manufacturing share of GDP increased over time in Tunisia from 8.1% in 1965 to 16.5% in 2010 it fell to 14.8% in 2019, and has remained about 10% lower than those of East Asia which have been increasing at almost the same rate. In the latter countries, industrial policies have been instrumental in supporting the private sector and achieving structural transformation, by using incentive systems based on performance and success in reaching the objectives.[22] Yet, nothing like this has occurred in Tunisia where in general its industrial and sectoral policies continued to be based on inputs and the ex-ante award of financial and non-financial benefits, and only rarely have positive performance incentives been used. As a result, in all too many cases, all that these policies have encouraged are further rent-seeking and the failure to innovate. Indeed, if anything, these policies have provided strong incentives primarily for maintaining the status-quo, for opposing reforms and for failing to adapt the system to changing conditions.

As explained in Chapters 3–5, over the period under study (1960–2020), Tunisia adopted numerous policies to encourage both exports and FDI. As a comparatively small country, Tunisia's share of exports and imports in GDP, a measure of trade openness, or simply non-oil merchandise exports in GDP, would be expected to be relatively high. Indeed, as shown in Table 4.8, Tunisia's shares in these respects are relatively high compared to a large East Asian country like China. Moreover, since the 1960s, Tunisia has managed to steadily increase its share of (non-oil) merchandise exports in GDP. Yet, in each period, these shares have been well below the East Asian averages and in growth terms Tunisia's non-oil merchandise exports have grown far slower than those of most East Asian countries but especially China, Korea, and Thailand. Tunisia failed to get out in a timely manner from the low-technology trap which resulted from the initially successful 'off-shoring' system introduced in the 1970s. Industrial policies, despite numerous attempts, remained fragmented and driven by immediate and incumbent interests. There was neither a private sector strong enough to lead the industrial transformation, nor a well-designed government policy capable of meeting the challenges of a fast-moving globalization and technological change. As suggested by Avina and Russell (2016), Information Technology training was a critical need for Tunisia and other MENA countries to be able to solve their youth unemployment problems and at the same time to stimulate technological change and growth.

As shown in Table 4.9, Tunisia had in general done even better than East Asia in attracting FDI in the early decades under review (1960–1990), yet unfortunately during the 1990s and especially since 2010 that advantage of Tunisia has turned into a deficit with respect to East Asia. From the comparative data on TFP growth from Tables 2.6a and 2.6b, moreover, there is little evidence that either its Exports growth or FDI growth had translated into higher TFP growth compared to the East Asian countries.

Another sign of Tunisia's lack of success in adapting its industrial policies is the tourism sector. Tunisia achieved at least partial success in overcoming its insufficient degree of outwardness by expanding this sector, as can be seen in the International Tourism Receipts (as % of GDP) in Table 2.3. In every period from the 1990s to present, Tunisia has done better in this respect than East Asia. But it has failed to upgrade and adapt to changing global conditions, as illustrated by the declining competitiveness and performance indicators shown in the discussion about Tables 2.3 and 2.4 in Chapter 2 and Section C.2 in the present Chapter.

Still other telling signs of lack of commitment to clear and transformative policies and private sector development have been rather obvious for a long time, especially arising from changes in policies over time and the rather imperfect reconciliation of the old and new policies which continue to exist to this day. As discussed above, a typical example of this is the 'off-shore' exports system, which was supposed to be temporary when created in the early 1970s, but which continued to co-exist for decades with old protection policies of the 1960s. The same problems in policy reconciliation between new and old policies have tended to arise since then. Meanwhile, and to make matters worse, throughout all periods, a large and inefficient public sector has continued to coexist with a sometimes expanding private sector, even in directly competitive activities.

A fourth and even more salient contributor to the weak development of the private sector is the ***weak development of the financial sector*** and how this was a direct result of the heavy hand of the state. The banking system continued to be dominated by state banks which have constituted a major share of assets available for credit provision. Together with the overall interventionism of the state, the domination of state banks has contributed to the stifling of competition in the banking sector, despite the liberalization efforts that have been taken in this sector since the 1980s, as well as to the lack of innovation in, and to weak growth and transformation of, the financial sector.

As shown in Table 5.3, in the 1960s and 1970s the shares of bank credit to the private sector in GDP were actually higher in Tunisia than in East Asia. The share of credit to the private sector as a percentage of GDP rose in Tunisia by an impressive 17 percentage points between the 1960s and 1980s. Yet, during the next three decades, the growth in that share slowed considerably, rising only an additional 14 percentage points as of 2019, despite the fact that the same share increased in the East Asian sample as a whole by 47 percentage points, and much more rapidly than that in China (a communist country), Korea, Malaysia, and Thailand. Table 5.4 shows that Tunisia has lagged even further behind East Asia in financing private sector development through stock markets. Since old firms can finance growth out of their profits, what these figures are showing is that new firms, typically SMEs which could grow rapidly over time and thus which could represent the more dynamic, new technologies and new ideas about suitable activities to invest in would be getting far less opportunity to make such investments and generate competition for existing firms in Tunisia than in East Asia. This problem has become much worse over time. This is demonstrated by the fact that, according to the randomized but representative sample of private firms included in the 2013 ES of the World Bank, and as shown in Table 6.4, no less than 50% of all firms in the sample were rating Political Instability to be the most serious obstacle to their business. With so much Political Instability, firms are quite naturally very unsure as to whether the rules and incentives in place at that point in time would still be in place in the next couple of years by the time their investment might come to fruition. It is this policy uncertainty pertaining to the economy which so seriously undermines new investments by the private sector and hence also the competitiveness of the economy in the years ahead.

As indicated in Chapter 5, there have long been pervasive state interventions in the development of the financial sectors in both Tunisia and East Asia. Indeed, with market failures widely recognized as being more prevalent in financial markets than in other markets due to the especially great asymmetries of information in access to credit, government intervention has been pervasive.[23] These asymmetries depend very heavily on firm size, and sector type, those being much greater in small firms about which little is known, and in sectors subject to greater policy uncertainty, such as those in which exporting or government procurement is important and the relevant policies subject to sudden change, and in countries (or regions thereof) where credit rating agencies or other mechanisms are lacking. Since SMEs are very prominent in Tunisia, and policy uncertainty, and the rigidities in labor regulations relatively strong and viewed as important obstacles to business by firm managers, all these problems are relevant and important. The relative success of governments in such interventions has to a large extent shaped their success in guiding diversification and innovation. All of the vertical or horizontal industrial policies tend to depend heavily on access to finance in the appropriate volume, form and quality and at the appropriate time and cost.

In general, on both bank credit and finance from the stock market, Tunisia's shortfall relative to other MENA countries and especially East Asian countries, has become larger since the 1980s and especially since the mid-1990s. It should be rather obvious that the political economy changes over this period must have contributed a great deal to this shortfall. The disaffection of the main labor organization from the government and the failure of the government to prevent rather severe political and economic crises from arising has made for very serious increases in policy uncertainties, discouraging further investments in specific sectors and their technological upgrading at a time when the East Asian countries were becoming increasingly involved in global value chains (GVC) and becoming technological leaders in high and medium technology industries. Without making this transition to increasing competitiveness in increasingly advanced technology industries by entering dynamic competitive GVCs, Tunisian firms have remained much more dependent on the state to deliver benefits to them directly in a more protectionist framework rather than being encouraged to become more competitive on their own and thereby to thrust themselves more deeply into international competition and innovation. With the withering stability of the state and lack of investment for expansion and upgrading, Tunisian firms quite naturally have remained dependent on preferential government support. This continuing dependence of private firms on favorable regulations or possibly finance from public sector banks and development banks of course has raised the benefits to firms and government of discriminatory regulatory policies, such as those to be exposed in Chapter 7 (to follow) that were conferred on firms owned by members of the Ben Ali family. But it has increasingly closed the doors to other firms over the period from 1990 on. The dramatic rise of corruption on the part of the state both impeded access of other Tunisian firms to finance, and thereby to increasing their output, upgrading their technology, and expanding their exports. Notably, while the very time this was happening in Tunisia was when the East Asian countries were already well on their way to accomplishing all these outcomes and thereby earning the 'East Asian Miracle' honor.

It should also be realized that the various market distortions are by no means likely to offset each other. For example, making use of data on firms based on the ESs for Morocco which are very similar to those reported above for Tunisia, Chauffour and Diaz-Sanchez (2021) have shown how insufficient access of SMEs to credit, biases in access to finance of political connected firms, and barriers to imports of intermediate goods all combine to explain why market distortions are especially high among SMEs, among those in non-exporting and ones where competition from state enterprises tends to play a substantial role.

Fifth, another a major contributor to Tunisia's weak private sector and overall development over the last two decades has been the ***weak labor market dynamics and skills mismatches.*** This has been reflected in its stubbornly high unemployment rates, especially for youth, women and those with tertiary education degrees. These were again the result of the weak growth and limited structural transformation, which in turn were the direct result of the heavy hand of the state and the lack of dynamism of the private sector. Government policies for education and training have failed to adequately match the needs of the evolving labor market, and at the same time Tunisia's economic policies and their achievements have failed to match the increasing educational levels of the youth, and fallen far short of what East Asian countries have achieved in these respects.

Sixth, the ***insufficient use of global markets*** is the result of the hesitant trade policies, with complex incentives trying to cater both to exports and import-competing activities, and of inadequate industrial policies. The government has been unable, despite some occasional successes, to provide sufficiently strong and effective incentives for export diversification, for improved logistics, and the provision of other services for trade.

Notes

1 For a useful debate on, and comparative evaluation of, these alternatives, see Onis (1991).
2 This agency was later separated into two entities: the 'Office National du Tourisme de Tunisie' (1956) and the 'Office National du Thermalisme de Tunisie.'
3 The two institutions merged in 1989 to become the Banque Nationale Agricole.
4 The problems with respect to rules of origin in the inter-Arab trade agreements contrast sharply with the Association Agreement that Tunisia has with the EU where the rules of origin were harmonized.
5 A nice illustration of the relevance of quality, rather than technical efficiency, as a source of competitiveness is provided by the interesting randomized control experiment reported on in the carpets industry in Egypt by Atkin et al. (2014) which showed experience in exporting actually lowered standard productivity measures like TFP but this was more than offset by the remarkable improvements in various dimensions of product quality which raised firm profits through the higher prices commanded by the higher quality of the goods.
6 Notably, the recovery in tourism since 2010 was artificial, because of the collapse in nights stayed of the average tourist of tourist nights and occupancy rates.
7 However, to some extent, the rise in unemployment among the well-educated may be expected to fall in the future given the fact that the demographic bulge of educated youths entering the labor force in ever larger numbers is perhaps now being reversed, Abdessalem (2011).

8 See World Bank (2004a, 212–218) for a discussion of this disconnect.

9 Cammett (2007) provides a fascinating demonstration of this point by comparing Tunisia with its neighbor Morocco in the same two industries, textiles, and clothing. In both countries, the two industries are very similar, with textiles more capital intensive and domestic market-oriented and clothing export-oriented and labor-intensive. She contrasts the ways in which firms from the two different sectors deal with each other and with the state and their preferences for policy changes in the two countries. In both cases, the interest of textile producers would be for protection and clothing producers for free imports of imported textile materials. Similarly, textile producers would not be interested in the efficiency of customs procedures, whereas clothing producers would be vitally interested in this given the importance of both imports and exports to their business. Because of the firms' heavy dependence on the state for credit, protection, tax exemptions, and the like, and past experience with harassment and blackmail in the form of selective tax audits of firms which criticize government policy, Tunisian firms in both sectors were generally very passive and not engaged in collective action. They were members of the aforementioned producers' association (UTICA) but the relevant chamber of this organization was dominated by the textile firms. As a result, the clothing producers felt powerless to have any influence over policy and, since they, too, were substantially benefited by tax exemptions and subsidized credit, they also did not have much incentive to seek that influence. While Moroccan firms had been similar until the emergence of new exporters in clothing, once they did emerge, they found themselves greatly disadvantaged by the dominance of the textile people who were well-entrenched and very close to the policy makers. Thanks to a much more independent and open business association that included businessmen from both sectors, the clothing entrepreneurs in Morocco were also much freer to complain about the existing discriminatory treatment and the need for improvements if they were to be able to succeed in international markets (again with subcontracting arrangements, etc.). While at first the two sectors found themselves on opposite sides, moderates among them soon saw that it would be in the interest of both groups to identify common ground where they could each benefit and speak to the government authorities with one voice. She went on to detail ways in which the resulting actions taken seemed to be putting Moroccan producers in a better position, given the rapidly changing conditions of the industry and international markets. No such actions occurred in Tunisia.

10 It should be noted that the data for Tunisia obtained from the World Bank WDI seem inaccurate for the years 1997–2010. For this reason, in Table 6.1, they are replaced by figures obtained from the Tunisia National Accounts for the years 2001–2017. Unfortunately, the data for 1998–2000 are missing.

11 Such numbers might well have been lower until recent years in China, but such data are unavailable.

12 European Bank for Reconstruction and Development, European Investment Bank and World Bank (2016).

13 See Schneider, (2007), Schneider et al. (2010), and Medina and Schneider (2018).

14 Notably also, data from the Tunisian Labor Market Panel Survey of 2014 showed that the income levels of workers in single worker firms were substantially higher on average than those in firms with 2–19 workers.

15 Delays of these two sorts could be a couple of factors contributing to the exceptionally high percentage of Senior Management Time needed to Spend on Government Regulations shown in the first column as well as to the high percentage of Tunisian firms choosing to be informal.

16 This is consistent with the theoretical conditions identified by Acemoglu and Pischke (1998) for when private training may be successful.

17 MENA governments have tried to fill the gap with training provided by the public sector or in academic institutions financed by the government. Yet, the benefits relative to costs of these programs have been shown to be minimal and rarely if ever oriented to dealing with the specific needs of individual private firms. See, for example, World Bank (2004a) and Abrahart et al. (2002).

18 For further discussion of this outside the MENA region, see Campos and Nugent (2018).

19 In an interesting study of Brazil, Almeida and Carneiro 2009 showed variations across different regions of Brazil supporting the relevance of regulations and their enforcement to on the job training.

20 The fact that Tunisia's CBR3 measure of rigidity in firing was especially high relative to GCC countries is attributable to the fact that the workers in GCC countries are largely foreign workers brought in from low wage countries in Asia.

21 The following ordered logit equation is used based on the firm-specific data on the entire sample in the 2013 Enterprise Survey for Tunisia:

$$Y_i = \alpha + \beta_1 X_1 + \ldots \beta_k X_k + \quad \varepsilon_i$$

where Y_i is the Severity of Obstacle i, measured on a 1-5 scale from least severe to most severe, X_1 through X_k are the k different firm circumstances deemed relevant, including age of the firm, experience of its top manager, Sector, Ownership characteristics, Region in Tunisia (Tunis, Sfax, Northeast, South Coast and Interior), and a few other firm characteristics (the percent of imported raw materials, exports, innovation, quality certificate, and subsidy).

22 For example, Korea became known for the generous way in which it opened up the supply of credit to industrial exporters but only after they had proven their efficiency and other capabilities by having exported in sufficient quantities (Kim and Nugent 1999) and Nugent and Nabli (1992).

23 These asymmetries in information and the complications they have posed for attempts to create effective means of supplying credit to SMEs have been carefully explained based on experience in such markets from all around the world in Armendariz de Aghion and Morduch (2005).

7 Uprisings, Democracy, and Transition

In the previous chapters, our analysis and assessment of the Tunisian experience and how it compared with both other MENA countries and the successful East Asian countries has focused mostly on the period from independence until 2010. Despite many political and policy changes, Tunisia remained relatively stable politically. The uprisings, which started on December 17, 2010 and led to the collapse of the political regime on January 14, 2011, was a major surprise and shock to almost all observers, and indeed went on to impact the whole region through contagion effects. These uprisings were widely perceived to have the potential both for becoming a 'revolution,' and leading to a long political transition process toward democracy. Even if not resulting in this definition of 'revolution,' it has been seen as a vehicle for changing policies and institutions in ways that could help bring about policies designed to more fully achieve long-term development.

The first part of this chapter reviews the major reasons and explanations for the collapse of the long-existing authoritarian regime. The second part assesses the impact of the political transition on Tunisia's economic performance and its development. This assessment leads to new questions about the explanations behind Tunisia's relative success or failure compared to other countries. In the third part of the chapter, we discuss the prospects of improved democracy scores leading to improved economic performance and greater well-being.

A. Uprisings and the Collapse of an Authoritarian Regime in 2010/2011[1]

The political, economic, and social modernization in Tunisia since its independence, as in most of MENA countries, had created the basis for a social contract whereby the authoritarian regimes committed themselves to provide their citizens with economic and social rights, in return for allowing these regimes to run their governments without having to grant the citizens with much in the way of political rights. This has come to be known in the literature as the 'authoritarian bargain'[2]. It is primarily applied to natural resource exporting countries such as the GCC countries and other major

DOI: 10.4324/9781003309550-7

oil exporting MENA countries like Algeria, Iran, Iraq, or Libya. While this characteristic is much less applicable to Tunisia, it should not be forgotten that in the 1970s Tunisia was at least a fairly significant producer of oil, and a significant exporter and processor of other natural resources like phosphates, which have been run by state enterprises, and that, even in recent years, its government has been trying to attract more foreign oil companies to explore for and subsequently produce more oil (Reuters 2021). While the credit for the applicability of the authoritarian bargain to Tunisia's own natural resources should not exaggerated, it should also be recognized that it is bordered by Algeria and Libya, which still are major oil exporters, and is also geographically and politically related (as members of the Arab League) to many other extremely large natural resource exporters (such as the GCC countries and Iraq), most of which have had (or still have) kings, generals or other autocrats, implying that Tunisia's autocratic character could also be attributed to the indirect influence from these neighboring countries in the Arab region. As noted below moreover, some analysts of the determinants of democracy (or of the lack thereof) in individual countries have attributed much influence to the extent of democracy among neighboring countries (Acemoglu et al. 2019; Madsen et al. 2015; Persson and Tabellini 2009).

As shown in previous chapters, significant economic and social gains and improvements in economic, social and human development outcomes were achieved in Tunisia during the 1960s and 1970s, reflecting a situation wherein those social and human development gains of the population could be seen as the benefits that its fairly autocratic government gave to its citizens in return for their partial compliance in accepting somewhat limited political rights.

This old social contract, however, started to come under strong pressure in the early 1980s, as its cost became increasingly difficult to finance. The government became unable to continue to deliver on the promises of subsidized consumption goods, free access to education and other social services, as well as access to highly cherished public sector jobs.

The 1980s, moreover, were turbulent times in Tunisia. There was a major social conflict, in January 1984 (in the wake of a previous one in January 1978), in which there was a violent confrontation between the country's major labor union (UGTT) and the government. This was followed by a major macroeconomic and financial crisis in 1985–1986, and a change in political regime in November 1987, with the peaceful removal of President Bourguiba from power and the takeover of his position as President by his Prime Minister at the time, Zine El Abidine Ben Ali.

The ability to maintain the authoritarian bargain in Tunisia was made more difficult by two other factors, (1) the decline in oil prices from the mid-1980s until after 2000 and (2) the effects of the demographic transition that led to the 'youth bulge' discussed in Section D of Chapter 2. With respect to factor (1), much of that influence was indirect, derived from the fact that the large oil countries of the GCC no longer had the kinds of funds available to invest in Tunisia and thereby generate more economic activity. With respect to factor (2), as shown in the youth share of the population data of Table 2.8, that share had been increasing rapidly through the year 2000, and along with it came an acceleration of the growth of the labor force. With declining capital inflows, and declining government revenues, it became much harder for the government to use government jobs as the means of fulfilling the authoritarian bargain. The rising shortage of public sector jobs combined with the very slow growth of the private sector led to the emergence of high unemployment rates. This meant that the youth bulge did not turn out to offer the benefits which potentially might have been possible and made it even more clear that the authoritarian bargain had become broken.

The old system, however, in the case of Tunisia was a little broader and did not collapse. Instead, it was reformed in a way that led to a slightly different new equilibrium and social coalition in power. Most of the same dominant groups continued to be part of the regime. Government and public sector employees and the middle class were the main constituency. The majority of the business community stayed committed to this coalition and in return continued to benefit heavily from trade protection and rent distribution, but as indicated in Chapter 6 had not increased their competitiveness. The security and military forces also generally continued to support this coalition.

Yet, by the turn of the century, clouds and vulnerabilities started to accumulate and accentuate.

1. The Warning Signs of Increased Vulnerability

As claimed by Deverajan and Ianchovicha (2017), the Arab uprisings in Tunisia and elsewhere in the MENA region beginning in 2011 were mostly the result of the failure of the existing autocratic regimes to maintain their part of the authoritarian bargain. This was a major underlying cause of the emerging vulnerabilities.

Even though these authors denied that other factors like rising inequality played a significant role in the impending demise of the authoritarian regime, this remains a subject of debate. Various researchers (e.g., Lipset 1959 and most recently Acemoglu and Robinson 2006) have shown that political leadership by dictators or narrow elites is not likely to lead to democracy unless inequality gets very high. Others point out that democracy offers greater advantages in working out compromises among groups when the groups are very distinct in terms of ethnic, religious or income differences. For this reason, Tunisia's ethnic and religious homogeneity, combined with a degree of income inequality that was never of crisis proportions and which, as shown in the last column of Table 1.2, has declined steadily and very substantially over time, has undoubtedly contributed to Tunisia's social and political stability and relatively successful development, but without democracy. One perceived threat to the Tunisian regime and other Arab countries in recent years came from Islamic fundamentalists, especially in the 1980s. In many Arab countries, such groups have tried to play an active role in social welfare provision to the poor. Yet, with periodic crackdowns on these fundamentalists by the Tunisian authorities (including in some cases with life imprisonment) and more importantly with the government being active in social welfare provision (El-Said 2008), this has been a far less serious threat in Tunisia than elsewhere in the region.

In any case, since the mid-2000s, a number of events signaled the vulnerability of the old political system in Tunisia. The radical opposition started a major mobilization campaign against the regime's proposal to change the constitution so as to allow the president to sit for a fourth term in 2004. This effort brought together for the first time the Islamist and modernist/secular oppositions in a so-called October 18, 2005 alliance to fight against authoritarianism. The influence of Islam was certainly not new since the vast majority of Tunisians were Muslims. The problem, as seen by Tunisian scholars, however, was that fundamentalists began to demand that Islamic religious ideology be embedded in the state, not simply in the minds of individuals.

The unrest was not limited to the political sphere. The sense of rebellion within the disenfranchised groups came to express itself in years prior to the winter of 2010/2011 in fights between hooligans at soccer games in Tunisia. The country also experienced major social movements, such as the events in the mining region, with uprisings in the town of Redeyef which were put down by very muscular repression in 2008. Yet, notably, this uprising did not spread rapidly to other areas.

Economic and social polarization was becoming a major feature of the development experience in almost all Arab countries. In the case of Tunisia, it was taking the form of major gaps between people in the coastal regions and those of the interior. In 2010, the average consumption expenditure per person was 35–40% lower in the regions of Center-West and North-West compared to the national average. Notably, Amara and Jemmali (2017) applied a method for decomposing the overall inequality into between-region and within-region components with detailed data on individual households in both 2005 and 2010. Their results showed that, while overall income and expenditure inequality fell slightly during this five-year period, the extent of between-region inequality increased sharply. Perhaps, even more disturbing is the demonstration by Jemmali (2016) that during this same period and with the same household level data, while there was overall improvement in access to both basic housing services for children (such as in access to improved water, sanitation facilities, and electricity) and education services (reaching 9th grade on time) in the country as a whole and in most regions, in at least one interior region (Center-West), such access declined overall and inequality in such access within that region increased. While in the case of educational access, a significant portion of this deterioration was due to household behavioral differences, such as poor families having more children than richer ones, it was more strictly geographic factors that were responsible for the gaps in access to basic housing services.

Similarly, the poverty headcount ratio in 2011 was as high as 42% in the Center-West and 36% in the North-West, compared to a national average of 20.5%, and only 11–15% in the more developed regions of the North and East.[3] There were also wide disparities in access to public services, such as education and health. Unemployment rates were also significantly larger in the interior regions than in the coastal regions. According to the 2014 Census data figures (Institut National de la Statistique 2017), the total unemployment rate was 19% in the interior regions compared to 12% in the coastal regions.

Another segment of Tunisian society and economy which was growing rapidly was the informal sector in the urban areas. As job opportunities in the formal sector weakened while the labor force growth peaked, the informal sector became almost the only option for an increasing fraction of the population in the search for jobs. Discontent and violence became evident among those in this group in the face of difficult working conditions and harassment from the authorities.

2. *Triggers and the Collapse of an Authoritarian Regime*

While vulnerabilities in the existing system and the non-sustainability of the political regime were increasingly recognized, it was still not possible to predict a specific reason or time for major change, or even collapse. In fact, one of the puzzling facts was that Tunisia, where the Arab uprisings started, had not appeared to be even among the most vulnerable countries. As noted earlier, it had been achieving moderate economic growth rates, improving standards of living, and significantly reducing poverty. It had also achieved quite favorable macroeconomic conditions with low inflation, deficits, and debt. Yet eventually a number of triggers could be identified which prompted the uprisings, led mainly by some underprivileged groups. It was the defection of some other major actors, however, which explains the speed and decisiveness of the collapse of the autocratic regime in Tunisia.

While Tunisia may not have been the most vulnerable country, we point to the following three major triggers that seem to have been most important in giving rise to the uprisings in the country.

The first such trigger was a rather gradually occurring and general one, namely, the declining ability of Tunisian economic growth to generate employment for its growing labor force. Ghazali and Mouelhi (2018) conducted a quantitative exercise quite different from that of Nabli and Véganzonès-Varoudakis (2007), which was drawn upon in Chapter 4 to identify some of the *positive* factors lying behind Tunisia's fairly successful growth over the long run. What Ghazali and Mouelhi (2018) did in their quantitative analysis was to examine the employment intensity of that growth and to see how this changed over time and differed across sectors. They pointed to a number of warning signs. One was that the employment elasticity of growth had been declining rather steadily over time from 0.61

in the 1980s to 0.57 in the 1990s and to 0.48 in the decade before the Arab Uprisings in 2011. Also, the few sectors with high and rising employment elasticities of growth, like agriculture, manufacturing and construction, were declining in shares (in great contrast to services). More importantly, they showed that over time the aggregate employment elasticities of growth were negatively related, not only to the inflation rate and nominal exchange rates that had been rising, but also to trade openness which government policy was trying to increase.

Given that youth unemployment was the greatest challenge facing the labor market in general, Stampini and Verdier-Chouchane (2011) examined the dynamics of youth employment and unemployment over the period 2005–2007. They showed that the greatest potential for growth in youth employment was in Services within the private sector, but also that this sector was failing to increase employment.

The ability of the economy to generate growth and employment worsened with the global financial crisis that started in 2008. As is well known, its impacts were substantial all over the world, but in Tunisia a major channel for this effect was the effect of the global financial crisis on significant declines in Tunisian exports, FDI inflows and the remittances from the Tunisians working in Europe and elsewhere, reducing Tunisia's GDP growth rate from 5.1% during 2005–2007 to 3.6% during 2008–2010 and raising both its unemployment rate from 13.8% in 2008 to 14.3% in 2009 and increasing other economic and social vulnerabilities.[4] Jordan was another MENA country badly impacted by the Global Financial Crisis of 2008–2009 and especially like Tunisia in that so much of this was through reduced exports to Europe and remittance inflows from its workers in Europe and the GCC. David and Marouani (2013) conducted comparisons of simulated effects of the GFC and subsequently also the beginning of the downturn in Tunisia emanating from its political transition crisis. These simulations showed that in both the 2008–2010 and 2011–2015 periods Tunisia's labor market and GDP growth were much more seriously affected than those of Jordan by the GFC. The total unemployment rates in Tunisia were increased by about 1% more in each period than in Jordan, and Tunisia's GDP per capita growth rates were reduced in both periods by almost 1%, in large part through lower investment rates and emigration rates (in the latter case with the impact much greater on the more highly skilled workers). These authors also went on to link their analysis with the aforementioned study of Stampini and Verdier-Chouchane (2011) by conducting another simulation on the possible consequences of a trade reform which would allow the same two countries to export more in the way of services. They showed that such a reform would have the effect of reducing unemployment rates in Tunisia in all skill categories by much more than in Jordan and especially among young and more highly skilled workers. These results highlight the interconnectedness of two of Tunisia's important policy shortcomings: its insufficient reforms in both the labor market and international trade.

The second, and a much more specific, trigger was that graduates of tertiary level education in Tunisia were facing unprecedentedly high levels of unemployment, especially in the underprivileged regions of the interior. While the overall rate of unemployment declined from 20.2% in 2000 to 13.8% in 2010, the unemployment rate among tertiary education graduates skyrocketed from 8.6% in 1999 to 23.3% in 2010. This was primarily the result of unusually easy admission to university education. The rate of admission,[5] which was around 30% in the 1990s, increased to 50–52% in 1999–2000 and further to 66% in 2003. As a result, the annual flow of new entrants to tertiary education jumped from about 4000 students in the 1990s to 91,000 in 2008, subsequently causing the flow of tertiary education graduates looking for jobs to balloon after the mid-2000s. With limited demand by firms for this ballooning number of university graduates, the unemployment rate among tertiary education graduates surged.

Since the beginning of 2010, the unemployed university graduates, just as in other Arab countries (such as Morocco), began to openly challenge the regime, with sit-in demonstrations in some of the most visible and symbolic areas of both Tunis and some interior cities. The youth challenge also gained some legitimacy in the broader population, since education had long been seen as a major channel for social promotion. That this channel could no longer be seen as leading to opportunities for its citizenry contributed to this being perceived to be one of the regime's most significant failures.

Two factors aggravated this situation. First, since the quality of education was deteriorating significantly, obtaining a degree was no longer providing such a positive and valid signal of achievement and potential. Second, the excess supply of university graduates was accompanied by a rise in the discriminatory, non-competitive way in which the privileged were locking in access to the available jobs. As a result, a sense of despair and frustration became pervasive among the many young university graduates who did not have that privileged access. Indeed, many of these university graduates could no longer see any prospects of employment that would come anywhere near matching their expectations.

The third trigger to the popular uprisings against the Ben Ali regime was the quickening pace and increasingly pervasive incidence of corruption from the early 2000s onwards. This corruption was increasingly concentrated within the ruling families and a limited circle of cronies (Maaloul et al. 2018) as was the case also in Egypt (Dang et al. 2018). There was an accelerating change in regulations favoring Ben Ali family members and other connected private firms at the expense of others. Making careful use of firm-level data over the period 1994–2010, Rijkers, Baghdadi, and Raballand (2017), Rijkers, Freund, and Nucifora (2017), and Baghdadi et al. (2019) have shown the following: (1) that Ben Ali and other 'connected' firms vastly outperformed other non-connected firms in employment, output, profits, output growth, and market share growth over this period of time, and (2) that the sectors, in which the connected and especially Ben Ali firms were entering most rapidly and becoming dominant in, were sectors in which authorizations for production were most necessary and restrictions on FDI were most severe. This implied that Tunisia's regulations were indeed being specifically changed so as to discriminate in favor of Ben Ali firms and identifying discrimination in the application of regulations as an important mechanism for generating the benefits for the connected firms. Bencheikh and Taktak (2017) revealed another mechanism for such discrimination which was through bank loans, especially in the form of short-term loans which could be frequently renewed and with lower costs than long-term loans and involving lower risk of default. Atiyas et al. (2021) identify two other mechanisms: privatization and trade policy. With respect to privatization, they found that, over the preceding years, 8 of the 84 public sector firms which were privatized wound up as Ben Ali firms. In the case of trade policy, the discriminatory treatment was detected by the fact that Ben Ali firms were on average operating in sectors protected by higher tariffs.[6] Baghdadi et al. (2019) demonstrated the impressive power of firms owned by the Ben Ali family resulting from these discriminatory treatments by showing (1) that, while these firms contributed only about 5% of private sector output, they generated some 15% of private sector profits and (2) that the ten largest of these firms generated 10% of gross profits in the entire economy. Notably, Maaloul et al. (2018) showed that the connected firms gained in performance and value, not only by the favors and advantages they obtained directly from their patrons, but also from the fact that other investors (minority investors) would want to invest in these enterprises so as to gain some of the benefits for themselves.

But corruption extended well beyond the afore-mentioned specific regulations on industry and FDI. This rising corruption trend had three important effects. First, it contributed to the defection of those members of the business community who had been discriminated against by the Ben Ali regime actions, and at the same time reduced the level of private investment. Second, that trend and the public's increasing awareness of it (which derived from the many high profile cases of corruption and cronyism) served to further delegitimize the regime in the population as a whole.[7] Third, the costs of corruption trickled down to the community level as (1) parents of children in public schools found it necessary to pay the teachers for private tutoring or simply to pass exams, and (2) patients in public hospitals found it necessary to pay bribes to medical staff in order to receive needed services.[8]

These triggers led to turmoil and uprisings especially in the interior regions, but the arrival and widespread availability of the social media made it possible for web dissidents to organize and to share information with people in urban and more highly developed areas at very low cost (Breuer et al. 2015), and for the movement to spread quickly throughout the country. Since the contributions of the internet and youth to these rebellions are often underestimated, to better understand the contribution of the Internet' it is useful to compare the situation at this time after the spread of social media with that a few years earlier such as was the case in the aforementioned example of government suppression of labor uprisings in Tunisia's mining region of Redeyef before social media access and internet access had become so widespread and without leadership from educated youths who became so good at using the internet and social media. Indeed, the rise of, and the increased access to, the internet and cyber-dissidence, and especially among the growing youth share in the population, made it much easier to organize these uprisings and more difficult to put them down. While these new uprisings first arose in Tunis, they spread easily and quickly to other regions within Tunisia, and soon thereafter to other Arab countries.[9]

3. The Defection of Major Critical Support Groups from the Old Regime

While a number of factors, including the rebellion of underprivileged groups and the increasing popular aversion to the regime due to the unbridled corruption that had become apparent at high levels, created a very favorable environment for triggering the uprisings, they, alone, were not sufficient to explain the collapse of the regime. Indeed, the regime could well have suppressed the uprisings with the use of force, as it had long been doing. Instead, it was the defection of major components of the coalition, including the middle class, the business community, and trade unions, who had previously supported the regime that explains the speed and decisiveness of the regime's collapse in Tunisia.

Notably, the middle class had played a critical role during the national liberation movement against Tunisia's colonial power. Then, after independence, that middle class had come to constitute an even larger part of the support to the new political elite which carried out economic and social modernization. These elites had moved progressively toward accepting an autocratic system via the authoritarian bargain, which reduced the political participation of the middle class in return for being sufficiently benefitted by the regime. Although, beginning as early as the late 1960s, some members of the middle class served as leaders of opposition movements to the autocratic regimes in the region, these were mostly students and intellectuals and their actions mainly limited to student movements and the like. A strong majority among the emergent middle class, however, had come to accept the autocratic bargain. That middle class majority included traditional groups, such as the employees of the civil service and of public enterprises. New groups within the middle class, such as the employees of the formal private sector, as well as professionals and other successful independent entrepreneurs, were also growing. They, too, had become the beneficiaries of the economic system with secure jobs, social security protection and improving standards of living. They valued the stability and security they received from the regime and accepted the constraints on political activity and freedoms that were part of the 'authoritarian bargain.'

The democratic transitions that occurred during the decade of the 1990s in various other developing countries, along with the extension of the democratic system at the global level, had important impacts on the middle class in the Arab region. Specifically, it made democratic values more attractive to its members. In his study on Egypt, Diwan (2013) identified this shift and the conversion of the middle class to democracy. The combination of deterioration in the economic and social benefits of the middle class, and their increased democratic aspirations moved the middle class away from its traditionally conservative position and brought it to a pro-democratic viewpoint.

The defection of the middle class from the existing regime in Tunisia can also be attributed to the impact of economic crisis at different levels of society. First, the rise of unemployment, especially for young educated people, contributed to the decrease in the perceived legitimacy of the political regime. Second, the deterioration in the quality of both health and education services contributed significantly to the dissatisfaction and growing discontent among the middle class. The middle class was also alienated from the regime by the increased level of corruption and crony capitalism which affected not only businesses and the workers in those businesses, but, as indicated above, also at the level of household activities and education and health services.

The business community as a whole was another important group defecting from its earlier support for the regime. Beginning in the 1990s but increasingly since the 2000s, the business community had come to suffer from unfair competition from the connected groups and crony capitalism (as it was also in Egypt at the same time according to Diwan and Schiffbauer 2018). This was the result of a large upswing of extortion, which reached very high levels. At the same time, the non-insider groups were more and more crowded out by the insiders and groups connected to the regime. While it was difficult for this community to express its political dissidence vocally, its response to the increased uncertainty took the form of declining investments. Despite some market-oriented reforms and incentives to the private sector, including a major new investment code which aimed at reducing constraints and improving incentives to private investment,[10] domestic investment remained weak and at levels which were much lower than those experienced in other successful developing countries (see Chapter 6). This breakdown of private investment, moreover, contributed to the failure of the existing economic and political model.

Other major players in the uprisings, in Tunisia, were the trade unions. Since Tunisia's independence, there was only the large major labor union (UGTT) which was also associated with the International Trade Union Federation. Its relations with the ruling party were complex. While early on after independence it had been quite close to the regime, in the 1980s when the ruling party tried to strengthen its hegemony over the trade union, the union resisted and became a vocal opposition force and supported civil society mobilization for a democratic transition. During the 1990s, the regime had been able to reduce the dynamism of the labor union and especially the *central* leadership of the trade union movement. Indeed, that central leadership of the unions surrendered to the autocratic regime. Yet, the *regional* and *sectoral* unions, stayed more independent and during Tunisia's so-called 'Jasmine Revolution,' they joined the unrest very quickly, playing a key role in the uprisings.

The uprisings, which started on December 17, 2010, following the self-immolation of a fruit-seller (operating in the informal sector), in the small city of Sidi Bouzid, one of the most under-privileged regions, quickly spread to other neighboring towns and regions. Repression did not stop the movement which gained in strength and soon reached coastal cities, and the capital city. Indeed, thanks especially to the spread of news and the ability to mobilize by the rapid spread and open access to internet and cell phones, by January 14, 2011, that is, in less than one month, the protests reached unprecedented levels, and the Ben Ali political regime collapsed. The country entered a new phase of political transition toward democracy.

B. Tunisia's Economic Collapse during the Political Transition Period

But why could not a smooth transition process be accomplished? Zartman (2015) and Ben Hafaiedh and Zartman (2015) have viewed the answer to be consistent with many other transitions in regimes in which there was no process of negotiating regime change between those in the old regime and those involved in the uprisings. For a successful transition, they argued that there needs to be a serious negotiation between the outgoing regime and those involved in the uprisings as might be the case when one political party loses out to another. Both parties are organized and can negotiate a settlement for what the old regime has to give up and what the new one wants to get. But, since all the old regimes in the Arab countries with Uprisings were so discredited by both their failure to resolve any of the existing and ever-deepening economic problems and inequities and their increasing practice of horrendous corruption in favor of families of the old regime, none of the incoming groups would be willing to have any negotiations with that old regime. For this reason, after the collapse of the old autocratic regime in early 2011, Tunisia entered into a period of political turmoil and of transition toward a democratic regime but without the benefit of a systematic way of setting up the new rules about how the new regime would be run based on the necessary negotiations with the outgoing regime.

While we admit that negotiations can be extremely useful in accomplishing a smooth transition, we point to the way in which the uprisings in Tunisia's (and also Egypt) had succeeded to some extent.[11] The success of the uprisings in both Tunisia and Egypt was largely the result of the amazing extent to which, during the uprisings, all elements of the growing oppositions to their old regimes stayed together in successful collective action despite their underlying religious, economic, and political differences. Since each group had different specific goals and desired programs, they could not afford to free ride by not participating intensively in the uprisings to oust the regime.

Yet, once their old regimes were thrown out, it left Egypt and especially Tunisia without any vision of a logical way to arrive at a new coalition rallying around a specific set of policy reforms. Virtually every different political or economic group had a different view of where it wanted to go once it became free of that regime. Hence, there was no longer the same large incentive for success in collective action in any particular program at the national level. As a result, Tunisia (and Egypt) became increasingly polarized into numerous different agendas.[12] Even among labor unions, divisions increased between the traditional UGTT and others, some of Islamist orientation, making it harder to agree on a common set of labor market policies (Pfeifer 2015). All this fractionalization, of course, greatly increased concerns about policy uncertainty and the potential for rapid policy changes, not only among outside specialists but also among private businessmen, leaving firm managers very unsure of future policies, thereby greatly increasing investment risks. While eventually Egypt returned to political dominance by the military and a relatively stable set of policies, Tunisia remained democratic but also very splintered and subject to great uncertainty about economic policy. In both cases, there was little incentive to come together to reach a consensus as Ben Hafaiedh and Zartman (2015) have also argued. In Tunisia, the few attempts to reach consensus resulted eventually in failures, as there was no sufficient trust between parties to sustain a consensus.

In this process, Tunisia has indeed progressed in the direction of satisfying some of the component measures of democracy (Table 7.1a) and in achieving political transformation (Table 7.1b). As shown in Table 7.1a, according to the Polity IV index, Tunisia has been considered democratic since 2014, with a score of 7 in that year, and of 8 by the municipal elections of 2018. Despite some security threats, the country has remained peaceful, and three different elections, each generally considered to be open and democratic, have been held since January, 2011. Even in 2011 itself, there was an election for a Constitutional Assembly, which drafted a new constitution, which, when adopted in early 2014, provided major gains in terms of freedom of expression, individual rights and open political activity. Toward the end of 2014 there was an election for Parliament and a President. In both 2018 and 2019 there were more elections for local councils, then for a new President and a new Parliament. In the last column of Table 7.1a are the scores across the same set of countries on the Freedom House Index (0–100) showing that similarly to the Polity IV scores, by 2019 on the Freedom House Index Tunisia had attained a level above that of any other MENA country and approximately comparable to the four democratic East Asian countries

Table 7.1a Democracy Indexes from Polity IV and Freedom House, 1960–2019

	Indexes from polity IV (0–10)								***Freedom house score (0–100)***
Country	***1960***	***1970***	***1980***	***1990***	***2000***	***2010***	***2017***	***2018***	***2019***
MENA non-major oil exporters	**0.8**	**0.6**	**0.0**	**0.2**	**1.0**	**1.8**	**2.7**	**2.7**	**30**
Djibouti		0	0	0	3	3	3	3	26
Egypt, Arab Rep.	0	0	0	0	0	1	0	0	22
Jordan	0	0	0	1	2	2	2	2	37
Lebanon	4	5	−77	−77	−66	6	6	6	45
Morocco	1	0	0	0	0	0	1	1	30
Syrian Arab Republic	−66	0	0	0	0	0	0	0	0
Tunisia	**0**	**0**	**0**	**0**	**1**	**1**	**7**	**7**	**69**
West Bank and Gaza									11
Yemen	0	0	0	−88	1	1	−77	−77	11
MENA major oil exporters	**0.0**	**0.0**	**0.0**	**0.3**	**1.0**	**1.8**	**3.0**	**3.0**	**23**
Algeria		0	0	1	0	3	3	3	34
Iran, Islamic Rep.	0	0	−88	0	4	0	0	0	18
Iraq	0	0	0	0	0	4	6	6	32
Libya	0	0	0	0	0	0	−77	−77	9
MENA GCC	**0.0**	**0.0**	**0.0**	**0.0**	**0.0**	**0.2**	**0.0**	**0.0**	**20**
Bahrain	0	0	0	0	0	1	0	0	12
Kuwait	0	0	0	−66	0	0	0	0	36
Oman	0	0	0	0	0	0	0	0	23
Qatar	0	0	0	0	0	0	0	0	25
Saudi Arabia	0	0	0	0	0	0	0	0	7
United Arab Emirates	0	0	0	0	0	0	0	0	17
East Asia	**4.0**	**2.5**	**1.3**	**4.0**	**6.0**	**5.8**	**5.2**	**5.3**	**50**
China	0	0	0	0	0	0	0	0	11
Indonesia	0	0	0	0	7	8	9	9	62
Korea, Rep.	8	4	0	7	8	8	8	8	83
Malaysia	10	3	5	5	4	6	6	7	52
Philippines	6	4	0	8	8	8	8	8	61
Thailand	0	4	3	4	9	5	0	0	30
Other Countries	**6.7**	**8.3**	**5.3**	**6.5**	**6.3**	**6.5**	**3.8**	**3.8**	**51**
Israel	10	9	9	7	7	7	7	7	78
Sudan	0	−88	0	0	0	1	0	0	7
Turkey	−88	8	2	9	8	8	0	0	31
United States	10	8	10	10	10	10	8	8	86

Sources and Notes:

Polity IV indexes from Polity IV Project data, 'Political Regime Characteristics and Transitions 1800–2018.'

Scores: 0 low, 10 high, −66 foreign intervention, −77 interregnum or anarchy, −88 transition.

Freedom House score from Freedom in the World Report 2019.

Scores: from 0 to 100. For Gaza and West Bank are given separately, 11 for Gaza and 25 for West Bank.

(Indonesia, Korea, Malaysia, and the Philippines) and the United States among democratic countries outside these two regions.

Even though the Polity IV and Freedom House Indexes of democracy shown in Table 7.1a are the most commonly used indexes, as with so many institutional indexes, they can be quite sensitive to the specific components considered in these indexes. In order to examine the robustness of our conclusions of the differences across countries in democracy scores to different components of such indexes, in Table 7.1b we present the same comparisons among the different MENA countries including Tunisia and the six East Asian countries based on a quite different and more recently developed kind of democracy index. This one is called the Bertelsmann Political Transformation Index. In the first four columns of the table labeled (1) are the values for this index for the years 2006 (the first year for which this index was created), 2010, 2018 and 2020 (the most recent observation from any of these indexes). Then, in the next five columns (labeled 2) are the 2020 scores for each country of the five different components of this index ("Stateness", Political Participation, Rule of Law, Stability of Political Institutions, and Political and Social Integration), each of which would seem to capture a component which most people would consider to be important for high quality democratic government. Not surprisingly, any given country can be expected to score higher on some of these components than on others. Note, for example, that the GCC monarchies all score quite high on "Stateness" but quite low on "Political Participation" and "Stability of Political Institutions". While there are some quite small differences in the trends of the comparable period from about 2000 to 2018 between this table and those in Table 7.1a, the general patterns across countries are quite similar. In particular, in every year indicated, the East Asian countries scored higher than any of the MENA subregion averages. Second highest among the sub-regions in all years is the MENA Non-Major Oil Exporters including Tunisia. The rise of Tunisia on this political Transformation Index is especially impressive, starting in 2006 well below that sub-region's average but rising by 2020 to be by far the highest in this region, and even considerably above the East Asian average. From the individual components of the overall Political Transformation Index in (the columns under section (2) of the table, it can be seen that Tunisia was rated especially high in Political Participation and surprisingly also in Stability of Political Institutions, ranking above all other countries in the table except the Republic of Korea. Note also from the columns in section (3) of the table that the same research organization did not find any corresponding jump in Tunisia's Economic Transformation Index.

Nevertheless, these democratic gains in Tunisia have not brought either political stability or improvements in governance and other institutional measures. Indeed, during the period from early 2011 to end of 2021, the country has seen a succession of 5 Heads of State, 10 heads of government, and 14 governments. The political crises have involved repeated attempts to reach a settlement on a new constitution which would clarify the role of

Table 7.1b Bertelsmann Political and Economic Transformation Indexes, 2006–2020

	Political transformation index				***2020 political transformation index***					***Economic transformation Index***	
	(1)				*(2)*					*(3)*	
Country	***2006***	***2010***	***2018***	***2020***	***Stateness***	***Political participation***	***Rule of law***	***Stability of political institutions***	***Political and social integration***	***2010***	***2020***
MENA Non-major oil exporters	**4.14**	**4.26**	**3.82**	**3.8**	**5.55**	**3.55**	**3.09**	**2.81**	**4.06**	**5.3**	**4.58**
Djibouti	n.a.	n.a.	n.a.	3.78	6.5	3	3	2.5	3.7	n.a.	6.75
Egypt, Arab Rep.	4.12	4.2	3.7	3.5	6.3	2.3	3	2	6	5.43	4.89
Jordan	4	4.02	4.37	4.32	6.5	4	4.3	2.5	4.3	6.29	5.9
Lebanon	5.6	6.35	4.82	5.3	5.5	6	4.8	5	5.3	6.18	3.97
Morocco	4.48	4.05	3.8	3.68	6.8	2.8	3.3	2	3.7	4.89	5.7
Syrian Arab Republic	3	3.23	1.75	1.8	3	1.5	1.5	1	2	4.54	1.71
Tunisia	**3.83**	**3.78**	**6.5**	**6.55**	**7.8**	**7.5**	**3.5**	**6.5**	**5.5**	**6.18**	**6.21**
West Bank and Gaza	n.a.	n.a.	n.a.	n.a.	n.a.	n.a.	n.a.	n.a.	n.a.	n.a.	n.a.
Yemen	4	4.23	1.8	1.5	2	1.3	1.3	1	2	3.73	1.54
MENA major oil exporters	**3.36**	**3.79**	**3.46**	**3.38**	**4.77**	**3.68**	**3.3**	**3.08**	**3.5**	**4.67**	**3.72**
Algeria	4.03	4.39	4.75	4.7	7.5	4.3	4.3	5.3	5	5.36	5.36
Iran, Islamic Rep.	3.75	3.45	2.92	2.88	5.3	2.3	2.3	2	2.7	3.86	2.79
Iraq	2.68	4.12	3.6	3.47	4.5	5.3	3.8	3	3.3	3.68	4.11
Libya	3	3.2	2.57	2.45	1.8	2.8	2.8	2	3	5.79	2.64

(Continued)

Table 7.1b Bertelsmann Political and Economic Transformation Indexes, 2006–2020 *(Continued)*

	Political transformation index				*2020 political transformation index*					*Economic transformation Index*	
	(1)				*(2)*					*(3)*	
Country	*2006*	*2010*	*2018*	*2020*	*Stateness*	*Political participation*	*Rule of law*	*Stability of political institutions*	*Political and social integration*	*2010*	*2020*
MENA GCC	**3.56**	**4.05**	**3.5**	**3.48**	**7.36**	**2.03**	**3.33**	**1.92**	**3**	**7.4**	**6.85**
Bahrain	4.92	4.4	3.23	3	6.3	1.5	2.8	1.5	3	7.68	6.25
Kuwait	n.a.	4.68	4.5	4.7	7.8	3.8	5	3	4	7.54	7.18
Oman	n.a.	3.98	3	2.9	7.3	1.5	1.8	2	3	7.07	5.54
Qatar	n.a.	4.2	3.73	3.9	8.5	2.3	3.8	2	3	7.93	7.89
Saudi Arabia	2.57	2.87	2.57	2.45	5.8	1.3	2.3	1	2	6.39	6.21
United Arab Emirates	3.2	4.15	4	3.9	8.5	1.8	4.3	2	3	7.5	8
East Asia	**6.19**	**5.97**	**5.43**	**5.55**	**7.77**	**5.02**	**5.1**	**4.58**	**5.02**	**6.7**	**6.94**
China	3.05	3.37	3.28	3.33	8.8	1.8	2.5	1	2.7	6.21	6.75
Indonesia	6.3	7	6.5	6.45	6.5	6.5	6	6.5	6.8	5.79	6.15
Korea, Rep.	8.9	8.9	8.45	8.6	10	8.5	8.5	8.5	7.5	8.54	8.71
Malaysia	5.07	5.28	4.78	5.85	8	5.5	5.5	5	5.3	7.07	7.29
Philippines	6.95	5.9	6.3	5.75	6.5	6.3	4.8	5.5	5.8	6.27	6.43
Thailand	6.85	5.35	3.25	3.3	6.8	1.5	3.3	1	4	6.32	6.32

Source: Bertelsmann Stiftung: Bertelsmann Transformation Indexes: https:/bti-project.org/en/index.

Notes: The components of the Political Transformation Index are given under heading (2). The components of the Economic Transformation Index include Level of Socioeconomic Development, Organization of Market and Competition, Monetary and Fiscal Stability, Private Property, and Welfare.

religion in politics and encourage coalition governments that would reflect the balance of power between political parties, labor unions and business groups.[13] The fragmentation of the political views and of the elected parliamentarians made it difficult for the parliament to pass most reform bills. Not only were there changes in party coalitions but there were also movements of deputies between different blocs and coalitions (Yerkes and Ben Yahmed 2019) all within the context of the deep-seated cleavage between the Islamic party Ennahda and the secular parties, the latter divided into progressives and remnants of the old regime. Periods of growing political and economic crises led on two occasions to national dialogues and consensus, one in October 2013 and another known as the Carthage Agreement in July 2016. The one in 2013 was the culmination of the National Dialogue Quartet constructed from the collaboration among four different civil society organizations, the aforementioned labor and business associations UGTT and UTICA, the Tunisian Human Rights League and the Tunisian Order of Lawyers. Indeed, the work of the National Dialogue Quartet was deemed so important, not only for Tunisia, but also for the sake of democracy in the world as a whole, as to be awarded by Norway's Nobel Peace Prize Committee the Nobel Peace Prize for 2015.[14]

While these consensus periods, in which power tended to be shared more fully across groups, reduced political turmoil, they did not contribute to badly needed economic reforms. Indeed, Jouini (2021) made use of detailed data on parliamentary voting and implementation on 468 different reform bills between 2012 and 2019 to show that the periods of consensus were accompanied by greater delays and even total failures to get those reform bills passed and implemented. His statistical results, moreover, were shown to be quite robust to the use of different modeling assumptions.

Lying behind the continuing turmoil and no doubt contributing to the failure to successfully undertake other institutional or economic policy reforms seems to have been declining trust. Spierings (2017) took advantage of detailed Arab Barometer and World Value Surveys (WVS) of individuals before and after the 2011 uprisings in as many MENA countries as possible, of course including Tunisia, although in this case only from the beginning of 2011. The focus in this study was on three main questions in these surveys, political-institutional trust, interpersonal trust, and ethno-religious tolerance. In general, the results showed that political institutional trust as well as interpersonal trust had been very low in the years of crony capitalist authoritarian regimes immediately prior to the political uprisings. But, trust of both types was found to increase sharply immediately after the successful overthrows in Egypt, Tunisia, and even Algeria where an important political reform in the direction of democracy had also been carried out. In each of these three countries, however, in the absence of other institutional reforms and so may remaining economic problems, these trust indexes declined sharply thereafter, at least through 2014 (the last year included in that study). At the same time, ethno-religious tolerance was also declining.

In addition to political and social instability, the country has been rocked with both major and less serious terrorist attacks, with ongoing fights against terrorist groups in a few remote areas of the country. Indeed, as a result of polarization and the subsequent inability to generate successful collective action, the country has seen little improvement in its ability to deal with its most serious problem, corruption. Indeed, according to the scores from ICRG in Table 4.12 for Control of Corruption, its score which was 3.0 in 2000, fell to 2.8 in 2010, and again further to 2.5 in 2015. Even more specific on this point are data obtained from a questionnaire conducted by Transparency International in November 2013, showing that no less than 61%of Tunisian respondents thought that corruption in the country 'had increased a lot' in the two years since the 2011 uprisings despite the fact that before that corruption under the old regime was, as indicated above, one of the important triggers giving rise to the uprisings.

Many of the other governance and institutional quality measures in Table 4.12 have also shown declines over much of the same period. The scores on Control of Religious Tensions fell from 5 or more between 2000 and 2010 to 4.0 in 2015, those on Government Stability fell from between 10.9 and 11.0 during 2000–2010 to 6.25 in 2015, those on Socioeconomic Conditions fell from a range of 5.4 to 6.0 during 2000–2010 to 5.04 in 2015, and those on Internal Conflict fell from a range of 10.2 to 11 during 2000–2010 to 7.08 in 2015. Not surprisingly, therefore, Tunisia's increasing polarization after its success in installing a more democratic political regime led, not only to the declining values of its various important institutional indicators of relevance to economic progress, but also to the aforementioned declines in economic performance.

In the remainder of this section, we turn from the more general institutional factors to more specific economic dimensions differentiating Tunisia's economic performance from those of other countries in the wake of the uprisings. In Section B-1, we focus on the new effects on Tunisia. Then, in Section B-2 we go on to how these and other developments affect the comparison of Tunisia with other MENA and East Asian countries. In Section B-3, we revisit the factors lying behind the overall comparison in economic performance across countries and over time. [15] Finally, in Section B-4 we return to the impact of the transition on economic outcomes, with a focus on private sector development, given the increasing evidence from the existing literature that what is holding back economic growth in MENA countries (including Tunisia) is their inability to remove the most important obstacles to private sector firms.[16]

1. Tunisia's Economic Performance in the Wake of the Uprisings

A first and more serious adverse effect stemmed from the domestic insecurity and political uncertainty that resulted from the post-regime downfall period in which a multiplicity of different religious and other groups emerged, each now trying to push its own objectives. This, moreover, was in a suddenly polarized setting that included extremist groups, some of which had been engaged in specific terrorist events elsewhere in the MENA region. The terrorism and other conflict threats triggered an increase in the allocation of resources for beefing up the security apparatus and carrying out the continuous fight against terrorist groups. Above all, there were the many changes in government referred to above taking place from 2011 to the present in Tunisia. In the presence of so many different groups supporting the political transition, but without any organized way of arriving at a consensus on the economic policies to be followed, policy uncertainty increased, making the economic policies to be followed less predictable, weakening governance and other institutions, and thereby raising the risks in investments by private firms. Not surprisingly, therefore, one important change in economic outcomes was a sharp decline after 2010 in investment and especially in that of the private sector. The share of gross fixed capital formation, which had averaged 25–27% of GDP during the previous decades, declined to 20.2% during 2011–2019, reaching a low of 18.3% in 2019 (See Table 5.1).

Second, the rising political and social instability and insecurity led to major losses in three critical sectors of Tunisia's economy, namely, phosphates extraction and transformation, oil and gas extraction, and tourism, mainly through disrupting production in those facilities. In each of these sectors, the losses were also reflected, not only in production and employment declines, but also in terms of declines in balance of payments receipts, placing more constraints on the use of monetary and fiscal policies.

The killings of important politicians in 2013 and the terrorism events of 2015, and the prioritization of security to which these events gave rise, moreover, had significant additional adverse effects. Indeed, Meddeb (2021) has revealed that much of Tunisia's imports of its highly demanded consumer goods switched from formal sources in Western Europe to Turkey and China through much more informal sources and using informal finance, such as informal letters of credit, so as to avoid being detectable from bank transactions. The informality of such imports has allowed them to arrive without having to pay the official import duties and other taxes and to enter by way of informal channels in Tunisia, even though many of them were associated with rich elites and political insiders as they had been under the old Ben Ali regime.

Third, the uprisings in Libya (Tunisia's neighbor to the east) and the ensuing collapse of the Libyan regime and outbreak of civil war in that country have had a significant impact on Tunisia in as much as, prior to that, economic links between the two countries had been strengthening in trade, tourism, health services, movements of people, and investment for some time. The crisis in Libya led to a disruption in those links and major losses. Estimates show that the total losses from these four sources have been huge and recurrent throughout the years since 2011, ranging from 5.9 to 10.8% of GDP per year (Nabli 2019).

All of these shocks have had the effects of severely damaging Tunisia's current account balances and increasing its foreign debt. As shown in Table 4.4, Tunisia's Current Account deficit increased from 5.2% of GDP in 2010 to 10.7% in 2019, at a time in which a majority of MENA countries and all East Asian countries except the Philippines were generating Current Account surpluses. The right-hand side of the same table shows that just the amount paid by Tunisia to service its foreign debt (as a percent of total exports) rose from 10.5% in 2010 to 16.7% in 2017 and 17.3% in 2019. Finally, as shown in Table 4.3, Tunisia's External Debt as a % of GDP, which had been steadily falling from 74% in the 1980s to 53.5% in 2010, increased to an all-time high of 100.8% in 2019.

While these shocks and losses, which turned out to be permanent and recurrent, called for some important adjustments in terms of policies and institutions, appropriate adjustments were not forthcoming, leaving the main policy response to be expansive fiscal policies. Faced with continuous social pressures, successive governments in the country have increased many different types of expenditures to meet all sorts of demands. These have included demands for public sector salary increases, greater hiring for the public sector, increased subsidies for both basic food commodities and energy products, and demands for increased public investments. As a result, total public expenditures (excluding debt service) as a percentage of GDP increased continuously from 22.4% of GDP in 2010 to 28.4% in 2019. Government sector wages increased from 10.7% of GDP in 2010 to 14.6% in 2019, accounting for no less than 70% of the total increase in public expenditures. The budget deficits, which were small or even in a small surplus in 2010, deteriorated rapidly, reaching an average yearly rate of 4.9% of GDP during the period 2017–2019.

Notably, these measures seem to have allowed Tunisia to continue to make gains on the social and human development front. Life expectancy increased further, while illiteracy and mortality rates declined (Table 1.1). Moreover, the poverty rate fell from 20.5% in 2010 to 15.2% in 2015 and the Gini index of income inequality declined from 35.8 to 32.8 over the same period (Table 1.2).

Yet, at the same time Tunisia's overall economic performance weakened dramatically, with a collapse in economic growth and entrance into a macroeconomic crisis. Total GDP growth, which had reached 4.2% per annum during 2001–2010, collapsed to 1.8% during the period 2011–2019, and GDP growth per capita, which had been 3.5% in that earlier decade, dropped to 0.9% in the latter period (Table 1.6). The unemployment rate increased between these same periods from an average of 13.4% to 16.3% (Table 2.10).

In addition to the aforementioned increases in current account and fiscal deficits, external debt, and debt service, inflation accelerated from 4.3% in 2010, and 3.5% in 2011 to 7.5% in 2018, and notably the Tunisian dinar depreciated by over 50% over the period 2010–June 2019.

These deteriorating macroeconomic conditions led the Tunisian government to enter into a special program with the IMF in 2013. Since that program was not completed successfully, this led to the adoption of a second four-year program between the IMF and the next Tunisian government in 2016. This second program was not completed either and was cancelled in March 2020. Even so, the country has remained mired in political instability and crisis, with continuing and accumulating major macroeconomic imbalances and low growth. Not surprisingly, the financial constraints arising from its rapidly increasing external debt and the IMF program induced the government to undergo a number of actions that made it even more difficult for private firms. From the Doing Business Surveys, which showed that most countries around the world were undertaking various reforms to make it easier for private firms to do business, the surveys showed that in 2014 Tunisia raised the cost to firms of registration and becoming formal, further inducing private firms to remain informal, and thus unable to access the credit and the technology that could allow them to grow.[17]

2. *Comparing Tunisia's Performance to Other MENA and East Asian Countries*

What are the implications of this post-uprisings experience for our comparison of Tunisia's performance with those of other MENA and East Asian countries? Even with such a disappointing experience during the last decade, Tunisia's performance still has ranked favorably among most MENA countries, (even though weaker than it had been in the preceding decades). However, it was now much weaker than the East Asian comparator countries than it had been earlier.

The former finding was attributable to the fact that economic performance deteriorated in almost all MENA countries in the period following the Arab uprisings compared to the previous decade. Except for Iraq, which was recovering from civil war, and the UAE and Bahrain, which were recovering from financial crises, growth in GDP per capita declined in all other MENA countries. Growth collapsed even more extremely in those MENA countries which experienced post-2010 conflicts, such as Yemen, Syria, and Libya. It fell significantly in all other countries, including Jordan and Lebanon (which have had to bear substantial proportions of refugees from Syria) and Egypt and Morocco which have been less affected by conflict. Tunisia's growth performance was similar to that during the 1980s, and its relative performance in MENA remained relatively favorable despite its large deterioration in absolute terms.

During the 2010s East Asian countries continued their strong economic growth despite some slowdown in China, Korea and Thailand (Table 1.6). GDP per capita growth improved in Indonesia, Malaysia and the Philippines. Overall, their growth rates over this period ranged from 2.4% in Korea to 6.7% per annum in China, which were much higher than

Tunisia's GDP per capita growth of 0.9% per annum. Also, unemployment rates were much lower and declining in East Asian countries, but high and increasing in Tunisia (Table 2.10).

In terms of poverty reduction, Tunisia achieved significant progress even during this recent period. In particular, using the $3.2/day poverty line, its headcount index declined from 9.1% in 2010 to 3.2% in 2015. Yet, Asian countries and especially China, Indonesia and the Philippines, achieved similar or even better progress in this and other poverty rates during the same period (Tables 1.2 and 1.3).

3. *Revisiting the Factors Lying Behind the Relative Performance*

As we have shown in the previous subsection, after the collapse of the political regime in early 2011, Tunisia's performance in economic and social development has taken a turn to the worse. In only two areas did Tunisia continue to perform relatively well. The first such area was its continued high levels of not only investments in human capital, but also in promoting equity and equality of opportunity. The second was in its leveraging of global markets in the form of trade in goods and services as reflected in the strong and even higher rates of economic openness to trade shown in Table 4.8.

At the same time, Tunisia has lost ground compared to other MENA countries in almost all other features, including some of those which had given it an advantage in the previous decades.

One important area in which Tunisia lost much of its earlier lead was its previously strong leadership, combined with a broadly shared vision and strong state capacity. Since the uprisings, Tunisia has been having a very fragmented political landscape, with weak and short-lived leadership. The democratic political environment has failed to produce a shared vision for the future, and state capacity has weakened very considerably. The country has also lost its advantage in terms of macroeconomic stability with higher inflation, more substantial exchange rate depreciation, large deficits, and skyrocketing debt levels. Hence, the lack of vision and strong political leadership in its leaders has translated into repeated attempts to resolve tensions through increased public expenditures of particular types, including subsidies but at the cost of increased indebtedness. Political instability and weak political leadership have also led to greater unpredictability in the economic policies and adaptive policies which had earlier given Tunisia an advantage relative to other countries.

4. *Transition to Democracy, Economic Growth, and Private Sector Development*

Tunisia's disadvantages with respect to East Asia have continued and even grown greater in some respects. The outcome was that Tunisia's economic dynamics continued with the same fundamental characteristics as in the pre-uprisings period, but which worsened to a large extent thereafter. Among the especially disappointing characteristics of Tunisia during this most recent decade were its limited structural transformation, low productivity growth, weak dynamics in its labor markets, and the failure of it private sector to become formal and to grow.

At the aggregate level, the process of structural transformation appears to have stalled, with declines in both the share of manufacturing in GDP (Table 2.1), and the share of tourism in GDP (Table 2.4). The only real exception to the failure to diversify and grow its manufacturing sector was some growth in higher technology exports, although to some extent this came at the expense of its traditional clothing manufactures. In particular, the share of medium-technology exports in total manufacturing exports increased from 30.2% in 2010 to 41.5% in 2017, while that of high-technology exports increased from 15.2% to 16.4%, while during this same period, the share of low-technology exports fell from 54.5% to 42.1% (Ghali and Nabli 2020).

The fundamental factors, discussed in Chapter 6, behind Tunisia's not achieving a performance comparable to that of the most successful East Asian countries remained in place. The Tunisian state continued to exert a heavy hand, but with weaker state capacity, and more corruption, the outcomes have become worse and the private sector's role has declined and become more inconsistent. As a result, the extent of Tunisia's use of markets and competition in the allocation of resources has not improved and may even have worsened. Inefficiencies have increased, with less reliability in access to various public goods and services, credit, and enforcement of the law, but at the same time greater social tensions and greater interference by the state. Its losses in exports of phosphates and tourism triggered real exchange rate depreciation, allowing Tunisian exports of manufacturing and agricultural products to continue to expand, but without indications of improving productivity.

One harmful effect of the rising political instability in Tunisia post 2010 was the impact of political risk on bank stability and bank risk. According to data from the IMF, the ratio of non-performing loans in total bank loans, which had fallen quite steadily in preceding years, rose from 11.5% in 2011 to 14.3% in 2015. Undoubtedly much of this can be traced to the rising importance of policy uncertainty, making increasing percentages of firm borrowers with intentions to invest in a particular sector or for a purpose unable to repay their loans. This is consistent with the empirical findings of Al-Shboul et al. (2020) for banks throughout the MENA region, showing that each of several different types of bank risks and instability (credit, risk, liquidity risk, leverage risk, portfolio risk, and especially insolvency risk) have been significantly raised by political instability.[18]

TFP growth was practically zero during 2011–2019 from Table 2.6a, and negative from Table 2.6b. Tunisia was not alone in this respect as in fact there was declining TFP growth in all MENA countries during this period.

Indeed, the TFP growth rate became strongly negative in countries such as Algeria, the GCC, Jordan, Iran, Iraq, Lebanon, and Yemen.

One important change over this recent decade was a major slowdown in the growth of Tunisia's working age population. As shown in Table 2.9, this fell from 2.6% per annum in the 1990s to 1.8% per annum in the 2001–2010 period and to 0.7% per year during 2011–2019, the lowest rate ever in the region.[19] This decline, while not favorable to aggregate growth, did help ease the enormous labor supply pressures, and supported a slight increase in the employment rate, as well as a slight increase in the female labor force participation rate. Yet, as shown in Table 2.11, the latter remained extremely low compared to East Asian countries. Other labor market indicators for Tunisia, however, deteriorated, in particular its high and increasing unemployment rates, and especially those of tertiary education graduates (Table 2.13) and of youths and women (Table 2.14).[20] Tunisia's investment rate declined further during the 2010s, and its savings rate collapsed while the situation continued to be strong in East Asia (See Table 5.1). The contribution to the decline in investment was by both the public and the private sectors (Table 6.1).

Despite the respectable recovery in finance through bank credit to the private sector after 2010 shown in Table 5.3, that increase was not as large as the relative percentage increases in the GCC countries, Lebanon, Morocco, China, Thailand and even Algeria, Iran, Iraq, and Libya.[21] But more than offsetting this promising change in the supply of bank credit to the private sector was the disappointing decline in finance through the stock exchange as shown in Table 5.4. This was despite the very specific advice given by the OECD (2012) and Amico (2014) on how to improve governance and other institutional impacts in Tunisia's Stock Exchange. Even more disappointing was the especially sharp decline in the share of FDI in GDP shown in Table 4.9 which contrasted with the impressive increases in these shares in each of the regions shown in the table. This decline may be deemed especially disappointing due to the well-recognized characteristic that FDI can serve as a convenient channel for increasing technical efficiency and also facilitating a country's firms entering into Global Value Chains (GVCs).

Perhaps the clearest way to detect what the deteriorating governance since the 'successful' uprisings in Tunisia has done to private firms in terms of both constraints on their business and performance outcomes is to compare private firm responses to the World Bank's Enterprise Surveys that were examined in Table 6.5a and which had been compared with other countries in Table 6.4. The data reported in those tables show that of all the some 20 different obstacles to business that private firm managers were asked to rank in terms of seriousness to their business in Tunisia's 2013 Enterprise Survey, 50% of them identified Political Instability as the most severe obstacle, thereby more serious than Corruption, Access to Finance, Courts and the Legal System, Labor Regulations, Licensing, Customs and Crime that are commonly named as serious ones. With this political instability lasting all through the decade until the present day, it is easy to understand why firms, both large and small, would find it difficult to commit to significant new investments, technological innovations or market niches. Since the most recent Enterprise Survey for Tunisia, that for 2020, has just been released by the World Bank, in Table 7.2, we compare the average responses of sampled private Tunisian firms to relevant and identical questions between the two years. While there is undoubtedly considerable overlap in the samples of the two years, the samples for 2013 and 2020 do not constitute a panel survey. Nevertheless, the sampling procedure was largely identical in the two surveys, the sample sizes fairly similar (although slightly larger in 2020 than in 2013) and we focus on the responses to questions which were identical in the two surveys.

We present in Table 7.2 the comparisons of answers to three different types of questions, first, the severity (on a 0–4 scale) of some 16 different obstacles to their individual firm's business, second, some 7 different indicators of firm innovation and quality, and finally, 7 indicators of the firm's financial development. For each separate response indicator, the table shows both the number of firms which responded to the relevant question in each survey, and the range of possible responses. These are 0–4 in the case of the severity of each obstacle to business measure, 0–1 in the case of most innovation and quality indicators, and 0–100 in those questions (mostly about financial indicators) in which the firm was asked to identify percentages. For each year of the survey the table also includes in the columns indicated the mean values of the responses of all firms as well as the standard deviations (S.D.) of these responses.

Focusing, first, on the obstacles to each firm's business in the top part of the table, it can be seen that for each and every one of the 16 different obstacles, the means of their severity scores were larger in 2020 than in 2013. In some cases, especially that for Political Instability, the increase in the sample mean was very minimal, a result which is not surprising given earlier evidence from Table 6.5a and related text that Political Instability was already regarded as a big problem because it made it impossible for firms to know what the relevant rules and incentives for production export and finance would be like in the near future, thereby substantially raising investment risk. Yet, very notable is the fact that for no less than six of these obstacles to business, namely, Access to Electricity, Access to Transportation, Customs and Trade Regulations, Access to Land, Business Licensing and Permits and Courts, the means of these severity measures had more than tripled over this 8 year period, and that those of Access to Finance, Crime, Theft and Disorder, and Labor Regulations, some of which were already quite important, more than doubled during that same period.

Then, turning to the indicators of innovation and quality in the second section of the table, the corresponding comparisons show that for five of the seven such measures the scores declined between 2013 and 2020 according to the Enterprise Surveys. Notably, for both Product and Process

Table 7.2 Tunisia Enterprise Surveys: Comparisons in Mean Responses of Firms between 2013 and 2020

			2013			*2020*		
Variables	***Min***	***Max***	***N***	***Mean***	***S.D.***	***N***	***Mean***	***S.D.***
Severity of obstacle to business								
Access to electricity	0	4	592	0.549	1.072	614	2.083	1.355
Access to transportation	0	4	588	0.541	0.961	611	2.322	1.272
Customs and trade regulations	0	4	581	0.599	1.005	571	1.977	1.321
Competition from informal sector	0	4	566	1.337	1.505	570	2.414	1.462
Access to land	0	4	589	0.421	0.927	567	1.899	1.402
Access to finance	0	4	592	1.144	1.368	606	2.421	1.266
Crime, theft, and disorder	0	4	592	0.590	1.094	615	1.735	1.316
Tax rates	0	4	586	1.123	1.220	581	2.096	1.275
Tax administration	0	4	590	1.007	1.187	580	1.722	1.246
Business licensing and permits	0	4	592	0.392	0.782	591	1.788	1.285
Political instability	0	4	591	2.455	1.240	607	2.471	1.325
Corruption	0	4	591	1.814	1.384	601	2.491	1.358
Courts	0	4	591	0.316	0.465	578	1.393	1.357
Labor regulations	0	4	592	0.590	0.926	614	1.637	1.368
Inadequately educated labor force	0	4	574	1.666	1.264	584	2.158	1.292
Indicators of innovation and quality								
Important product innovation	0	1	592	0.272	0.445	612	0.116	0.321
Important process innovation	0	1	591	0.254	0.436	610	0.044	0.206
Research and development spending	0	1	592	0.203	0.402	612	0.064	0.244
Innovation	0	1	592	0.127	0.333	615	0.166	0.372
Having a quality certificate	0	1	555	0.243	0.429	580	0.290	0.454
Exporting	0	1	590	0.510	0.500	605	0.413	0.493
Percentage of imported materials	0	100	329	54.810	40.470	595	37.330	39.970
Financial indicators								
% Purchased on credit	0	100	588	61.150	38.150	578	53.990	36.930
% Sold on credit	0	100	587	71.710	31.070	578	55.540	36.700
% Working capital financed by retained earnings	0	100	585	60.490	35.710	543	61.130	31.710
Purchased fixed assets	0	1	592	0.485	0.500	599	0.302	0.460
Firm has overdraft facility	0	1	592	0.713	0.453	602	0.556	0.497
Firm has credit line	0	1	592	0.574	0.495	602	0.413	0.493
Accounts audited by external auditor	0	1	592	0.784	0.412	597	0.303	0.460

Sources: European Bank for Reconstruction and Development, European Investment Bank and World Bank (2016, 2020). https://www.enterprisesurveys.org.

Innovation and also for R&D Spending, these scores all declined by more than 50% over this same period. The only two such indicators to reflect increases were those for Having Had an Innovation and Having a Quality Certificate, both of which could increase over time simply by the firm being in existence longer.

Finally, and even more alarmingly, in the bottom portion of the table, it can be seen that all seven of the indicators of financial development and credit use by Tunisian private firms revealed some decline. Both purchases and sales on credit fell significantly between the two years. The likelihood that the firm Purchased Fixed Assets, Had an Overdraft Facility or Credit Line all declined. The one indicator in the table which rose slightly between the two years was the Percent of Working Capital Financed by Retained Earnings, which is of course an inverse measure of financial development and credit. Worst of all, and consistent with the apparent rise of Corruption, Tax Rates and Tax Administration, Courts and Labor Regulations as obstacles to the firms' businesses, note that there was a fall from over 78% of the firms to only 30.3% of the firms in their propensity to have their Accounts Audited by an External Auditor.

The picture that emerges from these responses by individual firms between 2013 and 2020 could hardly be worse. While Political Instability remained the most severe obstacle to a firm's business in Tunisia, its severity actually increased a little and all other obstacles got more severe. So, too, the Innovation and Quality Measures of the firm's included in the Enterprise Surveys declined substantially as did the extent to which firms are able to make use of credit markets.

Hence, from both aggregate indicators and the special firm surveys, it is quite clear that the weaknesses of and difficulties facing the private sector worsened, supporting the view that, lying behind much of what has gone wrong, has been the failure of Tunisia and many other MENA countries to get their private sectors to engage successfully in meeting the increasing challenges of globalization in the 21st century and the many opportunities that globalization can provide. As discussed in relation to Table 4.13b, in terms of changes between 2015 and 2019 for all of the indexes included, progress was much greater in many MENA countries than in Tunisia. This is despite the fact that the uprisings in several other MENA countries triggered civil wars or other serious conflicts that more seriously affected economic outcomes there than in Tunisia.

As far as the character of the business elites and how it may have changed after the regime change, Oudenal and Ben Hamouda (2018) point to what happened in the aftermath of the confiscation and disposal of the Ben Ali family assets. They showed that these assets were largely purchased by groups of elite business people, some of which were also becoming more politically active. While we know of no signs of this yet, one has to worry that the rise of this new political elite could eventually lead to a repeat of the same Ben Ali accumulation and discriminatory regulations experience.

C. Democracy and Prospects for Economic Growth and Well-being

After 10 years of democratic transition, the economic and social outcomes seem to have been disappointing in Tunisia. But what are the prospects for the future? Could the country's improved scores on democracy open the way for a better future? And what would be the implications for the well-being of the population and what will be the new challenges and risks?

1. What Does Tunisia's Improved Democracy Score Imply for Other Institutions and Both Political Stability and Growth?

One direction to which democracy is often thought to lead that is relevant to these questions is by increasing information availability. This would seem especially likely, and badly needed, given that so much of the corruption that had arisen both during and after the overthrow of the Ben Ali regime occurred under the cloak of secrecy. Yet, given all the corrupt things that had been going on under that government, one can easily imagine that many people in the government might try to prevent such information from becoming available so as to avoid being penalized for the misdeeds that had occurred. Yet, if information availability about the government and its spending and other actions improved, it could be presumed to lead to pressures to increase efficiency and the responsiveness of government to the problems identified. A recent edited volume by Beschel and Yousef (2021) contains short evaluations of public sector reforms in several different countries of the MENA region, including ones like Tunisia, hit by the Arab Uprisings events.

The chapter by Dreisbach (2021) investigates the interesting and commendable initiative taken in Tunisia to increase transparency in government and its budget. Tunisia reacted very quickly. Soon after the ousting of the Ben Ali regime, a lawyer working in the provisional prime minister's office drafted the text of a decree declaring that it was the right of citizens to access administrative documents produced by the executive branch of government. Soon after that the Prime Minister's Office drew on other agencies within the government to plan how to put 'open government' into practice and by May 2011, well before there was a newly elected parliament, the president formally issued the Access to Information Decree. Dreisbach's evidence on how it started and evolved was largely based on interviews with relevant government officials. Getting that far so soon was attributed in part to the presence in the civil service of a sizable number of mostly young, internet-familiar government employees who, not only believed in such openness, but also were able to open e-government platforms offering access to information about government to the citizenry and on how to register to potential investors. All ministries and agencies were informed of the need to disclose relevant information and to respond to requests for more information and to establish a website on which relevant information would be provided by May 2013. After the first set of elections and with a new prime minister, by May 2012 relatively detailed guidelines were provided on how the open government was to be implemented. By late 2012 an overall website allowing users to access documents and at least small data sets had been created. As the challenges to its implementation continued, a foreign consulting team was selected to manage the open data portal and over time many of the individual ministries including the Statistics Institute, and the Ministries of Finance, Energy and Mines, Industry, and Culture opened their own websites. Encouraged to do so by the World Bank, Tunisia joined the Open Government Partnership, a multilateral initiative pushing for Open Governance around the world which provided additional insights and encouraged greater enthusiasm from within government circles. Such networking and the progress on opening up government action to the public also influenced at least partial attempts in this direction in Egypt and perhaps other countries of the MENA region.

Yet, the enthusiasm for complying with the Open Government Decree varied across ministries, and the ability to coordinate and to implement the resulting actions plans were delayed by the many crises that started to occur, some of them terrorist incidents, other political conflicts, and the many turnovers from one government to another that took place. Staff capable of responding appropriately to requests for information and knowledge about how to be sure that they were living up to international standards was limited, even after international donors and the African Development Bank helped overcome these problems with financial support. Even so, getting the acceptance of Tunisia's very politically divided Parliament required many rounds of redrafting so as to reach agreement on the few exceptions that would be allowed to full information provision. This was finally accomplished in 2016. Even so, its websites did not get rated highly in technical terms and usage remained low. Yet, at least according to the analysis of Dreisbach (2021), the evidence, suggesting that the transition from corrupt aristocracy to democracy could lead to greater information access of the kind which could help government better and more efficiently supply societal demand, was quite impressive. One of the biggest disappointments, however, was that the demand of users for such information was lower than expected, among other things implying that only relatively few potential investors were interested in accessing the information.[22]

Therefore, we want to go further and ask 'could democracy improve the prospects for growth and development in Tunisia?' Is it a sustainable and effective governance mechanism in such a country? Should Tunisia continue to make strong efforts to encourage and deepen it? The answers to these questions are remarkably controversial in all areas of the world. For example, while democracy has been lauded in the United States throughout its history, even in 2020, a respected American political economy scholar has just published a major new book arguing that '10% less democracy would be desirable and greater trust given to elites at the expense of the masses'

(Jones 2020). Such a response is not unique to the United States and is common in the Arab world with many examples commonly cited where the overthrows of monarchies and dictators have led to even worse institutions, and as a result, to lower economic growth and greater inequality. It should also be realized that all of the East Asian countries, especially in the earlier years where they were in the midst of the East Asian Miracle, were far from democratic.

Empirical evidence on the relationships between democracy and income or income growth rates has been controversial. While it has long been claimed that higher levels of income or income growth rates are positively related to democracy,[23] there have also been many papers with results contradicting such findings and also questioning the direction of causality in this relationship. Indeed, Addison and Baliamoune-Lutz (2006) showed that there can be substantial non-linearities in the effect of democracy indexes on growth, both directly and through their interactions with desirable reforms, such as trade and financial reforms, so that modest improvements in democracy may reduce income growth. Moreover, Addison and Baliamoune-Lutz (2006) showed this to be the case specifically for Tunisia and its Maghreb neighbors Algeria and Morocco when they used panel data for these three countries with common geographic locations and legal and other institutional heritage to examine these relationships over the period 1972–2000. As they see it: 'Since the adjustment costs associated with reform are likely to vary depending on what stage a country has reached in building its institutional quality, governments (together with the IMF and the World Bank) need to be more careful in the timing, sequencing, and pace of reforms to avoid unintended and negative output and employment effects. Otherwise, economic reform will show early failure before the longer-term benefits of trade and financial reforms arrive, and the fall in income associated with reform failure will imperil efforts to improve institutional quality.' (p. 1040).

More recently many authors including Rodrik and Wacziarg (2005), Persson and Tabellini (2006), Papaionnou and Siourounis (2008) and Acemoglu et al. (2019) have all used further improved panel data analyses to show that democracy raises economic growth rates. In the latter paper, Acemoglu et al. (2019) have suggested that previous results could well be biased by their failure to account for either dynamics in the process or for time-varying unobservables. In particular, they have claimed that most existing studies (either positive or negative in their support for a positive effect of democracy on economic growth) have failed to account for both (a) the tendency for the growth rate of GDP to fall in the 15 years prior to a country's democratization, and (b) the fact that democracy can spread among countries of a particular region as well as from the effects of common economic shocks across countries of a given region through trade and other mechanisms. For this reason, Acemoglu et al. (2019) use a variety of methods designed to mitigate these biases and show that their findings reveal *causality* between democracy and economic growth in the long run and demonstrate that their quantitative estimates of that causal long run effect on economic growth rates are quite robust across the different methods used.

An especially impressive method they have used is to construct an instrument for democracy based on regional democratization waves. In doing so, they make use of an especially large data set comprised of 175 countries from 1960 to 2010 and making use of more than one existing source of democracy measure, including those of both Polity IV and Freedom House. They also make use of a more conservative measure, wherein the country is not considered to be democratic unless it is classified as such by all the sources used. After demonstrating causality from democracy to growth, they also go on to identify the channels through which these positive effects on growth are realized, finding them to be: (a) higher investment rates, (b) encouragement of economic and institutional reforms, (c) improved health and education, and (d) a reduction in social unrest.

They also consider possible heterogeneity in these effects across different types of countries in either direction. As far as the effect of income on democracy is concerned, numerous authors (including Andersen and Ross 2014; Ross 2001, 2012) have claimed that resource-rich countries (especially oil countries), which are of course fairly common in the MENA region, are subject to a curse. Yet, Haber and Menaldo (2011) and subsequently O'Connor et al. (2018), using more advanced time series techniques for long term estimation, have produced results denying the existence of a negative oil curse effect on democracy in the long run. Notably, as indicated in the last column of Table 7.1a, Kuwait's score on the Freedom House Index of Democracy in 2019 was fourth highest among MENA countries.[24]

Acemoglu et al. (2019) have gone on to investigate the possibility of other heterogeneous effects between democracy and growth, depending on the level of per capita income and the level of education, both sometimes thought of as minimal requirements for a well-functioning democracy. Yet, they have not found any clear evidence of any kind of heterogeneity in such effects.

As Ross (in those aforementioned papers and book) and more recently Makdisi (2019, 2021) have indicated, the countries of the Middle East and North Africa have constituted something of an anomaly in the overall relationship between income (or income growth) and democracy. This is because its regional average score for Democracy (on virtually all indexes) ranks as the lowest in the world, below even Sub-Sahara Africa, despite having levels of GDP per capita and growth rates thereof averaging slightly above those in the world as a whole. As shown in Table 7.1a, because of the failure of virtually every country experiencing the Arab Uprisings to improve its democracy score after 2010, were it not for Tunisia, there would not have been even a tiny increase in democracy in the region as a whole resulting from the Arab Uprisings between 2010 and 2018. Yet, Tunisia has indeed been a notable exception in that its score on the Polity IV index has risen from 1 in 2010 to 7 beginning in 2014, qualifying it since that time as a 'flawed democracy,' tied with Israel, and ranked just below the United States whose Polity IV and other democracy scores have fallen in recent years. Note that Tunisia's 2018 score on the Polity IV is well over 2 times as large as the non-major oil exporting MENA average and even well above the East Asian average, and that its Freedom House score is almost as high in relative terms.as the aforementioned democracy score on the Polity IV Index.

During and even after the transition to its current level of democracy, and as discussed above, the most direct measures of economic growth and growth-related measures for Tunisia show declines. Among these are (1) the sharp decline in growth during 2011–2019 compared to the preceding two decades in Table 1.6[25], (2) the increases in unemployment rates among those with secondary and tertiary levels of education in Table 2.13, (3) the declines in both manufacturing and tourism receipt shares of GDP in Tables 2.1 and 2.3, and (iv) especially the decline in TFP growth rates in Tables 2.6a and 2.6b. Common among the explanations for this, among important witnesses to these events, have been the growing disappointment with democracy due to the continuous fractionalization between and within the more important political parties and hence their failure to adopt policies that would strengthen growth and reverse some of the recent declines identified below. Some political pundits, such as Grewal (2019), believe that the resulting widespread disappointment and frustration with results to date of the increase in its democracy index might well be likely to trigger a strong leader to emerge and bring about a return to autocratic rule.

Although the time since the Arab Uprisings events (2011) has not been long enough, given both the remarkably sharp increase in Tunisia's democracy index since 2010, and the aforementioned finding of Acemoglu et al. (2019) that rising investment rates, health and educational investments, and economic and institutional improvements were important mechanisms for linking improvements in democracy to subsequent economic growth, it would seem useful to further review whether or not Tunisia's rising democracy score has been accompanied by improvements in such variables as shown in the various tables discussed above. If so, such findings might make us more optimistic that Tunisia's jump in democracy might well raise economic growth in coming years.

There are a few promising indicators in some of the tables, the further improvements in health and education in Table 1.1, the continuing declines in income inequality and poverty rates in Table 1.2[26], the declines in its indexes of gender inequality in Table 2.14, the continuing increases in female labor force participation rates in Table 2.11, health expenditure shares of GDP in Table 4.5, and in all the Doing Business Survey indicators in Tables 4.13a and 4.13b.

But there are also many other less promising indirect measures suggesting that economic growth may be declining and that greater crises might lie ahead. First, as shown in Table 4.9 FDI as a percentage of GDP has fallen in the 2011–2019 period to its lowest level since the 1980s. Second, as shown in Table 5.1, both investment and savings rates have fallen during the

2011–2019 period to their lowest levels ever (at least since the 1960s). Factors lying behind these declines may well be the decline in the IPRI Property Rights Index in Table 4.11, and in virtually all the institutional indexes of the ICRG (except Democratic Accountability itself) in Table 4.12 and the unusually high percentages of private firms in Table 6.4 identifying Political Instability as the most serious obstacle to their business and the enormous percentage of time that managers have to spend on government regulations. While there has been a large increase since 2010 in bank deposits and domestic credit to the private sector in Table 5.3 thanks to a considerable easing of monetary policy, international debt as a share of GDP has exploded from 37.4% in 2010 to 74.3% in 2018 and the current account balance as a share of GDP has fallen from over 4.8% of GDP in 2010 to –11.1% of GDP in 2018 (and –8.4% in 2019, again an apparently all-time high in its deficit.

While on balance these post-2010 changes would seem to be not very promising as far as indicators of the effects of Tunisia's at least temporary increase in Democracy on the country's future economic growth, one should take into consideration the finding of Acemoglu et al. (2019) that real GDP growth has typically declined before, and perhaps even shortly after, democratization across the world and over time. Second, while Tunisia's increased democratization index reflects the fact that elections have taken place for President and Parliament repeatedly over the last several years and according to the rules spelled out in the new constitution of 2014 and monitored by an independent national election commission (and without the horrible consequences in terms of conflict and reversals in democracy that have characterized many other Arab Uprisings countries), many have pointed out several notable remaining deficiencies in the country's constitution which may impede institutional reform and administrative efficiency. For example, Boughzala and Romdhane (2017) have pointed to the need for much greater strengthening of the rule of law, and the ability to form coalition governments, and to raise voter turnout. McCarthy (2019), among others, has pointed to the existence of limitations on the types of responsibilities of the president, leaving many policy reforms exclusively in the hands of the parliament but which has been rendered quite ineffective by the extreme fractionalization of groups within parliament and its seeming inability to construct effective coalitions. This has resulted in the fact that, even as recently as 2019, 'Trust in Parliament and Trust in Political Parties' have been no higher than 14% and 9%, respectively, in Tunisia according to a recent Arab Barometer Survey.

Tunisia's municipal elections of 2018 allowed some 7200 local officials to be selected to represent 350 municipalities. However, as noted by Yerkes and Muasher (2018, 2), such local level 'elections will be meaningless without a strong legal framework for decentralization that clearly delineates power and responsibility between the national and local levels. The process will also require the political will to implement decentralization at both the national and local levels.' This legal framework has been introduced but its implementation faces major practical challenges. We would add that, if this were to be accomplished, it could eventually also lower the extreme disadvantages of firms located in the Interior of the country in accessing finance and technology relative to firms in Tunis, Sfax and other coastal locations as pointed out in Chapter 6.[27] As El-Haddad (2020, 1) put it, 'Tunisia is finding its way to an even more inclusive development model, but is still struggling for consensus for a clear economic policy direction and remains threatened by extremist elements.'

At present, however, Tunisians seem very disappointed in the outcome of their 'Revolution.' In December 2020 it was ten years since the street peddler Muhammad Bouazizi set himself on fire in protest to his punishment by local police, and their bribery demands in the interior city of Sidi Bouzid. Because that act provided such an important trigger to popular uprisings not only in Tunisia but also in several countries throughout the MENA region, Bouazizi has become much revered by many. But, at the same time because of as yet, the lack of any desirable outcome, as noted recently by The Economist (2020), based on some interviews at that time, attitudes seem to be very mixed with only a few locals regarding it as a success:

> Yet in Bouazizi's hometown of Sidi Bouzid, deep in the hinterland, few people plan to commemorate him. "He escaped to his maker and left us with his misery" says Haroun Zawawi, one of several young jobless men sitting near the roundabout where Bouazizi lit the match. On a nearby wall someone has mockingly scrawled "revolution" upside down. "People don't feel it has improved their lives" said the city's Member of Parliament. (41)

On the other hand, as was suggested by El Ouardani and Makdisi (2018) and Makdisi (2019), what all this represents is that the next decade is likely to be of great importance in determining, not only the sustainability and improvement of Tunisia's infant democracy, but also and indeed especially whether or not that democracy can bring about the boost in long run growth performance that has been alleged by Acemoglu et al. (2019).

The experience with previous episodes of rising democracy elsewhere in the region also has hardly led to optimism for the effects of democratization in Tunisia in the long run. For example, the international agreement that implemented a stability enhancing equitable power-sharing arrangement among Lebanon's different sectarian groups and which made Lebanon somewhat democratic (previously the most democratic country in the region) did help that country to grow out of the long-term economic decline that had resulted from its earlier civil war. Yet, more recently, that source of stability has come to be blamed for the low quality of institutions, gravely threatening both its remaining democratic characteristics and hopes of avoiding financial insolvency and returning to positive growth. The experience of other Arab Uprisings transition countries, such as Egypt,

Libya, Bahrain, Syria, and Yemen, have also not gotten anywhere in terms of either democracy or rekindled economic development and in some cases have led to greater repression, even worse economic performance, and in the case of both Syria and Yemen to some of the world's leading humanitarian disasters.

To obtain a broader yet more detailed comparative perspective of how the subjective views of Tunisians and other Arab countries have varied over time from just before the Arab Uprisings to the latest years available, Table 7.3 presents the percentages of individual respondents answering several different questions. Since some of these questions were deemed too controversial, they were not asked in some countries, accounting for the many blanks in this table. Note that answers to all 8 of the questions listed in the top row of the table were provided in the case of Tunisia. In most columns one can see both substantial differences in the answers across countries and over the decade.

From the first column of questions, it can be seen Tunisia started with the smallest percentage of respondents (27%) rating the current economic situation as 'good or very good' but it also ended the decade in 2018 with a still lower such percentage (7%). While these percentages had fallen further in Algeria (from 43% to 13%) and in Jordan (from 55% to 23%), even in 2018 Tunisia's percentage was the lowest of all. From column (2) it can be seen that at the beginning of the Arab Uprisings in 2011 78% said that they thought the economy would be at least somewhat better. Notably, by 2018 this percentage had fallen to 33%, though in both cases a little higher than the same percentages in Algeria, Lebanon, and Morocco. From column (3) it can be seen that 69% of Tunisians viewed Corruption as at least a problem of 'medium' severity in 2011 but, as more and more information became available, by 2018 this percentage had gone up to 90% (although still a little bit lower than Lebanon's 95%). While at the very start of the Arab Uprisings in 2011, as shown in column (4), 62% of Tunisians said they had 'quite a bit of Trust in Government by 2018 that percentage had fallen to 20%, lower than all countries except again Lebanon with 8%. So too, column (5) shows that while in 2011 34% of Tunisians thought that the government was doing at least a good job in creating employment activities by 2018 this had fallen to 17%, though slightly above the comparable assessments of people in Algeria and Palestine. Column (6) presents the percentages of respondents saying that they had thought about emigrating, showing that among Tunisians this percentage increased gradually from 22% in 2011 to 33% in 2018, while it had fallen sharply in Algeria. While questions about democracy were seldom asked in the Arab Barometer Surveys of other countries, well over 70% of Tunisians 'agreed that democracy has its problems but is better than the alternatives' which is considerably higher than the responses in Kuwait and Palestine. From the last column in the table it can be seen that the percentage of Tunisians agreeing that indecision is a characteristic of democracy has risen rather sharply with the aforementioned difficulties in enacting and

Table 7.3 Responses of Individuals to 8 Important Political Economy Questions across the Arab Uprisings Period in Arab Countries (%), 2006–2019

Countries/years		***(1) Percent of evaluations of current economic situation as good or very good***	***(2) Percent saying economy will be at least somewhat better in 2–3 Years***	***(3) Percent saying that corruption is at least a medium problem***	***(4) Percent saying they have at least quite a bit of trust in government***	***(5) Percent saying that govt. performance in creating employment opportunities is at least Good***	***(6) Percent saying that they thought about emigrating***	***(7) Percent agreeing that democracy has problems but it is better than other institutions***	***(8) Percent agreeing that indecision is a characteristic of democracy***
Algeria	2006	43	50				52		
	2011	32	39			31	42		
	2013	66	63				32		
	2016	27	27				22		
	2019	13	22			11	30		
Egypt	2011	23			99	25			
	2013	7			22	7			
	2016	30			85	13			
	2018	41			66	22			
Iraq	2011						24		
	2013						21		
	2018				86	93	33		
Jordan	2006	55			66		27		
	2010	44		60	72		34		
	2012	45		81	64		27		
	2016	48		79	54		22		
	2018	23		89	38		45		
Kuwait	2014			64					
	2019			82	47			38	

(Continued)

Table 7.3 Responses of Individuals to 8 Important Political Economy Questions across the Arab Uprisings Period in Arab Countries (%), 2006–2019 *(Continued)*

Countries/years		*(1) Percent of evaluations of current economic situation as good or very good*	*(2) Percent saying economy will be at least somewhat better in 2–3 Years*	*(3) Percent saying that corruption is at least a medium problem*	*(4) Percent saying they have at least quite a bit of trust in government*	*(5) Percent saying that govt. performance in creating employment opportunities is at least Good*	*(6) Percent saying that they thought about emigrating*	*(7) Percent agreeing that democracy has problems but it is better than other institutions*	*(8) Percent agreeing that indecision is a characteristic of democracy*
Lebanon	2010			86	31				
	2012			95	22				
	2016	9		95	14		30		
	2018	14	10	41	8		26		
Libya	2014				90		15		
	2019				92	10	21		
Morocco	2008		54				52		
	2013		51		83		32		
	2016		61				27		
	2018		30		71		44		
Tunisia	2011	27	78	69	62	34	22	70	19
	2013	12	54	69	39	29	27	70	50
	2016	14	48	90	33	28	25	85	69
	2018	7	33	90	20	17	33	79	51
West Bank	2011	40			54		25		
	2013	27			47		9		
	2016	33			29		18		
	2018	32		84	27	11	20	54	
Gaza	2011	33			48		30		
	2013	48			55		17		
	2016	20			37		48		
	2018	12		81	42	16	36	43	

Source: Arab Barometer Wave V Reports from Different Countries.

implementing coherent programs and reforms and any degree at all of political stability.

2. *Perceptions of Well-Being and of Frustrations*

It has been increasingly recognized, in the wake of the rising populism in both advanced and emerging countries, and the frequent uprisings in many developing countries in MENA and beyond, even in those thought to be highly successful economically such as Chile, that one has to go beyond the traditional macro-indicators of economic progress and inequality to understand them. Indeed, subjective perceptions of one's (1) relative position compared to others, (2) future expectations about that position, (3) attitudes towards cooperation with others, and (4) sense of security or insecurity have all been found to be major motivations for actions taken by individuals in their voting behavior and other public action including street protests. The same levels of measured inequality may induce different degrees of political action, depending on one's perceptions about the extent of fairness or unfairness of the observed outcomes in relative wealth.

The root cause of the political collapse of the regime in 2010/2011 and the subsequent economic collapse in Tunisia since the uprisings are clearly related to many of these factors. The sense of unfairness in the observed outcomes, both between social groups and between regions, have resulted in major disruptions in the extraction and transformation of natural resources, with large losses in production, exports, and budget revenues. Pressures by various socio-economic groups, often through the actions of labor unions, have led to large increases in wages and salaries, especially in the public sector, but have resulted in large budget deficits, lower competitiveness of private firms, and large debt increases.

An analysis by Gallup (2011) revealed a major disconnect between rising incomes before 2010 and souring perceptions of well-being and satisfaction with living conditions. This was reflected in the low score and ranking of Tunisia in the subjective measures of happiness, as measured by the Gallup World Poll surveys. Table 7.4 reports the scores and rankings of the countries in our MENA and East Asian samples in the World Happiness Reports[28]. The overall score for Tunisia was a low 4.826 (on a 0–10 scale) in 2010–2012, ranking it 104th among 156 countries. It was lower than the scores of almost all countries in our MENA and East Asian samples, exceptions being those which were in considerable turmoil or conflict at the time, such as Iraq, Yemen, Syria, Iran, and Egypt. Yet, by 2017–2019 Tunisia's score on this index had declined further to 4.392 according to the World Happiness Report 2020, ranking it as 128th among the 153 countries evaluated, representing a decline in the rankings of 24. Notably, although in both of the latter periods Tunisia's scores on the Happiness Index were above those of Egypt which had also gone through regime change, the decline in Tunisia was larger than that for Egypt. More importantly, this put Tunisia's

Table 7.4 Happiness Index, 2008–2019

Country	*Happiness index 2008–2012*		*Happiness index 2016–2018*		*Happiness index 2017–2019*	
	Score	*Rank*	*Score*	*Rank*	*Score*	*Rank*
MENA non-major oil exporters	**4.667**	**110**	**4.423**	**119**	**4.446**	**123**
Djibouti						
Egypt, Arab Rep.	4.413	130	4.166	137	4.151	138
Jordan	5.49	74	4.906	101	4.633	119
Lebanon	4.955	97	5.197	91	4.772	111
Morocco	4.875	99	5.208	89	5.095	97
Syrian Arab Republic	3.892	148	3.462	149		
Tunisia	**4.854**	**104**	**4.461**	**124**	**4.392**	**128**
West Bank and Gaza	4.614	83	4.601	113	4.553	125
Yemen	4.242	142	3.38	151	3.527	146
MENA major oil exporters	**5.185**	**93**	**4.930**	**101**	**4.988**	**102**
Algeria	5.462	73	5.211	88	5.005	100
Iran, Islamic Rep.	4.735	115	4.548	117	4.672	118
Iraq	4.787	105	4.437	126	4.785	110
Libya	5.755	78	5.525	72	5.489	80
MENA GCC	**6.500**	**35**	**6.359**	**33**	**6.382**	**34**
Bahrain	5.427	79	6.199	37	6.227	40
Kuwait	6.535	32	6.021	51	6.102	48
Oman	6.853	23				
Qatar	6.666	27	6.374	29		
Saudi Arabia	6.443	33	6.375	28	6.406	27
United Arab Emirates	7.075	14	6.825	21	6.791	21
East Asia	**5.478**	**66**	**5.543**	**73**	**5.612**	**71**
China	4.873	93	5.191	93	5.124	94
Indonesia	5.29	76	5.192	92	5.286	84
Korea, Rep.	6.017	41	5.895	54	5.872	61
Malaysia	5.694	56	5.339	80	5.384	82
Philippines	4.902	92	5.631	69	6.006	52
Thailand	6.094	36	6.008	52	5.999	54

Source: Helliwell et al. (2013, 2015, 2019, 2020).

Note: Life evaluations are on a scale from 0 to 10.

ranking on well-being or happiness well below its rankings in terms of GDP per capita (rank 84), or of life expectancy (rank 67). Although in the interest of space and since the results are quite similar, we do not present further evidence here, we have also made use of still another major source of Life Satisfaction scores, namely, those of the WVS for waves 3–7 for some 98 countries in which the scores for Tunisia have also been found to have been declining in the most recent waves and is scored well below all the East Asian countries and all the MENA countries (including even Libya and Yemen) except for Iraq, Morocco and Palestine (West Bank and Gaza) with only marginally lower scores on Life Satisfaction. In this case these same relative rankings appear after controlling for GDP per capita and other standard measures.

Hence, by 2017–2019, there was clearly a major gap between the standard economic and social performance indicators and the subjective perceptions of well-being on the part of Tunisia's population.[29] One possible explanation for this could be the existence of a 'frustration gap' between people's expectations and their daily life experience.[30] The Tunisian citizen has come to expect a lot from the state, but the state has been increasingly unable to deliver on these expectations. Instead, its performance in the delivery of public services has deteriorated and it has come to fail quite seriously in ensuring the citizenry with opportunities for jobs and improved living conditions. This gap has even widened further subsequent to its Arab Uprisings and the very optimistic expectations that had been created for overcoming the problems and difficulties, seemingly proving them to have been illusory, leading to the emergence of populism as a major political force in the last 2019 elections. The consequence of this for Tunisia is that the present and near future are full of substantial risks and uncertainties, further limiting the prospects for generating positive growth and innovation in Tunisia's private sector.

Notes

1 This chapter draws heavily on Nabli and Ben Hammouda (2015), where a more detailed analysis of these issues may be found.
2 See especially, Mahdavy (1970) and Beblawi (1987).
3 Institut National de la Statistique (2012).
4 In the case of remittances, Sridi and Ghardallou (2021) show that, even when the remittances rise, they have the effect of increasing standard country-level economic risk and thereby lowering growth in the long run, calling attention to the need to find the best way to handle remittances which as noted above have been especially important in the case of Tunisia. Hlasny and AlAzzawi (2018) use labor market panel surveys for Egypt, Jordan, and Tunisia to show that the outcomes of emigrant remittances in Tunisia may have been more adverse than those in Egypt and Jordan because Tunisia's emigrants were more highly concentrated in Europe which was much more directly affected by the GFC, whereas many more of Jordan's emigrants were in GCC countries which subsequently benefitted from rising oil prices.
5 This is the success rate at the nationwide end of secondary schooling examination, called Baccalauréat.
6 Notably, these authors argue this opportunity for corruption in favor of the privileged political elite was especially prominent in Tunisia and other MENA countries because, in contrast to the situation in Latin America and other parts of the world, economic policies had been liberalized in the 1990s but without the kind of political liberalization that occurred in these other regions.
7 For articulate and nicely researched documentations of the extent and nature of this corruption, see Hibou (2006) and World Bank (2014).
8 See Ghanem and Shaikh (2013, 11) who showed this to be happening in both Tunisia and Egypt, but notably that the situation was worse in Egypt than in Tunisia.
9 See, for instance, Delaney (2011).

10 The New Investment Code was adopted via Law No. 71-2016 on September 30, 2016.

11 Masri (2017) provides a full review of the experience of uprisings and their aftermath.

12 As such, this could be attributed to the theory of collective action articulated by Olson (1965), who pointed to the numerous characteristics of groups that may either strengthen or weaken collective action according to their differing degrees of vulnerability to 'free-riding.' Notably, Nabli and Nugent (1989), even in the pre-uprisings period of the 1980s, demonstrated the ability of such theory to explain various different institutional arrangements in Tunisia, and especially variations in the collective action in a number of separate studies. These included variations in the success of Tunisia's different producer organizations (Nugent 1989), labor organization (Zouari 1989), market institutions (Azabou, Kuran and Nabli 1989), state enterprises (Grissa 1989), and the groups involved in financial markets (Bechri 1989).

13 For a detailed account of the frustrations arising from the repeated failures to succeed in achieving consensus and stability on either of these fronts between 2012 and 2014, see Ben Hafaiedh and Zartman (2015) and for the years after that see Jouini (2021).

14 See, Nobel Peace Prize (2015). As the peace prize committee made clear in its declaration, the prize was not to any one of these organizations but rather to their collective 'National Quartet.'

15 The rest of this chapter draws heavily on Nabli (2019), which provides an extensive review of these developments.

16 See especially, Noland and Pack (2007), Devlin (2010), Henry and Springborg (2010), and more recently European Bank for Reconstruction and Development, European Investment Bank and World Bank (2016).

17 Only in 2019, did the Tunisian government, perhaps under increased pressure from the business community, introduce some reforms of the type deemed by the Doing Business Reports to make it easier for private firms to do business, by making it easier to register and transfer property, to protect minority investors, and finally to eliminate that new corporate income tax it had introduced in 2018.

18 In another study on risk-taking behavior of politically connected banks and firms in MENA countries, Braham et al. (2020) have shown that in conditions of high risk, MENA banks (including those of Tunisia) tend to lend especially heavily to politically connected firms, which themselves engage in risky investments, thereby also indirectly raising the financial fragility of banks and constraining credit especially to SMEs.

19 The low rates during the same period in Libya and Syria were related to their civil conflicts and emigration.

20 Jebili and Belkacem (2015) use a sequential special analysis across regions of Tunisia over the period 2004–2011 to show that the spatial sequences of changing labor force growth across regions and new attempts at sectoral diversification across regions interacted in such a way as to increase unemployment slightly as suggested by Lilien (1982).

21 From Table 4.13c, it would seem that considerable credit for Tunisia's improvement in terms of credit to the private sector should be given to the sharp increase in credit registry coverage, and to the remarkably short time it was reported in 2020 to take to successfully conclude an investigation of insolvency cases, and the remarkably high recovery rates in such cases.

22 For this reason, in their conclusion comparing the degree of success of reforms initiated in many countries of the region investigated in their book, Beschel and Yousef (2021) characterize it as only 'Mostly Successful,' that is, below some 'Clear Success' cases but above some 'Mixed Success,' 'Moderately Unsuccessful,' and 'Unsuccessful' cases. Makdisi and Soto (forthcoming) call

attention to the numerous very fundamental institutional reforms that will be necessary to make for a successful return to both peace and stability and a well-functioning economy not only in Tunisia but throughout the region.

23 For example, see Lipset (1959), Przeworski and Limongi (1993) and Przeworski et al. (2000).

24 Kuwait's relatively high democracy index stems in part from a coalition between business elites and minor members of the country's royal family that had also been backed by the British (Herb 2014).

25 Indeed, according to the most recent data on per capita GDP growth for Tunisia between 2017 and 2019, it has become negative in per capita terms.

26 It should be noted, however, that although data on the distribution of assets (on which Piketty (2014) and Alvarado and Piketty (2014) put so much emphasis for being the more important and most seriously increasing form of inequality) are very limited, Hlasny and AlAzzawi (2018) show estimates of asset inequality for Tunisia in 2014, showing inequality in the distribution of assets to have been higher in Tunisia than in either Egypt or Jordan at about the same time. Their results also showed considerably larger urban-rural, educated-non-educated, employed-unemployed, and employer-worker wealth gaps in Tunisia than in either Egypt or Jordan at that time.

27 See also Yerkes and Ben Yahmed (2018).

28 See Helliwell et al. (2013, 2015, 2019, 2020).

29 In an attempt to prove whether or not the Arab Uprisings experience caused lower happiness and life satisfaction, Hawash and AlAzzawi (2020) make use of respondents' answers to questions about Happiness and Life Satisfaction as well as attitudinal measures like Importance of Politics, Interest in Politics, Importance of Democracy Pride of Nationality and Importance of Income Inequality taken from a large sample of individuals in the *World Value Surveys* taken both before and after the Arab Uprisings. In both cases, they want to explain the changes between before and after the Arab Uprisings after controlling for many individual characteristics, such as age, gender, marital status, number of children in the household, education, health status, income, and social status, generally found to be appropriate for explaining these variables. While, for data availability reasons, they do so for Egypt rather than Tunisia, they argue that, because of the similarity of their experiences at least in the first year after the Arab Uprisings, the results should be similar. They compare and contrast the before and after Arab Uprisings results for Egypt with those for two other nearby Arab countries which did not go through much in the way of Arab Uprisings, namely, Jordan and Morocco. While some of their most interesting results were those obtained from interactions between the post-Arab Uprisings dummy and those other evaluations of the importance of politics, democracy, equality in income and pride in nationality, their difference -in -difference analysis of the effects of the post Arab Uprisings dummy in Egypt with those in Jordan and Morocco showed that both happiness and life satisfaction were lowered significantly more in Egypt than in either Jordan or Morocco. Again, for Egypt, and for an extremely small sample, Ibrahim (2021) makes use of a rather special questionnaire she administered, in this case to the same individuals, in two neighborhoods in Egypt, one rural and one urban, but both very poor. The comparisons in this case were between 2006 and 2015, but showed that, despite the fact that poor living conditions were a major motive for the Arab Uprisings among Egypt's poor, their reports on both these conditions (in terms of jobs, income, children's needs, housing, health, etc.) and their unfulfilled aspirations had all declined significantly, and especially among females over that decade.

30 See Ocampo (2019).

8 Conclusions

In this book we have reviewed 60 years of economic development experience in Tunisia and compared it with other countries in the MENA and East Asia regions. We have pointed out the successes and failures in terms of outcomes, as well as in the relative strengths and weaknesses in its institutions and policies. In Section A of this chapter, we summarize our main findings from the review of this experience and provide an explanation of the fundamental factors behind them.

Looking forward, we go on to ask: What are the lessons and implications of these findings? It is no longer possible to directly apply the lessons and draw policy implications from our findings to the situation of Tunisia today and in the years ahead because in the last 10 years the situation has changed completely. Not only its institutional and policy fundamentals and its performance indicators have changed rather remarkably, but major new challenges have emerged, each with major implications for the country's prospects. Taking into consideration this fundamentally changed situation, in Section B we go on to present some lessons and implications for the future drawn from our findings.

A. Looking Back, Understanding the Past

Many of the adverse circumstances and major shocks which have hindered development in so many different countries in the MENA region and elsewhere, and the complexities making these circumstances difficult to treat, such as recurrent conflicts, political strife, and large international financial crises, were not present in Tunisia, at least until very recently. Notably also, until recently, the country has been characterized by relatively little in the way of social and political fragmentation and heterogeneity, and the virtual absence of civil strife and conflict. Very remarkably, it has also experienced very little in the way of military intervention in its power struggles, and enjoyed a relatively peaceful regional neighborhood allowing it to avoid the wars that have stricken so many other parts of the region and the world. Together with the pre-existence of a relatively favorable state capacity, the absence of these negative factors, at least until 2010, explains to a

DOI: 10.4324/9781003309550-8

large extent the relative success of Tunisia's experience, especially relative to other MENA countries. Yet, in performance terms, in the last decade or so Tunisia's superior performance relative to other MENA countries has essentially disappeared, except with respect to the countries like Syria, Yemen, Iraq, and Libya that have been most directly and severely affected by conflict and like Lebanon and Jordan which have borne the brunt of the adverse externalities arising from these conflicts reflected in their enormous influxes of refugees.

The other striking feature of Tunisia's experience over the long term has been its relative political stability, compared not only with other countries in the region but also with East Asian countries. There has been little in the way of serious political crises and only rather limited political violence. Yet, unfortunately, Tunisia has not established a well-functioning constitutional process to manage the relatively few political transitions it has experienced, causing these political transitions to develop into political crises related to the issue of 'succession.' That same constitutional deficiency has resulted in the inability to handle its several underlying distributional problems. Indeed, the country has gone through three major political crises since independence: at the end of the 1960s, in the mid-1980s, and in the early 2010s. The last of these took the form of popular uprisings, leading to the subsequent collapse of the country's long-standing and impressively stable political regime.

Each of these political crises has been associated with a macroeconomic crisis, such as those arising in the mid and late 1960s, during the mid-1980s, and especially after the uprisings of 2010/2011. As a result, these political crises and related instabilities and macroeconomic crises have certainly negatively impacted the development performance of Tunisia, interrupting its periods of very satisfactory growth with downward cycles. During one politically stable period, 1970–1985, Tunisia showed that it could achieve Asian-like growth, averaging more than 7% per year in real GDP growth. This was followed, however, by Tunisia's 1985–1990 period of economic crisis and political transition. Yet, even after that crisis was over, during its slightly longer politically stable period between 1990 and 2010, GDP growth did not exceed 5% per year in any year, and even trended downwards at the end of that period. Hence, Tunisia's big economic shortcoming is that it has not been able to sustain high growth rates over sufficiently long periods of time as the East Asian countries have managed to do.

In addition to the several fortuitous factors mentioned above, Tunisia did not suffer from any major institutional weaknesses. Until the last decade at least, state capacity and institutional conditions have been quite continuously improved and strengthened. As we discussed in the context of Tables 4.11 and 4.12 Tunisia's institutions, including protection of property rights, bureaucratic quality, and various other indicators were either favorable or improving until around 2000. They did not constitute a major handicap compared to East Asian countries. Tunisia benefitted on the policy front from many other favorable factors: an overall stable macroeconomic environment (even in the face of a few crises), its pursuit over the long term of an open policy toward trade and investment and at least a reasonable leveraging of global markets, a developmental state which invested heavily in human capital and infrastructure and pursued active economic and social policies which were broadly predictable and adaptive. All these factors help explain the country's relatively good economic performance. Its very active social and redistributive policies have also supported major social progress, leading to both reductions in poverty and gender inequality and substantial improvement in several social indicators, and no doubt contributing to its political and economic stability and gradually improving institutions until the 2000s.

But an old question remains: why was Tunisia not able to achieve successful East Asian-type economic performance despite satisfying most of the conditions commonly identified as favorable to growth?

In trying to answer that question, we have highlighted a number of important differences between the experiences of Tunisia and the more successful East Asian countries. The first such difference is actually a set of symptoms or contributing factors, such as the limited structural transformation in Tunisia compared to East Asia, its lower rates of savings and physical capital accumulation, its slower productivity growth, higher unemployment rates, its very low female labor force participation rates, and the pervasiveness of its inefficiencies.

The second major, and even more fundamental, difference, highlighted in Chapter 6, was the heavy hand of the Tunisian state which has continued to hinder private sector development. Tunisia failed to create a favorable climate for the growth of the private sector that would allow it to become a dynamic actor in investment, innovation, economic growth, and structural transformation. While the state continued throughout the decades to actively and positively play its role in the provision of public goods, such as infrastructure, education, health, and other services, it has failed in creating the appropriate environment for a thriving private sector. The managers of private firms have had to spend unreasonably large portions of their time dealing with government regulations and many of these regulations have induced an unusually large percentage of its firms to remain informal. These informal firms, moreover, have created unfair competition for the formal private firms that have satisfied the costly requirements of formality.

Just think how this has contrasted with the evolution of China's policies to private business. China started out in the 1960s as a communist economic regime led by state-owned enterprises in industry and collective farms in agriculture. It closed down an existing association of private businesses, but in 1979 it allowed it to be re-created. By the 1980s, farming had become privatized and by the late 1990s, not only had the private sector been re-created, but also China had joined the WTO and has since become one of the world's largest traders and investors. By about 2005, its large association of private businesses had well over 3.5 million members and during the Global Financial Crisis of 2008–2009, that association collaborated with the government in the successful implementation of policies aimed at avoiding that crisis. This accounted, in part at least, for why China was the only country in the world not to have seen a fall in its exports during the Global Financial Crisis of 2008–2009 (Lei and Nugent 2018). In 2013, China launched its gigantic Belt and Road Initiative (BRI) that is transforming the group of countries stretching from East Asia to Africa and Eastern Europe, which had been linked by trade in ancient times, into an integrated network of countries with modern infrastructure and led by China's advanced technology and massive outward FDI flows (Nugent and Lu 2020). In this BRI-led transformation, China's industrial structure has been transformed from labor-intensive textiles and clothing and polluting heavy industry into one focused on high tech and innovation.

But identifying such differences does not provide a more fundamental explanation for the emergence of these differences. Tunisia had many of the same structural features observed in the successful East Asian countries: a developmental state and strong state capacity. It followed the same broad policy directions and policies we observe in East Asia, such as a focus on human capital, pragmatism and adaptability in policy, market orientation, and a strong outward orientation in its trade and investment policies. As demonstrated in previous chapters, despite these similarities, what have been missing in the Tunisian experience have been the abilities to foster stronger private sector development, higher levels of capital accumulation, higher productivity growth, deeper structural transformation, and greater efficiency in the allocation of resources, through business associations and their links to government policy.

In the following paragraphs, we identify three different hypotheses derived from what has been presented in preceding chapters which we believe contribute to *a more fundamental explanation* of the relative failure of Tunisia to match the East Asian performance.

1. Disappearance of Leadership Capable of Leading Macroeconomic Growth

One hypothesis is the eventual disappearance of a political leadership capable of coordinating future expectations, and projecting a credible future outlook, which would motivate higher savings, greater investments in physical and human capital, and innovation. Successful East Asian countries have benefitted from the emergence and further strengthening of such leadership over time. While Tunisia did benefit from the emergence of such leadership in the 1950s through the 1970s, the country has lacked such leadership since the 1980s and has been marred by political uncertainty, especially after political Islam emerged as a challenging force, reducing the credibility and trust of the political leadership. Tunisia's political leadership has also failed to create an environment capable of providing any kind of optimistic outlook for the future! Indeed, if anything, the country's underlying political and social tensions have increased over time, thereby greatly undermining confidence in and the credibility of policy reforms.

This shortcoming has been reflected in many of the tables presented. Indeed, the lack of success in projecting a better and more optimistic outlook since the 1980s is reflected in terms of Savings. As shown in Table 5.1, Tunisia's Gross Savings as a % of GDP was equal to that of East Asia in the 1970s, but Tunisia's Gross Savings rate has fallen in each subsequent decade while that of East Asia has increased so that by the 2010–2019 period Tunisia's Gross Savings ratio was almost 22 percentage points below that of East Asia. At the same time, from the same table, it can be seen that, while Tunisia remained on a par with East Asia in Gross Fixed Capital formation through the 1980s, by 2010–2019, it was a full 9 percentage points behind the East Asian average. The lack of leadership focused on long-term economic development is also reflected in the exaggeration of government consumption spending and the inability to maintain fiscal balance. Table 4.2 showed that, while Tunisia's leadership was able to maintain Tax Revenues to GDP averaging about 20% or higher over most of the 1980–2010 period, Government Expenditures increased significantly (with the surge in phosphates and oil revenues during the 1970s), as to reach 40% of GDP by the early 1980s. While they declined significantly with the oil shocks of the late 1970s and mid-1980s, Government Expenditures remained higher than 30% of GDP. As a result, significant budget deficits accumulated, and there was clearly no leadership which was able to reach a consensus on how to accommodate the various pressures other than by way of debt accumulation. With the exception of the late 1990s, when the Asian Financial Crisis erupted in some of the East Asian countries in our sample, as shown in Table 4.3, Tunisia's external debt burden has been much larger than that of East Asia, indeed more than double that of East Asia since 2010.

This failure of its leadership to provide a stronger outlook for the future is also apparent with respect to human capital. As shown in Table 1.1, since 1960 health (measured by e.g., Life Expectancy) has risen in Tunisia and mortality rates of children under 5 in Tunisia have fallen by even more than in East Asia. Yet, in terms of education Tunisia has not done as well as East Asia. The latter is reflected in Tunisia's consistently higher percentages of illiterates and lower average years of schooling in the population over 15 than the averages of these in East Asian countries. This is not to say that Tunisia has not greatly improved even in education. Indeed, its average years of schooling in the population over 15 years of age have increased from 3.7 in 1970 to 9.1 in 2010. Also, as shown in Table 4.5, Tunisia has actually spent consistently larger percentages of its GDP on education than have the East Asian countries. Yet, it is quite clear that, despite its greater public expenditures on education, the social benefits of these expenditures have been substantially undermined by each of the following (a) its apparently lower quality (reflected in Tunisia's much lower scores than East Asia on the international comparable PISA test scores), (b) the fact that unemployment rates of those with both intermediate and higher levels of education have been consistently much higher (and even grown over time) in Tunisia relative to East Asia, and (c) that as shown in Table 2.11 the labor force participation rates of females (whose levels of education have recently come to exceed those of males), have in every decade been less than half those in East Asia. All three of these outcomes suggest that much of Tunisia's investments in human capital have been wasted.

At the same time, Tunisia's unemployment rates over the whole period from 1980 have averaged over 15% whereas those of East Asia have averaged less than 4%. While Tunisia's poverty and income inequality indexes have fallen slightly over the same period, those of East Asia have fallen slightly more.

While the successful leadership in East Asia was able to coordinate and project success in terms of matching educational skills with employment, reducing unemployment rates, and reducing poverty; Tunisia's leadership was left with accumulating failures in terms of rising unemployment rates for the educated youth, low and declining rates of both returns to education and poverty reduction. Not surprisingly, and even though comparable happiness scores across countries and time are available only for fairly recent years, as shown in Table 7.4, Tunisia's scores have been significantly lower than those of the East Asian average and have been falling over time whereas those of East Asia have been rising.

Similarly, with respect to innovation, and technological change, Tables 2.6a and 2.6b showed that, while TFP growth had been higher than that in East Asia in the 1960s and 1970s, since 2000 Tunisia's TFP growth rates have fallen well behind those of East Asia.

Hence, even after rather favorable starts on all the important ingredients of aggregate growth, Tunisia's leadership has ever since then been unable to allow Tunisia to match East Asian countries in any of them, that is, savings and capital formation, human capital (especially education and its use), technical efficiency and TFP growth.

2. *Limited Adaptation, Resistance to Change, and Middle-Income Trap*

A second hypothesis is that in Tunisia the strength of special interests and political inertia have resulted in resistance to change prevailing in the area of economic and social policies. Two widely recognized, and very possibly interrelated, contributors to resistance to such change and the lack of, or insufficient adoption of economic and social policies to changing internal and external conditions are (a) the blocking of the process of creative destruction and (b) the middle-income trap (MIT) (Aghion et al. 2021; Kharas and Gill 2020). Political systems can have a tendency to protect and preserve incumbent firms and existing activities which, once the economy has reached the Middle-Income Trap, may become non-competitive, thereby undermining the process of innovation and creation of new more dynamic and productive firms. When that happens, the normal growth process in which countries gradually converge to higher income growth via a standard Solow growth model would no longer work. Economic convergence, and the productivity growth and structural transformation lying behind the convergence process, become either stalled or slowed down.

While Tunisia, as amply discussed in Chapter 2, had in the 1960s–1980s demonstrated a real capacity to adapt to change and to evolve in its policies, in the last two or three decades, it has proved much less capable of doing so. The discussion in Chapter 6 showed that, subsequent to that, greater resistance to change and limited adaptation have prevailed in Tunisia. The important contributors to this decline may have been that Tunisia's policymakers had become insufficiently committed to either a sufficiently strong outward orientation or growth driven by the private sector and the fostering of competitive markets. Instead, the heavy hand of the state has continued to dominate in Tunisia, restricting competition, controlling entry, and limiting trade and capital flows. Rent-seeking has continued to be pervasive, and the public sector has remained present everywhere and especially in finance, where the majority of banks and the larger ones are public sector banks and so many different kinds of regulations have remained very constraining to different kinds of firms. Especially in recent decades, there has been a large gap between the policies *announced* for the purpose of promoting the private sector, competition, and markets, and the policies and practices of these sorts that were *actually carried out*. Often, many of the policies actually carried out severely constrained the promotion of all of these desirable objectives.

As mentioned above, the Middle-Income Trap has been pointed to as a set of phenomena that have come together in countries which attained middle income status at some point but then, after growth slowdowns or other phenomena, even 20 or 30 years later have been unable to converge toward the higher income countries as had been suggested in the Solow growth model. In other words, they have gotten caught in the MIT. While most of the literature on the MIT has been concerned with countries in the 'upper-middle income group' which have been failing to break through to higher-income status, the concept is more broadly applicable to middle-income countries. According to World Bank data Tunisia reached low-middle income country status during its high growth spurt during the 1960s, since by 1965 its GNI per capita in 2010 constant dollars was $1083, while the threshold for this category using World Bank criteria for 2010 was $1005 (in GNI per capita Atlas Method). Despite a reasonable GDP growth performance, Tunisia remained in this category of developing countries for almost 50 years. It was only in the World Development Report of 2012, based on 2010 data, that Tunisia was classified as an upper-middle income country when its GNI per capita (according to the Atlas method) reached $4130, slightly above the threshold of $3975 (as of the World Development Report of 2012).[1] While Tunisia temporarily breached the lower end of the threshold of upper-middle income status during the early 2010s, it quickly reversed back to lower-middle income status with major losses in its level of income per capita afterwards. As a result, Tunisia has remained far away from even approaching higher income status and can be said to be stuck in the lower-MIT.

Such an assessment was also reached by Felipe et al. (2012), who applied the concept of income trap to various categories of countries: low, lower-middle, and upper-middle income countries. These authors based their analysis on data for the period 1950–2010 using GDP per capita data at 1990 PPP prices. They identified thresholds of $2000 to reach lower-middle income country status, $7250 to reach upper-middle income status and $11,750 for higher income. Based on their data (on GDP per capita at 1990 PPP international Prices), they determined that Tunisia reached lower-middle income status in 1971, where it remained for 39 years until 2010 thereby, classifying Tunisia as being in a lower-middle income trap by 2010.[2] It should be noted that, according to Felipe et al. (2012), four of the six Asian countries in our comparator group did succeed in transitioning from lower-middle to upper-middle income: China, Korea, Malaysia, and Thailand, with Korea graduating to the higher-income group by 1995. They also classified the Philippines as in the lower-middle income trap and Malaysia in the upper-middle income trap. Indonesia was deemed to be not yet in a middle-income trap. Using a different approach, which tests for convergence of the relative income of a given country to that of a reference country (the United States) toward a long-term steady-state trend which is within the middle-income range, Robertson and Ye (2013) have also determined Tunisia to be a country caught in the MIT. An even broader survey of MIT papers was carried out in 2016 by Glawe and Wagner (2016) which identified Tunisia as having gone through a serious growth slowdown in the late 1970s (and of course again after their study, between 2011 and 2019, as indicated in Table 1.6). Therefore, there would seem to be agreement that Tunisia has become stuck in the MIT, in contrast to most East Asian countries.

While there is considerable agreement on the applicability of the MIT to different middle-income countries, the literature varies more from study to study with respect to identifying factors lying behind the MIT and the failure to converge toward the higher income countries. One study which, although not focused on the Tunisian experience, we believe has special relevance to Tunisia is that of Agénor and Canuto (2015). These authors pointed to the limited product diversification, low productivity growth, misallocation of labor, and limited access to advanced infrastructure (including logistics) as the most common and fundamental contributors to the MIT, all characteristics which in this study we have pointed to as serious shortcomings in Tunisia's growth in recent years. Aiyar et al. (2018) used an unusually large sample of countries (135) at all levels of development and regions, including Tunisia and 17 other MENA countries, as well all six of our East Asian countries (plus seven others). It identified periods of serious growth slowdowns and then used regression models that included many possible factors to identify those most frequently seen as contributing to these slowdowns. It confirmed the MIT by showing that these slowdowns are far more likely to occur in middle-income countries than in other countries. Among the factors considered as possible contributors to a country's likelihood of falling victim to the MIT were a number of demographic factors, institutional factors, infrastructure, macroeconomic (both environment and policies), economic structure, trade structure, and other factors like ethnolinguistic fractionalization, religion, wars, and conflict. Among the factors found most likely to lead to the growth slowdowns and the MIT were measures which we have referred to as the 'heavy hand of government,' rigid regulations, lack of openness to trade and FDI, public debt, weak sectoral diversification, weak export diversification, weak regional integration, wars, and conflicts. Note that except for the wars and conflicts, we have identified several of these as having been especially relevant to the slowing growth performance in Tunisia. In a shorter rewrite of their 2013 paper (Aiyar et al. 2018), the authors went on to detail how some East Asian countries have done better on many of these same factors, allowing them to escape the MIT.

Somewhat similarly, in a still more up-to-date survey of MIT, Aghion et al. (2021) have argued that countries are most likely to get stuck in a MIT when they fail to adapt their institutions in such a way as to move from a catch-up model of growth to an innovation-based model. During the catch-up phase, policies which restrict entry and limit competition, limit access to financial markets and prevent foreign firms from entering the domestic market may not necessarily hinder growth and may even support it. But, at some point sticking with that same set of institutions and policies will eventually lead to a growth slow-down, implying that a movement to a rather different 'innovation-based' strategy would be required in order to be successful in overcoming the MIT. The innovation-based strategy for getting out of the MIT requires more competition, more FDI, and better access to capital markets. A process of creative destruction needs to be allowed to operate actively. To that end, Kharas and Gill (2020) argued that a Schumpeterian model of creative destruction is very relevant for understanding how middle-income countries may succeed in sustaining growth. Such an approach would mean adopting a three-pronged strategy 'involving: (i) putting in place mechanisms for increasing investment in physical and human capital, (ii) creating the incentives for innovation, and (iii) creating the institutions to ensure they affect timely transitions from accumulation to innovation.' They suggest that the effects of policies are very non-linear and very context-specific, which makes it difficult for middle-income countries to navigate the transition towards higher income status. For instance, the extent to which competition policy may stimulate investment or productivity is difficult to predict. Also, to manage any economic crises that may arise may quite appropriately require additional institutional reforms which are very context-specific and therefore cannot easily be identified even by simply examining past successes.

Although very much in line with this MIT literature in many respects, Doner and Schneider (2016) argue that any such transitions from middle-income traps are likely to be more about politics than about economics. Middle-income countries are likely to be more sharply divided into various income, sectoral, investor (foreign and domestic), and regional groups than are other countries. These inequities make it less likely that the political elites will be able to manage the kind of efficient transition to institutions and policies needed to steer the economy in healthy directions. Those healthy directions would include upgrading the secondary and higher educational systems so as to provide the labor force with the greater skill and technological capabilities needed to raise TFP in a sustained way. This would be in contrast to what so many middle-income countries do in that respect, which is allowing their informal sectors to dominate. The fact that in the last decade Tunisia has lost many aspects of a functioning government that could implement policies to upgrade technology and better align its educated work force with relevant jobs may help explain why Tunisia seems to be serving as a prime example of MIT difficulties.

3. The Neighborhood Effect

A third hypothesis is about the neighborhood in which Tunisia has operated. It could be argued that, if Tunisia were in a geographic neighborhood like that of East Asia, it could have achieved much stronger economic growth performance and technological upgrading. Tunisia did not have the opportunities offered in the East Asian region of being integrated into much more highly integrated regional networks and supply chains. Moreover, the networks that it did have did not undergo the dynamics that those of East Asia did. East Asia had an initially well developed and very dynamic Japan, but followed over time at different stages of the region's development, with the emergence of Korea in the 1970s and especially China beginning in the 1990s, each playing the leading roles in this process. Intra-regional trade and investment played substantial and indeed transformative roles, but always very much within openly competitive systems, in which many positive externalities could be generated. By contrast, Tunisia has operated in an environment wherein its closest neighbors have long been of similar income levels and economic structures.

For economies like Tunisia's, one trade strategy that has been used successfully is opening up free trade arrangements among nearby countries and by encouraging intra-industry trade and taking advantage of different kinds of within-sector specializations. Yet, as we saw in Chapter 5, Tunisia's attempts to engage in trade agreements of this sort with neighboring countries have proved not to be successful.

The two neighborhoods had therefore been very different. Tunisia and its neighbors were always at fairly similar levels of development and reflected quite similar comparative advantages. On the other hand, as stressed by

Studwell (2013), the East Asian countries were remarkably heterogeneous in terms of income per capita, institutional development, and economic structure, Japan, Korea, and later China being industrial, the small island states like Singapore and Hong Kong serving as Service Sector hubs, and Indonesia as a natural resource hub. Comparative advantages, therefore, were very much in evidence and proved to be taken advantage of throughout the period under study. Without clear comparative advantages among Tunisia and its most immediate neighbors, trade did not develop very substantially. While Tunisia and some of its neighbors took some steps toward somewhat closer integration with the European Union in the 1990s, over time Europe started to pay much more attention to trade with Eastern Europe after this, and the MENA countries that did sign agreements with European countries did not do much in the way of integration among each other as the European Union had hoped. Indeed, the so-called Maghreb Customs Union to which Tunisia was supposed to work out with Algeria, Morocco, Libya, and Mauritania has never been implemented, reflecting lack of cooperation among their respective governments. Even the much more recently formed Agadir Agreement involving Tunisia, Morocco, Jordan, and Egypt as noted above has failed to achieve any effective integration based on comparative advantages. More broadly, the attempt to form a broader and more encompassing trade agreement among Arab countries (GAFTA) has not succeeded.

Another key difference between the two neighborhoods, that is, Tunisia and the countries bordering it, Algeria and Libya, and the East Asian countries, arise from the importance of subsidies on key products traded in the MENA region but the general absence of subsidies among the goods traded in East Asia. Some of the largest subsidies are in commodities like petroleum products whose prices in Algeria and Libya are highly subsidized for nationals of these countries so as to comply with the authoritarian bargain in those countries. Since Tunisia and other surrounding countries which are not major exporters of petroleum products do not subsidize such products, there is naturally a large incentive for smuggling the subsidized items from Algeria and Libya into Tunisia and other neighboring countries like Egypt and Morocco. A straightforward way of doing business through formal channels would be for Algeria and Libya to collect tolls on these products at the border. In the case of land borders, however, since there can be many border crossing points, making it extremely difficult to monitor them, and thereby collect the appropriate taxes, informal trade or smuggling is a very common practice. Even so, it is a costly and inefficient process, the smuggled items generally being transported in very small, hard to detect shipments. Ayadi et al. (2013) did a study on Tunisia's land trade with Algeria and Libya. Despite the small size of the different shipments at these land borders, in both cases, the total official trade between them was only a fraction of the total trade (formal plus informal). The illegality of this trade makes its management and closely related provision of security to people near these land borders rather problematic.

As Henry and Springborg (2001, 43) pointed out long ago, even though Tunisia has achieved somewhat higher intra-industry trade index scores than its neighbors, its scores have remained well below half those of both Asian and European Union countries.

One part of Tunisia's neighborhood which does possess considerable differences in factor endowments and the potential for taking advantage of comparative advantages through trade is the bloc of countries immediately to the south, such as Chad, Mali, Mauritania, and Niger, and along the coast to the South and West such as Senegal, Gambia, Cameroon, Guinea, Sierra Leone, Ghana, and Nigeria. Since many of these countries are French-speaking like Tunisia, this should also be trade facilitating. But to accomplish this, Tunisian firms and policymakers will need to become much better acquainted with institutional rules and to be in a position to bargain for changes where needed. A major step in that direction would be for Tunisia to sign onto the African Continental Free Trade Area and for that free trade area to come into existence. De Melo et al. (2021) provide an up-to-date assessment of where things stand, showing that much progress has been made but also that there is need for further harmonizing on Rules of Origin, tariff rates on relatively high tariff items and ensuring that the rules turn out to be 'business friendly rather than business-owned in the sense of penalizing small firms by their complexity' (p. 7).

It is most likely that all factors identified in these hypotheses did play, at least some role, in this disappointing outcome. The most serious challenge is to quantify their relative importance and the extent to which and how they may have changed over time.

Until such time in the years ahead that we can see if Tunisia's neighborhood can be changed in a positive direction and Tunisia can overcome the various aforementioned factors that seem to have held it in a MIT, it leaves us with two even more challenging new questions. First, why, despite its relative success, did Tunisia become the first country in the MENA region to experience the political upheaval and uprisings in the early 2010s which led to the collapse of its political regime? And then second, how and why has Tunisia's engagement into a slow and difficult political transition toward democracy led to a major economic collapse?

In a way, it could be argued that it was the failure to achieve a performance on par with successful East Asian countries which adopted a new innovation-based growth path that was a major factor in the occurrence of the uprisings. The moderate economic growth during the 1990s, its slowdown during the 2000s, and further decline following the great recession led to not only higher unemployment and pressures in the labor markets but also to higher rates of informality among private firms. The limited structural transformation and weak demand for higher skills in recent years, despite an increasingly educated youth work force and the expressed need of firms to employ more skilled workers resulted not in the kind of transition to an innovation-oriented economy that would have been desirable but only to even higher unemployment rates for the tertiary education graduates, inducing larger portions of the workforce to accept the only available jobs in the informal sector. Weak growth reduced the ability of government to pursue stronger redistribution policies aimed at helping those left behind, including those in lagging regions of the country. Those were the immediate triggers of the uprisings and which resulted in the collapse of the political regime.

Such an argument fails to recognize that these problems and challenges were not worse in Tunisia than in other countries, and that some social progress indicators were much better in Tunisia than elsewhere, such as reduced poverty, improved health and education, higher life expectancy, and even lower inequality as measured traditionally. Even with lower growth, these indicators continued to improve.

So, what went wrong in Tunisia? In a nutshell, what we have seen is that the population's perceptions about well-being soured in Tunisia at the time of the uprisings, and they have only worsened since then. The lack of trust in political and state institutions, especially the trust in courts, in government and private services resulting from alarming increases in corruption, has led even further to more instability, turmoil and, even more recently, the emergence of populism in the wake of the 2019 elections (Brumberg 2021; International Crisis Group 2020). Tunisia continues its struggle to reconcile economic and social progress with democracy, and at the same time to improve the well-being of its citizens.

B. Looking Forward, Lessons, and Implications

As the writing of this book was being completed at the end of 2021, Tunisia entered a new and more turbulent phase of its history, with a major new political shock. This shock illustrates the continuing struggle of the country to maintain its democratic gains, and at the same time to undertake a badly needed economic recovery. On July 25, 2021, President Kais Saied, who was elected democratically with a large majority in 2019, but with limited constitutional powers, took drastic and unprecedented measures. These measures included suspending ('freezing' in the official terminology) the Parliament and dismissing the Government (elected by Parliament), accusing them of corrupt practices, utter mismanagement, and failure to deal with the country's many problems, including the highest rate of COVID deaths per capita in the MENA region during the first half of 2021. In September, he issued a decree giving himself all powers, effectively suspending the Constitution. The democratic process was brought to a halt, and another political reform process has been started. This turn of events has jeopardized any claims that Tunisia was still on the path of a democratic transition. The country continues to be mired in an all-encompassing political, economic, and social crisis. The populist and autocratic tendencies and temptations of the President are taking the country on an uncertain path.

The country is now far from its search of an East Asian-type economic miracle. The elusive search is over, and the country is in deep crisis, with its institutions in disarray, and its capacity to meet the challenges weakened. Tunisia has lost most of the favorable conditions which helped the country to achieve over the 1960–2010 period better results than most of MENA countries and even attempt to match some of the successful East Asian countries. Political instability and uncertainty have been the norm over the last decade. State capacity is weaker than it used to be, most institutions have been undermined, and its social fabric is under stress. Its macroeconomic environment is at a critical state with recurrent large budget deficits and very high public and external debt indicators. The country is in the middle of a public finance crisis. Many of its past successes, at the core of its human development achievements, such as the educational, the health, or the social protection systems, are under strain as well.

In the last decade, the contrast between the East Asian and MENA countries including Tunisia has widened considerably. Two severe shocks have been affecting growth and in particular trade: increasing protectionism and the COVID-19 which has affected long distance trade. As demonstrated by Arezki et al. (2020), these effects have been more serious on Tunisia and other neighboring MENA countries than on East Asia. For one thing, Tunisia's advantage from its integration with the EU has fallen considerably in the last 15 years since the tariff reductions on Tunisian and other Southern Mediterranean countries had all occurred by 2006, whereas since then the EU has lowered its tariffs on many other countries. Also, between 2000 and 2020, non-tariff measures including special regulations on food and other agricultural products of relevance to Tunisia were shown to have tripled and technical barriers including pre-shipment inspections relevant to manufactures to have doubled. Arezki et al. (2020) identify the SSA region as the most promising region for Tunisia and other Maghreb countries to liberalize with (because of the geographic proximity and different comparative advantages) but show that tariff barriers between these two sets of countries have increased significantly. Even more than intra-MENA and MENA-SSA regional integration, they point to the need for greater GVC participation They see greater GVC participation by Tunisia and other neighboring countries as a means of achieving each of the following growth and welfare improving mechanisms: (1) raising youth employment and raising the value of educated youth, (2) attracting FDI, (3) increasing employment of the region's blue collar workers that are engaged in its manufacturing, (4) increasing access to information and technology and thereby raising Tunisia's currently low share of high technology exports. To accomplish these improvements, they identify the following pre-conditions to be satisfied: to reduce and homogenize tariffs and non-tariff barriers across products and countries, to improve political stability (so as to reduce policy uncertainty and thereby its harmful effects on long-term investments), raise efficiency in customs and the quality of logistics (Tunisia's said to be some 30% below that of China), reduce trade costs by investing in ICT, and integrate the numerous SMEs and new entrepreneurs into the GVCs to take better advantage of different comparative advantages across firms and sectors. Many of these pre-conditions have already been accomplished in the successful East Asian countries.

The weaknesses which have been identified compared to East Asia have become deeper. Economic growth is anemic, productivity growth is lower, and rates of savings and investment are at an all-time low. Inefficiencies, distortions, and rent-seeking continue to prevail. Structural transformation and industrial upgrading have stalled. The levels of unemployment are extremely high, especially for youth and women, and regional and social inequalities are deepening. The heavy hand of the state, with its increased inefficiencies, and the weakness of the private sector have become even more stark. Lying behind many of these inefficiencies, is the absence of active networking among firms, such as business associations and other low-cost means of reducing the deficiency of information about other possible business partners and lowering the high transaction costs of inter-firm transactions, especially in circumstances where courts are increasingly seen as obstacles to business. If China, even as a communist country, could manage to allow its private firms to join in a large business association which has led to very considerable collaboration between government and private firms on the one hand and more importantly among private firms allowing several of them to become among the most impressive high-tech firms in the world, why can't Tunisia do at least something like this? As noted above, China's business association seems to have contributed substantially to explaining why China was the only country in the world whose exports and GDP growth did not fall at all during the Global Financial Crisis of 2008–2009 (Lei and Nugent 2018).

One cannot but hypothesize that the same *fundamental weaknesses* identified above in this chapter as the sources of the failure to achieve success in the earlier decades (since the 1980s), and which led to the collapse of the political regime in 2011, are also the source of the more recent events leading to the current dismal situation. The recent period has also lacked strong and visionary leadership. Short-term politics, which focused on gaining and keeping power, have become the rule, with loyalty as the main incentive. This has meant that reforms were stalled, and public expenditures were the main instrument used by politicians to gain support. The failure to change, adapt, and reform its policies and institutions to join the bandwagon of the successful countries, which was behind the uprisings and the collapse of the regime, continued to prevail. The political institutions remained weak and ineffective, and the management of the economy disastrous. The country accumulated the failures, leading to the new populist phase with its very uncertain and dangerous consequences. During the recent period the regional neighborhood for Tunisia has been mired in conflict, instability, and economic stagnation. Neighboring Libya, one of its main trading and investment partners, has been in civil war, affecting Tunisia in significant ways, economically, politically and in terms of security.

It would be tempting to draw direct lessons from our analysis and findings and suggest that Tunisia just needs to adjust and correct its weaknesses by following the 'successful' past experiences of East Asia. This could involve reforms to strengthen the role of markets and that of the private sector. It could be about better industrial policies or a stronger financial sector, and any of the other policies and institutions which differentiated the Tunisian experience from the more successful East Asian countries.

But this would be a serious mistake. Looking forward, we do not think this is the main message of the book. The situation is very different today, as the country has already lost most of its favorable conditions, and is under tremendous pressures, as it struggles with its democratic transition, and faces serious political, social, economic, and institutional difficulties. While its demographics are changing more favorably, with a much lower rate of growth in the labor force,[3] new challenges, and risks are emerging. Three major challenges stand out as the most significant and critical going forward: technological change and digital transformation, the changing context of globalization, and climate change.

Digitalization is changing the landscape and potential for development, all over the world. New technologies are taking over, driven by automation, artificial intelligence, and robotization. These technologies are disruptive, and in both advanced and emerging countries, are changing the way production and distribution of products and services are organized, the structure and shape of GVCs, global trade, and the nature of work, with potentially huge but uncertain implications in terms of productivity, employment, and inequality. While the economic impact of these changes on the Arab countries has been limited until now, it could become significant over the coming period (Fardoust and Nabli 2022), and business associations or other linking mechanisms could play an important role in this.

Tunisia has made progress in terms of infrastructure and access to digital services (Ben Youssef 2021). This has been the case especially for those individuals making greater use of digital platforms and the internet. But, as in most MENA countries, the adoption of digital technologies by businesses has been very limited. Expansion of e-commerce and Fintech has progressed little, and the digitalization of production in most sectors remains weak. As a result, the impact of digitalization on productivity and employment is still hardly observable, despite the dynamism shown by start-ups in the ICT sector. Tunisia has lagged very far behind the most advanced and successful East Asian countries. Tunisia needs to harness these technologies as the world economy changes, creating both opportunities and challenges.

But digitalization could also play an important role in the public sector and the miss-match between employee skills and job requirements. As Assaad and Barsoum (2019) have pointed out, Tunisia like other MENA countries has been experiencing considerable aging of the public sector workforce, which provides an opportunity to upgrade the skills in public administration as hirings pick up, With digitalization being increasingly useful in public sector activities, it would make sense that much more emphasis should be given to digital capabilities in such hiring, and thereby giving greater emphasis to the importance of teaching digital skills at all levels of education.

The second major challenge, which is also to a large extent related to digitalization, concerns the ongoing changes in the *context of globalization*. From the 1970s to the mid-2000s, the East Asian countries, benefitted from the ability to access international markets without restrictions in a way which was quite exceptional. The expansion of trade in manufacturing products and thereby being inserted into GVCs, allowed those countries to take advantage of their lower cost of labor. Yet, low-cost labor may no longer be a main driver for exports growth for developing countries, especially since much of the world has become much more protective. Technological, political, and geopolitical factors are changing the shape of international relations and globalization. This will make avoiding the Middle-Income Trap and achieving convergence much more difficult.

The third major challenge for Tunisia is *climate change*. The country is ranked 64th out of 181 countries based on an index of vulnerability to climate change in 2019 (World Bank 2021). Climate change is likely to imply for Tunisia increased temperatures, less precipitation, increased aridity, and rising sea levels. This may have dramatic impacts on the availability of water, food production and security, and economic sectors dependent on climate, such as fishing and tourism.

The new challenges and the changed domestic political situation are such that the tasks facing Tunisia are daunting. There are no easy and straightforward answers. There are, however, a few fundamental lessons which can be drawn from our comparative analysis of Tunisia's experience with other MENA and with East Asia and which remain useful going forward. Assuming the country succeeds in regaining stable and effective political institutions, and in overcoming the current fiscal crisis, the following are a few such lessons which can be advanced.

First, the country needs to make sure it has a *long-term vision* which guides its policies and reform agenda. This requires empowering *a visionary leadership,* and actively dealing with the major challenges of digitalization, and more generally of rapid technological change, in facing the new challenges in globalization and climate change.

Second, Tunisia needs to *preserve or regain the major fundamental strengths* it has so successfully achieved in the past. These include three major pillars: (i) to focus on human capital accumulation, along with sufficient upgrading and reforms of institutions, and especially those in health and education so as to better match them with the needs of their firms in the years ahead, (ii) to focus on inclusive social policies and the reduction of inequalities (including regional ones), and (iii) to maintain macroeconomic stability.

Third, the country needs to develop and empower institutions which make it agile in adapting in time to changing circumstances and to ensure that it does not get stuck with old choices and institutions. All too often, Tunisia's institutions have failed to change or adapt to changing conditions.

Fourth, the country needs to make sure that there is always a continuing balance between the roles of the state and markets, and not to let one dimension dominate over the other. The country still needs, even more than before, a strong state and a very active one. The country must *rebuild its state capacity*, make it stronger and more effective, but it should become less heavy-handed. But, it will also need to provide for a greater role for markets and the private sector so as to be able to adapt and take advantage of the rapidly evolving global context for technological change and GVCs.

Fifth, the country needs a strong and dynamic industrial policy which would combine the strength of the state and the private sector, and would focus on basic objectives rather than on particular policy instruments. Such a strategy would focus on structural transformation, innovation, and the 'creation of good jobs.'

Notes

1 The GNI Atlas method in 2010 of $4130 is to be compared to GNI per capita in 2010 constant prices of $3947.

2 Having been in that category for more than 28 years, which is the threshold defined as the median number of years it has taken the 9 countries who since 1950 have transitioned from lower-middle income to upper-middle income countries.

3 According to the UN Population Prospects, the working-age population (15–64 years old) will increase by 0.5–0.6% per year during the 2020–2040 period, compared to a rate of increase of 3.3% per year during 1980–1990, 2.6% during 1990–2000, 1.8% during 2000–2010 and 0.7% during 2010–2020 (see Table 2.9).

References

Abadie, Alberto, Alexis Diamond and Jens Hainmuller, 2015. "Comparative Politics and the Synthetic Control Method", *American Journal of Political Science*. 59 (2), pp. 495–510.

Abdallah, Ali and Philippe Adair, 2007. "The Paradox of Investment in the Tunisian Tourism Sector: Overcapacities, Rent and Governance". Paper presented at the 6th International Conference of the Middle East Economic Association, Dubai, March.

Abdelbary, Islam, 2021. *Reviving Arab Reform: Development Challenges and Opportunities*. London: Emerald.

Abdessalem, Tahar, 2011. "Scope, Relevance and Challenges of Financing Higher Education: the Case of Tunisia", *Prospects: Quarterly Review of Comparative Education*. XLI (41), 1/157, pp. 135–155, UNESCO.

Abedini, Javad and Nicolas Peridy, 2008. "The Greater Arab Free Trade Area (GAFTA): an Estimation of Its Trade Effects", *Journal of Economic Integration*. 23 (4), pp. 848–872.

Abrahart, Alan, Iqbal Kaur and Zafiris Tzannatos, 2002. "Government Employment and Active Labor Market Policies in MENA In a Comparative International Context", in Heba Handoussa and Zafiris Tzannatos (editors), *Employment Creation and Social Protection in the Middle East and North Africa*. Cairo: American University in Cairo Press.

Acemoglu, Daron, Philippe Aghion and Fabrizio Zilibotti, 2006. "Distance to the Frontier, Selection and Economic Growth", *Journal of the European Economic Association*. 4 (1), pp. 37–74.

Acemoglu, Daron and Jorn-Steffen Pischke, 1998. "Why Do Firms Train? Theory and Evidence", *The Quarterly Journal of Economics*. 113 (1), pp. 79–119.

Acemoglu, Daron and James A. Robinson, 2006. *Economic Origins of Dictatorship and Democracy*. Cambridge: Cambridge University Press.

Acemoglu, Daron and James A. Robinson, 2012. *Why Nations Fail: The Origins of Power, Prosperity and Poverty*. New York: Crown Publishers.

Acemoglu, Daron, Suresh Naidu, Pascual Restrepo and James A Robinson, 2019. "Democracy Does Cause Growth", *Journal of Political Economy*. 127 (11), pp. 47–101.

Adams, Richard H. Jr. and John M. Page, 2003. "Poverty, Inequality and Growth in Selected Middle East and North Africa Countries", *World Development*. 31 (12), pp. 2017–2048.

Adams, Zoe, Louise Bishop and Simon Deakin, 2016, "CBR Labour Regulation Index: Dataset of 117 Countries". Cambridge: Centre for Business Research.

Addison, Tony and Mina Baliamoune-Lutz, 2006. "Economic Reform When Institutional Quality Is Weak: The Case of the Maghreb", *Journal of Policy Modeling.* 28 (9), pp. 1029–1043.

African Development Bank (AfDB), 2011. *The Middle of the Pyramid: Dynamics of the Middle Class in Africa*, Market Brief, April 20.

African Development Bank (AfDB), 2012. *Distortions to Agricultural Policy Incentives in Tunisia: A Preliminary Analysis*, Economic Brief.

Agénor, Pierre-Richard and Karim Al-Aynaoui, 2003. "Labor Market Policies and Unemployment in Morocco: A Quantitative Analysis", World Bank Policy Research Working Paper No. 3091. July.

Agénor, Pierre-Richard and Otaviano Canuto, 2015. "Middle Income Growth Traps", *Research in Economics.* 69 (4), pp. 641–660.

Aghion, Philippe, Céline Antonin and Simon Bunel, 2021. *The Power of Creative Destruction: Economic Upheaval and the Wealth of Nations.* Cambridge and London: The Belknap Press of Harvard University.

Aiyar, Shekhar, Romain Duval, Damien Puy, Yiqun Wu and Longmei Zhang, 2018. "Growth Slowdowns and the Middle Income Trap", *Japan and the World Economy.* 48 (C), pp. 22–37.

Alaya, Marouane, 2020. "A Spatial Analysis of Regional Economic Growth in MENA Countries". Paper prepared for the 26th Annual Conference of the Economic Research Forum, (which was supposed to be held in Luxor, Egypt, March 28, 2020 but postponed).

Almeida, Rita and Pedro Carneiro, 2009. "Enforcement of Regulation, Informal Employment, Firm Size and Firm Performance", *Journal of Comparative Economics.* 37 (1), pp. 28–46.

Alphin, Henry C. Jr. and Jennie Lavine, 2016. "Higher Education and Philanthropy Potential in the GCC States: Analysis of Challenges and Opportunities for FDI and Venture Philanthropy in the MENA Region", Munich Personal RePEc Archive (MPRA) Paper 70781.

Al-Shboul, Mohammad, Aktham Maghyereh, Abul Hassan and Phillip Molyneux, 2020. "Political Risk and Bank Stability in the Middle East and North Africa", *Pacific Basin Finance Journal.* 60 (C), pp. 335–371.

Alvarado, Facundo and Thomas Piketty, 2014. "Measuring Top Incomes and Inequality in the Middle East", Economic Research Forum, Working Paper #832.

Amara, Mohamed and Hatem Jemmali, 2017. "On the Decomposition of Economic Inequality: A Methodology and an Application to Tunisia", Economic Research Forum Working Paper 1096.

Amico, Alissa, 2014. "Corporate Governance Enforcement in the Middle East and North Africa: Evidence and Priorities", OECD Corporate Governance Working Papers No. 13 (www.oecd.org/daf/corporateeaffairs/wp).

Amsden, Alice H., 1992. *Asia's Next Giant: South Korea and Late Industrialization.* New York: Oxford University Press.

Andersen, Jorgen J. and Michael L. Ross, 2014. "The Big Oil Change: A Closer Look at the Haber-Menaldo Analysis", *Comparative Political Studies.* 47 (7), pp. 993–1021.

Anderson, Lisa, 1986. *The State and Social Transformation in Tunisia and Libya, 1830–1980.* Princeton: Princeton University Press.

Anglo Tunisian Oil and Gas, 2010. *Foreign Oil Giants no longer interested in Tunisian Oil.* (https://anglotunisianoilandgas.com/tunisia).

Arab Barometer, 2019. *Wave V Country Reports: Algeria, Egypt, Iraq, Jordan, Kuwait, Lebanon, Libya, Morocco, Tunisia.* (https://www.arabbarometer.org/).
Arezki, Rabah, Blanca Moreno-Dodson, Rachel Yuting Fan, Romeo Gansey, Ha Nguyen, Minh Cong Nguyen, Lili Mottaghi, Constantin Tsakas and Christina Wood, 2020. *Trading Together: Reviving Middle East and North Africa Regional Integration in the Post-Covid Era.* Washington, DC: World Bank Middle East and North Africa Region.
Armendariz de Aghion, Beatriz and Jonathan Morduch, 2005. *The Economics of Microfinance.* Cambridge: MIT Press.
Arroyo, Dennis, 2008, "The Political Economy of Successful Reform: Asian Stratagems", Working Paper No. 356, Center for International Development, Stanford University.
Asian Development Bank (ADB), 2010. *Key Indicators for Asia and the Pacific 2010*, Manila, Philippines.
Asian Development Bank (ADB), 2020. *Asia's Journey to Prosperity: Policy, Market and Technology Over 50 Years.* Manila, Philippines.
Assaad, Ragui and Ghada Barsoum, 2019. "Public Employment in the Middle East and North Africa: Does a Changing Public Sector Workforce in the MENA Region Provide an Opportunity for Efficient Restructuring?", *IZA World of Labor.* Issue 463, Institue of Labor Economics (IZA).
Atiyas, Izak, Adeel Malik and Ishac Diwan, 2021. "A Pyramid of Privilege: How Cronyism Shapes Business-State Relationships in the Middle East", Chapter 20 in Hassan Hakimian (editor), *The Routledge Handbook on the Middle East Economy.* London: Routledge.
Atkin, David, Amit Khandelwal and Adam Osmani, 2014. "The Impact of Exporting: Evidence from a Randomized Trial", *Quarterly Journal of Economics.* 132 (2), pp. 557–615.
Avina, Jeffrey M. and Peter Russell, 2016. "IT Solution to Arab Youth Unemployment", *Middle East Institute Policy Focus* 2016-5, January 2016. (http://www.jstor.org/stable/resrep17593).
Ayadi, Lotfi, Nancy Benjamin, Sami Bensassi and Gael Raballand, 2013. "Estimating Informal Trade across Tunisia's Land Borders". World Bank Policy Research Working Paper 6731.
Ayres, Kelly, Ariel R. Belasen and Ali M. Kutan, 2014. "Does Inflation Targeting Lower Inflation and Spur Growth?, *Journal of Policy Modelling.* 36 (2), pp. 373–388.
Ayyagari, Meghana, Asli Demirguc-Kunt and Vojislav Maksimovic, 2011. "Small vs. Young Firms across the World: Contribution to Employment, Job Creation and Growth". World Bank Policy Research Working Paper 5631.
Ayubi, Nazih, 1997. "Etatisme Versus Privatization in Nine Arab Countries", in Heba Handoussa (editor), *Economic Transition in the Middle East: Global Challenges and Adjustment Strategies.* Cairo: American University in Cairo Press, pp.125–166.
Azabou, Mongi, Timur Kuran and Mustapha Kamel Nabli, 1989. "The Wholesale Market of Tunis and Its Porters: A Tale of Market Degeneration", in Mustapha Kamel Nabli and Jeffrey B. Nugent (editors), *The New Institutional Economics and Development: Theory and Applications to Tunisia.* Amsterdam: North Holland, pp. 352–374.
Baghdadi, Leila, Hassan Arouri and Bob Rijkers, 2019. "How Do Dictators Get Rich? State Capture in Ben Ali's Tunisia", in Ishac Diwan, Adeel Malik and Izak

Atiyas (editors), *Crony Capitalism in the Middle East: Business and Politics from Liberalization to the Arab Spring*. Oxford: Oxford University Press.

Bahmani-Oskooee, Mohsen, Thouraya Hadj Amor, Majid Maki Nayeri and Farhang Niroomand, 2019. "On the Link between Real Effective Value of Tunisia's Dinar and Its Sectoral Trade with the Rest of the World: New Evidence from Asymmetry Analysis", *The Quarterly Review of Economics and Finance*. 73 (C), pp. 111–118.

Barro, Robert and Jong-Wha Lee, 2013. (Updated in 2018). "A New Dataset of Educational Attainment in the World, 1950-2010", *Journal of Development Economics*. 104, September, pp. 184–198.

Baslevent, Cem and Ozlem Onaran, 2004. "The Effect of Export-Oriented Growth on Female Labor Market Outcomes in Turkey", *World Development*. 32 (8), (August), pp. 1375–1393.

Baud, Isabelle Suzanne Antoinette, B.H. Evers, Gerard A. Groot and Willy Wagenmans, 1977. *Jobs and Values: Social Effects of Export-Oriented Industrialization in Tunisia*. (Based on research done in Tunisia during the winter of 1976-77). Development Research Institute.

Bauluz, Luis, Yajna Govind and Filip Novokmet, 2020. Global Land Inequality World Inequality Database 10, pp. 1–24. (https://wid.world/).

Beblawi, Hazem, 1987. "The Rentier State in the Arab World", Chapter 2 in Hazem Beblawi and Giacomo Luciani (editors), *The Rentier State*. London: Routledge.

Bechri, Mohamed Z., 1989. "The Political Economy of Interest Rate Determination in Tunisia", in Mustapha Kamel Nabli and Jeffrey B. Nugent (editors), *The New Institutional Economics and Development: Theory and Applications to Tunisia*. Amsterdam: North Holland, pp. 375–403.

Bechri, Mohamed Z. and Sonia Naccache, 2007. "The Political Economy of Development Policy in Tunisia", in Jeffrey B. Nugent and Hashem Pesaran (editors), *Explaining Growth in the Middle East*. Amsterdam: Elsevier, pp. 307–334.

Bechri, Mohamed Z., Tijani Najah and Jeffrey B. Nugent, 2001. "Tunisia's Lending Program to SMEs: Anatomy of an Institutional Failure", *Small Business Economics*. 17 (4), pp. 293–308.

Beck, David and Paul Dyer, 2016. "Demographic Transitions Across the Middle East and North Africa", in Edward A. Sayre and Tarik M. Yousef (editors), *Young Generation Awakening: Economics, Society and Policy on the Eve of the Arab Spring*. Oxford: Oxford University Press, pp. 16–34.

Belev, Boyan, 2001. "Privatization in Egypt and Tunisia: Liberal Outcomes and/or Liberal Policies", *Mediterranean Politics*. 6 (2), pp. 68–103.

Bellin, Eva, 1994. "The Politics of Profit in Tunisia: Utility of the Rentier Paradigm?, *World Development*. 22 (3), pp. 427–436.

Bellin, Eva, 2002. *Stalled Democracy: Capital, Labor and the Paradox of State-Sponsored Development*. Ithaca: Cornell University Press.

Bellin, Eva, 2004. "The Robustness of Authoritarianism in the Middle East: Exceptionalism in Comparative Perspective", *Comparative Politics*. 36 (2), pp. 139–157.

Ben Braham, Mehdi and Mohamed Ali Marouani, 2016. "Determinants of Contribution Density of the Tunisian Pension System: A Cross Sectional Analysis", Economics Research Forum Working Paper 1005.

Ben Cheikh, Nidhal and Sami Bibi, 2017. *Evaluation de la Performance des Programmes d'Assistance Sociale en Tunisie: pour optimiser le ciblage des pauvres et freiner l'avancée de l'informalité*. Tunis: Centre de Recherches Economiques et Sociales (CRES).

Bencheikh, Fayrouz and Neila Boulila Taktak, 2017. "Political Connections and Debt Access: The Case of Tunisian Firms", *International Journal of Economics and Financial Issues*. 7 (3), pp. 180–185.
Ben Jelili, Riadh, 2005. "Technological Progress and in Tunisian Manufacturing Firms: Evidence from Firm-Level Panel Data", *Journal of Development and Economic Policies*. 7 (2), June.
Ben Hafaiedh, Abdelwahab and I. William Zartman, 2015. "Tunisia: Beyond the Ideological Cleavage: Something Else", in I. William Zartman (editor), *Arab Spring: Negotiating in the Shadow of the Intifadat*. Athens and London: University of Georgia Press, pp. 50–79.
Ben Khalifa, Adel, 2018. "Government Supports and Technology Adoption: Evidence from Tunisia", *Journal of Economic Development*. 43 (4), pp. 51–69.
Ben Naceur, Sami and Mohamed Omran, 2011. "The Effects of Bank Regulations, Competition, and Financial Reforms on Bank's Performance", *Emerging Market Review*. 12 (1), pp. 1–20.
Ben Salha, Ousama, 2013a. "Labor Market Outcomes of Economic Globalization in Tunisia: A Preliminary Assessment", *The Journal of North African Studies*. 18 (2), pp. 349–372.
Ben Salha, Ousama, 2013b. "Economic Globalization, Wages and Wage Inequality in Tunisia: An ARDL Bounds Testing Approach", *Review of Middle East Economics and Finance*. 9 (3), pp. 321–356.
Ben Salha, Ousama, 2013c. "Does Economic Globalization Affect the Level and Volatility of Labor Demand by Skill? New Insights from the Tunisian Manufacturing Industries", *Economic Systems*. 37 (4), pp. 572–597.
Ben Youssef, Adel, 2021. "Digital Transformation in Tunisia: Under which Conditions Could the Digital Economy Benefit Everyone?", Economic Research Forum Working Paper No. 1512, November.
Berger, Helge, Jakob de Haan and Sylvester C.W. Eijffinger, 2008. "Central Bank Independence: An Update of Theory and Evidence", *Journal of Economic Surveys*. 15 (1), pp. 3–36.
Bernanke, Ben S., 1983. "Irreversibility, Uncertainty and Cyclical Investment", *The Quarterly Journal of Economics*. 98 (1), February, pp. 85–106.
Bertelsmann Stiftung: Bertelsmann Transformation Indexes (https:/bti-project.org/en/index).
Beschel, Robert P. Jr and Tarik M. Yousef, 2021. "Conclusion: Making Sense of It All", in Robert P. Beschel Jr and Tarik M. Yousef (editors), *Public Sector Reform in the Middle East and North Africa: Lessons of Experience for a Region in Transition*. Washington, DC: Brookings Institution Press.
Besley, Timothy and Torsten Persson, 2009. "The Origins of State Capacity: Property Rights, Taxation and Politics", *American Economic Review*. 99 (4), pp. 1218–1244.
Birdsall, Nancy and Richard H. Sabot, 1993. "Virtuous Circles: Human Capital Growth and Equity in East Asia", Background paper for World Bank, The East Asian Miracle 1993.
Bivand, Roger and Rolf Jens Brundstad, 2006. "Regional Growth in Western Europe: Detecting Spatial Misspecification using the R Environment", *Papers in Regional Science*. 85 (2), pp. 277–297.
Blonigen, Bruce A., Ronald B. Davies, Glen R. Waddell and Helen T. Naughton, 2007. "FDI in Space: Spatial Autoregressive Relationship in Foreign Direct Investment", *European Economic Review*. 51 (5), pp. 1303–1325.

Bloom, Nicholas, 2014. "Fluctuations in Uncertainty", *Journal of Economic Perspectives*. 28 (2), Spring, pp. 153–176.

Bockstette, Valerie, Areendam Chanda and Louis Putterman, 2002. "States and Markets: The Advantage of an Early Start", *Journal of Economic Growth*. 7 (4), New York: Springer, pp. 347–369.

Boughanmi, Houcine, 1995. "Les Principaux Volets des Politiques agricoles en Tunisie: évolution, analyse et performances agricoles", in Mahmoud Allaya (editor), *Les Agricultures Maghrébines à l'Aube de l'An 2000*. Montpellier: CIHEAM, pp. 127–138 (Options Méditerranéennes: Série B, Etudes et Recherches, n. 14).

Boughrara, Adel, 2007. "Can Tunisia Move to Inflation Targeting?", *The Developing Economies*. XLV (1), pp. 27–62.

Boughrara, Adel, Mongi Boughzala and Hassouna Moussa, 2008. "Inflation Targeting and Financial Fragility in Tunisia", Chapter 6 in David Cobham and Ghassan Dibeh (editors), *Monetary Policy and Central Banking in the Middle East and North Africa*. London: Routledge.

Boughzala, Mongi, 2001. "Budget Institutions and Expenditure Performance in Tunisia", University of Tunis El Manar, Working Paper. January.

Boughzala, Mongi, 2018. "Employment and Functioning of the Labor Market", in Ragui Assaad and Mongi Boughzala (editors), *The Tunisian Labor Market in an Era of Transition*. Oxford: Oxford University Press, pp. 61–85.

Boughzala, Mongi and Saousen Ben Romdhane, 2017. "Tunisia: The Prospects for Democratic Consolidation", in Ibrahim Elbadawi and Samir Makdisi (editors), *Democratic Transitions in the Arab World*. Cambridge: Cambridge University Press.

Boughzala, Mongi and Hassouna Moussa, 2011. "The Uncertain Journey Toward Inflation Targeting in Tunisia", Chapter 10 in Mongi Boughzala and David Cobham (editors), *Inflation Targeting in MENA Countries: An Unfinished Journey*. London: Palgrave Macmillan.

Boulakia, Jean David C., 1971. "Ibn Khaldun: A Fourteenth-Century Economist", *Journal of Political Economy*. 79 (5), pp. 1105–1118.

Boularès, Habib, 2011. *Histoire de la Tunisie: les Grandes Dates de la Préhistoire à la Révolution*. Tunis: Cérès Editions.

Braham, Rihem, Christian de Peretti and Lotfi Belkacem, 2020. "The Role of Political Patronage on Risk-Taking Behavior of Banks in the Middle East and North Africa Region", *Research in International Business and Finance*. 53, Amsterdam: Elsevier, pp. 1–14.

Breuer, Andrea, Todd Landman and Dorothea Farquhar, 2015. "Social Media and Protest Mobilization: Evidence from the Tunisian Revolution", *Democratization Journal*. 22 (4), pp. 764–792.

Brown, Leon Carl, 1964. "Stages in the Process of Change", in Charles A. Micaud (editor), *Tunisia: The Politics of Modernization*. New York: Praeger.

Brumberg, Daniel, 2021. *As 2021 Begins, Rival Populisms Menace Tunisia's Democracy*. Washington DC: Arab Center, January.

Bsaies, Abdeljabbar, 1989. "Educational Change and the Ulama in the 19th and Early 20th Centuries", in Mustapha Kamel Nabli and Jeffrey B. Nugent (editors), *The New Institutional Economics and Development: Theory and Applications to Tunisia*. Amsterdam: North Holland.

Bustos, Sebastian and Muhammed Ali Yildirim, 2017. *Tunisia's Manufacturing Sector*. The Lebanese Center for Policy Studies, Policy Paper, August.

Cammett, Melani Claire, 2007. *Globalization and Business Politics in Arab North Africa*. Cambridge: Cambridge University Press.

Campos, Jose Edgardo and Hilton L. Root, 2001. *The Key to the Asia Miracle: Making Shared Growth Credible.* Washington, DC: The Brookings Institution.
Campos, Nauro F. and Jeffrey B. Nugent, 2018. "The Dynamics of the Regulation of Labour in Developing and Developed Countries Since 1960", in Nauro Campos, Paul de Grauwe and Yuemei Ji (editors), *The Political Economy of Structural Reforms in Europe.* Oxford: Oxford University Press, pp. 75–89.
Carruth, Alan, Andy Dickerson and Andrew Henley, 2000. "What Do We Know About Investment Under Uncertainty", *Journal of Economic Surveys.* 14 (2), pp. 119–154.
Charrad, Mounira, 2001. *States and Women's Rights: The Making of Postcolonial Tunisia, Algeria and Morocco.* Berkeley: University of California Press.
Chauffour, Jean-Pierre and Jose L. Diaz-Sanchez, 2021. "Tackling Market Distortions to Rise Productivity: A Study Using Firm-Level Manufacturing Sector Data from Morocco", *Middle East Development Journal.* 13 (1), pp. 172–190.
Chebbi, Ali, 2019. "How to Enlarge the Fiscal Space and Gain Efficiency When Adopting Automatic Fuel Pricing Mechanisms? The Tunisian Case", *The Quarterly Review of Economics and Finance.* 73, August, pp. 34–43.
Chen, Shaohua and Martin Ravallion, 2008. "The Developing World is Poorer than We Thought, but No Less Successful in the Fight Against Poverty", World Bank Policy Research Working Paper 4703, August. (Source of data cited in Table 1.2).
Cherif, Reda and Fuad Hasanov, 2019. "The Return of the Policy that Shall Not be Named: Principles of Industrial Policy", International Monetary Fund Working Paper WP/19/74.
Chockri, Adnen and Ibticem Frihka, 2011. "La Portée de la Politique de Ciblage d'Inflation: Approche Analytique et Empirique pour le Cas Tunisien", *Panoeconomicus.* 1, pp. 91–111.
Commission on Growth and Development, 2008. *The Growth Report: Strategies for Sustained Growth and Inclusive Development.* Washington, DC: International Bank for Reconstruction and Development.
Conseil du Marché Financier, 2002. *Etude de Diagnostic et de Recommandations pour le Développement des Marchés de Capitaux en Tunisie.* Report by "Smart Finance" and "GMA Capital Markets". May, Tunis.
Conseil du Marché Financier, 2003–2019. *Annual Reports.* Tunis.
Corden, W. Max, 1984. "Booming Sector and Dutch Disease Economics: Survey and Consolidation", *Oxford Economic Papers.* 36 (3), pp. 359–380.
Cottani, Joaquim A., Domingo F. Cavallo and M. Shahbaz Khan, 1990. "Real Exchange Rate Behavior and Economic Performance in LDCs", *Economic Development and Cultural Change.* 39 (1), pp. 61–76.
Cukierman, Alex, Stephen B. Webb and Bilin Neyapti, 1992. "Measuring the Independence of Central Banks and Its Effect on Policy Outcomes", *World Bank Economic Review.* 6, pp. 353–398.
Dang, Vinh Q.T., Erin P.K. So and Isabel K.M. Yan, 2018. "The Value of Political Connection: Evidence from the 2011 Egyptian Revolution", *International Review of Economics and Finance.* 56, pp. 238–257.
Dasgupta, Sukti and Ajit Singh, 2005. "Will Services Be the New Engine of Indian Economic Growth", *Development and Change.* 36 (6), pp. 1035–1057.
David, Anda and Mohamed Ali Marouani, 2013. "The Impact of Labor Mobility on Unemployment: A Comparison between Jordan and Tunisia", Fourth Conference

of the GDRI-DREEM Evaluation of Economic Policies and Institutional Changes in Mediterranean Countries 2013/09, Florence, Italy.

Dee, Philippa and Ndiame Diop, 2010. "The Economy-Wide Effects of Further Trade Reforms in Tunisia's Services Sectors", World Bank, Policy Research Working Paper 5341.

Deininger, Klaus, 2003. *Land Policies for Growth and Poverty Reduction.* A World Bank Policy Research Report, Oxford University Press.

Deininger, Klaus, Songqing Jin and Hari Nagarayan, 2007. "Land Reforms, Poverty Reduction and Economic Growth: Evidence from India", World Bank Policy Research Working Paper #4448, December.

Deininger, Klaus and Lyn Squire, 1998. "New Ways of Looking at Old Issues: Inequality and Growth", *Journal of Development Economics.* 57 (2), pp. 259–287.

Delaney, Colin, 2011. "How Social Media Accelerated Tunisia's Revolution: An Inside View", (https://www.huffpost.com/entry/how-social-media-accelera_b_821497#).

De Melo, Jaime, Dzmitry Kniahin, Julien Gourdon and Mondher Mimouni, 2021. "Harmonizing Rules of Origin for the African Continental Free Trade Area", The Forum, Economic Research Forum, June 22.

Deverajan, Shantayan and Elena Ianchovicha, 2018. "A Broken Social Contract, Not High Inequality, Led to the Arab Spring", *Review of Income and Wealth.* 64 (s1), pp. 5–25.

Devlin, Julia C., 2010. *Challenges of Economic Development in the Middle East and North Africa Region.* New Jersey: World Scientific.

Devlin, Julia C., 2016. *Economics of the Middle East: Development Challenges.* New Jersey: World Scientific.

Dhaoui, Souad and Iheb Samoud, 2016. "Investissement Direct Etranger et Transfert de Technologie: Cas des Industries Manufacturières en Tunisie", Notes et Analyses no. 35, Institut Tunisien de la Compétitivité et des Etudes Quantitatives.

Dillman, Bradford, 1998. "The Political Economy of Structural Adjustment in Algeria and Tunisia", *The Journal of North African Studies.* 3 (3), pp. 1–24.

Diwan, Ishac, 2013. "Understanding Revolution in the Middle East: The Central Role of the Middle Class", *The Middle East Development Journal.* 5 (1). (https://doi.org/10.1142/S1793812013500041).

Diwan, Ishac and Marc Schiffbauer, 2018. "Private Banking and Crony Capitalism in Egypt", *Business and Politics.* Cambridge: Cambridge University Press, pp. 1–20.

Diwan, Ishac, Zafiris Tzannatos and Tarik Akin, 2018. "Debunking Myth: Economic Values in the Arab World Through the Prism of Opinion Polls", *The Middle East Development Journal.* 10 (1), pp. 31–63.

Dixit, Robert K. and Robert S. Pindyck, 1994. *Investment Under Uncertainty.* Princeton: Princeton University Press.

Doner, Richard F. and Ben Ross Schneider, 2016. "The Middle-Income Trap: More Politics than Economics", *World Politics.* 68 (4), October, pp. 608–644.

Dreher, Axel, 2006. "Does Globalization Affect Growth? Evidence from a New Index of Globalization", *Applied Economics.* 38 (10), pp. 1091–1110.

Dreher, Axel and Noel Gaston, 2008. "Has Globalization Increased Inequality?, *Review of International Economics.* 16 (2), pp. 516–536.

Dreisbach, Tristan, 2021. "Enhancing Transparency in Post-Revolutionary Tunisia", Chapter 7 in Robert P. Beschel and Tarik M. Yousef (editors), *Public Sector Reform in the Middle East and North Africa: Lessons of Experience for a Region in Transition.* Washington, DC: Brookings Institution Press, pp. 139–166.

Duc, Cindy and Emmanuelle Lavallée, 2006. "Do Euro-Med Agreements Improve Democracy and the Quality of Institutions in EU Partner Countries?". Paper Presented at the Fifth International Conference of the Middle East Economic Association, Sousse, Tunisia.

Durupty, Michel, 1986. "La Vie Administrative à l'Etranger: La Restructuration du Secteur Public en Tunisie", *La Revue Administrative*. 39ème Année, No. 231, pp. 285–287, Mai-Juin, Presses Universitaires de France.

Easterly, William and Ross Levine, 1997. "Africa's Growth Tragedy: policies and ethnic divisions", *The Quarterly Journal of Economics*. 112 (4), Oxford: Oxford University Press, pp. 1203–1250.

Economic and Social Commission for West Asia (ESCWA), 2011. *Central Bank Independence and Its Effect on Inflation in the ESCWA Countries*. Beirut: United Nations ESCWA.

Economic and Social Commission for West Asia (ESCWA), 2014. *Arab Middle Class: Measurement and Role in Driving Change*. Beirut: United Nations.

Economic and Social Commission for West Asia (ESCWA), 2016. *Social Protection Country Profile: Tunisia*. November, Beirut: United Nations.

Edwards, Sebastian, 1988. "Real and Monetary Determinants of Real Exchange Rate Behavior: Theory and Evidence from Developing Countries", *Journal of Development Economics*. 29 (3), pp. 311–341.

El-Araby, Ashraf, 2011. "A Comparative Assessment of Higher Education Financing in Six Arab Countries", *Prospects*. 41 (1), 1/157, pp. 9–21.

Elbadawi, Ibrahim and Hoda Selim (editors), 2016. *Understanding and Avoiding the Oil Curse in Resource-Rich Arab Countries*. Cambridge: Cambridge University Press.

El-Haddad, Amirah, 2008. "Vertical Integration and Institutional Constraints on Firm Behavior: The Case of the Garment Industry in Egypt", Economic Research Forum, Working Paper 383.

El-Haddad, Amirah, 2010. "Egypt Versus South Korea: Divergent Paths to Industrialization", in Abdullah Shehata (editor), *Role of the State in a Mixed Economy*. Cairo: Partners in Development.

El-Haddad, Amirah, 2013. "Political Patronage and Economic Opportunity: The Case of Vertical Integration in the Egyptian Clothing Industry", Economic Research Forum Working Paper 797.

El-Haddad, Amirah, 2020. "Redefining the Social Contract in the Wake of the Arab Spring: The Experiences of Egypt, Morocco and Tunisia", *World Development*. 127 (C), March. (https://doi.org/10.1016/j.worlddev.2019.104774).

El Ouardani, Hajer and Samir Makdisi, 2018. "Autocracy, Democracy and Populism in the Arab region with Reference to Tunisia", *Orient*. IV (59), pp. 70–77.

El-Said, Hamed, 2008. "Faith-Based Organizations and Welfare Provisions in the Arab World: The Cases of Jordan and Morocco". Paper presented at the Development without Developmental States: Latin America and MENA Compared at the University of California, San Diego, April 25–26.

Englehart, Neil A, 2009. "State Capacity, State Failure, and Human Rights", *Journal of Peace Research*. 46 (2), pp. 163–180.

Epstein, Stephan R., 2000. *Freedom and Growth: The Rise of States and Markets in Europe*. London: Routledge, Taylor and Francis Group.

Erdle, Steffen, 2011. "Industrial Policy in Tunisia", German Development Institute Discussion Paper 1, Bonn.

Esfahani, Hadi Salehi and Lyn Squire, 2007. "Explaining Trade Policy in the Middle East and North Africa", *The Quarterly Review of Economics and Finance*. 46 (5), pp. 660–684.

European Bank for Reconstruction and Development, European Investment Bank and World Bank, 2016. *What's Holding Back the Private Sector in MENA? Lessons from the Enterprise Survey*. London, Luxembourg and Washington, DC.

European Bank for Reconstruction and Development, European Investment Bank and World Bank, 2020. *Tunisia 2020: Country Profile*. Washington, DC: World Bank.

Evans, Peter, 1995, *Embedded Autonomy: States and Industrial Transformation*. Princeton: Princeton University Press.

Farazi, Subika, Erik Feyen and Roberto Rocha 2011. "Bank Ownership and Performance in the Middle East and North Africa Region", World Bank Policy Research Working Paper 5620, April.

Fardoust, Shahrokh and Mustapha Kamel Nabli, 2022. *Growth, Employment, Poverty, Inequality, and Digital Transformation in the Arab Region: How Can the Digital Economy Benefit Everyone?*. UNDP-ERF Policy Report. (https://erf.org.eg/programs/growth-employment-poverty-inequality-and-digital-transformation-in-the-arab-region/).

Fay, Marianne, Hyoung Lee Il, Massimo Mastruzzi, Sungmin Han and Moonkyoung Cho, 2019. "Hitting the Trillion Mark: A Look at How Much Countries are Spending on Infrastructure?", World Bank Policy Research Working Papers 8730, February.

Feenstra, Robert C., Marcel P. Robert Inklaar and Timmer, 2015. "The Next Generation of the Penn World Table", *American Economic Review*. 105 (10), pp. 3150–3182, (www.ggdc.net/pwt).

Felipe, Jesus, Arnelyn Abdon and Utsav Kumar, 2012. "Tracking the Middle-Income Trap: What Is It, Who Is in It and Why?", Levy Economics Institute of Bard College, Working Paper #715, April.

Fernandez, Raquel and Dani Rodrik, 1991. "Resistance to Reform: Status Quo Bias in the Presence of Individual-Specific Uncertainty", *America Economic Review*. 81 (5), pp. 1146–1155.

Ferreira, Francisco H.G., Philippe George Leite and Martin Ravallion, 2010. "Poverty Reduction Without Economic Growth?: Explaining Brazil's Poverty Dynamics, 1985-2004", *Journal of Development Economics*. 93 (1), pp. 20–36.

Fingleton, Bernard and Enrique López-Bazo, 2006. "Empirical Growth Models with Spatial Effects", *Papers in Regional Science*. 85 (2), pp. 177–198.

Food and Agriculture Organization (FAO), 2021. *Global Review of Census Methodologies and Results (2006–2015), World Programme for the Census of Agriculture 2010*. FAO Statistical Development Series No. 18, Rome.

Freedom House, 2008. Map of Freedom 2008 and Freedom in the World Survey 2008. (http://www.freedomhouse.org).

Freund, Caroline and Alberto Portugal-Perez, 2012. "Assessing MENA's Trade Agreements", World Bank Working Paper Series 55, World Bank.

Gallup, 2011. "Tunisia: Analyzing the Dawn of the Arab Spring: Examining Public Perceptions Leading up to the First Regional Uprising", (https://news.gallup.com/poll/157049/tunisia-analyzing-dawn-arab-spring.aspx).

Garriga, Ana Carolina and Cesar M. Rodriguez, 2020. "More Effective than We Thought: Central Bank Independence and Inflation in Developing Countries", *Economic Modelling*. 85, pp. 87–105.

Gasiorek, Michael and Sami Mouley, 2018. *Analyzing the Impact of a EU-Tunisia DCFTA on Tunisian Trade and Production*. FEMISE Research Program Report FEM 43-16.
Gazdar, Kaouthar and Mondher Cherif, 2015. “Institutions and the Finance-Growth Nexus: Empirical Evidence from MENA Countries”, *Borsa Istanbul Review*. 15 (3), pp. 137–160.
Gehlbach, Scott and Philip Keefer, 2007. *Investment Without Democracy: Ruling-Party Institutionalization and Credible Commitment in Autocracies*. Madison: Mimeo, Political Science Department, University of Wisconsin.
Ghafar, Adel Abdel and Anna L. Jacobs, 2019. “Beijing Calling: Assessing China’s Growing Footprint in North Africa”, Report, Brookings Doha Center.
Ghali, Khalifa H., 1999. “Financial Development and Economic Growth: The Tunisian Experience”, *Review of Development Economics*. 3 (3), pp. 310–322.
Ghali, Sofiane, 2018, *Dépenses Publiques et Innovation*. Université de Tunis, September.
Ghali, Sofiane and Pierre Mohnen, 2004. “Restructuring and Economic Performance: The Experience of the Tunisian Economy”, in Hassan Hakimian and Jeffrey B. Nugent (editors), *Trade Policy and Economic Integration in the Middle East and North Africa: Economic Boundaries in Flux*. London and New York: Routledge Curzon Press, pp. 101–118.
Ghali, Sofiane and Mustapha Kamel Nabli, 2020. “Export Diversification and Sophistication and Industrial Policy in Tunisia”, Economic Research Forum Working Paper #1415, December, Cairo.
Ghali, Sofiane and Habib Zitouna, 2018. “Labor Demand in Tunisia: Size, Structure and Determinants”, in Ragui Assaad and Mongi Boughzala (editors), *The Tunisian Labor Market in an Era of Transition*. Oxford: Oxford University Press, pp. 39–60.
Ghanem, Hafez and Salman Shaikh, 2013. *On the Brink: Preventing Economic Collapse and Promoting Inclusive Growth in Egypt and Tunisia*. Washington, DC: The Brookings Project on U.S. Relations with the Islamic World, U.S.-Islamic World Forum.
Ghazali, Monia and Rim Mouelhi, 2018. “The Employment Intensity of Growth: Evidence from Tunisia”, *Journal of Economic Development*. 43 (3), pp. 85–117.
Ghura, Dhaneshwar and Thomas Grennes, 1993. “The Real Exchange Rate and Macroeconomic Performance in Sub-Saharan Africa”, *Journal of Development Economics*. 42 (1), pp. 155–174.
Gisolo, Enrico, 2008. “The Degree of Legal Central Bank Independence in MENA Countries: International Comparisons and Macroeconomic Implications”, Chapter 3 in David Cobham and Ghassan Dibeh (editors), *Monetary Policy and Central Banking in the Middle East and North Africa*. Routledge, pp. 27–64.
Glawe, Linda and Helmut Wagner, 2016. “The Middle-Income Trap: Definitions, Theories and Countries Concerned- A Literature Survey”, *Comparative Economic Studies*. 58 (4), pp. 507–538.
Gomez, Edmond Terence and K.S. Jomo, 1997. *Malaysia’s Political Economy: Politics, Patronage and Profits*. Cambridge: Cambridge University Press.
Grewal, Sharan, 2019. *Tunisian Democracy at a Crossroads*. Policy Brief, Brookings Institution, February.
Grissa, Abdessatar, 1973. *Agricultural Policies and Employment: Case Study of Tunisia*. Paris: OECD.
Grissa, Abdessatar, 1989. “An Interest Group Analysis of Tunisia’s Public Enterprises”, in Mustapha Kamel Nabli and Jeffrey B. Nugent (editors), *The New*

Institutional Economics and Development: Theory and Applications to Tunisia. Amsterdam: North Holland, pp. 404–427.

Guellouz, Azzedine, 2010, "La Tunisie Husseinite au XVIIIè Siècle", in Azzedine Guellouz, Abdelkader Masmoudi and Mongi Smida (editors), *Histoire Générale de la Tunisie, Tome III: Les Temps Modernes*, Tunis: Sud Editions.

Gutierrez, Eva, 2003. "Inflation, Performance and Constitutional Central Bank Independence: Evidence from Latin America and the Caribbean". International Monetary Fund Working Paper 03/53, March.

Gygli, Savina, Florian Haelg, Niklas Potrafke and Jan-Egbert Sturm, 2019. "The KOF Globalisation Index–Revisited", *Review of International Organizations.* 14 (3), pp. 543–574. (https://doi.org/10.1007/s11558-019-09344-2).

Haan, Jacob de and Willem J. Kooi, 2000. "Does Central Bank Independence Really Matter? : New Evidence for Developing Countries Using a New Indicator", *Journal of Banking and Finance.* 24 (4), pp. 643–664.

Haber, Stephen and Victor Menaldo, 2011. "Do Natural Resources Fuel Authoritarianism? A Preappraisal of the Resource Curse", *American Political Science Review.* 105 (1), pp. 1–26.

Hakimian, Hassan (editor), 2021. *The Routledge Handbook on the Middle East Economy.* London: Routledge.

Hakimian, Hassan and Jeffrey B. Nugent (editors) 2004. *Trade Policy and Economic Integration in the Middle East and North Africa: Economic Boundaries in Flux.* London and New York: Routledge Curzon.

Hansen, Bent, 1991. *The Political Economy of Poverty, Equity and Growth: Egypt and Turkey.* Oxford: Oxford University Press.

Hausmann, Ricardo, Caesar Hidalgo, Sebastian Bustos, Michele Coscia, Alexandre Simoes and Muhammed Ali Yildirim, 2014. *The Atlas of Economic Complexity: Mapping Paths to Prosperity.* Cambridge, MA: MIT Press.

Hawash, Ronia and Shireen AlAzzawi, 2020. "Happily Ever After? Did Life Satisfaction Increase After the Arab Spring?", Middle East Economic Association Annual Meeting, January.

Helliwell, John F., Richard Layard and Jeffrey D. Sachs (editors), 2013, 2015, 2019, 2020. *World Happiness Reports.* New York: Sustainable Development Solutions Network.

Henry, Clement M., 1996. *The Mediterranean Debt Crescent: Money and Power in Algeria, Egypt, Morocco, Tunisia and Turkey.* Gainesville: University Press of Florida.

Henry, Clement M. and Robert Springborg, 2001. *Globalization and the Politics of Development in the Middle East.* Cambridge: Cambridge University Press.

Henry, Clement M. and Robert Springborg, 2010. *Globalization and the Politics of Development in the Middle East*, Second Edition. Cambridge: Cambridge University Press.

Herb, Michael, 2014. *The Wages of Oil: Parliaments and Economic Development in in Kuwait and the UAE.* Ithaca, NY: Cornell University Press.

Hermalin, Benjamin E., 1998. "Toward a Theory of Leadership: Leading by Example", *American Economic Review.* 88 (5), pp. 1188–1206.

Hertog, Steffen, Giacomo Luciani and Marc Valeri (editors) 2013. *Business Politics in the Middle East.* London: Hurst and Co.

Hibou, Beatrice, 2006. "Domination and Control in Tunisia: Economic Levers for the Exercise of Authoritarian Power", *Review of African Political Economy.* 33 (108), pp. 185–206.

Hill, Hal, 2013. "The Political Economy of Policy Reform: Insights from Southeast Asia", *Asian Development Review*. 30 (1), pp. 108–130.
Hirschman, Albert O., 1958. *The Strategy of Economic Development*. New Haven: Yale University Press.
Hlasny, Vladimir and Shireen AlAzzawi, 2018. "Return Migration and Socioeconomic Mobility in MENA", United Nations University UNU-WIDER, Working Paper 2018/35, March.
Holz, Carsten A., 2011. "The Unbalanced Growth Hypothesis and the Role of the State: the Case of China's State-Owned Enterprises", *Journal of Development Economics*. 96 (2), November, pp. 220–238.
Hrenko, Zachary and Jeffrey B. Nugent, 2021. "Collateral Reforms and Access to Finance: Evidence from the West Bank and Gaza", University of Southern California. Presentation at the Western Economic Association International June 27.
Huntington, Samuel, 1991. *The Third Wave: Democratization in the Late Twentieth Century*. Norman: University of Oklahoma Press.
Ibn, Khaldun, 1967. *The Muqaddimah: An Introduction to History*. Translated and introduced by Franz Rosenthal. Princeton: Princeton University Press.
Ibrahim, Solava, 2021. "The Dynamics of the Egyptian Social Contract: How the Political Changes Affected the Poor", *World Development*. 138 (February), pp. 267–299.
Institut National de la Statistique (INS), 2012. *Measuring Poverty, Inequalities and Polarization in Tunisia 2000-2010*. Tunis.
Institut National de la Statistique (INS), 2017. *Recensement Général de la Population et de l'Habitat 2014, Volume 9 Caractéristiques Economiques de la Population*. Tunis.
Institut Tunisien de la Compétitivité et des Etudes Quantitatives (ITCEQ), 2010. *Evaluation du Programme de Mise à Niveau: Résultats de la Sixième Enquête sur le Programme de Mise à Niveau*. Tunis: Février.
International Crisis Group, 2020. "Avoiding a Populist Surge in Tunisia", Briefing No. 73, March.
International Institute of Agriculture, 1939. *The First World Agricultural Census: Volume 1 (1930)*. Rome: Villa Umberto.
International Monetary Fund, 2018. "Manufacturing Jobs: Implications for Productivity and Inequality", Chapter 3 in *World Economic Outlook*. Washington D.C.: International Monetary Fund.
Ismail, Ayman, Thomas Schott, Abbas Barzagan, Basheer Salaytah, Hamad Al-Kubaisi, Majdi Hassen, Ignacio de la Vega, Nihel Chabrak, Abier Annan, Mike Herringto and Penny Kew, 2018. "The MENA Region National Entrepreneurial Framework Conditions", in Nezameddin Faghih and Mohammad Reza Zali (editors), *Entrepreneurship Education and Research in the Middle East and North Africa (MENA. Contributions to Management Science*. New York: Springer, pp. 73–102.
Issawi, Charles, 1982. *An Economic History of the Middle East and North Africa*. New York: Columbia University Press.
Jebili, Walid and Lotfi Belkacem, 2015. "Sectoral Shifts, Diversification, Regional Unemployment on the Eve of Revolution in Tunisia: A Sequential Spatial Panel Approach", Economic Research Forum, Working Paper 952.
Jemmali, Hatem, 2016. "Inequality of Opportunities among Tunisian Children over Time and Space", Economic Research Forum (ERF) Working Paper 1048.

Joekes, Susan P., 1982. *Female–led Industrialization: Women's Jobs in Third World Manufacturing – The Case of the Moroccan Clothing Industry.* Sussex: Institute for Development Studies.

Jomo, K.S., Chen Yun Chung, Brian C. Folk, Irfan ul-Haque, Pasuk Phongpaichit, Batara Simatupang and Mayuri Tateishi, 1997. *Southeast Asia's Misunderstood Miracle.* Boulder: Westview.

Jones, Garett, 2020. *10% Less Democracy: Why You Should Trust Elites a Little More and the Masses a Little Less.* Redwood City, California: Stanford University Press.

Joong-Woong, Kim, 1988. "Economic Development and Financial Liberalization in the Republic of Korea: Policy Reforms and Future Prospects", in Miguel Urrutia (editor), *Financial Liberalization and the Internal Structure of Capital Markets in Asia and Latin America.* Tokyo: United Nations University, pp. 137–171.

Jorgenson, Dale W., Mun S. Ho and Kevin J. Stiroh, 2005. *Information Technology and the American Growth Resurgence.* Cambridge: MIT Press.

Jouini, Nizar, 2021. "Political Consensus, Economic Reforms, and Democratic Transitions: Evidence from Voting Tunisian Reform Bills". Paper presented at the 2021 Annual Conference of the Western Economic Association International, June.

Jouini, Nizar, Nora Lustig, Ahmed Moummi and Abebe Shimeles, 2018. "Fiscal Policy, Income Distribution and Poverty Reduction: Evidence from Tunisia", *Review of Income and Wealth*, Series. 64 (S1), October, pp. 225–248.

Kadria, Mohamed and Mohamed Safouane Ben Aissa, 2014. "The Inflation Targeting Policy in Tunisia: Between Perception and Reality", Munich Personal RePEC Archive (MPRA) Paper No 61442.

Kalinowski, Thomas, 2015. "Crisis Management and the Diversity of Capitalism: Fiscal Stimulus Packages and the East Asian (Neo-) Developmental State", *Economy and Society.* 44 (2), pp. 244–270.

Khanna, Tarun and Yishay Yafeh, 2007. "Business Groups in Emerging Markets: Paragons or Parasites", *Journal of Economic Literature.* 45 (2), pp. 331–372.

Kharas, Homi and Intermit S. Gill, 2020. "Growth Strategies to Avoid the Middle-Income Trap", Duke Global Working Paper Series #17, January.

Kheir-El-Din, Hanaa and Heba el-Laithy, 2006. "An Assessment of Growth, Distribution, and Poverty in Egypt: 1990/91-2004/05". Cairo: The Egyptian Center for Economic Studies (ECES). (Source of data cited in Table 1.2).

Kim, Linsu and Jeffrey B. Nugent, 1999. "Korean SMEs and Their Support Mechanisms", Chapter 4 in Brian Levy, Albert Berry and Jeffrey B. Nugent (editors), *Fulfilling the Export Potential of Small and Medium Firms.* Boston: Kluwer Academic Publishers, pp. 115–167.

King, Stephen J, 1998. "Economic Reform and Tunisia's Hegemonic Party: The End of the Administrative Elite", *Arab Studies Quarterly.* 20 (2), Spring, pp. 59–86.

Khodeir, Aliaa Nabil, 2017. "Intra-Trade in Arab Manufacturing Industries as a Determinant of the Technological Progress", *Arab Economic and Business Journal.* 12 (1), pp. 1–12.

Kobeissi, Nada and Xian Sun, 2010. "Ownership Structure and Bank Performance: Evidence from the Middle East and North Africa Region", *Comparative Economic Studies.* 52 (3), Palgrave, pp. 287–323.

Kohli, Atul, 2004. *State-Directed Development: Political Power and Industrialization in the Global Periphery.* Cambridge: Cambridge University Press.

Koopman, Robert, William Powers, Zhi Wang and Shang-Jin Wei, 2010. "Give Credit Where Credit is Due: Tracing Value Added in Global Production Chains?", National Bureau of Economic Research (NBER) Working Paper 16426.

Kourtelis, Christos, 2021. "The Agadir Agreement: The Capability Traps of Isomorphic Mimicry", *World Trade Review*. 20 (3), pp. 306–320.

Krugman, Paul, 1994. "The Myth of Asia's Miracle", *Foreign Affairs*.73 (6) (November/December), pp. 62–78.

Lacouture, Jean, 1970. *The Demigods*. 1st ed. New York: Random House.

Lahouel, Mohamed, 1998. "Competition Policies and Deregulation in Tunisia", in Nemat Shafik (editor), *Economic Challenges Facing Middle Eastern and North African Countries: Alternative Futures*. New York: St. Martin's Press, pp. 25–49.

Lahouel, Mohamed, 2007. "The Success of Pro-Poor Growth in Rural and Urban Tunisia", in Timothy Besley and Louise J. Cord (editors), *Delivering on the Promise of Pro-Poor Growth, Insights and Lessons of Pro-Poor Growth*. London: Palgrave Macmillan.

Lahouel, Mohamed and Keith Maskus, 2000. "Competition Policy and Intellectual Property Rights in Developing Countries", *World Economy*. 23 (04), pp. 595–611.

Lee, Keun and Hochul Shin, 2021. "Varieties of Capitalism and East Asia: Long-Term Evolution, Structural Change, and the End of East Asian Capitalism", *Structural Change and Economic Dynamics*. 56 (C), Amsterdam: Elsevier, pp. 431–437.

Lei, Zhenhuan and Jeffrey B. Nugent, 2018. "Coordinating China's Economic Growth Strategy via Its Government-Controlled Association for Private Firms", *Journal of Comparative Economics*. 46 (4), pp. 1273–1293.

Levy, Brian, Albert Berry and Jeffrey B. Nugent (editors), 1999. *Fulfilling the Export Potential of Small and Medium Firms*. Boston, Dordrecht: Kluwer Academic Publisher.

Lewis, W. Arthur, 1954. "Economic Development With Unlimited Supplies of Labour", *Manchester School of Economic and Social Studies*. 20, pp. 105–138.

Liaqat, Zara and Jeffrey B. Nugent, 2015. Under-Provision of Private Training by MENA Firms: What to Do About It?", *IZA Journal of Labor & Development*. 4 (2), pp. 1–29.

Liaqat, Zara and Jeffrey B. Nugent, 2016. "When Do Firms Choose to Train? The Roles of Labor Regulations, Their Enforcement, and Firm and Industry Characteristics", *Journal of Development Studies*. 52 (2), pp. 224–241.

Lilien, David M., 1982. "Sectoral Shifts and Cyclical Unemployment", *Journal of Political Economy*. 90 (4), pp. 777–793.

Limam, Imed and Abdelwahab BenHafaiedh, 2017, "Education, Earnings and Returns to Schooling in Tunisia", Economic Research Forum Working Paper 1162.

Lin, Justin Yifu, 1988. "The Household Responsibility System in China's Agricultural Reform: A Theoretical and Empirical Study", *Economic Development and Cultural Change*. 36 (3) Supplement, pp. S199–S224.

Lin, Justin Yifu, 1990. "Collectivization and China's Agricultural Crisis in 1959–1961", *Journal of Political Economy*. 98 (6), pp. 1228–1252.

Lin, Justin Yifu, 2009. *Economic Development and Transition: Thought, Strategy and Viability*. Cambridge: Cambridge University, Marshall Lectures.

Lin, Justin Yifu, 2012a. *New Structural Economics: A Framework for Rethinking Development and Policy*. Washington DC: World Bank.

Lin, Justin Yifu, 2012b. *Demystifying the Chinese Economy*. Cambridge: Cambridge University Press.

Lin, Justin Yifu, 2012c. *The Quest for Prosperity: How Developing Countries Can Take Off.* Princeton: Princeton University Press.

Lipset, Seymour M., 1959. "Some Social Prerequisites for Democracy: Economic Development and Political Legitimacy", *American Political Science Review.* 53 (1), pp. 69–105.

Lougani, Prakash and Nathan Sheets, 1997. "Central Bank Independence, Inflation and Growth in Transition Economies", *Journal of Money, Credit and Banking.* 28 (3), August.

Lowe, Markus, 2006. *Middle East/North Africa and the Millennium Development Goals: Implications for German.* Development Cooperation. (DOI:10.2139/ssrn.2218863).

Lu, Jiaxuan and Jeffrey B. Nugent, 2021. "China's Outward Foreign Direct Investment in the Belt and Road Initiative: What Are the Motives for Chinese Firms to Invest?", *China Economic Review.* 68, August.

Lybek, Tonny, 1999. "Central Bank Autonomy and Inflation and Output Performance in the Baltic States, Russia and Other Countries of the Former Soviet Union, 1995–97", International Monetary Fund Working Paper 99/4.

Maaloul, Anis, Raida Chakroun and Sabrine Yahyaoui, 2018. "The Effect of Political Connections on Companies' Performance and Value: Evidence from Tunisian Companies after the Revolution", *Journal of Accounting in Emerging Economies.* 8 (2), pp. 185–204.

Madsen, Jacob B., Paul A. Raschky and Ahmed Skali, 2015. "Does Democracy Drive Income in the World, 1500–2000", *European Economic Review.* 78 (C), pp. 175–195.

Magruder, Jeremy R., 2013. "Can Minimum Wages Cause a Big Push? Evidence from Indonesia", *Journal of Development Economics.* 100 (1), Elsevier, pp. 48–62.

Mahdavy, Hossein, 1970. "The Patterns and Problems of Economic Development in Rentier States: The Case of Iran", in M.A. Cook (editor), *Studies in Economic History of the Middle East.* London: Oxford University Press, pp. 427–467. Reprinted by Routledge, 2002.

Makdisi, Samir, 2019. "The Arab Uprisings, Autocracy, Democracy and Sustainable Development", RIEME Conference.

Makdisi, Samir, 2021. "Arab Development and the Transition to Democracy", Chapter 19 in Hassan Hakimian (editor), *The Routledge Handbook on the Middle Eastern Economy.* London: Routledge.

Makdisi, Samir and Raimundo Soto, forthcoming. "On the Causes of Conflict and the Premises for Reconstruction", in Samir Makdisi and Raimundo Soto (editors), *Aftershock of the Arab Uprisings: Reconstruction, National Peace and Democratic Change.* Cairo: Economic Research Forum.

Malinvaud, Edmond and Mustapha Kamel Nabli, 1997. "The Future Role of Planning in Market Economies", Chapter 4 in Edmond Malinvaud and Amartya E. Sen (editors.), *Development Strategy and Management of the Market Economy,* Volume I. Oxford: Clarendon Press.

Malkawi, Bashar H., 2017. "Reforming Rules of Origin in Greater Arab Free Trade Area for Effective Economic Integration", Economic Research Forum Policy Brief No. 29.

Mankiw, N. Gregory, David Romer and David N. Weil, 1992. "A Contribution to the Empirics of Economic Growth", *Quarterly Journal of Economics.* 107 (May), pp. 407–437.

Marouani, Mohamed Ali and Michelle Marshalian, 2019. "Winners and Losers in Industrial Policy 2.0: An Evaluation of the Impacts of the Tunisian Industrial Upgrading Program", Economic Research Forum Working Paper No 1302.

Masri, Safwan M., 2017. *Tunisia: An Arab Anomaly*. New York: Columbia University Press.

Matoussi, Wided and Paul Seabright, 2014. "Cooperation Against Theft: A Test of Incentives for Water Management in Tunisia", *American Journal of Agricultural Economics*. 96 (1), pp. 124–153.

McCarthy, Rory, 2019. "The Future of Democracy in Tunisia", *New York Times*. Opinion Section September 24.

Medina, Leandro and Friedrich Schneider, 2018. "Shadow Economy All Around the World: What Did We Learn over the Last 20 Years". IMF Working Paper 18/17.

Meddeb, Hamza, 2021. "The Hidden Face of Informal Cross-Border Trade in Tunisia after 2011", Carnegie Endowment for International Peace, May 2021.

Meon, Pierre-Guillaume and Khalid Sekkat, 2004. "Does the Quality of Institutions Limit the MENA's Integration in the World Economy", *The World Economy*. 27 (9), pp. 1475–1498.

Miniesy, Rania S., Jeffrey B. Nugent and Tarik M. Yousef, 2004. "Intra-Regional Trade Integration in the Middle East: Past Performance and Future Potential", in Hassan Hakimian and Jeffrey B. Nugent (editors), *Trade Policy and Economic Integration in the Middle East and North Africa*. London: Routledge Curzon, pp. 41–65.

Ministry of Education, 2016. *The White Book*. Republic of Tunisia (http//www.echos.education.gov.tn/2016-05-20/LivreBlanc.pdf).

Moalla, Mansour, 1992. *L'Etat Tunisien et l'Indépendance*. Tunis: Cérès Productions.

Mohaddes, Kamiar, Jeffrey B. Nugent and Hoda Selim (editors), 2019. *Institutions and Macroeconomic Policies in Resource-Rich Arab Economies*. Oxford: Oxford University Press.

Montenegro, Claudio E. and Harry A. Patrinos, 2014. "Comparable Estimates of Returns to Schooling Around the World", World Bank Policy Research Working Paper 7020, September.

Moore, Clement H., 1965. *Tunisia since Independence*. Berkeley and Los Angeles: University of California Press.

Moore, Clement H., 1991. "Tunisian Banking: Politics of Adjustment and the Adjustment of Politic", in I. William Zartman (editor), *Tunisia: The Political Economy of Reform*. Boulder, Colorado: Lynn Reinner, pp. 67–97.

Morikawa, Masayuki, 2016. "What Types of Policy Uncertainties Matter for Business?", *Pacific Economic Review*. 21 (5), pp. 527–540.

M'Rabet, M'hamed Ali, 2008, "L'Ifriqya à l'Epoque Hafside", in Hichem Djaït, Mohamed Talbi, Farhat Dachraoui, Abdelmajid Dhouib and M'hamed Ali M'Rabet (editors), *Histoire Générale de la Tunisie, Tome II: Le Moyen-Age*, Tunis: Sud Editions.

Muller, Christophe and Chistophe J. Nordman, 2011. "Intra-Firm Human Capital Externalities in Tunisia", *Journal of Development Studies*. 47 (4), pp. 657–675.

Murphy, Emma C., 1999. *Economic and Political Change in Tunisia*. New York: St. Martin's Press.

Murphy, Emma C., 2006. "The Tunisian Mise à Niveau Programme and the Political Economy or Reform", *New Political Economy*. 11 (41), pp. 519–540.

Murphy, Kevin M., Andrei Shleifer and Robert M. Vishny, 1989. "Industrialization and the Big Push", *Journal of Political Economy*. 97, pp. 1003–1026.

Nabli, Mustapha Kamel, 1981. "Trade Strategies and Employment in Tunisia", in Anne O. Krueger, Terry Monson and Narongchai Akrasanee (editors), *Trade and Employment in Developing Countries: Individual Studies*. Chicago: University of Chicago Press, 90 pages.

Nabli, Mustapha Kamel, 1997. "Planning: Between Mitigating Market and Government Failures", Chapter 7 in Richard Sabot and Istvan Székely (editors), *Development Strategy and Management of the Market Economy*, Volume II. Oxford: Clarendon Press.
Nabli, Mustapha Kamel, 2019. *J'y Crois Toujours: Au-delà de la débâcle ... une Tunisie démocratique et prospère*, Tunis: Sud Editions.
Nabli, Mustapha Kamel, and Hakim Ben Hammouda, 2015. "The Political Economy of the New Arab Awakening", in Justin Y. Lin and Celestin Monga (editors), *The Oxford Handbook of Africa and Economics*. Oxford: Oxford University Press.
Nabli, Mustapha Kamel and Jeffrey B. Nugent (editors), 1989. *The New Institutional Economics and Development: Theory and Applications to Tunisia*. Amsterdam: North-Holland, Contributions to Economic Analysis.
Nabli, Mustapha Kamel, Carlos Silva-Jaurugui and Ahmet Faruk Aysan, 2008. "Authoritarianism, Credibility of Reforms and Private Sector Development in the Middle East and North Africa", in, *Institutions and Economic Development: Selected Papers from the ERF 14th Annual Conference*. Cairo: Economic Research Forum.
Nabli, Mustapha Kamel and Marie-Ange Véganzonès-Varoudakis, 2004. "Exchange Rate Regime and Competitiveness of Manufactured Exports: The Case of MENA Countries", in Hassan Hakimian and Jeffrey B. Nugent (editors), *Trade Policy and Economic Integration in the Middle East and North Africa: Economic Boundaries in Flux*. London and New York: Routledge Curzon, pp. 66–83.
Nabli, Mustapha Kamel and Marie-Ange Véganzonès-Varoudakis, 2007. "Reform Complementarities and Economic Growth in the Middle East and North Africa", *Journal of International Development*. 19, pp. 17–54. Also in Mustapha Kamel Nabli*: Breaking the Barriers to Higher Economic Growth: Better Governance and Deeper Reforms in the Middle East and North Africa*. Volume of Collected Papers, World Bank.
Nabli, Mustapha Kamel, Medja Bahlous, Mohamed Z. Bechri, Marouane El Abbassi, Riadh El Ferktaji and Bechir Talbi, 2002. "Trade, Finance and Competitiveness in Tunisia", in José Maria Fanelli and Rohinton Medhora (editors), *Finance and Competitiveness in Developing Countries*. London and New York: Routledge, pp. 222–256.
Naccache, Sonia, 2009. "The Political Economy of Trade Policy in Tunisia", *Middle East Development Journal*. 1 (1), pp. 31–58.
Nobel Peace Prize, 2015. Tunisia: National Dialogue Quartet. (NobelPrize.org).
Noland, Marcus and Howard Pack, 2007. *The Arab Economies in a Changing World*. Washington, DC: Peterson Institute for International Economics.
Nugent, Jeffrey B., 1989. "Collective Action in Tunisia's Producer Organizations: Some Variations on the Olsonian Theme", in Mustapha Kamel Nabli and Jeffrey B. Nugent (editors), *The New Institutional Economics and Development: Theory and Applications to Tunisia*. Amsterdam: North Holland, pp. 289–322.
Nugent, Jeffrey B., 1997. "From Import Substitution to Export Led Development: Some Institutional and Political Economy Conditions for Success", in Heba Handoussa (editor), *Economic Transition in the Middle East: Global Challenges and Adjustment Strategies*. Cairo: American University in Cairo Press, pp. 89–105.
Nugent, Jeffrey B., 2016. "Does Labor Law Reform Offer an Opportunity for Reducing Arab Youth Unemployment", Chapter 10 in Edward A. Sayre and Tarik M. Yousef (editors), *Young Generation Awakening: Economics, Society and Policy on the Eve of the Arab Spring*. Oxford: Oxford University Press, pp. 188–203.

Nugent, Jeffrey B., 2021. "Explaining Growth in the Middle East", Chapter 1 in Hassan Hakimian (editor), *The Routledge Handbook on the Middle East Economy*. London: Routledge.

Nugent, Jeffrey B. and Abla M. Abdel Latif, 2009. "A Quiz on the Net Benefits of Trade Creation and Trade Diversion in the QIZs of Jordan and Egypt". Paper presented at the 16th Annual Conference of the Economic Research Forum, Cairo, November.

Nugent, Jeffrey B. and Jiaxuan Lu, 2020. "Does the All-China Federation of Industry and Commerce Align Private Firms With the Goals of People's Republic of China's Belt and Road Initiative?", *Asian Development Bank Review*. 37 (2), pp. 45–76.

Nugent, Jeffrey B. and Mustapha Kamel Nabli, 1992. "Development of Financial Markets and the Size Distribution of Manufacturing Establishments: International Comparisons", *World Development*. 20 (10) October, 1489–1499.

Nugent, Jeffrey B. and Hashem Pesaran (editors), 2007. *Explaining Growth in the Middle East*. Amsterdam: Elsevier.

Nugent, Jeffrey B. and Tarek Yousef, 2005. "Does MENA Defy Gravity? How MENA has Performed in its Intraregional, EU and Other Trade: Implications for EU and Intra-MENA Trade Agreements", European University Institute Working Papers (Florence) (http://cadmus.eui.eu// handle/1814/3248).

Nunn, Nathan, 2005. *Slavery, Institutional Development, and Long-Run Growth in Africa, 1400-2000*. (https://ideas.repec.org/s/wpa/wuwpit.html).

Nurkse, Ragnar, 1953. *Problems of Capital Formation in Underdeveloped Countries*. New York: Oxford University Press.

O'Brien, Patrick, 2005. "Fiscal and Financial Preconditions for the Rise of British Naval Hegemony, 1485–1815", in Jurgen Backhaus and Nicholas M. Rodger (editors), *Navies and State Formation*. New York: Springer.

Ocampo, Emilio, 2019. "The Economic Analysis of Populism: A Selective Review of the Literature", Working Paper No. 694, Universidad del CEMA, Buenos Aires, Argentina, May.

O'Connor, Kelsey, Luisa Blanco and Jeffrey B. Nugent, 2018. "Does Oil Really Curse Democracy? A Long-Run Time-Series Analysis of 127 Countries", *Resources Policy*. 57 (C), Elsevier, pp. 264–277.

OECD, 2005a. Indicators of Regulatory Conditions in the Professional Services, 2 December.

OECD, 2005b. Indicators of Regulatory Conditions in Seven Non-manufacturing Sectors, December.

OECD, 2005c. Modal Estimates of Services Barriers TD/TC/WP (2005) 36 OECD, Paris.

OECD, Organization for Economic Cooperation and Development, 2012. *The Role of MENA Stock Exchanges in Corporate Governance* (www.oecd.org/daf/corporateaffairs/mena).

OECD, Organization for Economic Cooperation and Development, 2018. *Morocco in Global Value Chains: Results and Strategic Recommendations from the Integration of Morocco in the Trade in Value Added Database*. (https://www.oecd.org/mena/economies/morocco/Morocco-Global-Value-Chains-TiVA.pdf).

Onis, Ziya, 1991. "The Logic of the Developmental State", *Comparative Politics*. 24 (1), pp. 109–126.

Oudenal, Mohamed and Houda Ben Hamouda, 2018. "The Political Economy of Business Elites in Tunisia: Actors, Strategies and Identities", ERF Working Paper No. 1273, December.

Olson, Mancur, 1965. *The Logic of Collective Action: Public Goods and the Theory of Groups*. Cambridge: Harvard University Press.
Owen, Roger, 1992. *State, Power and Politics in the Making of the Modern Middle East*. 2nd Edition. London: Routledge.
Owen, Roger and Sevket Pamuk, 1999. *A History of Middle East Economies in the Twentieth Century*. Cambridge: Harvard University Press.
Ozler, Sule, 2000. "Export Orientation and Female Share of Employment: Evidence from Turkey", *World Development*. 28 (7), 1239–1248.
Page, John M., 1994. "The East Asian Miracle: Four Lessons for Development Policy" National Bureau of Economic Research.
Panagariya, Arvind, 2008. *India: The Emerging Giant*. Oxford: Oxford University Press.
Papaionnou, Elias and Gregorius Siourounis, 2008. "Democratization and Growth", *Economic Journal*. 118 (532), pp. 1520–1551.
Perkins, Kenneth J., 1997. *Historical Dictionary of Tunisia*. 2nd ed. Lanham, MD and London: The Scarecrow Press, Inc.
Persson, Torsten and Guido Tabellini, 2006. "Democracy and Development: The Devil in the Details", *American Economic Review*. 96 (2), pp. 319–324.
Persson, Torsten and Guido Tabellini, 2009. "Democratic Capital: The Nexus of Political and Economic Change", *American Economic Journal: Macroeconomics*. 1 (2), pp. 88–126.
Pfeifer, Karen, 2015. "Rebels, Reformers and Empire: Alternative Economic Programs for Egypt and Tunisia", *Middle East Report*. 274 (Spring), Middle East Research and Information Project.
Piketty, Thomas, 2014. *Capital in the Twenty-First Century*. Cambridge: Belknap Press of Harvard University Press.
Piro, Timothy J., 1998. *The Political Economy of Market Reform in Jordan*. Lanhan: Rownan and Littlefield Pub. Inc.
Potrafke, Niklas, 2015. "The Evidence of Globalization", *The World Economy*. 38 (3), pp. 509–551.
Powell, John Duncan, 1970. "Peasant Society and Clientelist Politics", *American Political Science Review*. 64 (2), pp. 411-425.
Przeworski, Adam and Fernando Limongi, 1993. "Political Regimes and Economic Growth", *Journal of Economic Perspectives*. 7 (3), pp. 51–69.
Przeworski, Adam, Michael Alvarez, José Antonio Cheibub and Fernando Limongi, 2000. *Democracy and Development: Political Institutions and Well-Being in the World, 1850–1990*. New York: Cambridge University Press.
Rachdi, Houssem and Sami Mensi, 2013. "Does Institutions Quality Matter for Financial Development and Economic Growth Nexus? Another Look at the Evidence from MENA Countries", *International Journal of Financial Economics*. 1 (1), pp. 1–15.
Rama, Martin, 1998. "How Bad Is Unemployment in Tunisia? Assessing Labor Market Efficiency in a Developing Country", *The World Bank Research Observer*. 13 (1), pp. 59–97.
Reuters, 2021. *Foreign Oil Giants no longer interested in Tunisia* (https://www.reuters.com/article/tunisia-oil).
Richards, Alan and John Waterbury, 1990. *A Political Economy of the Middle East: State, Class and Economic Development*. Boulder: Westview.
Rijkers, Bob, Leila Baghdadi and Gael Raballand, 2017. "Political Connections and Tariff Evasion: Evidence from Tunisia", *The World Bank Economic Review*. 31 (2), pp. 459–482.

Rijkers, Bob, Caroline Freund and Antonio Nucifora, 2017. "All in the Family: State Capture in Tunisia", *Journal of Development Economics*. 124 (C), pp. 41–59.

Robertson, Peter E. and Longfeng Ye, 2013. "On the Existence of a Middle-Income Trap", University of Western Australia Economics Discussion Paper 13–12, February.

Rocha, Nadia and Deborah Winkler, 2019. "Trade and Female Labor Force Participation: Stylized Facts Using a Global Dataset", Background Paper, World Bank World Trade Organization Trade and Gender Report, World Bank, Washington, DC (https://openknowledge.worldbank.org/handle/10986/33106. License: CC BY 3.0 IGO).

Rocha, Roberto, Subika Farazi, Rania Khouri and Douglas Pearce, 2011. "The Status of Bank Lending to SMEs in the Middle East and North Africa Region: Results of a Joint Survey of the Union of Arab Banks and the World Bank", World Bank Policy Research Working Paper 5607.

Rodrik, Dani, 2008. "Industrial Policy: Don't Ask Why, Ask How", *Middle East Development Journal*, Demo Issue (2008), pp. 1–29.

Rodrik, Dani, 2009. "Growth After the Crisis", Working Paper No. 65, Commission on Growth and Development, World Bank.

Rodrik, Dani, 2016. "Premature Deindustrialization", *Journal of Economic Growth*. 21 (1), pp. 1–33.

Rodrik, Dani and Romain Wacziarg, 2005. "Do Democratic Transitions Produce Bad Economic Outcomes?, *American Economic Review*. 95 (2), pp. 50–55.

Ross, Michael L., 2001. "Does Oil Hinder Democracy?, *World Politics*. 53 (3), Cambridge University Press, pp. 325–361.

Ross, Michael L., 2008. "Oil, Islam and Women", *American Political Science Review*. 102 (1), pp. 1–17.

Ross, Michael L., 2012. *The Oil Curse: How Petroleum Wealth Shapes the Development of Nations*. Princeton: Princeton University Press.

Saadani, Yousef, Zsofia Arvai and Roberto Rocha, 2011. "A Review of Credit Guarantee Schemes in the Middle East and North Africa Region", World Bank Policy Research Working Paper 5612.

Salehi-Isfahani, Djavad, 2016. "Schooling and Learning in the Middle East and North Africa", in Edward A. Sayre and Tarik M. Yousef (editors), *Young Generation Awakening: Economics, Society and Policy on the Eve of the Arab Spring*. Oxford: Oxford University Press.

Samoud, Iheb and Souad Dhaoui, 2019. "The Tunisian Integration into Global Value Chains: The Role of Offshore Regime and FDI". EMNES Working Paper No. 21, February.

Sayre, Edward A. and Tarik M. Yousef, 2016. "Introduction", in Edward A. Sayre and Tarik M. Yousef (editors), *Young Generation Awakening: Economics, Society and Policy on the Eve of the Arab Spring*. Oxford: Oxford University Press, pp. 1–15.

Schnabl, Gunther and Fran Asziska Schobert, 2009. "Monetary Policy Operations of Debtor Central Banks in MENA Countries", Chapter 4 in David Cobham and Ghassan Dibeh (editors), *Monetary Policy and Central Banking in the Middle East and North Africa*. London: Routledge, pp. 65–84.

Schneider, Friedrich, 2007. "Shadow Economies and Corruption all Over the World: New Estimates for 145 Countries", *Economics*, 2007–09, July.

Schneider, Friedrich, Andrea Buehn and Claudio E. Montenegro, 2010. "Shadow Economies All Over the World: New Estimates for 162 Countries for 1999–2007", World Bank, Policy Research Working Paper No 5356.

Selim, Hoda, 2019. "Does Central Bank Independence in Arab Oil Exporters Matter?", Chapter 5 in Kamiar Mohaddes, Jeffrey B. Nugent and Hoda Selim (editors), *Institutions and Macroeconomic Policies in Resource-Rich Arab Economies*. Oxford: Oxford University Press, pp. 119–148.

Sen, Amartya K., 1985a. "Well-Being, Agency and Freedom: The Dewey Lectures 1984", *Journal of Philosophy*. 82 (4), pp. 169–221.

Sen, Amartya K., 1985b. *Commodities and Capabilities*. Amsterdam: North Holland.

Sen, Amartya K., 1988. "The Concept of Development", Chapter 1 in Hollis B. Chenery and T.N. Srinivasan (editors), *Handbook of Development Economics*. Volume 1. Amsterdam: North Holland, pp. 9–26.

Sen, Amartya K., 1999. *Development as Freedom*. New York: Anchor Books.

Sheng, Andrew, 1988. "Financial Opening in Malaysia", in Miguel Urrutia (editor), *Financial Liberalization and the Internal Structure of Capital Markets in Asia and Latin America*. Tokyo: United Nations University, pp. 172–179.

Shin, Yang-Ha, 1976. "Land Reform in Korea, 1950", *Bulletin of the Population and Development Studies Center*. 5 (September), pp. 14–31.

Smida, Mongi, 2010, "La Tunisie Husseinite au XIXè Siècle", in Azzedine Guellouz, Abdelkader Masmoudi and Mongi Smida (editors), *Histoire Générale de la Tunisie, Tome III: Les Temps Modernes*, Tunis: Sud Editions.

Solow, Robert M., 1956. "A Contribution to the Theory of Economic Growth", *Quarterly Journal of Economics*. 70 (1), February, pp. 65–94.

Solow, Robert M., 1957. "Technical Change and the Aggregate Production Function", *Review of Economics and Statistics*. 39 (3), August, pp. 312–320.

Solt, Frederick, 2020. "Measuring Income Inequality Across Countries and Over Time: The Standardized World Income Inequality Database", *Social Science Quarterly*. SWIID Version 9.0, October.

Spierings, Niels, 2017. "Trust and Tolerance across the Middle East and North Africa: A Comparative Perspective on the Impact of Arab Uprisings", *Politics and Governance*. 5 (2), pp. 4–15.

Sridi, Dorsaf and Wafa Ghardallou, 2021. "Remittances and Disaggregated Country Risk Ratings in Tunisia: an ARDL Approach", *Middle East Development Journal*. 13 (1), pp. 191–211.

Stampini, Marco and Audrey Verdier-Chouchane, 2011. "Labor Dynamics in Tunisia: The Issue of Youth Unemployment", IZA Discussion Paper 5611.

Stiglitz, Joseph E., 2002. *Globalization and Its Discontents*. London: Penguin Books.

Strauss, John and Duncan Thomas, 1995. "Human Resources: Empirical Modeling of Household and Family Decisions", in Jere R. Behrman and T.N. Srinivasan (editors), *Handbook of Development Economics*. Amsterdam: Elsevier, pp. 1883–2023.

Studwell, Joe, 2013. *How Asia Works: Success and Failure in the World's Most Dynamic Region*. New York: Grove Press.

Symbiotics, 2017. *Symbiotics MIV Survey: Market Data and Peer Group Analysis*, 11th Edition, September. (www.findevgateway.org/paper/2017/09/2017-symbiotics-miv-su).

Szirmai, Adam and Bart Verspagen, 2015. "Manufacturing and Economic Growth in Developing Countries, 1950–2005", *Structural Change and Economic Dynamics*. 34 (C), pp. 46–59.

Testas, Abdelaziz, 2000. "The Contribution of EU Investment to Tunisia's Economic Development", *The Journal of North African Studies*. 5 (2), pp. 9–24.

The Economist, 2020. "Tunisia: Ten Years after the Revolution", *The Economist*. August 13, 2020, pp. 41–42.

Thomas, Duncan and John Strauss, 1997. "Health and Wages: Evidence on Men and Women in Urban Brazil", *Journal of Econometrics*. 77, pp. 159–185.

Tilly, Charles, 1990. *Coercion, Capital, and European States, ADS 900-1990*. Oxford: Blackwell.

Timmer, Marcel P. and Gaaitzen J. de Vries, 2009. "Structural Change and Growth Acceleration in Asia and Latin America: A New Sectoral Dataset", *Cliometrica*. 3 (2), pp. 165–190.

Tzannatos, Zafiris, Ishac Diwan and Joanna Abdel Ahad, 2016. "Rates of Return to Education in 22 Arab Countries: An Update and Comparison between MENA and the Rest of the World", Economic Research Forum, Working Paper 1007, May.

United Nations, 2002. *World Population Prospects: The 2000 Revision*. New York: United Nations, Department of Economic and Social Affairs.

United Nations, 2004. National Report on Millennium Development Goals: Tunisia, United Nations.

United Nations, Food and Agricultural Organization (FAO), 1994. *Etude Multidimensionnelle et Comparative des Régimes de Tenures Foncières Communales et Privées en Afrique: Le Cas de la Tunisie, 1994*, 21.

Wade, Robert, 1990. *Governing the Market: Economic Theory and the Role of Government in East Asian Industrialization*. Princeton: Princeton University Press.

Walter, Andrew and Xiaoke Zhang, 2012. "Debating East Asian Capitalism: Issues and Themes", in Andrew Walter and Xiaoke Zhang (editors), *East Asian Capitalism: Diversity, Continuity and Change*. Oxford: Oxford University Press, pp. 1–20.

Waterbury, John, 1989. "The Political Management of Economic Adjustment and Economic Reform", in Joan Nelson (editor), *Fragile Coalitions: The Politics of Economic Adjustment*. Washington, DC: Overseas Development Council.

White, Gregory, 2001. *A Comparative Political Economy of Tunisia and Morocco: On the Outside Looking In*. Albany: State University of New York Press.

Williamson, Oliver E., 1979. "Transaction Cost Economics: The Governance of Contractual Relations", *Journal of Law and Economics*. 22 (2), pp. 233–262.

World Bank, 1993. *The East Asian Miracle: Economic Growth and Public Policy*. New York: Oxford University Press.

World Bank, 1995. *Republic of Tunisia Poverty Alleviation Preserving Progress While Preparing for the Future*. Washington, DC, 1.6.

World Bank, 1996. *Republic of Yemen: Poverty Assessment*. Report No. 15158-YEM. Washington DC: The World Bank. (cited Table 1.2).

World Bank, 1999. *Democratic and Popular Republic of Algeria: Poverty Update*, (In Two Volumes) Volume 1: Main Report. Report No. 18564-AL. Washington, DC: The World Bank. (cited in Table 1.2).

World Bank, 2002. *Republic of Yemen: Poverty Assessment*. Report No. 24422-YEM. Washington DC: The World Bank. (cited in Table 1.2).

World Bank, 2004a. *Unlocking the Employment Potential in the Middle East and North Africa-Toward a New Social Contract*. Washington, DC: World Bank.

World Bank, 2004b. *Doing Business in 2004: Understanding Regulation World Bank*. Washington, DC: International Finance Corporation; Oxford: Oxford University Press.

World Bank, 2008a. *The Road Not Traveled: Education Reform in the Middle East and North Africa*. Washington, DC: World Bank.

World Bank, 2008b. *Tunisia's Global Integration: Second Generation of Reforms to Boost Growth and Employment*. Washington, DC: World Bank Draft Report No. 40129-TN.

World Bank, 2014. *The Unfinished Revolution: Bringing Opportunity, Good Jobs, and Greater Wealth to All Tunisians*, Development Policy Review. Washington, DC.

World Bank, 2015. *Consolidating Social Protection and Labor Policy in Tunisia: Building Systems, Connecting to Jobs*. Report 103218-TN, December, Washington, DC.

World Bank, 2018. *Connecting to Compete 2018: Trade Logistics in the Global Economy*. Washington DC. (https://lpi.worldbank.org).

World Bank, 2019. *Secured Transactions, Collateral Registries and Movable Asset-Based Financing: Knowledge Guide*. World Bank. (https://doi.org/10.1596/32551).

World Bank, 2020. *World Development Report 2020: Trading for Development in the Age of Global Value Chains*. Washington, DC: World Bank Group. World Development Report.

World Bank, 2021. *Climate Risk Country Profile: Tunisia*. Washington, DC.

World Bank and Islamic Development Bank, 2005. *Tunisia: Understanding Successful Socioeconomic Development: A Joint World Bank-Islamic Development Bank Evaluation of Assistance*. Washington, DC and Jeddah, Saudi Arabia.

World Economic Forum, 2014. *The Global Competitiveness Report 2014-2015*. World Economic Forum.

World Trade Organization, 2018. *Factual Presentation: Arab Mediterranean Free Trade Agreement (Agadir Agreement) between Egypt, Jordan, Morocco and Tunisia (Goods)*. WT/COMTD/RTA/11/1, Geneva: World Trade Organization.

Yanikkaya, Halit and Abdullah Altun, 2020. "The Impact of Global Value Chain Participation on Sectoral Growth and Productivity", *Sustainability*. 12 (12) (DOI: 10.3390/su12124848).

Yerkes, Sarah and Marwan Muasher, 2018. "Decentralization in Tunisia: Empowering Towns, Engaging People", Carnegie Endowment for International Peace, Paper, May 17, 2018 Paper.

Yerkes, Sarah and Zeineb Ben Yahmed, 2018. "Tunisians' Revolutionary Goals Remain Unfulfilled", Carnegie Endowment for International Peace, Article, December 6.

Yerkes, Sarah and Zeineb Ben Yahmed, 2019. "Tunisia's Political System: From Stagnation to Competition", Carnegie Endowment for International Peace, Working Paper, March.

Yotopoulos, Pan A. and Jeffrey B. Nugent, 1973. "A Balanced Growth Version of the Linkage Hypothesis: A Test", *Quarterly Journal of Economics*. 87, pp. 157–171.

Young, Alwyn, 1995. "The Tyranny of Numbers: Confronting the Statistical Realities of the East Asian Growth Experience", *Quarterly Journal of Economics*. 110 (3), pp. 641–680.

Young, Crawford, 1994. *The African Colonial State in Comparative Perspective*. New Haven: Yale University Press.

Yousef, Tarik M., 2004. "Development, Growth and Policy Reform in the Middle East and North Africa Since 1950", *Journal of Economic Perspectives*. 18 (3), pp. 91–116.

Zartman, I. William, 2015. "Negotiations in Transitions: A Conceptual Framework", in I. William Zartman (editor), *Arab Spring: Negotiating in the Shadow of the Intifadat*. Athens, Georgia and London: The University of Georgia Press, pp. 1–49.

Zhang, Xiaoke and Richard Whitley, 2013. "Changing Macro-Structural Varieties of East Asian Capitalism", *Socio-Economic Review*. 11 (2), pp. 301–335.

Zouache, Abdallah and Mohamed-Cherif Ilmane, 2008. "Central Bank Independence in a MENA Transition Economy: The Experience of Algeria", Chapter 5 in David Cobham and Ghassan Dibeh (editors), *Monetary Policy and Central Banking in the Middle East and North Africa*. London: Routledge, pp. 85–105.
Zouari, Abderrazak, 1989. "Collective Action and Governance Structure in Tunisia's Labor Organization", in Mustapha Kamel Nabli Mustapha and B. Nugent Jeffrey (editors), *The New Institutional Economics and Development: Theory and Applications to Tunisia*. Amsterdam: North Holland, pp. 323–351.
Zouari-Bouatour, Salma, 1998. "L'enseignement Supérieur en Tunisie: Les enjeux," in Jean Michel Plassard and Said Ben Sédrine (editors), *Enseignement Supérieur et Insertion Professionnelle en Tunisie*. Toulouse: Presses de l'Université des Sciences Sociales.
Zouari-Bouatour, Salma, Lazhar Boudhraa and Sami Zouari, 2014. "Evolution of Rates of Return to Schooling in Tunisia: 1980-1999", *Eurasian Journal of Social Sciences*. 2 (3), pp. 28–47.
Zrelli Ben Hamida, Nadia, Salwa Trabelsi and Ghazi Boulila, 2017. "The Impact of Active Labor Market Policies on the Employment Outcomes of Youth Graduates in the Tunisian Governorates", *Economics, Management and Sustainability*. 2 (2), pp. 62–78.

Index

For Product Safety Concerns and Information please contact our EU
representative GPSR@taylorandfrancis.com
Taylor & Francis Verlag GmbH, Kaufingerstraße 24, 80331 München, Germany

www.ingramcontent.com/pod-product-compliance
Ingram Content Group UK Ltd.
Pitfield, Milton Keynes, MK11 3LW, UK
UKHW020155200926
475702UK00016B/2724
9781032314006